2500

D1208807

a gift...

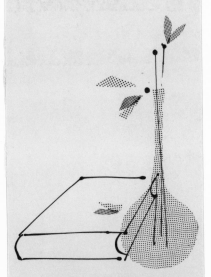

saint paul public library

from

Mr. & Mrs. Paul E. Miller
in memory of
Edward J. Miller

HENRY PURCELL
1659–1695

HENRY PURCELL

1659–1695

An analytical catalogue of his music

BY

FRANKLIN B. ZIMMERMAN

798561

ST MARTIN'S PRESS

1963

ST. PAUL PUBLIC LIBRARY

Copyright © Franklin B. Zimmerman 1963

REFERENCE
ML
134
P95Z5

MACMILLAN AND COMPANY LIMITED
St Martin's Street London WC 2
also Bombay Calcutta Madras Melbourne

THE MACMILLAN COMPANY OF CANADA LIMITED
Toronto

ST MARTIN'S PRESS INC
New York

PRINTED IN GREAT BRITAIN

To RACHEL

for her indispensable help and encouragement in the
compilation of this memorial to her great
countryman, Henry Purcell.

FOREWORD

It is no depreciation of the labours of past scholars to say that a catalogue of Purcell's works is urgently necessary. A great deal of spade-work was done by men like G. E. P. Arkwright and W. Barclay Squire; and without their researches as a foundation Professor Zimmerman's task would have been much more difficult. But many new sources have been discovered since these men were writing—sources which often enable us to establish a more reliable text and also in some cases to distinguish what is genuine from what is spurious. A thematic catalogue is the only satisfactory way of listing any composer's works: it enables us to recognize at once what we already know and it also draws our attention to places where a composer has used the same material in more than one composition. Many of Purcell's borrowings have been recorded before, but mainly in a haphazard way. I think it is fair to say that this is the first time that all the evidence has been presented.

The editor of a work of this kind has to do a good deal of original research: the pages that follow will show how extensive this has been in preparing the present volume. But he has also to solve problems of arrangement, if he wants his catalogue to be not only comprehensive but also usable. The reader who first glances at Professor Zimmerman's work may be bewildered by an elaborate system of numerical references. But once he studies the system he is bound to find, as I have, that it is a model of clarity. The re-editing of the volumes of the Purcell Society, now in progress, will benefit substantially from the information contained in this work. But there will also be many musicians who will want to know where they can find the original sources of any particular work, or at a more modest level may simply want to know where they can find a practical edition which they can use for performance.

If it is true that the labour we delight in physics pain, I can only assume that Professor Zimmerman has enjoyed compiling a work which must have involved an enormous amount of drudgery. It must be some satisfaction to him to know that the work is completed—at least for the time being, since new material is bound to appear from time to time. But an even greater reward will be the gratitude of those who will be constantly turning to this volume for guidance—if not on their own shelves, at least in a library. English scholars need feel neither shame nor regret that the work has been done by an American. There are no frontiers in research, and Purcell's music is valued as much on the other side of the Atlantic as it is in England. I hope this latest contribution to a knowledge of his works will find an equal welcome in both countries.

Sir Jack Westrup

AUTHOR'S PREFACE

THIS catalogue originated as an appendix to the study of Purcell's life and works, which I began in 1955. During the first stages of my research I encountered so many unanswered questions on authenticity, accurate chronology, and the various versions of Purcell's compositions, that it seemed only logical to deal with these as fully as possible before continuing work on the biography itself. My subsequent efforts to survey all extant manuscript and edited sources, and to evaluate ascriptions have brought this catalogue to its present proportions.

Even though I cannot claim that it will provide the last, or even the latest word on various problems which confront modern editors, performers and publishers of Purcell's music, I offer it to these, and in general to any Purcellians 'who carry musical souls about them', as a contribution to existing knowledge of the origins, the backgrounds and the intrinsic characteristics of Purcell's compositions. If it proves as useful after publication as it has been before (both to me and to others), I shall feel well rewarded for the time and energy it has required.

CONTENTS

CONTENTS

ACKNOWLEDGEMENTS

BEFORE outlining the method of this catalogue, I should explain that it is by no means the first attempt of its kind. In 1832 or thereabouts, Vincent Novello compiled a thematic catalogue of Purcell's sacred works (presumably in conjunction with his editing of the music), which may now be seen in the British Museum (Add. *MS* 9074). More recently, the late Gerald M. Cooper compiled a slip-catalogue of Purcell's works, which I consulted frequently during the early stages of my own work. However, differences in our general aims, as well as in methods, soon made it clear that I would have to begin anew, so that responsibility for the present compilation is entirely my own.

For various kinds of assistance I am indebted to many persons, most of whom I can only name here, even though gratitude urges a fuller account. First of all I wish to acknowledge very generous help from Thurston Dart of Cambridge, Professor of Music in the University. Mr. Dart has given me continuous encouragement and numerous valuable suggestions which have brought about many improvements in the catalogue. After reading the whole of the typescript, Mr. Dart undertook the laborious task of examining galley and page-proofs in detail—a service for which both the publishers and I are indeed grateful.

Secondly, I must thank Sir Jack Westrup, Heather Professor of Music in the University of Oxford. He was the first, during a visit to the University of Southern California in 1952, to encourage my enthusiasm for Purcell's music. Subsequently, his expert supervision at Oxford was invaluable in guiding me along the way towards a better understanding of English music of Purcell's century.

My thanks are due also to Mr. Denis W. Stevens, who brought this catalogue to the attention of the musical adviser to Macmillan & Co., Ltd., the late Eric Blom, whom I wish also to thank here publicly, though, alas, posthumously. His generous interest and sympathetic advice have left both my wife and myself with many warm memories of a cherished friendship, however brief.

Furthermore I must thank Mr. Walter Emery and the firm of Novello & Co., Ltd., for permission to consult copy and proofs of the recent series of the Purcell Society Edition volumes before publication. Among Purcell Society editors, I wish particularly to thank Dr. Nigel Fortune, Lecturer in the Department of Music in the Barber Institute of Fine Arts, University of Birmingham, Professor Anthony Lewis, Professor of Music in the University of Birmingham, Mr. Arnold Goldsbrough of Tenbury

ACKNOWLEDGEMENTS

Wells, and, indeed, the whole of the Purcell Society Editorial Board for their friendly co-operation.

Having dedicated this catalogue to my wife, Rachel, I would like also to acknowledge the valuable help lent by her sister, Judith Phillips. Through their perseverance and teamwork, they made possible the completion of several indexing and cross-referencing tasks which I could scarcely have finished alone. Here I want also to mention gratefully Mr. and Mrs. Ivor Phillips, my parents-in-law, and Peter, their son, for putting up with many inconveniences with hospitable forbearance, during several lengthy periods while the catalogue was in preparation.

During my stay in Oxford, I was also helped by the following persons: Dr. Egon Wellesz, University Reader in Byzantine Music, and Lecturer in the History of Music; Mr. Ralph Leavis of Lincoln College; Mr. W. G. Hiscock, Assistant Librarian, Christ Church College Library; Dr. R. W. Hunt, Keeper of Western Manuscripts, Bodleian Library, Miss Margaret Crumm and Messrs. Harris, Hughes, Moon, and Long of the Bodleian staff; Miss Valerie Elliot (now Mrs. Elliot Leach), Music Faculty Librarian; Dr. Bernard Rose, Choirmaster, and Dr. Neil Ker, Librarian, Magdalen College, and all the librarians and staff at other Oxford institutions listed in Appendix III.

In Cambridge I am indebted to Mr. Charles Cudworth, Pendlebury Librarian in the Faculty of Music; Dr. Peter le Huray, Fellow of St. Catherine's College; Miss Phyllis Giles, Music Librarian in the Fitzwilliam Museum; Mrs. Jill Vlasto, Music Librarian in the Rowe Library, King's College; and Dr. Margaret Laurie, now of Glasgow University Library.

At the British Museum I owe special thanks to Mr. A. Hyatt King, Keeper of Printed Music, Mr. O. W. Neighbour, Assistant Keeper, Miss Pamela Willetts, Assistant Keeper in the Department of Manuscripts, and Mr. Edward Croft-Murray, Keeper of Prints and Drawings. To the last-named I am grateful also for a great many favours, which include the loan of the still-life from which the jacket for this book was reproduced, and several periods of very gracious hospitality.

Elsewhere in London I received kind assistance from Miss Barbara D. Banner, Librarian, The Royal College of Music; Dr. MacD. Emslie, Lecturer in the Department of English, University College; Mr. S. O. Freer, Archivist in the National Register of Archives; Mr. Max Hinrichsen, Editor, Hinrichsen Editions, Ltd.; Miss Pemberton, Music Librarian at Westminster Central Public Library; Mr. Lawrence E. Tanner, Librarian, and Mr. N. H. MacMichael, Assistant Librarian at Westminster Abbey; Mr. Maurice Bevan, Lay Clerk, and the Dean and Chapter of St. Paul's Cathedral; Mr. W. H. Stock, Librarian at the Royal Academy of Music; and the Committees of the Guildhall and of Gresham College.

Elsewhere in England, I must thank the Warden of St. Michael's College, Tenbury Wells; and, especially, Mr. H. Watkins Shaw, who most kindly assisted me with the manuscripts both at St. Michael's and at Worcester Cathedral; the Reverend Canon

Pocock and the Dean of Worcester Cathedral; the Reverend Canon Fendick of Gloucester Cathedral; the Reverend Canon Parks of Stonleigh Abbey; the Very Reverend Dean of Christ Church Cathedral, Dublin, and Mr. Rafter, Lay Clerk; Mr. William O'Sullivan, Assistant in charge of *MSS*, Trinity College Library, Dublin; Mr. Pollard, Assistant Librarian, Archbishop Marsh's Library, Dublin; Mr. MacKenna, University Librarian, Glasgow University; Dr. Michael Tilmouth of the Faculty of Music at Glasgow University; Miss Jane Cooling, Assistant to the Librarian, Durham Cathedral, and Mr. Alec Harman of the Music Faculty, Durham College; the Reverend Canon Cant, Librarian, York Minster; Mr. George Dodgson; Mr. Jack Pilgrim; Mr. Donald J. Cox, Assistant Organist at Lichfield Cathedral; Mr. F. C. Morgan and Miss Penelope Morgan, and the Reverend Canon Moreton at Hereford Cathedral; Dr. Gordon Slater, Organist, the Reverend Canon Synge, Mr. Charles Clark, Librarian, Mr. Clifford Hewis and the Reverend Canon Cooke at Lincoln Cathedral; Professor Gerald Abraham and Mr. R. A. Markus, Sub-Librarian in the Faculty of Arts, University of Liverpool; Mr. E. H. Fletcher, Assistant Organist, Peterborough Cathedral; and Mr. Layton Ring of Haslemere.

On the continent, I am happy to acknowledge the assistance of M. François Lesure, Librarian of the Music Department of the Bibliothèque Nationale in Paris, M. Jean Jacquot of the National Centre for Scientific Research; in Brussels, M. Albert van der Linden, Librarian at the Conservatoire Royal de Musique; in Barcelona, Señor Don Miguel Querol Gavaldá of the Institute of Musicology; and Professor Otto Erich Deutsch of Vienna, who was also generous with advice and encouragement.

In Canada I wish to thank Mr. Hugh McLean, Lecturer in Music at the University of British Columbia; and in the United States, Dr. Vincent Duckles and Mrs. Harriet Nicewonger of the Music Library in the University of California at Berkeley; Mrs. Edna Davis, Reference Librarian, William Andrews Clarke Library, Los Angeles; Miss Mary Isobel Fry, Reference Librarian, Huntington Library, San Marino, California; Dean Raymond Kendall, Dr. Pauline Alderman, Emeritus Professor of Music, and Professor Halsey Stevens, School of Music, the University of Southern California; Professor Theodore M. Finney, Music Department, University of Pittsburgh; the late Richard Hill of the Music Division, Library of Congress; Miss Dorothy Mason, Reference Librarian, Folger Shakespeare Library, Washington, D.C.; Miss Ruth Watanabe, Music Librarian in the Eastman School of Music, Rochester, N.Y.; Mr. Sidney Beck, Reference Librarian and Sivart Poladian, Librarian in the New York Public Library; and Dr. Lawrence Moss, Assistant Professor at Yale University.

Finally, I must thank the publishers of this catalogue, without whose confidence and generosity it would never have materialized, and wish to acknowledge with particular gratitude the patient assistance of Mr. Harry Cowdell.

EXPLANATORY NOTES

BECAUSE so few of Purcell's works can be dated accurately, the systematic arrangement of this catalogue is based upon the various musical forms and performing media for which Purcell composed. These are arranged alphabetically under the four headings shown in the Table of Contents. The nomenclature of these forms has to a certain extent determined the numbering of the individual works. On the principle that the soundest terminology would be that with fewest anachronisms, I have eschewed the terms 'cantata' and 'motet', for which I could find no well-established usage in seventeenth-century England. On the other hand, I have employed the term 'ode' because it was used in the seventeenth century, though not exactly in its modern sense.

The numbering system is self-explanatory, except, perhaps, for the gaps in the numerical sequence, occurring at the end of each category. These were left to accommodate newly-discovered works, or works now doubtfully ascribed to Purcell which may later prove authentic. Gaps occurring elsewhere are due to the removal of a work from the authentic to the doubtful or spurious category, as, for instance, No. 398. One work ('Stript of their green our groves appear', No. 444) was removed to the doubtful category on grounds that seemed sufficient at one time. Later evidence made it apparent that this was Purcell's work after all, for which reason it was re-assigned a new number at the end of its category, out of alphabetical sequence. The numbers for such works are prefixed with the letter 'N' to explain their appearance out of alphabetical order, which will allow for their deletion should they not stand the test of time as authentic compositions by Purcell.

In the main body of the catalogue, the number and title of each work appear in bold-face, followed by volume and page-number in the Purcell Society Edition (or title and page-number in another modern edition). Next in order appear sub-title, date, author (or translator or adaptor) and source and date of publication of the text, if known. For each piece, the voices and instruments necessary for performances are symbolized by the following abbreviations:

Verse (in lower-case italics)
s: verse or solo soprano.
a: verse or solo alto (or counter-tenor).
t: verse or solo tenor.
b: verse or solo bass (or upper singing bass).

Chorus (in italic capitals)
S: chorus soprano.
A: chorus alto (or counter-tenor).
T: chorus tenor.
B: chorus bass.

Instruments (*in italics*)

Fl: Flute (*i.e.* recorder).

Ob: Oboe.

T.Ob: Tenor oboe.

Bn: Bassoon.

Tpt: Trumpet.

Flatt Tpts: Slide trumpets and trombones.

Kdr: Kettledrum.

Vn: Violin.

Va: Viola.

Str: 2 Violins, Viola and Bc.

Bc: Gamba and Keyboard Continuo. (For individual sections, this combination is as present unless omission is mentioned. In works for strings, the rubric ' *Bc* ' stands for 'cello (or ' Bass violin ' as Purcell would have called it), double bass and keyboard (or possibly bass lute or theorbo) continuo. In church music without string accompaniments, *Bc* denotes organ alone. In the chamber works it stands for organ or harpsichord continuo.

At present, evidence relating to instrumentation of the fantasias is insufficient to establish firmly that they were written either for viols or violins. As Mr. Thurston Dart has pointed out, Purcell may have intended them for violins (G clefs), lyra-viols (C clefs) and bass viols (F clefs). It is even possible that Purcell intended some for performance with basso continuo. At any rate, any indications of performing media for the fantasias would be misleading, for which reason I have omitted them.

For the first section of each work (or the first instrumental and vocal sections in larger works) all parts involved are represented in compressed score, except where the bass is stationary or silent, in which case it may be omitted. For subsequent sections, simplified incipits are shown on one staff, even for canons. However, canonic incipits do show, by use of various clefs, the melodic and rhythmic intervals of the entries of the subject. Two-stave incipits are given also for grounds (in which the ground bass and its melody are ' telescoped ', the latter enclosed in square brackets) and for the opening pieces of major sections of operas and larger works. Ties in square brackets beneath the staff (as shown in No. 10 on page 9 for instance) indicate that the basso-continuo sustains the note or notes so shown. Other markings in square brackets are editorial except for rubrics taken from autographs where square brackets indicate that the rubric is held over from a previous section. Ornaments have been omitted.

Each musical incipit appears under a heading which includes the title (editorial, if it appears in square brackets) and performers required. With each incipit that can be related to an extant autograph copy, Purcell's rubrics are given above in quasi-facsimile, and his original note-values are shown, although reduced, or otherwise altered note-values elsewhere follow those shown in the Purcell Society Edition, or some other modern edition. His time-signatures, with the source from which they are taken, are entered immediately beneath the editorial time-signature which appears in the staff. Square brackets around symbols for performing media indicate a later entry on the same theme for which the preceding unbracketed symbols are given. Where the closing passage of a solo or verse section is repeated in a choral setting as, for instance, in No. 8/5b, the relationship is shown.

After the last incipit for each work, the 'apparatus' begins with a census of manuscripts (dating from before *ca.* 1765) in which the work is to be found. Complete copies, and incomplete copies which include more than half the work in question, are represented first (the latter shown with the suffix '(inc)'), after which copies of individual sections are listed. All these are symbolized by numbers which refer to the *MSS* listed alphabetically by source in Appendix III, those in bold-face type representing autograph copies. A single number may also represent a set of part-books, in which case the individual books are represented by lower-case letters. Manuscript copies of which portions are missing are listed as 'fragments'.

For transcriptions, the abbreviation '(Trans)' is added to the manuscript number. Songs or instrumental melodies to which new texts have been fitted are indicated by the abbreviation '(Mock)', which follows the number of the manuscript in which they occur.

Next follows a selective representation of the publications in which the work appeared before *ca.* 1850. As in Claudio Sartori's *Bibliografia della musica strumentale Italiana* (Florence: Olschki, 1952), the symbol for each work indicates or approximates the year in which it was published. Here the abbreviations 'Mock' and 'Trans' signify 'Mock-song' and 'transcription', respectively, as described above for *MSS*. As in Day and Murrie's *English Song-Books 1651–1702* (London: Bibl. Soc., 1940) 'mnp' stands for 'music not printed'. In these sections also, complete or nearcomplete editions are represented first, references to publications of individual pieces following afterwards.

The Commentary, containing information on provenance, source, historical data relevant to chronology, information on first performances, notes on literary sources and descriptions of Purcell's borrowings of his own melodies, or pieces, follows next. The persons, places, and subjects mentioned in these are classified in Index IV.

The section under the heading 'Literature' provides a bibliography of books and articles in which the work is discussed. Although I have attempted to omit no article or book of vital importance, the bibliography represented in this catalogue is quite selective; a fuller bibliography will appear with the above-mentioned biography. To avoid a great deal of unnecessary repetition within the various sections headed 'LITERATURE', I list here those general studies which discuss a considerable number of works:

Arundell, Dennis, *Henry Purcell*, London: O.U.P., 1927

Cooper, Gerald M., 'The Chronology of Purcell's Works', *Musical Times*, July–Dec., 1943

Cummings, W., *Purcell*, in *The Great Musicians* series, London: Sampson Low, Marston & Co. Ltd., 1903

Demarquez, Suzanne, *Purcell*, Paris: La Colombe, 1951

Dupré, Henri, *Purcell*, Paris, 1927. English translation by Catherine A. Phillips & Agnes Bedford, New York, 1928

Holland, A. K., *Henry Purcell: The English Musical Tradition*, London: Penguin Books, 1948

Meinardus, Wolfdieter, *Die Technik des Basso Ostinato bei Henry Purcell*, Unpublished Dissertation, Cologne, 1950

Reichlin, Gerhart, *Continental Influences on the Work of Henry Purcell*, Unpublished Doctoral Dissertation, Princeton University, 1960: In Progress

Runciman, John F., *Purcell*, London: George Bell, 1909

Sietz, R., *Henry Purcell, Zeit, Leben, Werk*, Leipzig: Breitkopf & Härtel, 1955

Walker, E., *History of Music in England*, 3rd edition, revised by J. A. Westrup, Oxford: Clarendon, 1952

Westrup, J. A., *Purcell*, in *Master Musicians* series, London: Dent, 1947. [All references in the catalogue refer to this edition, even though a fourth edition has since appeared (in 1960).]

References less than a paragraph in length have been ignored, and page-numbers appear only for books not indexed. At the end of each category pertinent books and articles are listed under the heading ‘ General Literature ’. Some editions of Purcell’s music also present significant musicological information. To avoid misleadingly listing these among books and articles, and to avert unnecessary proliferation of small appendices, I list them here. In addition to various volumes of the Purcell Society Edition, which offer a wealth of this kind of information, the following items represent this new, happily burgeoning category of Purcellian bibliography:

[2] ‘ Behold, I bring you glad tidings ’ (A Christmas Anthem), ed. Alfred Mann, Rutgers University Press, 1953

[231] ‘ Evening Service in G Minor ’, ed. Maurice Bevan, London: O.U.P., 1959

[328] ‘ Hail, bright Cecilia ’ (Ode for St. Cecilia’s Day, 1692), ed. Michael Tippett and Walter Bergmann, London: Schott & Co., Ltd., 1955

[626] ‘ Dido and Aeneas ’ [Vocal score, ed. Edward J. Dent], London: O.U.P., 1925

[626] ‘ Dido and Aeneas ’ [Vocal score, ed. Margaret Laurie and Thurston Dart], London: Novello & Co., Ltd., 1961

[731] ‘ Fantasia: Three Parts Upon a Ground ’, ed. Denis Stevens and Thurston Dart, London: Hinrichsen Editions, 1953

[732–43, ‘ Fantazias and In Nomines ’, ed. Thurston Dart, London: Novello & 745-47] Co., Ltd., 1959

[780] ' Trio-sonata for Violin, Bass-viol and Continuo ', edited and reconstructed by Thurston Dart, London: Novello & Co., Ltd., 1959

[780] ' Sonata in G Minor for Solo Violin ', ed. Howard Ferguson, London: Hinrichsen Editions, 1958

[807] ' Sonata No. VI in G Minor', ed. Robert Donington and Walter Emery, London: Novello & Co., Ltd., 1959

[810] ' Sonata No. IX in F Major (" The Golden Sonata ") ', ed. Robert Donington and Walter Emery, London: Novello & Co., Ltd., 1959 [published together with the foregoing]

[860] ' March and Canzona for the Funeral of Queen Mary, 1695 ', ed. Thurston Dart, London: O.U.P., 1958

The following is a list of books and documents which are often referred to in commentaries, but not included under the heading ' LITERATURE ' throughout the catalogue, since they make no specific reference to Purcell's music. References to these in the commentaries have been made by author's name alone:

Akerman, J. Y., ed., *Money Received and Paid for Secret Services of Charles II and James II from 30th March, 1679, to 25th Dec. 1688*, London: printed for the Camden Society, 1851

Burnet, Gilbert, *Bishop Burnet's History of His Own Time*, Oxford: Clarendon Press, 1823

Cibber, Colley, *An Apology for the Life of Mr. Colley Cibber, Comedian*, 2nd ed., London: printed by John Watts for the Author, 1740

Day, C. L., and Murrie, E. B., *English Song Books 1651–1702*, London: Bibl. Soc., 1940

Downes, John, *Roscius Anglicanus*, ed. Montague Summers, London: The Fortune Press (Facsimile of the original edition of 1708), n.d.

Evelyn, John, *John Evelyn's Diary*, ed. William Bray, London: Dent, 1920

Genest, John, *Some Account of the English Stage*, Bath: printed by H. E. Carrington, sold by Thomas Rodd, London, 1832

Heywood, E., *Watermarks*, Hilversum: The Paper Publications Society, 1950

Lafontaine, Henry Cart de, *The King's Musick*, London: Novello, 1909

Langbaine, Gerald, *The Lives and Characters of English Dramatick Poets*, London: printed for Tho. Leigh & William Turner, 1699

Luttrell, Narcissus, *A Brief Relation of State Affairs from September 1678 to April 1714*, Oxford, 1857

Nicoll, Allardyce, *A History of Restoration Drama*, 2nd ed., Cambridge University Press, 1928

Pepys, Samuel, *Pepys Diary*, ed. Lord Braybrooke, London: Newnes, 1825

Rimbault, E. F., *The Old Cheque-Book of the Chapel Royal*, London, 1872

Summers, Montague, *The Playhouse of Pepys*, London: Kegan Paul, Trench, Trubner & Co., 1935

In each section of the main body of the catalogue, I have entered cross-references to titles in corresponding categories of Appendices I and II. I have entered cross-references also where similarity of first lines, or other considerations might give rise to confusion as to the proper category for a work. Since there is a first-line index, however, I have kept these to a minimum to avoid redundancy. In listing original and 'transcribed' keyboard works separately (the latter with the prefix 'T') I have also entered cross-references to the transcriptions in the list of original compositions.

Appendix I lists works which can be attributed to Purcell only with considerable doubt, because of stylistic incongruities, or lack of reliable evidence of authenticity. The numbers for these are prefixed with the symbol 'D'. Future research may qualify some of these for inclusion in the main catalogue, or relegate others to Appendix II, which lists works spuriously ascribed to Purcell (prefixed 'S'), and gives the name of their actual composers.

Appendix III lists *MSS* dating from before about 1765, at which time printed anthem collections began to supplant *MS* part-books in cathedrals and churches. The Japanese collection (concerning which Mr. Hugh McLean has generously provided me with information) and those in Lichfield and in the *Deutsche Staatsbibliothek* in Marburg, Germany, are the only collections which I have not examined for myself. *MS* 370 turned up too late for inclusion in numerical sequence. Although I circularized all the institutions listed in the *British Union Catalogue of Early Music*, and afterwards visited many of those which had reported no pertinent holdings on first inquiry, I have no doubt that other *MSS* could have been located if time and financial means available to me had permitted a broader search. I have ignored late transcripts like that of the *Te Deum and Jubilate* in the Guernsey Public Library, and those in the Canterbury Cathedral Archives, to name only two by way of example.

These *MSS* are listed according to place names, which are arranged alphabetically. These are sub-divided under the names of individuals or institutions holding collections, which again are arranged alphabetically, as in the *British Union Catalogue*. Within each of these sub-divisions, *MSS* are listed in the numerical order indicated by their call-number or of press-mark, without regard to literal prefix. MS No. 370 (Bri. Mus. MS Eg. 3767) appears out of numerical order, however, since it was acquired only after this catalogue was in galley proofs. (The abbreviations following the running numbers in the left-hand column are included for reference in my forthcoming biography, and are not referred to elsewhere in the '*MSS Sections*' which follow most of the entries in the main body of the catalogue.)

In the heading for each *MS* I have given the type of music copy involved (*i.e.* score, part-book, organ book, etc.), the date or approximate date of copying, where ascertainable, and the book-plate, name or inscription of important early owners. Actual dates or inscriptions from the *MSS* themselves are shown in quotation marks. Works by Purcell which each *MS* contains, or doubtful or spurious ascriptions, are listed for each entry by the work-numbers appearing in the main body of the catalogue. Numbers in bold-face type represent autograph copies; those prefixed by the symbol 'T', transcriptions; by 'M', mock-songs (see p. xix for an explanation of this term); by 'D', doubtful ascriptions, and by 'S', spurious ascriptions. Sections from larger works are represented by numbers given in the catalogue proper, these numbers being separated from the work numbers with which they appear by an oblique stroke, as for example in *MS* 456, where two selections from *Don Quixote* are represented by the symbol 578/1, 3.

Appendix IV is a list of publications printed before 1850, selective for the last century, but containing editions printed before 1750, save for collections of catches and glees, better dealt with by someone whose bibliographical skill is greater than mine. The list is also incomplete in that I have not attempted to catalogue all extant broadsheets and single-sheet editions of Purcell's works, although a few bound collections of these are listed (see, for instance, Edition 1704a). I have attempted to list one representative single-sheet edition for each work so edited, but I shall not be surprised to discover omissions. In fact, until a trained bibliographer sorts out this bibliographical tangle, a definitive list of Purcell's single-sheet editions will scarcely be practicable.

I have made no attempt to furnish complete titles, though I have tried in every case to provide sufficient data for certain identification. Titles enclosed in square brackets represent editions no longer extant, or editions which were registered, but never published. As in the list of *MSS*, Purcell's works appearing in these editions are represented by their catalogue numbers. At the end of Appendix IV are listed undated editions, and after these, several editions which came to my attention too late for inclusion in this edition.

Appendix V is a tentative chronology incorporating evidence afforded by the position of various works in the autographs. In my forthcoming biographical study, stylistic evidence will be adduced in an attempt further to refine this chronology, which now rests almost entirely (and, I feel, unsatisfactorily) upon so-called 'external evidence'.

Appendix VI, a list of works by other composers copied out by Purcell, is self-explanatory.

Index I lists first lines, titles and sub-titles in the conventional manner. Where several works fall into the same category (such as the Welcome Songs and Birthday Odes), these are listed in chronological order, or in the order in which they were first published. If neither of these rules applies, works are listed by their keys, in alphabetical order. Where a title is also the first line of the second or third section of a work, the section number is appended in square brackets, as follows:

Blessed are they that fear   5/[2]

Index II, pertaining to instrumental forms and titles, is also largely self-explanatory. However, I should point out that Purcell himself was by no means consistent in using the terms ' Overture ', ' Sonata ' and ' Symphony '. The pieces to which he attached these titles cannot always be distinguished from one another either as to style or form. For instance, in *The Fairy Queen*, Purcell himself labelled the eighteenth section as an ' Overture ' but saw it through the press in the first edition as a ' Symphony '. Later in the same ' opera ', the ' Sonata while the Sun rises ' (as it is called in the first edition) appears as a ' Symphony ' in the partial autograph. Therefore these three terms (' Overture ', ' Sonata ' and ' Symphony ') which were not mutually exclusive in Purcell's day, are more or less interchangeable in this catalogue.

That is to say, the actual music appearing under the heading ' Overture ' in the theatrical compositions differs in name only from the ' Symphonies ' for Anthems and Odes, and in only name and performing medium from many of the ' Sonatas '. Therefore these terms have been entered in the index neither as hard-and-fast formal labels nor as mutually exclusive stylistic designations. In fact, their component sections have been listed indiscriminately as belonging to either ' Overture ', ' Sonata ' or ' Symphony ' (see, for instance, under ' Adagio '). Names of forms or formal components not given in an early source are enclosed in square brackets. Modified names are entered under the first substantive, with a cross-reference to the complete title. (See, for instance, ' Slow Air ' and ' Poco Largo ' which appear under main entries for ' Air ' and ' Largo ' respectively.) The same method applies to sub-titles or sobriquets, such as ' Bell-Barr ', for which the main entry is ' Almand '. Variant spellings of forms and titles have been recorded in the catalogue as they appear in various sources with no attempt to render them consistent. In Index II, however, I have listed these under their English versions, retaining authentic Purcellian orthography insofar as such is possible. (See, for instance, ' Borry ', for ' Borrée ', and ' Almand ' for ' Allemande ' and so forth.)

Index III which lists authors, translators, paraphrasers and Biblical and other literary sources is largely self-explanatory.

Index IV is a general index to the persons, places and subjects mentioned in the commentaries, where these cannot be included in any of the foregoing indices.

ANTHEMS

1. Awake, put on thy strength

(XIV, 41) *ca.* 1683; *Isaiah* 51: 9–11

Verse: *aab*   2 *Vns, Va, Bc*   Chorus: missing

(1) Symphony: *Str*
   (a) [Grave]   (b) [Canzona]   (2) Awake, put on thy
                                                        strength: *b*

C: LK 20.b.8   *Vers solo*

                                                   A-wake, a-wake, put on thy strength

(3) Ritornello: *Str*   (4) Therefore the redeem'd: *aab*   (5) = 1b

                          Vers:
                          3 There-fore the re-deem'd

(6) Alleluia: *aab*   (7) Ritornello: *Str*   (8) Section indicated 'Chorus'.
                                                      Neither music nor number
                                                      of parts is given.

3 Al - le - lu - ia   *Ritor*

MSS: 453 (inc; partly autograph)

EDITIONS: XIV, 41

COMMENTARY: The manuscript source ends with the seventh section. No indication is given as to
the overall length of the work, but it is probable that a final alleluia for chorus on the same
ground as that underlying the seventh section would end the work:

Awake up my glory (See D1)

2. Behold, I bring you glad tidings

(XXVIII, 1) not later than 1687; *Luke* 2: 10-11, 14

Verse: *atb*   2 *Vns, Va, Bc*   Chorus: *SATB*

(1) Symphony: *Str*   (2a) Behold, I bring you:
   (a) [Grave]   (b) [Canzona]   *atb*

(2b) Glad tidings: *atb,*   (2c) Ritornello: *Str*   (2d) Glory to God: *aatb, SATB*
   SATB, Str

(3a) And on earth peace: (3b) Ritornello: *Str*   (3c) = 2d   (3d) = 3a   (3e) = 2d
   atb

(3f) Ritornello: *Str*   (4) Alleluia: *atb*   (5) = 2d: *SATB*

MSS: 1, 15, 48, 64a, 65, 81, 82, 84, 85, 86, 121, 158, 160, 163ace, 164adg, 166gh, 180, 186, 187, 194a to
   c, e to g, 195, 196, 197, 200b, 203, 245ace, 248, 255, 273, 301 (inc), 303, 326, 369, 403, 410, 430a to f,
   500a to e, 501, 505a to f, 506, 509acd, 510, 511, 513, 589, 694, 735, 743, 746a, 753, 755, 771, 803,
   808acdfgh, 810a, 813, 815, 818, 822, 827, 828, 829, 830, 831, 833, 836, 848b, 850adeh, 855

EDITIONS: XXVIII, 1, 1724d ?1769b, 1773, 1828[-44]

COMMENTARY: The text is the second lesson for Matins, Christmas Day.

LITERATURE: Watkins Shaw, 'A Contemporary Source of English Music of the Purcellian Period,'
   Acta Musicologica, vol. XXXI, 1, 1959, pp. 38-44.

3. Behold, now praise the Lord

(XIIIA, 49) *ca.* 1680; *Psalm* 134: 1–3 with *Doxology*

Verse: *atb*　　　　　　　　　2 *Vns, Va, Bc*　　　　　　　Chorus: *SATB*

(1) Symphony: *Str*　　　　　　　　　　　　　　　　(2) Behold, now praise: *atb*
  (a) [Grave]　　　　　　　(b) [Canzona]

(3) Ritornello: *Str*　　　　(4) Lift up your hands: *atb*　　　(5) Ritornello: *Str*

(6) Glory be to the Father: *atb, Str, SATB*

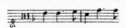

MSS: **326,** 410, 833

EDITIONS: XIIIA, 49,　1828[–44]

COMMENTARY: This anthem appears in Purcell's autograph in the second of the 'Flackton MSS' (British Museum MS Add. 30932, f.121v). The first three staves are written on an inserted slip under which is copied Michael Wise's catch 'When Judith laid Holofernes to bed'. On the back of this slip are written twenty-two irregular bars, which constitute a fragment of the second flute (i.e. recorder) part for the Fantasia 'Three Parts upon a Ground' (see No. **731**), which appears also in the British Museum MS Royal Music 20.h.9, in a version for three violins, marked 'play'd 2 notes higher for flutes'.

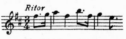

This melody (erroneously given a third lower in the Purcell Society Edition, vol. XIIIA) could be played in its violin key (D major) without transposition. The player had only to alter the clef and reckon the necessary changes for key signature and accidentals.

As for the anthem itself, A. Hughes-Hughes ('Henry Purcell's Handwriting', *Musical Times*, Feb. 1896, p. 81) and, after him, G. E. P. Arkwright ('Purcell's Church Music', *Musical Antiquary* I, July 1910, p. 242) have dated it comparatively early in Purcell's career. Their main arguments are based upon calligraphic evidence, particularly upon the appearance of the backward 'e' (ɘ) which Purcell used only in his early years.

4. Be merciful unto me

(XXVIII, 28) not later than 1687; *Psalm 56: 1-7, 10-11*

Verse: *atb*   *Bc*   Chorus: *SATB*

(1) Be merciful unto me: *atb*   (2) Mine enemies are daily: *b*

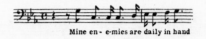

(3a) I will praise: *atb*   (3b) the same: *SATB*   (4) They daily mistake: *t*

   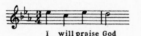   

(5) They hold all together: *atb*   (6) In God's word: *atb*   (7) Alleluia: *SATB*

MSS: 15, 64a, 70, 77, 78, 80, 81, 84, 85, 86, 121, 159, 160, 162, 163acde, 164ab, 166adeghi, 180, 184, 192, 195, 196, 202, 203, 220, 245bce, 248, 272, 301, 303, 306, 325, 403, 430a to f, 478e, 500abde, 501, 505b to f, 506, 509abcd, 511, 514, 517, 589, 603, 647a to e, 666, 694, 746ac, 751, 753, 755, 808a, 809cd, 810a, 811gh, 813, 815, 818, 820, 821, 822, 823, 825, 826, 832, 836, 855

EDITIONS: XXVIII, 28, 1768, ?1790b, 1828[-44]; Section 6: Undated publications nos. 1 and 2.

COMMENTARY: Although it appears in several fairly early MSS (e.g. Christ Church Library, Oxford, MSS 1220-4, Royal College of Music, London, MS 1068, and British Museum MS Add. 30931) no autograph copy of this anthem is known. Nor can any of these copies be dated precisely. G. E. P. Arkwright ('Purcell's Church Music', *Musical Antiquary* I, July 1910, p. 245) judged it to be a fairly late work. However, Harold Watkins Shaw has advanced convincing arguments for a date of composition not later than 1687 in his article in *Acta Musicologica* listed below.

LITERATURE: C. Burney, *A General History of Music*, London: Foulis & Co. Ltd., 1935, II, 384; Watkins Shaw, 'A Contemporary Source of English Music of the Purcellian Period,' *Acta Musicologica*, vol. XXXI, 1, 1959, pp. 38-44.

5. Blessed are they that fear the Lord

(XXVIII. 42) before January 29th, 1688; *Psalm 128: 1-3, 5, 6, 4*

Verse: *ssab*   *2 Vns, Va, Bc*   Chorus: *SATB*

(1) Symphony: *Str*

(a) [Grave]

(b) [Canzona]

(2) Blessed are they: *ssab*

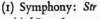

C: L Add 30931

Blessed, blessed are they

Be: [

(3) Ritornello: *Str*

(4a) For thou shalt eat the labour: *b*

For thou shalt eat the la - bour

(4b) O well is Thee: *ssab*

(5a) The Lord thy God: (5b)=4b *b, Str*

(6) Yea, thou shalt see: *a*

O well is Thee,   O

The Lord thy God

Yea, thou shalt see

(7a) O well is Thee: *ssab*

(7b) Lo, thus shall the man: *ssab*

(7c) Ritornello: *Str*

C   O well is Thee,   O well is Thee

Lo thus, thus, thus shall the man

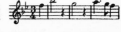

(7d) = 7b: *ssab*

(8) Alleluia: *ssab*

(9) Alleluia: *SATB, Str*

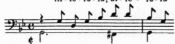
Al - le - lu - ia, al - le - lu - ia

Cho:
Al - le - lu - ia, al - le - lu - ia

MSS: 183, 255, **325**, 457, 516, 759

EDITIONS: XXVIII, 42,   1790a, ?1790b, 1828[-44]

COMMENTARY: The following note appears above the copy of this anthem in the Gostling part-books in York Minster Library: 'Composed for the Thanksgiving appoint'd to be observed in London and 12 miles around and upon the 29th over England following for the Queen's [Queen Mary of Modena] being with child.' In the *Book of Common Prayer*, this Psalm, or *Deus Misereatur* is given to be read or sung as part of the service for Matrimony.

6. Blessed be the Lord, my strength

(XXVIII, 60) before 1683; *Psalm* 144: 1-8

Verse: *atb*   *Bc*   Chorus: *SATB*

(1) Blessed be the Lord, my strength: *b*

(2a) Lord, what is man?: *atb*   (2b) Man is like a thing: *atb*

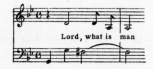

(3) His time passeth away: (4) Bow Thy heav'ns,   (5) Send down Thine hand: *SATB*
   SATB   O Lord: *atb*

MSS: 42, 304, 326, 353, 850bdfh

EDITIONS: XXVIII, 60, 1828[-44]

7. Blessed is he that considereth the poor

(XXVIII, 71) *ca.* 1688; *Psalm* 41: 1-3 with *Doxology*

Verse: *atb*   *Bc*   Chorus: *SATB*

(1) Blessed is he: *atb*   (2) The Lord preserve him: (3) The Lord comfort him:
                                               a   *atb*

(4) Make Thou all: *atb*   (5) Glory be to the Father: (6) Alleluia: *SATB*
    atb

Make Thou all his bed

Glo - ry be to the Father

Al - le - lu - ia, al - le - lu - ia

MSS: 69, 121, 131, 138, 164c, 167bd, 203, 245e, 255, 276, 430c (last chorus), 503, 516, 518, 590, 743, 746c, 752, 759, 773, 848d

EDITIONS: XXVIII, 71,   1703e, 1714b, 1726a, 1730c, 1765b, 1778, 1800b, 1828[-44]

COMMENTARY: As the Purcell Society editor has suggested, the final chorus to this anthem, the style of which is not characteristic of Purcell, may have been added in the eighteenth century.

8. Blessed is he whose unrighteousness is forgiv'n

(XIIIA, 71) *ca.* 1680-2; *Psalm* 32: 1-7, 10, 11

Verse: *ssattb*   Bc   Chorus: *SATB*

(1) Blessed is he whose unrighteousness is forgiv'n: *ssattb*

Bles - sed is   he whose un-right-teous-ness is for-giv'n,   And whose

C: CFM 88   Bles - sed is   he whose un -

(2a) For while I held: *b*   (2b) = 3:*b*   (3) I will acknowledge my sin:
                                                          SATB

For while I held my tongue,

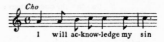

I will ac-know-ledge my sin

(4) I said, I will: *atb*   (5a) Thou art a place: *t*   (5b) = 6:*t*

I said, I will con-fess

Thou art a place to hide

(6) Thou shalt compass: *SATB*   (7) Great plagues remain: *ss*

Thou shalt com-pass me

Great, great plagues re-main

(8) Be glad, O ye righteous: *ssattb*   (9) Alleluia: *SATB*

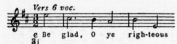

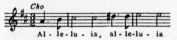

MSS: **41**, 42, 825, 827, 828, 829, 830, 831

EDITIONS: XIIIA, 71, 1828[–44]

9. Blessed is the man that feareth the Lord

(XXVIII, 83) *ca.* 1688; *Psalm* 112: 1–5, 9

Verse: *atb*   Bc   Chorus: *SATB*

(1) Symphony: *Bc*   (2) Blessed is the man: *atb*

(3) His seed shall be: *atb*   (4) Riches and plenteousness: *atb*

(5) Unto the Godly: *atb* (6a) Alleluia: *atb* (6b) the same: *SATB*

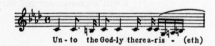

MSS: 1, 64a, 163b to e, 164aeghi, 167cf, 183, 184, 193, 245a to e, 248, 255, 301 (organ intro. somewhat altered), 334, 500e, 503, 505bcefg, 506, 509abcd, 510, 511, 515, 518, 737, 743 (inc), 752, 753,
759, 813, 815, 818, 820, 821, 822, 823, 825, 826, 832, 836, 848ef, 855
Section 6: 201

EDITIONS: XXVIII, 83, 1750a, 1828[–44]

COMMENTARY: Misunderstanding Tudway's remarks on the anthem sung at Queen Mary's funeral,
Vincent Novello described this work as a 'Funeral Anthem'—a most unlikely designation in
view of the unsuitability of the text for such an occasion. According to the W. K. Gostling MS
(now unavailable) this anthem was written for a Founder's Day celebration at Charterhouse.
The event took place on December 12 (the day on which this celebration was traditionally held
unless the 12th fell on Sunday) probably in the year 1688. The ceremony consisted, then as now
(as I am advised by Mr. John Wilson, Music master of the present-day Charterhouse at Godalming,

Surrey) of a 'Solemn Service' with a sermon given in the chapel, followed by a 'Feast' in some neighbouring hall. In Purcell's time the organist was Nicholas Love, the Masters were William Erskine and the Reverend Thomas Burnet, and the preacher was the Reverend John Patrick. The latter also was the author of several of the versified texts of Psalms to which Purcell composed music. (See Nos. 133, 136, 137, 139, *etc.*)

Evidence from several MSS suggests that Purcell wrote an earlier version which differed from that represented above mainly in that it required only two solo voices (tenor and bass) and no four-part chorus. According to one of Sir Frederick Bridge's Gresham lectures as recorded in *Musical News* for May 23, 1903 (p. 486), the William Kennedy Gostling MS (see Appendix III, No. 255) gives the following remark on this anthem:

> ' " Blessed is the man that feareth the Lord " Purcell. Anthem for the Charterhouse sung upon the Founder's Day by Mr. Barincloe and Mr. Bowman. This is a duet, but an extra part for the tenor is inserted into the book.'

Without examining the MS itself, it is impossible to say how much of this information was taken directly from it. Probably, though, Bridge was quoting verbatim all but the last sentence, which was his own. Evidence from other sources tends to substantiate the hypothesis that there was an earlier, simpler version. Thus Tenbury MSS 1172–82 lack the Tenor part; British Museum MS Harl. 7340, (f. 260) lacks the chorus, as does Tenbury MS 1029 (p. 279) and Worcester MS A.3.10 (p. 121). The copy in MS M7319745 in the library of the Department of Music, University of California at Berkeley, is an arrangement for soprano and bass, also lacking the four-part Alleluia chorus.

An additional *Alleluia* for *SATB* is given in the Purcell Society edition, vol. XXVIII, 95:

10. Blow up the trumpet in Sion

(XXVIII, 96) *ca.* 1681; *Joel* 2: 15–17

Verse: *(cantoris) saatb*	*Bc*	Chorus: *(cantoris) SAATB*
(decani) ssatb		*(decani) SSATB*

(1) Blow up the trumpet: *(can.) sa*
(dec.) ssatb

(2) Sanctify a fast: *(can.) sa*
(dec.) ssatb

(3) = 1:
(can.) SAATB
(dec.) SSATB

(4) Assemble the elders: *(can.) sa*
(dec.) ssatb

(5a) Let them weep: *(can.) sa*
(dec.) ssatb

(5b) And let them say: *(can.) sa*
(dec.) ssatb

(5c) =6: *(can.) sa*
(dec.) ssatb

(6) Spare Thy people:
SSAATTBB

(7) Wherefore should they: (8) the same:
(can.) sa   *SSAATTBB*
(dec.) ssatb

Spare Thy peo-ple,   Spare Thy peo-ple

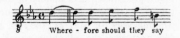

Where - fore should they say

MSS: 481, 850a to h

EDITIONS: XXVIII, 96

COMMENTARY: In York MSS M.1/1–8.S, this anthem is copied into the part-books under the following headings: (1) Medius cantoris (2) Medius decani (3) Medius decani (4) Contratenor cantoris (5) Tenor cantoris (6) Contratenor decani (7) Tenor decani (8) Tenor cantoris (9) Bassus cantoris (10) Bassus decani. However, the fifth of these is written in alto clef with the annotation: 'The contratenor and tenor for this anthem are here to sing together.' This part is actually in alto range throughout, and has been so indicated in the scheme of abbreviations for modern choral nomenclature shown with the above incipits. As may be seen here, Purcell did not write antiphonally for *cantoris* and *decani* groupings as separate and contrasting choirs, but rather intermixed voices from each in various ensembles, even though the verse sections are divided nominally between cantoris soprano and alto on the one hand, and decani soprano, soprano, alto, tenor, and bass on the other.

11. Bow down Thine ear, O Lord

(XIII, 103) *ca.* 1680–2; *Psalm* 86: 1, 3–5, 8, 10–12

Verse: *satb*   *Bc*   Chorus: *SATB*

(1a) Prelude   (1b) Bow down Thine ear: *satb*

Bow   down Thine ear, O   Lord, and hear me

Vers / Organ / Bow

C: CFM 88

(2) Be merciful unto me: *t*   (3a) For Thou, Lord: *atb*   (3b) the same: *SATB*]

Be mer-ci-ful un-to me

For Thou,___ Lord, art good

For Thou, Lord art good

(4) Among the gods: *b*   (5) Teach me Thy way: (6) And I will thank Thee:
                                        satb   *SATB*

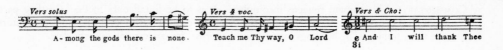

(7) =6: *SATB*

MSS: **41,** 42, 825, 827, 828, 829, 830, 831

EDITIONS: XIII, 103,   1828[–44]

COMMENTARY: Neither of the two earliest sources (Cambridge, Fitzwilliam Museum MSS 88 and 117)
shows whether the opening section of this anthem should be sung by 'chorus' or 'verse'.
The Purcell Society editor, following Vincent Novello's precedent, has chosen to indicate the
latter procedure.

By the waters of Babylon (See S1)

Christ is risen (See S2)

Come, honest Sexton (See S3)

12. Give sentence with me, O God

(XXXII, 117) *ca.* 1687? *Psalm* 48: 1–3, 5

Verse: *sab*   Bc   Chorus: ? (missing in MS)

(1a) Give sentence with me: *sab*   (1b) And why go I so   (2) Ritornello
                                              heavily: *b*   (missing)

   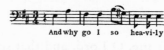

(3a) **Why art thou:** *b*   [(3b) O put thy trust: *sb*

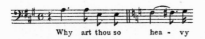   

(4) Alleluia: *SA*[*T?*]*B*

MS: 850a

EDITION: XXXII, 117

COMMENTARY: This anthem remains incomplete. It is to be found only in the 'Gostling part-books' at York Minster, where only the Soprano cantoris, Alto cantoris and Bass cantoris are to be found. The headings 'verse' and 'chorus' are conjectural, as is the date.

Glory be to God on high (See D2)

God sheweth me His goodness (See S4)

Great is the Lord, Hymn (See S5)

13A. Hear me, O Lord, and that soon

(XIIIA, 87) *ca.* 1680–2; *Psalm* 143: 7

Verse: *satb*   *Bc*   Chorus: *SATB*

(1) Hear me, O Lord: *satb*

MSS: 42, **324** (inc), 389, 758

EDITION: XIIIA, 87

COMMENTARY: In the autograph (British Museum MS Add. 30930, f.23v) the work is entitled a 'Vers'. This title implies that it may have been intended as part of a full-scale anthem with alternate verses and choruses, not merely an optional section for No. 13B.

13B. Hear me, O Lord, and that soon

(XIIIA, 90) *ca.* 1680–2; *Psalm* 143: 7–11

Verse: *satb*   *Bc*   Chorus: *[S]SATB*

(1) Hear me, O Lord: *satb*

(2a) O let me hear: *sb*   (2b) Show Thou me: *sb*   (3) Deliver me: *satb*

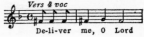

(4) =3: *SATB*   (5) Teach me to do: *at*   (6) Quicken me, O Lord: *satb*

(7) Glory be to the Father: *SSATB*

MSS: **41**, 303

EDITION: XIIIA, 90, 1828[–44]

COMMENTARY: This version is similar to the foregoing until about the middle of the first section. From there on it is quite different, according to the edition published by Vincent Novello, who edited it from a manuscript (now missing) belonging to 'Mr. Richard Guise, Master of the Choristers at Westminster'.

14. Hear my pray'r, O God

(XXVIII, 125) before 1683; *Psalm 55*: 1–2, 4–8, 16–17

Verse: *atb*   Bc   Chorus: *SATB*

(1) Hear my pray'r: *atb*   (2) My heart is disquieted: *atb*

(3a) And I said: *t*   (3b) Lo, then would I get me away: *atb*

(4) I would make haste: *atb*   (5) I will call upon God: *SATB*

I would make haste_____ to es-cape

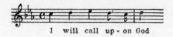

I will call up - on God

MSS: 158, 166gi, 304 (inc), 818, 819, 821, 822

EDITIONS: XXVIII, 125

15. Hear my prayer, O Lord

(XXVIII, 135) *ca.* 1680–2; *Psalm* 102: 1–   Incomplete

Full: *SSAATTBB*   *Bc*

(1) Hear my prayer, O Lord

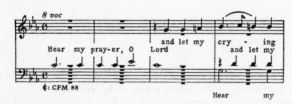

MSS: 41 (inc), 166gh, 820

EDITIONS: XXVIII, 135, 1828[–44]

COMMENTARY: In the autograph copy Purcell did not close off this anthem with the customary complete double bar and flourishes. Since there are a number of blank pages following, it seems likely that this is but a fragment of a work he did not finish composing or copying. In the *Book of Common Prayer* this is given as one of the Funeral sentences.

LITERATURE: E. H. Fellowes, *English Cathedral Music*, London: Methuen, 1941.

Hosanna to the Prince of light, Hymn (See S6)

How pleasant is Thy dwelling place, Hymn (See S7)

I am the resurrection (See S8)

If the Lord himself (See No. N66)

I heard a voice (See S9)

16. In Thee, O Lord, do I put my trust

(XIV, 53) *ca.* 1683; *Psalm* 71: 1, 2, 5, 6, 20, 22, 23

Verse: *atb*   2 *Vns, Va, Bc*   Chorus: *SATB*

(1a) Symphony: *Str*

3: O Mus. C26

(1b) In Thee, O Lord: *atb*

In Thee, O Lord, do I put my trust
In Thee

(1c) Ritornello: *Str*

(1d) For Thou, O Lord God: *at*

(2) Through Thee: *atb*

For Thou, O Lord God

Through Thee have I been hold (en)

(3) Symphony: *Str*

(4a) O what great troubles: *b, 2 Vns*

(4b) Ritornello: *Str*

 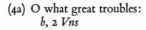  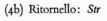 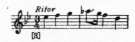

O what great trou-bles

(5a) Therefore will I: *atb, 2 Vns*

(5b) Ritornello: *Str*

(6a) My lips shall be: *a*

  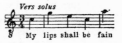

Verse 5 parts (Violins)

There-fore will I praise Thee

My lips shall be fain

(6b) Ritornello: *Str*

(7a) Alleluia: *atb*

Al - le - lu - ia, al - le - lu - ia

(7b) Ritornello: *Str*

(7c) Alleluia: *SATB, Str*

 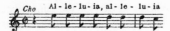

Al - le - lu- ia, al - le - lu - ia

MSS: 303, 386, 410, **453, 581**, 833

EDITIONS: XIV, 53, 1828[-44]

COMMENTARY: There are two autograph sources for this anthem. The earlier (Oxford, Bodleian MS Mus. C 26, f.10) may have been a corrected version from which the latter (British Museum

Royal Music MS 20.h.8, f.17v) was copied. The ground bass for the opening symphony is the same as that for ' O Solitude, my sweetest choice ' (See No. **406**). For the last chorus, only one violin part is written out in the autographs. Presumably, second violin and viola parts doubled the treble and counter-tenor voices. This Psalm is given to be read in the ' Form for the Visitation of the Sick ' in the *Book of Common Prayer*.

17A. In the midst of life

(XIIIA, 1) before 1682; First Version; *The Book of Common Prayer*, 1660

Full: *SATB*, with Verse: *satb*

(1) In the midst of life: *SATB*   (2) Yet, O Lord: *satb* [*SATB*]

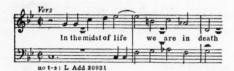 

MSS: 503

EDITIONS: XIIIA, 1

COMMENTARY: This sentence from the Burial Service (apparently the first version which Purcell set) is to be found by itself in the British Museum MS Add. 30931. In the autograph score in the Fitzwilliam Museum, Cambridge, MS 88, however, another setting of this sentence follows *Man that is born* (see No. **27**) with no other indication than the section-heading ' Verse '. It is in turn followed without interruption by the anthem *Remember not, Lord, our offenses* (see No. **50**). Two notes of sufficient interest to be included here are to be found in the British Museum autograph MS Add. 30931 on f.81v:

    (a) ' The following verses of Mr. Henry Purcell's composition seem to have been alter'd, and in some instances not for the better. The first verse viz " Man that is born of a woman " is here wanting to complete the anthem, for as such it was evidently composed and not intended as a funeral service. I have the whole perfect in a large collection of anthems transcrib'd in the year 1683 at Windsor. Phil Hayes August 1784.'

    (b) ' I have since the doctor's remarks above, found the first verse—viz " Man that is born of a woman " &c—in Mr. Gostling's hand-writing bound at the end of a common prayer-book with other anthems &c, number 265 cat. 1785 which said: number 265 is since sold to Dr. Arnold. W.F.' [W. Flackton[. This copy of the prayer-book has not yet come to light.

Vincent Novello suggests that Purcell composed these sentences from the Burial Service to complete Raylton's service for the same office. He based his opinion upon a note in the MS from which he edited Raylton's sentences. (See EDITION 1828[–44], Appendix 47.)

17B. In the midst of life

(XXVIII, 215) before 1682; Second Version; See **Man that is born of a woman,** No. **27**, Sections 2 to 4

MSS: **41**, 183

COMMENTARY: Alterations which differentiate this version from the foregoing were made by Purcell himself, and are shown in the autograph score-book, Cambridge, Fitzwilliam Museum MS 88, f.102.

18. It is a good thing to give thanks

(XIV, 1) *ca.* 1682; *Psalm* 92: 1–6

Verse: *atb*   2 *Vns, Va, Bc*   Chorus: *SATB*

(1) Symphony: *Str*   (2a) It is a good thing: *atb*

(a) [Grave]   (b) [Canzona]

(2b) Ritornello: *Str*   (3a) To tell of Thy loving kindness: *atb*   (3b) Ritornello: *Str*

(4) For Thou, Lord: *atb*   (5)=1b   (6) O Lord, how glorious: *b*

(7)=4   (8a) Alleluia: *atb*   (8b) Ritornello: *Str*

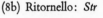

(9)=2a   (10)=2b   (11) Alleluia: *SATB*

MSS: 81, 84, 85, 86, 183, 304, 430bdf, **453,** 516, 759, 813, 818, 820, 822, 833, 868

EDITIONS: XIV, 1, 1828[–44]

17

2B

19. I was glad when they said unto me

(XIV, 97) *ca.* 1683–4; *Psalm* 122: 1–8

Verse: *atb* 2 Vns, Va, Bc Chorus: *SATB*

(1) Symphony: *Str*
(a) [Grave] (b) [Canzona] (2a) I was glad: *a*

  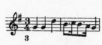 

(2b) Ritornello: *Str* (3a) Jerusalem is built: *atb* (3b) Ritornello: *Str*

  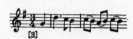

(3c) For there is the seat: *t* (4) [Symphony]: *Str* (5) O pray for the peace: *atb*

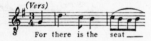 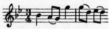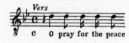

(6) Peace be within: *SATB* (7) For my brethren: *atb* (8)=6

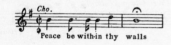 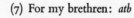

MSS: 2, **13**, 42, 64ab, 66, 77, 78, 81, 83, 84, 86, 98, 118, 119, 121, 131, 140 (in F major), 150, 151, 153, 160, 162, 163cde, 164ad, 166adeghi, 180, 187, 194a to dfg, 195, 196, 197, 201, 202, 203, 220, 245acde, 246, 248, 275, 276, 300, 329, 370, 403, 410, 430a to f, **453**, 478bde, 500abd, 503, 505a to f, 506, 509abcd, 510, 511, 513, 517, 518, 589, 603, 647a to e, 648, 653, 694, 735, 745, 752, 753, 755, 762, 771, 773, 795abc, 796b, 802, 809cd, 810a, 811gh, 813, 815, 818, 820, 821, 822, 826, 833, 834, 835, 837, 850bceg (index only) h, 855, 858.

EDITIONS: XIV, 97,   1703e, 1714b, 1724d, 1726a, 1730c, 1770a, 1785a, ?1790b, 1800b, 1828[–44]

COMMENTARY: This was the first of nine anthems sung during the ceremonies attending King James II's coronation. Francis Sandford, in *The History of the Coronation of James II and Queen Mary* (London: 1687), described the part of the ceremony in which this anthem figured as follows:
' By this time [i.e. after the peers and peeresses were seated] the King and Queen being entered the church were received by the Dean and Prebendaries, who with the choir of Westminster, proceeding a little before their majesties, sung the full [*sic*] anthem following.'

Sandford added, in a marginal note: 'composed by Mr. Hen. Purcell, a Gentleman of the *Chapel-Royal*, and *Organist* of St. Margarets Westminster.' There is no other mention of Purcell's appointment at St. Margaret's. The inclusion of this anthem in the so-called 'Blow MS' (Cambridge, Fitzwilliam Museum MS 117) has given rise to the theory that Purcell must have written it at least two years before this coronation, as the manuscript is dated 1683. However, this does not necessarily follow. The anthem may have been copied, or inserted into Blow's volume after he had dated it. Its position in the autograph, Royal Music MS 20.h.8, suggests that it was copied into fair score about 1683–4.

LITERATURE: Watkins Shaw, 'A Contemporary Source of English Music of the Purcellian Period,' *Acta Musicologica*, vol. XXXI, 1, 1959, pp. 38–44.

20. I will give thanks unto Thee, O Lord

(XVII, 47) *ca.* 1685; *Psalm* 138: 1–8

Verse: *ssatb*   2 *Vns, Va, Bc*   Chorus: *SATB & SSATB*

(1) Symphony: *Str*   (2a) I will give thanks: *ssatb*
  (a) [Grave]   (b) [Canzona]

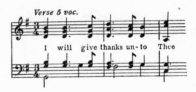

(2b) Ritornello: *Str*   (3) I will worship: *s*

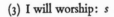

(4) When I called: *ssatb*   (5) Ritornello: *Str*   (6)=2:   (8) All the kings: *atb*
                                                      SATB
                                                      (7)=1ab

(9) Ritornello: *Str*   (10) For though the Lord: *b*   (11) The Lord shall: *ssatb, Str, SSATB*

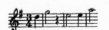

MSS: 369, **453** (inc)

EDITIONS: XVII, 47

COMMENTARY: The music for the second line in Section 8 is missing in the autograph, as in the Purcell Society Edition. It is to be found in British Museum MS Add. 47845, ending as follows:

LITERATURE: E. H. Fellowes, *English Cathedral Music*, London: Methuen, 1941.

21. I will give thanks unto the Lord

(XXVIII, 139) ?1685; *Psalm 111: 1-4, 6-9*

Verse: *tbb*   2 *Vn, Bc*   Chorus: *SATB*

(1a) Prelude: *Str*   (1b) I will give thanks: *tbb*

 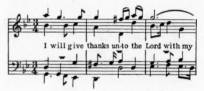

(2) Symphony

  (a)   (b)   (c)

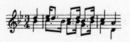 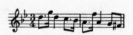

(3a) The works of the Lord: *b*   (3b) Ritornello: *Str*   (3c) His work is worthy: *tbb*

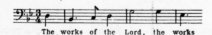 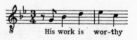

(4a) The merciful and gracious: *SATB*   (4b) the same: *ttb*   (4c)=4a   (5)=2

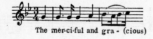

(6) He hath shewed:
   t, 2 Vn

(7) They stand fast:
   tbb, 2 Vn

(8) Holy and reverend:
   tbb [SATB, 2 Vn]

He hath shew-ed His peo-ple

They stand fast ___ for-ev-er

Ho - ly,   ho - ly and

MSS: 410, **453** (index only), 833

EDITIONS: XXVIII, 139, 1828[–44]

COMMENTARY: This anthem was probably written about the time of Charles II's last illness. Purcell's index of the anthems in his fair-copy autograph score (once called ' the Buckingham Palace autograph,' now British Museum Royal Music MS 20.h.8.) includes this work, and, ironically, *O Lord grant the King a long life,* neither of which he copied in.

I will love Thee, O Lord (See No. N67)

22. I will sing unto the Lord

(XXVIII, 165) before 1683; *Psalm* 104: 33–5

Full: *SSATB,* with Verse: *ssatb*

(1) I will sing: *SSATB*

(2) My joy shall be: *SSATB*

I will sing un-to the Lord as long as I live

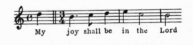
My   joy shall be   in the   Lord

(3a) As for sinners: (3b) the same:
   ssatb   *SSATB*

(4) And the ungodly:
   ssatb

(5) But praise ye the Lord
   SSATB

As   for sin-ners, they shall be

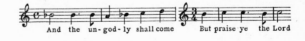
And the un-god-ly shall come   But praise ye   the Lord

MSS: 42, 77, 80, 156, 160, 162, 163acde, 164adf, 166aceghi, 167a, 304, 478bde, 500a to e, 503 505abdef (f is missing), 589, 647a to e, 650, 744, 850a to egh

EDITIONS: XXVIII, 165, 1828[–44]

COMMENTARY: No autograph copy of this anthem is known at present. The most authoritative source is in the so-called ' Blow' manuscript (Cambridge, Fitzwilliam Museum, MS 117), which, with some uncertainty, dates the work *ca.* 1683. It is, in fact, a ' full anthem,' written in an older style than that of the verse anthems, and may therefore have been written earlier.

23. Let God arise

(XXVIII, 173) after 1683; *Psalm* 68: 1–3, 7–8

Verse: *tt*   *Bc*   Chorus: *SATB*

(1) Let God arise: *tt*   (2) But let the righteous: *SATB*

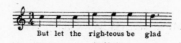

(3) O God, when Thou: *tt*   (4) Ev'n as Mount Sinai also: *SATB*

MSS: 42, 166ghi, 185, 304, 478bde, 850bdfh

EDITIONS: XXVIII, 173, 1828[–44]

COMMENTARY: According to G. E. P. Arkwright ('Purcell's Church Music', *Musical Antiquary*, July 1910, p. 245), Purcell may have written this anthem during his choir-boy days. This is scarcely probable, since the anthem is quite Italianate in style, which suggests a date after 1683 (when Purcell publicly announced his liking for Italian music in the preface to his first set of Trio-Sonatas). Furthermore, most of the anthem is given to very florid passage-work for two tenors, which is more consistent with the style of Purcell's later works than with anything from his early period.

LITERATURE: G. E. P. Arkwright, 'Purcell's Church Music,' *Musical Antiquary*, July 1910, p. 245.

24. Let mine eyes run down with tears

(XXIX, 1) ?1682; *Jeremiah* 14: 17–22

Verse: *ssatb*   *Bc*   Chorus: *SATB*

(1a) Let mine eyes: *ssatb*   (1b) If I go forth: *b[ssatb]*

(2) We acknowledge: *SATB*   (3) Do not abhor us: *ssatb*

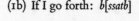

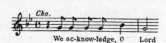

(4) Therefore will we wait: *ssatb* [*SSATB*]

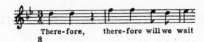

There-fore, there-fore will we wait

MSS: 478bde, 481, **581**

EDITIONS: XXIX, 1

COMMENTARY: In the Bodleian autograph, MS Mus. C.26. f.4, an earlier version of Section 3 begins as follows:

Do___not ab-hor___us for Thy

(Other variant passages are described in the Commentary to the Purcell Society Edition, vol. XXIX, p. 191.) At the end of this copy, Purcell has written: 'Ye Triple again for ye Chorus & so conclude.' There is no indication as to whether all five parts of the tripla (*i.e.* movement in triple meter) are to be sung by the chorus, or four only, as in other choral sections of the work.

25. Lord, how long wilt Thou be angry

(XXIX, 19) *ca.* 1680–2; *Psalm* 79: 5, 8, 9, 13

Full: *SSATB*, with Verse: *atb*   Bc

(1) Lord, how long: *SSATB*   (2) O remember not: *atb*

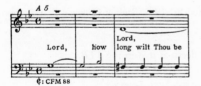

Lord, how Lord, long wilt Thou be

Ȼ: CFM 88

O ___ re-mem-ber not
Vers
O ___ re- mem-ber not our

(3) Help us, O God: *SSATB*   (4) So we that are: *SSATB*

Help us, O God, help us

So we, that are Thy peo - ple,

MSS: **41**, 47, 183, 300, 303, 503, 713, 739, 851, (and Royal College of Music, London, MS 518, too late for inclusion in the appendix)

EDITIONS: XXIX, 19, 1828[–44]

26. Lord, who can tell how oft he offendeth?

(XXIX, 28) *ca.* 1678; *Psalm* 19: 12–14, with *Doxology*

Verse: *ttb*   Bc   Chorus: *SATB*

(1a) Prelude   (1b) Lord who can tell: *ttb*   (2) Keep Thy servant: *ttb*

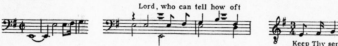

(3) Let the words: *ttb*   (4) Glory be to the Father: *SATB*

MSS: 42, 181 (anon), 430a to f (lacking soprano chorus part), 478bde

EDITIONS: XXIX, 28   1828[–44]

COMMENTARY: Dated not later than 1683 by reason of its inclusion in the so-called Blow MS
(Cambridge, Fitzwilliam Museum MS 117, p. 233), this work is also to be found in the set of
Chapel Royal part-books now in the Music Room at the British Museum (Royal Music MS
23.m.1–6). According to the researches of H. Watkins Shaw, Purcell wrote this work at a date
probably not later than 1678.

LITERATURE: Watkins Shaw, 'A Contemporary Source of English Music of the Purcellian
Period,' *Acta Musicologica*, vol. XXXI, 1, 1959, pp. 38–44.

27. Man that is born of a woman

(XXIX, 36) *ca.* 1680–2; *Job* 14: 1–2 and Funeral Sentences (*The Book of Common Prayer*, 1660)

Full: *SATB*, with Verse: *satb*   Bc

(1a) Man that is born: *satb*   (1b) He fleeth as it were: *SATB*

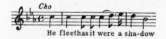

   (2) In the midst of life: *satb*

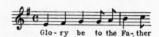

(3) Yet, O Lord: *satb* [*SATB*]   (4a) Thou knowest, Lord: *SATB*

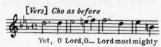   

(4b) But spare us, Lord: *SATB*

(5) Suffer us not: *satb, SATB*

3⅜ But   spare   us,   Lord

Suf-fer us not at our last hour

MSS: **41** (partly autograph), 42, 131, 201, **325** (section 2 only), 509abcd (first two sections only), 511, 516, 613, 754, 759, 825, 827, 828, 829, 830, 831, 861

EDITIONS: XXIX, 36, 1828[–44]

COMMENTARY: In British Museum MS Add. 17839, on f.209v, this work is ascribed to John Blow. In the revised version of his edition (Stainer & Bell, 1962), Thurston Dart has suggested that sections 4 and 5 may well have been added by John Blow to Purcell's setting of sections 1–3. The documentary evidence in the two Fitzwilliam MSS seems to favours this view. However, a similar, apparently earlier setting of these settings in Purcell's own hand exists (See No. **58A**). Furthermore, there are a number of independent copies of the above version—sufficient to establish its separate identity—which are definitely ascribed to Purcell. (See No. **58B**.) For further information on sections 1–3, see Nos. **17AB**.

28. My beloved spake

(XIIIA, 24) before 1683; *The Song of Solomon* 2: 10–13, 16

Verse: *atbb*   2 *Vns, Va, Bc*   Chorus: *SATB*

(1) Symphony: *Str*

3i: L Add 30932

(2a) My beloved spake: *atbb*

My be-lov-ed spake and said un - to me

(2b) Ritornello: *Str*

(3a) For lo! the winter: *atbb*   (3b) Ritornello: *Str*   (4) The flow'rs appear: *atbb*

3 For lo! the win-ter is past

The flow'rs ap-pear up - [on]

(5a) And the time: *SATB*   (5b) Ritornello: *Str*   (5c) = 5a: *atbb*

3 And the time of the sing - ing of

(5d) Alleluia: *atbb*   (5e) Ritornello: *Str*   (6) And the voice: *atbb*

(7) = 1   (8a) The fig tree: *t, Vn*   (8b) = 2b   (9) My beloved is mine: *atbb*

(10) Ritornello: *Str*   (11) Alleluia: *atbb*   (12) Ritornello: *Str*

(13a) = opening of 9: *SATB*   (13b) Alleluia: *atb, [SATB]*

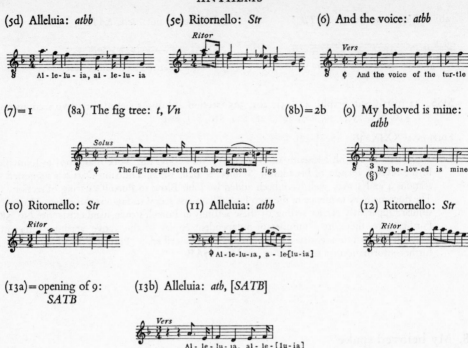

MSS: 20, 42, 186, 299, 304, **326**, 505bcef, 749, 753, 754, 769

EDITIONS: XIIIA, 24, 1828[–44]

COMMENTARY: This anthem, one of the earliest with string accompaniments, occurs in the 'Flackton' MS (British Museum MS Add. 30932), which bears the note: 'By Henry Purcell; in his own handwriting: the original score. "Signed:" P. Hayes 1785.' Purcell seems to have revised this anthem more than once. Certain revisions are marked in the autograph copy, while others based on a reputed autograph (now missing) are indicated in Vincent Novello's edition. A revised version of this work in the so-called 'Blow MS' (Cambridge, Fitzwilliam Museum MS 117), is said to be the same as that in the manuscript upon which Vincent Novello based his edition. Novello's edition is essentially the same as that of the Purcell Society except for the following differences. The opening symphony begins as follows:

And for the ritornello after Section 6, Section 5e rather than Section 1 recurs. Novello based his edition on 'a copy in which there was a note stating that it was transcribed from an MS volume written by the late Dr. Hayes from the original in Purcell's own handwriting, which latter copy was afterwards deposited by Dr. Hayes in the King's Library.' This MS is now untraceable, but Novello's version is much the same as that in the Tudway MS (see MS 299).

LITERATURE: E. H. Fellowes, *English Cathedral Music*, London: Methuen, 1941.

29. My heart is fixed, O God

(XIV, 112) *ca.* 1684; *Psalm* 57: 7–11

Verse: *atb*   2 *Vns, Va, Bc*   Chorus: *SATB*

(1) My heart is fixed: *atb*   (2a) Awake up my glory: *atb:* [Str]

(2b) I myself will awake: *atb*   (3) Ritornello: *Str*

(4) I will give thanks: *atb*   (5)=3   (6) Set up Thyself:
                                                    atb, 2 *Vns*

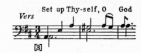

(6b) Ritornello: *Str*   (6c)=6a   (6d) Ritornello: *Str*

(7a) Alleluia: *atb*   (7b) Ritornello: *Str*   (7c) Alleluia: *SATB*

MSS: **13**, 46, 303, 410, **453**, 739, 833

EDITIONS: XIV, 112, 1828[–44]

30. My heart is inditing

(XVII, 69) April 23, 1685; *Psalm* 45: 1, 9b, 14, 15, 10 and 17; and *Isaiah* 49: 23

Verse: *ssaattbb*   2 *Vns, Va, Bc*   Chorus: *SSAATTBB*

(1) Symphony: *Str*   (2a) My heart is inditing:
   (a) [Grave]   (b) [Canzona]   *SSAATTBB*

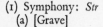

2: LK 20.h.s.

(2b) Ritornello: *Str*   (3) At his right hand: *SSAATTBB, Str*

(4a) She shall be brought: *ssaatb*   (4b) With joy and gladness: *ssaatbb.*
                                    [*SSAATTBB, Str*]

(5) = 1a, b   (6a) Hearken, O daughter: *ssaattbb*   (6b) Ritornello: *Str*

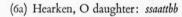
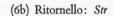

(7a) Praise the Lord: *SSAATTBB, Str*   (7b) Ritornello: *Str*

(8) Alleluia, Amen: *SSAATTBB, Str*

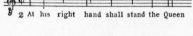
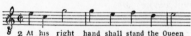
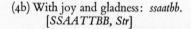

MSS: 410, **453**, 833

EDITIONS: XVII, 69 1828[–44]

COMMENTARY: This anthem was sung at the coronation of James II, for which occasion it was
    presumably composed. Sandford in his *History of the Coronation of James II and Queen Mary*,
    p. 101, has described the ceremony in the following passages: ' The Queen being thus Anointed

and Crowned, and having received all the Royal Ornaments, the Choirs sung the following Verse-Anthem, performed by the whole Consort of Voices and Instruments. Anthem IX *Psalm* 45 *Verse* 1: " My heart is Inditing of a good Matter " etc. As soon as this Anthem began, the Queen arose from Her Faldstool, & being supported by the Two Bishops, & Her Train born, and attended as before, went up to the Theatre; and as She approached towards the King, bowed Her Self reverently to His Majesty sitting upon His Throne; and so was Conducted to Her Own Throne on the Left Hand of the King, where She reposed Her Self till the Anthem was ended.'

This is the last work which Purcell copied into British Museum Royal Music MS 20.h.8. There is some evidence of haste in the copying, as Purcell made a great many more mistakes and omissions than usual. He used the Symphony again for *Celestial Music* (see No. **322/1**).

LITERATURE: E. H. Fellowes, *English Cathedral Music*, London: Methuen, 1941; F. Sandford, *The History of the Coronation of James II and Queen Mary*, London: 1687.

My heart rejoiceth in the Lord (See S10)

31. My song shall be alway

(XXIX, 51) ?1688; *Psalm* 89: 1, 5–9, 13–15

Verse: *b* (or *s*)   2 *Vns, Va, Bc*   Chorus: *SATB*

(1) Symphony: *Str*
  (a) [Grave]   (b) [Canzona]   (2) My song shall be: *b* (or *s*)

(3) O Lord, the very heav'ns: *b* (or *s*)   (4a) Prelude=4b   (4b) For who is he: *b* (or *s*)

(5) God is very greatly: *b* (or *s*)   (6) Alleluia: *SATB, Str*   (7)=1

(8a) O Lord God of hosts: *b* (or *s*)   (8b) Thou rulest the raging: *b* (or *s*)

(8c) Ritornello: *Str*   (9) Thou hast a mighty arm: *b* (or *s*)

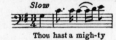

(10) Mercy and truth: *b* (or *s*)   (11) Alleluia: *b* (or *s*)   (12)=6

MSS: 1, 46 (inc), 64b, 65, 77, 80, 81, 84, 85, 86, 97, 98, 105, 132, 140 (in F Major), 150, 154, 158, 160,
   163d, 166ghi, 181, 184, 185, 194abfg, 195, 196, 197, 198, 200b, 202, 219, 245de, 248, 249, 255,
   299, 306, 320 (for soprano), 325, 344 (for soprano), 362, 370, 391, 430abcdef, 478e, 489, 500d,
   503, 505b (inc), 509acd, 592, 613, 631, 646, 665, 667 (bass part), 691, 692, 693, 694, 695, 735, 743,
   745, 746e, 771, 795d, 802, 804, 807, 808a, 810e, 811h, 815, 818, 820, 822, 823, 825, 827 (Alleluia;
   chorus only), 832, 834, 836, 837, 855

EDITIONS: XXIX, 51,   1703e, 1714b, 1726a, 1730c, 1828[–44]

COMMENTARY: In the manuscript and printed sources this anthem is to be found in several keys,
   written either for soprano or bass voice.   Among manuscript sources, there are a few more
   versions for bass than for soprano, but in the early printed sources, beginning with *Harmonia
   Sacra* of 1703, versions for the latter are predominant.   For the most part, the key is G major,
   but some sources give this work in F, B-flat, or A major.   Westrup suggests that the anthem was
   written for the Italian castrato, Siface, since no other virtuoso soloist was available at the Chapel
   Royal in 1688.   Other authorities maintain that the anthem was written for a bass soloist,
   Hawkins (IV, 522) going so far as to state that it was written expressly for John Gostling,
   without advancing any proof.   The date 1688 is conjectural, being deduced from the position of
   this anthem in the MS formerly in the possession of William Kennedy Gostling, now unavailable.
   In the Bodleian MS, Mus. Sch. c 61, it is dated 1690, a date which probably has nothing to do
   with the date of its composition.   In this same MS one finds other inscriptions from books by
   Mace, Bassani, *etc.* which are also dated.   These obviously are mere copy-work and have little
   or nothing to do with the chronological position of the MS itself, much less of the works it
   contains.

LITERATURE: Michael Howard, 'An Anthem by Henry Purcell', *Monthly Musical Record*, vol. 83,
   No. 945, pp. 66–9.

O be joyful (See D3)

O come, loud anthems (See S11)

32. O consider my adversity

(XXIX, 68) *Psalm* 119 (*Resh*): 153–160, with Doxology

Verse: *atb*   *Bc*   Chorus: *SATB*

(1a) O consider: *atb*

(1b) Ritornello

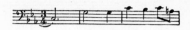

(2a) Avenge Thou my cause: *atb*

(2b) O quicken me: *atb*

(2c) Health is far from the ungodly: *t*

(3a) Great is Thy mercy: *atb*

(3b) = 2b

(4a) Great is Thy mercy: *SATB*

(4b) O quicken me: *SATB*

(5) Many there are: *b*

(6a) It grieveth me: *atb*

(6b) Consider, O Lord: *atb*

(6c) = 2b

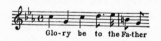

(7) Thy word is true: *atb*

(8) Glory be to the Father: *SATB*

MSS: 186, 191, 192

EDITIONS: XXIX, 68, 1828[-44]

33. O give thanks unto the Lord

(XXIX, 88) 1693; *Psalm* 106: 1, 2, 4, 5, 48

Verse: *satb*

2 *Vn, Bc*

Chorus: *SATB*

(1a) O give thanks: *atb, SATB*   (1b) For He is   (1d) And His mercy: *SATB*
                                   gracious: *atb*

§/2: CFM 152   (1c) = 1a

(1e) = 1b   (1f) Ritornello: 2 *Vn, Bc*   §(2a) Who can express: *ab*

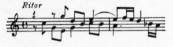

(2b) Ritornello: 2 *Vn, Bc*   (3) Remember me, O Lord: *satb [SATB]*

(4a) Ritornello: 2 *Vn, Bc*   (4b) That I may see: *a*

(5) Ritornello: (6a) Blessed be the Lord: (6b) And let all the people:
   2 *Vn, Bc*   *satb [SATB]*   *satb SATB*

MSS: 1, **46** (mainly autograph), 64b, 69, 75, 80, 81, 84, 85, 86, 104, 118, 131, 150, 151, 158, 160, 162,
    163ade, 164ad, 166adeghi, 167b, 180, 189, 194g, 197, 200c, 203, 245acde, 248, 255, 273, 301, 306,
    325, 334, 357, 360, 400, 403 (supposititious autograph; treble missing), 43cabcdf, 478bde, 500a to
    e, 503, 505a to f, 506, 509abcd, 510, 511, 513, 518, 603, 634, 647a to e, 653, 665, 666, 735, 743,
    746c, 751, 752, 753, 754, 762, 771, 773, 795a, 808a, 811gh, 812f, 813, 815, 818, 820, 821, 822, 823,
    826, 832, 836, 837, 848ef, 850ab, c (index only) de, f (index only) g (index only) h
    Section 2a: 105

EDITIONS: XXIX, 88, 1703e, 1730c, 1750b, 1765b, 1773, 1779a, 1780, 1795, 1828[-44]

COMMENTARY: The copy of this anthem in Fitzwilliam Museum, Cambridge, MS 152, is partially in
    Purcell's hand. However, from bar 191 to the end, it is copied in an 18th century hand. An
    exact date was given in the so-called W. K. Gostling MS, which is missing.

LITERATURE: E. H. Fellowes, *English Cathedral Music*, London: Methuen, 1941; Watkins Shaw,
    'A Contemporary Source of English Music of the Purcellian Period,' *Acta Musicologica*, vol.
    XXXI, 1, 1959, pp. 38-44.

34. O God the King of glory

(XXIX, 108) before 1683; *Collect for the Sunday after Ascension*

Full: *SATB*

(1) O God the King: *SATB*

(2) But send to us Thine Holy Ghost: *SATB*

MSS: 481, 850bdfh

EDITIONS: XXIX, 108,   1828[-44] (Preface only, mnp)

COMMENTARY: For his edition of Purcell's sacred music, Vincent Novello edited this anthem from a Westminster Abbey manuscript, now apparently lost. It may be a section from a longer work.

O God, they that love Thy name (See D4)

35. O God, Thou art my God

(XXIX, 111) *ca.* 1680-2; *Psalm* 63: 1-4, 7

Full: *SATB, (decani and cantoris)* with Verse: *ssatb*   Bc

(1) O God, Thou art: *SATB*

(2) My soul thirsteth: *atb*

(3) Thus have I look'd: *SATB*

(4) For Thy loving-kindness: *ssa*

(5) As long as I live: *SATB (full, dec. & can.)*

(6) Alleluia: *SATB (dec., can. & full)*

MSS: **41** (inc), 42, 77, 81, 83, 84, 85, 86, 99, 116, 120, 126, 131, 156, 160, 162, 163acde, 164acdf, 166adeg (inc) hi, 167d, 182, 188, 198, 200e, 245bcd, 246, 247, 271, 272, 274, 300, 303, 307, 330, 403, 411 (bass only w/o text), 430 (abcdef), 500b to c, 503, 504, 505a to f, 509acd, 512, 513, 514, 517, 603, 652, 746d, 759, 761, 765, 809e, 810a, 811b, 812bf, 813, 816, 818, 820, 821, 822, 823, 831, 836, 848f, 850acegh (index only), 851

EDITIONS: XXIX, 111, 1768, ?1790b, 1828[-44]

COMMENTARY: The autograph copy (Cambridge, Fitzwilliam MS 88, f.89) is incomplete, ending with the first few words of the text only of Section 5. Enough space has been left for the remainder of the anthem. However, in the same library, MS 117 (the so-called 'Blow MS,' which is not certainly in Blow's hand, as Mr. Harold Watkins Shaw affirms) contains a complete copy which must have been taken from another autograph or contemporary MS. It bears the heading: 'To Mr. Purcell's B-mi Service.' (Incipits 5 and 6 above were taken from this MS.) In the Chapel Royal part-books in the Music Room, British Museum (Royal Music MS 23.m.1–6) this anthem appears between the *Nunc dimittis* and the *Cantate Domino* of the Service in B-flat by Purcell, as if it might have been performed in conjunction with this Service.

LITERATURE: C. Burney, *A General History of Music*, London: Foulis & Co. Ltd., 1935, II, p. 383; Watkins Shaw, 'A Contemporary Source of English Music of the Purcellian Period,' *Acta Musicologica*, vol. XXXI, 1, 1959, pp. 38–44.

36. O God, Thou hast cast us out

(XXIX, 120) *ca.* 1680–2; *Psalm* 60: 1–2, 11–12

Full: *SSAATB*, with Verse: *ssaatb*   *Bc*

(1a) O God, Thou hast: *SSAATB*

(1b) Thou hast moved: *SSAATB*

(2) O be Thou our help: *ssaatb*

(3) Through God will we do: *SSAATB*

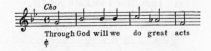

MSS: **41**, 42, 51 (missing), 77, 79, 81, 83, 84, 85, 97, 116, 120, 125, 131, 156, 160, 162, 163 acde, 164adf, 166aeg (inc) hi, 183, 200e, 220, 245bcd, 271, 274, 300, 303, 307, 330, 360, 401, 403, 430a to f, 500a to e, 503, 505abdef, 506, 510, 513, 514, 542, 603, 650, 666, 713, 738, 745, 759, 761, 765, 809e, 810a, 811b, 812bf, 813, 816, 821, 822, 823, 831, 836, 850aceg, h (index only, part copied into 'g'), 851

EDITIONS: XXIX, 120, 1768, 1828[–44]

LITERATURE: C. Burney, *A General History of Music*, London: Foulis & Co. Ltd., 1935, II, p. 384;
Watkins Shaw, 'A Contemporary Source of English Music of the Purcellian Period,' *Acta Musicologica*, vol. XXXI, 1, 1959, pp. 38–44.

O God, wherefore art Thou (See S12)

37. O Lord God of hosts

(XXIX, 130) *ca.* 1680–2; *Psalm* 80: 4–7, 18

Full: *SSAATTBB*, with Verse: *ssaatb*   Bc

(1) O Lord God: *SSAATTBB*

(2a) Thou feedest them: *ssaattb*

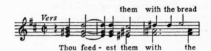

(2b) Thou hast made us: *SSAATTBB*

(3) Turn us again: *ssaab*

(4) And so will we not: *SSAATTBB*

MSS: **41**, 116, 303, 430ad

EDITIONS: XXIX, 130, 1768, 1828[–44]

COMMENTARY: In the contra-tenor decani book of the Chapel Royal part-books in the British
Museum (Royal Music MS 23.m.1) this anthem is copied in after *O God, Thou art my God*, as if
it may also have been sung within the sections of the evening service. As suggested by the
Chapel Royal part-books, Purcell may have intended that the anthem be performed by decani
and cantoris choirs.

LITERATURE: C. Burney, *A General History of Music*, London: Foulis & Co. Ltd., 1935, II, p. 384;
Watkins Shaw, 'A Contemporary Source of English Music of the Purcellian Period,' *Acta Musicologica*, vol. XXXI, 1, 1959, pp. 38–44.

O Lord God of my salvation (See S13)

38. O Lord, grant the King a long life

(XXIX, 141) ?1685; *Psalm* 61: 6, 7; *Psalm* 132: 18

Verse: *atb*   2 *Vn, Bc*   Chorus: *SATB*

(1) Symphony: *Str*   (2) O Lord, grant the King: *atb, SATB*   (3)＝1

O Lord, grant the King a long life

(4a) He shall dwell: *atb, 2 Vns*   (4b) Ritornello: *Str*

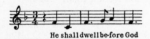

He shall dwell be-fore God

(5a) O prepare: *atb*   (5b) Ritornello: *Str*

O,   O—pre - pare

(6a) As for His enemies: *atb*   (6b) Amen: *SATB*

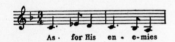

As · for His en - e-mies

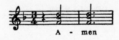

A - men

MSS: **453** (index only), 771

EDITIONS: XXIX, 141, 1828[–44]

COMMENTARY: In Purcell's autograph index to British Museum Royal Music MS 20.h.8, this anthem is listed, but has not been copied in. The last anthem copied in this score book is dated 1685. As Charles II died in the spring, it may be that Purcell was too late in finishing this anthem for it to be used at the Chapel Royal under Charles II. This seems all the more probable since he replaced it in the score-book with the anthem written for James II's coronation.

39. O Lord, our Governor

(XXIX, 152) before 1683; *Psalm* 8: 1–9, with Doxology

Verse: *sssbb*   *Bc*   Chorus: *SATB*

(1a) Prelude

(1b) O Lord, our Governor: *b*

(2) Out of the mouths: *sss*

Out of the mouths of

(3) For I will consider: *bb*

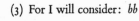

For I will con-si-der

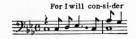

(4) The moon and the stars: *bb [SATB]*

The moon and the stars

(5) Lord, what is man: *b*

Lord,   Lord_ what is man

(6) Thou mad'st him: *sssbb*

Thou mad'st him low-er thanthe An-gels

Thou mad'st him   low-er

(7a) All sheep and oxen: *SATB*

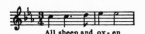

All sheep and ox-en

(7b) The fowls of the air: *SATB*

The fowls of the air, and the fish-es

(8) O Lord, our Governor: *bb*

O Lord,   O Lord,ourGov-er-nor

O Lord,   O Lord   our

(9) Glory be to the Father: *SATB*

Glo-ry be to the Fa-ther

MSS: 42, 303, 739, 850a to d, f to h

EDITIONS: XXIX, 152,   1828[-44]

COMMENTARY: The only authentic contemporary sources now known for this anthem are the so-called 'Blow MS' (Cambridge, Fitzwilliam Museum MS 117, p. 242) and the 'Gostling' part-books at York Minster.

O Lord, our Governor, Sacred Part Song (See No. 141)

40. O Lord, rebuke me not

(XXIX, 168); *Psalm 6: 1–7*

Verse: *ss*   *Bc*   Chorus: *SATB*

(1a) O Lord, rebuke me not: *ss*

(1b) Ritornello

(1c) Have mercy upon me: *ss*

(2) Turn Thee, O Lord: *ss*

(3)=2: *SATB*   (4) For in death: *ss*

(5)=2   (6)=3

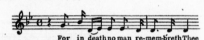

MSS: 158, 166ghi, 365 (inc), 509abcd, 743

EDITIONS: XXIX, 168, 1828[–44]

COMMENTARY: Novello remarks that in some copies this composition is attributed to Weldon. He may have been thinking of the work listed herein as S14.

O Lord, rebuke me not, Sacred Song (See S14)

41. O Lord, Thou art my God

(XXIX, 179) *ca.* 1680–2; *Isaiah 25: 1, 4, 7–9*

Verse: *atb*   *Bc*   Chorus: *SATB*

(1) O Lord, Thou art my God: *b*

(2) For Thou hast been: *at*

(3) And He will destroy: *b*

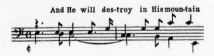

(4) He will swallow up death: *atb*

He will swal-low up death in— vic-to-ry

(5) O Lord, Thou art my God: *SATB*

O Lord, Thou art my God

(6) And it shall be said: *atb*

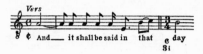

And— it shall be said in that day

(7) Alleluia: *atb*

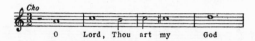

Al-le-lu-ia al-le-lu-ia

(8) Alleluia [*SATB*]

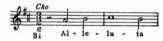

Al-le-lu-ia

MSS: **41**, 666, 713, 825, 826, 827, 828, 829, 830, 831

EDITIONS: XXIX, 179, 1828[-44]

O miserable man, Sacred Song (See S15)

42. O praise God in His holiness

(XIV, 21) *ca.* 1683; *Psalm* 150: 1–6

Verse: *atbb*   2 *Vn, Va, Bc*   Chorus: *SATB*

(1) Symphony: *Str*
   (a) [Grave]   (b) [Canzona]   (2a) O praise God: *atb*

(2b) Praise Him in the firmament: *atb*

Praise Him in the firm-a-ment

(3) Ritornello: *Str*

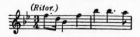

39

(4a) Praise Him in His noble acts: *atbb*   (4b) Praise Him according: *atb*

 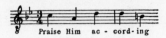

(5) Ritornello:
    Str   (6) Praise Him in the sound: (7) Praise Him in the cymbals:
                          atbb, Vn obbligato   *a*

(8)＝1b   (9a) Praise Him on the well-tuned   (9b) Ritornello: *Str*
                          cymbals: *b, Vn*

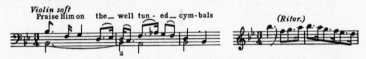

(10) Let ev'rything that hath breath: *atbb, SATB, 2 Vn*

MSS: 293, 303, 410, **453**, 739, 833

EDITIONS: XIV, 21, 1828[–44]

COMMENTARY: The anthem is dated conjecturally from its relative position in Royal Music MS 20.h.8.

LITERATURE: E. H. Fellowes, *English Cathedral Music*, London: Methuen, 1941.

43.   O praise the Lord, all ye heathen

(XXXII, 1) *ca.* 1682; *Psalm* 117: 1–2 with Doxology

Verse: *tt*   *Bc*   Chorus: *SATB*

(1) O praise the Lord: *tt*   (2) Alleluia: *SATB*

(3) Glory be to the Father: *tt*   (4) = 2

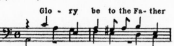

Glo - ry   be   to the Fa- ther

MSS: 149, 166cdeghi, 167a, 293, 322, 850ef (complete), bdh (chorus only)

EDITIONS: XXXII, 1, 1828[-44]

COMMENTARY: The Alleluia is to be repeated as the final section according to a note in British Museum MS Add. 30478.

O pray for the peace (See D5)

44. O sing unto the Lord

(XVII, 119) 1688; *Psalm 96*: 1-3, 6, 4, 5, 9, 10

Verse: *satbb*   2 *Vn, Va, Bc*   Chorus: *SATB*

(1) Symphony: *Str*   (2a) O sing unto the Lord: *b, Bc*
  (a) [Grave]   (b) [Canzona]

Vers: *upper bass*

O   sing un-to the Lord

C: LK 20.h.8

(2b) Alleluia: *SATB, Str*   (2c) Sing unto the Lord all the   (2d) Alleluia: *SATB, Str*
                                        whole earth: *b*

Al - le - lu - ia

(2e) Ritornello: *Str*   (2f) Sing unto the Lord: *satb*

                                        Sing un-to the Lord, sing____

(3a) Declare His honour: *b, Str*   (3b) Glory and worship: *SATB, Str*

De-clare His hon- our   Glo - ry and wor-ship   go   be-fore Him

41

C

(4) The Lord is great: *sa*

The Lord is great—

(5) Ritornello: *Str*

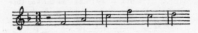

(6) O worship the Lord: *satbb*, [*SATB, Str*]

(7a) Tell it out: *b, SATB*

(7b) The Lord is King: *SATB, Str*

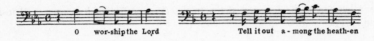

O wor-ship the Lord   Tell it out a - mong the heath-en

(7c) And that it is He: *b*

(7d) 'Tis He who hath made: *SATB, Str*

(7e) And how that He shall: *b*

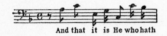

And that it is He who hath

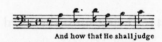

And how that He shall judge

(7f) He shall judge: *SATB, Str*

(8) Alleluia: *sabb*, [*SATB, Str*]

Al - le - lu - ia

MSS: 255, 303, 453, 739, 759

EDITIONS: XVII, 119, 1828[–44]

COMMENTARY: The alteration and re-arrangement of the verses of the text to this anthem suggests that it may have been an occasional composition. Ordinarily, Purcell followed the biblical text rather closely as far as the original order was concerned. The work is incomplete in British Museum Royal Music MS 20.h.8, f.67. It is also incorrect, for which reason the Purcell Society editor used the William Kennedy Gostling MS (now unavailable) for his edition. He dated the work from a note at the end of this MS which reads: 'Composed by Mr. Purcell 1688.'

LITERATURE: E. H. Fellowes, *English Cathedral Music*, London: Methuen, 1941.

O that mine eyes would melt, Hymn (See S16)

45. Out of the deep have I called

(XXXII, 8) *ca.* 1680; *Psalm* 130: 1–7

Verse: *sab*   *Bc*   Chorus: *SATB*

(1) Out of the deep: *sab*

Out of the deep have I call-[ed]

C: L Add 30931

(2) But there is mercy: *sab* [*SATB*]

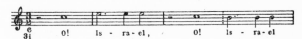

.3 But there is mer-cy, is mer-cy—with Thee

(3) I look for the Lord: *b*

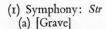

Sola. I look for the Lord

(4) O! Israel, trust in the Lord: *sab* [*SATB*]

O! Is - ra - el, O! Is - ra - el

MSS: **325,** 713

EDITIONS: XXXII, 8, ?1790b, 1800b, 1828[–44]

COMMENTARY: In British Museum MS Add. 30931 (on f.70v) appears the following marginal note in the hand of William Flackton: ' This is an Original. Supposed by Mr. Purcell & by some to be his handwriting, tho' somewhat unlike the foregoing anthem [" Blessed are they &c "] as two different papers & also different pens & wrote at diverse times may make a seeming difference in any man's hand writeing. W. Flackton.' Actually, the copy is in Purcell's hand.

Peace be within thy walls (See D6)

46. Praise the Lord, O Jerusalem

(XVII, 146) *ca.* 1688; *Psalm* 147: 12, with *Isaiah* 49: 23, *Psalm* 48: 8 and *Psalm* 21: 13

Verse: *ssatb*　　　　　　　　　　2 *Vn, Va, Bc*　　　　　　　　　　Chorus: *SSATB*

(1) Symphony: *Str*　　　　　　　　　　　　　　(2a) Praise the Lord: *ssatb, Str*
 (a) [Grave]　　　　　　　　(b) [Canzona]

Praise the Lord, praise

(2b) Ritornello: *Str*　　　　(2c) For Kings shall be: *SATB*　　　　(2d)=2a (altered)

(3a) Prelude: *Str*　　　　　　　　　　　　(3b) As we have heard: *atb*,
　　　　　　　　　　　　　　　　　　　　　　　[*SSATB, Str*]

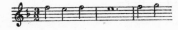

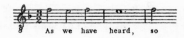

As we have heard, so

(4a) Ritornello: *Str*

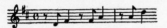

(4b) Be Thou exalted: *ssatb, SSATB, Str*

Be Thou ex-al - ted, Lord, in Thine own

(5) Alleluia: *SSATB, Str*

Al - le - lu - ia

MSS: 453

EDITIONS: XVII, 146,   1895 (see Commentary)

COMMENTARY: This was probably an occasional composition, since it is based on several Biblical
texts. The opening verse is from the Psalm proper to Evensong, Sunday next before Advent.
The anthem was first printed for performance at the Purcell bicentenary festival held in
Westminster Abbey on November 21st, 1895. H. E. Wooldridge edited it from British Museum
Royal Music MS 20.h.8, a unique copy in the hand of an amanuensis or copyist.

LITERATURE: E. H. Fellowes, *English Cathedral Music*, London: Methuen, 1941.

47. Praise the Lord, O my soul, and all that is within me

(XIV, 131) *ca.* 1684–5; *Psalm* 103: 1–4, 8–14, 22

Verse: *ssttbb*   2 *Vn, Va, Bc*   Chorus: *SATB*

(1) Symphony: *Str*
  (a) [Grave]

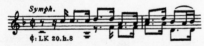

🎼: LK 20.h.8

(b) [Canzona]

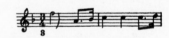

(2a) Praise the Lord: *ssttbb*

Verse on the close

Praise   the   Lord, praise the Lord

(2b) Ritornello: *Str*

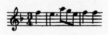

(2c) Praise the Lord: *ssttbb*

Vers

Praise   the Lord, praise the Lord

(2d) Ritornello: *Str*

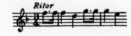

Ritor

(3) The Lord is full: *ttb*   (4) He hath not dealt: *t*   (5)＝1b

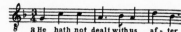

(6) For look, how high: *b*   (7a) O speak good: *ssttbb*   (7b) Praise thou the Lord: *ssttbb*

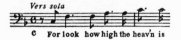

(7c) Ritornello: *Str*   (7d) Praise thou the Lord: *SATB*

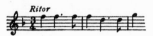

MSS: 369, 410, **453**, 833

EDITIONS: XIV, 131, 1828–[44]

COMMENTARY: An incomplete copy of this anthem exists in Purcell's fair copy-book (British Museum Royal Music MS 20.h.8, f.81), written in the hand of a copyist. The primary source used for correcting the rather careless version given there has been unavailable since the sale of some of the effects of W. Kennedy Gostling by Sotheby's in 1935.

48. Praise the Lord, O my soul, O Lord my God

(XVII, 166) 1687; *Psalm* 104: 1–3, 5–8, 14, 15, 19, 20, 24, 25, 27–31

Verse: *ab*   2 *Vn, Bc*   Chorus: *SATB*

(1) Symphony: 2 *Vn, Bc*

  (a) [Grave]   (b) [Canzona]   (2) Praise the Lord: *b*

(3a) He laid the foundations: *b*   (3b) Ritornello: 2 *Vn, Bc*   (3c) He bringeth forth grass: *ab*

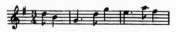

(4a) That He may bring food: *ab*

That He may bring food out of the earth

(4b) Ritornello: 2 *Vn, Bc*

(5) He appointeth the moon: *a*

He ap - point - eth the moon

(6) O Lord, how manifold: *ab [SATB]*

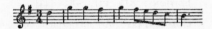

O___ Lord,　O___ Lord how ma-ni-fold

(7) = 1

(8) The earth is full: *ab*

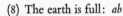

The earth is full of Thy rich-es

(9) Ritornello: 2 *Vn, Bc*

(10a) When Thou hidest: *ab*

When Thou hi - dest Thy face

(10b) Ritornello: 2 *Vn*

(11) The glorious Majesty: *ab*

(12) The Lord shall rejoice: *ab*　　(13) = 6:
　　　　　　　　　　　　　　　　　　　　SATB

Slow

The　glo - - - rious Ma - jes-ty　　The Lord shall re - joice___

MSS: 64a, 185, 255, 293, 300, 334, 453 (inc.), 516, 759

EDITIONS: XVII, 166, 1828[–44]

COMMENTARY: In the autograph score-book (British Museum Royal Music MS 20.h.8) this anthem
appears in the hand of a later copyist. It is, however, incomplete, coming to an end just after
the word 'die' in Section 10 of the anthem. At the end the copyist has written: 'Composed
by Mr. Hen. Purcell—1687.' In St. Michael's College, Tenbury, MSS 1176–82, a simpler melodic
line suggests that there may have been an earlier version.

Praise the Lord ye servants (See No. N68)

49. Rejoice in the Lord alway

(XIV, 155) *ca.* 1684–5; *Philippians* 4: 4–7

Verse: *atb*　　　　　　　　　　2 *Vn, Va, Bc*　　　　　　　　　Chorus: *SATB*

(1) Prelude: *Str*

(2) Rejoice in the Lord alway: *atb*

(3) Symphony: *Str*
(a)   (b)

(4)=2   (5) Let your moderation: *atb*

(6) Rejoice in the Lord: *SATB*

(7)=3   (8a) Be careful for nothing: *atb*

(8b) And the peace of God: *atb*   (8c) Ritornello: *Str*   (9)=2   (10)=3   (11)=6

MSS: 118, 119, 121, 127, 157, 166f, 183, 184, 200b (missing), 272, 300, 303, 306, 334, 410, **453,** 509, 511, 666, 694, 743, 749 (text: 'Laudate Dominum'), 753, 773, 808a, 810a, 811gh, 818, 820, 822, 823, 860

EDITIONS: XIV, 155, 1775b, 1779a, 1828[–44]

COMMENTARY: The autograph copy (British Museum, Royal Music, MS 20.h.8) is incomplete, lacking the inner parts almost throughout. The origin of the subtitle 'the Bell Anthem' is explained by the following note from British Museum MS Add. 31445, f.42: 'Rejoice in the Lord, Conr. Tenor & Bass, with a Symphony, imitating Bells, (it was originally call'd ye Bell Anthem:)—Purcell.' The editor for the Purcell Society Edition has added an instrumental bass part, which is not in any of the sources.

LITERATURE: E. H. Fellowes, *English Cathedral Music*, London: Methuen, 1941.

50. Remember not, Lord, our offences

(XXXII, 19) *ca.* 1680–2; From the *Litany*

Full: *SSATB*   Bc

MSS: **41**, 42, 183, 303, 503, 739

EDITIONS: XXXII, 19,   1828[–44]

LITERATURE: D. Arundell, *Henry Purcell*, London: O.U.P., 1927, p. 37; E. H. Fellowes, *English Cathedral Music*, London: Methuen, 1941.

COMMENTARY: The text for this anthem is also included as part of the ' Order for the Visitation of the Sick ' in the *Book of Common Prayer*, and the anthem itself sometimes considered as one of the ' funeral sentences '. (See No. 17A/Commentary.)

51. Save me, O God, for Thy Name's sake

(XIIIA, 64) *ca.* 1680–2; *Psalm* 54: 1–4, 6–7

Verse: *ssatb*   Bc   Chorus: *SSATTB*

(1a) Save me, O God: *ssatb*   (1b) Behold, God is my helper: *SSATTB*

(2) An off'ring of a free heart: *ssa*   (3a) For He hath deliver'd me: *SSATB*

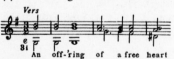

(3b) And mine eyes: *SSATB* (canon 5 in 1)

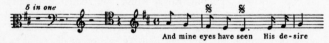

MSS: 2, **41**, 42, 300, 303, 333, 713, 759, 760, 795bd, 850a to d, f to h, 851
     Section 3b: 327

EDITIONS: XIIIA, 64,   1828[–44]

52. Sing unto God, o ye kingdoms of the earth

(XXXII, 23) 1687; *Psalm 68: 32-35*

Verse: *b*   Bc   Chorus: *SATB*

(1) Sing unto God: *b*

Sing, sing ———— un-to God

(2) Alleluia: *SATB]*   (3) Who sitteth in the   (4) Ascribe ye the pow'r: *b*
                                  heav'ns: *b*

Al-le-lu-ia, al-le-lu-ia   Who sit-teth in the heav'ns   As-cribe ye the pow'r to God

(5)=2   (6) O God, wonderful art   (7a) Blessed be God: *b*   (7b) Amen: (8ab) the
            Thou: *b*   SATB   same

O —— God, O ——   Bless-ed, bless - ed be God   A - men

MSS: 78, 180, 194bf, 255, 430a to e, 478bde, 509abcd, 590, 739, 743

EDITIONS: XXXII, 23, 1828[-44]

LITERATURE: Watkins Shaw, ' A Contemporary Source of English Music of the Purcellian Period,'
Acta Musicologica, vol. XXXI, 1, 1959, pp. 38-44.

COMMENTARY: In a Nanki Library MS (see Appendix III, No. 540) the bass part of the alleluia
choruses and final ' amens ' appears under the title: ' Sing unto the Lord, O ye kingdoms . . .'.
The fragment, which appears to be autograph, shows the following scheme:

Vincent Novello evidently found yet another version when editing this anthem ' From a very
rare and unpublished M.S. in the possession of Mr. Hawes, Gent.ⁿ of the Chapel Royal '. In his

edition (*The Cathedral Services, Anthems, Hymns, and other Sacred Pieces Composed by Henry Purcell*, London: J. Alfred Novello, n.d., vol. I, p. 128) the three words 'O give praises' appear in place of the four syllables of ' Alleluia '.

Sing unto the Lord, O ye kingdoms (See No. 52/Commentary)

Sing we merrily unto God (See D7)

The Lord is King and hath put on (See No. N69)

53. The Lord is King, be the people never so impatient

(XXXII, 36) ?after 1690; *Psalm* 99: 1–3, 5 with Doxology;

Verse: *ss*   Bc   Chorus: *SATB*

(1) The Lord is King: *ss*

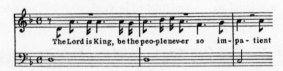

The Lord is King, be the peo-ple nev-er so im-pa-tient

(2) The Lord is great: *ss*   (3) O magnify: *SATB*

The Lord is great ___ The Lord   O   mag-ni-fy the Lord, our God

(4) Glory be to the Father: *ss*   (5) Alleluia: *SATB*

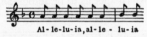

Glo - ry be to the Fa-ther   Al-le-lu-ia, al-le-lu-ia

MSS: 166ghi, 245d, 306, 401, 500a to e, 505e, ?666

EDITIONS: XXXII, 36

54. The Lord is King, the earth may be glad

(XXXII, 44) 1688; *Psalm* 97: 1–6, 10–12

Verse: *b*   Bc   Chorus: *SATB*

(1) Prelude

(2) The Lord is King: *b*

(3) Clouds of darkness: *b*

Clouds of dark-ness are round

(4) There shall go before Him: *b*

There shall go be - fore Him

(5) The hills melted: *b*

The hills melt - [ed]

(6) The heav'ns have declared: *SATB*

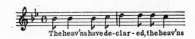

The heav'ns have de-clar-ed, the heav'ns

(7) O ye that love: *b*

O, O, O ye that love

(8) There is sprung up: *b*

There is sprung up a light

(9) Rejoice in the Lord: *b*

Re - joice, re-joice, re - joice

(10) Alleluia: *SATB*

Al - le - lu - ia, al - le - lu - ia

(11) Rejoice and give thanks: *b*

Re-joice, re-joice, re - joice

(12) = 9

MSS: 64a, 71, 158, 166ag, 181, 184, 186, 192, 196, 255, 325, 500bce, 505bce, 509abcd, 516, ?666, 759, 764

EDITIONS: XXXII, 44, 1769a, ?1781, *ca.* 1789–98, 1828[–44]

COMMENTARY: The following notes appear in British Museum MS Add. 30931 on f.75, in the hand of William Flackton, ' This copied from an original copy of Mr. Purcell's own handwriting '; on f.78v, ' This copied from a MS in the Revd. Mr Jon. Gostling's possession & of Mr. Purcell's handwriting. 1776 '; on f.78v, ' Now in my possession, Phil. Hayes.'

55. The Lord is my light

(XIV, 78) *ca.* 1683–4; *Psalm 27:* 1, 3–6

Verse: *atb*   2 *Vn, Va, Bc*   Chorus: *SATB*

(1) Symphony: *Str*
 (a) [Grave]   (b) [Canzona]

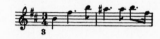

(2a) The Lord is my light: *atb*   (2b) Ritornello: *Str*

(3a) Though an host: *b*   (3b) Ritornello: *Str*   (3c) For in the time of trouble: *atb*

   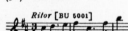   

(4) = 1b   (5a) And now shall He lift: *a*   (5b) Ritornello: *Str*

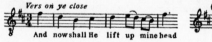

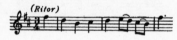

(6) Therefore will I offer: (7a) Alleluia: *atb*   (7b) Ritornello: *Str*
      atb

(7c) Alleluia: *SATB*

MSS: **13,** 303, 410, **453,** 739, 833

EDITIONS: XIV, 78, 1828[-44]

The Lord my pasture, Hymn (See S17)

56. The way of God is an undefiled way

(XXXII, 58) 1694; *Psalm* 18: 30–32, 34, 38–42, 49–51

Verse: *aab*   *Bc*   Chorus: *SAAATB*

(1) Prelude

(2) The way of God: *aab*

(3a) It is God that girdeth me: *aab*

(3b) He teacheth my hands: *aab*

(3c) Thou hast girded me: *b*

(4) For this cause will I: *aa*

(5) Alleluia: *aab [SAAATB]*

(6) Thou hast made mine enemies: *b*

(7) They shall cry: *aa*

(8) The Lord liveth: *b*

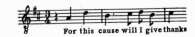

(9) Great prosperity: *aab*

(10) It is He that hath: *b*

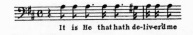

(11) Great prosperity: *aab*

(12) = 5: *aab, SAAATB*

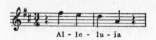

MSS: 188, 255, 330, 501, 509abcd, 510, 511a, 513, 515, 516, 603, 759, 855, 861

EDITIONS: XXXII, 58, 1828[–44]

COMMENTARY: This anthem was probably written for the celebration of the return of William IV
    from Flanders in 1694. It is dated 'IIth Nov. 1694' in the 'W. K. Gostling' manuscript,
    which has the marginal note: 'King William then returned from Flanders.'

57. They that go down to the sea

(XXXII, 71) after February 6th, 1685; *Psalm* 107: 23–32

Verse: *ab*   2 *Vn, Bc*   Chorus: *SATB*

(1) Symphony: 2 *Vn, Bc*   (2) They that go down: *b*, 2 *Vns*
    (a) [Grave]   (b) [Canzona]

(3) Ritornello: 2 *Vn, Bc*   (4) So when they cry: *ab*   (5) Ritornello:
                                                                            2 *Vn, Bc*

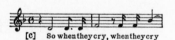

(6) Then are they glad: (7) Ritornello: (8) O that men would
    ab, 2 *Vn*   2 *Vn, Bc*   therefore: *ab*

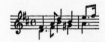

(9) Ritornello: 2 *Vn, Bc*   (10) O, praise the Lord: *SATB*

MSS: 64ab, 71, 77, 78, 81, 116, 117, 124, 161, 163ade, 164aci, 167cf, 180, 187, 193, 194ab, 195, 196 (index only), 202, 245ade, 247, 299 (with variant ritornelli), 303, 304, 330, 334, 369, 403 (Bass; inc), 430a to f, **453** (inc), 478de, 501, 505bce, 590 (another version), 647ce, 649, 694, 735, 746b, 762, 805, 811gh, 812f, 813, 815, 818, 821, 822, 824, 827, 831, 832, 834, 835, 836, 837, 850c (index only)

EDITIONS: XXXII, 71, 1730c, 1773, 1828[–44]

COMMENTARY: The autograph copy of this work (British Museum, Royal Music MS 20.h.8, f.52) is incomplete. According to Hawkins (IV, p. 498), ‘ the anthem “ They that go down to the sea in ships ” was composed at the request of the Rev. Sub-dean Gostling, who being at sea with the King & the Duke of York in the Fubbs yacht and in great danger of being cast away, providentially escaped.’ However, according to Hawkins, the King died before hearing the work, which indicates that it was probably first performed after February 6th, 1685. (See also p. 359 in the same volume for a more detailed account of the adventure.) The ‘ Fubbs yacht ’ was the King’s newly-built vessel, named, because of its broad beam, after one of his mistresses, the Duchess of Portsmouth, who was nicknamed ‘ Fubbs ’. Vincent Novello published this anthem in two versions in the Musical Antiquarian Edition of *The Cathedral Services, Anthems, Hymns, and Other Sacred Pieces composed by Henry Purcell* (vol. I, pp. 147 and *147 respectively). However, the second ‘ version ’ which Boyce had published in his edition of *Cathedral Music* (1768) is actually the same as the first, without the opening symphony and the ritornelli between verses, which Boyce either omitted, or adapted for the organ. Richard Clark reported to Vincent Novello that John Gostling wrote a verse upon this anthem, which verse S. Webbe Sr. set as a glee—one of his best, he thought.

LITERATURE: J. Hawkins, *A General History of the Science and Practice of Music*, London: Novello, 1853, IV, 498; Watkins Shaw, ‘ A Contemporary Source of English Music of the Purcellian Period,’ *Acta Musicologica*, vol. XXXI, 1, pp. 38–44.

58A. **Thou know’st, Lord, the secrets of our hearts** [First setting, first version]

(XIIIA, 6) before 1683; *The Book of Common Prayer*, 1660

Full: *SATB*   Bc

(1) Thou know’st Lord: *SATB*   (2) But spare us, Lord: *SATB*

(3) Suffer us not: *SATB*

MSS: **325,** 749

EDITIONS: XIIIA, 6

58B. Thou knowest, Lord, the secrets of our hearts [First setting, second version]

(XXXII, 88) *ca.* 1683; *The Book of Common Prayer,* 1660

Verse: *satb*   *Bc*   Chorus: *SATB*

(1) Thou knowest, Lord: *satb*   (2) But spare us: *satb*

(3) Suffer us not: *satb* [*SATB*]

MSS: 42, 166b, 167ef, 613

EDITIONS: XXXII, 88

COMMENTARY: For a discussion of the authenticity of this work and its other versions, see **No. 27/** Comm.

58C. Thou knowest, Lord, the secrets of our hearts [Second setting]

(XXXII, 88) 1695; *The Book of Common Prayer,* 1660

Full: *SATB*   '*Flatt trumpets,*' *Bc*

(1) Thou knowest, Lord: *SATB*   (2) But spare us, Lord: *SATB*

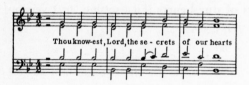

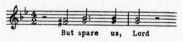

(3) Suffer us not: *SATB*

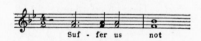

MSS: 69, 96, 99, 104, 156, 164af, 167b, 296, 301, 334, 359, 500a to e, 505abef, 632, 796ab, 828, 829, 831, 848c

EDITIONS: XXXII, 88, 1724a, 1828[–44], (undated publication No. 2)

COMMENTARY: This third version of the funeral sentence was composed for the burial service of Queen Mary, which took place in Westminster Abbey, on March 5th, 1695, accompanied by 'flatt mournful trumpets' (i.e. slide trumpets). The work was used later that same year for Purcell's own funeral. (See also No. **860.**)

LITERATURE: E. H. Fellowes, *English Cathedral Music,* London: Methuen, 1941; W. B. Squire, 'Purcell's Music for the Funeral of Mary II,' *S.I.M.G.,* IV, pp. 225–233.

59. Thy righteousness, O God, is very high

(XXXII, 124) *Psalm* 71: 19

Full: ?*SATB*   *Bc*

(1a) Thy righteousness, O God: *SATB*   (1b) And great things are they: *SATB*

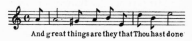

MSS: 162, 166hi

EDITIONS: XXXII, 124

COMMENTARY: This anthem is represented by only two manuscript sources in the Durham Cathedral
Library (C28 and A33). The first of these is a Bass book of 1705 or earlier, the second an organ
book. These two MSS, however, provide a fairly adequate basis for reconstruction of the anthem
as a whole, until such time as a complete source may come to light. The authenticity of the
work is by no means assured.

60. Thy way, O God, is holy

(XXXII, 91) 1687; *Psalm* 77: 13, 14 and 15 (elided), 16–18

Verse: *ab*   *Bc*   Chorus: *SATB*

(1) Thy way, O God: *ab*   (2) Ritornello

(3) Thou art the God: *ab*   (4)=1   (5)=2   (6) The voice of Thy thunder: *ab*,

(7)=2   (8)=3   (9)=1   (10) Alleluia: *SATB*

MSS: 81, 116, 152, 158, 160, 163ade, 164agh, 167b, 184, 185, 194eg, 197, 200bd, 220, 245acde, 248, 255, 310 (in c-minor), 430abcef, 478bde, 500e, 503, 505a to e, 509bcd, 511, 590, 805, 811gh, 813, 815, 818, 825, 826, 827, 831 (chorus only), 832, 850b (index only) c (index only) deh
Section II: 201

EDITIONS: XXXII, 91, 1724d, 1730c, 1768, 1792, 1828[–44]

LITERATURE: C. Burney, *A General History of Music*, London: Foulis & Co. Ltd., 1935; Watkins Shaw, 'A Contemporary Source of English Music of the Purcellian Period,' *Acta Musicologica*, vol. XXXI, 1, 1959, pp. 38–44.

61. Thy word is a lantern

(XXXII, 101) not later than 1687; *Psalm* 119: (Nun) 105–108, 110–111

Verse: *atb*   *Bc*   Chorus: *SATB*

(1) Thy word is a lantern: *atb*   (2) I have sworn: *atb*

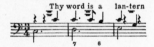

Thy word is a lan-tern

I have sworn and have stead-fast-ly pur-pos-ed

(3) I am troubled: *atb*   (4) Quicken me, O Lord:
                                                 atb [*SATB*]

I am troub - led a-bove mea-sure

Quick-en me, quick-en me, O Lord

(5) Let the freewill off'rings: *atb*   (6) The ungodly have laid: *a*

Let the free-will off-'rings of my mouth

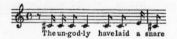

The un-god-ly have laid a snare

(7) They are the very joy: *atb*   (8) Alleluia: *SATB*

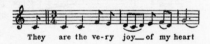

They are the ve-ry joy—of my heart

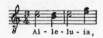

Al - le - lu - ia,

MSS: 64ab, 69, 75, 121, 158, 166aeghi, 181, 187, 194abdef, 195, 196, 197, 198, 272, 430a to f, 500abde, 503, 505a to f, 506, 509abcd, 510, 511, 513, 518, 666, 691, 692, 693, 694, 695, 743, 745, 753, 771, 772, 773, 812bf, 818, 820, 821, 835, 848h, 850ad (inc) h (inc), 855

EDITIONS: XXXII, 101, 1773, 1792, 1828[–44]

LITERATURE: Watkins Shaw, 'A Contemporary Source of English Music of the Purcellian Period,' *Acta Musicologica*, vol. XXXI, 1, 1959, pp. 38–44.

To celebrate Thy praise, O Lord, Psalm (See S18)

Turn Thee again, O Lord (See D8)

Turn Thou us, O good Lord (See S19)

62. Turn Thou us, O good Lord

(XXXII, 111) *ca.* 1682–5; (*The Third Collect for the 30th of January, on the Martyrdom of King Charles*)

Verse: *atb* Bc Chorus: *SATB*

(1) Turn Thou us: *t* (2) Spare Thy people: *atb*

(3) the same: *SATB* (4) Hear us, O Lord: *t* (5)=2 (6)=3

MSS: 325

EDITIONS: XXXII, 111, 1828[–44]

COMMENTARY: At the end of the copy in British Museum MS Add. 30931, in the hand of the copyist, is the note, 'Mr. Hen. Pursell of Westminster.' In the *Book of Common Prayer*, this Psalm also occurs in the Commination Service. In his article 'Purcell's Church Music' (*Musical Antiquary*, Jul., 1910), Arkwright classified this as a doubtful work.

63. Unto Thee will I cry, O Lord

(XVII, 20) *ca.* 1684–5; Psalm 28: 1–3, 5–7

Verse: *atb* 2 Vn, Va, Bc Chorus: *SATB*

(1) Symphony: *Str*
(a) [Grave]

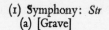

(b) [Canzona]

(2a) Unto Thee: *b, Str*

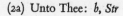
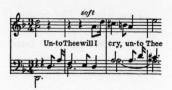

Un-to Thee will I cry, un-to Thee

(2b) Ritornello: *Str*

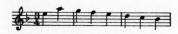

(3a) Hear the voice: *atb*

Hear the voice, O hear the voice of my

(3b) When I hold up: *atb*

When I hold up my hands

(3c) Ritornello: *Str*

(4a) O pluck me not
away: *atb*

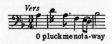

O pluck me not a-way

(4b) Ritornello: *Str*

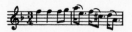

(5a) Prelude: *Str*

(5b) Praised be the Lord: *atb*

Prais-ed be the Lord, prais-ed be

(5c) the same: *atb,*
SATB, Vn obbligato

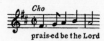

prais-ed be the Lord

(6) The Lord is the strength: *a Str*

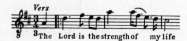

The Lord is the strength of my life

(7a) [Prelude]: *Str*

(7b) Alleluia: *atb*

Al-le-lu-ia

(7c) Ritornello: *Str*

(7d) Alleluia=7b: *SATB, Str*

MSS: 410, **453**, 823, 833

EDITIONS: XVII, 20, 1828[–44]

64. Who hath believed our report?

(XIIIA, 11) *ca.* 1679–80; *Isaiah* 53: 1–8 (altered)

Verse: *attb*   *Bc*   Chorus: *SATB*

(1) Who hath believed: *attb*

Vers Who   who— hath be-liev-ed our re-port

𝄞: L Add 30932

(2) He hath no form: *t*

He hath no form nor come-li-ness

(3) He is despised: *t*

He is des-pi-sed and re-jec-ted

(4) Surely He hath born: *b*

Sure-ly,   sure-ly He hath born our griefs

(5a) All we like sheep: *attb*   (5b) the same: *SATB*

(6a) He was oppressed: *attb*

All we like sheep have gone a-stray   He was op-press - ed

(6b) He is brought: *t*

He is brought as a lamb

(7) For He was cut off: *t*

e For He was cut off
31

(8) = 5b

MSS: **326**

EDITIONS: XIIIA, 11, 1828[–44]

65. Why do the heathen so furiously rage?

(XVII, 1) *ca.* 1684–5; *Psalm* 2: 1–12

Verse: *atb*   2 *Vn, Va, Bc*   Chorus: *SATB*

(1) Symphony: *Str*
   (a) [Grave]

Symph.

𝄞: LK 20, h. 8.

[(b) [Canzona]

3

(2) Why do the heathen: *b*

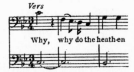

Vers
Why,   why do the heath-en

(3a) The kings of the earth: *atb*

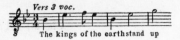

(3b) Let us break the bonds: *atb*

(3c) Ritornello: *Str*

(4a) But He that dwelleth: *b, Vn*

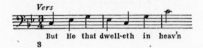

(4b) Then shall He speak: *at*

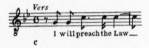

(4c) Yet have I set: *atb*

³(5) = 1b

(6) I will preach: *t*

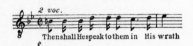

(7) Thou art my Son: *b*

(8) Be wise now: *at*

(9a) Serve the Lord: *atb*

(9b) Kiss the Son: *atb*

(9c) Blessed are all they: *atb*

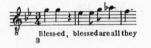

(9d) Ritornello: *Str*

(10) Blessed are they: *SATB*

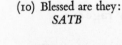

(11) Alleluia: *SATB*

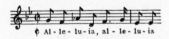

MSS: 293, 410, **453,** 759, 833

EDITIONS: XVII, 1, ?1790b, 1828[−44]

COMMENTARY: In the commentary to the Purcell Society Edition, vol. XVII, variants between Purcell's text and that of the *Authorized Version* are noted. The editor has altered Purcell's text in one such instance, and let it stand in two others. As he suggests, Purcell probably intended that appropriate instruments accompany the voice parts, even though no instrumental parts are written, or mentioned in the manuscripts. As A. K. Holland has pointed out (*Henry Purcell*, London: Penguin Books, 1948, p. 128) the overture superficially resembles that for *Dido and Aeneas*.

N66. If the Lord himself

Psalm 124: 1–4(?)

Verse: [?]   [?*Vn, Va*] *Bc*   [?*SAT*]*B*

(1) Symphony: [?*Str*] (missing in the only known source, although time-signature, clef, and key-signature are given in MS 540 on p. 28 as follows:

(2a) 'vers' If the Lord himself: [?] (missing in the only known source)

(2b) 'cho' If the Lord himself: [?*SAT*]*B*

If   the   Lord   him - self   had   not   been

(2c) Ritornello: [?*Str*] (missing in the only known source)

(3) 'vers': [?] (missing in the only known source)

(4) Symphony: [?*Str*] (missing in the only known source; possibly the same as 1)

(5a) 'vers' Alleluia: [?] (missing in the only known source; possibly similar to 5c)

(5b) Ritornello: [?*Str*] (missing in the only known source)

(5c) 'cho' Alleluia: [?*SAT*]*B*

Al - le - lu - ia,   al - le - lu - ia

MSS: 540

COMMENTARY: Although there is but one source for this anthem, the authenticity of this is such that the work may be ascribed to Purcell with scarcely any serious doubt. Should other part-books containing parts for this anthem come to light, the following copy of the bass choral part in the Nanki MS may possibly be of use in reconstructing the anthem as a whole:

N67. I will love Thee, O Lord

(XXVIII, 157) *ca.* 1679(?); *Psalm* 18: 1–6, 16–18

Verse: *b*   *Bc*   Chorus: *SATB*

(1) I will love Thee: *b*   (2) I will call upon the Lord: *b*

(3) They prevented me: *SATB*   (4) The sorrows of death: *b*

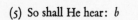

(5) So shall He hear: *b*   (6) He shall send down: *b*   (7) = 3

MSS: 153 (missing), 249, 590, 613 (Chorus only)

EDITIONS: XXVIII 157, 1828[–44] (mentioned in the Preface as missing)

COMMENTARY: I discovered this anthem in one of the Charles Badham score-books (MS Mus. Sch. C.40, p. 26) in the Bodleian Library, Oxford. Later I found the chorus in the Christ Church Library, Oxford (MS 22, f.88) in an anonymous copy bearing a pencilled ascription to Purcell. Recently, yet another source has come to light in Gloucester Cathedral Chapter Library, in a bass book carefully copied in a nearly contemporary hand. In Durham Cathedral Library MS A.15 a setting of the same text is ascribed to Purcell in the index, but the composition itself has been torn out and is missing.

LITERATURE: F. B. Zimmerman, 'A Newly Discovered Anthem by Purcell,' *The Musical Quarterly*, vol. XLV, No. 3, July 1959, p. 302.

N68. Praise the Lord, ye servants [Fragmentary]

Psalm 113: 1–9

Verse: [?*att*]*b*   [?2 *Vn*, *Va*,]   *Bc*   [?*SAT*]*B*

(1) Symphony: [?*Str*] (missing in both known sources, but beginning with time signature, clef, and key-signature in MS No. 540 as follows:

(2a) 'vers solus': Praise the Lord, ye servants: ?*t* (missing in both known sources).

(2b) 'cho': Praise the Lord, ye servants: [?*SAT*]*B* (taken from MS No. 540 only)

Praise the Lord, ye   ser - vants

(3a) 'vers 4 voc': ?*attb*: (missing in both known sources; probable text: 'Blessed is the name of the Lord').

(3b) Ritornello: *Str* (missing in both known sources).

(4) 'cho' The Lord's name is praised: [?*SAT*]*B* (from MS No. 540 only)

The   Lord's name   is   prais - ed

(5) 'vers': (12 bars, missing in both known sources; probable text: 'From the rising of the sun.')

(6) 'cho': The Lord is high above: [?*SAT*]*B* (from MS No. 540 only)

(7) 'Symphony': [?*Str*] (missing in both known sources; possibly the same as (1))

(8a) 'vers' (missing in both known sources; probable text: 'Who is like unto our Lord')

(8b) Ritornello: [?*Str*] (missing in both known sources)

(9) 'vers' (missing in both known sources; probable text: 'Who humbleth himself to behold: ?*attb*)

(10a) 'vers': He taketh up the simple: [?*att*]*b* (from MS No. 20 only)

(10b) Ritornello [?*Str*] (10 bars missing in both known sources)

(11a) 'vers': That he may set him with princes: [?*att*]*b* (from MS No. 20 only)

(11b) Ritornello: [?*Str*] (7 bars, missing in both known sources)

(11c) 'vers': Even with the princes: [?*att*]*b* (from MS No. 20 only)

(12a) 'cho': He maketh the barren women: [?*SAT*]*B* (from both MSS, Nos. 20 and 540)

(12b) And to be a joyfull mother: [?*SAT*]*B* (from both MSS, Nos. 20 and 540)

MSS: 20, 540

EDITIONS: 1828[-44] (listed in the Preface as missing)

COMMENTARY: In the first MS source that came to light (in the collection of Mr. Richard Border, of Pulborough, Sussex) only a verse and a chorus bass part were to be found, the text and musical setting beginning in the middle of *Psalm* 113 at the words: 'He taketh up the simple out of the dust' (See section 10a, above). The title, therefore, was then only conjectural, although it corresponded to that of the missing anthem for three voices listed by Vincent Novello in the prefatory volume to his edition of *Purcell's Sacred Music*, London: Alfred Novello, n.d., p. iii.

    The discovery (by Mr. Hugh McLean) of another source in the Nanki Library (in Japan, near Tokyo) clearly establishes the title as that of an authentic work by Purcell. This new source also opens up the possibility that there may have been more than one version of the anthem. Unlike the work Novello described, this one was written for four soloists. Furthermore, sections 10a, 10b, 11a, 11b, and 11c are not represented in the Nanki MS, although their existence is clearly indicated in the Border MS. Incidentally, both these MSS appear to have been copied by the same hand, which is also similar to one that may be found in the Chapel Royal part-books, British Museum R.M. 23.m.1-6.

To facilitate the reconstruction of this anthem in the event that other parts are discovered, or for collation should a score be found, the relevant portions of the material provided by these two MSS are reproduced here. (NB: The text is reproduced in quasi-facsimile. That is to say, obvious editorial accidentals have not been introduced, although abbreviations in the underlay have been expanded, and short-hand realized):

(A) *Praise the Lord ye Servants:* Bass part (chorus) from MS No. 540

Mr. Henry Purcell

(B) *Praise the Lord, ye Servants:* incomplete solo (and chorus) bass part from MS No. 20, p. 33

The remainder of the music copied for this Anthem in MS No. 20 is virtually the same as that given under (A) above. The extreme lowness of the range for solo part suggests that this may have been another Purcellian anthem written to suit the extraordinary voice of John Gostling.

N69. The Lord is King, and hath put on glorious apparel

(XXXII, 30); *Psalm* 93: 1–5 (with Doxology)

Verse: *sb*   *Bc*   Chorus: *SATB*

(1) The Lord is King: *s,* [*SATB*]   (2) He hath made: *s,* [*SATB*]

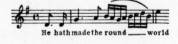

(3) The floods are ris'n: *s*

(4) Thy testimonies, O Lord: *s*

(5) Glory be to the Father: *SATB*

MSS: 201

EDITIONS: XXXII, 30

COMMENTARY: This anthem, only recently discovered, can neither be confirmed nor denied as
Purcell's work without further evidence. It is one of his less inspired works, if it is indeed his.

GENERAL LITERATURE

G. E. P. Arkwright, 'Purcell's Church Music,' *The Musical Antiquary*, I, Jan. 1910, pp. 63–72; Biblio-
graphy, *ibid.*, July, 1910, pp. 234–48; J. Bumpus, *A History of English Cathedral Music, 1549–1889*, London;
T. Werner Laurie, n.d.; E. H. Fellowes, *English Cathedral Music*, London: Methuen, 1941; G. Marco,
'The Variety in Purcell's Word Painting,' *The Music Review*, XVIII, pp. 1–3; V. Novello, *Purcell's
Sacred Music* (prefatory volume), London: J. A. Novello, 1842; F. de Quervain, *Der Chorstil Henry
Purcells*, Bern & Leipzig: Paul Haupt, 1935; H. O. Statham, 'Purcell's Church Music,' *Musical Times*,
May 1924; J. A. Westrup, *Purcell*, London: J. M. Dent & Sons, 1947.

CANONS

101. Alleluia ('Canon 4 in 2, *recte et retro*')

AABB

Al - le - lu - ia, al - le - lu - ia

MSS: 327

EDITIONS: 1828–[44]

COMMENTARY: As Vincent Novello pointed out in his edition (*The Cathedral Service, Anthems, Hymns and other Sacred Pieces Composed by Henry Purcell*, vol. III, p. 831), 'This very curiously constructed canon is adapted to secular words ("Joy, Mirth, Triumphs I do defy") in the original copy.' The copy to which he was referring was a rare MS in the possession of the Revd. Joshua Dix of Faversham, now Br. Mus. MS Add 30933.

Alleluia [in C Major] (See No. N110)

Alleluia [in B♭ Major] (See D15)

And ascended into heaven ('Canon 4 in 1') (See No. 230C/6f)

And mine eyes have seen his desire ('Canon 5 in 1') (See No. 51/3b)

And Thou, child, shalt be called ('Canon 4 in 1') (See No. 230M/2b)

102. Domine non est exaltatum cor meum (Incomplete)

(XXXII, 172) *ca.* 1680

AT   Bc

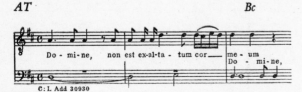

Do - mi - ne,   non est ex-al-ta - tum cor___ me - um
                                           Do - mi - ne,

C: L Add 30930

MSS: **324**

EDITIONS: XXXII, 172

COMMENTARY: The conjectural date is based on the position of this work, which is near the front of Purcell's autograph copy, MS Add. 30930 in the British Museum. The MS title-page is dated '1680'. As indicated in the Purcell Society Edition, this is probably an unfinished motet, even though the imitation begins rather strictly.

103. Gloria Patri et Filio

(XXXII, 163) *ca.* 1680; 'From Dr. Patrick's version.'

SATB

(a) Gloria Patri et Filio

C: L Add 30930

(b) Sicut erat in principio

MSS: **324,** 389, 630, 758

EDITIONS: XXXII, 163, 1828[–44]

COMMENTARY: Neither of the two sections of this work is a strict canon. For the reasoning behind the conjectural date given above, see **No. 102**/Commentary. (This work appears on f.7v of the autograph.)

104. Gloria Patri et Filio ('Canon 3 in 1')

(XXXII, 159)

SAB   *Bc*

MSS: **327**

EDITIONS: XXXII, 159, 1828[–44]

105. Gloria Patri et Filio (' Canon 4 in 1 *per arsin et thesin* ')

(XXXII, 161)

SSTB

MSS: 327, 454

EDITIONS: XXXII, 161, 1828[-44]

Gloria Patri in d minor (See No. 870D1)

106. Glory be to the Father (' Canon 4 in 1 ')

(XXXII, 168)

SATB

MSS: 327

EDITIONS: XXXII, 168, 1828[-44]

Glory be to the Father (' Canon 2 in 1 by inversion ') (See No. 230M/2f)

Glory be to the Father (' Canon 2 in 1 ') (See No. 230M/3j)

Glory be to the Father (' Canon 4 in 2 ') (See No. 230E/8c)

Glory be to the Father (' Canon 3 in 1 ') (See No. 230E/7g)

Glory be to the Father (' Canon 3 in 1 by inversion ') (See No. 230E/9i)

Glory be to the Father (' Canon 4 in 1 by inversion ') (See No. 230E/10h)

Glory be to the Father (' Canon 4 in 2 ') (See No. 231/2c)

Glory be to the Father (' A Canon Four in One ') (See No. 870D3)

Glory be to the Father [in D Major] (See D21)

107. God is gone up (' Canon 7 in 1 at the unison ')

(XXXII, 170)

7 voices

MSS: 454

EDITIONS: XXXII, 170

Joy, mirth, triumphs, all farewell (See No. 101/Commentary)

108. Laudate Dominum (' Canon 3 in 1 ')

(XXXII, 170)

SAB

MSS: 327, 587

EDITIONS: XXXII, 170,   1828[–44]

Laudate Dominum (' Canon 3 in 1 ') (See D22)

109. Miserere mei (' Canon 4 in 2 ')

(XXXII, 171), 1687

SATB

D

MSS: 454

EDITIONS: XXXII, 171, 168a, 1694c, 1697b, 1718a

COMMENTARY: In British Museum Royal Music MS 20.h.9 (f.1ᵛ), the opening line begins: 'Miserere nostri.' (See also **No. 870D2,** where the same canon is shown in original clefs.)

O go your way into His gates ('Canon 4 in 2 per arsin and thesin') (See No. 230M/4c)

O go your way into His gates ('Canon 4 in 1') (See No. 232/2e)

Vouchsafe, O Lord, to keep us ('Canon 4 in 2') (See No. 230M/1g)

N110. Alleluia (Canon)

SSATB

EDITIONS: 1728a, 1731e, 1750b

COMMENTARY: This *Alleluia* is ascribed to Purcell in Michael Broome's *A Choice Collection of Twenty-four Psalm Tunes* (1728), where it appears as part of the anthem 'Great is the Lord' (*Psalm* 48) by Thomas Everett, a man otherwise unknown. The *Alleluia* appears under the same conditions in William Corbett's *The Second Edition of the First Book of the Voice of Melody* ... (William East, Waltham, Leicestershire, 1750) without ascription to Purcell. Its authenticity must remain uncertain until confirmation is provided by other sources.

CHANTS

120. Chant No. 1 [in a minor] (XXXII, 174)

SATB

MSS: 73, 141, 194c (in b minor), 359, 619, 648, 649, 666, 852 (in b minor), 853 (in b minor), 863

EDITIONS: XXXII, 174, 1765a (anon), 1767a, 1828[-44]

COMMENTARY: In the various manuscript sources, this chant appears in several versions. The variants consist mainly in the division into smaller rhythmic units of the note-values given above. However, a few sources (Cambridge, King's College MSS 9-17 and York Minster MSS 3 and 5) give this chant in b minor. In 1765, John Arnold published it anonymously as the 'Uxbridge Tune' for *Psalm* XXX. It is also identified as the 15th tune (Proper Tune) in Oxford, Christ Church MS 48.

121. Chant No. 2 [in G Major] (XXXII, 173)

SATB

[sic]

MSS: 194c, 359, 863

EDITIONS: XXXII, 173

COMMENTARY: In the 'Copy in ordinary notation of the Tunes to the Psalms in Richard Ayleward's MS Book' belonging to Dr. A. H. Mann (see Cambridge, King's College MSS 9-17, p. 12, rev.) the following marginal note is to be found: 'Well-known (in Boyce's *Cathedral Music*) and is attributed to Henry Purcell and also to Daniel Purcell.' In British Museum MS Add. 37027 it is ascribed to Purcell (without Christian name) in pencil in a later hand.

122. Chant No. 3 [in G Major] (XXXII, 174)

SATB

MSS: 169 (alto only), 587, 648

EDITIONS: XXXII, 174, 1828[–44]

COMMENTARY: This chant is very similar to that attributed to Thomas Purcell by Boyce (see D33), by Vincent Novello, and by Burney (II, 380), except that it is in G Major.

123. Chant No. 4 [in d minor]

SATB

MSS: 357, 359 (in a minor), 649, 848i, 852, 853

EDITIONS: 1767a, 1828[–44]

COMMENTARY: In Oxford, Christ Church Library MS 1229 this chant is ascribed to Edward Purcell, as it is in C. & S. Thomson, *Fifty Double Chants*, 1767; this ascription is probably correct. In British Museum MS Add. 37027, f.51v, it is set to the words: 'Come let us sing.'

124. Chant No. 5 [in G Major]

SATB

MSS: 852, 853

COMMENTARY: The authenticity of this work is not established.

125. Chant No. 6 [in g minor] (The 'Burford' Psalm-tune) XXXII, 173

SATB

MSS: 314 (in a minor), 331, 871 (bass only)

EDITIONS: XXXII, 173, 1718c, 1730g, 1765a, 1772-4, 1790c,? 1798, 1800a (see Commentary), 1828[-44], ca.1830 (see Commentary), 1831, Undated publ. No. 4

COMMENTARY: Tradition associates this chant with the historic old church in Burford, Oxfordshire. A connection with Burford parish in Shropshire may be equally probable, if, indeed, any connection is indicated at all, which is doubtful. As for the history of the tune itself, the ascription to Purcell is based (according to Lightwood, *Hymn-tunes and their Story*, p. 93) on an anecdote describing a fire at Epworth Vicarage in 1709. Among other relics, one scorched bit of paper was rescued from the flames, on it a hymn 'Behold the saviour of mankind' set to a tune by Purcell called the 'Burford'. Apparently John Wesley discovered it there years later. The tune first appeared in print in *A Book of Psalmody, containing a Variety of Tunes for all the Common Metres of the Psalms in the Old and New Versions...*' John Cheltham, 1718, where neither place nor composer is named. The name 'Burford' appears to have been first used by Nathaniel Gawthorn in his *Harmonia Perfecta* (early 18th century) where he did not name Purcell as the composer. The earliest known book in which Purcell is mentioned as the composer is Cotterill's *Christian Psalmody* printed in 1831, although one Dr. Miller printed it in his *Psalms of David* (1790) with the note: 'said to be Purcell's.' In an early American publication (*The Village Harmony, or New England Repository of Sacred Music*, ?1798) the tune appears in the tenor in a setting of the words 'How shall the young secure their hearts.' The tune is labelled 'Burford' and is ascribed to Purcell. The tune also appears under the place-name 'Norwich' in the 10th edition of Watson's collection, ca. 1830. In a footnote to the version of this work printed in his *Cathedral Services &c*, Vincent Novello speaks of a book of 'Purcell's Psalms', mentioned earlier by Croft. Croft may have been referring to the publication listed herein as Edition 1694b (which contains no works by Purcell, although it was edited by him) or, as Novello surmised, to a collection of Purcell's Psalm-tunes now lost. In my opinion, the ascription to Henry Purcell is very doubtful. Not only are the sources which ascribe it to him suspiciously late, but the melody itself does not strike me as 'Purcellian.' The setting beginning as follows (copied in 1814 by J. W. Windsor, Organist of Bath—see London, Royal College of Music MS 667) is perhaps somewhat more Purcellian in style. It appears under the heading 'Psalm 71, verses 1, 2, 3, and 9th':

Chant [in A Major] (See D30)

Chant [in C Major] (See D31)

Chant [in G Major] (See D32)

Chant [in g minor] (See D33)

Chant [in g minor] (See D34)

Venite [chant in G Major] (See D35)

Chant [in g minor] (See D36)

Chant [in B♭ Major] (See D37)

Chant [in g minor[(See D38)

HYMNS, PSALMS, AND SACRED PART-SONGS

130. Ah! few and full of sorrows

Hymn (XXX, 109) 1680; George Sandys: a paraphrase of *Job* 14: 1

Verse: *tb*   *Bc*   Chorus: *SATB*

(1) Ah! few and full of sorrows: *SATB*

ϕ: L Add 30930

(2) Wilt thou thine eyes: *t*

(3) O! that thou would'st: *b*

(4) I will expect until my change: *SATB*

MSS: **324**, 389, 601, 758

EDITIONS: XXX, 109, 1828[–44]

COMMENTARY: The text alone occurs in John Gibson's Commonplace Book (British Museum MS Add. 37719, f.18v), but no author is named. This manuscript dates from about 1655–60. The autograph and all known sources break off at bar 66, Novello's edition ending with a pause on the chord of C Major, which seems strangely inappropriate. Purcell may have left the work in fragmentary form, for the autograph copy ends just after a new time signature; and he left the following one and a half pages blank. Seventeen and a half lines of text remain to complete the poem (as printed in George Sandys' *A Paraphrase upon the Divine Poems*, Folio, 1638) from where Purcell left off. However, this need not all have been set, for Purcell had skipped over lines earlier in the text. Possible first-lines for further sections—if, indeed, Purcell did set more of Sandys' poem—might have been: 'Can man recover his departed breath?' or, 'Thy wrath prevails against him everyday.' See **No. 102**/Commentary for the reasoning behind the above conjectural dating. (This work appears on f.15ᵛ in the autograph.)

131. Beati omnes qui timent Dominum

Latin Hymn (XXXII, 137) 1680; *Vulgate: Psalm 127: 1–4*

Verse: *sb*   *Bc*   Chorus: *SSAB*

(1) Beati omnes qui timent Dominum: *SSAB*

(2a) Labores manuum tuarum: *SSAB*   (2b) Uxor tua sicut vitis: *b*

 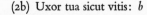

(2c) Filii tui sicut novellae olivarum: *s*

(3) Ecce, sic benedicitum homo: *SSAB*   (4) Alleluia: *SSAB*

MSS: **324,** 389, 630, 758

EDITIONS: XXXII, 137, 1828[–44]

COMMENTARY: Note the similarity of the beginning motif to the ritornello in *Why, why are all the Muses mute?* (No. **343/9**). The date is based on the position of the work in the autograph, Br. Mus. MS Add. 30930, f.11.

132. Early, O Lord, my fainting soul

Sacred part-song (XXX, 117) after 1680; ?Psalm 63 (paraphrase), John Patrick: *A Century of Select Psalms*, 1684

Verse: *sb*   *Bc*   Chorus: *SSAB*

(1) Early, O Lord: *SSAB*

(2a) I long t'appear: *s*

(2b) For life itself: *SSAB*

(3) When others sleep: *b* (4) Danger, whilst Thou art near: *SSAB*

MSS: **324,** 348, 389, 601, 630, 758

EDITIONS: XXX, 117, 1684c (mnp), 1828[-44]

COMMENTARY: The date is conjectured from the position of the work in the autograph, on f.26.

Far from me be all false ways, Hymn (See D40)

Great is the Lord, Hymn (See S5)

133. Hear me, O Lord, the great support

Sacred part-song (XXX, 127) 1680-2; *Psalm* 4: 1-8, John Patrick: *A Century of Select Psalms, 1684*

Verse: *at* Bc Chorus: *ATB*

(1) Hear me, O Lord: *ATB* (2) Know that the Lord: *t*

(3) Sin not, but fear: *ATB* (4) Tho' others in distrust: *ATB*

D2

(5) Thy love more cheers: *a*

(6) Down will I lie: *ATB*

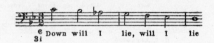

MSS: **324**, 389, 399, 601, 758

EDITIONS: XXX, 127, 1684c (mnp), 1828[–44]

COMMENTARY: Novello's edition was based on a manuscript, now missing, formerly in the possession of a Reverend I. Parker. The approximate date was deduced from the position of this piece in the autograph (itself dated 1680) on f.28.

Here the weary cease from labour, Hymn (See No. 191/2, 3)

Hosanna to the Prince of light, Hymn (See S6)

How pleasant is Thy dwelling place, Hymn (See S7)

134. In guilty night

Sacred Oratorio (XXXII, 128) before 1693; 'Saul and the Witch of Endor,' a paraphrase of *Samuel* 28: 8–20

Verse: *sab*   Bc   Chorus: *SAB*

(1) In guilty night: *SAB*

(2a) Woman, arise, call: *a*

(2b) Why should'st thou wish: *s*

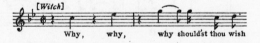

(2c) Woman, be bold: *a*

(2d) Whom shall I raise: *sa*

(2c) Who's he that comes?: *sa*

Who's   he that comes?

(3) Why hast thou robb'd me?: *b*

Why,   why hast thou robb'd me?

(4) O! I'm sore distressed: *a*

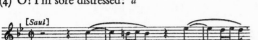

O!   O!

(5) Art thou forlorn: *b*

Art thou for-lorn of God?

(6) O! Farewell: *SAB*

Fare - well,   fare - well

MSS: 214, 310, 359, 528, 614, 758, 848de, 872 (inc, corrupt)

EDITIONS: XXXII, 128,   1693b, 1714a, 1714b, 1805, 1828[-44]

COMMENTARY: The text alone is to be found anonymously in John Gibson's Commonplace Book
(British Museum MS Add. 37719, f.189ᵛ). It was probably copied into the manuscript between
the years 1656 and 1660, while Gibson was a Royalist prisoner at Durham Castle. The same
text had been set earlier by Robert Ramsey (British Museum MS Add. 11608, f.23v), by Benjamin
Lamb (British Museum MS Add. 31453 f.187), and by Nicholas Lanier (MS Add. 22100, f.105).

135. Jehova, quam multi sunt hostes

Latin Psalm (XXXII, 147) 1680; *Vulgate*: Psalm 3

Verse: *tb*   *Bc*   Chorus: *SSATB*

(1a) Jehova, quam multi: *SSATB*

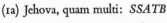

Je - ho - va,
Je - ho - va,   quam mul-ti sunt hos-tes
Je - ho - va,

¢ : L Add 30930

(1b) Quam multi dicunt: *SSATB*

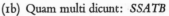

Quam___   mul - ti di-cunt de
Quam___   mul-ti di - cunt de   a - ni-ma

(2a) At Tu, Jehova, clypeus es: *t*

At Tu, Je - ho - va, cly-pe-us es

(2b) Gloria mea et extollens: *t*

Glo-ri-a   me - a,

(3a) Voce mea ad Jehovam: *SSATB*

(3b) Ego cubui et dormivi: *SSATB*

(4a) Non timebo a myriadibus populi: *b*

(4b) Surge, Jehova: *b*

(4c) Qui percussisti omnes inimicos: *b*

(5) Jehova est salus: *SSATB*

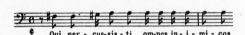

MSS: **324,** 389, 630, 758, 787

EDITIONS: XXXII, 147, 1828[–44]

COMMENTARY: Novello based his edition on a manuscript belonging to Mr. Hawes, Gentleman of the Chapel Royal. He collated this with a manuscript in Christ Church Library, Oxford (probably MS 628, p. 135).

LITERATURE: E. H. Fellowes, *English Cathedral Music*, London: Methuen, 1941.

136. Lord, I can suffer Thy rebukes

Sacred part-song (XXX, 136) after 1680; *Psalm 6*: 1–10; John Patrick, *A Century of Select Psalms,* 1684

Verse: *ssab*   *Bc*   Chorus: *SSAB*

(1) Lord, I can suffer: *s*

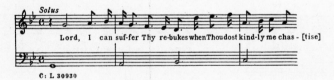

C: L 30930

(2) Pity my languishing estate: *SSAB*

(3a) Lord, for Thy goodness: *b*

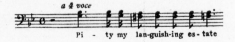

(3b) See how I pass: *ss*

See how I pass my wea-ry days

(3c) Depart, ye wicked foes: *ab*

De - part,—— ye wick-ed foes

(4) The Lord hath heard: *SSAB*

The Lord hath heard, hath heard

(5) Alleluia: *SSAB*

Al - le-lu - ia, al - le - lu - ia,

MSS: **324**, 389, 601, 758

EDITIONS: XXX, 136, 1684c (mnp), 1828[-44]

COMMENTARY: The date has been conjectured from the position of this work in the last section of the front end of the autograph, Br. Mus. Add. MS 30930, f.22.

137. Lord, not to us

Sacred part-song (XXX, 146) *ca.* 1680; *Psalm* 115; John Patrick, *A Century of Select Psalms*, 1684

Bc

ATB

(1) Lord, not to us: *ATB*

Lord, not to us, But to Thy name

:L Add 30930

MSS: **324** (inc), 389, 758

EDITIONS: XXX, 146, 1684c (mnp), 1828[-44]

COMMENTARY: Purcell may have left this as a fragment, for so it exists in all extant sources. The position of this piece fairly near the beginning of the autograph (Br. Mus. Add. MS 30930, f.14) provides the basis for the conjectural dating.

138. O, all ye people, clap your hands

Psalm (XXX, 148) 1680; *Psalm* 47: 1-3, 5-7; John Patrick, *A Century of Select Psalms*, 1684

Bc

SSTB

(1) O, all ye people: *SSTB*

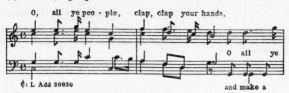

(2a) In a triumphant state: *SSTB*

(2b) Trumpets proclaim our joys: *SSTB*

(2c) Sing cheerful praises: *SSTB*

(3) God o'er the heathen: *SSTB*

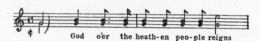

MSS: 157, **324**, 347, 348, 389, 544, 601, 630, 758

EDITIONS: XXX, 148, 1684c (mnp), 1828[–44]

COMMENTARY: This is the second work to have been copied into the autograph, dated 1680 at this end of the MS.

O God, sole object of our love (See D41)

139. O happy man that fears the Lord

Sacred part-song (XXX, 157); *Psalm* 112: 1–10; John Patrick, *A Century of Select Psalms*, 1684
SSAB

(1) O happy man that fears the Lord: *SSAB*

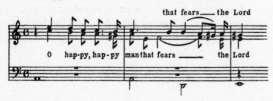

MSS: 601

EDITIONS: XXX, 157, 1684c (mnp), 1828[–44]

COMMENTARY: This work is incomplete in the earliest extant manuscript source (Oxford, Bodleian MS Mus. C. 28, f.122) and in Novello's edition and manuscript copy (Br. Mus. Add. MS 9076, f.48) which derive either from this MS or one like it. Novello states that he based his edition on a score in Purcell's own handwriting in the possession of the Reverend James Pears of Bath. The Oxford MS, though not an authentic autograph, has been so described, and is the only extant MS which this description comes near to fitting.

140. O, I'm sick of life

Sacred part-song (XXX, 160) after 1680; George Sandys

Verse: *at*   *Bc*   Chorus: *ATB*

(1) O, I'm sick of life: *ATB*

C: L Add 30930

(2) What, should Thy wrath: *a*   (3) What, are Thy days as frail: *ATB*

(4) Cannot my known integrity: *t*   (5) O, since I have so short: *ATB*

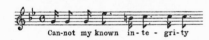   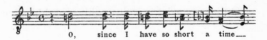

MSS: 14, **324**, 389, 399, 601, 630, 758

EDITIONS: XXX, 160, 1828[–44]

COMMENTARY: Novello printed his edition from a manuscript belonging to Dr. Hawes, which may be one of the above. If not, it is another of those which are missing. In the front end of the autograph (begun in 1680, according to the inscription on the title-page) this work appears on f.20ᵛ.

141. O Lord, our Governor

Psalm (XXX, 167) *ca.* 1680; *Psalm* 8: 1–9; John Patrick, *A Century of Select Psalms*, 1684

Verse: *b*   *Bc*   Chorus: *SSAB*

(1) O Lord, our Governor: *SSAB*   (2) From the weak pow'r of babes: *SSAB*

(3) When I to heav'n: *b*   (4) Tho' lower than the angels: (5) = 1
                                                  SSAB

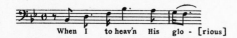   

MSS: **324,** 389, 601, 630, 758

EDITIONS: XXX, 167, 1684c (mnp), 1828[–44]

COMMENTARY: As the ninth piece at the front end of the autograph, this work has been dated
   conjecturally as of 1680, the date when that MS was begun.

O Lord, rebuke me not, Sacred Song (See S14)

O miserable man, Sacred Song (See S15)

O that mine eyes would melt, Hymn (See S16)

O that my grief was throughly weigh'd, Hymn (See D42)

142. Plung'd in the confines of despair

Part-song (XXX, 180) 1680; *Psalm* 130; John Patrick, *A Century of Select Psalms,* 1684

Verse: *tb*   *Bc*   Chorus: *TTB*

(1) Plung'd in the confines of despair: *TTB*

(2a) Should'st Thou against each: *b*

(2b) But Thou forgiveness dost proclaim: *b*, [*TTB*]

(3a) My soul less brooks: *t*

(3b) The frailty of our state: *TTB*

MSS: **13**, 14, **324**, 347, 389, 399, 601, 630, 758

EDITIONS: XXX, 180, 1684c (mnp), 1828[–44]

COMMENTARY: Being the first piece copied into the front end of the British Museum autograph, this work has been dated as of the year 1680, when this part of the MS was begun.

Put me not to rebuke, O Lord, Psalm (See D43)

143. Since God so tender a regard

Sacred part-song (XXX, 187) after 1680; *Psalm* 116; John Patrick, *A Century of Select Psalms*, 1684
Verse: *tb*   *Bc*   Chorus: *TTB*

(1) Since God so tender: *t*

(2) Assail'd with grief: *TTB*

89

(3a) Nor do I cry to God: *b*

(3b) God and thyself, my soul: *TTB*

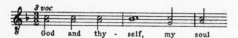

(4a) The solemn payment: *t*

(4b) By all engagements, Lord: *TTB*

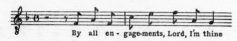

MSS: 14, **324**, 348, 389, 399, 544, 601, 630, 758

EDITIONS: XXX, 187, 1684c (mnp), 1828[-44]

COMMENTARY: This work appears fairly near the end of the front section of the autograph; therefore it can be dated some considerable time after that MS was begun in 1680.

The gracious bounty of our God, Hymn (See D44)

The Lord my pasture shall prepare, Hymn (See S17)

To celebrate Thy praise, O Lord, Psalm (See S18)

Walsall, Hymn (See D45)

Westminster Abbey, Hymn (See D46)

144. When on my sick bed I languish

Sacred part-song (XXX, 194) 1680; Thomas Flatman, 'A Thought on Death,' *Poems and Songs*, 1674
Verse: *tb*   *Bc*   Chorus: *TTB*

(1a) When on my sick bed: *TTB*

(1b) Fainting, gasping, trembling: *TTB*

(2) O tell me: *b*

(3) Be not fearful: *TTB*

(4) Think with thyself: *t*

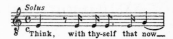

(5) Like Caesar with assurance: *TTB*

MSS: 14, **324,** 347, 348, 389, 544, 601, 630, 758

EDITIONS: XXX, 194

COMMENTARY: As the third work to have been copied into the front end of the autograph, this song
may be dated shortly after 1680, when that part of the MS was begun, according to the date on
the title-page.

SACRED SONGS AND DUETS

Arise, great dead, for arms renown'd (See D69)

Arise, my darken'd melancholy soul (See D70)

181. Awake, and with attention hear

(XXX, 1), *ca.* 1685; a paraphrase by Abraham Cowley of *Isaiah* 34
Solo: *b*   *Bc*

(1) Awake, and with attention hear: *b*

(2) God does a solemn sacrifice prepare: *b*   (3) So will they fall: *b*

(4) And know, O cursed land: *b*   (5) As one who buys: *b*

MSS: 343, **453**, 724

EDITIONS: XXX, 1, 1688c, 1703e, 1714b, 1828[–44]

182. Awake, ye dead

(XXX, 98), 1685; Nahum Tate, ' A Hymn upon the last day'
Soli: *bb*   *Bc*

(1) Awake, ye dead: *bb*

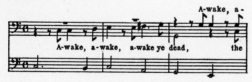

(2) The virtuous soul alone appears humor'd: *tb*

MSS: 69, 381, 758, 848e, 863

EDITIONS: XXX, 98, 1693b, 1714a, 1714b, 1792, 1828[–44]

183. Begin the song and strike the living lyre

(XXX, 18) *ca.* 1687–8; Abraham Cowley

Solo: *b*   *Bc*

(1) Begin the song: *b*

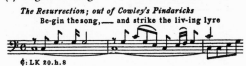

The Resurrection; out of Cowley's Pindaricks
Be-gin the song,___ and strike the liv-ing lyre

♮: LK 20.h.8

(2) Then shall the scatter'd atoms crowding come: *b*

(3) And where th'attending soul naked and shivering stands: *b*

MSS: **453** (inc)

EDITIONS: XXX, 18, 1693b, 1714a, 1714b, 1828[–44]

184. Close thine eyes and sleep secure

(XXX, 105) 1688; Francis Quarles, ' A Good-Night,' *Divine Fancies*, 1632

Soli: *sb*   *Bc*

(1) Close thine eyes: *sb*

Close___ thine eyes and sleep,___ sleep___ se - cure

(2) The music and the mirth of Kings: *sb*

MSS: 381, 758

EDITIONS: XXX, 105, 1688c, 1703e, 1714b, 1805, 1828[–44]

COMMENTARY: The text for this work has been traditionally attributed to King Charles I. However, the poem is given in its entirety in *The Complete Works in Prose and Verse of Francis Quarles*, ed. A. B. Grosart (Chertsey Worthies' Library) II, 1880, p. 243, with no indication that it is not one of Quarles' own poems. The original version of the poem differs in the wording of the first line ('Close now thine eyes and rest secure') as in other parts of the poem.

185. Full of wrath His threatening breath

(XXX, 28); Jeremy Taylor, ' On the conversion of St. Paul '

Solo: *s*   *Bc*

(1a) Prelude　　　　　　　　　　　(1b) Full of wrath: *s*

MSS: 326

EDITIONS: XXX, 28, 1828[–44]

COMMENTARY: Novello printed this work 'from the original MS by Purcell in the possession of the Revd. Joshua Dix of Faversham' Its whereabouts are not known at present.

186. Great God and just

(XXX, 33) 1688; Jeremy Taylor, 'A penetential hymn'

Verse: *s*　　　　　　　　　　　　　　*Bc*　　　　　　　　　　　　　Chorus: *SSB*

(1) Great God and just: *s*

(2) Then will we sing: *SSB*

MSS: 14

EDITIONS: XXX, 33, 1688c, 1703e, 1714b, 1828[–44]

187. Hosanna to the highest

(XXX, 38), 'The words by Dr. Fuller, late Lord Bishop of Lincoln'

Verse: *b*　　　　　　　　　　　　　　*Bc*　　　　　　　　　　　　　Chorus: *AB*

(1a) Prelude　　　　　　　　　　　(1b) Hosanna to the highest joy: *b*

(2) Be ravish'd, earth, to see this contract driven: *AB*

MSS: 503

EDITIONS: XXX, 38

188. How have I stray'd

(XXX, 44) ?1688; Dr. Fuller, Bishop of Lincoln

Verse: *s*   *Bc*   Chorus: *SB*

(1) How have I stray'd: *s*

(2) 'Tis Thou, O Lord, must bring: *SB*

EDITIONS: XXX, 44, 1688c, 1703e, 1714b, 1828[-44]

189. How long, great God

(XXX, 48) ?1688; William Norris, 'The Aspiration', 'The words by Mr. Norris of Wadham College, Oxon'

Solo: *s*   *Bc*

(1) How long, great God: *s*

(2) Would'st Thou, great love: *s*

MSS: 343, 348, 349, 867

EDITIONS: XXX, 48, 1688c, 1703e, 1714b, 1828[-44]

190. In the black, dismal dungeon of despair

(XXX, 53) 1688; 'The words by Dr. William Fuller, late Lord Bishop of Lincoln'

Solo: *s*   *Bc*

In the black, dismal dungeon of despair: *s*

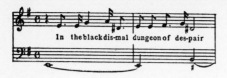

MSS: 343

EDITIONS: XXX, 53, 1688c, 1703e, 1714b, 1828[-44]

It must be done, my soul (See D71)

191. Let the night perish (Job's Curse)

(XXX, 57) *ca.* 1683; Jeremy Taylor: a paraphrase of *Job* 3. ' The words translated by Dr. Taylor '

Verse: *s*　　　　　　　　　　　　　*Bc*　　　　　　　　　　　Chorus: *SB*

(1) Let the night perish: *s*

(2) Here the weary cease from labour: *s*　　　(3) the same: *SB*

MSS: 14, 343, 348, 381, **453**

EDITIONS: XXX, 57, 1688c, 1703e, 1714b, 1805, 1828[-44]
　　　Section 2: *ca.* 1791, ?1796

COMMENTARY: Sections 2 and 3 appear as a single composition in two late 18th century publications as indicated above.

192. Lord, what is man?

(XXX, 62) 1693; William Fuller, a paraphrase on *Psalm* 8: 4, ' Words by Dr. William Fuller, Lord Bishop of Lincoln '

Solo: *s*　　　　　　　　　　　　　*Bc*

(1) Lord, what is man?: *s*

(2) Reveal the glorious spirit: *s*   (3) O for a quill: *s*

(4) Alleluia: *s*

MSS: 581

EDITIONS: XXX, 62, 1693b, 1714a, 1714b, 1828[–44]

COMMENTARY: The version in MS 581 (Bodleian Library, Oxford, MS Mus. C.26, f.2ᵛ) begins as
follows:

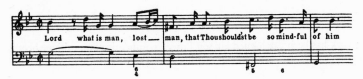

This copy has been bound so that the final alleluia appears to come before the song itself.

My op'ning eyes are purg'd (See D72)

193. Now that the sun hath veiled his light

(XXX, 70) 1688; William Fuller, 'An evening hymn,' 'The words by Dr. William Fuller, late
Lord Bishop of Lincoln'

Solo: *s*   Bc

(1) Now that the sun hath veiled his light: *s*

(2) Alleluia: *s*

MSS: 196, 343, 587 (ground only)

EDITIONS: XXX, 70, 1688c, 1703e, 1714b, 1828[–44]

O give thanks unto the Lord (See D73)

O Lord, rebuke me not (See S14)

194. O Lord, since I experienced have

Solo: *s*   Bc

(1) O Lord, since I experienced have: *s*

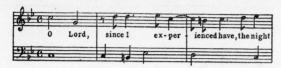

(2) But whilst I remain within this house of clay: *s*

MSS: 14

COMMENTARY: This work has been catalogued among Purcell's authentic compositions because the source in which it appears is very trustworthy, and because the style seems quite authentic.

O miserable man (See S15)

O praise the Lord, laud ye the name (See D74)

Praise the Lord, O my soul, and all (See D75)

195. Sleep, Adam, and take thy rest

(XXX, 75) ?1683

Solo: *s*   *Bc*

(1) Sleep, Adam, and take thy rest: *s*

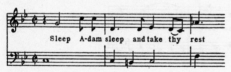

(2) Flesh of thy flesh, bone of thy bone: *s*

MSS: 95

EDITIONS: XXX, 75, 1683b, 1695j, 1772–4

Soon as the morn salutes your eyes (See D78)

196. Tell me, some pitying angel

(XXX, 77) ?1693; Nahum Tate, 'The blessed Virgin's expostulation,' a paraphrase of *Luke* 2: 42

Solo: *s*   : *Bc*

(1) Tell me, some pitying angel: *s*

(2) She Judah's daughter once caressed: *s*   (3) Now fatal change: *s*

(4) How shall my soul its motions guide: *s*   (5) How shall I stem the various tide: *s*

(6) For whilst of thy dear sight beguil'd: *s*

EDITIONS: XXX, 77,   1693b, 1714a, 1714b, 1828[–44]

197. The earth trembled, and heav'n closed

(XXX, 85) 1688; Francis Quarles, ' The Crucifixion: On our Saviour's passion '
Solo: *b* (or *s*)   *Bc*

(1) The earth trembled: *b* (or *s*)

(2) Can senseless things do this: *b* (or *s*)

MSS: 14, 150, 724
EDITIONS: XXX, 85,   1688c, 1703e, 1714b, 1828[–44]

The Lord, even the most mighty (See D76)

The night is come (See D77)

198. Thou wakeful shepherd

(XXX, 88) ?1688; William Fuller, ' A morning hymn '
Solo: *s*   *Bc*

(1) Thou wakeful shepherd: *s*

(2) With joy I'd sing: *s*

MSS: 343

EDITIONS: XXX, 88, 1688c, 1703e, 1714b, 1828[–44]

199. We sing to Him whose wisdom form'd the ear

(XXX, 91) ?1688; Jean Ingelow

Verse: *s*   *Bc*   Chorus: *SB*

(1) We sing to Him whose wisdom form'd the ear: *s*

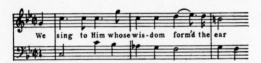

(2) And whilst we sing, we consecrate: *s*   (3) the same: *SB*

MSS: 309 (treble), 867

EDITIONS: XXX, 91, 1688c, 1703e, 1714b, 1828[–44]

200. With sick and famish'd eyes

(XXX, 94) *ca.* 1683; George Herbert, ' A religious elegy '

Solo: *s*   *Bc*

With sick and famish d eyes: *s*

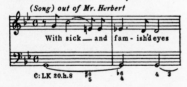

MSS: 14, 349, **453**

EDITIONS: XXX, 94, 1688c, 1703e, 1714b, 1828[–44]

GENERAL LITERATURE

J. A. Westrup, *Purcell*, London: J. M. Dent and Sons, 1947.

SERVICES

Sanctus (See D90)

230. Service [in B♭ Major] (Morning, Communion and Evening Services)
before Oct., 1682

M. MORNING SERVICE [IN B♭ MAJOR]

(XXIII, 1)

(1) TE DEUM LAUDAMUS ('The Song of St. Ambrose') English translation, from a Latin hymn by (?) Nicetas, Bishop of Remesiana, *ca.* 400.

Verse: *satb(decani) satb(cantoris)*   *Bc*   Chorus *SATB*

(a) We praise Thee, O God: *SATB*

(b) To Thee all angels cry: *ssatb(dec. & can.)*   (c) Holy, holy, holy: *SATB(dec. & can.)*

(d) The Father of an infinite majesty: *ssatb(dec. & can.)*   (e) When Thou took'st upon Thee: *ssatb(dec. & can.)*

(f) Thou sittest at the right hand of God: *SATB*   (g) Make them to be numbered: *satb(dec.) sa(can.)*

(h) Day by day we magnify Thee: *SATB*

(i) Vouchsafe, O Lord ('Canon 4 in 2'): *sab(dec. & can.)*

(j) O Lord, let Thy mercy: *sa(dec.) s(can.)*   (k) O Lord, in Thee: *SATB(dec. & can.)*

(2) BENEDICTUS *Luke* 1: 68 ('The Song of Zacharias')

Verse: *satb(dec. & can.)*   *Bc*   Chorus: *SATB(dec. & can.)*

(a) Blessed be the Lord God of Israel: *SATB*

(b) As He spake: *ssaatb(dec. & can.)*

(c) To perform the mercy: *SATB(dec. & can.)*

(d) And thou, child, shalt be called the prophet ('Canon 4 in 1'): *SATB*

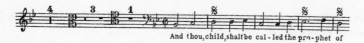

(e) To give knowledge: *ssaatb(dec. & can.)*

(f) Glory be to the Father ('Canon 2 in 1 by inversion'): *SATB(dec. & can.)*

(3) BENEDICITE OMNIA OPERA *Daniel* 3: 52–58 ('The song of the Three Children')

Verse: *ssaatb*   *Bc*   Chorus: *SATB(dec. & can.)*

(a) O all ye works of the Lord: *b*   (b) Bless ye the Lord: *SATB*

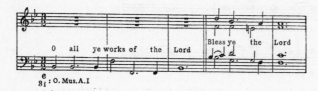

(c) O ye sun and moon: *ssatb(dec. & can.)*   (d) O ye fire and heat: *SATB (dec. & can.)*

(e) O ye nights and days: *ssatb(dec. & can.)*   (f) O let the earth bless the Lord: *SATB*

(g) O ye mountains and hills: *SATB(dec. & can.)*   (h) O ye seas and floods: *ssatb(dec. & can.)*

(i) O ye priests of the Lord: *ssatb(dec. & can.)*

(j) Glory be to the Father ('Canon 2 in 1'): *SATB*

Glo - ry be to the Fa - ther__ and to__ the Son

(4) JUBILATE DEO   *Psalm* 100: 1–5

Verse: *satb(dec.) atb(can.)*   Bc   Chorus *SATB*

(a) O be joyful in the Lord: *SATB*   (b) Be ye sure that the Lord: *SATB*

O__   be   joy - ful, be   joy - ful

(c) O go your way into His gates ('Canon 4 in 2 *per arsin et thesin*'): *satb(dec.)*

O, go your way   in - to   His gates with thanks-giv-ing

(d) For the Lord is gracious: *atb(can.)*   (e) Glory be to the Father: *SATB*

MSS: 21 (inc), 42, 42 (inc), 77, 79, 82 (inc), 83, 85, 87, 97 (inc), 115 (inc), 119 (inc), 123 (inc), 151 (inc)
   161 (inc), 162 (inc), 163d, 164abcefhi (all inc), 165ab (inc) cd (inc) e (inc), 167bcdefgij (all
   inc), 181 (Section 3 only, inc), 188, 194b (inc) e, 232 (inc), 245a (inc) c (inc), 246 (inc), 272,
   300 (inc), 301, 303, 304, 363, 370 (MI and 2 only), 430a to f, 454 (inc), 478a (inc) c (inc), 500a to e
   (all inc), 503, 505a to f (all inc), 517, 541 (MI and 2 only), **586** (Section 3 only), 616, 651 (inc),
   694, 757 (inc), 806, 811d to h, 813 (inc), 814 (inc), 817 (inc), 820, 821, 822, 823, 826, 832, 848a
   (inc) h (Section 4 only), 849 (inc), 850a to h

EDITIONS: XXIII, 1, 1773, 1779a, 1828[–44]

   Section 2d: 1737c

   Section 2f: *ca.*1790

C. Communion Service [in B♭ Major]

(XXIII, 43)

(5) Kyrie Eleison

Full: *SATB (dec. & can.)*

Lord have mercy upon us: *SATB*

(6) Nicene Creed

Verse: *satb(dec. & can.)*   Bc   Chorus: *SATB*

(a) I believe in one God: *b* (b) The Father almighty: *SATB*

(c) And in one Lord: (d) Very God of very God: (e) Who for us men:
   satb(dec.) st(can.)   *SATB*   *satb(dec.) sa(can.)*

(f) And ascended into Heav'n ('Canon 4 in 1'): *SATB(dec. & can.)*

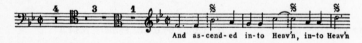

(g) And I believe in the Holy Ghost: *satb(dec.) sa(can.)*

(h) And I believe in one Catholic and Apostolic: *satb(dec.) sa(can.)*

(i) And I look for the Resurrection: *SATB(dec. & can.)*

MSS: 42, 82 (Section 6 only), 97 (inc), 115 (inc), 119, 123, 162, 165e, 167gij, 188, 194b (inc) e,
    232 (inc), 301, 303, 304, 363 (inc), 478ac, 500a to e, 503, 505a to f, 616, 757, 811d to h,
    850a to h, 859 (Section 5 only)

Editions: XXIII, 43, 1773, 1828[-44]

E. EVENING SERVICE [IN B♭ MAJOR]
(XXIII, 52)

(7) MAGNIFICAT. *Luke* 1: 46–55 ('The Song of Blessed Marie')

Verse: *satb(dec. & can.)*   Bc   Chorus: *SATB(dec. & can.)*

(a) My soul doth magnify the Lord: *SATB*   (b) For He hath regarded:
                                                        sa(can.) satb(dec.)

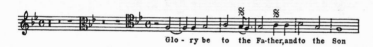

My soul doth mag-ni - fy the Lord

(c) And His mercy is on them:
      SATB(dec. & can.)

(d) He hath shewed strength:
      sa(can.) satb(dec.)

(e) He rememb'ring His mercy:
      SATB(dec. & can.)

(f) As He promised:
      a(dec.) atb(can.)

(g) Glory be to the Father ('Canon 3 in 1'): *SATB(dec. & can.)*

Glo - ry be to the Fa-ther, and to the Son

(8) NUNC DIMITTIS *Luke* 2: 29–32 ('The Song of Simeon')

Verse: *satb(dec.) sa(can.)*   Bc   Chorus: *SSATB*

(a) Lord, now lettest Thou Thy servant depart in peace: *SSATB*

Lord__ now let-test Thou Thy ser - vant de - [part]

(b) For mine eyes have seen: *satb(dec.) sa(can.)*
(c) Glory be to the Father ('Canon 4 in 2'): *SATB*

Glo - ry be to the Fa - ther__ and to__ the Son

Glo - ry be to the Fa-ther and to the Son and to the

105

E

(9) CANTATE DOMINO   *Psalm 98: 1–9*

Verse: *satb(dec. & can.)*   *Bc*   Chorus: *SATB(dec. & can.)*

(a) O sing unto the Lord a new song: *SATB*

(b) The Lord declared His salvation: (c) O shew yourselves joyful:
     satb(dec.) sa(can.)   *SATB(dec. & can.)*

(d) Praise the Lord upon the harp: (e) With trumpets also: *SATB*
     atb(can.), SATB

(f) Let the sea make a noise: *SATB*   (g) Let the floods clap their hands: *sa(dec.)a(can.)*

(h) With righteousness shall He judge: *atb(dec.)a(can.)*

(i) Glory be to the Father ('Canon 3 in 1 by inversion'): *SATB*

(10) DEUS MISEREATUR   *Psalm 67: 1–7*

Verse: *satb(dec. & can.)*   *Bc*   Chorus: *SATB(dec. & can.)*

(a) God be merciful unto us: *SATB*

(b) That Thy way may be known: (c) Let the people praise Thee:
     sa(dec.)s(can.)   *SATB(dec. & can.)*

(d) O let the nations rejoice: *atb(can.)*   (e) =c [except for opening harmony]: *SATB*

(f) Then shall the earth: *sa(dec.)s(can.)*   (g) God shall bless us: *atb(dec.)a(can.)*

(h) Glory be to the Father ('Canon 4 in 1 by inversion'): *SATB*

MSS: 21 (inc), 42, 42 (inc), 77, 79, 82, 83, 85, 87, 97 (inc), 103 (inc), 115 (inc), 119 (inc), 122 (inc), 123, 161 (inc), 162 (inc), 163d, 164acefhi (all inc), 165a (inc) bcd (inc) e (inc), 167bcdefgij (all inc), 182, 188, 194e, 200a, 232 (inc), 245a (inc) c (inc), 246 (inc), 272, 300 (inc), 301 (inc), 303, 304, 363, 370 (E7 and 8 only), 430a to f, 454 (without text), 478a (inc) c (inc), 500a to e (all inc), 503, 517, 616 (inc), 651 (inc), 694, 757 (inc), 806, 811d to h, 813 (inc), 814 (inc), 817 (inc), 820, 821, 822, 823, 826, 832, 848a (inc), 849 (inc), 850a to h, 851, 860

EDITIONS: XXIII, 52, 1773, 1828[–44]

COMMENTARY: A payment to Purcell for copying this work appears in the account ending Michaelmas, 1682, now preserved in the Westminster Abbey Treasury Papers. In several manuscripts this work is divided into two sections, the *Benedicite, Jubilate, Cantate* and *Deus Misereatur* being called 'Mr. Purcell's Second Service in B mi.' (See British Museum MS Add. 38648 and others.) For the purposes of this catalogue, however, it has been found useful to list the canticles in their usual order. The *Te Deum, Benedictus, Benedicite* and *Jubilate* (principal and alternate sections) make up the Morning Service (symbolized by 'M' in the manuscripts and Editions lists); the *Kyrie* and *Credo* make up the Communion Service (symbolized by 'C'); and the *Magnificat, Nunc Dimittis, Cantate Domino* and *Deus Misereatur* make up the principal and alternate sections of the Evening Service ('E'). Only the incipits of the 10 major sections of the service are given, sub-sections being merely listed, excepting for canons, printed in short form. The *Deus Misereatur* is given as an alternate to be sung in the 'Form for the Solemnization of Marriage' in the *Book of Common Prayer*. (See also the Commentary for 'O God, Thou art my God', No. **35**.) English sub-titles are taken from the *Book of Common Prayer*.

LITERATURE: J. Bumpus, *A History of English Cathedral Music, 1549–1889*, London: T. Werner Laurie, n.d., p. 153; C. Burney, *A General History of Music*, London: Foulis & Co. Ltd., 1935, II, p. 385; W. H. Cummings, 'On the Mutilation of a Masterpiece', *P.M.A.*, 30th Session, 1903–4, pp. 113–127; E. H. Fellowes, *English Cathedral Music*, London: Methuen, 1941; Watkins Shaw, 'A Contemporary Source of English Church Music of the Purcellian Period,' *Acta Musicologica*, vol. XXXI, 1, 1959, pp. 38–44; J. A. Westrup, 'Purcell's Benedicite, a Restoration,' *The Times*, 25th Feb., 1938.

231. Evening Service [in g minor]

(XXIII, 80)

(1) MAGNIFICAT *Luke* 1: 46–55 ('The Song of Blessed Marie')

Verse: *ssa(dec.) atb(can.)* or 'full'   Bc   Chorus: *SATB*

(a) My soul doth magnify the Lord: *SATB*

My soul doth mag-ni-fy the Lord

(b) For behold, He hath regarded: *atb(can.) ssa(dec.)*

(c) Holy is His name: *SATB* [echoing preceding verse]

(d) And His mercy is on them: *atb(can.) ssa(dec.)*

(e) He hath put down the mighty: *atb(can.)*[& 'full']

(f) He rememb'ring His mercy: *atb(can.) ssa(dec.)*

(g) Glory be to the Father: *SATB*

(2) NUNC DIMITTIS   *Luke* 2: 29–32 (' The Song of Simeon ')

Verse: *satb*   *Bc*   Chorus: *SATB*

(a) Lord now lettest Thou Thy servant depart: (b) For mine eyes have seen: *ssa(dec.)*;
    SATB   [*atb(can.)*]

(c) Glory be to the Father (' Canon 4 in 2 ' incomplete): *satb* (' full ')

(d) As it was in the beginning: *b, SATB*

MSS: 167e, 860, 861

EDITIONS: XXIII, 80, 1828[–44]

COMMENTARY: Novello's edition was taken from a manuscript in York Minster, which is said to
    have been later destroyed in a fire. Several of the passages in his edition appear to have been
    tampered with. Another copy of the work (in York Minster Library MS M.14.S.) has the
    following note written at the top of page 193, on which the Gloria to the *Nunc Dimittis* begins:
    ' Gloria Patri compos'd by Mr. Roseingrave Jr.' The ' Gloria ' does not seem to be in the same
    style as the rest of the composition.

LITERATURE: J. Bumpus, *A History of English Cathedral Music, 1549–1889*, London: T. Werner
    Laurie, n.d., p. 153; E. H. Fellowes, *English Cathedral Music*, London: Methuen, 1941;
    E. Walker, *History of Music in England*, 3rd edition, revised by J. A. Westrup, Oxford: Clarendon,
    1952.

Te Deum in C (See D91)

232. **Te Deum and Jubilate [in D Major]** (Morning Service)

(XXIII, 90) 1694;

(1) TE DEUM LAUDAMUS (' The Song of St. Ambrose ') (?) An English translation of a Latin Hymn by
    Nicetas, Bishop of Remesiana: *ca.* 400(?)

Verse: *ssaatb*   2 *Tpt, 2 Vn, Va, Bc*   Chorus: *SSATB*

(a) Prelude: 2 *Tpt, Str*

(b) We praise Thee, O God:
atb[*SATB, Str, 2 Tpt*]

(c) To Thee Cherubin and Seraphin:
ss, SSATB

(d) The glorious company of the Apostles:
atb[*SATB, Str*]

(e) The Father of an infinite Majesty:
ssaa, 2 Vn

(f) Thou art the King of Glory:
SSATB, 2 Tpt, 2 Vn

(g) When Thou took'st upon Thee: *ab*

(h) Thou sittest at the right hand: *ss, atb*[*SATB*]

(i) O Lord save Thy people: *atb*

(j) Day by day we magnify Thee: *SATB, Str*

(k) Vouchsafe, O Lord, to keep us this day:
a, 2 Vn

(l) O Lord, in Thee have I trusted:
SATB, 2 Tpt, Str

MSS: 131, 159 (in C Major), 164a (inc) di, 165abce, 167bcdhj, 302, 306, 378, 500a to e, 505a to f, 588, 591, 602, 625 (inc, in C Major; Bass part only), 671, 672, 701, 740, 795abc, 796b, 813, 814, 817, 820, 821, 822, 823, 862

EDITIONS: XXIII, 90, 1697c, 1702c, 1707d, 1708b, 1720l, 1731a, 1755b, 1778, 1784, 1785b, 1795, 1799, 1828[-44] (with additions and accompaniment by Boyce)

(2) JUBILATE DEO   *Psalm* 100: 1–5

Verse: *sab*   2 *Tpt, 2 Vn, Va, Bc*   Chorus: *SSATB*

(a) Prelude: *Tpt*

(b) O be joyful in the Lord: *a, Tpt*

(c) O be joyful: *SATB, 2 Tpt, Str*[*a*]

(d) Be ye sure that the Lord He is God: *sa*

(e) O go your way into His gates ('Canon 4 in 1'): *SATB, Str*

(f) For the Lord is gracious: *ab, Str*

(g) Glory be to the Father: *SATB, Str*

MSS: 159 (in C Major), 164di, 165abce, 167bcdhj, 302, 306, 315 (Section e only), 500a to e, 505a to f, 588, 602, 625 (inc, in C Major; Bass part only), 671, 672, 701, 740, 795abc, 796b, 813, 814, 817, 820, 821, 822, 823, 862

EDITIONS: XXIII, 90, 1697c, 1702c, 1707d, 1708b, 1720l, 1731a, 1755b, 1784, 1785b, 1795, 1799, 1828[-44] (with Boyce's accompaniments)

COMMENTARY: In the preface to his sixth volume (British Museum MS Harl. 7342) Tudway states that Purcell composed the *Te Deum* and *Jubilate* ' principally against the opening of St. Paul's, but did not live till that time '. This statement may have given rise to the traditional belief—probably unfounded—that the work had been commissioned for that occasion. However, the composer's widow printed the work in 1697 as ' Made for St. Cecilia's day, 1694 '. It was no doubt written for the annual meeting of the Sons of the Clergy, as Hawkins, and others after him, have maintained.

LITERATURE: F. Bridge, *Twelve Good Musicians*, London: Kegan Paul, Trench, Trubner & Co., 1920, p. 134; J. S. Bumpus, *A History of English Cathedral Music, 1549–1889*, London: T. Werner Laurie, n.d., p. 154; C. Burney, *A General History of Music*, London: Foulis & Co. Ltd., 1935, II, p. 386; T. Busby, *A General History of Music*, London: Printed for G. and W. B. Whittaker, 1819; W. H. Cummings, ' The Mutilation of a Masterpiece ', *P.M.A.*, 30th Session, pp. 113–127; E. H. Fellowes, *English Cathedral Music*, London: Methuen, 1941 (*Te Deum* only); J. Hawkins, *A General History of . . . Music*, London: Novello, 1853, p. 745; W. H. Husk, *An Account of Musical Celebrations on St. Cecilia's Day*, London: Bell & Daldy, 1857, p. 34; V. Novello, *Purcell's Church Music* (prefatory volume), London: J. A. Novello, 1842; F. de Quervain, *Der Chorstil Henry Purcells*, Bern und Leipzig: Paul Haupt, 1935; J. F. Runciman, *Purcell*, London: George Bell, 1909 (*Te Deum* only); H. O. Statham, ' Purcell's Church Music ', *Musical Times*, May 1, 1924.

CATCHES

240. A health to the nut-brown lass

(XXII, 5) before 1685; John Suckling, 'The Goblins': Samuel Sheppard's *Committee Man Curried*, 1647, also in *Wits Interpreter*, (anon), 1655

3 *voices* (12-bar interval)

EDITIONS: XXII, 5, 1684d (mnp), 1685c, 1686a, 1687e, 1701b, 1707e, 1707f, 1720n, 1724c, 1726c, 1731b, 1733a, 1740g

COMMENTARY: The text, which also appeared in Samuel Sheppard's *Committee Man Curried* (1647) is bowdlerized in the Purcell Society Edition.

241. An ape, a lion, a fox and an ass

(XXII, 1) 1686

3 *voices* (8-bar interval)

MSS: 866

EDITIONS: XXII, 1, 1701b, 1704c, 1707e, 1707f, 1709e, 1711a (Flute), 1720n, 1724c, 1726c, 1731b, 1733a, 1740g, ?1750

COMMENTARY: The source of the text is unknown, but there is a copy in Bodleian MS Montague 13, ff.96ᵛ–97: 'A copy of verses after 1747.' Another early MS source for the text is to be found in British Museum MS Add. 28253, f.65ᵛ.

As now we're met (See **I gave her cakes** (No. 256), of which this is an adaptation.)

242. As Roger last night

(XXII, 1) 'Roger and Jenny'

3 *voices* (8-bar interval)

MSS: 45

EDITIONS: XXII, I, 1701b, 1707e, 1707f, 1710a, 1720n, 1724c, 1726c, 1731b, 1733a, 1740g

COMMENTARY: The text is bowdlerized in the Purcell Society Edition.

At the close of the evening (See **The Knight of Malta**, No. 599)

243. Bring the bowl and cool Nantz

(XXII, 1) 1693–4; ' A Punch Catch '

3 *voices* (12-bar interval)

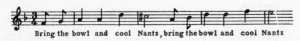

Bring the bowl and cool Nantz, bring the bowl and cool Nantz

MSS: 168, 598, 673, 866

EDITIONS: XXII, I, ?1693c, 1701b, 1704c, 1707e, 1707f, 1709e, 1711a (Flute), 1720n, 1724c, 1726c, 1731b, 1733a, 1740g

COMMENTARY: This catch was introduced into the play *The Richmond Heiress*, in Act IV (See No. **608**/Commentary), first produced in 1693.

244. Call for the reck'ning

(XXII, 2) ' The Careless Drawer '

3 *voices* (11-bar interval)

Call for the reck'ning, and let us, and let us be gone

MSS: 310, 317, 866

EDITIONS: XXII, 2, 1701b, 1707e, 1707f, 1720n, 1724c, 1726c, 1731b, 1733a, 1740g

COMMENTARY: In the early manuscript and printed sources there is no signature for f♯, but the use of a natural sign for f♮ (actually shown as ' f flat ') later on shows that there should have been.

245. Come, let us drink

(XXII, 2) Alexander Brome's *Songs and Other Poems*, 1661

3 *voices* (12-bar interval)   Bc

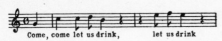

Come, come let us drink, let us drink

MSS: 866

EDITIONS: XXII, 2, 1701b, 1704c, 1707e, 1707f, 1709e, 1720n, 1724c, 1726c, 1731b, 1733a, 1740g, 1748a

COMMENTARY: This catch, like **Jack, thou'rt a toper** (No. **574/10**) and **Prithee ben't so sad and serious** (No. **269**) is unusual in having basso continuo accompaniment.

246. Come, my hearts, play your parts

(XXII, 3) 1685; 'A Loyal Catch': J. Playford's *Wit and Mirth*, 1684

3 *voices* (9-bar interval)

Come my hearts, play———— your parts with your quarts

MSS: 315, 863

EDITIONS: XXII, 3, 1684d (mnp), 1685c, 1686a, 1687e

Come pull away boys (See S52)

247. Down with Bacchus

(XXII, 3) 1693

3 *voices* (12-bar interval)

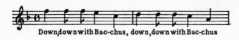

Down,down with Bac-chus, down,down with Bac-chus

MS: 866

EDITIONS: XXII, 3, 1693k

248. Drink on, till night be spent

(XXII, 4) 1686; Philip Ayres, *Lyric Poems*, 1687

3 *voices* (7-bar interval)

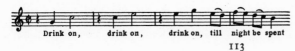

Drink on,   drink on,   drink on, till night be spent

MSS: 317, 318, 598, 866

EDITIONS: XXII, 4, 1686a, 1687e, 1701b, 1704c, 1707e, 1707f, 1709e, 1711a (Flute), 1720n, 1724c, 1726c, 1731b, 1733a, 1740g

Fie, nay prithee, John (See D100)

Fill all the glasses (See S53)

249. Full bags, a brisk bottle

(XXII, 18) 1686; Colonel Jacob Allistree

3 *voices* (8-bar interval)

Full bags, a brisk bot - tle

EDITIONS: XXII, 18, 1686a, 1687e, 1701b, 1707e, 1707f, 1720n, 1724c, 1726c, 1731b, 1733a, 1740g

COMMENTARY: This catch appeared anonymously in the *Pleasant Musical Companion*, II, of 1686. The text has been bowdlerized for the Purcell Society Edition.

250. God save our sov'reign Charles

(XXII, 4) 1685

3 *voices* (6-bar interval)

God save our sov-'reign, Charles our faith's de - fen - der

EDITIONS: XXII, 4, 1685c

251. Great Apollo and Bacchus

(XXII, 4) *ca.* 1682–1690

3 *voices* (8-bar interval)

Great A - pol - lo and Bac-chus one night

MSS: 318

EDITIONS: XXII, 4

COMMENTARY: The conjectural dating of this work is based on the date given for British Museum MS Add. 29397.

Had she not care enough (See S54)

Hail happy words (See D101)

Hang sorrow (See S55)

Hark, Harry, 'tis late (See S67)

Hark the bonny Christ Church bells (See S56)

252. Here's a health, pray let it pass

(XXII, 5)

4 *voices* (4-bar interval)

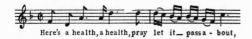

Here's a health, a health, pray let it — pass a - bout,

MSS: 598

EDITIONS: XXII, 5, 1701b, 1707e, 1707f, 1711a (Flute), 1720n, 1724c, 1726c, 1731b, 1733a, 1740g

253. Here's that will challenge all the Fair

(XXII, 5) 1673; ' Bartholomew Fair '

3 *voices* (8-bar interval)

Here's that will chal-lenge all the fair, come buy my

MSS: 309, 317, 405, 673, 866

EDITIONS: XXII, 5, 1673a, 1682d (mnp), 1684d (mnp), 1685c, 1686a, 1686d (trans), 1687e, 1701b, 1704c, 1707e, 1707f, 1709e, 1711a (Flute), 1720n, 1724c, 1726c, 1731b, 1733a, 1740g, 1805

COMMENTARY: The authenticity of this work is open to question. If Henry Purcell did compose it, he would have then been but fourteen years of age.

254. He that drinks is immortal

(XXII, 4) 1686

3 *voices* (7-bar interval)

He that drinks is im - mor-tal, he that drinks

MSS: 673, 866

EDITIONS: XXII, 4, 1686 (Harvard), 1701b, 1707e, 1707f, 1720n, 1724c, 1726c, 1731b, 1733a, 1740g

COMMENTARY: The printed source of 1701 gives a c sharp in the key signature. This is missing in the manuscript source, which is correct. According to Day and Murrie, this catch also appears in a unique print of the 1686 edition of *The Second Book of the Pleasant Musical Companions* in the Library at Harvard.

255. If all be true that I do think

(XXII, 6) 1689; ?Dean Aldrich, ' An adaptation of an epigram by Jean Sirmond '

3 *voices* (5-bar interval)

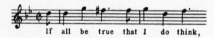

If all be true that I do think,

MSS: 310, 317, 866

EDITIONS: XXII, 6, 1689b, 1701b, 1704c, 1707e, 1707f, 1709e, 1711a (Flute), 1720n, 1724c, 1726c, 1740g

COMMENTARY: The text alone appears in a contemporary MS in the British Museum, MS Add. 30982, f.104. Entitled ' Causa bibendi ', and usually attributed to Aldrich, the complete Latin text (as printed in John Bingley, *Musical Biography*, London: Henry Colburn, 1814, p. 240) is as follows:

> Si bene quid memini, causae sunt quinque bibendi,
> Hospitis adventes, praesens sitis, atque futura,
> Aut vini bonitas, aut quaelibet altera causa.

256. I gave her cakes and I gave her ale

(XXII, 6) 1690

3 *voices* (8-bar interval)

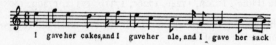

I gave her cakes, and I gave her ale, and I gave her sack

MSS: 317

EDITIONS: XXII, 6,   1690b, 1700dd, 1701b, 1707e, 1707f, 1720n, 1724c, 1726c, 1731b, 1733a, 1740g, 1805

COMMENTARY: This same catch appears as a setting of the words 'As now we're met' in British Museum MS Add. 30273, f.30ᵛ, a manuscript of too late a date for inclusion in Appendix III.

Insecta precauta (See No. 266)

257. Is Charleroi's siege come too?

(XXII, 6) 1692; 'A catch upon Charleroy'

3 *voices* (12-bar interval)

MSS: 543 (without text), 673

EDITIONS: XXII, 6,   ?1693c, 1701b, 1707e, 1707f, 1720n, 1724c, 1726c, 1731b, 1733a, 1740g

COMMENTARY: The Purcell Society editor has stated that this catch probably refers to the siege of Charleroi laid by the Prince of Orange in 1677. However, Luttrell's entry for October 15, 1692, records the actual event in celebration of which Purcell probably composed this catch: 'Harwich letters say, a boate put in there from Holland belonging to sir Henry Furnace, and brought letters to him; but he kept the contents secret, and made great advantage thereof by laying wagers, taking 4 to 1 that Charleroy would not be taken this year, and has wonn above 2000 l.: for now we have account that the queen has an expresse from the king, that the French, after some bombs thrown into the place, quitted the same without formally beseiging the same; and withdrew their troops, leaving behind them 5 or 6 cannon, which they had not time to carry off, the confederate forces being at the heels of them.'

Jack, thou'rt a toper (See No. 574/10)

Joy, mirth, triumphs (See No. 101/Commentary)

Let's live good honest lives (See D102)

258. Let the grave folks go preach

(XXII, 7) 1685; 'The Jovial Drinker'

3 *voices* (16-bar interval)

MSS: 309

EDITIONS: XXII, 7, 1685c, 1702f, 1707c, 1707e, 1707f, 1709c, 1710a, 1720n, 1724c, 1726c, 1740g

COMMENTARY: In British Museum MS Add. 19759 the title runs: 'Let the grave fools go preach.'

259. Let us drink to the blades

(XXII, 7) ?1691

3 *voices* (9-bar interval)

Let us drink, let us drink to the blades

MSS: 543, 673, 866

EDITIONS: XXII, 7, ?1693c, 1701b, 1707e, 1707f, 1720n, 1724c, 1726c, 1731b, 1733a, 1740g

COMMENTARY: This was probably written in honour of the siege of Limerick in 1691.

260. My lady's coachman John

(XXII, 8) 1687

3 *voices* (5-bar interval)

My la-dy's coach-man John, whose sight is al-most gone

MSS: 543 (without text), 673

EDITIONS: XXII, 8, 1688b, 1701b, 1707e, 1707f, 1710a, 1720n, 1724c, 1726c, 1731b, 1733a, 1740g

COMMENTARY: The text has been bowdlerized for the Purcell Society Edition.

My wife has a tongue (See No. 594)

261. Now England's great council

(XXII, 8) 1676; 'A catch made in time of Parliament, 1676': J. H., *A Choice Compendium*, 1681

3 *voices* (13-bar interval)

Now Eng-land's great coun-cil's as-semb-led to make laws

EDITIONS: XXII, 8, 1684d (mnp), 1685c

COMMENTARY: The text has been bowdlerized for the Purcell Society Edition.

262. Now we are met and humours agree

(XXII, 9) 1687

3 *voices* (10-bar interval)

Now, now we are met and hu-mours a-gree,

MSS: 317, 673, 866

EDITIONS: XXII, 9, 1688b, 1688d, 1701b, 1704c, 1707e, 1707f, 1709e, 1711a (Flute), 1720n, 1724c, 1726c, 1731b, 1733a, 1740g, ?1750, *ca.* 1790, 1800c

COMMENTARY: The text (without music) occurs in British Museum MS Add. 27407, f.1. The MS containing verses in favour of Parliament, dates from the mid-seventeenth century.

263. Of all the instruments that are

(XXII, 9) 1693; ' A catch for three voices in commendation of the viol '

3 *voices* (5-bar interval)

Of all, all the in-stru-ments, all, all, all the in-struments that are,

MS: 543 (without music)

EDITIONS: XXII, 9, 1693a, 1701b, 1707e, 1707f, 1720n, 1724c, 1726c, 1731b, 1733a, 1740g

COMMENTARY: Hawkins (IV, 505, 1st edition) has recorded the following anecdote in connection with this round: ' The reverend Mr. Subdean Gostling played on the viol da gamba, and loved not the instrument more than Purcell hated it. They were very intimate as must be supposed, and lived together upon terms of friendship; nevertheless, to vex Mr. Gostling, Purcell got some one to write the following mock-eulogium on the viol, which he set in the form of a round for three voices.'

264. Once in our lives let us drink to our wives

(XXII, 9) ?1680; anon, ' A Farewell to Wives ': J. Playford's *Wit and Mirth*, 1684

3 *voices* (4-bar interval)

Once in our lives let us drink to our wives,

MSS: 43, 317, 598, 866

EDITIONS: XXII, 9, 1684d (mnp), 1686a, 1687e, 1701b, 1704c, 1707e, 1707f, 1709e, 1710a, 1720n, 1724c, 1726c, 1731b, 1733a, 1740g, 1740i

COMMENTARY: The inclusion of this catch in Fitzwilliam Museum MS 118 suggests the possibility that it may have been written as early as 1680. Another setting by Michael Wise appears in *Catch That Catch Can* (1685).

265. Once, twice, thrice I Julia tried

(XXII, 10)

3 *voices* (9-bar interval)

Once,   twice,   thrice   I   Jul   -   ia tried

MSS: 310, 317, 598, 866

EDITIONS: XXII, 10, 1701b, 1704c, 1707e, 1707f, 1709e, 1710a, 1711a (Flute), 1720n, 1724c, 1726c, 1731b, 1733a, 1740g, 1740i

COMMENTARY: The original text has been bowdlerized in the Purcell Society Edition.

266. One industrious insect

(XXII, 10) Mr. Tomlinson 'A rebus upon Mr. Anthony Hall who keeps the Mermaid Tavern in Oxford, and plays his part very well on the violin'

3 *voices* (8-bar interval)

One in - dus - tri-ous   in - sect and the sweet-ness of   th'oth- er

MSS: 673

EDITIONS: XXII, 10, 1701b, 1707e, 1707f, 1720n, 1724c, 1726c, 1731b, 1733a, 1740g

COMMENTARY: In the earliest edition, the text is also given in a Latin translation, which begins: 'Insecta praecauta, alterius merda ...' Anthony Hall (1679–1723) was a Fellow of Queens College, Oxford, and an antiquary in that city. If he actually was the man referred to in the catch, the ascription to Purcell would seem somewhat doubtful, for when Purcell died, Hall would have been only 16 years of age. Perhaps these words were fitted to Purcell's music at some later date.

267. Pale faces, stand by

(XXII, 10) 1688; Mr. Taverner: C. Gildon's *Miscellany Poems*, 1692, p. 45

3 *voices* (8-bar interval)

Pale fa - ces, stand by and our bright ones a - dore

MSS: 673, 866

EDITIONS: XXII, 10, 1688f, 1701b, 1704c, 1707e, 1707f, 1709e, 1710a 1711a (Flute), 1720n, 1724c, 1726c, 1731b, 1733a, 1740g, *ca.* 1790

COMMENTARY: The text has been bowdlerized in the Purcell Society Edition.

268. Pox on you for a fop

(XXII, 11)

3 *voices* (18-bar interval)

(Belch) Pox on you, (belch), pox on you

MSS: 673

EDITIONS: XXII, 11, 1701b, 1704c, 1707e, 1707f, 1709e, 1720n, 1724c, 1726c, 1731b, 1733a, 1740g

COMMENTARY: The text has been bowdlerized in the Purcell Society Edition.

269. Prithee ben't so sad and serious

(XXII, 11) Alexander Brome's *Songs and Other Poems*, 1661

3 *voices* (16-bar interval)   Bc

Pri - thee ben't so sad — and se - rious

EDITIONS: XXII, 11, 1701b, 1707e, 1707f, 1720n, 1724c, 1726c, 1731b, 1733a, 1740d?, 1740g, 1740i, ?1750

COMMENTARY: The text has been bowdlerized in the Purcell Society Edition.

270. Room for th' express

(XXII, 12) 1694; ' Written on the fall of Limerick, July, 1694 '

3 *voices* (14-bar interval)

Room, room, room, room, room for th' ex - press!___

MSS: 317, 673, 866

EDITIONS: XXII, 12, 1701b, 1704c, 1707e, 1707f, 1709e, 1711a (Flute), 1720n, 1724c, 1726c, 1731b, 1733a, 1740g, ?1750

Say, good master Bacchus (See D103)

Say what you please (See S62)

271. Since the Duke is return'd

(XXII, 12) ?1682; ' On the Duke's return '

3 *voices* (16-bar interval)

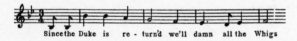

Since the Duke is re - turn'd we'll damn all the Whigs

MSS: 309

EDITIONS: XXII, 12, 1684d (mnp), 1685c

COMMENTARY: In the one manuscript source (British Museum MS Add. 19759 f.39ᵛ) this is labelled ' A Catch for 4 voc:' The date of composition may have been shortly after June, 1682, when the Duke of York returned to London from Scotland. Percy Scholes (in the *Oxford Companion to Music*, 9th Edition, p. 412) has pointed out that the setting of the phrase ' God save the King ' is exactly the same as the beginning of the tune for the British National Anthem. A more striking correspondence is that between this melody and the tune for **Hey, then, up go we.** (cf. No. 344/5 bass.)

272. Since time so kind to us does prove

(XXII, 12) *ca.* 1682–90

3 *voices* (6-bar interval)

Since time so kind to us does prove

MSS: 317, 318, 543 (without text), 673, 866

EDITIONS: XXII, 12, 1700dd, 1701b, 1707e, 1707f, 1720n, 1724c, 1726c, 1731b, 1733a, 1740g

Since women so false and so jiltish are grown (See D104)

273. Sir Walter enjoying his damsel

(XXII, 13)

3 *voices* (8-bar interval)

Sir Wal-ter en - joy-ing his dam-sel

MSS: 317, 318, 543 (without text), 866

EDITIONS: XXII, 13, 1701b, 1707e, 1707f, 1710a, 1740h, 1740i

COMMENTARY: The text has been bowdlerized in the Purcell Society Edition.

274. Soldier, take off thy wine

(XXII, 13)

4 *voices* (5-bar interval)

Sol-dier, sol-dier take off thy wine

MSS: 310, 317, 486, 673, 866

EDITIONS: XXII, 13, 1701b, 1704c, 1707e, 1707f, 1709e, 1710a, 1711a (Flute), 1720n, 1724c, 1726c, 1731b, 1733a, 1740a, 1740g, 1740h, 1740i, ?1750, 1767b, 1775a, *ca.* 1790, 1805

275. Sum up all the delights

(XXII, 13) 1687

3 *voices* (21-bar interval)

Sum up all the de - lights, sum up all

MSS: 317, 866

EDITIONS: XXII, 13, 1688b, 1688d, 1701b, 1704c, 1707e, 1707f, 1709e, 1711a (Flute), 1720n, 1724c, 1726c, 1731b, 1733a, 1740g, 1748a, ?1750, *ca.* 1790

COMMENTARY: In British Museum MS Add. 31463, the first note is 'a', rather than 'c' (as in the Purcell Society Edition); 'a' is preferable.

The glass was just tim'd (See D105)

276. The Macedon youth left behind

(XXII, 8) 1686; Sir John Suckling, *Brennoralt*, 1646

4 *voices* (7-bar interval)

The Ma - ce-don youth left be-hind him this truth,

MSS: 317, 866

EDITIONS: XXII, 8, 1686a, 1687e, 1701b, 1707e, 1707f, 1720n, 1724c, 1726c, 1731b, 1733a, 1740d?, 1740g, 1740i, 1805

COMMENTARY: This catch is a setting of the second stanza of Suckling's song in *The Tragedy of Brennoralt*.

277. The miller's daughter riding to the fair

(XXII, 19) 1686

3 *voices* (7-bar interval)

The mil-ler's daughter rid-ing to_ the fair

MSS: 317, 673

EDITIONS: XXII, 19, 1686a, 1687e, 1688b, 1701b, 1704c, 1707e, 1707f, 1709e, 1710a, 1720n, 1724c, 1726c, 1731b, 1733a, 1740g

COMMENTARY: Although ascribed to John Blow by John Carr in *A Small Collection of the Newest Catches*, 1688, p. 1, the earliest edition, and all those following it ascribe the catch to Purcell. The text has been bowdlerized for the Purcell Society Edition.

278. The surrender of Lim'rick

(XXII, 14) 1691

3 *voices* (12-bar interval)

The sur - ren - der of Lim-'rick and the flight_____

MSS: 317

EDITIONS: XXII, 14

COMMENTARY: Another catch written on the fall of Limerick in 1691 (See also No. **259**). The earliest MS containing this catch dates from 1762, while Walsh's *Catch Club* of 1760 is the earliest printed source.

279. 'Tis easy to force

(XXII, 14) ?1681; ' A catch on a horse '

4 *voices* (8-bar interval)

'Tis ea - sy to force to the wa - ter your horse

MSS: 43, 309 (treble)

EDITIONS: XXII, 14, 1685c, 1686a, 1687e

COMMENTARY: Since it is included in British Museum MS Add. 19759, this catch may have been written as early as the year 1681. Its presence in Fitzwilliam Museum MS 118 strengthens this possibility.

280. 'Tis too late for a coach

(XXII, 14) 1686

3 *voices* (8-bar interval)

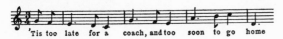

'Tis too late for a coach, and too soon to go home

MSS: 317, 543 (without text), 673, 866

EDITIONS: XXII, 14, 1686a, 1687e, 1701b, 1704c, 1707e, 1707f, 1709e, 1710a, 1711a (Flute), 1720n, 1724c, 1726c, 1731b, 1733a, 1740g, 1740k, 1790d

281. 'Tis women makes us love

(XXII, 14) 1685 (or, possibly *ca.* 1681)

4 *voices* (4-bar interval)

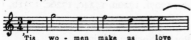

'Tis wo - men make us love

MSS: 43, 317, 866

EDITIONS: XXII, 14, 1685c, 1686a, 1687e, 1701b, 1707e, 1707f, 1720n, 1724c, 1726c, 1740g, ?1750, 1805

COMMENTARY: This work has been variously attributed to Blow, Purcell and Forcer. The version ascribed to Forcer in Fitzwilliam Museum MS 118 varies somewhat from the published versions (which are ascribed to Purcell) and may have been his work. This version, at least, probably dates from *ca.* 1681. One bar-line is omitted in the Purcell Society Edition.

282. To all lovers of music

(XXII, 15) 1687; John Carr, 'A catch by way of epistle': Carr's *Comes Amoris*, I, 1687

3 *voices* (16-bar interval)

MSS: 318, 543 (without text), 598, 673

EDITIONS: XXII, 15, 1687c, 1701b, 1707e, 1707f, 1720n, 1724c, 1726c, 1731b, 1733a, 1740g

COMMENTARY: This catch is prefixed to *Comes Amoris*, I, 1687, 'by way of epistle to the reader.' It is the usual publisher's advertisement set in musical form.

Tom making a mantua for a lass (XXII, 19) (See D106)

283. To thee and to a maid

(XXII, 15) 1685

3 *voices* (5-bar interval)

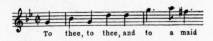

MSS: 317, 543 (without text)

EDITIONS: XXII, 15, 1685c, 1686a, 1687e, 1701b, 1707e, 1707f, 1720n, 1724c, 1726c, 1731b, 1733a, 1740g

COMMENTARY: The text has been bowdlerized in the Purcell Society Edition.

284. True Englishmen drink a good health

(XXII, 15) *ca.* 1689; words written 1689; 'Song with music on the 7 Bishops'

3 *voices* (8-bar interval)

True Eng-lish-men, drink a good health,

MSS: 317, 543 (without text), 866

EDITIONS: XXII, 15, 1701b, 1704c, 1707e, 1707f, 1709e, 1711a (Flute), 1720n, 1724c, 1726c, 1731b, 1733a, 1740g, ?1750

COMMENTARY: The 'seven who supported our cause' were the seven Bishops imprisoned by James II in the tower in 1688. The text alone appears in British Museum MS Sloane 1731.A, f.155.

285. Under a green elm lies Luke Shepherd's helm

(XXII, 16) 1686

4 *voices* (7-bar interval)

Un-der a green elm,   lies Luke Shep-herd's helm

MSS: 673

EDITIONS: XXII, 16, 1686a, 1687e, 1701b, 1707e, 1707f, 1720n, 1724c, 1726c, 1731b, 1733a, 1740g

COMMENTARY: Some later editions read: 'Under a great elm.'

286. Under this stone lies Gabriel John

(XXII, 16) 1686; 'An old epitaph'

3 *voices* (8-bar interval)

Un - der this stone lies Ga - bri-el   John

MSS: 233, 317, 468, 529, 673, 866

EDITIONS: XXII, 16, 1686a, 1687e, 1701b, 1704c, 1707e, 1707f, 1709e, 1710a, 1711a (Flute), 1720n, 1724c, 1726c, 1731b, 1733a, 1740g, ?1750, ?1779, 1805

Well rung, Tom boy (See D107)

287. When V and I together meet

(XXII, 16) 1686

3 voices (8-bar interval)

When V and I to-geth-er meet,

MSS: 866

EDITIONS: XXII, 16, 1686a, 1687e, 1687f, 1701b, 1707e, 1707f, 1710a, 1720n, 1724c, 1726c, 1740g, ?1750, 1767b

288. Who comes there? Stand!

(XXII, 16) 1685

3 voices (16-bar interval)

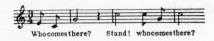

Who comes there?   Stand! who comes there?

MSS: 317, 318, 598, 673, 866

EDITIONS: XXII, 16, 1684d (mnp), 1685c, 1686a, 1687e, 1701b, 1707e, 1707f, 1709e, 1709f, 1711a (Flute), 1720n, 1724c, 1726c, 1731b, 1733a, 1740g, 1805

289. Wine in a morning makes us frolic

(XXII, 17) 1686; Tom Brown

3 voices (12-bar interval)

Wine, wine in a morn-ing makes us frol-ic

MSS: 318, 543 (without text), 598, 673, 866

EDITIONS: XXII, 17, 1686a, 1687e, 1701b, 1707e, 1707f, 1720n, 1724c, 1726c, 1740g

290. Would you know how we meet

(XXII, 17) 1685; ?Thomas Otway

3 voices

Would you know how we meet o'er our jol-ly full bowls

MSS: 233, 310, 317, 405, 543 (without text), 866

EDITIONS: XXII, 17, 1685e, 1686a, 1687e, 1695j, 1701b, 1704c, 1707e, 1707f, 1709e, 1710a, 1711a (Flute), 1719b, 1720n, 1724c, 1726c, 1731b, 1733a, 1740g, 1740k, 1800c, 1805

COMMENTARY: The author of the text is given as Otway in the Purcell Society Edition and in other modern sources, although the poem does not appear in Ghosht's *Otway*. The same text occurs anonymously in Bodleian MS 196, f.5v. In earlier editions it is said that the words are by Otway.

291. Young Collin cleaving of a beam

(XXII, 17) 1691; Thomas D'Urfey, *New Poems*, 1690, translated from the Latin of George Buchanan

3 *voices* (18-bar interval)

, Young Col - lin cleav - ing of - a beam,

MSS: 293, 866

EDITIONS: XXII, 17, 1691e, 1701b, 1704c, 1707e, 1707f, 1709e, 1711a (Flute), 1719a, 1719b, 1719c, 1720n, 1724c, 1726c, 1731b, 1733a, 1740g

COMMENTARY: The text has been bowdlerized in the Purcell Society Edition.

292. Young John the gard'ner

(XXII, 18) 1683

4 *voices* (5-bar interval)

Young John the gard-her hav - ing late - ly got

MSS: 309, 317, 318 (in B♭)

EDITIONS: XXII, 18, 1683g (in B-flat), 1685c, 1686a, 1687e, 1701b, 1707e, 1707f, 1710a, 1720n, 1724c, 1726c, 1731b, 1733a, 1740g

COMMENTARY: The text has been bowdlerized in the Purcell Society Edition.

GENERAL LITERATURE

D. Arundell, *Henry Purcell*, London: O.U.P., 1927; C. Burney, *A General History of Music*, London: Foulis & Co. Ltd., 1935, II, p. 399; E. F. Hart, 'The Restoration Catch', *Music & Letters*, XXXIV, 1953, p. 289; R. Sietz, *Henry Purcell: Zeit, Leben, Werk*, Leipzig: Breitkopf & Härtel, 1955, pp. 156 ff; J. A. Westrup, *Purcell*, London: J. M. Dent and Sons, 1947.

ODES, BIRTHDAY SONGS, WELCOME SONGS, AND OTHER OCCASIONAL VOCAL WORKS

' Address of the Children of the Chapel Royal ' (See D120)

320. Arise, my muse

(XI, 36) ' Birthday song for Queen Mary ' April 30th, 1690; Thomas D'Urfey: *Poems on Affairs of State, III,* 1698

Solo: *aatb*   2 *Fl,* 2 *Ob,* 2 *Tpt,* 2 *Vn,* 2 *Va, Bc*   Chorus: *SATB*

(1) Symphony: 2 *Tpt,* 2 *Vn,* 2 *Va*
  (a) [Grave]

(b) [Canzona]

(2a) Arise, my muse: *a,* 2 *Vn,* 2 *Va*

(2b) Ritornello: 2 *Vn,* 2 *Va*

(3a) Ye sons of music: *SATB,* 2 *Vn,* 2 *Va*

(3b) Ritornello: *2 Tpt, 2 Vn, 2 Va* (4a) Then sound your instruments: *tb*

Then sound your in — stru-ments
3: O MS Mus C 26

(4b) the same: *SATB, 2 Tpt, 2 Vn, Va*

(5) See how the glitt'ring ruler: *a*

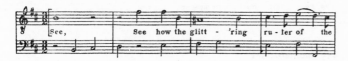

See, See how the glitt - 'ring | ru - ler of the

(6a) Hail, gracious Gloriana, hail: *aa*

Hail, gra-cious Glo-ri - a - na, hail

Hail, gra-cious Glo-ri - a - na

(6b) All hail, Gloriana: *SATB, 2 Ob, 2 Vn, 2 Va* (6c) Ritornello: *2 Ob, 2 Tpt*

All hail, Glo-ri - a - na, all hail

(7a) And since the time's distress: *b, 2 Vn* (7b) Only to rise: *b, 2 Vn*

And since the time's dis - tress On - ly to rise,— to rise,—

(8a) Prelude: *Bc* (8b) To quell his country's foes: *atb*

 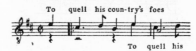

To quell his coun-try's foes

7 # To quell his

(9a) But ah! I see Eusebia: *a, 2 Fl* (9b) Ah! wretched me: *a, 2 Fl*

But ah! ah! I see, I see— Eu - se - bia Ah! wretch-ed me

(9c) But Glory cries: *b, 2 Vn*   (9d) the same: *SATB, 2 Vn, 2 Va*

(9e) = 9c

But Glo - ry cries, "Go on"

(9f) No Fate must some meaner force: *a, 2 Fl*   (9g) = 9c: *SATB, Str*

No, no,   no, no,   Fate must some mean - er

MSS: 336, 342 (inc), 396, 453 (inc), 462, 581

EDITIONS: XI, 36,

　　Section 2a: 1719a (mnp), 1719b (mnp), 1719c (mnp)

COMMENTARY: Purcell did not set the last fifteen lines of D'Urfey's poem, omitting the verse begin-
　　ning: 'See, all Europe bend their eyes,' and the chorus: 'Exalt your voice high.' Goodison
　　printed the symphony as the 'original overture' to **King Arthur,** as did the Purcell Society
　　Editor (See No. 628/4). The Purcell Society Edition also gives these as the same. The text
　　without music is copied anonymously in British Museum MS Harl. 7319 (ff. 335-7), dating from
　　about 1703.

321. Celebrate this festival

(XXIV, 36) 'Birthday song for Queen Mary' April 30th, 1693; Nahum Tate

Solo: *ssatb*　　　　　　　　　2 *Ob, 2 Tpt, 2 Vn, Va, Bc*　　　　　　Chorus: *SSAATTBB*

(1) Symphony: 2 *Ob, 2 Tpt, Str*

　　(a) [Grave]　　　　　　　　　　　　　　　　(b) [Canzona]

(2a) Celebrate this festival: *ssatb*　　　　　　(2b) the same: *SATB, 2 Ob, Tpt, Str*

Ce - le-brate this | fes - ti-val, | cel-e-brate this

(3) Britain now thy cares beguile: *ss*   (4a) Prelude: 2 *Ob*

Bri-tain now,   now,now,   now,now,   now, now   thy cares be-guile

(4b) = 2b   (5) 'Tis sacred, bid the trumpet: *s, Tpt [SATB]*

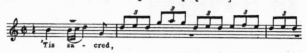

'Tis   sa -   cred,

(6a) Prelude: 2 *Vn*   (6b) Let sullen discord smile: *s*

Let sul -   len dis - - - - - - - cord smile

(6c) Devote this day to Peace: *SATB, 2 Ob, Str*

De-vote   this   day   to Peace

(7) Crown the altar, deck the shrine: *a*   (8a) Prelude: 2 *Vn*

Crown   the   al -   tar,   deck — the shrine

(8b) Expected Spring at last: *b, 2 Vn*   (8c) She waited for Maria's day:
                                                     SATB, 2 Ob, Str

Ex - pec - ted Spring at   last   is   She wait - ed   for   Ma - ri - a's   day

(9a) **April, who till now:** *a*   (9b) Ritornello: *Str*

Ap - ril who till now, who till now
2: LG VI.5.6

(10a) Departing thus: *a*

De-part-ing,   thus,   thus   you'll hear

(10b) I envy not the pride of May: *a*

I en-vy not—the pride—of May

(11a) Ritornello: *2 Ob*

(11b) Happy realm: *atb*

Hap-py,hap-py, hap-py realm

(12a) While for a righteous cause: *b, Tpt*

While for a right-eous cause he arms

(12b) Let guilty monarchs shun: *b, Tpt*

Let guil - ty, let guil - ty mon-archs shun

(13a) Prelude: *2 Fl, Ob, Str*

(13b) Return, fond muse:
     a, 2 Fl, 2 Ob, Str

Re - turn,— fond muse

(13c) Repeat Maria's name: *a, SSAATTBB, Str*

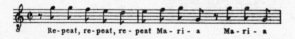

Re-peat, re-peat, re - peat Ma - ri - a   Ma - ri - a

(14a) Kindly treat Maria's day: *s*

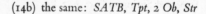

(14b) the same: *SATB, Tpt, 2 Ob, Str*

Kind - ly treat Ma - ri - a's day

MSS: 215, 305, 336, 386, 397, 398, 458, 461 (inc), 601, 626a to c (inc), 671, 766, 790
     Sections 1 to 7: 614
     Section 2ab: 45, 219, 310, 341, 460
     Section 2a (in F major, for flute), 605
     Section 4a: 354 (in c minor)
     Section 5: 341, 460
     Section 9a: **442** (in c minor)
     Section 12a: 39
     Section 13b: 39
     Section 14a: 354
     Section 14ab: 310, **442** (in B flat), 460, 614, 724

EDITIONS: XXIV, 36, 1693g (mnp), ?1790b

> Section 2ab: 1694d, 1698d, 1700g, 1705b, 1705d, 1706a, 1706b, 1710e, 1721a, 1725c, 1726b, 1745c, 1805, 1809 [all for solo soprano]
> Section 3: 1702d, 1711b, 1712a, 1721a
> Section 6b: 1706a, 1706b, 1721a
> Section 7: 1702d, 1711b, 1712a, 1721a
> Section 9a: 1702d, 1711b, 1712a, 1721a
> Section 10b: 1694d
> Section 11: 1706a, 1706b, 1721a
> Section 12: 1706a, 1706b, 1721a
> Section 13ab: 1706a, 1706b, 1721a
> Section 14ab: 1693g, 1694d

COMMENTARY: Luttrell's entry for May 2nd, 1693, reads as follows: ' Sunday last being the Queen's birthday, the guns were discharged at the tower as usual; and the next day the nobility congratulated her majestie thereon; and at night was a great ball at court.' In British Museum Royal Music MS 24.e.4, the names of the original performers are given as: Mrs Ayliff, ' the boy' (Jemmy Bowen), Turner, Snow, Edwards, Howell, Bowman, Damascene, Bouchier, Roberts, and Woodeson. The overture is the same as that for **Hail, bright Cecilia** (see No. **328**), transposed from D to C Major. Nahum Tate's text, as printed in the *Gentleman's Journal* for April 1692, begins with the lines:

> ' Hark, hark, the Muses and the Graces call
> To celebrate this festival . . .'

An adaptation of Section 10b appears in D Major as No. **376** in this catalogue.

322. **Celestial music did the gods inspire**

(XXVII, 29) August 5th, 1689; ' A Song that was perform'd at Mr. Maidwell's a schoolmaster on ye 5th of August 1689 ye words by one of his scholars '

Solo: *satb*　　　　　　　　2 *Fl*, 2 *Vn*, *Va*, *Bc*　　　　　　　Chorus: *SATB*

(1) Symphony: *Str*
(a) [Grave]　　　　　　　　　　　　　　(b) [Canzona]

(2a) Celestial music: *b, Str*　　　　　　(2b) Ritornello: *Str*

(2c) Hence he by right the God of wit: *Str, SATB*

Hence   he   by right the   God of wit   shall be

(3a) Her charming strains: *a, 2 Fl*

Her   charm - - - [ing]

(3b) Ritornello: *2 Fl*

(4) Thus Virgil's genius lov'd the country best: *s*

Thus   thus   Vir - gil's   ge - nius   lov'd _____   the coun - try best

(5a) Whilst Music did improve Amphion's song: *ab*

Whilst   Mu - sic   did   im - prove

(5b) Ritornello: *Str*

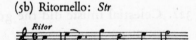

(6) When Orpheus sang all nature did rejoice: *a, Str*

When Or - pheus sang _____

(7a) Let Phillis by her voice: *atb*

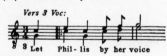

Let   Phil - lis   by her voice

(7b) the same: *Str, SATB*

MSS: 351 (inc), 390, 453 (largely not autograph)

EDITIONS: XXVII, 29

COMMENTARY: The Symphony is the same as that for the anthem **My heart is inditing** (No. **30/1**)

136

323. Come ye sons of art away

(XXIV, 87) 'Birthday song for Queen Mary' April 30th, 1694

Solo: *saab*　　　　　　　　2 *Ob, Tpt, Kdr,* 2 *Vn, Va, Bc*　　　　　　　Chorus: *SATB*

(1) Symphony: *Tpt, Ob, Str*
　　(a) [Grave]　　　　　　　　　　　　(b) [Canzona]: *Tpt, Ob, Str*

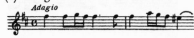

　　　　　　　　　　　　　　　　　　(c) Adagio: *Str*

(2a) Prelude: *Ob, Str*　　　(2b) Come ye sons of art: *a*　　　(2c) the same: *SATB,*
　　　　　　　　　　　　　　　　　　　　　　　　　　　　　　2 *Ob,* 2 *Tpt, Str*

(3) Sound the trumpet 'till around: *aa*　　　　　　(4a)＝2a　　　　(4b)＝2c

(5a) Strike the viol, touch the lute: *a,* 2 *Fl*　　　　(5b) Ritornello: 2 *Fl, Str* (on
　　　　　　　　　　　　　　　　　　　　　　　　　　　　the foregoing ground)

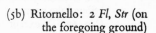

3: LG VI.5.6

(6a) Prelude: *Str*　　　(6b) The day that such a blessing: *b, Str*　(6c)＝6b: *SATB, Str*

F　　　　　　　　　　　137

(7) Bid the Virtues, bid the Graces: *s, Ob*

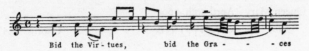

Bid the Vir-tues,   bid the Gra - - - ces

(8) These are the sacred charms: *b*

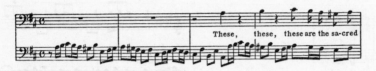

These,   these, these are the sa-cred

(9a) See Nature, rejoicing, has shown us: *sb*   (9b) the same: *SATB, 2Ob, 2 Tpt, 2 Kdr, Str*

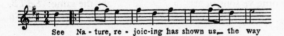

See Na - ture, re - joic-ing has shown us,_ the way

MSS: 395
> Section 3: 215
> Section 5a: 219, **442** (without flutes)

EDITIONS: XXIV, 87
> Section 3: 1706a, 1706b, 1721a, ?1755a
> Section 5a: 1694j, 1698d, 1706a, 1706b, 1721a

COMMENTARY: Luttrell's entry for May 1, 1694, reads: 'Yesterday was her Majestie's birthday, when she was 33 years old, and it was observed.' The only extant manuscript copy of the complete work is in the Royal College of Music, London, MS 993. However, Section 3 is to be found in Folger Library, MS F.474.5 and Section 5a in Gresham College London, MS VI.5.6 (autograph) and in Folger Library MS F.1634.4. The only singer mentioned in an early source (the Gresham autograph) is Mr. Damascene, although Mr. Howell probably sang the alto in 'Sound the trumpet.' The overture is the same as that to the second act of **The Indian Queen** (No. **630**/5), except that it lacks the final 9/8 section, and has been transposed from D to C Major.

LITERATURE: G. L. Mayer, 'The Vocal Works of Henry Purcell: a Discography,' *The American Record Guide*, Special Silver Jubilee Issue, May 1959, pp. 588–591, 670–687 (passim).

324. Fly bold rebellion

(XV, 116) 'The Welcome Song perform'd to his Majesty in the year 1683' (September ?9th)

Solo: *ssaatbb*   2 *Vn, Va, Bc*   Chorus: *SSAATTBB*

(1) Symphony: *Str*
(a) [Grave]

(b) [Canzona]

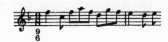

(2a) Fly bold rebellion: *aatbb*

(2b) Ritornello: *Str*

(2c) The plot is displayed: *b*

(3) Then with heart and with voice: *SATB*

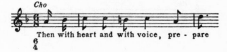

(4) Ritornello: *Bc*

(5a) Rivers from their channels: *a*

(5b) Ritornello: *Str*

(6) For Majesty moves: *SATB*

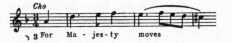

(7) If then we've found: *b*

(8a) But kings, like the sun: *t*

(8b) Ritornello: *Str*

(9a) But heaven has now dispelled those fears: *ssa*

(9b) Ritornello: *Str*

(10a) Come then, change your notes: *atb*

139

(10b) But with heart and with
voice: *SATB*

(11a) Be welcome then, great Sir: *a*

(11b) Ritornello: *Str*

(12) Welcome to all those wishes: *ssaatbb*,
[*SSAATBB*]

(13) Thus let united duty pray: *SSAATTBB, Str*

MSS: 351, **453**

EDITIONS: XV, 116

COMMENTARY: No date nor occasion for this composition is given in any of the sources. However, the line ' The plot is displayed and the traitors some flown and some to Avernus thrown down' suggests that the ode was written to celebrate the foiling of the Rye House Plot. The actual date on which the composition was performed was probably September 9th as indicated in the following account in Luttrell, I, 279:

> ' The 9th, being the day appointed by his majesties declaration as a thanksgiving for his deliverance from the late conspiracy, was observed accordingly: '

325. From hardy climes

(XXVII, 1) ' A Song that was perform'd to Prince George upon his Marriage with the Lady Ann '
(later Queen Anne), July 28th, 1683

Solo: *b*   2 *Vn, Va, Bc (Harpsichord)*   Chorus: *SATB*

(1) Symphony: *Str*
  (a) [Grave]   (b) [Canzona]

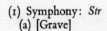

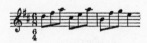

(2) From hardy climes: *b*

(3a) Hail, welcome Prince: *b*

(3b) the same: *Str, SATB*

(3c) Ritornello: *Str*

(4a) Prelude: *Harpsichord*

(4b) As Fame, great Sir: *a*

(5a) For since Heaven pleas'd: *ss*

(5b) Ritornello: *Str*

(6a) Wake then my muse: *b*

(6b) To celebrate the joys: *Vn, SATB*

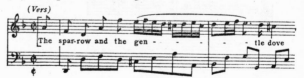

(7) Ritornello: *Str*

(8a) The sparrow and the gentle dove: *t*

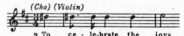

(8b) Ritornello: *Str*

(9a) So all the boons: *atb*

(9b) Ritornello: *Str*   (10a) Hence without scheme or figure: *s*

(10b) the same: *SATB*   (10c) Do we foretell: *s*   (10d) the same: *SATB*

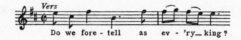

MSS: 351, **453**

EDITIONS: XXVII, I
    Section 8a: 1706a, 1706b, 1721a

COMMENTARY: Luttrell's entry for July 19th 1683 reads: ' The 19th in the afternoon, Prince George, brother to the King of Denmark, arrived at Whitehall, and was kindly received by their majesties and royal highnesses, being come to make his addresses to the Lady Ann. . . . The 28th in the evening was celebrated at St. James by the Bishop of London, the marriage between Prince George and the Lady Ann, his majestie's niece.'
    The Ritornello which appears as the seventh section is the same as the eighth of the instrumental tunes (a Minuet in D) in **The Gordian Knot Unty'd** (No. **597**/8).

326. From those serene and rapturous joys

(XVIII, I) ' On the King's Return to White-hall, after his Summer's Progress, 1684. SONG. Set by Mr. *Henry Purcell*.' [September 26th, 1684]; Thomas Flatman: *Poems and Songs*, 1686

Solo: *ssatb*   2 *Vn, Va, Bc*   Chorus: *SATB*

(1) Symphony: *Str*
    (a) [Grave]   (b) [Canzona]

(2a) From those serene and rapturous joys: *a*   (2b) Ritornello: *Str*

(3a) Behold, th'indulgent Prince: *b, 2 Vn*

(3b) Ritornello: *Str*

(4) Welcome home: *SATB, 2 Vn*

(5) Not with an helmet: *ss*

(6) Ritornello: *Str*

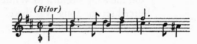

(7) Welcome as soft refreshing showers: *b*

(8) Welcome home: *SATB, 2 Vn*

(9a) Welcome, more welcome does he come: *t*

(9b) Ritornello: *Str*

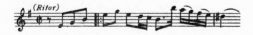

(10a) Nor does the sun more comforts bring: *ab, Str*   (10b) Ritornello: *Str*

(11a) Ritornello: *Str*   (11b) With trumpets and shouts: *a*

With trum - - - - pets and shouts

(11c)=11a   (11d)=11b: *SATB, 2 Vn*

MSS: 351, 397, 398, **453**
  Section 11a: 628 (treble and bass)

EDITIONS: XVIII, 1

COMMENTARY: In Thomas Flatman's *Songs and Poems*, the text of this work appears under the caption:
'On the King's return to Whitehall after his Summer's progress, 1684.' The occasion for which
Purcell set the song was therefore probably Charles II's return from Winchester in September
that year. (See Luttrell, *Diary*: 5th April, 1684, 26th August, 1684, and September, 1684.)

327. Great parent, hail

(XXVII, 59) 'Commemoration Ode performed at Christ Church, Dublin, January 9th, 1694';
Nahum Tate

Solo: *satb*   2 *Fl, 2 Vn, Va, Bc*   Chorus: *SATB*

(1) Symphony: *Str*
  (a) [Grave]   (b) [Canzona]

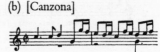

(2a) Great parent, hail: *atb*   (2b) All hail to thee: *Str, SATB*

great,great,great

greatgreat, great
Great, great,great   great,great

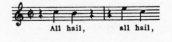

All hail,   all hail,

(2c) Who hast thro' last distress: *SATB*   (2d) To see this joyful year: *SATB, Str*

Who   hast thro' last dis - tress

Who hast thro' last dis - tress   To   see this joy - - - ful

(3) Another century commencing: *a*

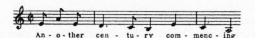

An - o - ther   cen - tu - ry   com - menc - ing

(4a) Ritornello: *Str*

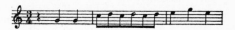

(4b) After war's alarms: *at*

Af - ter   war's _____ a - larms _____

(5) Awful Matron, take thy seat: *b, Str*

Aw - ful Ma - tron

(6a) She was the first who did inspire: *t, SATB*

She   was   the   first   who   did   in - spire _____

(6b) Whose deathless memory the soul: *t*

Whose   death - less   me - mo - ry, The   soul __

(7) Succeeding Princes next recite: *ab*

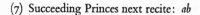

Suc - ceed - ing   Prin - ces   next,

(8) But chiefly recommend to fame: *Str, SATB*

But chief-ly re-com-mend to   fame

(9a) Symphony: *2 Fl, Va*

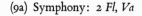

(9b) The royal Patron's sung: *s, 2 Fl*

The   roy - al   roy - - - al   Pa - tron's sung

(10) Then a second Ormond's story: *s*   (11) With themes like these: *Str, SATB*

Then   a   se - cond, then   a   se - cond   With   themes   like   these,   ye   Sons   of   Art

MSS: 336, 380, 396, 462

EDITIONS: XXVII, 59, ?1790b

    Section 5: 1805

COMMENTARY: Commissioned for the centenary celebration of Trinity College, Dublin, this work was first performed at Christ Church Cathedral in Dublin on January 9th, 1694. A contemporary source (*Some Account of My Conversation in Ireland*, 1699, by John Dunton) gives the following report: ' In the afternoon, there were several orations in Latin spoke by the Scholars in praise of Queen Elizabeth and the succeeding Princes; and an Ode made by Mr. Tate (the Poet Laureate) who was bred up in this College ...'

328. Hail, bright Cecilia

(VIII, 1) ' A Song for St. Cecilia's Day ' November 22nd, 1692; Nicholas Brady

Solo: *saatbb*   2 *Fl, B.Fl,* 2 *Ob,* 2 *Tpt, Kdr,* 2 *Vn, Va, Bc*   Chorus: *SATB*

(1) Overture: 2 *Ob,* 2 *Tpt, Str*
    (a) [Grave]   (b) [Canzona]

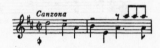

(1c) Adagio: 2 *Ob, Str*   (1d) Allegro: 2 *Ob,* 2 *Tpt,*
                                                                   Kdr, Str

(1e) Adagio: 2 *Ob, Str*   (2a) Hail, bright Cecilia: *b, Str*

(2b) Hail, bright Cecilia: *SATB,* 2 *Ob, Str*   (2c) Fill ev'ry heart: *SATB,* 2 *Ob, Str*

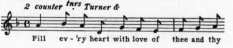

(2d) That thine and music's sacred love: *at, SATB, 2 Ob, Str*

(2e) Ritornello: *2 Ob, Str*

(3a) Prelude: *2 Fl, B.Fl, Str*

(3b) Hark each tree its silence breaks:
ab, 2 Fl, B.Fl, 2 Vn

(4) 'Tis Nature's voice: *a*

(5) Soul of the world: *SATB, 2 Ob, Str*

(6a) Symphony: *2 Ob*

(6b) Thou tun'st this world: *s, 2 Ob*

(6c) the same: *SATB, 2 Ob, Str*

(7) With that sublime celestial lay: *aa, b*

(8a) Prelude: *2 Ob*

(8b) Wond'rous machine; *b, 2 Ob*

(9) The airy violin and lofty viol: *a, 2 Vn*

(10a) Prelude: *2 Fl*   (10b) In vain the am'rous flute: *at*

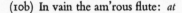

(11a) Prelude: *2 Tpt, Kdr*   (11b) The fife and all the harmony:
                                          a, 2 Tr, Kdr

(12) Let these among themselves contest: *bb*

(13) Hail, bright Cecilia:
     SATB, 2 Ob, 2 Tr, Bn, Kdr, Str   (14) With rapture of delight: *aatb*

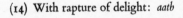

MSS: 44 (inc), 259, 270, 294, 319, 336, 337, 341, 376, 386, 395, 409, 463 (in C), **581** (largely autograph), 582 (inc), 585, 615 (inc), 736, 770, 862 (inc)

Section 1: 95
Section 1abc: 645
Section 2a: 95, 856 (inc)
Section 4: **442** (transposed to D Major, for soprano), 737
Section 6b: **442,** 856 (inc)
Section 8: 39, 487
Section 9: 487
Section 11b: 39, 105, **442** (transposed to A Major, for soprano)

EDITIONS: VIII, 1, 1847, 1848

Section 3b: 1702d, 1711b, 1712a, 1721a
Section 4: 1693m, 1693n, 1696b, 1698d, 1704a, 1706a, 1706b, 1721a
Section 6: 1706a, 1706b, 1721a
Section 8: 1702d, 1711b, 1712a, 1721a
Section 9: 1706a, 1706b, 1721a
Section 10b: 1711b, 1712a, 1721a
Section 11b: 1706a, 1706b, 1710z, 1721a

COMMENTARY: *Gentleman's Journal* for November 1692 had the following notice of **Hail, bright Cecilia** ... ' The following ode was admirably set to music by Mr. Henry Purcell, and perform'd twice with universal applause, particularly the second stanza, which was sung with incredible graces by Mr. Purcell himself. Though I was enjoyned not to name the author of the Ode, I find a great reluctancy to forbear letting you know whom you must thank for so beautifull a poem....' In the issue for January 1692/3 the poet was identified as ' Mr. B—y, whose Ode for St. Cecilia's Day you liked so well.' The symphony is the same as that for **Celebrate this festival**, except that the latter is in C Major. Singers mentioned in Oxford, Bodleian Library MS Mus. C 26 include Mr. Howell (in place of Mr. Turner, whose name has been struck out), Mr. Damascene, Mr. Edwards, Mr. Freeman, Mr. Snow, Mr. Bouchier, Mr. Woodson (in place of Mr. George Hart, whose name has been erased), Mr. George Wilkins and Mr. Pate, who evidently also sang ' 'Tis Nature's voice' with Purcell's ' incredible graces.' In the final chorus, the fugal subject is the same as that for ' All creatures of our God and King.' Daniel Purcell borrowed passages from the Opening Overture for his Symphony to *The Judgement of Paris.*' The setting for Section 6b uses the same melody as that for ' No watch, dear Celia' (see No. **401**). The bass motive with which Section 10 (' In vain the am'rous flute ') opens is the same as the ground which Purcell used for Dido's lament.

LITERATURE: H. C. Colles, *Voice and Verse*, London: O.U.P., 1928; W. H. Husk, *An Account of the Musical Celebrations on St. Cecilia's Day*, London: Bell and Daldy, 1857, pp. 27, 162; G. L. Mayer, ' The Vocal Works of Henry Purcell: A Discography,' *The American Record Guide*, Special Silver Jubilee Issue, May 1959, pp. 588–591, 670–687 (passim).

329. **Laudate Ceciliam**

(X, 44) ' A Latin Song made upon St. Cecilia, whose day is commerated [sic] yearly by all Musitians.'
November 22, 1683

Solo: *atb*   2 *Vn, Bc*   Chorus: ?

(1) Symphony: *2 Vn, Bc*

(a) [Grave]   (b) [Canzona]

(2) Laudate Ceciliam: *atb*

(3a) Modulemini psalmum novum: *atb*   (3b) Ritornello: *2 Vn, Bc*

(4) Quia preceptum est in Ecclesia sanctorum: *b*   (5)=2   (6)=1ab

(7) Dicite Virgini, canite martyri: *at*

(8a) Adeste Cælites: *atb*   (8b) Nobiscum martyri alternate: *atb*   (9)=2

MSS: **453**

EDITIONS: X, 44

COMMENTARY: The author of the text is unknown, but it has been presumed that Purcell may have taken the words from some Italian collection. Where it was performed cannot be determined, although it may have been intended for performance in Queen Catherine's chapel.

LITERATURE: W. H. Husk, *An Account of the Musical Celebrations on St. Cecilia's Day*, London: Bell and Daldy, 1857, p. 16; E. Walker, *History of Music in England*, 3rd edition, revised by J. A. Westrup, Oxford: Clarendon, 1952.

330. Light of the world   Missing

'Hymn to the Sun Set by Dr. Purcell and sung before Their Majesties on New-Years Day, 1693/4'; Matthew Prior

Purcell's setting for this Hymn has not been discovered. Michael Tilmouth ('The Technique and Forms of Purcell's Sonatas,' *Music and Letters*, XL, No. 2, p. 109) suggests that the Trumpet Sonata may have been the overture to this ode. (See No. **850**). The full text of Prior's poem may be seen in H. B. Wright and M. K. Spear's edition, *The Literary Works of Matthew Prior*, Oxford: O.U.P., 1959, vol. I, p. 125.

331. Love's goddess sure was blind

(XXIV, 1) 'Birthday song for Queen Mary,' April 30th, 1692; Sir Charles Sedley

Solo: *saatb*   2 *Fl*, 2 *Vn*, *Va*, *Bc*   Chorus: *SATB*

(1) Symphony: *Str*
  (a) [Grave]   (b) [Canzona]

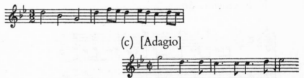

                                       (c) [Adagio]

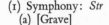

(2a) Love's goddess sure: *a*   [(2b) Ritornello: *Str*

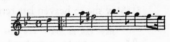

(3a) Those eyes, that form: *b, Str*   (3b) Ritornello: *Str*

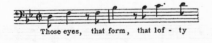

(4) Sweetness of Nature: *aa*, [2 *Fl*]

(5a) Long may she reign: *s* (5b) the same: (6a) Ostinato: *Bc*
  SATB, Str

Long may she reign

(6b) May her blest example chase: *s* (6c) Ritornello: *Str*

May her blest ex - am - ple chase___

['Cold and Raw']

(7a) Many such days may she behold: *aa*

Ma - ny, ma - ny, ma - ny such days may she

(7b) Ritornello: *Str*

(8) May she to heaven late return: SATB, Str

May she to hea - ven late re - turn

And choirs of an - gels

(9a) As much as we below shall mourn: *atb* (9b) Our short but their eternal choice: SATB, Str

As much as we

As much as we be - low Our short, our short, but their e - ter - nal

MSS: 336, 396, 462
  Section 6c: 308

EDITIONS: XXIV, 1

Section 6: (The following have the melody which is used as the bass part: 1688b, 1693a, ?1693c, ?1700, 1702d, 1706e, 1707g, 1709h, 1711b, 1712a, 1720s, 1721a)
Section 7a: 1702d, 1711b, 1712a, 1721a

COMMENTARY: Luttrell's entry for April 30, 1692, reads: 'This being the Queen's birthday, a new ode was sung before her on the occasion: the nobility and gentry, with the Lord Mayor and aldermen of this citty, attended to compliment thereon.' Hawkins (1853, II, p. 564 fn.) relates that Purcell composed the song 'May her blest example' using the Scots song 'Cold and raw' as a bass because he had been nettled by the Queen's preference of that piece to his own work one afternoon when he, Arabella Hunt and John Gostling entertained her with music. The tune appears in a broadside in the Bodleian Library, Oxford, with the alternate title, 'Stingo', as a setting of the words, 'Ho! broder Teague . . . &c', which also appear in connection with 'Lilliburlero' (see No. 646). The Overture is the same as that for **The Rival Sisters** (see No. 609/1ab).

332. Now does the glorious day appear

(XI, 1) 'Birthday song for Queen Mary' April 30th, ?1689; Thomas Shadwell: *Poems on Affairs of State*, II, 1697

Solo: *satbb*   3 *Vn, Va, Bc*   Chorus: *SATB*

(1) Symphony: 3 *Vn, Va*
   (a) [Grave]

   (b) [Canzona]

(2a) Now doth the glorious day appear:
     SATB, 3 *Vn, Va*

(2b) Ritornello: *Str*

(3) Not anyone such joy could bring: *tb*

(4a) This does our fertile isle: *t*

This, this does our fer - tile isle

(4b) Ritornello: *Str* (5) = 2ab

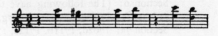

(6) It was a work of full as great: *b*

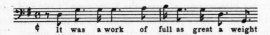

It was a work of full as great a weight

(7a) By beauteous softness: *a*

[By beau — teous soft - - - - [ness]

(7b) Ritornello: *Str*

(8) Her Hero to whose conduct: *bb*

Vers 4 voc

3 Her He - ro to whose con - duct

(9) Our dear religion: *sat*

Our dear re - li - gion, our

(10) No more shall we the great Eliza: *t*

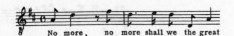

No more, no more shall we the great

(11) Symphony: *Str*

(12a) Now with one united voice: *SATB, 3 Vn, Va* (12b) Io Triumphe:

Now, now with one u - ni - ted voice   I - o Tri - um - - -[phe]

MSS: 453, 601

EDITIONS: XI, 1

COMMENTARY: No date is given in the manuscript sources for this work, but from its position in British Museum Royal Music MS 20.h.8, and from the fact that all other years in Queen Mary's reign are already represented by birthday songs, 1689 seems most probable.

333. Of old when heroes thought it base

(I, 1) 'The Yorkshire Feast Song' March 27th, 1690; Thomas D'Urfey, *Songs Compleat Pleasant and Divertive*, 1719

Solo: *aatbb*   2 *Fl*, 2 *Ob*, 2 *Tpt*, 2 *Vn*, *Va*, *Bc*   Chorus: *SSATB*

(1) Symphony: 2 *Tpt*, *Str*

  (a) [Grave]   (b) [Canzona]

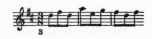

C: L Eg 2956

(2) Of old when heroes: *b*, 2 *Vn*

(3a) Ritornello: 2 *Tpt*, *Str*   (3b) Brigantium, honour'd with a race divine: *ab*

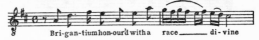

(4a) Prelude: 2 *Fl*   (4b) The bashful Thames: *t*, 2 *Fl*

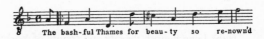

(5)=4b: *SATB*

(6a) Ritornello: 2 *Ob*, *Str*   (6b) The pale and the purple Rose: *a*, *Str*

(7ab) And in each tract of glory: *tb*, [*SATB*]   (8)=1

(9a) And now when the renown'd Nassau: *aa, 2 Tpt*

(9b) Ritornello: *2 Tpt*

And now when the re-nown'd, the re-nown'd Nas-sau

(10) They did no storms nor threat'nings fear: *bb*

They did no storms _____ nor threat'nings fear, nor threat'nings fear

(11a) Prelude: *Str*
[Ground]

(11b) So when the glitt'ring Queen of night: *t, Str*

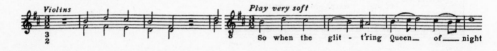

Play very soft

So when the glit - t'ring Queen ___ of ___ night

(12) Let music join in a chorus: *SSATB, Str*

Let mu - sic join in a cho-rus

(13a) Sound, trumpet, sound, beat every drum: *a*

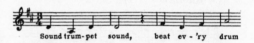

Sound trum-pet sound, beat ev - 'ry drum

(13b) Ritornello: *2 Tpt, Str*

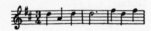

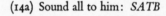

(14a) Sound all to him: *SATB*

Sound all, sound _____

(14b) Long flourish the city and county of York: *SATB, 2 Tpt, Str*

Long flour-ish the ci - ty and coun - ty of York

MSS: 44 (inc), 54, **289**, 297, 336, 342 (inc), 383, 395 (corrupt), 397, 398, 453, 461, 584, 736, 758, 763
    Section 6b: 39
    Section 7: 45, 219, 460, 847

EDITIONS: I, 1, ?1790b

    Section 2: 1719a (mnp), 1719b, 1719c
    Section 3b: 1702d, 1711b, 1712a, 1721a
    Section 4: 1702d, 1711b, 1712a, 1721a
    Section 6: 1702d, 1711b, 1712a, 1721a, 1748a, ?1750, ?1790

Section 7: 1693k, 1698d, 1700c, 1705b, 1706a, 1706b, 1710c, 1719a, 1719b, 1719c, 1720b, 1721a, 1725c, 1726b, 1731c, 1744, 1745c, 1745d, ?1755a
Section 9: 1706a, 1706b, 1721a
Section 10: 1706a, 1706b, 1721a, 1805
Section 11: 1702d, 1711b, 1712a, 1721a
Section 13a: 1706a, 1706b, 1721a

COMMENTARY: This work (entitled 'a song') was written for an annual festival of the Yorkshire Society in London scheduled to be held on February 14th, 1690, but postponed until March 27th. D'Urfey, in his *Pills to Purge Melancholy*, gives the text of the song with the heading: 'An Ode on the Assembly of the Nobility and Gentry of the City and County of York, at the Anniversary Feast, March the 27th, 1690. Set to Musick by Mr. Henry Purcell. One of the finest compositions he ever made, and cost 100 l, the performing.' As this year agrees with those above, as announced in the *London Gazette*, it is obvious the 'Ode' was written about the time of the first anniversary of the 'Glorious Revolution', not during its course, as suggested elsewhere.

LITERATURE: R. E. Loveless, 'Yorkshiremen in London,' *Yorkshire Post*, 17th Feb., 1949.

334. Raise, raise the voice

(X, 26) 'A Song for St. Cecilia's day' November 22nd, ?1683; (?Christopher) Fishburn

Solo: sb   2 Vn, Bc   Chorus: **STB**

(1) Symphony: 2 Vn, Bc
  (a) [Grave]

(b) [Canzona]

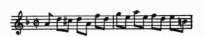

(2a) Raise, raise the voice: b (or t)

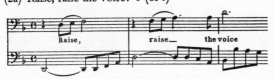

(2b) the same: *STB*, 2 *Vn*

(3) Ritornello: 2 Vn, Bc

(4) The god himself says: s

(5a) Crown the day with harmony:
    stb, STB

(5b) And let every generous heart: *STB*

(6) Ritornello: *2 Vn, Bc*

(7a) Mark how readily each pliant string: *s, 2 Vn*

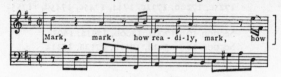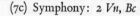

(7b) Then altogether all in one: *STB, 2 Vn*

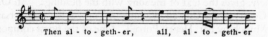

(7c) Symphony: *2 Vn, Bc*

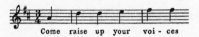

(8) Come raise up your voices: *STB, 2 Vn*

MSS: 351 (inc), 386, 459, 626c (Bass part), 638

EDITIONS: X, 26

COMMENTARY: The date was taken from two manuscripts formerly in the possession of W. H. Cummings. Their whereabouts is now unknown, and the date is somewhat unlikely since No. **339** is the St. Cecilia Ode for this year. The ritornello-minuet (Section 6) is the same as the Minuet in d minor for harpsichord, No. **T688**.

335. Sound the trumpet, beat the drum

(XVIII, 121) 'Birthday Song for King James' October 14th, 1687

Solo: *aattbb*   *2 Vn, Va, Bc*   Chorus: *SATB*

(1) Symphony: *Str*
  (a) [Grave]   (b) [Canzona]

(2a) Sound the trumpet:
  ab, SATB, Str   (2b) Ritornello: *Str*

(2c) Caesar and Urania come: *SATB, Str*   (2d) Ritornello: *Str*
(2e)=2c: *SATB, Str*   (2f) Bid the Muses haste: *b*
(2g)=2a: *SATB, Str*

(3) Crown the year and crown the day: *t*

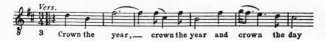

Crown the   year,___   crown the year and   crown   the day

(4) To Cæsar all hail: *SATB, Str*

To   Cae - sar   all___ hail,   all   hail

(5a) Let Cæsar and Urania live: *aa*

Let Cae - sar and   U - ra - nia   live,   Let   all

(5b) Ritornello: *Str*

(6a) What greater bliss can Fate bestow: *tb*

What   great - er   bliss___   can   Fate___   be - stow?

(6b) With plenty surrounding: *SATB, Str*

With   plen - ty   sur - round - - - [ing]

(7) Chaconne: *Str*

(8a) While Cæsar, like the morning star: *b, Str*

While Cae - sar, like the morn - ing star,   our

(8b) His fame like incense mounts: *b, Str*

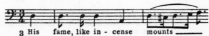

His   fame, like in - cense   mounts___

(9a) To Urania and Cæsar delights without measure: *atb*   (9b) the same: *SATB, Str*

MSS: 44 (inc), 53, 336, 351, 392 (inc), 397, 398, **453**, 461
    Section 5a: 45, 219, 347, 460, 489

EDITIONS: XVIII, 121
    Section 2: 1702d, 1711b, 1712a, 1721a, ?1790
    Section 3: 1702d, 1711b, 1712a, 1721a
    Section 5a: 1698d, 1706a, 1706b, 1720k, 1726b, 1744, 1745c, 1745d, ?1755a, 1763, ?1765,
    ca. 1780, ?1790, 1805

COMMENTARY: Purcell set this ode (by an unknown author) as the last of his birthday songs 'For King James II for the royal celebration on October 14, 1687.' There were 'no bonefires; being so particularly commanded', according to Luttrell. In British Museum Royal Music MS 24.e.7 appears the note: 'After Mr. Purcell's death other words were adapted to the music and it was performed as a Welcome Song on King William's return from Flanders.' The text for this occasion has not been discovered.

    Contemporary performers mentioned in the early manuscripts include Mr. Abell and Mr. Robert (in British Museum MS Add. 31447), Mr. Marsh and Mr. Bowman (in Cambridge, Fitzwilliam Museum MS 30.h, in British Museum MSS Add. 31447 and Add. 33287). 'Crown the year' (Section 3) appears in *Orpheus Britannicus* (2nd edition) in another version in g minor 'Let Cæsar and Urania live' also is given here in another version in c minor for two soprano voices. Yet another version of this duet is printed as an appendix in the Purcell Society Edition (XVIII, 164). This version, based on British Museum Royal Music MS 24.e.7, reverses the order of the verse and ritornello. Purcell also used the Chaconne for Section 7 in **King Arthur** (see No. **628**/1a), transposing it into minor for Section 1b.

336. Swifter, Isis, swifter flow

(XV, 24) 'A Welcome Song in the Year 1681 For the King' [Charles II] before August 27, 1681
Solo: *ssatb*   2 Fl, Ob, 3 Vn, Va, Bc   Chorus: *SATB*

(1) Symphony: *Str*
  (a) [Grave]   (b) [Canzona]

(2a) Swifter, Isis: *a*

(2b) the same: *SATB, Str*

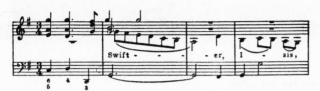

(2c) Ritornello: *Str*

(3a) Charles, the mighty sov'reign: *SATB*

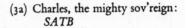

(3b) Ritornello: *Str*

(4a) Prelude: *2 Fl*

(4b) Land him safely on her shore: *b, 2 Fl*

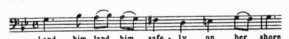

(4c) He with joy her walls: *b, Str*

(5a) Prelude: *Str*

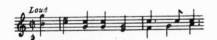

(5b) Hark! just now my list'ning ears: *a*

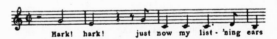

(5c) Ritornello: *Ob, 3 Vn, Va*

(6ab) Welcome, dread Sir: *atb, [SATB]*

(6cd) Though causeless jealousy: *atb [SATB]*

(7) But with as great devotion: *b*

(8ab) Your Augusta he charms: *t*, [*SATB*]

(8c) Ritornello: *Str*

(9) The king, whose presence like the spring: *ss*

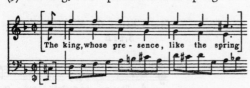

(10a) Then since, Sir: *SATB*

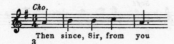

(10b) May no harsher sounds: *s*

(10c) No trumpet be heard: *SATB, Str*

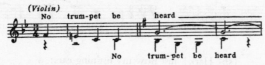

MSS: 351, **453**

   Section 1: 454

EDITIONS: XV, 24

COMMENTARY: Authorities differ as to the date of the occasion for which this piece was written. The Purcell Society editor specifies Charles II's return from Newmarket on 12th October, 1681. But since the text specifically refers to a return by river, it is more likely that the occasion was Charles's return from Windsor at the end of August—as recorded by Luttrell in his entry for August 27th, 1681. The Purcell Society Edition (XXXI, 79) reprints a concert version of the Overture as a separate instrumental work, as it is to be found in MS No. 454, on f. 113 (rev.).

337. The summer's absence unconcerned we bear

(XV, 83) 'A Welcome Song for his Majesty at his return from New Market October the 21—1682'

Solo: *ssaatbb*   2 *Vn, Va, Bc*   Chorus: *SATB*

(1) Symphony: *Str*
  (a) [Grave]

Symphony

¢: LK 20.h.8

(b) [Canzona]

(c) [Adagio]

(2) The summer's absence: *b*

Vers sola

The summer's ab-sence un - con-cern'd we bear

(3) Shine thus for many years:
  atb, [SATB]

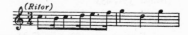

3 voc.

Shine _____ thus

(4) Ritornello: *Str*

(Ritor play each strain twice)

(5a) And when late from your throne: *a*

Vers

And when late from your throne Heaven's call you at - tend, in

(5b) Let no sham pretences: *a*, [SATB]

Let no sham pre - ten - ces give

(5c) Ritornello: *Str*

(Ritor)

(6) Ah! had we, Sir, the pow'r: *b*

Vers

C Ah! ___ had we, Sir, the pow'r ___ or art

(7a) All hearts should smile: *ss*

All hearts should smile, as at that hour

(7b) Then would we conclude: *SATB*

Cho

Then would we con - clude that our

(8a) Prelude: *Bc*

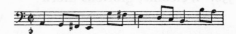

(8b) Happy while all her neighbours bled: *aabb*　　　　　(8c) Ritornello: *Str*

(9) So happily still you your counsels: *t*

(10a) These had by their ill usage: *a*　　　　　(10b) Ritornello: *Str*

(11) But those no more shall dare: *t*

(12) Britannia shall now: *SATB*

MSS: 351, **453**

EDITIONS: XV, 83

　　Section 5c: 1689c (in C Major)

COMMENTARY: Luttrell's entry for October 21st, 1682 (I, 230) chronicles the return of Charles II and his company from Newmarket, the event which this welcome song celebrated. The ground bass which accompanies Section 10 is very similar to that for Section 25 in *Dido* (see No. **626**/25).

338. Welcome, glorious morn

(XI, 72) ' Birthday song for Queen Mary ' April 30th, 1691

Solo: *satbb*　　　　　2 Ob, 2 Tpt, 2 Vn, Va, Bc　　　　　Chorus: *SATB*

(1) Symphony: 2 *Ob*
  (a) [Grave]

(b) [Canzona]

(2a) Welcome, glorious morn: *a, 2 Ob*

(2b) the same: *SATB, 2 Ob, Str*

Wel-come, wel-come, wel-come

(3a) At thy return the joyful earth: *ab*

(3b) Ritornello: *2 Ob*   (4)=2b

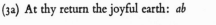

At thy re-turn the joy-ful earth

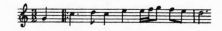

(5) Welcome as when three happy
    kingdoms strove: *ab*

(6a) Prelude: *Str*

Wel-come, wel-come as when

(6b) The mighty goddess of this wealthy isle: *t, Str*

(7a) Full of wonder and delight:
        atb

The migh-ty, migh-ty, migh - - - - ty god-dess   Full of won - der

(7b) the same: *SATB, Str*

(8) Ritornello: *2 Tpt, Str*   (9a) And lo! a sacred fury: *b*

And lo! a sac-red fu - - - ry

(9b) To lofty strains: *b*

(9c) the same: *SATB, Str*

To lof - ty strains,

To lof - ty strains, to lof - ty

(10a) My pray'rs are heard: *s*

My pray'rs are heard, Heav'n has at last be-stow'd

(10b) I see the round years: *s*

I see the round ____ years

(10c) Then our sad Albion: *SATB, Str*   (11) He to the field by honour call'd: *bb*

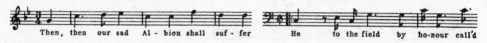

Then, then our sad Al - bion shall suf - fer   He to the field by ho-nour call'd

(12) Whilst undisturb'd his happy Consort: *t*

Whilst un - dis - turb'd his hap - py—

(13a) Sound all ye spheres: *t, 2 Tpt*   (13b) the same: *SATB, 2 Tpt, Str*

Sound all ye spheres, sound all ye spheres

MSS: 336, 396, 462

    Section 9a: 866

EDITIONS: XI, 72

    Section 9a: 1702d, 1711b, 1712a, 1721a

    Section 10a: 1702d, 1711b, 1712a, 1721a

339. Welcome to all the pleasures

(X, 1) 'A song for St. Cecilia's Day' November 22nd, 1683; Christopher Fishburn

Solo: *ssatb*   2 *Vn, Va, Bc*   Chorus: *SATB*

(1) Symphony: *Str*

  (a) [Grave]   (b) [Canzona]

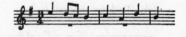

(2a) Welcome to all the pleasures: *atb*

(2b) Hail, great assembly: *SATB*

(2c) Ritornello: *Str*

(3ab) Here the Deities approve: *a*

(3c) Ritornello: *Str*

(4a) While joys celestial: *sat*

(4b) Ritornello: *Str*

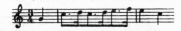

(5) Then lift up your voices: (6) the same: (7) Symphony: *Bc*
      b   *SATB*

(8a) Beauty, thou scene of love: *t*

(8b) Ritornello: *Str*

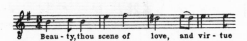

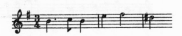

(9a) In a consort of voices: *t*

(9b) the same: *SATB, Str*

MSS: 53, 56 (bass part), 214, 337, 350 (organ part), 351, 395, 581 (inc)
      Section 3: 59, 142, 219, 330 (inc), 460

EDITIONS: X, 1, 1684a
      Section 3: 1698d, 1706a, 1706b, 1721a

COMMENTARY: This appears to be the first of the series of major compositions written for St. Cecilia's Day celebrations, which became popular in the last two decades of the 17th century in England. In a copy of the first edition in the W. A. Clark Library in Los Angeles are annotations and figured-bass symbols said to be in Purcell's hand. The hand does not appear to be Purcell's. Section 3 appears in another version as a harpsichord work (see No. T682).

LITERATURE: W. H. Husk, *An Account of the Musical Celebrations on St. Cecilia's Day*, London: Bell & Daldy, 1857, p. 13.

340. Welcome, Vicegerent of the mighty King

(XV, 1) 'Welcome song for Charles II' September 9th, 1680

Solo: ssatb   2 Vn, Va, Bc   Chorus: SATB

(1) Symphony: Str
  (a) [Grave]

(b) [Canzona]

(2) Welcome, Vicegerent: SATB, Str

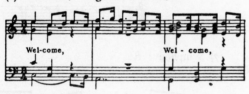

(3a) Ah! mighty Sir: ab

(3b) Ritornello: Str

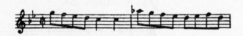

(4) But your blest presence: SATB

(5) Ritornello: Str

(6) Your influous approach: t, [SATB]

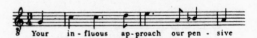

(7) Ritornello: Bc

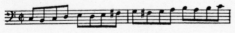

(8) When the summer in his glory: ss

(9) All loyalty and honour: *SATB*

(10a) Music, the food of love: *t*

All loy - al - ty and ho - nour be

Mu - sic the food of love

(10b) the same: *SATB*

(10c) Touch with a joyful sound: *t*

(10d) the same: *SATB* (10e) Ritornello: *Bc* (10f) Ritornello

(11) His absence was Autumn: *ab, SATB*

(12) Then all that have voices: *ab, SATB, Str*

His ab - sence was Au - tumn, his pre - sence

Then all that have voi - ces

MSS: 311, 336

EDITIONS: XV, I

COMMENTARY: Although described as 'A song to welcome home his majesty from Windsor in 1680' in Luttrell (I, 54), in British Museum MS Add. 31447, f.107 (an 18th-century manuscript), it is given as 'A Welcome Song at the Prince of Denmark's coming home.' The instrumental accompaniment to the opening chorus (Section 2) is the same as the second section of the symphony (Section 1b). The first ritornello (Section 3b) is constructed upon a motive taken from the final phrase of the previous section.

341. **What shall be done in behalf of the man**

(XV, 52) 'A Welcome Song for his Royall Highness at his return from Scotland Year 1682.' ? 27th May, 1682

Solo: *ssatb* 2 *Fl*, 2 *Vn*, *Va*, *Bc* Chorus: *SATB*

(1) Symphony: *Str*
   (a) [Grave]

(b) [Canzona]

2 & ¢: LK 20.h.8

G

(2) What shall be done: *b, 2 Fl*

Sola (For Flutes)

What, what shall be done in be - half

(3a) His foes shall all tremble: *atb*

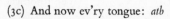

(a 2)

His foes shall all trem [ble]

(3b) And the mobilé crowd: *t*

And the mo - bil - é crowd

(3c) And now ev'ry tongue: *atb*   (3d) the same: *SATB*

3 Voc

[3]And now ev - 'ry tongue

(3e) Ritornello: *2 Fl, Str*

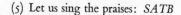

(4a) All the grandeur he possesses: *a*

Vers

All the gran - deur he pos - ses - ses

(4b) Ritornello: *Str*

(5) Let us sing the praises: *SATB*

Cho

3 Let   us,   let us   sing   the prai - ses

(6) Mighty Charles, though joined: *b*

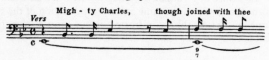

Vers

Migh - ty Charles,   though joined with thee

(7) But thanks be to Heaven: *SATB*

(8) Long live great Charles: *satb, SATB*

Cho   But thanks be to Heaven

But thanks be to Heaven, he's now

Long live great Charles, the gen-ius of this land

(9) = 3e (*2 Fl, 2 Vn, Va*)

(10a) May all factious troubles: *sa*

Vers

May all fac - tious trou - bles cease

(10b) the same: *SATB*

MSS: 351, 453

EDITIONS: XV, 52

    Section 4b: 1691b

COMMENTARY: This work was written either for the occasion of the Duke of York's return from Scotland, where he had been High Commissioner since 1679 (i.e. March 4th to 10th, 1682), or, more likely, for May 27th, when he had returned from a shorter trip to Scotland. Luttrell's entry for this occasion reads, in part: 'at night were ringing of bells, and bonefires in severall places, and other publick expressions of joy.' The ritornello, (3e), is to be found also in No. 344/9k. The song 'All the grandeur' and its ritornello (Section 4) reappear as Air No. 2 in *The Gordian Knot Unty'd* (see No. 597). 'Long live King Charles' had a prototype with the same title which appeared in *Catch that Catch Can* for 1663. A final note, in Purcell's hand in British Museum Royal Music MS 20.h.8 instructs performers to sing the 'Cho. again as before leaving out the Interlude of the Instrumental part between & sing it thro', each strain twice, so conclude. Finis.'

342. Who can from joy refrain?

(IV, 1) 'A Birthday song for the Duke of Gloucester' July 24th, 1695; ?Nahum Tate

Solo: *ssaab*   2 *Ob, T.Ob(?), Tpt, 2 Vn, Va, Bc*   Chorus: *SSATB*

(1) Symphony: 2 *Ob, Tpt, Str*

  (a) [Grave]   (b) [Canzona]   (c) [Adagio]

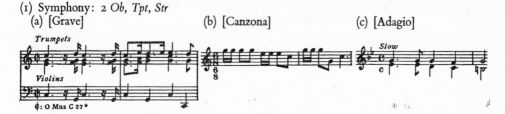

(2a) Prelude *Bc*   (2b) Who can from joy: *a*

(2c) Wond'rous day: *atb, SSAB, Tpt, 2 Ob(?), Str*   (2d)=2b

(2e) For tho' the sun: *ab*

(3a) A Prince of glorious race: *a*

(3b) Ritornello: *Str*

(4a) Prelude: 2 *Vn*

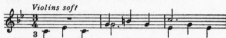

(4b) The father brave as e'er was Dane: *b*, 2 *Vn*

(5a) Prelude: 2 *Ob*

(5b) The Graces in his mother shine: *s*, 2 *Ob*

(6) Sound the trumpet, beat the warlike drum: *a*, *Tpt*

(7) 'Chaconne': 2 *Ob*, *T.Ob*(?), *Tpt*, *Str*

(8a) If now he burns: *ss*

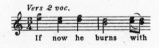

(8b) Ritornello: *Str*

(8c) From pole to pole: *ss*

(8d) Ritornello:
    2 *Ob*, *Tpt*, *Str*

(8e) Then Thames shall be Queen:
    ssaab

(8f) Ritornello: 2 *Ob*, *Str*

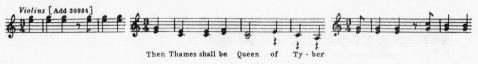

(8g) = 8e: *SATB, 2 Ob, Tpt, Str*

MSS: 44 (inc), 52, **328**, 336, 340, 380, 386, 397, 459, **583**, 679, 766
 Section 2d: 866
 Section 4: 39

EDITIONS: IV, 1
 Section 2ab: 1702d, 1711b, 1712a, 1721a
 Section 2e: 1702d, 1711b, 1712a, 1721a
 Section 3a: 1702d, 1703b, 1711b, 1712a, 1721a
 Section 4: 1702d, 1711b, 1712a, 1721a

COMMENTARY: W. H. Cummings mentions 'Overture with a jigg in 5 short movements,' which seems to have disappeared. It is possible that the Suite in G Major (see No. **770**), which just fits this description, could be the music to which Cummings alluded. The Overture given above is the same as that for *Timon of Athens* (see No. **632/1**) and as that appearing as a keyboard transcription in No. **T691**, being transposed to C Major. In Oxford, Oriel College Library MS U^a 37^a there is another version of Section 8d. In British Museum MS Add. 30934, Mr. Freeman's name is written (as the singer) over Mr. Damascene's, which has been struck through in Section 6.

343. **Why, why are all the muses mute?**

(XVIII, 37) 'Welcome Song 1685 being ye first Song performed to King James ye 2d' October 14th, 1685

Solo: *ssatbb*   2 *Vn, Va, Bc*   Chorus: *SSATB*

(1a) Why, why are all the muses mute?: *s*   (1b) Awake, 'tis Cæsar: *a, SATB*

(2) Symphony: *Str*
 (a) [Grave]   (b) [Canzona]

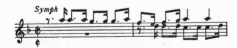

(3a) When should each soul: *t*   (3b) Cæsar, Earth's greatest good: *t*

(4a) For Cæsar's welcome we prepare: *SSATB. Vn*

Cho. (Violin)

For Cae - sar's wel - come, for Cae - sar's wel - come

(4b) Ritornello: *Str*

(Ritor)

(5a) Britain, thou now art great: *a*

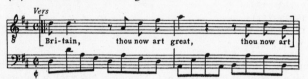

Vers

Bri - tain, thou now art great, thou now art

(5b) Ritornello: *Str*

Ritor

(6a) Look up, and to our isle: *atb*

Look up, and to our isle

Vers

Look up, and to

(6b) Great Cæsar's reign with conquest: *atb, [SATB, Vn]*

Great Cae - sar's reign with con-quest

(7a) Accursed rebellion reared his head: *b, 2 Vn*

Violins soft

Ac-cursed re-bel-lion reared his head

(7b) Prelude: *Str*

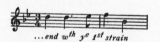

(7c) But when Cæsar from on high: *b, Str*

But when Cae - sar from on high

(8) So Jove scarce settled: *ss*

So Jove scarce set - tled

So Jove scarce set - - - - tled

(9) Ritornello: *Str*

...end wth y^e 1st strain

(10a) Cæsar for milder virtues: *ab, Vn*

Violins soft

Cae - sar for mild - er - vir - tues
Vers solus

(10b) Secured by his victorious arms: *ab, Vn, [Str.]*

Se-cured by his vic-tor-ious arms

(11) The many-headed beast is quelled: *t, [SATB]*

The ma - ny head - ed beast is quelled

(12) In the equal balance laid: *bb*

(13a) O how blest is the isle: *a*　　　　　(13b) Symphony: *Str*　　(13c)=13a: *SSATB*

[... *turn over to ye Symphony*]

MSS: 351, **453**

EDITIONS: XVIII, 37

COMMENTARY: The subtitle, as given in British Museum Royal Music MS 20.h.8., (f.171 rev.) is 'Welcome Song, 1685, being ye first song perform'd to King James 2d,' the work evidently being written after the suppression of Monmouth's rebellion, and probably performed at the first official celebration of King James II's birthday on October 14th, 1685. Luttrell's entry for this date describes the 'publick demonstrations of joy, as ringing of bells, store of bonefires, &c.' Evelyn heard a work performed at court at this time, and had the honour of discussing it with James himself. It may well have been this work of Purcell's (see Evelyn's *Diary*, October 15th, 1685). Section 9 (a ritornello) reappears in **The Gordian Knot Unty'd** as a Rondeau-Minuet. It is also somewhat similar to the beginning of **Beati omnes**. (See No. **597**/3 and No. **131**.)

344. **Ye tuneful muses, raise your heads**

(XVIII, 80) 'Birthday Song for King James II' October 14th, ?1686

Solo: *ssatb*　　　　　　　2 *Fl, Kdr*(?), 2 *Vn, Va, Bc*　　　　　Chorus: *SATB*

(1) Symphony: *Str*
　(a) [Grave]　　　　　　　　　　　　　　　　　　　(b) [Canzona]

2: LK 20.h.8

(2) Ye tuneful muses: *bb*　　　　　　　　(3) Ritornello: *Str*

Ye tune-ful mus-es, raise

175

(4) This point of time ends all your grief: *a, SATB, Vn*

Cho
This point of time ends all, ends all

(5a) Be lively, then and gay: *a*   (5b) the same: (5c) Ritornello: *Str*
                                               SATB, Vn

Be live - ly, then and gay, all signs   Ritor

(6) In his just praise your noblest song: *b, 2 Vn*

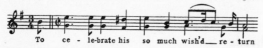

Play soft
In his just praise, in his just praise

(7a) Try ev'ry strain: *SATB, Vn*   (7b) Tune all your strings: *SATB, Vn*

Try, try ev-'ry strain   Tune all your strings

(7c) To celebrate his so much wish'd return: *SATB, Vn*

To ce - le-brate his so much wish'd re - turn

(8) Ritornello: *Str*   [(9a) Prelude: *Str*

(9b) Ritornello: *Str*   (9c) From the ratt'ling of drums: *t*

   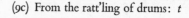
                                               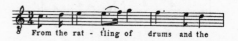

From the rat - tling of drums and the

(9d) the same: *SATB, Vn*   (9e) The best protectors: *ssb*
(9f) = 9d   (9g) By which he glory first: *atb*
(9h) = 9d   (9i) = 9b   (9j) = 9d   (9k) Ritornello

(10) To music's softer but yet kind: *aab, 2 Fl*

> To mu - sic's soft - er, but yet kind — and pleas - ing

(11a) With him he brings the partner: *a*

> With him he brings the part - ner of — his throne, that

(11b) Ritornello: *Str*

(12) Happy in a mutual love: *ss*

> 2 Hap - py in — a — mu - tual love

(13) Whilst in music and verse: *t, [SATB]*

> Whilst in mu - sic and verse
> 3

MSS: 351, 453

EDITIONS: XVIII, 80
    Section 11a: 1706a, 1706b, 1721a

COMMENTARY: This song may have been written for James II's birthday celebration on October 14th, 1686, for which occasion Luttrell has recorded: 'The 14th, being his majesties birth day, was observed with great solemnity: in the morning his majesties four troops of guards were drawn up in Hide park, all new clothed very finely; and the day concluded with ringing of bells, bonfires, and a ball at court.' However, at the passage in the text beginning, 'Happy in a mutual love,' there is the suggestion that the ode may have had something to do with a wedding ceremony or anniversary.

    The bass to the chorus 'Be lively, then, and gay' is the tune 'Hey then, up go we!' A variant of this tune appears in a hand very much like that of Purcell in the New York Public Library copy of *Ayres of 3 parts* once belonging to Thomas Britton. Section 5c appears as one of the movements in the suite in G Major (see No. **770/4**). The 'Ritornello', 9k, appears also in No. **341/3e**. The ground for Section 11 is the same as that in the Ground for harpsichord, No. **T681**.

GENERAL LITERATURE

J. Herbage, 'The Purcell Welcome Songs,' *The Listener*, May 5th, 1937, p. 892; A. K. Holland, 'The English Court Ode,' *The Listener*, Sept. 1st, 1955, p. 353; P. Scholes, 'Purcell in Praise of Princes,' *Musical Times*, October 1915, p. 519; E. Walker, *History of Music in England*, 3rd edition, revised by J. A. Westrup, Oxford: Clarendon, 1952; J. A. Westrup, *Purcell*, London: J. M. Dent & Sons, 1947.

G2

SOLO SONGS

351. Aaron thus propos'd to Moses

1688

Aa - ron thus pro - pos'd to Mos - es

MSS: 543 (without text, *bis*), 598

EDITIONS: 1688f, 1700dd, 1701b, 1707e, 1707f, 1710a, 1720n, 1724c, 1726c, 1731b, 1733a, 1740g

COMMENTARY: Although printed as a catch in several early prints, this song is decidedly not a catch, as W. Barclay Squire has pointed out. Melodically, it is similar to Nos. **353** and **T694**. Arthur Somervell, the editor of volume XXV of the Purcell Society Edition was wrong, I think, in considering the ascription of this work to Purcell as very doubtful.

352. Ah! cruel nymph! you give despair

(XXV, 1)

Ah! cru-el, cru-el, Ah! cru-el

3: LGC VI.5.6

MSS: **442**

EDITIONS: XXV, 1, 1702d, 1711b, 1712a, 1721a

353. Ah! how pleasant 'tis to love

(XXV, 4) 1688

Ah! how pleas-ant 'tis to love

EDITIONS: XXV, 4, 1688e, 1688f

COMMENTARY: The author of the text is unknown, but see Dryden's 'Ah! how sweet it is to love' from *Tyrannic Love* (cf. No. **613**); see also Oxford, Bodleian Library MS Rawl. Poet. 173 f.87a for a text which is similar: 'Ah! how dull it is to love.' The piece also appeared as a 'Song tune' for harpsichord in *Musick's Handmaid* (see No. **T694**).

354. Ah! what pains, what racking thoughts

(XXV, 4) William Congreve

s   ? *Bc*

Ah! ——————————————— what   pains__
3 : LGC VI.5.6

MSS: **442** (inc; voice-part only)

EDITIONS: XXV, 4

A lass there lives upon the green (See S50)

355. Amidst the shades and cool refreshing streams

(XXV, 6) 1683

s   *Bc*

(*Song.*)

A-midst the shades and cool   re-fresh-ing streams

C: LK 20.h.8   ♮3   4   6
                                             5

MSS: **14** ('Among the shades'), **453**

EDITIONS: XXV, 6, 1687d, 1695j, 1805

356. Amintas, to my grief I see

(XXV, 9) 1679

s   *Bc*

A - min-tas, to   my │ grief I see, with│

EDITIONS: XXV, 9, 1679

357. Amintor, heedless of his flocks

(XXV, 10) 1681

s   Bc

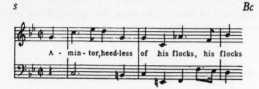

A - min - tor, heed-less of his flocks, his flocks

EDITIONS: XXV, 10, 1681

A quire of bright beauties (See D130)

358. Ask me to love no more

(XXV, 11) 1694; Anthony Hammond

s   Bc

Ask me to love no more, no more

MSS: 466

EDITIONS: XXV, 11, 1694i

As unconcerned and free as air (See D131)

359. A thousand sev'ral ways I tried

(XXV, 178) *ca.* 1681

s   Bc

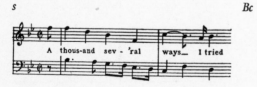

A thous-and sev - 'ral ways__ I tried

MSS: 43, 309

EDITIONS: XXV, 178, 1684b, 1695j, 1707g, 1712c, 1719b

COMMENTARY: The accepted date for this work has been 1684. However, it occurs in British Museum MS Add. 19759, which is dated *ca.* 1681.

Away fond love, thou foe to rest (See D132)

360. Bacchus is a pow'r divine

(XXV, 13)

b   Bc

MSS: 219

EDITIONS: XXV, 13, 1698d, 1706a, 1706b, 1721a

361. Beware, poor shepherds!

(XXV, 18) 1684; 'The Caution'

s   Bc

EDITIONS: XXV, 18, 1684b, 1695j

362. Cease, anxious world, your fruitless pain

(XXV, 19) *ca.* 1684–5; Sir George Etherege

s   Bc

MSS, 219, **453**

EDITIONS: XXV, 19, 1687d, 1695j, 1698d

363. Cease, O my sad soul

(XXV, 21) 1678; Charles Webbe

s   Bc

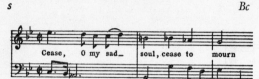

EDITIONS: XXV, 21,   1678

364. Celia's fond, too long I've lov'd her

(XXV, 22) 1694; Peter Anthony Motteux (' The words fitted to the tune)

s   Bc

EDITIONS: XXV, 22, 1694k

COMMENTARY: According to a note in the *Gentleman's Journal* for July 1694, the words were fitted
to the tune by Motteux.   No other source for the tune is known.

365. Corinna is divinely fair

(XXV, 24) 1692; Verse by ' A person of Honor '

s   Bc

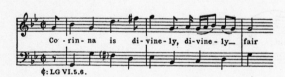

♦: LG VI.5.6.

MSS: **442**

EDITIONS: XXV, 24, 1692i, 1706a, 1706b, 1721a

366. Corinna when you left the town (Missing.)

The words only are given in D'Urfey's *Miscellany Poems*, 1690, which provides the sub-title: 'To pretty Mrs. H. D. An Ode upon the sight of her picture standing amongst others at Mr. Kneller's, and excellently set to Musick by Mr. Henry Purcell.' Mr. Edward Croft-Murray makes the suggestion that the wife of Charles D'Avenant may have been the subject of the picture in question, for there exists an engraving made from her portrait, painted by Kneller. (See John Smith, *British Mezzotint Portraits*, III, 1162.) Another possible subject would be the Mrs. Davies who is recorded as having sung in Crowne's masque *Calisto* in 1674 (see Allardyce Nichol, *A History of Restoration Drama*, p. 321). In neither case can the Christian name be ascertained.

Crown your bowles, loyal souls (See MT678)

367. Cupid, the slyest rogue alive

(XXV, 26) 1685; *Miscellany Poems* (after Anacreon)

Cu-pid, the sly-est rogue a-live, one day was plun-d'ring of a hive

EDITIONS: XXV, 26, 1685e, 1695j

Drunk was I last night (See M574/6)

368. Farewell, all joys!

(XXV, 32) 1685

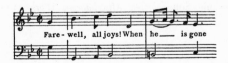

Fare-well, all joys! When he__ is gone

EDITIONS: XXV, 32, 1685d, 1695j

369. Fly swift, ye hours

(XXV, 39) 1692

[Ground]

MSS: 45, 349, 592

EDITIONS: XXV, 39, 1692c, 1698d, 1705b, 1706a, 1706b, 1710l, 1710m, 1721a, 1725c, 1726b, 1745c

COMMENTARY: The author of this text is unknown, but in Oxford, Bodleian Library MS Rawl. Poet. 222 there is a similar poem by Richard Duke: 'Fly, swift, ye hours, ye sluggish minutes fly.'

Forth from the dark and dismal cell (See S68)

370. From silent shades and the Elysian groves

(XXV, 45) *ca.* 1683; 'Bess of Bedlam'

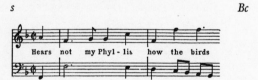

MSS: 43, 45, 219, 287, 310, 318, 347, 460, 595, 620, 670, 724, 724 (in B♮ Major)

EDITIONS: XXV, 45, 1683b, 1695j, 1698d, 1705b, 1706a, 1706b, 1710p, 1720c, 1720d, 1720e, 1721a, 1725c, 1726b, 1736a, 1737a, 1737b, 1745c, ?1779, 1805, 1809

COMMENTARY: An early copy of the text alone occurs in British Museum MS Lansd. 740, f.171v. On f.140 in this manuscript appears the date 1655.

371. Hears not my Phyllis

(XXV, 58) 1695; Sir Charles Sedley, 'The Knotting Song': *The Miscellaneous Works*, 1702 (first printed 1694)

MSS: 358

EDITIONS: XXV, 58, 1695k, 1707g, 1714c, 1719b

COMMENTARY: Motteux prefaced the text in *Gentleman's Journal*, August & September, 1694, p. 233, with the following words: 'Happy the lover who with all his art can warm one of these cold beauties into pity, principally now the fit of Knotting (to speak in a lover's phrase) possesses the best part of the finer half of human kind, and leaves them as unconcerned for sighs and vows as the fair subject of this song.'

372. He himself courts his own ruin

(XXV, 57) 1684

EDITIONS: XXV, 57, 1684b, 1695j, 1707g, 1712c, 1719b

Honours may crown (See M627/21)

373. How delightful's the life of an innocent swain

(XXV, 65) Abraham Cowley

MSS: 318

EDITIONS: XXV, 65

How happy are they (See S57)

374. How I sigh when I think of the charms of my swain

(XXV, 66) 1681

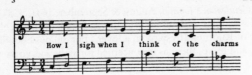

EDITIONS: XXV, 66, 1681

How peaceful the days are (See D133)

How well doth this harmonious meeting prove (See S58)

375. I came, I saw, and was undone

(XXV, 67) *ca.* 1685 ; Abraham Cowley, ' The Thraldom ' from *The Mistresse*, 1647

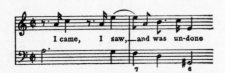

MSS: 219, 291, **453** (title only)

EDITIONS: XXV, 67, 1698d

COMMENTARY: The second section of this song (beginning ' I am thy slave ') is, no doubt, the missing
song referred to in Sotheby's catalogue no. 1398, for the Rimbault sale in July, 1877. The MS in
which it occurred, presented by the catalogue as an autograph, is also missing.

376. I envy not a monarch's fate

(XXV, 72) 1693

MSS: 466

EDITIONS: XXV, 72, 1693i

COMMENTARY: This song is Purcell's own adaptation of the song 'I envy not the pride of May' from
Queen Mary's Birthday Song, **Celebrate this festival**. The original is in E Major. (See
No. **321**/10b).

377. I fain would be free

(XXV, 73)

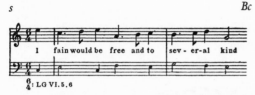

$\frac{6}{4}$: LG VI.5.6

MSS: **442** (voice part only)

EDITIONS: XXV, 73

COMMENTARY: The voice part only appears in the autograph copy of this song (London, Gresham
College Library MS VI.5.6), which is its unique source. In the Purcell Society Edition the bass
is editorial, as shown in the small notes printed above.

378. If grief has any pow'r to kill

(XXV, 82) 1685

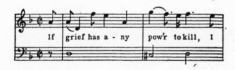

EDITIONS: XXV, 82, 1685e, 1695j

379A. If music be the food of love (First version)

(XXV, 83) 1692; Colonel Henry Heveningham

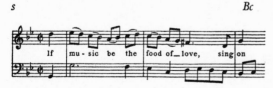

EDITIONS: XXV, 83, 1692f

379B. If music be the food of love (Second version)

(XXV, 84) 1693; Colonel Henry Heveningham

EDITIONS: XXV, 84, 1693a, 1699e, 1707g, 1714c, 1719b

379C. If music be the food of love (Third version)

(XXV, 85) 1695; Colonel Henry Heveningham

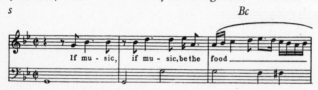

MSS: 341, 737

EDITIONS: XXV, 85, 1695b, 1698d, 1705f, 1706a, 1706b, 1721a, 1725c, 1726b, 1745c

380. If pray'rs and tears

(XXV, 89) *ca.* 1685

MSS: 26, 45, 219, 453

EDITIONS: XXV, 89, 1698d

381. I lov'd fair Celia

(XXV, 77) 1693; Bernard Howard

EDITIONS: XXV, 77, 1702d, 1711b, 1712a, 1721a

COMMENTARY: This is not the same as the setting by Courteville, though there are similarities. The music is the same as that for **We now, my Thirsis** (see No. **427**), so the date of the music itself should read ' 1693, or before.'

382. I love and I must

(XXV, 74) ' Bell Barr '

s   *Bc*

3:LGC VI. 5.6

MSS: **442**

EDITIONS: XXV, 74

COMMENTARY: The subtitle is yet to be explained satisfactorily. There is a hamlet called ' Bell-Bar ' at the south end of Hatfield Park, which fact provides the likeliest explanation. The slight similarity between the bass motto of the piece and the bass of the Almand in the Suite in d minor for harpsichord (No. **668**) has been remarked upon elsewhere, but the similarity can scarcely be said to indicate any connection between the two works.

383. Incassum, Lesbia, incassum rogas

(XXV, 97) after 28th Dec. 1694; George Herbert, ' The Queen's Epicedium '

s   *Bc*

EDITIONS: XXV, 97, 1695o

COMMENTARY: Purcell's setting is taken from *Three Elegies upon the Much Lamented Loss of Our Late Most Gracious Queen Mary*. This piece was published with *O dive custos*, at the beginning of May, 1695. It is a translation of ' No, Lesbia, no you ask in vain,' the first of the three elegies set by Blow, also in 1695.

In Cloe's sparkling eyes (See D134)

384. In Cloris all soft charms agree

(XXV, 95) 1684; John Howe: *Miscellany*, 1685

EDITIONS: XXV, 95,   1684b, 1695j, 1707g, 1712c, 1719b

385. In vain we dissemble

(XXV, 96) 1685

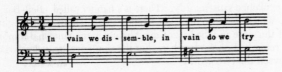

MSS: 219

EDITIONS: XXV, 96,   1685d, 1693a, 1695j

386. I resolve against cringing

(XXV, 79) 1679

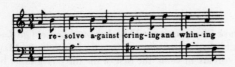

EDITIONS: XXV, 79,   1679

387. I saw that you were grown so high

(XXV, 80) 1678

s   Bc

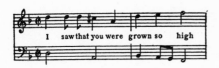

EDITIONS: XXV, 80, 1678

388. I take no pleasure in the sun's bright beams

(XXV, 81) 1681

s   Bc

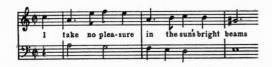

EDITIONS: XXV, 81, 1681

COMMENTARY: The text, without music, appears in British Museum MS 14047, f.126ᵛ, where it
    appears under the heading 'Some of my dear Mother Chamberlaine's Verses.' The MS is
    composed of poems and pieces copied in the late 17th century at Winchester College and
    (Oxford?) University.

389. Leave these useless arts in loving

(XXV, 102) 1694

s   Bc

no t-s: LG VI. 5.6

MSS: 442

EDITIONS: XXV, 102, 1706a, 1706b, 1748b

COMMENTARY: See **Epsom Wells** (No. **579**) in which there is a two-part version of this same song.

390. Let each gallant heart

(XXV, 103) 1683; John Turner

s   Bc

Let each gal-lant heart, un-touch'd with love's dart

[Ground]

EDITIONS: XXV, 103,   1683b, 1695j

391. Let formal lovers still pursue

(XXV, 105) 1687

s   Bc

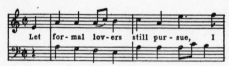

Let for-mal lov-ers still pur-sue, I

EDITIONS: XXV, 105,   1687f

392. Love arms himself in Celia's eyes

(XXV, 108)

s   Bc

Love arms

MSS: 219

EDITIONS: XXV, 108,   1698d, 1706a, 1706b

393. Love is now become a trade

(XXV, III) 1685

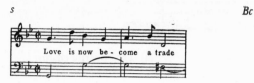

EDITIONS: XXV, III,   1685d, 1695j

394. Lovely Albina's come ashore

(XXV, 117) 1695; 'The last song that Mr. Purcell set before he dy'd'

MSS: 45, 219, 628 (Soprano part only)

EDITIONS: XXV, 117,   1696n, 1698d, 1706a, 1706b, 1745c

COMMENTARY: There is a theory that the words refer allegorically to the reconciliation between Princess Anne and the King. The text is to be found in a manuscript (British Museum MS Add. 30303) which may well be earlier than this event.

395. Love's pow'r in my heart shall find no compliance

(XXV, 117) 1688

EDITIONS: XXV, 117,   1688e, 1706e, 1707g, 1709h, 1720s

396. Love, thou can'st hear, tho' thou art blind

(XXV, 112) 1695; Sir Robert Howard

s   Bc

(1) Love, thou can'st hear

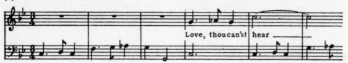

Love, thou can'st hear

(2) She is unconstant [Ground]   (3) = 1   (4) The pow'rful charms

MSS: 219, 460

EDITIONS: XXV, 112, 1695a, 1698d, 1706a, 1706b, 1721a

397. More love or more disdain I crave

(XXV, 120) 1678; Charles Webbe: Banister and Low's *New Airs and Dialogues,* 1678

s   Bc

More love or more dis - dain I crave

EDITIONS: XXV, 120, 1678

COMMENTARY: See also Carew's *Give me more love or more disdain,* in which the text is quite similar.

Musing I late on Windsor Terras sate (See D135)

398. Vacant

399. My heart, whenever you appear

(XXV, 123) 1685

s   Bc

My heart, when-ev - er you ap-pear

EDITIONS: XXV, 123, 1685d, 1695j

400. Not all my torments can your pity move

(XXV, 130)

C:LGC VI.5.6

MSS: 442

EDITIONS: XXV, 130

401. No watch, dear Celia, just is found

(XXV, 128) 1693

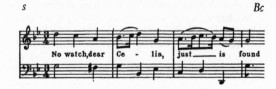

EDITIONS: XXV, 128, 1693f

COMMENTARY: Purcell's setting for these words is based on the tune he used for 'Thou tun'st this world' in the St. Cecilia Ode for 1692 (see No. **328**/6bc).

Now comes joyful Peace! (See M631/5b)

Ode to an expiring frog (See S60)

402. O! fair Cedaria, hide those eyes

(XXV, 132)

s   Bc

(1) O! fair Cedaria

(2) Such beauty and charms [Ground]   (3) Then pity me

EDITIONS: XXV, 132, 1702d, 1711b, 1712a, 1721a

Of noble race was Shinkin (See D136)

403. O! how happy's he, who from bus'ness free

(XXV, 136) ?1694; William Mountfort

EDITIONS: XXV, 136, 1691b, 1693c, 1706e, 1707g, 1709h, 1720s, 1720s (Mock, mnp)

COMMENTARY: The date generally assigned to this work is probably too late. An instrumental transcript published in *Apollo's Banquet*, II (1691, No. 3) would date it at least as early as 1691. The tune itself appears in **Dioclesian** (see No. **627**/4), a fact which sets the date back yet another year. The Purcell Society Editor probably took his bass from this source, for it is lacking in all others shown above. The same tune also appeared in *The Dancing Master* (8th edition, 1695) as ' The Siege of Limerick.' There is a corollary text in Oxford, Bodleian Library, MS Rawl. Poet. 196, f.35. Probably this is a case where the words were fitted to the tune, as in numerous other mock songs. In D'Urfey's *Pills to Purge Melancholy*, vol. VI, 1719–20, the name of the author of the text appears along with the title as follows: ' The Loyal Delights of a contented mind, The Words by Mr. Mumford. Set by Mr. H. Purcell.' (Mountfort was killed in 1692, but this event sheds little light on the problem as to when the words were adapted to the tune.)

404. Olinda in the shades unseen

(XXV, 141)

MSS: **442**

EDITIONS: XXV, 141

One long Whitsun holiday (See D137)

405. On the brow of Richmond Hill

(XXV, 142) 1692; Thomas D'Urfey, 'An Ode to Cynthia, walking on Richmond Hill'

s   Bc

On   the brow of   Rich-mond Hill

EDITIONS: XXV, 142,   1692c, 1702d, 1711b, 1712a, 1719a, 1719b, 1719c, 1721a, 1805

406. O solitude, my sweetest choice

(XXV, 137) 1687; Katherine Philips, 'Solitude': *Poems*, 1667

s   Bc

Very slow   0   sol - i-tude, my   sweet - est choice

e
3 i : LK 20.h.8

[Ground]

MSS: 45, 219, 310, 318, 348 (partly autograph), 349, 358, 453 (in a minor), 724

EDITIONS: XXV, 137,   1687c, 1687d, 1695j, 1698d

COMMENTARY: The sobriquet 'Matchless Orinda' was that used by Katherine Philips in the 'Society of Friendship' in which the members all adopted fantastic names. The meetings were held in the Philips' home at the Priory, Cardigan, until her death of smallpox in 1664. The ground is the same as that appearing in the anthem 'In Thee, O Lord' (see No. 16). In British Museum Royal Music MS 20.h.8 this song is copied partially in Purcell's hand, partially in the hand of an anonymous copyist.

407. Pastora's beauties, when unblown

(XXV, 144) 1681

s   Bc

Pas - to - ra's beau-ties when un-blown

EDITIONS: XXV, 144,   1681, 1719b

408. Phyllis, I can ne'er forgive it

(XXV, 145) 1688

s   Bc

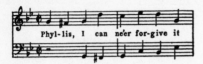

Phyl-lis, I   can ne'er for-give it

EDITIONS: XXV, 145,   1688e, 1706e, 1707g, 1709h, 1720s

409. Phyllis, talk no more of passion

(XXV, 146) 1685

s   Bc

Phyl-lis, talk no   more of pas-sion

EDITIONS: XXV, 146,   1685e, 1695j

410. Pious Celinda goes to pray'rs

(XXV, 148) 1695; William Congreve: *Miscellany Poems V*, 1704

s   Bc

Pi - ous Ce - lin - da__ goes to

EDITIONS: XXV, 148,   1695a, 1695l, 1695q, 1702d, 1711b, 1712a, 1721a

411. Rashly I swore I would disown

(XXV, 150) 1683

s   Bc

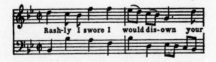

Rash-ly I swore I   would dis-own   your

EDITIONS: XXV, 150,   1683b, 1695j

412. Sawney is a bonny lad

(XXV, 151) before 1692; Peter Anthony Motteux

s   Bc

2:LGC VI.5.6

MSS: 358 (in C Major), **442**, 466, 854 (without text)

EDITIONS: XXV, 151, ?1692, 1694g, 1694m, 1694n, 1699e, 1707g, 1714c, 1719b

COMMENTARY: This song was performed at a concert in honour of Prince Louis of Baden in York Buildings on January 25th, 1694, together with the Ode to St. Cecilia for 1692.

413. She loves and she confesses too

(XXV, 156) 1683; Abraham Cowley, 'A song upon a ground': *The Mistresse*, 1656

s   Bc

[Ground]

MSS: 43, 45, 95, 218, 219, 318, 347

EDITIONS: XXV, 156, 1683b, 1695j, 1698d

414. She that would gain a faithful lover

(XXV, 159) 1695

s   Bc

MSS: 628

EDITIONS: XXV, 159, 1695a

415. She who my poor heart possesses

(XXV, 161) 1683

S   Bc

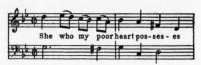

She who my poor heart pos-ses-es

MSS: 309

EDITIONS: XXV, 161, 1683b, 1695j

Since, Cloris, the pow'rs of your charms (See S63)

416. Since one poor view has drawn my heart

(XXV, 163) 1681

S   Bc

Since one poor view has drawn my heart

EDITIONS: XXV, 163, 1681

Smug, rich and fantastic (See D138)

417. Spite of the god-head, pow'rful Love

(XXV, 146) 1687; Mrs. Anne Wharton: *A New Miscellany*, 1701

S   Bc

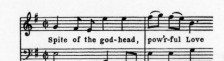

Spite of the god-head, pow'r-ful Love

EDITIONS: XXV, 146, 1687f

Stript of their green our groves appear (See No. 444)

Sunny, rich and fantastic (See D138)

418. Sweet, be no longer sad

(XXV, 169) 1678; Charles Webbe: Banister and Low's *New Airs and Dialogues*, 1678

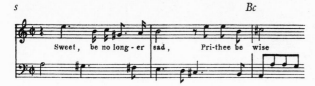

EDITIONS: XXV, 169, 1678

COMMENTARY: There is a curious resemblance to the opening phrase of Matthew Locke's anthem *Lord, let me know mine end.*

Sweet tyranness (See S70)

419. Vacant

420. Sylvia, now your scorn give over

(XXV, 162) 1688

EDITIONS: XXV, 162, 1688e, 1688f

COMMENTARY: A similar text appears anonymously in Oxford, Bodleian Library MS Rawl. Poet. 196, f.1ᵛ. The melody appears in a transcription for keyboard in No. **T695.**

421. The fatal hour comes on apace

(XXV, 36)

EDITIONS: XXV, 36, 1702d, 1711b, 1712a, 1721a

H

422. They say you're angry

(XXV, 171) *ca.* 1685; Abraham Cowley, 'The Rich Rival': *The Mistresse*, 1647

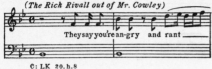

MSS: 219, **453**

EDITIONS: XXV, 171, 1685e, 1695j, 1698d

COMMENTARY: The versions given in the printed sources vary slightly.

423. This poet sings the Trojan wars

(XXV, 174) *ca.* 1686–7; after Anacreon, 'Anacreon's defeat'

MSS: 45, 168, 219, **453**

EDITIONS: XXV, 174, 1688d, 1698d, 1706a, 1706b, 1745c

'Tis vain to fly like wounded deer (See D140)

424. Through mournful shades and solitary groves

(XXV, 179) 1684; Anon.: Richard Duke's *Miscellany Poems*, 1693

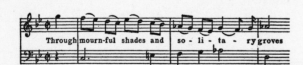

EDITIONS: XXV, 179, 1684b, 1695j

Tom and Will were shepherd swains (See M655)

425. Turn, then thine eyes

(XXV, 181) 1692; ?Elkanah Settle

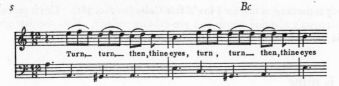

Turn,— turn,— then, thine eyes, turn , turn— then, thine eyes

MSS: **442**

EDITIONS: XXV, 181, 1721a

COMMENTARY: An adaptation from a two-part song in **The Fairy Queen** (see No. **629/50c**).

426. Urge me no more, this airy mirth

(XXV, 183)

Urge me no more, this air - y mirth

MSS: 95, 347, 620

EDITIONS: XXV, 183

View well those stars (See D141)

Was ever nymph like Rosamund (See S65)

427. We now, my Thyrsis never find

(XXV, 186) 1693; Peter Anthony Motteux

We now,— my Thyr - sis

MSS: 466

EDITIONS: XXV, 186, 1693h

COMMENTARY: The melody is the same as that for **I lov'd fair Celia** (see No. **381**). This is probably
another instance of Motteux's adapting words to a pre-existing melody. If so, the date given
for **I lov'd fair Celia** would have to be altered to 'before 1693.'

428A. What a sad fate is mine

(XXV, 188) 'A song on a ground'

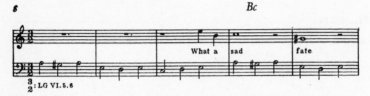

MSS: **442**

EDITIONS: XXV, 188, 1721a, 1726b, 1745c

COMMENTARY: The copy in the autograph manuscript in Gresham College (MS VI.5.6) is without the
bass, which has been supplied from early printed sources.

428B. What a sad fate is mine

(XXV, 191) 'A song on a ground'

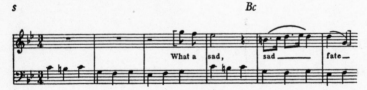

MSS: 310

EDITIONS: XXV, 191, 1698d, 1706a, 1706b

429. What can we poor females do?

(XXV, 194) 1694

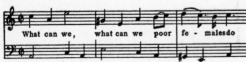

MSS: 442

EDITIONS: XXV, 194, 1694d

COMMENTARY: This is a solo version of the two-part song to the same text (see No. 517).

What ungrateful devil makes you come (See D142)

430. When first Amintas sued for a kiss

(XXV, 199) 1687; Thomas D'Urfey, 'A new song to a Scotch tune set by Mr. Henry Purcell':
A Compleat Collection, 1687

MSS: 60

EDITIONS: XXV, 199, 1687c, 1687d, ?1690, 1695j, 1697g, 1699e, 1707g, 1714c, 1719a (Mock),
1719b, 1719b (Mock)

COMMENTARY: The 'Scotch Tune' appears as 'Mr. Purcell's Jig' in various editions of *Apollo's
Banquet*. The 'Scotch' quality evidently derives from the Scotch snap in the instrumental
versions, and the considerable use of the flat seventh degree of the scale (see No. **N775**). D'Urfey
published another mock song to this same tune beginning 'Amintas one night had occasion' in
his *Songs Compleat* of 1719.

When first Dorinda's piercing eyes (See D143)

431. When first my shepherdess and I

(XXV, 201) 1687

EDITIONS: XXV, 201, 1687d, 1695j

432. When her languishing eyes said 'Love'

(XXV, 202) 1681

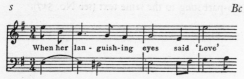

EDITIONS: XXV, 202, 1681

433. When I a lover pale do see

(XXV, 203) 1678; Anon: Banister and Low's *New Airs and Dialogues*, 1678

EDITIONS: XXV, 203, 1678

434. When my Acmelia smiles

(XXV, 204)

EDITIONS: XXV, 204, 1699b, 1699c, 1700gg, 1702d, 1711b, 1712a, 1721a

COMMENTARY: The correct spelling of the proper name is uncertain. The Purcell Society Edition gives 'Amelia' in the text, 'Acmelia' in the introduction. 'Acmelia' is probably no more than a misprint for 'Aemilia' or 'Æmilia'. In the September–December issue of *Mercurius Musicus* for 1699, the song is sub-titled: 'Song set by the late Mr. H. Purcell, never before publish'd.'

435. When Strephon found his passion vain

(XXV, 206) 1683

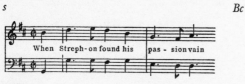

MS: 405

EDITIONS: XXV, 206, 1683b, 1695j

436. When Thyrsis did the splendid eye

(XXV, 207) 1675; *Westminster Drollery*, II, 1672

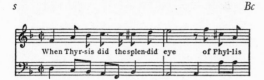

EDITIONS: XXV, 207, 1675, 1676

COMMENTARY: The authenticity of this work is not definitely established.

While Phyllis is drinking (See D144)

437. While Thyrsis, wrapt in downy sleep

(XXV, 208) 1685; 'A Pastoral Coronation Song'

EDITIONS: XXV, 208, 1685e, 1695j

438. Whilst Cynthia sung

(XXV, 209) 1686

EDITIONS: XXV, 209, 1686b

COMMENTARY: In Grove's *Dictionary*, 5th edition, this is given erroneously as 'While Celia sung . . .

439. Whither would my passion run   (Lost)

This appears as No. 11 of Matthew Prior's 'Songs Set to Music by the most eminent masters. Set by Mr. Purcell.' For a similar text see Oxford, Bodleian Library MS Rawl. D1095, ff.125v–6, 'The Arrest.'

440. Who but a slave

(XXV, 211)

s   Bc

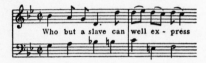

Who but a slave can well ex-press

MSS: 43

EDITIONS: XXV, 211

441. Who can behold Florella's charms

(XXV, 212) 1695; 'A new song . . . sung by Mrs. Siball'

s   Bc

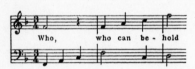

Who,   who can be-hold

MSS: 341, 624, 628

EDITIONS: XXV, 212, 1695a

Why does the morn (See S66)

442. Why so serious, why so grave?

(XXV, 214) Thomas Flatman, 'The Whim': *Poems and Songs*, 1674

s   Bc

Why   so   ser-i-ous, why so grave?

MSS: 405

EDITIONS: XXV, 214

COMMENTARY: The voice part only, signed 'H.P.' appears in the Royal College of Music, London, MS 1119, which is the only extant source for this song.

443. Ye happy swains whose nymphs are kind

(XXV, 215) 1685

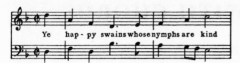

EDITIONS: XXV, 215, 1685d, 1695j, 1719b

COMMENTARY: The text is anonymous in all sources. But see Etherege: ' Ye happy swains whose hearts are free *etc.*'

Young Strephon he has woo'd me (See D145)

444. Stript of their green our groves appear

(XXV, 167) 1691/2; Peter Anthony Motteux

MSS: 45

EDITIONS: XXV, 167, 1692e, 1698d, 1710y, 1726b, ?1728, 1745c

SOLO SONGS WITH CHORUS

461. Beneath a dark and melancholy grove

(XXV, 16) *ca.* 1681

Solo: *s*   *Bc*   Chorus: *SB*

MSS: 14, 309

EDITIONS: XXV, 16

COMMENTARY: A similar text appears under the heading 'The Murmur' in Oxford, Bodleian Library MS Don. C.55, ff.5–5v. Another setting, attributed to 'Mr. Fishburn' in *Choice Ayres and Songs* (Book 5) of 1684 bears several similarities which suggest that Purcell may have known it. In British Museum MS Add. 19759, f. 30v, the melody appears without bass, and without a final chorus.

462. Draw near, you lovers

(XXV, 29) *ca.* 1683; Thomas Stanley, 'The Exequies': *Poems and Translations*, 1647

Solo: *s*   *Bc*   Chorus: *SB*

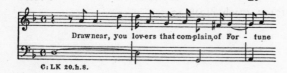

MSS: 453

EDITIONS: XXV, 29

463. Farewell, ye rocks, ye seas, ye sands

(XXV, 33) 1685; Thomas D'Urfey, 'The Storm'

Solo: *s*   *Bc*   Chorus : *SB*

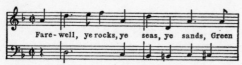

EDITIONS: XXV, 33, 1685b, 1719a, 1719b

464. Gentle shepherds, you that know

(XXV, 49) 1687; Nahum Tate, 'A Pastoral elegy on the death of Mr. John Playford'

Solo: s   Bc   Chorus: SB

MSS: 45, 219

EDITIONS: XXV, 49, 1687b, 1698d

COMMENTARY: According to Cummings, this elegy was composed on the death of John Playford, Jr., who died at 21, the youngest son of 'Honest John' the music publisher.

LITERATURE: E. Walker, *A History of Music in England*, 3rd edition, revised by J. A. Westrup, Oxford: Clarendon, 1952.

465. High on a throne of glitt'ring ore

(XXV, 59) 1690; Thomas D'Urfey, 'An Ode to the Queen': *New Poems*, 1690

Solo: s   Bc   Chorus: SB

MSS: 293

EDITIONS: XXV, 59, 1706a, 1706b, 1719a (mnp), 1719b (mnp), 1721a

466. Let us, kind Lesbia, give away in soft embraces

(XXV, 106) 1684

Solo: s   Bc   Chorus: SB

EDITIONS: XXV, 106, 1684b, 1695j

467. Musing on cares of human fate

(XXV, 121) 1685; Thomas D'Urfey, *Cynthia and Endimion*

s   *Bc*   Chorus : *SB*

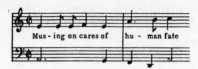

EDITIONS: XXV, 121, 1685e, 1695j

COMMENTARY: The text, in a slightly different version, appears in Thomas D'Urfey's opera *Cynthia and Endimion*, which was first produced in 1697, but written much earlier, probably in 1685.

LITERATURE: Cyrus L. Day, *The Songs of D'Urfey*, Harvard University Press, 1933, p. 21.

468. No, to what purpose should I speak?

(XXV, 124) *ca.* 1683; Abraham Cowley, 'The Concealment': *The Mistresse*, 1647

Solo: *s*   *Bc*   Chorus: *SB*

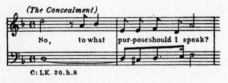

C: LK. 20.h.8

MSS: 26, **453**

EDITIONS: XXV, 124

469. Scarce had the rising sun appear'd

(XXV, 152) 1679

Solo: *s*   *Bc*   Chorus: *S*

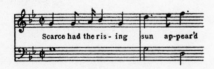

EDITIONS: XXV, 152, 1679

470. See, how the fading glories of the year

(XXV, 153) 1689

Solo: s   Bc   Chorus: SB

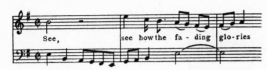

MSS: 219

EDITIONS: XXV, 153,   1689a, 1690b, 1698d, 1706a, 1706b, 1721a

471. Since the pox or the plague

(XXV, 164) 1679

Solo: s   Bc   Chorus: SB

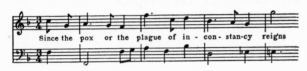

EDITIONS: XXV, 164,   1679

COMMENTARY: The first bar is as shown above in the only known early source.

472. What hope for us remains now he is gone?

(XXV, 196) 1677; ' On the death of his worthy friend Mr. Matthew Lock, musick-composer to his majesty, and organist of Her majestie's Chappel, who dyed in August 1677.'

Solo: s   Bc   Chorus: SB

MSS: 95 (inc)

EDITIONS: XXV, 196,   1679

LITERATURE: H. C. Colles, *Voice and Verse*, London: O.U.P., 1928; W. H. Cummings, *Henry Purcell*, London: Sampson Low, Marston & Co. Ltd., [1903], p. 26.

Young Strephon he has woo'd me (See D145)

473. Young Thyrsis' fate the hills and groves deplore

(XXV, 216) 1690; ?Nahum Tate, ' An elegy upon the death of Mr. Thomas Farmer'.

Solo: *s*   *Bc*   Chorus: *SB*

(1) Young Thyrsis' fate: *s*

(2) What makes the spring [Ground]: *s*   (3) What can the drooping sons: *s*

(4) While thus in dismal notes: *SB*

MSS: 293, 592 (fragment of the second part without text)

EDITIONS: XXV, 216,   1702d, 1711b, 1712a

COMMENTARY: Although Thomas Farmer died *ca.* 1690, this elegy was first published in 1702. It
was advertised in a Playford catalogue along with some of Farmer's own compositions: ' Mr
Farmer's second consort of Musick with his Elegy, set by Mr. Purcell.'

TWO-PART SONGS

480. Above the tumults of a busy state

(XXII, 150) *ca.* 1683
sb   Bc

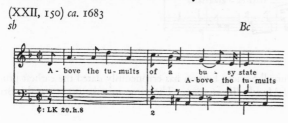

MSS: 348, **453**

EDITIONS: XXII, 150

481. A grasshopper and a fly

(XXV, 54) 1686; Thomas D'Urfey, ' A [*sic*] allegory ': *A Compleat Collection*, 1687
sb   Bc

MSS: 347

EDITIONS: XXV, 54, 1686b, 1719a, 1719b

482. Alas, how barbarous are we

(XXII, 153) Katherine Philips
sb   Bc

MSS: 14, 43, 347, 614

EDITIONS: XXII, 153

Cease the rovers (See S51)

483. Come, dear companions of th' Arcadian fields

(XXII, 40) 1686

sb   Bc

Come, dear— com-pan-ions of___ th'Ar-ca-dian fields

EDITIONS: XXII, 40,   1686b

COMMENTARY: The editor of the Purcell Society Edition has erroneously dated the earliest printed
source for this work (*Theater of Musick*, III) as 1685.   The same mistake occurs in the British
Museum Catalogue.

484. Come, lay by all care

(XXII, 21) 1685; ' Adieu to his mistress '

sb   · Bc

Come, lay by_ all_ care

MSS: 670

EDITIONS: XXII, 21,   1682d (mnp), 1684d (mnp), 1685c, 1686a, 1687e

COMMENTARY: The text is bowdlerized in the Purcell Society Edition.

Come pull away boys (See S52)

485. Dulcibella, whene'er I sue for a kiss

(XXII, 105) 1694; Anthony Henly

sb   Bc

Dul - ci - bel - la,   Dul - ci - bel - la,

MSS: 45, 219, 310, 460, 543, 863 (soprano only)

EDITIONS: XXII, 105,   1694l, 1698d, 1705b, 1706a, 1706b, 1710i, 1721a, 1725c, 1726b, 1744, 1745c,
1745d, ?1755a, ?1765, ?1790, 1805

486. Fair Cloe my breast so alarms

(XXII, 97) 1692; John Glanville: *Poems*, 1725

sb   *Bc*

3:LGC VI.5.6

MSS: 45, 219, 293, **442**, 460, 543, 598, 863 (soprano only)

EDITIONS: XXII, 97,   1692c, 1695c, 1698d, 1704a, 1706a, 1706b, 1710j, 1721a, 1725c, 1726b, 1735a, 1745c, 1748a, ?1750, ?1755a, ?1765, ?1790, 1805

COMMENTARY: The editor of the Purcell Society Edition, vol. XXII, mentions an autograph copy of this song in the Royal Library.   If this copy ever existed, it is now lost.

Fill all the glasses (See S53)

487. Fill the bowl with rosy wine

(XXII, 55) 1687; Abraham Cowley, ' The Epicure ': *Anacreontiques*, 1656

sb   *Bc*

MSS: 28

EDITIONS: XXII, 55,   1687c, 1687d, 1695j, 1805

COMMENTARY: This appears as part II of ' Oft am I by women ' as set by E.Y. in *New Ayres and Dialogues . . .* 1678, pp. 90–94.

488. For love ev'ry creature is form'd

(XXII, 118) 1691; John Dryden, *King Arthur*

sb   *Bc*

MSS: 45, 280, 460, 543

EDITIONS: XXII, 118, 1698d, 1706a, 1706b, 1720g, 1721a, 1745c, ?1755a

COMMENTARY: This version of the duet and chorus in *King Arthur* (see No. **628/**30ef) differs very
little from the original.

489. Go tell Amynta [Amintor], gentle swain

(XXII, 133) *ca.* 1684; John Dryden: *Miscellany Poems*, 1685

sb   *Bc*

MSS: 14, 215, 219, 321, **453**

EDITIONS: XXII, 133, 1706a, 1706b, 1719b, 1720j, 1721a, 1745c, ?1755a, ?1790

490. Haste, gentle Charon

(XXII, 172) *ca.* 1683 ; 'A dialogue between Charon and Orpheus'

bb   *Bc*

(1) Haste, gentle Charon: *b*   (2) Be still : *BB*

MSS: 26, 219, 311, 347, **453**

EDITIONS: XXII, 172, ?1755a

491. Has yet your breast no pity learn'd?

(XXII, 66) 1688; 'A dialogue between Strephon and Dorinda

sb   *Bc*

MSS: 14, 347

EDITIONS: XXII, 66, 1688d

492. Hence, fond deceiver

(XXII, 62) 1687; 'Love and Despair: A Dialogue'

sb   *Bc*

MS: 544

EDITIONS: XXII, 62,   1687d, 1695j

493. Here's to thee, Dick

(XXII, 69) *ca.* 1685; Abraham Cowley: *Miscellanies*, 1656

sb   *Bc*

MSS: 45, 219, 453

EDITIONS: XXII, 69,   1688d, 1698d

494. How great are the blessings

(XXII, 43) 1685; Nahum Tate, 'A health to King James': *Cuckold's Haven*, 1685

sb   *Bc*

MSS: 45

EDITIONS: XXII, 43,   1686a, 1687e, 1774b

495. How sweet is the air and refreshing

(XXII, 54) 1687

sb   Bc

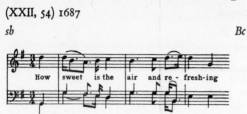

How sweet is the air and re - fresh-ing

EDITIONS: XXII, 54, 1687d, 1695j, 1774b, *ca.* 1790

496. In all our Cynthia's shining sphere

(XXII, 125) Elkanah Settle, 'A dialogue': *The World in the Moon*, first produced 1697

sb   Bc

In all our Cyn-thia's shin - - - - - ing sphere

EDITIONS: XXII, 125, 1706a, 1706b, 1721a

COMMENTARY: There is some doubt as to Purcell's authorship of this piece. Grove's *Dictionary* (5th Edition) attributes it to Daniel Purcell, possibly because of his connection with Settle's *The World in the Moon*. However, its inclusion in *Wit and Mirth* (1706) and in both the second and third editions of *Orpheus Britannicus* (see EDITIONS 1706a, 1706b and 1721a) as a work of Henry Purcell's would seem to indicate that it was his composition. Otherwise Daniel Purcell would have had ample opportunity for correcting the error, at least in the first two of the editions mentioned above.

497. In some kind dream

(XXII, 59) *ca.* 1685; Sir George Etherege

sb   Bc

In some kind dream up - on her slum- bers steal

¢: LK 20.h.8

MSS: 321, **453**, 544

EDITIONS: XXII, 59, 1687d, 1695j

498. I saw fair Cloris all alone

(XXII, 36) 1686; William Strode: Walter Porter's *Madrigales and Ayres* 1632

sb   Bc

EDITIONS: XXII, 36, 1686b, 1805

499. I spy Celia, Celia eyes me

(XXII, 141)

sb   Bc

EDITIONS: XXII, 141, 1702d, 1711b, 1712a, 1721a, 1725b, ?1755a, ?1790, 1805

500. Julia, your unjust disdain

(XXII, 139)

sb   Bc

MSS: 310

EDITIONS: XXII, 139, 1696b, 1702d, 1703f, 1711b, 1712a, 1721a, ?1750

501. Let Hector, Achilles, and each brave commander

(XXII, 82) 1689

MSS: 26, 45, 219, 460, 595, 863 (soprano only)

EDITIONS: XXII, 82, 1689a, 1690b, 1698d, 1706a, 1706b, 1725c, 1726b, 1745c, ?1755a, ?1790, 1805

COMMENTARY: The text alone, subtitled ' On Celia's Charms ' appears in British Museum MS Lansd.
740 on f.171. This MS dates from early in the seventeenth century.

502. Lost is my quiet forever

(XXII, 91) 1691

MSS: 45, 219, 231, 293, 310, 460, 543, 724, 863 (soprano only)

EDITIONS: XXII, 91, 1691e, 1698d, 1700x, 1705b, 1706a, 1706b, 1710v, 1725c, 1726b, 1745c,
?1750, ?1755a, ?1790, 1805

503. Nestor, who did to thrice man's age attain

(XXII, 88) 1689

MSS: 26, 45, 219, 460, 724, 870

EDITIONS: XXII, 88,   1689a, 1690b, 1698d, 1706a, 1706b, 1721a, 1745d, 1755a, 1763, ?1790, 1805

No word, Sir, no word I'll e'er give (See No. 588/Commentary)

504. O dive Custos Auriacae domus

(XXII, 112) after 28th December, 1694; Henry Parker, ' An elegy on the death of Queen Mary '

ss   *Bc*

(1) O dive Custos: *ss*   (2) Seu te fluentem: *ss*

(3) Maria musis flebilis: *ss*

EDITIONS: XXII, 112, 1695o

COMMENTARY: See **Incassum Lesbia** (No. **383**).

505. Oft am I by the women told

(XXII, 52) 1687; Abraham Cowley: *Anacreontiques, 1656*

sb   *Bc*

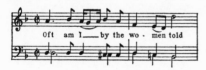

EDITIONS: XXII, 52, 1687c, 1687d, 1695j

Old Chiron thus preached (See S61)

506. O! what a scene does entertain my sight

(XXII, 166) *ca.* 1683–4

Solo: *sb*   *Vn, Bc*   Chorus: *SB*

(1) Symphony   (2a) O what a scene: *s*
   (a) [Grave]   (b) [Canzona]

(2b) How my senses all are courted: *S*   (2c) the same: *SB*

(3a) All creatures now are in a merry vein: *s*   (3b) The wanton lambs: *s*

(3c) Come, then let's strike up: *sb*

MSS: 351, **453**

EDITIONS: XXII, 166

COMMENTARY: Purcell did not prescribe an instrument for the symphony. Violin would seem the most likely choice, but the flute is also possible.

507. Saccharissa's grown old

(XXII, 46) 1686

sb   *Bc*

EDITIONS: XXII, 46, 1686a

508. See where she sits

(XXII, 157) Abraham Cowley

Solo: *sb*   2 *Vn, Bc*   [Chorus: *SB*]

(1a) [Prelude] 2 *Vn*   (1b) See where she sits: *sb*, 2 *Vn*

(2a) [Prelude] 2 *Vn*

(2b) As stars reflect on waters: *s*

As stars re-flect on wa-ters

(3a) Ne'er yet did I behold: *b*

Ne'er yet— did I be-hold so glo - rious

(3b) Ah! mighty love: *SB*

Ah! — migh-ty love, that it were in-ward heat,

MSS: 26, 351, **453**

EDITIONS: XXII, 157

COMMENTARY: Purcell's setting appears to bear a certain melodic relationship to Reggio's composition on the same text. The text alone appears in British Museum MS Add. 28644, f.36. The MS is dated 1671.

509. Sit down, my dear Sylvia

(XXII, 26) 1685; Thomas D'Urfey, 'A dialogue betwixt Alexis and Sylvia'

Solo: *sb* Bc Chorus: *SB*

Sit down, my dear Syl- via and then

MSS: 28

EDITIONS: XXII, 26, 1685b, 1687e, 1719a (mnp), 1719b (mnp)

510. Soft notes and gently rais'd accent

(XXII, 32) *ca.* 1683–4; (? Cowley) Charles Howe, 'A serenading song': *Poems by several hands*, 1685

Solo: *sb* 2 Fl, Bc Chorus: *SB*

(1) Symphony: 2 *Fl*, *Bc*

(a) [Grave]

(b) [Canzona]

(*A Serandeing* [sic] *Song Symphony for Flutes*)

¢: LK 20.h.8

(2) Soft notes and gently: *s*

Soft____ notes and gent-ly

(3) = 1b

(4) Thus feeble man: *s*

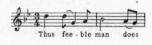

Thus fee-ble man does

(5) Ten thousand raptures: *SB*

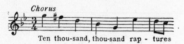

Chorus

Ten thou-sand, thou-sand rap-tures

MSS: 45, 219, 351, **453**

EDITIONS: XXII, 32, 1685e, 1695j, 1698d

COMMENTARY: The Purcell Society Edition attributes the poem to Tate, Grove's Dictionary (5th edition) to Cowley, but Day and Murrie (*English Song Books*) indicate that the text is taken from Howe's *Poems by Several Hands*, 1685. The latter ascription is probably correct.

511. Sylvia, thou brighter eye of night

(XXII, 155) *ca.* 1683-4; 'A serenading song'

sb   *Bc*

(1) Sylvia, thou brighter eye: *sb*

(2) Remember, remember: *sb*

A Seranading [sic] *Song*

Syl-via, thou bright-er__ eye of night

¢: LK 20.h.8

Re-mem-ber, re-mem-ber

(3) Did we the happy time: *sb*

Did we the hap-py time im-prove,__

MSS: 14, **453**

EDITIONS: XXII, 155

COMMENTARY: In the autograph copy (British Museum Royal Music MS 20.h.8) this is subtitled 'A serenading Song'.

512. Sylvia, 'tis true you're fair

(XXII, 38) 1686; 'A serenading song'

sb   *Bc*

EDITIONS: XXII, 38,   1686b

513. There ne'er was so wretched a lover

(XXII, 120) William Congreve

sb   *Bc*

MSS: 45, 219, 866

EDITIONS: XXII, 120,   1698d, 1706a, 1721a, 1745c

COMMENTARY: The text has been slightly bowdlerized in the Purcell Society Edition.

514. Though my mistress be fair

(XXII, 23) 1683–4

sb   *Bc*

3: LK 20.h.8

MSS: 45, **453**

EDITIONS: XXII, 23,   1685c, 1686a, 1687e, 1698d, 1706a, 1706b, 1721a, 1745c

To this place we're now come (See No. N526)

515. Trip it in a ring

(XXII, 132) 'A Song for two voices'

sb   Bc

Trip it, trip it, trip it, trip it,   trip it, trip it in a ring

EDITIONS: XXII, 132,   1711b, 1712a, 1721a

COMMENTARY: This duet is an arrangement from the solo version in the *Fairy Queen*. (See No. **629/5cd**).

516. Underneath this myrtle shade

(XXII, 100) *ca.* 1683; Abraham Cowley, 'The Epicure': *Anacreontiques*, 1656

Solo: sb   Bc   Chorus: SB

(1) Underneath this myrtle shade

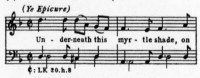

Un - der-neath this   myr - tle shade, on

(2) In this more than kingly state

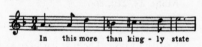

In   this more than king - ly state

(3) Why do we precious ointments

Why   do we pre-cious oint-ments show'r?

(4) Crown me with roses

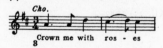

Crown me with   ros - es

MSS: 45, **453**, 791

EDITIONS: XXII, 100,   1692c, 1702d, 1711b, 1712a, 1721a

COMMENTARY: The supposed autograph copy in the Library of Congress, Washington D.C., is not
in Purcell's hand, but in that of an anonymous copyist, of the eighteenth century.

517. Were I to choose the greatest bliss

(XXII, 86) 1689

sb *Bc*

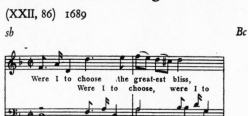

MSS: 45, 310, 543, 595, 670, 724

EDITIONS: XXII, 86, 1689b, 1696s (Mock), 1698d, 1706a, 1706b, 1710cc (Mock), 1720r, 1721a, 1744, 1745c, 1745d, ?1750, ?1755a, ?1765, ?1790, 1805, 1809

518. What can we poor females do?

(XXII, 104) ?1694

sb *Bc*

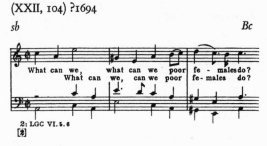

MSS: 45

EDITIONS: XXII, 104, 1694d, 1702d, 1711b, 1712a, 1721a

COMMENTARY: See also the solo version (No. **430**).

519. When gay Philander left the plain

(XXII, 20) 1684

sb *Bc*

EDITIONS: XXII, 20, 1684b, 1695j, 1707g, 1712c, 1719b

COMMENTARY: The text alone is to be found in a late seventeenth-century source, British Museum MS Add. 30303, f.8ᵛ.

520. **When, lovely Phyllis, thou art kind**

(XXII, 30) 1685

sb   Bc

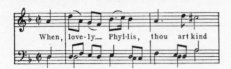

EDITIONS: XXII, 30, 1685e, 1695j, 1702d, 1711b, 1712a, 1721a, ?1750, ?1755a, ?1790

COMMENTARY: No separate instrumental bass is printed with the version of this song appearing in *The Theater of Musick*, II, 1685. The Purcell Society editor has supplied such a part because it is implied in certain passages.

521. **When Myra sings**

(XXII, 109) ?1695; George Granville, Lord Lansdowne, 1693

sb   Bc

MSS: 45, 310, 863

EDITIONS: XXII, 109, 1695b, 1698d, 1705b, 1705k, 1706a, 1706b, 1710ee, 1721a, 1725c, 1726b, 1745c, ?1750, ?1755a, ?1765, ?1790, 1805, 1809

COMMENTARY: A similar Latin text is to be found in Oxford, Bodleian Library MS Ballard 50, f.105: 'Ad Myram inter cantandum.'

522. **When Teucer from his father fled**

(XXII, 48) *ca.* 1685; Daniel Kenrick (or Kendrick), 'Teucer's Voyage' from Horace, *Odes*, Book I, No.7

sb   Bc

(1) When Teucer from his father: *sb*   (2) Cheer up my hearts: *sb*

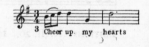

¢: LK 20.h.8

(3) Let us drink: *sb*

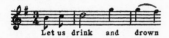

Let us drink and drown

MSS: 45, 60, **453**, 543, 724

EDITIONS: XXII, 48, 1686a, 1687e, 1698d, 1706a, 1706b, 1721a, 1745c, 1805

523. While bolts and bars my days control

(XXII, 130)

sb   *Bc*

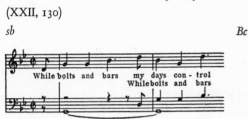

While bolts and bars   my days con - trol
While bolts and bars

EDITIONS: XXII, 130, 1706a, 1706b, 1721a, *ca.* 1790

524. While you for me alone had charms

(XXII, 146) *ca.* 1683; John Oldham (' The 9th Ode of Horace imitated: A dialogue betwixt the poet and Lydia ')

sb   *Bc*

(1) While you for me alone: *b* [*s*]   (2) Then cease all jealousies:

                                                        sb

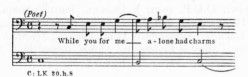

(Poet)

While you for me — a - lone had charms

Then cease, cease,

C: LK 20.h.8

MSS: 26, **453**

EDITIONS: XXII, 146

COMMENTARY: The text alone occurs in Oxford, Bodleian Library MS Rawl. Poet. 173, f.33; in Book 3 of the Ninth Ode of Horace: ' Donec eram gratus tibi ' . . . ' A dialogue of love and jealousy. Horace and Lydia. Oldham, John, Translator.'

525. Why, my Daphne, why complaining?

(XXII, 93) 1691; 'A dialogue between Thyrsis and Daphne'

sb   Bc

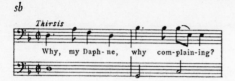

MSS: 293, 724

EDITIONS: XXII, 93,   1691e, 1702d, 1711b, 1712a, 1721a, ?1750

N526. To this place we're now come

sb   Bc

EDITIONS: '94 Songs by Henry Purcell, D. Purcell, Blow *et altri*' (See undated editions),   1720q, ?1755a, ?1790

GENERAL LITERATURE

D. Arundell, *Henry Purcell*, London: O.U.P., 1927; ——'The Songs of Purcell', *The Listener*, 13th Feb., 1929; J. F. Bridge, *Twelve Good Musicians*, London: Kegan Paul, Trench, Trubner & Co., 1920; B. Britten, 'On Realizing the Continuo in Purcell's Songs', *Henry Purcell 1659–1695: Essays on his Music*, London: O.U.P., 1959; C. Burney, *A General History of Music*, London: Foulis & Co. Ltd., 1935, II, p. 390; H. C. Colles, *Voice and Verse: a Study in English Song*, London: O.U.P., 1928; C. L. Day and E. B. Murrie, *English Song Books, 1651–1702*, London: O.U.P., 1940; E. Duncan, 'Purcell's Songs,' *Monthly Musical Record*, 1st May, 1903; R. Sietz, *Henry Purcell: Zeit, Leben, Werk*, Leipzig: Breitkopf & Härtel, 1955, p. 146 ff.; W. Barclay Squire, 'An Unknown Autograph of Henry Purcell', *The Musical Antiquary*, Oct., 1911, pp. 5–17; E. Walker, *History of Music in England*, 3rd edition, revised by J. A. Westrup, Oxford: Clarendon, 1952; J. A. Westrup, *Purcell*, London: J. M. Dent & Sons, 1947.

THREE- AND FOUR-PART SONGS AND LARGER VOCAL WORKS

A poor blind woman (See D171)

541. Hark, Damon, hark

(XXVII, 93) *ca.* 1683

Solo: *sb*   2 *Fl*, 2 *Vn*, *Bc*   Chorus: *SSB*

(1a) Symphony: *Str*   (1b) Canzona

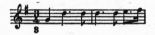

(2) Hark, Damon, hark: *s*

(3a) Orpheus perhaps is from the shades: *b*   (3b) Come, shepherds, come: *b*

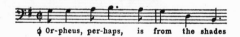

(4) Ritornello: 2 *Fl*   (5) I'll warrant you, boys: *SSB*

MSS: 311, 347, 351, **453**

EDITIONS: XXVII, 93

COMMENTARY: In British Museum MS Add. 33234, f.117v, this work is termed a 'dialogue'.

I

542. Hark how the wild musicians sing

(XXVII, 100) *ca.* 1683

Solo: *ttb*   2 *Vn, Bc*   Chorus: *TTB*

(1) Hark how the wild musicians sing: *ttb*

(2a) Prelude: 2 *Vn*   (2b) Look how the fields: *t*

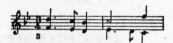

(2c) Ritornello: 2 *Vn*   (2d) See, fairest, see: *t*   (2e) Pleas'd Nature thus drest
                                                                     up: *TTB*, 2 *Vn*

(3a) Prelude: 2 *Vn*   (3b) Then why, Dorinda: *b*

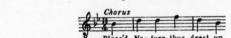

(3c) Ritornello: 2 *Vn*   (3d) We'll freely feast: *ttb*

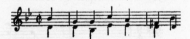

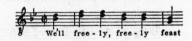

(3e) Ritornello: 2 *Vn*   (4) Though now your eyes: *t*

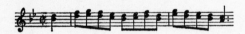

(5) Then let us not waste: *TTB*, 2 *Vn*

MSS: 351, **453**

EDITIONS: XXVII, 100

543. How pleasant is this flow'ry plain

(XXII, 74) *ca.* 1683; Abraham Cowley

Solo: *st*   2 *Fl, Bc*   [Chorus: *ST*]

(1a) Symphony [Grave]: 2 *Fl*   (1b) [Canzona]

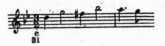

(2a) How pleasant is this flow'ry plain: *t*

(2b) The happy swain in these enamelled fields: *s*

(2c) No fears, no storms: *st*   (2d) Oft to the silent groves he does: *s*

(3a) Prelude: 2 *Fl*   (3b) Ah, happy life: *st*, 2 *Fl*

(4) No guilty remorse: *ST*, 2 *Fl*

MSS: 45, 219, 348, 349 (section 1 only: ascribed to John Blow), 351, **453**

EDITIONS: XXII, 74, 1688d, 1698d

COMMENTARY: The Introduction is given as a 'symphony in g minor for two flutes' ascribed to Blow, in British Museum MS Add. 33236 (f.64b). However, all other sources ascribe the work to Purcell.

LITERATURE: H. L. Clarke, *John Blow*, unpublished doctoral dissertation, Harvard University, 1947, p. 57.

544. If ever I more riches did desire

(XXVII, 118) *ca.* 1686–7; Abraham Cowley

Solo: *sstb*　　　　　　　　　　　　　2 *Vn, Bc*　　　　　　　　　　　Chorus: *STB*

(1a) Symphony [Grave]　　　　　　　　　　　　　　　　　(1b) [Canzona]

(2a) If ever I more riches: *s*　　　　　　　　　　　(2b) the same: 2 *Vn, STB*

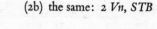

(3a) Upon the slippery tops: *b, 2 Vn*　　　　　　　(3b) Ritornello

(4) Me, O ye gods: *ss*

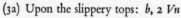
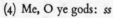

(5a) Here let my life with as much silence slide: *t, Vn*　(5b) An old plebeian let me die: *t, Vn*

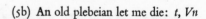

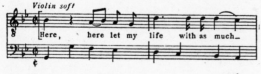
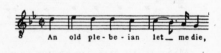

(5c) An old plebeian let me die: *2 Vn, STB*

(5d) Ritornello

(6ab) To him, alas, to him I fear: *s [STB, 2 Vn]*

MSS: 351, **453**

EDITIONS: XXVII, 118

COMMENTARY: John Gostling's name appears against the lowest bass solo part in British Museum Royal Music MS 20.h.9.

545. In a deep vision's intellectual scene

(XXVII, 140) *ca.* 1683; Abraham Cowley, ' The Complaint '

Solo: *ssb*   *Bc*   Chorus: *SSB*

(1) In a deep vision's intellectual scene: *b*

(2) She touch'd him with her harp: *SSB*

(3a) Art thou return'd: *s*

(3b) But when I meant: *s*

(3c) When I resolv'd: *s*

(3d) Go, renegado, cast up: *s*

(3e) Go on, twice seven years: *s*

(3f) But think how likely: *s*

(4) Thus spake the muse: *SSB*

237

(5a) Ah, wanton foe: *b*　　　　　　　　(5b) To all the ports: *b*

(5c) Whoever this world's happiness: *b*　　　(5d) Teach me not, then: *b*

(6) However, of all princes: *SSB*

MSS: 14, 26, 95 (mnp), 348, **453**, 601, 639

EDITIONS: XXVII, 140

Lightly tread, 'tis hallowed ground (See S59)

Sweet tyranness I now resign (See S69)

The owl is abroad (See S64)

546. 'Tis wine was made to rule the day

(XXII, 177) ' A drinking song with chorus for three voices '

Solo: *s*　　　　　　　　　　*Bc*　　　　　　　　Chorus: *SSB*

(1) 'Tis wine was made to rule the day: *s*　　(2) Wine is th' amazement of the old: *s*

(3) Let my Queen live forever: *SSB*　　　(4) Infus'd in wine, let's sink: *s* (melody = 1)

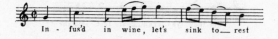

(5) = 3　　　(6) O! lull me, couch'd in soft repose: *s*　　　　　(7) = 3

MSS: 45

　　Section 3: 402

EDITIONS: XXII, 177, 1702d, 1711b, 1712a, 1721a, ?1750, ?1755a, ?1790, 1805

COMMENTARY: In the Library of the Royal College of Music, London, MS 1064, the third section of this song appears as an individual song thus:

Let my king live for - ev - er

No instrumental bass is printed in *Orpheus Britannicus*, II, but the lowest voice part is figured.

547. **We reap all the pleasures** (fragmentary)

(XXVII, 156) *ca.* 1683

Solo: ?   2 Fl, Bc   Chorus: *STB*

(1) [Symphony]
  (a) [Grave]   (b) [Canzona]

(*Symph. for Flutes*)

2: LK 20.h.8

(2) We reap all the pleasures: *STB*

Flute

Cho. We reap all the plea-sures, all, all the

MSS: **453**

EDITIONS: XXVII, 156

COMMENTARY: The autograph copy (British Museum Royal Music MS 20.h.8.) is incomplete, as is the only other extant source for the work (Royal College of Music, London, MS 518).

When the cock begins to crow (See D172)

INCIDENTAL MUSIC

570. Abdelazer, or the Moor's Revenge

(XVI, 1) 1695; Tragedy by Aphra Behn, 1677, derived from *Lust's Dominion, or the Lascivious Queen*, 1657, (erroneously attributed to Marlowe)

Solo: *s*   2 *Vn, Va, Bc*

(1) Overture: *Str*
  (a) [Grave]

(b) [Canzona: Allegro]

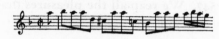

(2) Rondeau: *Str*

(3) Air: *Str*

(4) Air: *Str*

(5) Minuet: *Str*

(6) Air: *Str*

(7) Jig: *Str*

(8) Hornpipe: *Str*

(9) Air: *Str*

(10) Lucinda is bewitching fair: *s, Bc*

Lu- | cin- da is __ be- | witch- ing fair, Lu- [cinda]

¢: LGC VI.5.6   4   6 ♮

MSS: 22 (lacking Sections 7 and 10), 50 (lacking Section 10), 358 (lacking Sections 5, 8, and 10)
406 (lacking Section 10), 621 (iuc)

Section 1: 407, 612
Section 2: 596
Section 4: 594
Section 5: 59, 594
Section 6: 59, 408, 623
Section 7: 408
Section 8: 280, 310, 570 (Trans), 629
Section 9: 59, 408
Section 10: 219, **442** (without bass), 724

EDITIONS: XVI, 1, 1697a (lacking Section 10)

Section 2: ?1700
Section 3: ?1700, 1701d
Section 7: 1701c, 1703g
Section 8: 1698g, 1701c, 1703g, 1713b, 1716b, 1721b
Section 10: 1695g, 1695l, 1698d, 1706a, 1706b, 1745c

COMMENTARY: According to (?) Gildon in Langbaine, *The Lives and Characters of the English Dramatick Poets* (1699), the model for *Abdelazer* may have been Marlowe's *Lust's Dominion*. *Abdelazer* was first produced in 1676, possibly as early as April, at the Dorset Garden Theatre. The tradition existing before Barclay Squire's researches on the subject wrongly had it that Purcell's music was written for this early production. Since the earliest printed sources of any of Purcell's music for the play appeared in 1695, it is very likely that he composed it for a revival which, as Cibber reports, was mounted by the patentees of the Theatre Royal, Drury Lane, and Dorset Garden on April 4th, 1695, as their first joint attempt. This fact is corroborated by the caption printed with 'Lucinda is bewitching fair' in *Orpheus Britannicus* of 1698: 'Sung by Jemmy Bowen, at the opening of the Old Play-house.'

Apparently Purcell did not set the two songs given in the play ('Love in phantastick triumph sat' and 'Make haste, Amintas') nor provide music for those incidents in the play for which the stage directions required it. On the other hand, the text for 'Lucinda is bewitching fair' does not appear in any of the editions of the play.

Section 2 recurs as a 'Rondeau for harpsichord' (see No. **T684**). Section 6 is transcribed for keyboard as No. **T693**/2. Section 7 is transcribed for keyboard as No. **T686**. Section 8 has been arranged for harpsichord in British Museum MS Add. 22099 and in Fitzwilliam Museum, Cambridge, MS 52.b.7, where it appears as an 'Air' in C Major. The ninth section bears some relation to the tune by Lully which appeared in D'Urfey's *A New Collection of Songs* (see EDITION 1683e) and in other collections of the period. In British Museum MS Add. 35043, ff. 40v–44, the following order is to be found for these Tunes, which are copied under the heading: 'Mr. Purcell's tunes to Abdelazer': Air (Section 4), Air (Section 6), Jig (Section 7), Overture and Canzona (Sections 1ab, entitled a 'Courtain Tune'), Rondeau (Section 2) and Air (Section 3).

571. A Fool's Preferment, or the Three Dukes of Dunstable

(XX, 11) 1688; Thomas D'Urfey, derived from Fletcher's *Noble Gentleman*

Solo: *t*[*s*?]   *Bc*

(1a) I sigh'd and I pin'd: *t*   (1b) But now I'm a thing: *t*

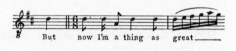

(2) There's nothing so fatal as woman: *t*   (3) Fled is my love: *t*

(4) 'Tis Death alone can give me ease: *t*   (5) I'll mount to yon blue coelum: *t*

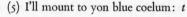

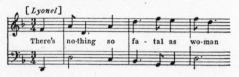

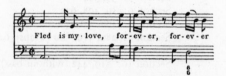

(6) I'll sail upon the dog-star: *t*   (7) Jenny, 'gin you can love: *s* or *t*

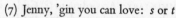

(8) If thou wilt give me back my love: *t*

Here's a health to the King (See D571/9)

MSS: 598 (lacking Section 8)
  Section 6: 45, 219, 870

EDITIONS: XX, 11, 1688a (lacking Section 5)
  Section 6: 1698d, 1700t, 1705b, 1706a, 1706b, 1720a, 1721a, 1725c, 1726b, 1745c, 1805

COMMENTARY: For all but one anachronistic scene (taken from a novel, *The Humours of Bassett*) of this play, D'Urfey rewrote Fletcher's *Noble Gentleman*, produced at Dorset Garden some time about April, 1688, when the play was published (see EDITION 1688a). D'Urfey evidently borrowed the text for the mad-song 'I'll sail upon the dog-star', since there is an earlier version, published in *The New Academy of Complements*, 1671. (See Cyrus Day, *The Songs of D'Urfey*, Cambridge: Harvard University Press, 1933, p. 135.) Purcell's eight songs appeared with this edition with separate title-page and pagination. Only three songs (Sections 1, 2 and 5 respectively) appear in the printed script of the play, which contains texts for two songs (' In yonder cow-slip' and 'I'll lay me down') for which no settings by Purcell are known. Sections 3 and 4 probably replaced these in the 1688 production. Except for the dialogue, the songs were all sung by Mountfort in the original performance.

572. Amphitryon, or the Two Sosias

(XVI, 21) 1690; John Dryden, after Plautus and Molière

Solo: *sb*   2 *Vn, Va, Bc*   Chorus: *SB*

(1) Overture: *Str*
  (a) [Grave]   (b) [Canzona]: Allegro

(c) [Adagio]   (2) Saraband: *Str*

(3) Hornpipe: *Str*   (4) Scotch tune: *Str*

(5) Air: *Str*   [(6) Minuet: *Str*

(7) Hornpipe: *Str*

(8) Bourrée: *Str*

[ACT THREE]

(9a) Celia, that I once was blest: *s*

(9b) Ritornello: 2 *Vn*

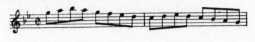

(10a) Symphony: 2 *Vn, Bc*

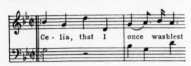

[ACT IV]

(10b) For Iris I sigh: *s*, 2 *Vn*

(11a) Fair Iris and her swain: *sb, Bc*

(11b) Thus at the height we love:
SB, Bc

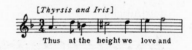

(N12) [Song tune]: [*Str?*]

MSS: 55, 214, 467 (lacking Sections 9 to 11)

    Section 1: 22, 50, 407, 612
    Section 2: 22, 50, 629
    Section 4: 22, 629, 741
    Section 5: 22, 50
    Section 6: 50
    Section 7: 22, 50, 629
    Section 8: 22, 50
    Section 9: 310, 598
    Section 10: 26
    Section 11: 293, 598, 724

EDITIONS: XVI, 21, 1697a (lacking Sections 9 to 11)

    Section 2: 1691b, ?1701–2
    Section 4: 1691b
    Section 5: 1691b
    Section 6: 1691b
    Section 7: 1691b
    Section 9: 1690a, 1691a, 1691b, ?1693c, 1700jj, 1707g, 1714c, 1719b, 1774a [Mock]
    Section 10: 1690a, 1691a, 1691b, ?1693c, 1707g (NYPL copy), 1714c, 1719b
    Section 10b: 1700jj, 1707g (British Museum copy)
    Section 11: 1690a, 1691a, 1702d, 1710k, 1711b, 1712a, 1721a, 1744, 1745c, ?1755a, ?1790
    Section N12: 1691b

COMMENTARY: Dryden's *Amphitryon: or the Two Sosias* was acted at the Theatre Royal in Drury
    Lane in April, 1690. The play was published that same year (see *London Gazette*, Oct. 30th–
    Nov. 3rd, 1690) with Purcell's songs, and re-issued in 1691, 1694 and 1706. In Cambridge,
    Fitzwilliam Museum MS 30.h., f.26, Mr. Bowman is named as having sung 'Celia, that I once
    was blest,' Mrs. Butler as having sung 'For Iris I sigh,' both joining in 'Fair Iris and her swain.'
    The hornpipe (Section 7) is printed in *Apollo's Banquet* (see EDITION 1691b) as 'A Dance in the
    Play of the Boarding School.'

573. Aureng-Zebe, or the Great Mogul

(XVI, 42) ?1692–4; John Dryden, 1675

Solo: *s*   *Bc*

(1a) Ground   (1b) I see she flies me: *s*   (1c) Were she but kind: *s*

(1d) = 1ab

MSS: 219, 310, **442**, 460

EDITIONS: XVI, 42, 1694d, 1695f, 1698d, 1700u, 1704a, 1706a, 1706b, 1710s, 1712b, 1721a, 1725c,
    1726b, 1745c

COMMENTARY: *Aureng-Zebe*, by Dryden, was first produced at the Theatre Royal in Drury Lane in
    November, 1675. 'I see she flies me' was probably written for one of the revivals in 1692 or
    1694. In 1695 it appeared as a single sheet printed by Thomas Cross with the heading: 'A Song
    in the Play call'd *Oranzebe* set to Musick and Sung by Mrs. Ayliff.'

574. Bonduca, or the British Heroine

(XVI, 45) 1695; A tragedy adapted from Fletcher's play by an anonymous friend of George Powell

Solo: *ssatb*   2 *Fl*, 2 *Ob*, *Tpt*, 2 *Vn*, *Va*, *Bc*   Chorus: *SATB*

(1) Overture: *Str*
　(a) [Grave]

　(b) [Canzona]

(c) [Adagio]

(2) Song-tune: *Str*

(3) Song-tune: *Str*

(4) Air: *Str*

(5) Hornpipe: *Str*

(6) Air: *Str*

(7) Hornpipe: *Str*

(8) Air: *Str*

(9) Minuet: *Str*

(10) Jack, thou'rt a toper: 3 *voices* (16-bar interval)

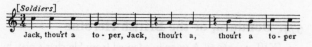

[Soldiers]

Jack, thou'rt a to - per, Jack, thou'rt a, thou'rt a to - per

(11a) Prelude: *Str*

(11b) Hear us, great Rugwith:
        satb, SATB

(12) Hear, ye gods of Britain: *b*

(13a) Symphony: *2 Fl, Bc*

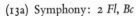

(13b) Sing ye Druids all: *ss, SATB*

(13c) Sing divine Andate's praise:
        SATB, Bc

(14) Divine Andate: *t*

(15a) Symphony: *Tpt*
        See (3)

(15b) To arms, your ensigns straight
        display: *ab [SATB?]*

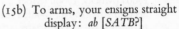

(16a) Prelude: *Tpt, 2 Ob*
        See (2)

(16b) Britons strike home:
        a, [SATB, Tpt, 2 Ob]

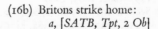

(17a) O lead me to some peaceful gloom: s

(17b) There let me soothe: s

MSS: 44 (inc), 216 (inc), 298, 336 (inc), 340, 377 (inc), 385, 406 (lacking Sections 10 to 17), 466 (inc), 601 (inc), 676, 736, 758

Section 1: 22, 50, 58, 310, 358, 407, 593, 612
Section 1ab: 59
Section 2: 50, 59, 280, 323, 368
Section 3: 22, 50, 59, 323, 368
Section 4: 22, 50, 59, 629, 741
Section 5: 22, 50, 59, 141, 593
Section 6: 22, 50, 310 (Mock), 323, 354 (Mock), 593, 629
Section 7: 22, 50, 59, 323, 593
Section 8: 22, 323, 408, 593
Section 9: 22, 50, 59, 323, 408, 593, 741
Section 10: 233, 310, 317, 598, 604, 673, 866
Section 11: 211, 342, 615
Section 12: 39
Section 13: 211, 615
Section 15: 45, 60, 141, 211, 310, 593, 607, 670
Section 15b: 607
Section 16: 22, 60, 141, 308, 310, 593, 607, 618, 623 (Tr), 670
Section 17: 45, 60, 219, 310, 341, 460

EDITIONS: XVI, 45, 1695n (inc), 1697a (lacking Sections 10 to 17), 1842

Section 2: ?1700, 1701d
Section 3: ?1700, 1701d
Section 6: ?1700 (in A Major), 1701–2 (in d minor), 1705c (Mock), 1706e (Mock), 1707g (Mock), 1709a (Mock), 1709h (Mock), 1710h (Mock), 1712c (Mock), 1715a (Mock), 1719b (Mock, mnp)
Section 10: ?1693c, 1696f, 1701b, 1704c, 1707e, 1707f, 1709e, 1710t, 1711a (Flute), 1720n, 1724c, 1726c, 1731b, 1733a, 1740a, 1740g, 1748a, ?1750, 1767b, 1775a, 1790e, ca. 1790
Section 11: ca. 1780, 1809
Section 12: 1702d, 1711b, 1712a, 1721a, 1805, 1809
Section 13: 1702d, 1711b, 1712a, 1721a, ca. 1780
Section 14: ca. 1780, 1805, 1809
Section 15: 1696n, 1706a, 1706b, 1710aa, 17200, 1720p, 1721a, 1725c, 1726b, 1730f, 1735e, 1737a, 1740j, 1744, 1745c, 1745d, 1747, ?1755a, 1758a, ?1765, 1767b, 1775a, ca. 1780, ?1790, 1797–1802, 1805, 1809
Section 16: 1696n, 1706a, 1706b, 1710aa, 1720p, 1721a, 1725c, 1730f, 1735e, 1740j, 1745c, 1745d, 1747, 1756, 1758a, ?1765, ca. 1780, ?1790, 1797–1802, 1805, 1809
Section 17: 1696f, 1696j, 1698d, 1704a, 1705b, 1705h, 1706a, 1706b, 1707g (Mock), 1712c (Mock), 1719b (Mock), 1721a, 1725c, 1726b, 1745c, ca. 1780, 1805, 1809

COMMENTARY: The *London Gazette* for October 24th–28th, 1695, advertised the publication of *Bonduca*, which was probably produced earlier that year at the Theatre Royal in Drury Lane. George Powell (who played the part of Caratach) signed the dedication (to Lord Jeffries), but indicated that the adaptation of Beaumont and Fletcher's play was carried out by an anonymous friend. The order of the first nine movements above is that found in *Airs for the Theatre*.

The Air (Section 4) appears in *The Double Dealer* as a 'Minuet, Slow Air' (See No. **592/6**). The Air (Section 6) was adapted to the song 'Celadon, when spring came on' by D'Urfey for the 1707 edition of *Wit and Mirth* as 'A Song in the Comedy call'd *The Country Miss with her Furbelo*, the words by Mr. Tho. D'Urfey, to a tune of the late Mr. Henry Purcell's, and sung by Mr. Leveridge.' In the 1709 edition of the same collection the same tune is used for a song with the heading: 'Drunk was I last night, a song, the words made to a tune of the late Mr. Henry Purcell's.' According to a marginal note in the John Travers manuscript at Tenbury (MS 338), the duet 'To arms' was to be sung 'first as a duet then as a chorus.' However, since no version for chorus is known (unless a two-part chorus were meant), this direction cannot easily be followed. In this MS the same note precedes the next section: 'Britons, strike home,' indicating that the 'verse' preceding the chorus should have been a duet rather than a chorus. Since the song appears in *Orpheus Britannicus* (I, 76) for soprano and bass, it is possible that Rimbault and the Purcell Society editor were wrong in assigning the song to solo alto.

Singers mentioned in the earliest sources include Messrs Freeman and Edwards (for Section 15) and Miss Cross (for Section 17). The catch Section 10 was probably introduced into the play, not written for its first performance. Cummings (*Henry Purcell*, p. 84) quotes Arne's note to the effect that Purcell himself wrote the words of this catch, no proof being given. In July, 1778, Samuel Arnold arranged Purcell's music from *Bonduca*, adding a march of his own.

LITERATURE: C. Burney, *A General History of Music*, London: Foulis & Co., Ltd., 1935, II, p. 398.

Bussey d'Ambois, or the Husband's Revenge (See D620)

575. Circe

(XVI, 95) 1685; Charles D'Avenant, 'A rhymed tragedy'

Solo: *satb*   2 *Vn, Va, Bc*   Chorus: *SATB*

[ACT I, SCENE 4]

(1a) Prelude: *Str*

(2a) Their necessary aid you use: *tb, Str*

(3a) Come ev'ry demon: *t*

(1b) We must assemble: *b, SATB*

(2b) The air with music gently wound: *a, [SATB, Str]*

(3b) Circe the daughter of the sun: *t, [SATB, Str]*

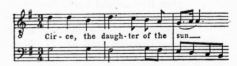

(3c) You who hatch factions: *a*

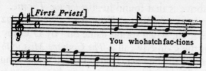

You who hatch fac-tions

(3d)=3b: *SATB, Str*

(4a) Lovers who to their first embraces go: *s*

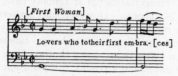

Lo-vers who to their first em-bra-[ces]

(4b) In speed you can outdo: *s*

In speed____ you can out-do,

(4c) Behold, quick as thy thought: *a*

Be-hold, quick as thy thought

(4d) Great minister of fate:
     SATB, Str

Great min-is-ter of fate

(4e) At your dread word: *a*

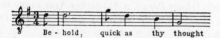

At your dread word they fly____

(4f)=4d

(5) Magician's dance: *Str*

(6) Pluto, arise!: *b, Str*

Plu-to, a-rise, a-rise, - a-rise, a-[rise]

MSS: 62 (see Commentary), 217, 336 (inc), 381, 397, 398, 678
    Section 5: 22

EDITIONS: XVI, 95

COMMENTARY: According to Downes, this rhyme tragedy (which he calls 'opera', although this term does not appear on the title-page of the first quarto edition, printed by Tonson in 1677) was first performed between 1678 and 1681. A warrant dated June 29, 1677 (L.C. 5/142, p. 81, in P.R.O.) indicates that on May 12 the Lord Chamberlain paid £20 for the acting of *Circe* 'at double price.' Downes states that the music for this original production was written by Banister. However, only three of Banister's songs for the play survive: 'Cease, valiant hero' from Banister and Low's *New Ayres and Dialogues* of 1678; 'Give me my lute' from Anne Godbid and John Playford's *Choice Ayres and Songs*, 1679; and 'Young Phaon strove' which appears in this same collection as well as in D'Urfey's *Wit and Mirth* (1700, 1707 and 1712) and *Songs Compleat* (1719 &c...). None of his instrumental music appears to have any connection with the play.

Although various commentators (notably Langbaine and the editor of *Biographia Dramatica*) state that the plot is after Ovid's *Metamorphoses* (Book 14), Genest is probably right in confuting this statement and in saying that the plot is founded on Euripides' *Iphigenia in Tauris*. Even so, the introduction of Circe as the wife of Thoas is rather an extreme use of adaptor's license.

Purcell's music for the play may have been connected with the production referred to in the Lord Chamberlain's order of November 7, 1690, to 'pay Mrs. Barry £25 for "Circe" acted by command' (L.C. 5/150, p. 170). His music for only the first act of the play exists, more or less complete, in seven MSS, but in no published source. Of the MSS, all but one (British Museum MS Add. 31447, *ca.* 1700) were written during the course of the 18th century, and may have been copied from a common source, as suggested by the omission of the same three notes in each for the beginning of the song 'You who hatch factions.' The 'Magicians' Dance' appears also as part of the incidental music to *The Married Beau* (see No. 603/2). In MS 87 in the Fitzwilliam Museum Library, Cambridge, the music to *Circe* is ascribed to Banister in a pencilled note. This might be in the hand of E. Rimbault, who published the work as by Banister in 1847, but later ascribed the music to Purcell in an article in *Concordia*. The first five notes of the setting for 'You who hatch factions' were supplied conjecturally by the Purcell Society editor from the setting for the preceding strophe.

576. Cleomenes, the Spartan Hero

(XVI, 120) 1692; John Dryden and Thomas Southerne

Solo: s   Bc

[ACT II]

No, no, poor suff'ring heart: s

3: LG VI. 5. 6

MSS: 313 (Trans), 358, **442**

EDITIONS: XVI, 120,   1693a, ?1693c, 1693d (Trans), 1706e, 1707g, 1709h, 1720h

COMMENTARY: This play was first acted at the Theatre Royal in the spring of 1692, after having been suppressed for some time (thus hastening the first performance of *The Fairy Queen*). Motteux first mentioned both the play and the opera in *Gentleman's Journal* for March, 1691/2, writing '. . . after Easter we are to have a new Opera; and Mr. Dryden's *Cleomenes* very shortly. . . .' However in the issue for the following month, he announced: 'I was in hopes to have given you in this letter an account of the acting in Mr. Dryden's *Cleomenes*; It was to have appeared upon the Stage on Saturday last, and you need not doubt but that the Town was big with the expectation of the performance; but orders came from her Majesty to hinder its being acted; so that none can tell when it shall be played.'

Before the appearance of the May issue, however, Dryden evidently had exonerated himself, for Motteux then published the following statement: ' Since that time the Innocence and merit of the play have raised it several eminent advocates, who have prevailed to have it acted, and you need not doubt but it has been with great applause.' In his preface, Dryden admits that he borrowed the plot from Plutarch. Purcell's song represents the only music that has survived, although the script requires other music in several places, particularly some incidental music in Act III.

From the dedication to *The Wives Excuse*, according to Genest, it appears that Southerne wrote half the last act of *Cleomenes*, and that it was not acted.

577. Distressed Innocence, or the Princess of Persia

(XVI, 122) 1690; Elkanah Settle (and William Mountfort)

2 Vn, Va, Bc

(1) Overture: *Str*
   (a) [Grave]

(b) [Canzona]

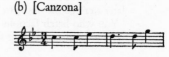

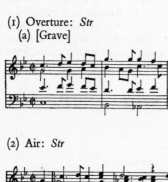

(2) Air: *Str*

(3) Slow air: *Str*

(4) Air: *Str*

(5) Hornpipe: *Str*

(6) Rondeau: *Str*

(7) [Second Music]: *Str*

(8) Minuet: *Str*

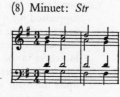

MSS: 22, 50 (lacking Section 6), 741 (inc)
    Section 1: 407, 612
    Section 2: 629
    Section 3: 629

Section 6: 408
Section 7: 467
Section 8: **324,** 467, 629

EDITIONS: XVI, 122, 1697a (lacking Section 8)

COMMENTARY: Elkanah Settle's play (founded on the story of Isdegerdes, King of Persia) was first produced at the Theatre Royal in Drury Lane in October, 1690, the text being published separately first in 1691. In the dedication Settle states that the last scene was written by William Mountfort, who also wrote the epilogue. As far as publications are concerned, Purcell's music is connected with the play only in *Airs for the Theatre* in 1697. The arrangement of the pieces for the play may have been that shown in Tenbury MS 785, with the following headings:

Section 6: ' ([1st] Musick) '
Section 7: ' (2d Musick) '
Section 8: [Blank]
Section 1: ' (Overture) '
Section 2: ' (First act Tune) '
Section 3: ' ([2d] Act Tune) '
Section 4: ' (3d Act Tune) '
Section 5: ' (4th Act Tune) '

This arrangement seems more logical than that in the Purcell Society Edition not only because it leaves the body of the incidental music in the same key, but also because it emphasises the optional nature of Sections 6, 7 and 8, the last of which appears as part of the unfinished suite in G Major in Purcell's autograph manuscript British Museum MS Add. 30930, f.54 (rev) and Royal College of Music MS 999, although in shortened form. For this suite, see No. **770.**

The ' Minuet ' (Section 8 above) appears also as No. **770**/3.

578. Don Quixote, [The Comical History of]

(XVI, 132) Parts I and II: 1694, Part III: 1695; Thomas D'Urfey, *The Comical History of Don Quixote* (after Cervantes)

Solo: *satb*   2 *Vn, Va, Bc, Tpt*   Chorus: *SBB*

PART I

[ACT II, SCENE I]

(1a) Sing all ye muses: *ab*   (1b) When a soldier's the story: *ab*

Sing, sing ———— all ye

(1c) Yet see how they seem: *ab*   (1d) They scale the high wall: *ab*

(1e) Though death's underfoot: *ab*   (1f) 'Till fate claps her wings: *ab*

(1g) Then happy's she whose face: *ab*

[ACT III, SCENE 2]

(2) When the world first knew: *b*

[*Galley slave (Gines de Passamonte)*]

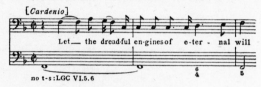

When the world first knew cre - a - tion

[ACT IV, SCENE 1]

(3a) Let the dreadful engines (Mad song): *b*   (3b) Or let the frozen North: *b*

[*Cardenio*]

Let— the dread-ful en-gines of e-ter - nal will

no t–s : LGC VI.5.6

(3c) Can nothing warm me: *b*   (3d) Ye powers, I did but use her name: *b*

(3e) Ah! where are now those flow'ry groves: *b*   (3f) Why must I burn?: *b*

(3g) Cool it then and rail: *b*   (3h) When a woman love pretends: *b*

(3i) And so I fairly bid 'em: *b*

[ACT V, SCENE 2]

(4a) Prelude: 2 *Vn*   (4b) With this sacred charming wand: *b*

[*Montesmo*]
Soft

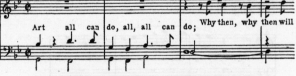

With this, this sac-red charm - ing wand

(4c) I from the clouds: *s*   (4d) I, when 1 please: *s*

(4e) Groves with eternal sweets: *SSB*   (4f) I can give bear / : *s*

(4g) Nature restore and life when spent: *s*   (4h) Art all can do, why then will mortals: *ssb*

(4i) See there a wretch: *b*

(4j) I've a little spirit yonder: *s*

(4k) No, that fate's too high: *SSB*

Art all can do, all, all can do; Why then, why then will

(5a) Appear ye fat fiends: *b* [*SSB, 2 Vn*]

[*Montesmo*]

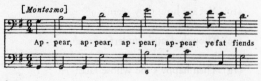

Ap - pear, ap-pear, ap - pear, ap-pear ye fat fiends

6

MSS: 601 (inc)
>   Section 1: 45, 456, 460, 489, 724, 863 (alto only)
>   Section 3: 45, 310, **442** (transcribed for soprano), 456, 460, 724

EDITIONS: XVI, 132,   16940, 1694p
>   Section 1: 1698d, 1706a, 1706b, 1719a (mnp), 1719b (mnp), 1719c (mnp), 1721a, 1725c, 1726b,
>   1740f, 1744, 1745c, 1745d, ?1755a, 1763, ?1765, ?1790, ca. 1790, 1805
>   Section 2: 1707g, 1712c, 1719a, 1719b
>   Section 3: 1694f, 1698d, 1704a, 1705b, 1706a, 1706b, 1710u, 1719a (mnp), 1719b (mnp), 1719c
>   (mnp), 1721a, 1725c, 1726b, 1745c, 1805, 1809
>   Section 4b: 1711b, 1712a, 1721a
>   Section 4h: 1706a, 1706b, 1721a, 1745c

PART II

[ACT IV, SCENE 3]

(6a) Since times are so bad: *sb*
    (A song sung by a clown and his wife)

(6b) Ambition's a trade: *SB*

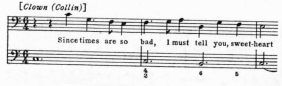

[ACT V, SCENE 2]

(7a) Prelude: *Tpt*

(7b) Genius of England: *t, Tpt*

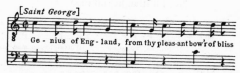

(7c) Then follow brave boys: *t, Tpt*

(8) Lads and lasses, blithe and gay: *s*

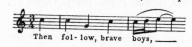

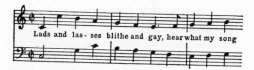

MSS: Section 6a: 45, 219, 341, 598, 601
>   Section 6b: 76, 219, 598
>   Section 7: 45, 394, 622
>   Section 7b: 310, 358 (Trans), 489
>   Section 8: 358

EDITIONS: XVI, 132,   1694q
>   Section 6a: 1698d, 1705b, 1705i, 1706a, 1706b, 1719a (mnp), 1719b (mnp), 1719c (mnp), 1721a,
>   1725c, 1726b, 1744, 1745c, 1745d, ?1755a, 1775a, ?1790, 1805
>   Section 6b: 1705b, 1725c

Section 7: 1700s, 1702d, 1705b, 1710q, 1711b, 1712a, 1719a, 1719b, 1719c, 1721a, 1725c, 1726b, 1735c, 1735e, 1745c, ?1755a, 1758a, *ca.* 1780, ?1790
Section 7b: 1700s, 1719a, 1719b, 1719c, 1721a
Section 8: 1694e, 1695k, 1699e, 1705l (Mock), 1707g, 1707g (Mock), 1710ff (Mock), 1714c, 1714c (Mock), 1719b, 1719b (Mock)

PART III

[ACT V, SCENE I]

(9) From rosy bow'rs (Mad song): *s*

  (a) [Movement: Love]
        From rosy bow'rs: *s*

  (b) [Movement: Mirthfully mad]
        Or if more influencing: *s*

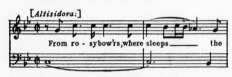

  (c) [Movement: Slow melancholy]   (d) [Movement: Passion]
        Ah! 'tis in vain: *s*   Bleak winds in tempests: *s*

  (e) [Movement: Swift frenzy]
        No, I'll straight run mad: *s*

MSS: 45, 310, 460, 622, 756

EDITIONS: XVI, 132, 1696i, 1698d, 1700q, 1700r, 1703d, 1705b, 1706a, 1706b, 1707a, 17100, 1719a (mnp), 1719b (mnp), 1719c (mnp), 1720i, 1721a, 1725c, 1726b, 1736a, 1737a, 1737b, 1745c, *ca.* 1760, 1805, 1809

COMMENTARY: *Part I.* The earliest announcement of the play appeared in the *Gentleman's Journal* for May 1694, when it was performed at Dorset Garden. Publication of the script was advertised in the *London Gazette* for July 2nd–5th of the same year. Only the Purcell songs shown above survive, although the play requires other music, such as a 'Dance of Milkmaids', 'Dance of Anticks', 'Dance of Spinsters', 'Dance of the Seven Champions' etc. In the first scene of Act II, Vincent introduces 'Sing all ye muses' with the line: 'Now sing the song in praise of Arms and Soldiery.' The text for 'Appear ye fat fiends' was not in the original version of the play.

    Part II. The second part, including song-settings by Eccles and Pack (especially the former's 'I burn . . .' which, as sung by Mrs. Bracegirdle, inspired Purcell's 'Whilst I with grief') was advertised in the *London Gazette* for July 19th–23rd, 1694. Performers mentioned in early printed sources include Reading, Mrs. Ayliff, Freeman, Mrs. Cibber, Mrs. Hudson and the trumpeter, John Shore. In D'Urfey's *Songs Compleat* (see EDITION 1719a) the dialogue is entitled 'A Dialogue. Highly diverting Queen Mary in the 4th Act of the second part of Don Quixote;

for a clown and his wife. Sung by Mr. Reading and Mrs. Ayliff. Set by Mr. Henry Purcell.'
In the play, Section 7 bears the caption: ' At the Duke's Entertainment by St. George and the
Genius of England: Sung by Mr. Freeman and Miss Cibber.'

Part III. The publication of Part III was not advertised until after Purcell's death, in the
London Gazette for December 12th–16th, 1695. Purcell's song was sung by Miss Cross for the
first production, which was unsuccessful, according to report, because the music was poorly
performed. The only singers named are Leveridge, Edwards, and Miss Cross. In the fourth
edition of *Wit and Mirth* (Book I, 1719), D'Urfey listed the five movements of the song as follows:

1. From rosie bowers: Sullenly mad
2. Or if more influencing: a swift movement: mirthfully mad
3. Ah! 'tis in vain: Melancholy madness
4. Or say, ye powers: Fantastically mad
5. No, no I'll run straight mad: Stark mad

(Note that D'Urfey's 4th section does not correspond with Purcell's.) Another arrangement of
the sections of this song is to be found in *The Comical History of Don Quixote as it was acted at the
Queens Theatre in Dorset Gardens* . . . Part III London: printed for John Darby, . . . 1729, where
the following scheme is given: ' Here Altisidora Sings:

In Five Movements:

1. Movement: From Rosy Bowers, where sleeps the God of Love,
               Hither ye little waiting Cupids fly.
               Teach me in soft, melodious strains to move
   Love.   With tender passion my heart's darling joy
               Ah! let the sound of Musick tune my voice
               To win dear Strephon, who my soul enjoys.

2. Movement: Or if more influencing
               Be something airy,
               With a hop and a bound,   ⎫
               And a Frisk from the round,⎬ Gayly
               I'll trip it like a Fairy.
               As when on Ida dancing,
               Were three celestial bodies,
               With an air and a face,
               And a shape and a grace,
               Let me charm like Beauty's Goddess.

3. Movement: Ah! 'Tis in vain, 'tis all, 'tis all in vain,
   Slow   Death & Despair must end the fatal pain.
               Cold, cold despair disguis'd, like Snow & Rain,
               Falls on my breast: Bleak winds in Tempests blow.
   Melancholy: My veins all shiver, and Fingers glow:
               My pulse beats a dead march for lost repose,
               And to a solid lump of ice my poor fond heart is froze.

4. Movement: Or say, ye Powers, my peace to crown,
               Shall I thaw myself, and drown
               Amongst the foaming billows,
   Passion: Increasing all with tears I shed?
               On beds of ooze, and Crystal Pillows,
               Lay down my Love-sick head?

5. Movement: No, no, I'll run straight mad,
   Swift   That soon my heart will warm;

> When once the sense is fled,
> Love has no Power to charm.
>
> Frenzy Wild thro' the woods I'll fly,
> And dare some savage Boar;
> A Thousand deaths I'll die,
> Ere thus in vain adore.'

LITERATURE: V. Espinós, 'Las realizaciones musicales del Quijote: Enrique Purcell y su " Comical History of Don Quixote ",' *Revista de la Biblioteca*, Madrid, 1932; J. Hawkins, *A General History of Music*, London: Novello, 1853 (discusses Section 7), p. 753; J. F. Runciman, *Purcell*, London: George Bell, 1909 (discusses Section 9).

579. Epsom Wells

(XVI, 221) 1693; Thomas Shadwell, *Comedy*

Solo: *sb*   Bc

Leave these useless arts in loving: *sb*

MSS: 45, 219, 543

EDITIONS: XVI, 221,   1693l, 1694m, 1694n, 1698d, 1706a, 1706b, 1721a, 1745c

COMMENTARY: According to William Barclay Squire, Purcell's song was probably written for a revival of the play in 1693, since it was printed as ' A New Song in *Epsom Wells.* . . .' (1694). In the Gresham College autograph (MS VI, 5.6), the wording of the first line is ' Leave these worthless arts in loving.' See also No. **389** in this catalogue: a setting of the same text for solo soprano (the bass and basso-continuo parts having been made into one) which represents the solo versions that are to be found in *Orpheus Britannicus* and in the Gresham autograph (now in the Guildhall Library).

580. Henry the Second, King of England

(XX, 38) 1692; (?)William Mountfort and (?)John Bancroft, *Tragedy*

Solo: *s*   Bc

(1a) In vain 'gainst Love I strove: *s*   (1b) Yet love more strong: *s*

¢: LGC VI.5.6   6

(2) Hornpipe: *Str* (See *King Arthur*, Section 18)

MSS: Section 1: **442**

EDITIONS: XX, 38

  Section 1: 1693a, 1693c, 1698d, 1706a, 1706b, 1721a, 1745c

COMMENTARY: *Henry the Second* was produced at Drury Lane in November 1692, and the play was published in 1692. The first performance may have been that attended by the Queen and the Maids-of-Honour on November 14, 1692, when a payment of £15 was made for a box for them (L.C. 5/151 p. 369). According to Gildon, John Bancroft (a surgeon) was the author. However, the actor William Mountfort (who signed the dedication to Sir Thomas Corke appearing with an edition of this play and of *Edward III* in 1720) may have had a hand in it. He disclaims sole authorship of the play. Neither the words nor music of the song appeared in the printed play, but in *Comes Amoris*, Book IV (1693), which refers to the play, naming Mrs. Dyer as the singer. With regard to the Hornpipe, the Purcell Society editor of *King Arthur* (in which it appears as Section 18) suggests that ' K.Hr ' may be a mistaken abbreviation for ' K.Ar ' in Royal College of Music, London, MS 1172. This is almost certainly the case, for all other capital ' A's ' in this hand are open at the top and look very much like ' H's ' (see ff. 22v, 23 and 21v), whereas capital ' H's ' have an extra serif. For this reason the Hornpipe is entered in *King Arthur* only, in this catalogue.

581. King Richard the Second, or the History of the Sicilian Usurper

(XX, 43) 1680; Nahum Tate, after Shakespeare

Solo: *s (or t)*   *Bc*

Retir'd from any mortal's sight [Song for the prison scene in the last Act]: *s*

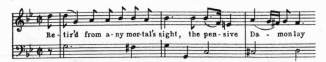

EDITIONS: XX, 43, 1683b, 1695j

COMMENTARY: An adaptation from Shakespeare, this play was first produced as *The Sicilian Usurper* in 1680. It was suppressed after one performance by an order from the Lord Chamberlain on December 14th, 1680 (L.C. 5/144, p. 28). It was first published in 1681. The script calls for two songs: ' Love's delights were past expressing ' and ' Retir'd from any mortal's sight.' Purcell set only the second, which was published with no indication of any connection with the play (see EDITION 1683b). (See also Oxford, Bodleian Library MS Rowe D.865, f.55c, where the poem is sub-titled ' Despair,' as it is in the second edition of Tate's published *Poems* of 1684.)

582. Love Triumphant, or Nature will Prevail

(XX, 70) 1693; John Dryden, *Tragi-Comedy*. The words of the song are by William Congreve

Solo: *s*   *Bc*

[ACT V]

How happy's the husband: s

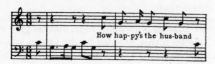

EDITIONS: XX, 70, ?1693c, 1693l, 1694m, 1694n, 1706e, 1707g, 1709h, 1720s

COMMENTARY: This tragi-comedy, its plot based on Fletcher's *King and no King*, was produced at Drury Lane around December 1693, and was published in 1694. The last of Dryden's plays, it was not a notable success. Of the music required (three songs and a dance), Purcell seems to have set only Congreve's song, 'How happy's the husband.' According to the versions printed in *Thesaurus Musicus* (see EDITION 1694m) and *Joyful Cuckoldom* (see EDITION ?1693c), Mrs. Ayliff sang the song, even though she is not mentioned in the cast.

Macbeth (See S100)

Neglected Virtue (See D200)

583. Oedipus

(XXI, 1) 1692; John Dryden and Nathaniel Lee, *Tragedy*

Solo: *atb*   2 *Vn, Bc*   Chorus: *ATB*

[ACT III, SCENE I]

(1a) Prelude: 2 *Vn*

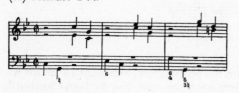

(1b) Hear, ye sullen powers below: *atb*

(1c) Till they drown: *atb*

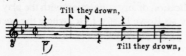

(1d) Ritornello: 2 *Vn*

(2) Music for a while: *a*

(3a) Come away, do not stay: *b, 2 Vn*

(3b) the same: (4) Laius, hear!: *atb, 2 Vn*   (5) = 3b
    ATB, 2 Vn

MSS: 44 (inc), 211 (inc), 213, 216, 336 (inc), 340, 342, 377, 385 (lacking Section 4), 395, 467 (inc), 568, 582 (inc), 615, 676, 736
    Section 1b: 480
    Section 2: 142
    Section 4: 480

EDITIONS: XXI, 1, ?1790b
    Section 2: 1702d, 1711b, 1712a, 1721a

COMMENTARY: Dryden and Lee's tragedy (which owes much to Seneca) was first played at Dorset Gardens in about January, 1678/9. According to Dryden's own statement (in *The Duke of Guise*, 1683), he wrote only the first and third acts, and 'drew the scenery of the whole play.' Purcell's music for *Oedipus*, which probably was commissioned in 1692 for one of many revivals, therefore had to do only with that portion of the play written by Dryden.

584. Oroonoko

(XXI, 38) 1695; Thomas Southerne
Solo: *ss*   *Bc*

Celemene, pray tell me: *ss*

MSS: 219, 337, 460, 624

EDITIONS: XXI, 38, 1696g, 1698d, 1699d, 1699f, 1700h, 1704a, 1706a, 1706b, 1719a (mnp), 1719b (mnp), 1719c (mnp), 1721a, 1726b, 1745c

COMMENTARY: Thomas Southerne's tragedy was first produced at Drury Lane in about November 1695, and was printed in the following year. In the preface, he acknowledges his indebtedness to Aphra Behn for the plot. Purcell's dialogue, which is the setting of a text by D'Urfey, was also inserted in *The Conquest of Granada* (probably in place of the song in two parts, 'How unhappy a lover am I') in Act IV, Scene 1 of Part Two. 'Celemene pray tell me' appears in *Deliciae*

Musicae, IV (see EDITION 1696g), as ' A Dialogue in Oroonoko, by the boy and girl.' However, a copy engraved before 1704 is sub-titled: ' A Dialogue in the Second Part of the Conquest of Granada. The words by Thomas D'Urfey.' It is impossible to say with certainty for which play Purcell wrote the music. However, in view of D'Urfey's borrowing ways, it might be assumed that he used Purcell's song at second hand.

585. Pausanias, the Betrayer of his Country

(XXI, 44) 1695; Norton

Solo: *st*   *Bc*

[ACT III, SCENE I]

(1) Sweeter than roses: *s*   (2) My dearest, my fairest: *st*

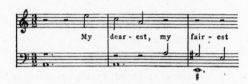

MSS: Section 1: 219
     Section 2: 543 (ascribed to Daniel Purcell)

EDITIONS: XXI, 44

     Section 1: 1698d, 1706a, 1706b, 1721a, 1745c
     Section 2: 1700z, 1745b, 1745c, ?1750, ?1755a, 1767b, ?1790

COMMENTARY: The play, written by one Norton, otherwise unknown, was staged at Drury Lane by Southerne in 1695, and published that same year. Purcell's songs in Act III are thus among his latest works. The first was first printed in *Orpheus Britannicus*, I, 1698, the second about 1700 as a single-sheet song, sung as a ' dialogue between Mr. Cook and Mrs. Hudgson by Mr. Henry Purcell.' This ascription is weakened by the clear ascription to Daniel Purcell in both the index and text of Nanki Library MS 0.O.10 (See MS No. 543).

586. Regulus, or the Faction of Carthage

(XXI, 51) 1692; John Crowne

Solo: *s*   *Bc*

[ACT II]

Ah me! to many deaths decreed: *s*

MSS: 293

EDITIONS: XXI, 51, 1692g, 1698d, 1706a, 1706b, 1721a

COMMENTARY: John Crowne's tragedy was first acted at Drury Lane in June 1692, but not printed
until 1694. Purcell's song, which first appeared in the *Gentleman's Journal* for August 1692, was
not connected with the play (though ascribed to Crowne) either here or in *Orpheus Britannicus*, I
(see EDITION 1698d). However, Motteux, in the former edition, wrote: 'The first of these
three songs which I send you is set by *Mr. Purcell* the *Italian* way; had you heard it sung by Mrs.
Ayliff, you would have owned that there is no pleasure like that which good notes, when so
divinely sung can create!' No setting is known for 'Down with your sprightly wine,' a song
in Act IV of the play.

587. Rule a Wife and Have a Wife

(XXI, 85) 1693; John Fletcher

Solo: *s*   *Bc*

There's not a swain on the plain: *s*

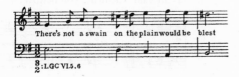

There's not a swain on the plain would be blest

$\frac{8}{2}$:LGC VI.5.6

MSS: **442**

EDITIONS: XXI, 85, ?1693c, 1694i, 1706e, 1707g, 1709h, 1720s (mnp)

COMMENTARY: Purcell's song was written for a revival of Fletcher's play which took place sometime
after 1692. After the merger of the King's and Duke's companies in 1682, according to Downes,
'the mixt company . . . revived the several old and modern plays that were the property of
Mr. Killigrew, as Rule a Wife and Have a Wife . . .' &c. *Gentleman's Journal* for April 1694
prints the song, entitling it 'A song, the notes by Mr. Henry Purcell, the words fitted to the tune
by N. Henley, Esq.' The tune is, in fact, the second part of the 'First Musick' in *The Fairy
Queen* (see No. **629**/1b). The existence of a copy of the song in Purcell's autograph (see Gresham
College Library MS VI.5.6) indicates that he may have had a share in the adaptation. This seems
all the more probable in view of the fact that the bass and the harmonic progressions differ.

588. Sir Anthony Love, or the Rambling Lady

(XXI, 87) 1690; Thomas Southerne, *Comedy*, with song by Major-General Sackville

Solo: *sb*   2 *Vn, Bc*

(1) Overture: 2 *Vn*
  (a) [Grave]   (b) [Canzona]   (c) [Adagio]

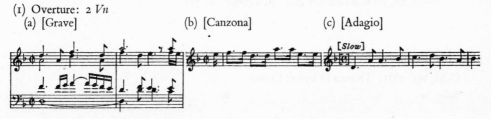

[ACT II]

(2a) Prelude: 2 *Vn*

(2b) Pursuing beauty men descry:
s, 2 *Vn*

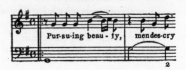

(2c) Be wise and do not try: *s*

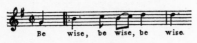

[ACT IV]

(3) No more, Sir, no more: *sb*

[ACT V]

(4) In vain, Clemene, you bestow: *s*

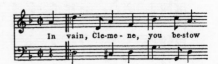

(5) Ground: *Vn*

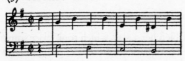

MSS: 741
    Section 5: 588 (attr. to Eccles)

EDITIONS: XXI, 87
    Section 3: 1691g
    Section 4: 1692c, 1706e, 1707g, 1709h, 1720s

COMMENTARY: Thomas Southerne's comedy—Nicoll aptly calls it a 'she-comedy'—was acted at Drury Lane some time about December 1690. According to Langbaine it met with extraordinary success. In the following year the play was published with the words of the songs printed at the end of the play. The text of 'In vain, Clemene' is by Major-General Sackville. The 'song in dialogue, "No more, Sir . . ." ' was sung by Mr. Bowman and Mrs. Butler, according to information given in *Vinculum Societatis*, III. The text of this is paraphrased in the mock song 'No word, Sir, no word I'll e'er give' in Tenbury MS 785.

589. Sir Barnaby Whigg, or No Wit Like a Woman's

(XXI, 103) 1681; Thomas D'Urfey, *Comedy*

Solo: *sa*   Bc   Chorus: *SB*

[ACT I, SCENE I]

(1a) Blow, Boreas, blow: *a, Bc*

Blow, blow,— Bo-reas, blow, and let thy sur-ly winds.

(1b) Then cheer my heart: *s*

Then cheer____ my heart,

(1c) Hey! how she tosses up: *s*

Hey, how she toss-es up,

(1d) With them we'll live: *s*

With them we'll live, with them

(1e) The flashes of lightning: *SB*

The flash-es of light-ning

MSS: 28, 219, 460, 670

EDITIONS: XXI, 103, 1683e, 1685b, 1698d, 1706a, 1706b, 1719a (mnp), 1719b (mnp), 1719c (mnp), 1721a

COMMENTARY: D'Urfey based his comedy upon Marmion's *The Fine Companion*, and, partly, upon the novel, *A Double Cuckold*. Purcell's song represents the only surviving music for the play, although two songs and several dances are required. The comedy was produced in about September 1681, being published later that year. The earliest extant manuscript source appears to be the late seventeenth-century score in the Brussels Conservatoire Library. In the New York Public Library copy of D'Urfey's *Wit and Mirth*, this song is subtitled 'The Storm.'

590. Sophonisba, or Hannibal's Overthrow

(XXI, 109) ?1685; Nathaniel Lee: *Tragedy*

Solo: *s*   *Bc*

(1a) Beneath the poplar's shadow
        (Mad song): *s*

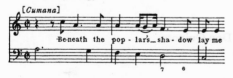

[*Cumana*]

Beneath the pop - lar's_ sha - dow lay me

(1b) I swell and am bigger:
        s

I swell____

(1c) I cannot, I will not: *s*

I can-not, I will not,

K

EDITIONS: XXI, 109, 1702d, 1711b, 1712a, 1721a

COMMENTARY: First produced at Drury Lane in April 1675 (and published in 1676), Lee's tragedy
was revived in 1681, 1685, 1691, 1693, 1697 and in later years. Although Mr. Sidney Lee (in
his article on Nathaniel Lee in the *Dictionary of National Biography*) states that Purcell wrote
for *Sophonisba* the earliest music he produced for the stage, he advances no convincing evidence.
Purcell's song was probably written for one of the revivals of the play; but it is impossible to
say which, for the earliest print of the song (in Pearson's *Orpheus Britannicus*) makes no mention
of the play. Other music called for in the text of the play (including soft music for Act I, a
Trumpet March for Act III, and another song in Act IV: 'Hark, hark, the drums rattle') has
not survived.

The Campaigners (See No. 611/Commentary)

591. The Canterbury Guests, or A Bargain Broken

(XVI, 87) 1694; Edward Ravenscroft, *Comedy*

Solo: *ssab*   Bc

[ACT III, SCENE 5]

Good neighbour, why do you look awry?: *ssab*

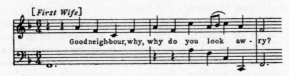

MSS: 358, 866

EDITIONS: XVI, 87, 1695k, 1707g (mnp), 1714c (mnp), 1719b (mnp)

COMMENTARY: Ravenscroft's five-act farce was produced in the autumn of 1694, according to
Gentleman's Journal for November of that year. The printed play (without the music) was
advertised in the *London Gazette* for December 17th–20th. Purcell's 'Dialogue' was probably
sung in Act III, Scene 5 of the play, in which stage directions call for a song and a dance. Purcell
does not seem to have set other songs called for in the play. The text of the song has been
bowdlerized in the Purcell Society Edition.

The Comical History of Don Quixote (See **Don Quixote**)

592. The Double Dealer

(XVI, 194) 1693; William Congreve, *Comedy*

Solo: *s*   2 *Vn, Va, Bc*

(1) Overture: *Str*
(a) [Grave]

(b) [Canzona]

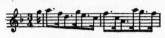

(c) [Adagio]

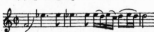

(2) Hornpipe: *Str*

(3) Minuet: *Str*

(4) Air: *Str*

(5) Hornpipe: *Str*

(6) Minuet (Slow Air): *Str*

(7) Minuet: *Str*

(8) Air: *Str*

(9) Air: *Str*

[ACT II, SCENE 1]

(10a) Cynthia frowns whene'er I woo her: *s*

(10b) Prithee, Cynthia, look: *s*

¢: LGC VI. 5, 6

MSS: 22 (lacking Section 10), 50 (lacking Sections 1 to 3 and 10), 467 (lacking Section 10)

    Section 1: 407, 612 (inc)
    Section 5: 623
    Section 8: 408
    Section 9: 629
    Section 10: 45, 219, 358 (in d minor), **442**

EDITIONS: XVI, 194, 1697a (lacking Section 10)

    Section 10: 1693l, 1694m, 1694n, 1694r, 1698d, 1703c, 1706a, 1706b, 1721a, 1745c

COMMENTARY: Congreve's comedy was first given at the Theatre Royal in Drury Lane in November 1693 (according to Malone) and published that same year, as advertised in the *London Gazette*, December 4th–7th, 1693. The song 'Cynthia frowns whene'er I woo her' (which in the Gresham College Library autograph MS VI.5.6, begins 'Celia frowns . . .') was sung by Mrs. Ayliff. The first Minuet (Section 3) has been transcribed for keyboard (No. **669/4**), as has the third Minuet (Section 7—see No. **T676**). The preceding minuet (Section 6 above) appears as an air in c-minor in *Bonduca* (See No. **574/4**).

593. The Double Marriage

(XVI, 211) ?1682–85; Fletcher and Massinger, *Tragedy*

?2 *Vn*, ?*Va*, *Bc*

(1) [First Music]: *Str*

(2) [First Music]: *Str*

(3) [Second Music]: *Str*

(4) [Second Music: Minuet]: *Str*

(5) Overture: *Str*
  (a) [Grave]

(b) [Canzona]

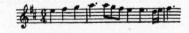

(c) [Adagio]

(6) Jig: *Str*

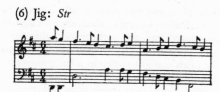

(7) Rondo: *Str*

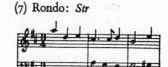

(8) [Minuet]: *Str*

(9) [Minuet]: *Str*

MSS: 406 (lacking Section 9)
  Section 3: 22

EDITIONS: XVI, 211

COMMENTARY: This tragedy by Fletcher and Massinger (attributed to Beaumont and Fletcher in the Purcell Society Edition, after Langbaine) was revived between 1682 and 1685. There are only two early sources of the music for the play, and neither provides sufficient evidence to establish Purcell's authorship beyond all doubt. The arrangement, as shown above, is almost certainly wrong. Although it seems to conform to the conventional pattern (i.e. ' 1st and 2nd Musick', consisting of two movements each, before the Overture), it does not in fact do so. The third incipit actually stands for an overture, consisting of three foreshortened movements, and so is most illogically placed. Furthermore, the main source (i.e. Royal College of Music, London, MS 1144) is none too reliable in its other ascriptions to Purcell (see especially the ascription of the pieces to *Timon of Athens*, as discussed in the Commentary to that work) and should be viewed with suspicion here. Altogether, the ascription to Purcell is doubtful.

594. The English Lawyer

(XVI, 221) *ca.* 1685? ; Edward Ravenscroft, from a Latin Comedy by George Ruggle, *Ignoramus*.

[ACT III]

My wife has a tongue: (' The Scolding Wife ')

3 *voices* (7-bar interval)

My wife has a tongue as good as e'er_____ twang'd

MSS: 318

EDITIONS: XVI, 221, 1684d (mnp), 1685c, 1686a, 1687e, 1701b, 1707e, 1707f, 1720n, 1724c, 1726c

COMMENTARY: Edward Ravenscroft's adaptation of a Latin comedy by George Ruggle (1575–1622) was performed at Drury Lane in about December 1677, and was printed early in 1678. (A translation of the same play in 1662 is tentatively ascribed to Robert Codrington by Langbaine on p. 518.) Purcell's catch may have been introduced into this performance, although as William Barclay Squire has pointed out, there is no place in the play where three voices could have been introduced naturally and easily. If the catch was introduced in a later, unrecorded revival, a possible clue to its date is to be found in the fact that the words are given in Playford's *Wit and Mirth* for 1684 under the heading ' New catches,' but do not appear in the earlier edition. The catch's connection with the play is tenuous at best. Although Day and Murrie list the song as appearing in the *Pleasant Musical Companion* of 1720, it is not to be found in the British Museum copy. Though ascribed to Purcell in the earliest edition (Playford's *Catch that Catch Can* of 1685), the song does not appear under his name in the later editions.

595. The Fatal Marriage, or the Innocent Adultery

(XX, 1) 1694; Thomas Southerne, *Tragedy*

Solo: s   Bc

[ACT III, SCENE 2]

(1) The danger is over: s   (2a) I sigh'd and owned my love: s

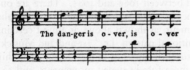

(2b) But, oh! her change: s   (2c) But while she strives: s

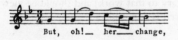

MSS: Section 1: 60, 358, 466

   Section 2: 442

EDITIONS: XX, 1

   Section 1: ?1693c, 1694h, 1699e, 1707g, 1714c, 1719b
   Section 2: 1695k, 1706a, 1706b, 1721a, 1745c

COMMENTARY: Southerne's very successful play was first produced at Drury Lane in February 1693/4 and was published the following month, according to the *Gentleman's Journal* for March 1694. Langbaine (1699 edition, p. 135) indicates that the basic idea for the play came from Aphra Behn's novel, *The Nun*.

596. The Female Virtuosos

(XX, 7) 1693; Thomas Wright, from Molière, *Les Femmes Savantes*. The words of the song are by Anne, Countess of Winchelsea, ' On Love ': *Miscellany Poems*, 1713

Solo: ss   Bc

[ACT V]

Love, thou art best of human joys: ss

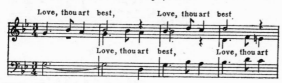

MSS: 45, 219, 310

EDITIONS: XX, 7, 1694d, 1698d, 1706a, 1706b, 1721a, 1745c, 1748b

COMMENTARY: *The Female Virtuosos*, adapted from Molière's *Les femmes savantes* by Thomas Wright (stage-machinist at the Theatre Royal), opened at Dorset Garden in April 1693 and was published that same year. (See *Gentleman's Journal* for May 1693.) Two songs are required for the play. Of the first (which should be a translation of Molière's ' Si le roi m'avait donné ') no setting is known. Purcell has set the second, required in Act V, which is sung by two characters not in the cast.

597. The Gordian Knot Unty'd

(XX, 23) 1691; Anon.

2 *Vn, Va, Bc*

(1) Overture: *Str*
  (a) [Grave]

                                      (b) [Canzona]

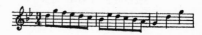

  (c) [Adagio]

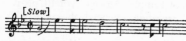

(2) Air: *Str*

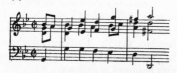

                                    (3) Rondeau Minuet: *Str*

(4) Air: *Str*

(5) Jig: *Str*

(6) Chaconne: *Str*

(7) Air: *Str*

(8) Minuet: *Str*

MSS: 22 (lacking Section 6), 50, 741

    Section 1: 407, 408, 612
    Section 2: 408
    Section 3: 408, 629
    Section 4: **324**
    Section 5: 308
    Section 7: 467
    Section 8: 467

EDITIONS: XX, 23, 1697a

    Section 2: 1691b, ?1700
    Section 5: 1691b
    Section 7: 1691b

COMMENTARY: The author (said to be a ' Gentleman who writ lately a most ingenious Dialogue concerning women, now translated into French ') and the date of performance of this play are unknown, although the latter has been supposed to have been some time in 1691. Motteux, in *Gentleman's Journal* for January 1691/2, strongly hints that Sir William Temple may have written this play. Jonathan Swift, in his preface to the edition of Temple's *Memoirs* (vol. III, pp. iv–xiv), elaborated on his reputation as a Francophile, while repeating a general objection (which he claims to have heard often) to Temple's affected use of French words and turns of expression. The Air (Section 2) is the same as the Symphony for ' All the grandeur ' in *What shall be done in behalf of the man* (see No. **341**/4b); the Rondeau-Minuet (Section 3) also appears in the ode *Why are all the muses mute* (see No. **343**/9); the Air (in G Major, Section 4) has been published as part of an Overture in G Major (see No. **770**/1c) by the Oxford University Press and by the Purcell Society in volume XXXI. The Jig (Section 5) has the tune ' Lilliburlero ' as its bass. The Chaconne is called ' First musick ' in the Richard Border MS songbook (see MS 22). The Minuet (Section 8) appears as a Ritornello in *From hardy climes* (see No. **325**/7). Therefore, this music, at least, dates from no later than July 28th, 1683. The original arrangement of these pieces in the play is probably that given in Tenbury MS 785, with headings as follows:

Section 6: 'Chacone (1st Musick)' (For a similar instance, see *King Arthur*, No. **628**/1)
Section 7: '2d Musick'
Section 8: 'Minuet'
Section 1: 'Overture'
Section 2: '1st Act Tune'
Section 3: '2nd Act Tune'
Section 4: '3d Act Tune'
Section 5: '4th Act Tune' (with 'Lilliburlero' written under the bass staff).

598. The Indian Emperor, or the Conquest of Mexico

(XX, 41) 1691; John Dryden and Sir Robert Howard, *Tragedy*

Solo: *s*   *Bc*

I look'd and saw within the book of Fate: *s*

C: LG VI.5.6

MSS: 45, **442**

EDITIONS: XX, 41, 1692c, 1696b, 1698d, 1706a, 1706b, 1721a, 1725c, 1726b, 1745c

COMMENTARY: *The Indian Emperor*, a sequel to *The Indian Queen*, was first produced at the Theatre Royal, Drury Lane, in April 1665, and published in 1667. Purcell's music was probably written for a revival in 1692—one of many—in which this song was sung by Mr. Pate (according to a single sheet edition of the song in the Royal College of Music, London). No music has been found for the 'Spanish dance' called for in the play.

599. The Knight of Malta

(XX, 44) ?1691; Beaumont and Fletcher

At the close of the ev'ning:

3 *basses* (12-bar interval)

EDITIONS: XX, 44, 1691b, 1691g, 1701b, 1707e, 1707f, 1720n, 1731b, 1733a

COMMENTARY: Purcell's catch may have served as the 'Song of the Watch' at the beginning of Act III in some later revival of the play, of the kind recorded among those acted by Killigrew's company at the Theatre Royal in 1668/9 (see Nicoll, *The Restoration Theatre*, p. 315). The text is given in the Bodleian Library, Oxford, MS Montague 14, ff. 15v–16. No connection with the play is indicated in any source before 1701 (see EDITION 1701b).

600. The Libertine, or the Libertine Destroyed

(XX, 45) ?1692; Thomas Shadwell, *Tragi-comedy*, 1676

Solo: *sab*   *Tpt, 4 Flatt Tpt, 2 Vn, Va, Bc*   Chorus: *SATB*

[ACT IV]

(1a) Prelude: *Str*

(1b) Nymphs and shepherds, come away: *s*

[*? Second Shepherd*]

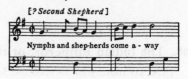

(1c) We come: *SATB*

(1d) In these delightful, pleasant groves: *SATB*

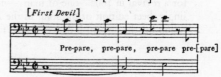

[ACT V]

(2a) Prelude: '*flatt trumpets*'

[*Flatt trumpets*]

(2bc) Prepare, prepare, new guests draw near: *sab*, [*SAB, Str*]

[*First Devil*]

(2d) Let 'em come: *SATB, Str*

(2e) In mischief they've all: *a* [*b, s*]

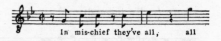

(2f) = 2c (in E♭ Major)

(2g) = 2d

(3a) Prelude: *Tpt*

(3b) To arms, heroic prince: *s, Tpt*

(3c) But battles: *s, Tpt*

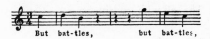

But bat-tles,   but bat-tles,

MSS: 44 (inc), 211 (inc), 213, 216, 297, 336 (inc), 342 (inc), 383, 397, 467 (inc), 584 (inc), 736
>   Section 1: 330
>   Section 3b: 105

EDITIONS: XX, 45
>   Section 1b: 1706a, 1706b, 1721a, 1745c, 1805
>   Section 1d: 1706a, 1706b, 1721a, 1805
>   Section 3b: 1695b, 1702d, 1711b, 1712a, 1721a

COMMENTARY: Shadwell's tragi-comedy in blank verse, a version of the Don Juan legend (Langbaine, 1699 edition, states that the plot is after Molière's *L'athée foudroyé*, but actually it derives from Dorimon's *Le Festin de Pierre*, according to Montague Summers in his edition of *The Complete Works of Thomas Shadwell*, London: 1927), was produced at Dorset Garden in June 1675, and published in the following year. Purcell probably wrote his music (confined to Acts IV and V) for a revival of 1692. (See *Biographia Dramatica*). No setting has been discovered for the song ' All th'inhabitants o' the wood . . . with a chorus and Dance' required in the text of the play. Purcell re-used the prelude to ' Prepare, prepare' for his funeral music for Queen Mary (see No. **851**). Several sources (*cf.* Day and Murrie) give ' Now ghosts' instead of ' new guests' in the opening line. ' To arms' was sung by ' the boy,' according to the information given in *Deliciae Musicae*, 1695 (see EDITION 1695b), who is identified as Jemmy Bowen in *Orpheus Britannicus* (see EDITION 1702d). The play does not provide an obvious place for the introduction of this song, which apparently achieved great popularity in its day.

601. The Maid's Last Prayer, or Any Rather Than Fail

(XX, 72) 1693; Thomas Southerne, *Comedy*

Solo: *ss*   *Bc*

[ACT IV]

(1) Though you make no return to my passion: *s*

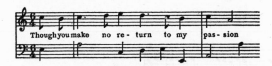

Though you make   no re - turn   to my   pas - sion

(2a) (Anthony Henly) No, resistance is
>   but vain: *ss*

No, no, no,

No, no,   no,   no,

(2b) A thousand ways: *ss*   (2c) Sometimes he sighs: *s*

(2d) The fierce with fierceness: *s*   (2e) The soft with tenderness: *ss*

(2f) The weak with pain: *ss*   (2g)=2a

[ACT V, SCENE I]

(3) Tell me no more I am deceiv'd: *s*

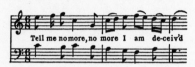

MSS: Section 1: 598
     Section 2: 45, 219, 460
     Section 3: 670

EDITIONS: XX, 72, 1684d (mnp)
     Section 1: ?1693c, 1693d (Trans), 1693e, 1693k, 1706e, 1707g, 1709h, 1720s
     Section 2: 1695a, 1698d, 1706a, 1706b, 1721a, 1745c
     Section 3: 1693d (Trans), 1693e, 1693k, 1699e, 1707g, 1714c, 1719b

COMMENTARY: This comedy was produced at Drury Lane in January 1692/3, and was printed that same year. The first two of the songs occur in Act IV at a 'Musick Meeting' at the house of Sir Symphony, a *fanatico per la musica*. The text Purcell set is a variant of that printed in the *Gentleman's Journal* for 1693. The text of the second song was written by Anthony Henly. The text of the third song, generally ascribed to Congreve, is said to be the work of Southerne himself in Oxford, Bodleian Library, MS Rawl. poet. 196, f.46v. The latter source may be in error, for this is named by Malone as Congreve's first acknowledged literary work. Mrs. Ayliff and Mrs. Hodgson sang in the original performance.

602. The Marriage-Hater Match'd

(XX, 84) 1692; Thomas D'Urfey, *Comedy*

Solo: *sb*   *Bc*

[ACT V]

(1a) As soon as the chaos was made: *sb*

(1b) They quickly did join: *sb*   (1c) For never, my friends: *sb*

[ACT II]

(2) How vile are the sordid intrigues of the town: s

How   vile   are the   Sor-did   in - trigues

MSS: 22

    Section 1: 45, 310, 460, 543, 724, 863
    Section 2: 358, 598, 606

EDITIONS: XX, 84

    Section 1: 1698d, 1700e, 1706a, 1706b, 1719a (mnp), 1719b (mnp), 1719c (mnp), 1721a, 1726b, 1774, 1745c, 1745d, ?1755a, ?1765, ?1790, 1805
    Section 2: 1693a, ?1693c, 1699e, 1707g, 1714c, 1719a, 1719b, 1719c, 1731g

COMMENTARY: D'Urfey's comedy was produced at Drury Lane in January 1691/2, and published that same year. It is mentioned by Motteux in the January–February issue of that year in the *Gentleman's Journal* as follows: 'I send you the Marriage-Hater Match'd, a new comedy by Mr. D'Urfey; it hath met with very good success, having been plaid six days together, and is a diverting play.' Of the several songs required for the play, Purcell set only the two given above. And there is some doubt about his authorship of the latter. Both Alan Gray (in the Purcell Society Edition, vol. XX, p. xvii) and Cyrus Day (*The Songs of Thomas D'Urfey*, p. 144) dismiss the many ascriptions to Purcell (in EDITIONS 1693c, 1699e, 1707g, 1714c, 1719a, 1719b and 1719c) in favour of that to D'Urfey himself (in EDITION 1693a), reasoning that the setting is unworthy of Purcell. This is an opinion with which I do not agree, since it seems to me that both the handling of the word-rhythms and the melodic freedom show far more musical finesse than D'Urfey could ever have demonstrated.

    The song was sung by Mrs. Lassells (as Berenice) in *The Marriage-Hater Match'd* in 1692, and by Mrs. Bracegirdle (as Fulvia) in *The Richmond Heiress* (Act II) in 1693.

    The words alone are printed in *The Compleat Academy of Complements* (1705, p. 143); *The Compleat English Secretary* (1714, p. 137); *A New Academy of Complements* (1715, p. 143); *A Complete Collection of Old English and Scotch Songs* (1736, IV, p. 129); and as a broadside ballad in British Museum MS C.39, k.6(12). In British Museum MS Add. 35043, f.6, the tune alone is copied under the heading: 'The Disconsolate Lady's Complaint—set by Mr. Purcell.'

603. The Married Beau, or the Curious Impertinent

(XX, 89) 1694; John Crowne

Solo: s   2 Vn, Va, Bc

(1) Overture: *Str*
   (a) [Grave]   (b) [Canzona]

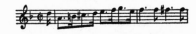

(2) Slow Air: *Str*

(3) Hornpipe: *Str*

(4) Air: *Str*

(5) Hornpipe: *Str*

(6) Jig: *Str*

(7) Trumpet Air: *Str*

(8) March: *Str*

(9) Hornpipe on a ground: *Str*

[ACT V]

(10) See where repenting Celia lies: *s, Bc*

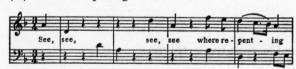

MSS: 22 (lacking Sections 2 and 10)
    Section 1: 407, 612
    Section 2: 50, 629
    Section 3: 50
    Section 6: 50, 741
    Section 7: 50
    Section 8: 50, 629 (inc)
    Section 9: 50
    Section 10: 219, 341 (in c minor)

EDITIONS: XX, 89, 1697a (lacking Section 10)

    Section 6: 1718b, 1728b
    Section 8: ?1700
    Section 10: 1695i, 1695k, 1698d, 1704a, 1706a, 1706b, 1721a

COMMENTARY: Crowne's comedy, with Purcell's music, was played at the Theatre Royal in Drury Lane early in 1694, and published that same year. The play is a farce taken from Cervantes' popular tale in *Don Quixote, Part One*. The 'Slow Air' (Section 2) also appears in *Circe* (see No. **575**/5). The Hornpipe (Section 3) is transcribed for harpsichord in No. **668**/3 as is the March (Section 8) in No. **T687**. The song (*cf.* Oxford, Bodleian Library MS Rawl. poet. 196, f.45, for a similar text) was sung by Mrs. Ayliff in the original production.

604. The Massacre of Paris

(XX, 106) 1689; Nathaniel Lee

Solo: *s* or *b*   *Bc*

[ACT V, SCENE I]

(A) (a) Thy genius, lo!: *b*   (b) And swift as thought: *b*

(c) She told thy story: *b*   (d) But Charles, beware: *b*

(B) Thy genius, lo!: *s*

MSS: A: 219

EDITIONS: XX, 106

    A: 1696b, 1698d, 1704a, 1706a, 1706b, 1721a, 1745c, 1805, 1809
    B: 1697f

COMMENTARY: Though written much earlier, Lee's tragedy was first performed at the Theatre Royal in Drury Lane in October 1689, and was published in 1690. The song, as given in this first publication, was sung by Mr. Bowman in the first version. The second version, probably written for a revival of the play, at some later date, was sung by Jemmy Bowen, 'the boy.'

605. The Mock Marriage

(XX, 113) 1695; Thomas Scott, *Comedy*

Solo: *s*   *Bc*

[ACT II]

(1) Oh! how you protest and solemnly lie: *s*

[ACT III]

(2) 'Twas within a furlong of Edinboro' town: *s*

(3) Man is for the woman made: *s*

MSS: Section 1: 598
    Section 2: 310 (Trans; attr. to Clarke), 313 (Trans), 354 (music only), 628

EDITIONS: XX, 113
    Section 1: 1696f, 1706e, 1707g, 1709h, 1719b
    Section 2: 1696o, 1696r (Trans), 1698g (Trans), 1699e, 1701c (Trans), 1703g (Trans), 1707g,
    1713b (Trans), 1714c, 1715a, 1716b (Trans), 1719b, 1721b (Trans), 1730h
    Section 3: 1696f, 1696r (Trans), 1698g (Trans), 1699e, 1701c (Trans), 1703g (Trans), 1707g,
    1713b (Trans), 1714c, 1716b (Trans), 1719b, 1721b (Trans), *ca.* 1790

COMMENTARY: This comedy by the obscure dramatist Thomas Scott—Gildon (in *A Companion
between the Two Stages*, 1702, p. 8) calls him ' A Young fellow of the town, a retainer and kind
of pensioner to the stage '—was acted at Dorset Garden some time about October 1695, and
published in the following year. ' O how you protest ' (sung by Mrs. Knight) was published
anonymously in *Deliciae Musicae* (see EDITION 1696f) but ascribed to Purcell in Oxford, Bodleian
Library, MS Mus Sch C.95 and elsewhere (see EDITIONS as above).
    The text alone of the second song appears anonymously in British Museum MS Sloane 1731A
on f.173, and in British Museum MS Add. 28095 on f.54. It is printed in *The Compleat English
Secretary* (1714) on p. 135; in *A New Academy of Complements* (1715) on pp. 142–3; in *The
Hive*, II (1733) on pp. 240–1; in *The Vocal Miscellany*, I (1734) on pp. 144–5; in *A Complete
Collection of Scotch and English Songs*, I (1735) on pp. 27–8; and in several other eighteenth-century

collections. It was also published as a broad-side ballad now to be found in the Earl of Crawford's collection: *Bibliotheca Lindesiana, Catalogue of a Collection of English Ballads*, 1890, No. 1221.

In British Museum MS Add. 22099, f.9, this setting is attributed to Clarke, but a near-contemporary single-sheet edition in the British Museum describes it as 'A Scotch Song, Sung by the Girl, in the Mock Marriage. Set by Mr. Henry Purcell, and sold at most Musick Shops in Town.'

The incidental music to the play was contributed by Morgan, an older contemporary of Purcell.

606. Theodosius, or the Force of Love

(XXI, 115) 1680; Nathaniel Lee, *Tragedy*

Solo: *satb*   2 *Fl, Bc*   Chorus: *SATB*

[ACT I, SCENE I]

(1) Prepare, the rites begin: *b*, [*ATB, 2 Fl*]

(2a) Can'st thou, Marina, leave: *atb*

(2b) Say, votaries, can this: *ATB*

(3a) The gate to bliss: *s*

(3b) Haste then: *ss*

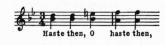

(4a) Prelude: 2 *Fl*   (4b) Hark, behold the heavenly   (4c) To the powers divine:
                                      choir: *b*, 2 *Fl*   *SATB*, [2 *Fl*]?

[AFTER ACT I]

(5) Now the fight's done: s

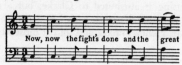

Now, now the fight's done and the great

[AFTER ACT II]

(6a) Sad as death at dead of night: s

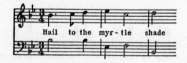

Sad as death at dead of night

(6b) Curse the night: b

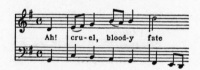

Curse the night, then curse the hour,

(7) Dream no more of pleasures past: s, [sa]

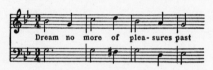

Dream no more of plea-sures past

[AFTER ACT III]

(8) Hail to the myrtle shade: a, [sa]

Hail to the myr-tle shade

[AFTER ACT IV]

(9) Ah! cruel, bloody fate: s

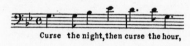

Ah! cru-el, blood-y fate

MSS: Section 1: 582
Section 2: 582
Section 3: 582
Section 4: 582

EDITIONS: XXI, 115, 1680 (lacking Sections 3, 4, and 7)
Section 5: 1681, 1682b (Trans), 1682c (Mock), 1683f, 1720s (Mock, mnp), 1774a (Mock)
Section 8: 1681, 1682a (Mock), 1683f, 1685a (Mock, mnp), 1694a (Mock, mnp), 1699e, 1707g, 1714c, 1719b, 1774a (Mock; bis)
Section 9: 1681, 1682b (Trans), 1685a (Mock), 1690c (Trans), 1694a (Mock), 1700jj, 1707g, 1714c, 1719b

COMMENTARY: Purcell evidently wrote his first stage music for Lee's tragedy, which was acted at Dorset Garden in about September 1680, and was published (with Purcell's music as an appendix) that same year. According to the following statement by Downes, it was quite successful: 'All the parts in't being perfectly perform'd with several Entertainments of Singing; Compos'd by the Famous Master Mr. Henry Purcell, (being the first he ever compos'd for the stage) made it a living and gainful play to the company.' As intimated here, Purcell's songs instead of Act Tunes were sung between the acts. The play was revived in 1684, 1692, 1697 and 1711.

The music for the Confirmation scene in Act III is now missing, although Burney (vol. III, p. 479) relates having heard it in his time. He may, of course, have confused it with the setting by Arne in British Museum Royal Music MS 21.c.46. The duet in Act V, 'Happy day, ah happy day,' is also missing. A mock-song 'Hail to the Knight of the Post' was printed in EDITION 1682a as a polemic against Titus Oates and the Whig faction. The text for 'Now the fight's done' appears in British Museum MS Add. 30303, f.4. In *Choyce Ayres and Songs* (EDITION 1681) the song begins as follows:

Now, now the fight's done, and the great &c.

The bass solo 'Curse the night' (Section 6b) has no accompaniment in EDITION 1680, the only known source.

607. The Old Bachelor

(XXI, 19) 1691; William Congreve, *Comedy*

Solo: *sb* 2 *Vn, Va, Bc*

(1) Overture: *Str*
  (a) [Grave]

(b) [Canzona]

(c) [Adagio]

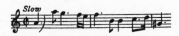

(2) Hornpipe: *Str*

(3) Slow Air: *Str*

(4) Hornpipe: *Str*

(5) Rondeau: *Str*

(6) Minuet: *Str*

(7) Boree: *Str*   (8) March: *Str*   (9) Jig: *Str*

(10) Thus to a ripe consenting maid: *s*   (11) As Amoret and Thyrsis: *sb*

3: LG VI.5.6

MSS: 22 (lacking Sections 1, 2, and 10), 50 (lacking Sections 1, 5, 10), 406 (lacking Sections 10 and 11)

    Section 1: 280, 612
    Section 2: 59
    Section 3: 59, 629
    Section 4: 60
    Section 5: 629
    Section 6: 741
    Section 8: 59, 629
    Section 9: 59
    Section 10: 358, **442**, 598
    Section 11: 219, 358

EDITIONS: XXI, 19, 1697a (lacking Sections 10 and 11)

    Section 2: 1691b
    Section 3: 1691b, 1691g
    Section 4: 1691b, 1691g, 1701c, 1703g
    Section 7: 1701–2
    Section 10: ?1693c, 1700ee
    Section 11: 1702d, 1706e, 1707g, 1709h, 1711b, 1712a, 1720s, 1721a, 1744, 1745d, ?1755a, ?1790

COMMENTARY: Congreve's comedy, which he wrote in his twenty-first year, was produced at Drury Lane in about January 1692/3 and was published that same year. The prologue was written by Anthony Cary, according to Montague Summers (see his edition of *The Complete Works of Thomas Otway*, I, xxiii). Motteux, in *Gentleman's Journal* for February 1692/3, reported that the play was very successful and had been printed three times. The third edition was in fact advertised in the *London Gazette* for March 23rd–27th, 1693. Other performances no doubt followed, as in the Lord Chamberlain's accounts for the following year appears the notice:

    'Order to pay Mrs. Barry £25 for "Ye Old Bachelor." April 16, 1694' (L.C. 5/151, p. 30)

The fourth piece (Hornpipe) exists also in a transcription for harpsichord (see No. **T685**). In Royal College of Music, London, MS 1144, this music appears under the heading 'Bussy d'Ambois', apparently indicating that it was used for D'Urfey's *Bussy d'Ambois* at one time or another. The text alone of Section 10 appears in British Museum MS Add. 30303, f.9v, and the text for Section 11 is given in British Museum MS Add. 19202, f.167v, under the subtitle: 'On a cheese.'

The Old Mode and the New, or the Country Miss with Her Furbelo (See M574/6)

608. The Richmond Heiress, or A Woman Once in the Right

(XXI, 53) 1693; Thomas D'Urfey, *Comedy*

Solo: *sb*   *Bc*

[ACT II]

(1a) Behold the man that with gigantic might
    ('*A Dialogue between a Mad Man and Mad Woman*'): *sb*

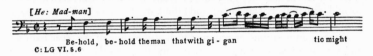

Be-hold, be-hold the man that with gi - gan   tic might
C: LG VI. 5. 6

(1b) Come on, ye fighting fools: *b*

(1c) Who's he that talks: *s*

Who's he that talks of   war, when   charm - ing,

(1d) When I appear: *s*

When I ap - pear the mar - tial

(1e) Ha! ha! now we mount: *b*

(1f) Drive 'em o'er: *b*

Drive 'em o'er__ the

(1g) By this disjointed: *s*

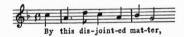

By this dis-joint-ed mat-ter,

(1h) Then mad, very mad: *sb*

Then mad, ve-ry mad let us be

(1i) My face has heav'n enchanted: *s*

(1j)=1h

(1k) I found Apollo singing: *s*

(1l)=1h

(1m) 'Tis true, my dear Alcides: *s*

(1n)=1h

(2) Bring the bowl and cool Nantz: 3 *voices* (See No. **243**)

(3) How vile are the sordid intrigues: *s* (See No. **602/2**)

MSS: 45, 219, 313 (inc, Trans), **442**, 460, 724, 862, 869, 870

EDITIONS: XXI, 53, 1698d, 1700f, 1705b, 1706a, 1706b, 1710d, 1719a (mnp), 1719b (mnp), 1719c (mnp), 1721a, 1725c, 1745c, ?1755a, ?1790

COMMENTARY: D'Urfey's sentimental comedy was first produced at Drury Lane, probably in February, 1692/3, and published that same year. According to Gildon (see *An Exact Account &c.*, pp. 51–2), it was well received. His statement is backed up by one written by D'Urfey himself which appeared in the second edition of the play (printed by D. Brown in 1718): ' The Entertainment of Songs and Dances in it, as they gave more Diversion than is usually seen in Comedies, so they were perform'd with universal applause; and I think my Enemies have cause to say, with greater than is ordinary; and though this had its Inconveniences by lengthening the whole piece a little beyond the Common time of action, which at this time of the Year I am sensible is a very great fault, yet the worst of Malice has granted me this, that there appeared no Defect of Genius, whatever there might be of judgement. . . .'

Of the several songs required in the play, Purcell is certainly the composer of two (' Behold the man that with gigantic might' in Act II; and ' Bring the bowl and cool Nantz' in Act IV), and possibly the composer of a third (' How vile are the sordid intrigues of the town') which was introduced from *The Marriage-Hater Match'd* (see No. **602**/Commentary). Another song in Act IV, ' Of noble race was Shinkin' has been ascribed to Purcell on insufficient grounds (see **D136**). ' Behold the man . . .' was sung by Mr. Reading and Mrs. Ayliff according to *Orpheus Britannicus*, I, 1698, 1706 &c., and as a mad dialogue by Mr. Leveridge and Mrs. Lyndsay in a later production, according to D'Urfey's *Songs Compleat* of 1719. A separate and slightly different version of the second stanza (see ii above) was copied into the ' Knight' MS at York (MS M.9.5) as follows:

My glance has heav'n en - chant - ed

No setting is known for the song in the last Act, ' All Europe is now in confusion.' The song ' Maiden fresh as a rose' printed in *The Merry Musician*, 1716, was probably composed for a later revival.

609. The Rival Sisters, or the Violence of Love

(XXI, 63) 1695; Robert Gould

Solo: *s*   2 *Vn, Va, Bc*

(1) Overture: *Str*
   (a) [Grave]   (b) [Canzona]

(1c) [Adagio]

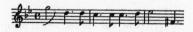

(2) Air: *Str*   (3) Jig: *Str*   (4) Air: *Str*

  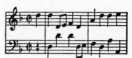

(5) Jig: *Str*   (6) Air: *Str*   (7) Minuet: *Str*

(8) Air: *Str*   (9) Air: *Str*

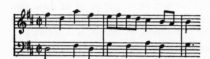 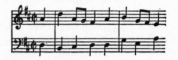

[ACT II, SCENE 1]

(10a) Celia has a thousand charms: *s*   (10b) But while the nymph: *s*

[ACT IV, SCENE 1]

(11) Take not a woman's anger   (12) How happy is she that early: *s*
ill: *t*

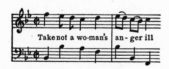 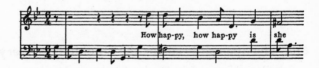

MSS: 358 (lacking Sections 10 to 12), 406 (lacking sections 10 to 12)
> Section 1: 408, 467
> Section 10: 310, 460, 598, 737, 767
> Section 11: 598, 628

EDITIONS: XXI, 63
> Section 2: 1696r, 1701c, 1703g, 1713b, 1716b, 1721b
> Section 3: 1696r, 1698g, 1701c, 1703g, 1713b, 1716b, 1721b
> Section 9: 1701c, 1703g, 1713b, 1716b, 1721b

Section 10: 1696d, 1696f, 1698d, 1704a, 1705b, 1706a, 1706b, 1710f, 1715b, 1720f, 1721a, 1725c, 1726b, 1745a, 1745c, 1746a, ?1786, 1805

Section 11: 1696f, 1696l, 1696r (Trans), 1697g (Trans), 1698g (Trans), 1699e, 1700cc, 1701c (Trans), 1703g (Trans), 1707g (mnp), 1713b (Trans), 1714c (mnp), 1716b (Trans), 1719b, 1721b (Trans), ca. 1790

Section 12: 1696f, 1698g, 1706e, 1707g, 1709h, 1720s

COMMENTARY: The instrumental music for this tragedy (produced in the autumn of 1695 and published the following year) can be traced only in two manuscript sources, in one of which (Royal College of Music, London MS 1172) the Overture alone is copied with the name 'Ridgley' at the end. This is probably John Ridgeley, one of the Royal Musicians after September 1694. The Overture is the same as that for *Love's goddess sure was blind* (see No. **331**/1), so Purcell's authorship of this piece is scarcely to be doubted. Furthermore Ridgeley's name occurs at the end of the gathering (ff. 1–29v inclusive) in the same hand that has copied the music onto these pages. It is possible that this was meant as a copyist's, not a composer's signature. It is true, however, that Sections 2–9 are musically much weaker than those generally attributed to Purcell. Pending the discovery of some MS with all parts complete, the question of authenticity must be left open for the time being. Whoever actually composed them, the order of these tunes in British Museum MS Add. 35043 (ff. 57–8) seems preferable to that of the Purcell Society Edition as given above. The order of the tunes, which are anonymous in this MS, is as follows:

    (1) 'First Lesson' (including Sections 6, 7 and 8 above)
    (2) Overture (Section 1abc above)
    (3) First Act [Tune] (Section 5 above)
    (4) Second Act [Tune] (Section 4 above)
    (5) Third Act [Tune] (Section 2 above)
    (6) Fourth Act [Tune] (Section 3 above)

In the 1695 production, 'Celia has a thousand charms' was sung by Jemmy Bowen, and 'Take not a woman's anger ill' by Leveridge. Blow set the dialogue in Act II. No setting has been found for the song 'Not though he fondly lies,' though the song is recorded in the Third Book of *Deliciae Musicae* for treble (see EDITION 1696f), as having been sung by Leveridge. Since he was a bass, there must have been another version, if this is true. Settings are wanting for several songs required by the text. One of these may have been replaced by Purcell's 'How happy is she,' the text for which does not appear in the printed play.

610. The Spanish Friar, or the Double Discovery

(XXI, 112) ?1694; John Dryden, 'A song on Mrs. Bracegirdle's singing "I burn ..." in the second part of "Don Quixote"'

Solo: *s*   *Bc*

[ACT V, SCENE 1]

(1a) Whilst I with grief did on you look: *s*   (1b) Marcella, then your lover prize: *s*

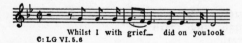

Whilst I with grief— did on you look
C: LG VI. 5.6

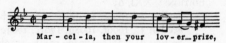

Mar - cel - la, then your lov - er— prize,

MSS: 358, **442**

EDITIONS: XXI, 112,   1695a, 1696p, 1696q, 1698d, 1706a, 1706b, 1721a, 1745c

COMMENTARY: One of Dryden's most successful comedies, *The Spanish Friar*, was produced at
Dorset Garden in March, 1679/80, and was published in 1681. There were revivals in 1686,
1690, 1695 and in later years. Purcell's music was probably written for one of the revivals after
1688, for the strongly Protestant spirit of the play would not have gone down well in official
circles before that date. (Charles II allowed the play, but James II suppressed it. See P.R.O.
Lord Chamberlain's Accounts 5/147, p. 239, dated December 8th, 1686.) It is said to have been
the first drama which Queen Mary saw after her accession. (According to Malone, she found
some parts of it embarrassing.)

Although other music is required for the play, Purcell's only contribution seems to have been
for the song in Act V, ' Whilst I with grief did on you look ', for which there is also a setting by
Godfrey Finger, in which the verse is attributed to D'Urfey.

611. The Virtuous Wife, or Good Luck at Last

(XXI, 148) 1694; Thomas D'Urfey, *Comedy*

2 *Vn, Va, Bc*

(1) Overture: *Str*
 (a) [Grave]

(b) [Canzona]

(2) Song tune: *Str*

(3) Slow Air: *Str*

(4) Air: *Str*

(5) Preludio: *Str*

(6) Hornpipe: *Str*

(7) Minuet: *Str*

(8) Minuet (Trumpet minuet): *Str*

(9) [?' 1st Act Tune ']: *Str*

MSS: 22 (lacking Sections 1, 4, 9), 50 (lacking Sections 1, 4, 9), 621

    Section 1a: 407, 408, 467, 593, 612
    Section 1b: 467 (Trans), 593
    Section 2: 408, 593
    Section 3: 59, 593, 629
    Section 4: 59, 593, 741
    Section 6: 59, 593
    Section 7: 59, 598 (Mock)
    Section 8: 280
    Section 9: 61 (Trans), 316 (Trans), 408, 593, 774

EDITIONS: XXI, 148, 1697a (lacking Section 9)

    Section 6: ?1700, 1701d
    Section 7: 1698b (Mock), 1698c (Mock), 1700aa (Mock), 1706e (Mock), 1707g (Mock), 1708c (Mock), 1709h (Mock), 1719a (Mock), 1719b (Mock)
    Section 9: 1696r, 1698g, 1700mm, 1701c, 1703g, 1711c (in a-minor), 1713b, 1716b, 1721b

COMMENTARY: D'Urfey's comedy was acted at Dorset Garden in about September 1679, and was published in the following year. Its plot was evidently inspired by Dryden's *Marriage à la Mode*, which had been acted at Lincoln's Inn Fields seven years earlier. Purcell's overture appears also as a keyboard piece (see No. **T693**/1ab). The song-tune (Section 2) is taken from 'Ah how sweet it is to love' in *Tyrannic Love* (see No. **613**/2). D'Urfey also used the minuet as a song-tune, to the words 'New reformation sweeps through the nation', a song which appeared in his play *The Campaigners: or, The Pleasant Adventures at Brussels*, which was acted at Drury Lane about November 1698 and published in that same year. In Royal College of Music, London, MS 1172, on f.3v, Section 9 is entitled '1 Act Tune.', and in EDITIONS 1711c, it is subtitled 'St. Martin's Lane' as in British Museum Add. MS 29371. In British Museum MS 35043, ff. 38v–9, several of the tunes appear in the following order: 612/5, 6, 4, 1ab, 9, 8, 2. The authenticity of Section 9 is doubtful. It enjoyed a wide circulation in 18th-century France, often under the title 'La Furstenburg': see N. Dufourcq in *Recherches 1960* (Paris: A. & J. Picard, 1960), pp. 209–13.

612. The Wives' Excuse, or Cuckolds Make Themselves

(XXI, 162) 1691; Thomas Southerne, *Comedy*

Solo: s   Bc

[ACT I, SCENE 2]

(1) Ingrateful Love! thus ev'ry hour to punish me: s

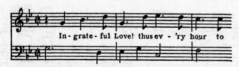

[ACT IV, SCENE 1]

(2) Say, cruel Amoret, how long in
    billet-doux?: t

(3) Corinna, I excuse thy face: s

[ACT IV, SCENE 3]

(4) Hang this whining way of wooing: *s*

Hang this | whin-ing way | of woo-ing

EDITIONS: XXI, 162

    Section 1: 1692c, ?1693c
    Section 2: ?1693c, 1706e, 1707g, 1709h, 1720s
    Section 3: 1692c, ?1693c, 1706e, 1707g, 1709h, 1720s
    Section 4: 1691b (Trans), 1692c, 1706e, 1707g, 1709h, 1720s

COMMENTARY: Southerne's comedy was acted at Drury Lane in December 1691, and although a failure, was published during the course of the following year. Music is required in several places in the play besides the four provided for by Purcell. In Act I, Scene 2, is shown a music meeting at the end of which an Italian song is sung (no text for this is given). Then follows Purcell's 'Ingrateful Love!', which is the setting of a text by Major-General Sackville. The text for Purcell's song in Act IV, Scene 1, 'Say, cruel Amoret' was written by 'a man of quality,' otherwise anonymous. It was sung by Mountfort. 'Corinna, I excuse thy face,' the text by Tho. Cheeke, Esq., was sung in this same scene, while 'Hang this whining way of wooing' was sung by Mrs. Butler in the third scene of the same act.

613. Tyrannic Love, or the Royal Martyr

(XXI, 135) 1695; John Dryden, *Tragedy*

Solo: *sb*   Bc

[ACT IV]

(1a) Hark my Damilcar: *b*   (1b) Let us go: *sb*

[Nakar]

Hark my Da-mil-car! hark! we're called

Let us go, let us go, let us go,

(1c) Merry we go: *sb*   (1d) But now the sun's down: *b*

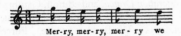

Mer-ry, mer-ry, mer-ry we

But now the sun's down

(1e) For you need not to fear 'em: *s[b]*   (1f) So ready and quick: *sb*

For you need not to fear em

So rea-dy, so rea-dy

291

(2) Ah! how sweet it is to love: s

MSS: Section 1: 45, 219, 310 (second part only with different text), 460, 863 (Soprano only)
Section 2: 310, **442**, 628

Editions: XXI, 135

Section 1: 1695a, 1698d, 1706a, 1706b, 1721a, 1730b, 1745c, ?1755a, ?1765, ?1790, 1805, 1809
Section 2: 1695a, 1696c, 1698d, 1704a, 1706a, 1706b, 1710b, 1721a, 1725c, 1726b, 1745c, 1805

Commentary: The song ' Ah ! how sweet it is to love ' is based on the ' song tune ' in **The Virtuous Wife** (see No. **611**/2). According to Burney (Mercer Edition, II, 394), there is in the music for *Tyrannic Love* ' a passage on which the late Mr. Bach has constructed a favourite movement in one of his *Quartetti Concertanti*.' He was probably referring to J. C. Bach, but the actual composition he had in mind has so far eluded efforts to find it.

Unidentified play

When Night her purple veil had softly spread (See D201)

GENERAL LITERATURE

D. Arundell, *Henry Purcell*, London: O.U.P., 1927; J. Bicknell, *Interdependence of Word and Tone in the Dramatic Works of Henry Purcell*, unpublished doctoral dissertation, Stanford, 1960; C. Burney, *A General History of Music*, London: Foulis & Co. Ltd., 1935, II, p. 388; E. J. Dent, ' Purcell on the Stage ', *Athenaeum*, 9th January, 1920; J. Downes, *Roscius Anglicanus* (ed. M. Summers), London: Fortune Press; n.d., A. Gray, ' Purcell's Dramatic Music ', *P.M.A.*, 43rd Session, 1916–17, pp. 51–62; J. Hawkins, *A General History of ... Music*, London: Novello, 1853; A. K. Holland, *Henry Purcell*, London: Penguin Books, 1948; R. Lamson, ' Henry Purcell's Dramatic Songs and the English Broadside Ballad ', *Publ. of the Mod. Lang. Assoc. of America*, LIII, No. 1, March 1938, pp. 148–161; A. M. Laurie, ' Purcell's Stage Works ', unpublished doctoral dissertation, submitted to University of Cambridge, 1962; J. Manifold, *The Music in English Drama*, London: Rockliffe, 1956; ' Theatre Music in the Sixteenth and Seventeenth Centuries,' *Music and Letters*, XXIX, No. 4, Oct., 1948, pp. 366–97; R. Moore, *Henry Purcell and the Restoration Theatre*, H.U.P., 1961; A. Nicoll, *A History of Restoration Drama*, 2nd edition, Cambridge University Press, 1928; E. Rendall, ' Purcell's Dramatic Music,' *Music and Letters*, Apr. 1920; R. Sietz, *Henry Purcell: Zeit, Leben, Werk*, Leipzig: Breitkopf & Härtel, 1955; W. Barclay Squire, ' Purcell's Dramatic Music,' *Sämmelbande I.M.G.*, Fünfter Jahrgang 1903–4; P. Stead, *Songs of the Restoration Theatre*, London: Methuen, 1948; W. Thorp, *Songs from the Restoration Theatre*, Princeton Univ. Press, 1934; E. Walker, *History of Music in England*, 3rd edition, revised Westrup, Oxford: Clarendon, 1952; J. A. Westrup, *Purcell*, London: J. M. Dent & Sons, 1947.

OPERA, SEMI-OPERAS ('AMBIGUES'), MASQUE

626. Dido and Aeneas

(III) ?1689; Nahum Tate (after Virgil)

Solo: *ssstb*   2 *Vn, Va, Bc* [*Guitars*]   Chorus: *SATB*
[Prologue]

[ACT I]

(1) Overture: *Str*
  (a) [Grave]   (b) [Canzona]

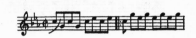

(2a) Shake the cloud from off your brow: *s*

(2b) Banish sorrow: *SATB*

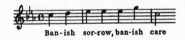

(3a) Ah! Belinda, I am prest: *s*   (3b) Ritornello: *Str*

(4) Grief increases by concealing: *ss*   (5) When monarchs unite: *SATB, Str*

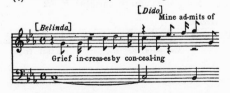

293

(6) Whence could so much virtue spring?: *ss*

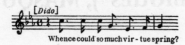

(7ab) Fear no danger: *ss*, [*SATB, Str*]

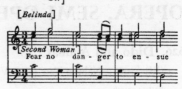

(8) See, your royal guest appears: *sst*

(9) Cupid only throws the dart: *SATB, Str*

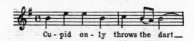

(10) If not for mine, for empire's sake: *t*

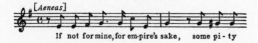

(11a) Prelude: *Str*

(11b) Pursue thy conquest, Love: *s, Str*

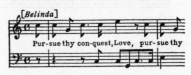

(12) To the hills and the vales: *SATB, Str*

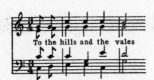

(13) Triumphing dance: *Str*

(14a) Prelude: *Str*

(14b) Wayward sisters, you that fright: *b, Str*

(15) Harm's our delight:
    SATB, Str

Harm's our de - light and

(16) The Queen of Carthage, whom we hate: *Str*

[*Sorceress*]

The Queen of Car - thage, whom we hate,

(17) Ho, ho, ho: *SATB, Str*

Ho ho

Ho ho ho ho ho ho ho ho

(18) Ruin'd ere the set of sun? *sss, Str*

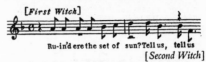

[*First Witch*]

Ru-in'd ere the set of sun? Tell us, tell us
[*Second Witch*]

(19) = 17 [in F Major]   (20) But ere we this perform: *ss, Str*

(21) In our deep vaulted
    cell: *SATB, Str*

[*First Witch*]   But ere we this per-form,

But ere we this per-form,   we'll con - jure
[*Second Witch*]

In our deep, vaul-ted cell

(22) Echo Dance of Furies: *Str*

[*Presto*]

[ACT II]

(23) Ritornello: *Str*

(24ab) Thanks to these lonesome vales:
    s, [SATB]

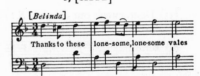

[*Belinda*]

Thanks to these | lone-some, lone-some vales

(24c) [Guitar ground a Dance: See
    Commentary]

(25a) Oft she visits this lone mountain: *s*

[*Second Woman*]

Oft she vis-its this lone moun-tain, oft she

(25b) Ritornello: *Str*

(26) Behold, upon my bended
    spear: *t*

[*Aeneas*]

Be-hold, up-on my bend-ed spear

(27) Haste, haste to town: *s, [SATB, Str]*

[*Belinda*]

Haste, haste, to town, haste, haste, haste, haste

(28a) Stay, Prince! and hear great Jove's command: *st*

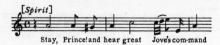

Stay, Prince! and hear great Jove's command

(28b) [The Sorceress and Witches; a chorus 'Then since our charms have sped' (see Commentary)]

(28c) [The Groves' Dance (see Commentary)]

[ACT III]

(29a) Prelude: *Str*

(29bc) Come away, fellow sailors: *s*, [SATB, Str]

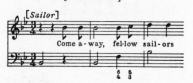

Come a-way, fel-low sail-ors

(30) The sailors' dance: *Str*

(31) See the flags and streamers: *s*

See, see, the flags and stream-ers

(32) Our next motion must be: *s*

Our next mo-tion must be

(33) Destruction's our delight: *SATB, Str*

Des-truc-tion's our de-light, de-light our great-est sor-row

(34a) The witches' dance: *Str*

(34b) *Str*

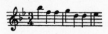

(34c) *Str*

(35a) Your counsel all is urg'd in vain: *s[st]*

Your coun-sel, all is urg'd in vain

(35b) But Death, alas!: *s*

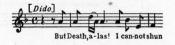

But Death, a-las! I can-not shun

(36) Great minds against themselves conspire: *SATB, Str*

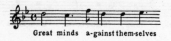

Great minds a-gainst them-selves

(37) Thy hand, Belinda: *s*

Thy hand, Be-lin-da, dark - - ness

(38a) Ground: *Bc*

(38b) When I am laid in earth: *s*

(38c) Ritornello: *Str*

(39) With drooping wings: *SATB, Str*

(40) Epilogue: All that we know the angels do above

MSS: 217 (inc), 339 (inc), 766 (inc)
    Section 3a: 168, 219, 460
    Section 7ab: 59, 215
    Section 29a: 59

EDITIONS: III, [For other editions, see explanatory notes, p. xx] ?1689 (mnp), 1700kk (mnp), 1841a,
    1814b, *ca.* 1843
    Section 3a: 1698d, 1706a, 1706b, 1721a
    Section 7ab: 1700p, 1700ff, 1700kk, 1788 (Mock), *ca.* 1790, 1800c, 1805
    Section 29bc: 1700ll

COMMENTARY: *Dido and Aeneas* was first performed at Josiah Priest's School for Young Ladies in
Chelsea, some time in 1689, according to W. Barclay Squire, who upset the traditional dating
of this opera in 1678, Purcell's nineteenth year. Eric Walter White (in his article ' Early
Theatrical Performances of Purcell's Operas,' *The Theatre Notebook*, Vol. XIII, No. 2) infers that
the performance of the opera could not have been before the 1688–9 Revolution, nor after
Nov. 1689, when D'Urfey's *New Poems* appeared with an Epilogue to *Dido* containing the
following lines:

> *Rome* may allow strange Tricks to please her Sons,
> But we are Protestants and *English* Nuns.

The earliest known source of Tate's libretto is the unique printed copy now in the Royal College
of Music Library. It is rather awkwardly bound in with a book of smaller librettos of the late
18th century, and is printed on sheets too long for the binding (being approximately 7" by
12½" in size). There is no evidence upon which to base the date of the edition except the paper,
which appears to be of English manufacture and not of the highest quality, and the watermark,
which, although it does not appear either in Heawood or Bricquet, is something like those of
the late 17th century which appear as nos. 314–17 in Heawood's book.

    The first professional performance on record appears to have taken place in 1700, when the
opera was incorporated as a series of musical entertainments in Thomas Betterton's production
of Shakespeare's *Measure for Measure* (as adapted by Charles Gildon) at Lincoln's Inn Theatre.
Gildon's version, complete with interpolated sections from *The Loves of Dido and Aeneas* (as it
was here entitled) with two short episodes added to the prologue and to Act II, and with the
17 dances of the original libretto reduced to ten. Four years later it was played as a separate
masque, ' The Masque of Dido and Aeneas', at Lincoln's Inn Theatre on January 29th and
April 8th, 1704.

L   .

No score seems to have been printed until 1841, when the Musical Antiquarian Society published MacFarren's edition, probably based on MS scores of the concert version which became popular during the course of the 18th century. (See, for instance, Br. Mus. Add. MS 31450, f.56: 'A masque . . . aetatis 19' transcribed by E. W. Smith about 1784); this was probably the source from which MS Add. 15979 was copied about 1788–96. A later copy in the hand of Edward Taylor, from about 1833, is the same in all details.

No setting of the prologue is known, and, apparently, Purcell composed neither this text, nor Aeneas's recitative, nor the ensemble which follows, nor the solo and chorus for witches: 'Then since our charms have sped'. Also missing are: 'The Country Maids' dance' at the end of the prologue, 'A Dance Gittars Chacony' in Act I, a 'Gittar ground A Dance' and 'The Groves' Dance in Act II, and a dance in which 'Jack of the Lanthorn' leads the Spaniards out of their way in Act III. Some modern editors (notably Thurston Dart and Margaret Laurie, and Benjamin Britten) have filled these gaps with other music by Purcell. Nor did Purcell set the Epilogue for D'Urfey's *New Poems* of 1689. The ground for Section 25 is very similar to that in No. 337/10.

The ground for Dido's lament was used also by Cavalli (*Didone*), by Lulli (scene of mourning in *Alceste*), and by J. S. Bach (in the 'Crucifixus' of the *B minor Mass*).

LITERATURE: D. Arundell, *The Critic at the Opera*, London: Benn, 1957, p. 147; H. C. Colles, *Voice and Verse*, London: O.U.P., 1928, p. 82; W. Cummings, 'Dido and Aeneas,' *Musical Times*, June 1910; H. Davey, *History of English Music*, London: Curwen & Sons, 1895, p. 356; E. J. Dent, 'English Opera,' *Proceedings of the Royal Musical Association*, 52nd Session, March 1926; 'Dramatic Music: Dido and Aeneas,' *Music and Letters*, April 1920; 'Dido and Aeneas,' *Musical Times*, Nos. 51 and 59; 'Dido und Aeneas,' *Musikblätter*, March 1924; 'Purcell's Dido: Belinda and Anna,' *Notes and Queries*, IV, i, and V, viii; 'Dido and Aeneas,' *Proceedings of the Royal Musical Association*, 1925; 'Didon et Enée,' *Revue Musicale*, May 1927; 'Purcell's Dido and Aeneas,' *Deutsche Kunstschau*, I (1934); P. Epstein, 'Gegen die Verbalhornung von Purcells Dido durch Bodansky,' *Zeitschrift für Musikwissenschaft*, 91 (1924); J. Hawkins, *A General History of the Science and Practice of Music*, London: Novello, 1853; P. Landormy, 'Didon et Enée,' *Le Ménestrel*, March 1927; Dr. A. M. Laurie, 'Purcell's Stage Works,' unpublished doctoral dissertation, University of Cambridge, 1962; G. L. Mayer, 'The Vocal Works of Henry Purcell—A Discography,' *The American Record Guide*, May 1959; A. H. Prendergast, 'Masques and Early Operas,' *English Music*, ed. F. J. Crowest, London: The Walter Scott Publishing Co, 1906; H. A. Scott, 'Purcell at Chelsea,' *Daily Telegraph*, June 26, 1937; E. Siegfried, 'Dido und Aeneas von Purcell,' *Musikalische Wochenblatt*, XLI, 1910; W. Barclay Squire, 'Purcell's Dido and Aeneas,' *Musical Times*, June 1918; E. Walker, *History of Music in England*, 3rd edition, revised by Westrup, Oxford: Clarendon, 1952; E. W. White, 'New Light on "Dido and Aeneas"', *Henry Purcell, Essays on His Music*, ed. Imogen Holst, London: O.U.P., 1959; E. W. White, *Rise of the English Opera*, London: Lehmann, 1951; E. W. White 'Early Theatrical Performances,' *Theatre Notebook*, XIII, 2, p. 2.

627. The Prophetess, or the History of Dioclesian

(IX) 1690; ?Thomas Betterton or ?John Dryden, from Fletcher and Massinger (Dances arranged by Josiah Priest)

Solo: *sattbb*　　　　2 Fl, 2 Ob, T.Ob, Bn, 2 Vn, Va, Bc　　　　Chorus: *SATB*

(1a) First music: *Str*　　　　　　　　　　　　　　　　(1b)

(2a) Second music: *Str, 2 Tpt, 2 Ob, T.Ob, Bn*

(2b) Trumpet tune

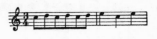

(3) Overture: *Str*
　(a) [Grave]

(b) [Canzona]

　(c) [Adagio]

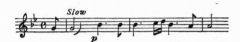

[ACT I]

(4) First Act tune: Hornpipe: *Str*

[ACT II]

(5a) Prelude: *Str*

(5b) Great Diocles the boar has
　　　killed: *b, Str*

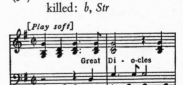

(5c) Sing Io's: *SATB, Str*

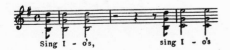

(5d) Praise the thund'ring Jove: *SATB, Str*

(6a) Prelude: 2 *Fl*

(6b) Charon the peaceful shade invites ('Second song, by a woman '): *s, 2 Fl*

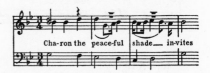

(7a) Sound all your instruments: *s*   (7b) Symphony: 2 *Tpt, Str*   (7c) [Canzona]

(8a) Let all mankind the pleasures share: *sb*

(8b) Sound all your instruments: *SATB* (voices alone)

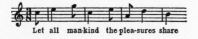

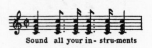

(8c) Flourish (' with all instruments in C fa ut key ')   (8d) = 8a: *SATB, 2 Tpt, 2 Ob, Str*

(9a) Prelude: *a, Ob*

(9b) Let the soldiers rejoice: *a*

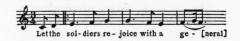

(9c) Rejoice with a general voice: *ATB, 2 Ob, Str*

(10) Ritornello: 2 *Tpt, 2 Ob* (between the verses of Section 9)

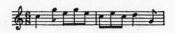

(11) To Mars let 'em raise: *atb* (tune=9b)

(12)=9b

(13a) Prelude: *2 Fl*

(13b) Since the toils and the hazards of war: *a, satb*, [*SATB, 2 Fl, 2 Ob, Str*]

Since the toils and the ha- zards of war's

(13c) With dances and songs ('Song on a ground'): *a, 2 Fl*

(13d) Ritornello: *2 Fl*

(13e) Let the priests with processions: *SATB, 2 Ob, T.Ob, Str*

[*A little faster*]

With dan-ces and songs,

Let the priests with pro-ces-sions

(14a) Prelude: *Str*

[*Soft music before the Dance*]

(14b) Dance of the Furies: *Str*

(15) Second Act tune: *Str*

[ACT III]

(16) Chaconne: *2 Fl*

(17) Chair dance: *Str*

(18a) Prelude: *2 Ob*

(18b) What shall I do?: *s, 2 Ob*

What shall I do to show

(18c)=18a

(18d) Since gods themselves (tune=18b)

[ACT IV]

(19) Third Act tune: *Str*   (20a)＝14a   (20b) Butterfly dance: *Str*

(21) Trumpet tune: *2 Tpt*   (22) Sound, Fame, thy brazen trumpet: *a, Tpt*

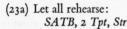

(23a) Let all rehearse:
      SATB, 2 Tpt, Str   (23b) All sing his story: *SATB, 2 Tpt, Str*

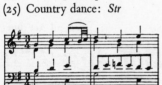

(24) Fourth Act tune＝21, arranged for strings

[ACT V]   [THE MASQUE]

(25) Country dance: *Str*   (26a) Prelude: *Str*

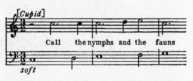

(26b) Call the nymphs and the fauns:
      s, Str [SATB]   (26c) Let the Graces and
                                  Pleasures: *s*

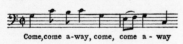

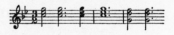

(27) Come away, no delay: *bb*   (28a) Prelude: *2 Ob, Str*

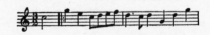

(28b) Behold, O mightiest of gods:
      SATB, 2 Ob, Str   (29) Paspe: *2 Tpt, Str*

(30) O, the sweet delights of love: *ss*

O, the sweet de-lights of love

(31) Let monarchs fight: *s*, [SATB, Str]

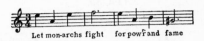

Let mon-archs fight for pow'r and fame

(32a) Prelude: 2 *Ob*

(32b) Make room for the great god of wine: *bb*, 2 *Ob*

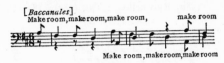

[*Baccanales*]
Make room, make room, make room,   make room

Make room, make room, make room

(32c) I'm here with my jolly crew: [SATB, 2 Ob, Str]

[*Bacchus*] I'm here   I'm here

[*play soft*]

(32d) Dance of Baccanals: 2 *Ob*, Str

(33a) Still I'm wishing: *s*, Str

[*Cupid's follower*]
Still I'm   wish-ing   still____ de-[siring]

(33b) Ritornello: *Str*

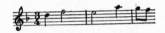

(33c) Can Drusilla give no more (tune = 33a)

(34) Canaries: *Str*

(35a) Tell me why, my charming fair: *sb*

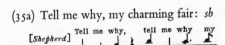

[*Shepherd*] Tell me why,   tell me why   my

(35b) O Mirtillo! you're above me: *s*

[*Shepherdess*]

O,____ Mir-til-____lo!

(35c) Could this lovely charming: *b*   (35d) O, how gladly we believe: *s*   (35e) = 35d: *sb*

[*Shepherd*]
Could this love-ly,   charm-ing____   O, how glad-ly we____

(36) Dance: *Str*

(37a) All our days and our nights: *t,*

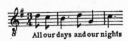

All our days and our nights

(37b) Begone, importunate reason: SATB, Str

Be-gone, be-gone, be-gone,

303

(37c) Wisdom and counsel: (37d) Dance: *Str*   (38a) Triumph, victorious Love: *atb*, [*SATB*,
SATB, Str   2 *Tpt*, 2 *Ob*, *Str*]

(38b) Ritornello: 2 *Tpt*, (38c)=38a (38d) Thou hast tam'd al-   (38e) Ritornello
      2 *Ob*, *T.Ob*, *Str*   mighty Jove: *atb*

(38f) Prelude: 2 *Tpt*, *Str*   (38g)=38a   (38h) Ritornello:
                                               2 *Tpt*, 2 *Ob*, *T.Ob*, *Str*

(39) Then all rehearse in lofty verse: *SATB*, 2 *Tpt*, 2 *Ob*, *T.Ob*, *Str*

(Appendix 1) When first I saw the bright Aurelia's eyes: *s*

(Appendix 2) Since from my dear Astrea's sight: *s*   (Appendix 3) Let us dance: *s*

   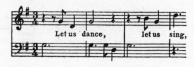

MSS: 342 (inc), 482, 766
    Section 1: 22, 50, 59
    Section 1a: 636
    Section 2b: 22, 50

Section 3: 407, 467, 612
Section 4: 22, 50, 606
Section 8: 310
Section 9a: 313, 629
Section 9b: 310 (Trans), 313 (Trans), 358, 570 (Trans), 670
Section 13b: 105
Section 15: 67, 74
Section 16: 644
Section 17: 67
Section 18: 598
Section 18b: 358 (Trans), 598, 606, 622
Section 19: 22, 50, 629
Section 21: 22, 59, 310 (Mock), 313, 323, 358, 629
Section 22: 105, 310, 323 (Trans), 598, 626a (Treble), 626b (Treble)
Section 24: 50, 59
Section 25: 22, 50, 323, 623
Section 26c: 624
Section 30: 45
Section 31: 59
Section 33: 598
Section 33a: 358
Section 34: 22, 50, 323, 629
Section 35: 219, 866
Section 38b: 626a (Treble)
Appendix 1: **442**
Appendix 2: 219, **442**

EDITIONS: IX (see the revised edition, by Margaret Laurie, published 1961), 1691f (inc), 1692a (inc)
    Sections 1 to 4: 1697a
    Section 5: 1805
    Section 6b: 1706a, 1706b, 1721a, 1745c
    Section 8: 1711b, 1712a, 1721a
    Section 9: ?1693c, 1700v, 1700w, 1700jj, 1707g, 1714c, 1719b, 1774a (Mock)
    Section 13: 1706a, 1706b, 1721a, 1745c
    Section 15: 1697a
    Section 18: 1691b, 1700jj, 1707g, 1714c, 1719b, 1774a (Mock; bis), 1805
    Section 19: 1697a
    Sections 19–27: 1805
    Section 21: ?1693c (Mock)
    Section 22: 1691c, 1696b, 1700bb, 1702d, 1704a, 1705b, 1710x, 1711b, 1712a, 1719a (mnp), 1719b (mnp), 1719c (mnp), 1721a, 1725c, 1726b, 1745c
    Section 24: 1697a
    Section 25: 1697a
    Section 30: 1702d, 1711b, 1712a, 1721a, 1744, 1745d, ?1755a, ?1790, 1805
    Section 31: ?1693c, 1700jj, 1707g, 1714c, 1719b
    Section 32b: 1805
    Section 33: 1691b, ?1693c, 1700jj, 1707g, 1714c, 1719b
    Section 34: 1697a
    Section 35: 1691d, 1698d, 1705b, 1706a, 1706b, 1721a, 1725c, 1726b, 1745c, 1805
    Section 38: 1805
    Appendix 1: ?1693c, 1693j, 1693l, 1694m, 1694n, 1698d, 1706a, 1706b, 1721a, 1745c

Appendix 2: ?1693c, 1693j, 1693l, 1694m, 1694n, 1698d, 1706a, 1706b, 1721a
Appendix 3: 1692h, 1693a, 1702d, 1711b, 1712a, 1721a

COMMENTARY: Thomas Betterton's version of *The Prophetess, or the History of Dioclesian* was performed at the Theatre Royal in Dorset Garden in June 1690, and was published that same year.
The music for this 'opera' (or play 'with Alterations and Additions after the manner of an
opera') was published separately under Purcell's name in March 1691. Langbaine had named
Dryden as the author of the version then produced, but Gildon (or whoever it was that corrected
this statement in the 1699 edition of Langbaine's work) gave the following entry under Beaumont
and Fletcher:

> ' *The Prophetess*, a Tragi-Comedy, fol. This is Reviv'd under the name of the Prophetess; or
> The History of Dioclesian, an Opera, 4to 1690. I know not what reasons Mr. Langbain has
> to attribute the revival to Mr. Dryden, when 'twas Mr. Betterton's. The true History you
> may find in *Nicephorus*, lib. 6 and 7. Eusebius lib. 8. Baronii An. 204 &c.'

Perhaps Langbaine was misled by the fact that Dryden wrote a prologue, which was suppressed
because of unflattering allusions to the 'female regency' and the campaign in Ireland. The
dedication (to Charles, Duke of Somerset) was probably also written by Dryden, although
published over Purcell's name. The whole is to be found in fair copy in Dryden's hand in
British Museum MS Stowe 755, f.34. Both Downes and Cibber report that the opera was a
success, contributed to in part by Josiah Priest's dances. The changing of the title of this opera
from 'The Prophetess' to 'Dioclesian' seems to have coincided with the appearance of G.
Finger's *The Virgin Prophetess* in 1701. Presumably, the change was made to distinguish
Purcell's work from this new opera by Finger.

The First Act Tune (see Section 4) has been adapted as a mock-song, 'O how happy's he'
(see No. **403**). The prelude to 'Great Diocles the boar has killed' may be the 'Symphony in
the Air' called for in the play-script. No other music for this situation is known. However,
three new instrumental pieces are ascribed to Purcell in Christ Church, Oxford, MS 468–9 as
follows:

The 'Trumpet tune' (Section 21) has been transcribed for keyboard (see **T697**) and appears in
MS 310 under the title, 'Honour's my crown', a popular mock-song of the times. A corollary
text for the song itself is to be found in the Bodleian Library, Oxford, in MS Rawl. Poet. 196,
f.28, signed 'M.N.' No setting has been found for the song 'With flowers let 'em strow'
called for in the play-script. The prelude to 'Since the toils and the hazards of war' (Section 13)
is, no doubt, the 'Symphony of Flutes in the air' called for in the stage direction. The 'Dead
March' mentioned at the end of Act II is also missing. The text of 'What shall I do' (Section
18b) has been ascribed both to Betterton and Dryden (*cf.* Day and Murrie, and Ault, *Seventeenth
Century Lyrics*, as well as others). The text of the song appears also (without music) in *Wit's
Cabinet* (?1700) and *The Compleat Academy of Complements* (1705 and ?1685). British Museum
MS Add. 30303, f.8v, gives the text, without music. Texts for the entry of Bacchus 'I'm here,
I'm here . . .' and for the following trio and chorus were not published with the play-script.
Nor did Purcell's setting of 'Let us dance, let us sing' appear in the original score he published.
According to the printed edition of the play, it should come between Sections 37 and 38 above.
Singers mentioned in early sources include Mrs. Ayliff, Mrs. Hudson and Mr. Freeman.

LITERATURE: J. Downes, *Roscius Anglicanus* (ed. Montague Summers), London: The Fortune Press,
[n.d.], p. 42; R. Ham, 'Dryden's Dedication for the Music of the Prophetesse, 1691', *P.M.L.A.*,
vol. L, No. 4, Dec. 1935, pp. 1065–1075; Dr. A. M. Laurie, 'Purcell's Stage Works,' unpublished
doctoral dissertation, University of Cambridge, 1962 (see also her preface to the new Purcell

Society Edition of Dioclesian (Vol. IX), London: Novello & Co. Ltd., 1961); R. McCutcheon, 'Dryden's Prologue to the Prophetess', *MLN*, vol. XXXIX (1924), p. 123; G. L. Mayer, 'The Vocal Works of Henry Purcell—A Discography,' *The American Record Guide*, May 1959: E. Walker, *History of Music in England*, 3rd edition, revised by Westrup, Oxford: Clarendon, 1952; E. W. White, 'Early Theatrical Performances of Purcell's Operas', *Theatre Notebook*, Vol. XIII, No. 2, 1959, p. 3.

628. King Arthur, or the British Worthy

(XXVI) 1691; John Dryden (Dances arranged by Josiah Priest)

Solo: *sssatb*   2 *Fl*, 2 *Ob*, 2 *Tpt*, 2 *Vn*, 2 *Va*, *BC*   Chorus: *SATB*

(1a) First Music: Chaconne: *Str*   (1b) [Chaconne] *Str*   (2) Second Music: *Str*
(a) Overture: [Grave]

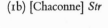

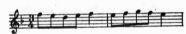

(b) [Canzona]   (3) Air

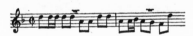

(4a) Overture: 2 *Tpt*, 2 *Vn*, 2 *Va*   (4b) Canzona: 2 *Tpt*, 2 *Vn*, 2 *Va*
[Grave]

[ACT I, SCENE 2]

(5a) Prelude: *Str*   (5b) Woden, first to thee: *tb, SATB, Str*
[?Grimbald]

Wo-den,   first to thee a milk-white steed

(6a) The white horse   (6b) To Woden thanks   (6c) the same: [at],
neigh'd: *at*   we render: *at*   *SATB*, 2 *Vn*, 2 *Va*

The white horse neigh'd a-loud, a-loud   To Wo-den thanks we rend-er,.   To Wo-den thanks we ren-der

(7a) The lot is cast: *s*, [*SATB, Str*]

The lot is cast and Tan - fan pleas'd

(7b) Brave souls: *SATB, Str*

Brave souls to be re-nown'd in sto - ry

(8) Die and reap: *SATB, Str*

[*Very Slow*]   Die—

Die — and reap

(9a) I call you all to Woden's hall: *a*

I call, I call, I call you all

(9b) To Woden's hall: *SATB, Str*

To Wo-den's hall, all,   all, to

(10a) Symphony: 2 *Tpt*, 2 *Ob, Str*

(10bc) Come if you dare: *t*, [*SATB, Str*]

Come if you dare, our trum-pets   sound

(10de) Now they charge on amain: *t*, [*SATB*]

Now they charge on   a - main

(10f) Ritornello: 2 *Tpt*, 2 *Ob*

(10g) The fainting Saxons: *t*, [*SATB, Str*]

The faint - ing   Sax - ons quit

(10h) Now the victory's won: *t*, [*SATB, Str*]

Now the vic - to-ry's   won

(11) First Act tune [Air]: *Str*

[ACT II]

(12a) Prelude: 2 *Ob, Str*

(12bc) Hither this way: *s*, [*SATB*, 2 *Ob, Str*]

[*Philidell*]

Hith-er, this way,   hith-er, this way

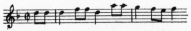

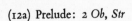

308

(13a) Let not a moon-born elf: *b*

(13b) Ritornello: *2 Vn*

(13c) = 12c

(14abc) Come follow me: *ssatb*,
  [*SSATB, Str*]

(14d) Ritornello: *Str*

(14ef) We brethren of air: *ssa*, [*SATB, Str*]

(15a) Dance: *Str*

(15b) How blest are shepherds: *t*

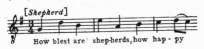

(15c) the same: *SATB, Str*   (15d) = 15b

(16a) Symphony: *2 Fl, 2 Ob*

(16b) Shepherd, leave decoying: *ss, 2 Fl,*
  2 Ob

(17a) Come, shepherds, lead up a
  lively measure: *SATB, Str*

(17b) Hornpipe: *Str*

(18) Second Act tune: *Str*

[ACT III, SCENE 2]

(19a) Prelude to 'Frost scene': *Str*

(19b) What ho! thou genius of this
  isle: *s*

309

(20a) Prelude while the Cold
Genius rises: *Str*

(20b) What pow'r art thou: *b, Str*

What pow'r art thou, who from be-[low]

(21) Thou doting fool,
forbear: *s*

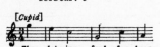

[Cupid]
Thou dot-ing fool, for-bear

(22) Great Love, I know thee
now: *b, 2 Vn*

[Cold Genius]
Great Love, I know thee now

(23) No part of my dominion:
s

[Cupid]
No part of my do-min-ion shall be waste

(24a) Prelude: *Str*   (24b) See, we assemble: *SATB* (24c) Dance: *Str*

[Cold People]
See, see, see, see, see we as-sem-ble

(25a) 'Tis I that have
warmed ye: *s*

[Cupid]
'Tis I, 'tis I, 'tis I, that have

(25b) Ritornello:
Str

(25c) 'Tis Love that has
warmed us: *SATB, Str*

[Cold People]
'Tis Love, 'tis Love

(26a) Prelude: *2 Vn*

(26b) Sound a parley: *sb, 2 Vn*

[Cupid]
Sound a par-ley, ye fair, and sur-
Cold Genius Sound, sound, sound, sound a

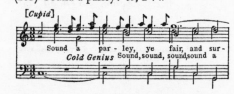

(27a)=25a   (27b)=25b   (27c)=25c   (27d)=25b

(28) Third Act tune: *Str*

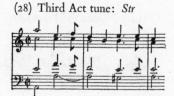

[ACT IV, SCENE 2]

(29) Two daughters of this aged stream: *ss*

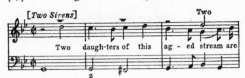

(30a) Passacaglia: *2 Ob, Str*

(30bc) How happy the lover: *a,*
[*SATB, Str*]

(30d) Ritornello: *2 Ob, Str*

(30ef) For love ev'ry creature is
form'd: *sb,* [*SATB, Str*]

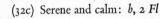

(30g) In vain are our graces: *sss*   (30h) Then use the sweet blessing: *atb*

(30i) No, no joys are above: *sss, SATB*

(31) Fourth Act tune (Trumpet tune): *Str*

[ACT V, SCENE 2]

(32a) Prelude: *Str*

(32b) Ye blust'ring brethren: *b, Str*   (32c) Serene and calm: *b, 2 Fl*

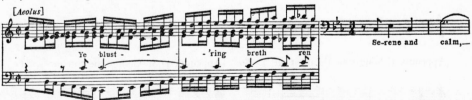

(33) Symphony: ?Tpt, ?2 Vn (?Ob ?Vn)

(34ab) Round thy coasts, fair nymph: sb, [SATB, Str]

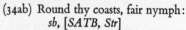
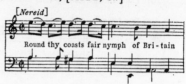

(35a) You say 'tis Love: sb

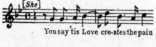

(35b) 'Tis not my passion: b

(35c) Love has a thousand:

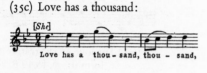

(35d) But one soft moment:

(35e) Let us love:

(36) For folded flocks: sb

(37ab) Your hay it is mow'd: t, [SATB]

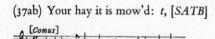

(38) Fairest isle: s

(39a) St. George, the patron of our isle: s

(39b) Our natives not alone appear: SATB, 2 Tpt, 2 Ob, Str

(40) Fifth act tune [Trumpet tune]: Str

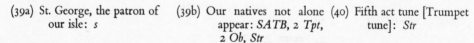

(Appendix 1) Song tune ('Come if you dare'): Str

(Appendix 2) Song tune ('Round thy coasts'): Str

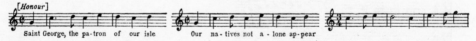
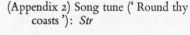
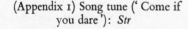

(Appendix 3) Song tune ('Fairest isle'): Str

(Appendix 4) St. George the patron: s, 2 Tr

MSS: 44 (inc), 215, 297 (inc), 336 (inc), 375, 384, 465, 677, 685 (inc), 736 (inc), 780 (inc)

Section 1: 22, 50
Section 2: 22, 50, 58, 612, 741
Section 2a: 392, 407
Section 3: 22, 50, 741
Section 4: 212
Section 4a: 741
Section 5b, 212, 741
Section 6: 212, 741
Section 7: 212, 741
Section 8: 22, 212, 741
Section 9a: 212, 741
Section 10: 212, 741
Section 10a: 323
Section 10bc: 45, 60, 406
Section 11: 22, 50, 59, 629
Section 12: 39, 351, 455
Section 15: 45
Section 15a: 22, 323, 406
Section 15b: 50
Section 16b: 633 (inc)
Section 17a: 623
Section 17b: 50, 406
Section 18: 22, 50, 406, 408
Section 19: 39
Section 20: 39
Section 21: 39
Section 22: 39
Section 23: 39
Section 24: 39
Section 25: 39
Section 26: 39, 45, 219, 460, 623, 863 (Soprano only)
Section 27: 39, 323 (Mock-Trans)
Section 28: 50
Section 29: 45, 219
Section 30bc: 347
Section 30ef: 347
Section 31: 22, 50, 323
Section 34: 406
Section 35: 45, 219, 349, 581, 866
Section 36: 45, 219, 342, 460, 543, 670
Section 37: 310 (Trans), 323 (in G)
Section 38: 45, 50, 219, 310, 366 (in G), 406, 635 (Treble only)
Section 40: 22, 50, 323
Appendix 1: 22, 50, 629
Appendix 2: 50
Appendix 3: 50, 280, 629
Appendix 4: 685

EDITIONS: XXVI, 1692a (inc), 1736b (mnp), 1770b (mnp), 1770d (inc), ?1773 (inc), 1781 (mnp), ?1790b, 1843,

Sections 1 to 3: 1697a

Section 6c: 1711b, 1712a, 1721a
Section 9a: 1706a, 1706b, 1710r, 1721a
Section 10: 1719b, 1805, 1809
Section 10a: 1697a
Section 10bc: 1691b, ?1693c, 1699e, 1707g, 1710g, 1714c
Section 11: 1697a
Section 12bc: 1706a, 1706b, 1721a, 1805, 1809
Section 13: 1805, 1809
Section 14: 1720u
Section 15a: 1691b, 1697a
Section 15bc: 1699e, 1707g, 1714c, 1719b
Section 16b: 1706a, 1706b, 1721a, ca. 1790, 1805
Section 17b: 1697a
Section 18: 1697a, ?1700, 1701d
Section 19: 1805
Section 19b: 1721a
Sections 19 to 25: 1809
Section 20b: 1721a, 1805
Section 21: 1691b (Trans), 1706a, 1706b, 1721a, 1805
Section 22: 1706a, 1706b, 1721a, 1805
Section 23: 1805
Section 24: 1805
Section 25: 1805
Section 26: 1693l, 1694m, 1694n, 1698d, 1702e, 1705b, 1706a, 1706b, 1710w, 1721a, 1725c, 1726b, 1744, 1745c, 1745d, ?1750, ?1755a, ?1765, ?1790, 1805
Section 27: 1691b (Trans), 1730h, 1731g
Section 28: 1697a
Section 29: 1695l, 1698d, 1706a, 1706b, 1710bb, 1721a, 1745c, 1745d, ?1755a, ?1765, 1779b, ?1790, 1805, 1809
Section 30bc: 1720s (Mock, mnp)
Section 30ef: 1763, ?1765, ?1790, ca. 1790
Section 31: 1697a
Section 34: 1697a
Section 35: 1696f, 1698d, 1706a, 1706b, 1721a, 1745c, 1748a
Section 36: 1698d, 1706a, 1706b, 1710n, 1721a, 1744, 1745c, 1745d, ?1750, ?1755a, 1763, ?1790, ca. 1790, 1805
Section 37: 1691b, 1692j, 1707g, 1714c, 1719b
Section 38: 1691b, 1698d, 1700o, 1706a, 1706b, 1706e, 1707g, 1709h, 1720s, 1721a, 1726b, 1731d, 1745c, 1746b, 1770c, 1771, 1790e, ca. 1790, 1805, 1809
Section 40: 1697a
Appendix 3: 1697a

COMMENTARY: Though advertised in the *London Gazette* for June 4th–8th, 1691, *King Arthur* was first produced sometime in the course of the previous month, according to Nicoll. Towards the end of the year, the first edition was brought out again with prologue and epilogue. This re-issue may have coincided with the production (reported in The Lord Chamberlain's Accounts 5/151, p. 369) for which the royal household spent £30 for two boxes for the Queen and her Maids-of-Honour on January 7th, 1691/2. Luttrell also reported for this date: ' The Queen and the Dowager Queen went this evening to the play of Mr. Dryden's opera.' Langbaine (p. 45) described the opera as being ' writ more for the sake of the singing part and machines than for any excellence of a dramatic piece; for in it shines none of Mr. Dryden's great genius, the incidents being all extravagant, many of them childish; the enchanted wood, as well as the rest of the wonders of Osmond's Art, he entirely owes to Tasso; where Rinaldo performs what Arthur does here.' Downes reports that the opera was both successful and profitable, but Cibber maintains that it was successful only.

No music survives for the following interludes, dances and songs—if, indeed, Purcell ever supplied them:

(a) Philidel's ' Masque of Airy Forms ' in Act III, Scene 2.
(b) ' We must work ' in Act III, Scene 2.
(c) Music for the following scene also in Act III, Scene 2:

> Man: O sight the mother of desire
> Woman: 'Tis sweet the blushing morn to view
> Chorus: This joy, all joys above
> Man: And if we may discover.

(d) New music before ' Frost scene ' when Osmond appears.
(e) Dance after Third Act Tune(?) when dancers and singers depart.
(f) ' Soft music and warbling of birds ' in Act IV, Scene 2.
(g) Song ' O pass not on but stay ' in Act IV, Scene 2.
(h) March and consort of trumpets after Section 32b, in Act V, Scene 2.
(i) ' Soft tune while island rises ' in Act V, Scene 2.
(j) After Section 37, a dance varied into a round country-dance in Act V, Scene 2.

Purcell used the first Chacone (Section 1ab) also in the ode *Sound the trumpet* (see No. **335**/7ab). In melodic outline, Section 3 of this opera is very similar to No. **796**/2. The Overture (Section 4) was also used in the birthday song *Arise my muse* (see No. **320**/1ab). The Second Act Tune has been misleadingly ascribed (see No. **580**/2) in one manuscript. Section 26a of this opera is very similar to Section 4 in *Timon of Athens*.

The three instrumental pieces in the appendix are transcriptions of songs from the opera. (Appendix 1 = ' Come if you dare,' Appendix 2 = ' Round thy coasts ' and Appendix 3 = ' Fairest Isle '.) Pending the discovery of the autograph copy of the score, or some complete and authentic contemporary source, it will be impossible to say whether these are actually parts of the opera as Purcell wrote it, or only transcriptions made afterwards. The Royal College of Music, London, MS 520, has been omitted from the list in Appendix III as being too late to be of value. In MS c. 353 in the Fitzwilliam Museum, Cambridge, the tune ' Fairest Isle ' (i.e. Appendix 3) is copied twice in the key of B♭. In the first version, in which the first line of text is underlaid, the controversial eighth note of the melody is given as A♭, in the second as A. Roger North wrote in glowing terms of a performance of *King Arthur* in which Mrs. Butler, in the part of Cupid, sang ' What ho! thou Genius of this isle ' in an unforgettable manner. (See *Roger North on Musick*, ed. John Wilson, London: Novello, 1959, p. 217.)

LITERATURE: ' Bucinator,' ' Purcell's " Come if you dare ",' *The Musical Antiquary*, II, Jan. 1911; C. Burney, *A General History of Music*, London: Foulis & Co. Ltd., 1935; E. J. Dent, ' Purcell's " King Arthur ",' *The Listener*, Dec. 4th, 1935; J. Downes, *Roscius Anglicanus* (ed. Montague Summers), London: The Fortune Press, [n.d.], p. 42; J. Fuller Maitland, ' Purcell's King Arthur,' *Studies in Music* (Robin Grey, ed.) NY: Scribner's Sons, 1901, pp. 185–198; J. Herbage, ' Dryden's " King Arthur ": Composed by Purcell,' *Radio Times*, Dec. 6th, 1946; A. H. D. Prendergast, ' Masques and Early Operas,' *English Music*, ed. F. J. Crowest, London: The Walter Scott Publishing Co., 1906; J. F. Runciman, *Purcell*, London: George Bell, 1909; P. Tiggers, ' " King Arthur " van Henry Purcell,' *Mens en Melodie*, Feb. 1954; E. Walker, *History of Music in England*, 3rd ed., revised by Westrup, Oxford: Clarendon, 1952; E. W. White, ' Early Theatrical Performances of Purcell's Operas,' *Theatre Notebook*, Vol. XIII, No. 2, 1959, pp. 3–4.

629. The Fairy Queen

(XII) 1692; ?Elkanah Settle, from Shakespeare's *Midsummer-Night's Dream*

Solo: *ssaatb*   2 Fl, 2 Ob, 2 Tpt, Kdr, 2 Vn, Va, Bc   Chorus: *SATB*

(1a) First music: Prelude: *Str*   (1b) Hornpipe: *Str*

C: LAM 1

(2a) Second music: Air: *Str*   (2b) Rondeau: *Str*

Roundeaux

[ACT I]

(3) Overture: 2 *Tpt, Str*
   (a) [Grave]   (b) [Canzona]

Overture Trumpets

Violins

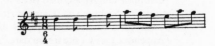

(4a) Prelude: 2 *Vn*   (4b) Come let us leave the town: *sb, 2 Vn*

Come, come, come, come,   Let us leave.
Come, come, come, come,

(5a) Prelude: *Str*   (5b) Fill up the bowl: (5cd) Trip it in a ring:
                                  ssb, [SATB, Str]   *s, [SATB, 2 Vn]*

[Drunken Poet]
Fi–, fi–, fi–, fill up the bowl

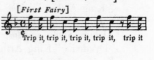
[First Fairy]
Trip it, trip it, trip it, trip it, trip it

(5e) Enough, enough: we must play: *b*   (5f) About him go: *s, [SATB, Str]*

(5g) Hold, you damned tormenting punk: *b*   (5h) I'm drunk: *b*

(5i) If you will know it: *b*

(5k) I confess: *b*

(5j) Pinch him for his crimes: *SATB, Str*

(5l) Drive 'em hence: *SATB, Str*

(6) First Act tune: Jig: *Str*

[ACT II]

(7a) Prelude: *Str*

(7b) Come all ye songsters: *a*

Come all, come all, all,all, come
C: LGC VI.5.6

(8a) Prelude: *2 Vn*

(8b) May the god of wit inspire: *atb*

May the god of wit in - - - - [spire]

(8c) Echo: *Tpt, Ob*

[Loud]

(9) Now join your warbling: *SATB, 2 Vn*

Now-join your warb - - - - - [ling]

Now join your warb - - ling

(10ab) Sing while we trip it: *s, [SATB, 2 Vn]*

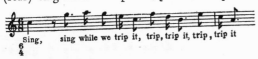

Sing,   sing while we trip it, trip, trip it, trip, trip it

(10c) = 10b: *Str* (For 'A Dance of Fairies')

(11a) Prelude: *Str*

[Violins with sourdines]

(11b) See, even Night herself
    is here: *s, Str*

[Night] See,   see,

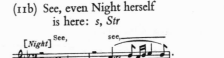

(11c) = 11a

(12) I am come to lock
    all fast: *s*

[Mystery]

2 I am come to lock all fast

(13a) Prelude:
    2 Fl

(13b) One charming night:
    a, 2 Fl

[Secrecy]

One charm-ing night gives more

(13c) = 13a

(14ab) Hush no more: *b, Str*
[*SATB*]

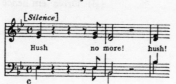

(15) Dance for the followers of
Night: *Str*

(16) Second Act tune: Air: *Str*

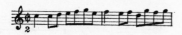

[ACT III]

(17a) Prelude: *Str*

(17bc) If love's a sweet passion: *s,*
[*SATB, Str*]

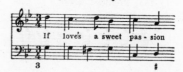

(18) Symphony (while the swans come forward): *Str*
(a) [Grave]

(b) [Canzona]

(19) Dance for the fairies: *Str*

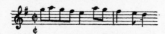

(20) Dance for the Green Men: *Str*

(21a) Ye gentle spirits of the air: *s*

(21b) Catch and repeat: *s*

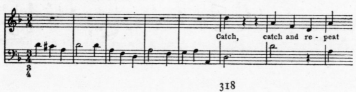

(22a) Prelude: 2 *Vn*   (22b) Now the maids and the   (22c) Nay, what do you
                                 men: *a* (Mr. Reading),   mean?: *ab*
                                 b (Mr. Pate), 'Dialogue
                                 between Corydon and
                                 Mopsa'

(23) When I have often heard: *s* (Mrs. Butler)

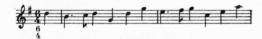

(24a) Dance for the haymakers: *Vn*   (24b) Dance for a Clown: [missing: See
                                             Commentary]

(25ab) A thousand ways we'll find: *a*, [SATB, Str]

(26) Third Act tune: Hornpipe: *Str*

[ACT IV]

(27) 'Sonata while the sun rises':
  (a) [Grave] 2 *Tpt, Kdr, Str*   (b) [Canzona]   (c) [Largo]: *Str*

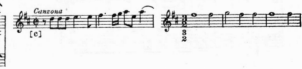

(d) [Allegro]: 2 *Tpt, Kdr, Str*   (e) [Adagio]: *Str*   (27f)=27d

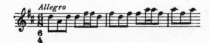
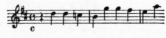

(28a) Now the night is chas'd away: *s*

(28b) All salute the rising sun: *SATB, Str*

(28c) Ritornello: *Str*

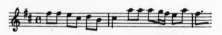

(29) Let the fifes and the clarions: *aa*

(30) Entry of Phoebus: *2 Tpt, Kdr, Str*

(31a) Prelude: *2 Vn*

(31b) When a cruel long winter: *t, 2 Vn*

(31c) 'Tis I who give life: *t*

(32a) Hail, great parent:
   SATB, 2 Tpt, 2 Ob, Kdr, Str

(32b) Light and comfort: *SATB, 2 Tpt, 2 Ob, Kdr, Str*

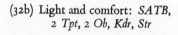

(32c) = 32a

(32d) Thou who giv'st all:
   SATB, 2 Tpt, 2 Ob, Kdr, Str

(33a) Prelude: *Str*

(33b) Thus the ever grateful spring: *s* (Mrs. Butler)

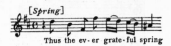

(34a) Prelude: 2 *Ob*

(34b) Here's the summer sprightly gay: *a* (Mr. Pate)

(35a) Prelude: *Str*

(35b) See my many colour'd fields: *t*

(36a) Prelude: *Str*

(36b) Next, winter comes slowly: *b, Str*

(37) = 32

(38) Fourth Act tune, Air: *Str*

[ACT V]

(39a) Prelude to Juno's song: *Str*

(39b) Thrice happy lovers (Epithalamium): *s*

[c: LGC VI.5.6]

(39c) Be to one another true: *s*

(40ab) O let me weep (' the Plaint '): s, Vn obbligato

O,   O,   let me,   O,   O,—   let me, let me weep

(41) Entry dance: Str   (42a) Symphony: (42b) [Symphony]   (42c) = 42a
                         2 Tpt, 2 Ob, Str

(43) Thus the gloomy world at first began to shine: a, Tpt, 2 Vn

[Chinese Man]

Thus, thus,   thus, thus the gloom-[y]

(44a) Prelude: Str   (44bc) Thus happy and free: s
                                          (Mrs. Ayliff) [SATB, Str]

[Simphony]

[Chinese Woman]

Thus hap-py and free, thus treat-ed are we

(45a) Ground: Bc   (45b) Yes Daphne [Xansi], in your looks I find: a

[Chinese Man]

Yes   Daph-ne,   yes   Daph-ne   in

no t-s   [¢:LGC VI.5.6]

(46a) Monkey's dance: Str   (46b) (the same) Str   (47a) Prelude: Str

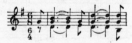  

[Prelude]

(47b) Hark how all things in one sound agree: a, Str

[First Woman]

Hark!   hark how

3: LGC VI.5.6

(48a) Prelude: *Tpt*

[¢: LGC VI.5.6]

(48bc) Hark! the ech'ing air: *s*, [*SATB*]

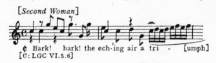

[*Second Woman*]

¢ Hark! hark! the ech'ing air a tri - [umph]
[¢: LGC VI.5.6]

(49a) Sure the dull god of marriage: *ss*

[*Second Woman*]

Sure the dull god of mar-riage does not hear
no t-s

(49b) Hymen! appear: *ss*

(49c) the same: *SATB, Str*

(49d) Our Queen of Night: *ss*

(49e) the same: *SATB*, [*Str*]

(50a) Prelude: *2 Vn*

3

(50b) See, I obey: *b, 2 Vn*

[*Hymen*] See, I o - bey, see, see,

c

(50c) Turn, then thine eyes: *ss*

[*First Woman*] [*Second Woman*]

Turn, turn, then thine eyes, Turn, turn, then thine
[$\frac{8}{12}$: LGC VI.5.6]

(50d) My torch indeed will from such
brightness shine: *2 Vn*

My torch in-deed will from such bright____
[*Hymen*]

¢

(50ef) They shall be as happy:
ssb, [*SATB, 2 Tpt, Str*]

They shall be as hap-py, hap-py

6
4

(51) Dance for the Chinese Man
and Woman: Chaconne:
Str

Chacone: Dance for Chinese Man and Woman

e
3i

(Appendix 1)= 8b: *SATB, 2 Vn, Va*

(Appendix 2)= 36a: (another version)

(Appendix 3)= 41

(Appendix 4) Entry Dance:
Str

MSS: 295 (partial text only), **373** (partial autograph), 385, 466 (inc)

    Section 1a: 22, 50, 323, 406, 407, 535, 741
    Section 1b: 22, 50, 323, 406, 535, 623
    Section 2: 22, 50, 323, 406, 535, 629
    Section 3: 22, 50, 392, 406, 407, 535, 612, 857
    Section 4a: 323
    Section 4b: 45, 308 (Paisible), 310, 358, **442**, 460, 598, 724
    Section 5cd: 215
    Section 6: 22, 50, 59, 323, 406, 408, 535
    Section 7: **442** (in B-flat)
    Section 7a: 406
    Section 8bc: 310, **442** (arranged for solo soprano in B-flat)
    Section 10ab: 406 (Trans), 535 (Trans)
    Section 10d: 22
    Section 12: 368 (Trans in g minor), 670
    Section 15: 50, 406, 407, 535
    Section 16: 22, 50, 406, 535
    Section 17: 598 (inc), 790
    Section 17a: 50, 323, 364 (Trans), 406, 535
    Section 17bc: 606 (Trans), 670
    Section 18: 22, 50, 323, 406, 535, 612, 741
    Section 18a: 407
    Section 19: 22, 50, 406, 535
    Section 20: 406
    Section 22b: 45, 59, 219, 358, **442** (in F Major), 460
    Section 23: 323 (Trans)
    Section 26: 22, 50, 323, 406, 535
    Section 27: 210 (inc)
    Sections 27 to 32: 380
    Sections 27 to 38: 396
    Section 28: **442** (slightly varied)
    Sections 28a to 32a: 210
    Section 29: 45
    Section 34a: 323
    Section 36: 39
    Section 38: 22, 50, 323, 406, 535
    Section 39b: **442**
    Section 40b: 219, 310, 460, 623, 626c (Bass)
    Section 41: 22, 50, 406
    Section 43: **442** (in B-flat)
    Section 44a: 22, 50, 323, 406, 629
    Section 45: **442** (transcribed for soprano), 535
    Section 46b: 535
    Section 47: **442**
    Section 48b: 105, 310, **442** (bass slightly varied)
    Section 50c: **442** (arranged for solo soprano; see No. 425)
    Section 50e: 406 (Trans)
    Section 51: 22, 50, 358, 406
    Appendix 4: 22, 406

EDITIONS: XII, 1692d (mnp), 16930 (mnp)

Sections 1 to 3: 1697a
Section 4b: 1694d, 1698d, 1700k, 1704a, 1706a, 1706b, 1721a, 1725c, 1726b, 1740b, 1744, 1745c, 1745d, ?1755a, 1763, ?1790
Section 6: 1693d, 1697a, 1700mm, 1733c
Section 7b: 1702d, 1711b, 1712a, 1721a
Section 8bcd: 1702d, 1711b, 1712a, 1721a, 1745d, ?1755a, ?1790, 1805
Section 10: 1693d (Trans), 1719b
Section 10a: 1692b, ?1693c
Section 10ab: 1699e, 1707g, 1714c
Section 10d: 1697a
Section 12: 1690c (Trans), 1692b, ?1693c, 1693d (Trans), 1706e, 1707g, 1709h, 1720s
Section 13: 1692b
Sections 15 to 19: 1697a
Section 17: ?1690 [MS], 1692b, ?1693c, ?1693 (Mock), 1693d (Trans), 1695e, 1699e, 1706e (Mock), 1707g, 1707g (Mock), 1709h (Mock), 1714c, 1719b, 1720s (Mock), ca. 1760, 1774a (Mock)
Section 21a: 1702d, 1711b, 1712a, 1721
Section 22b: 1692b, ca. 1692, 1694d (Mock), 1695h, 1698d, 1704a, 1705b, 1706a, 1706b, 1721a, 1725c, 1726b, 1745c, 1748a, ?1755a, ?1790
Section 23: 1692b, ?1693c, 1693d (Trans), 1706e, 1707g, 1709h, 1720s
Section 25a: 1692b
Section 26: 1693d, 1697a
Section 29: 1702d, 1711b, 1712a, 1721a, 1805
Section 31: 1702d, 1711b, 1712a, 1721a
Section 33b: 1692b, 1702d, 1711b, 1712a, 1721a
Section 34b: 1692b, ?1693c, 1702d, 1706e, 1707g, 1709h, 1711b, 1712a, 1720s, 1721a
Section 35: 1702d, 1711b, 1712a, 1721a
Section 36a: 1702d, 1711b, 1712a, 1721
Section 38: 1697a
Section 39b: 1702d, 1711b, 1712a, 1721a
Section 40b: 1698d, 1706a, 1706b, 1721a
Section 41: 1697a
Section 43: 1702d, 1711b, 1712a, 1721a
Section 44a: 1697a
Section 44b: 1692b, ?1693c, 1693d
Section 45b: 1702d, 1711b, 1712a, 1721a
Section 47b: 1702d, 1711b, 1712a, 1721a
Section 48b: 1702d, 1711b, 1712a, 1721a
Section 50c: 1693a, 1706a, 1706b
Section 50ef: 1711b, 1712a, 1721a
Section 51: 1697a
Appendix 4: 1697a

COMMENTARY: Nicoll gives April 1692 as the earliest date for the first performance of *The Fairy Queen*. Luttrell in his entry for Thursday, April 28, 1692, states: ' On Monday [*i.e.* May 2nd] will be acted a new opera, called the Fairy Queen: exceeds former playes: the clothes, scenes, and musick cost 3,000 l.' It may have been produced even earlier, for Motteux stated in *Gentleman's Journal* for January, 1691/2 ' ... we shall have speedily a New Opera, wherein something very surprising is promised us; Mr. *Purcel* who joyns to the Delicacy and Beauty of the *Italian* way, the Graces and Gayety of the *French*, composes the Music, as he hath done for the *Prophetess*, and the last Opera called *King Arthur*, which hath been plaid several times the last Month.' The first performance was hastened by the suppression of Dryden's *Cleomenes*, according to Motteux's statement in the same journal for April (p. 23) and May (p. 26) 1692 (see No. **576**/Commentary). The text was printed in 1692 (see EDITION 1692d) and re-issued in the following year with a few alterations and additional songs (see EDITION 1693n). The revised version incorporated a good many changes in Act I, added the air, ' Ye gentle spirits' (Section 21) to Act III, and ' The Plaint' (' O, let me weep ', Section 40) to Act V. The anonymous adaptor of Shakespeare's *A Midsummer Night's Dream* (who may have been Elkanah Settle, according to Nicoll, *Restoration Drama*, pp. 12, 150, 380) evidently borrowed the idea for the sequence beginning ' Pinch him black and blue ' from John Lyly's ' A Fairy Song ' in *Endimion*, 1592.

In Carr and Playford's *Some Select Songs . . . in the Fairy Queen* (see EDITION 1692b), Mrs. Ayliff is named as the singer of ' Sing whilst we trip it ' and ' Thus happy and free '; Mrs. Dyer for ' I am come to lock all fast ' and ' If love's a sweet passion '; Mr. Freeman for ' One charming night ' and ' A thousand ways we'll find '; Mrs. Butler for ' When I have heard ' and ' Thus the ever grateful spring '; and Mr. Pate for ' Here's the summer.' Mr. Pate and Mr. Reading, dressed as women, joined to sing ' Now the maids and the men,' as we know from a single edition of this song engraved by Thomas Cross in 1695 (see EDITION 1695h). A revival of the Fourth(?) Act in 1703 at Drury Lane (as advertised in the *Daily Courant* for January 29th) was performed with Leveridge, Laroon, Hughes, Mrs. Lyndsay and Mrs. Campion acting the chief parts.

The partial autograph score (see Royal Academy of Music, London, MS [1]) was lost for more than 200 years; (a reward was offered for its recovery in the *London Gazette* for October 9th–13th, 1701). However, music for the following situations required by the libretto is still missing, if Purcell did indeed ever supply any:

Dance: The Clowns' Dance   Act III
          (Note that space for this was left in the score; clefs, time-signatures and key-signatures being written in.)
Song: The woosel-cock so black of hue   Act III
Dance: Entry of the Four Seasons   Act IV
Dance: Dance of the Four Seasons   Act IV
Sonata: Composition in Imitation of a Hunt Act V
Symphony: Entry of Oberon, Titania, Robin
             and Fairies   Act V

The hornpipe in the ' First music ' provides the tune for ' There's not a swain ' (see No. **587**). A variant of the 1st Act tune is ascribed to J. Paisible in Br. Mus. Add. MS 17853, f. 7. The Air in the ' Second music ' also occurs as a dance in Act III of *The Indian Queen* (see No. **630**/12). The Overture (Section 3ab) is known also in a version for harpsichord (see No. **T692**). The dance called for at the end of Act I is missing, but these notes appear (rather dimly) where it should be in the partial autograph score:

' May the god of wit ' is set for four-part chorus in Royal Music MS 24, e. 12 (1), f.3v.; ' Now the maids and the men ' is given in the key of F in the Gresham autograph (see Gresham College Library MS VI.5.6). ' Next winter comes slowly ' appears in two versions. The second being listed here as ' Appendix 2 '. In the partial autograph score, the sequence of the pieces in Act V is as follows: Sections 39ab, 41, 46ab (not c), 43, 44abc, 45, 47ab, 18abc and 50abcdef. The Chaconne (Section 51) should probably be inserted between Sections 44 and 45. The ' Entry Dance' (Section 41) appears in *Ayres for Theatre* in a different version (for which no incipit is shown) listed here as ' Appendix 3 '. Sections 42b and 30 are similar in melodic contour. The song ' Yes, *Xansi* ' (Section 45b) begins: ' Yes Daphne' in the Gresham autograph as in the Royal Academy of Music, partial autograph. Within this same score, the following sections are in Purcell's hand: Sections 2a, 6, 26, 35 (partly), 38, 49a (partly), 49bcde and (?)51. The rest of the MS is in the hand of a copyist who appears to have worked under Purcell's supervision.

LITERATURE: J. Downes, *Roscius Anglicanus* (ed. Montague Summers), London: The Fortune Press, [n.d.], p. 42; G. L. Mayer, 'The Vocal Works of Henry Purcell—A Discography,' *The American Record Guide*, May, 1959; J. F. Runciman, *Purcell*, London: George Bell, 1909; W. Barclay Squire, 'Purcell's "Fairy Queen",' *Musical Times*, Jan. 1920; H. Stieber, *Henry Purcells Opernmusik 'The Fairy Queen' als festliche Begleitmusik zu Shakespeares 'Sommernachtstraum,'* Leipzig: Bühnenblatter, 1936/7; E. Walker, *History of Music in England*, 3rd ed., revised by Westrup, Oxford: Clarendon, 1952; E. W. White, 'Early Theatrical Performances of Purcell's Operas,' *Theatre Notebook*, Vol. XIII, No. 2, 1959, pp. 4–5.

630. The Indian Queen

(XIX, 1) ?1695; John Dryden and Sir Robert Howard

Solo: *ssatb*   2 Fl, 2 Ob, 2 Tpt, Kdr, 2 Vn, Va, Bc   Chorus: *SATB*

(1a) First music: Air: *Str*   (1b) Second air: *Str*

(2a) Second music: Hornpipe: *Str*   (2b) Hornpipe: *Str*

(3) Overture: *Str*
 (a) [Grave]   (b) [Canzona]

[PROLOGUE]

(4a) Trumpet tune: *Tpt, Str*   (4b) Wake, Quivera: *a*

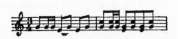   

327

(4c) Prelude: 2 *Fl*

(4d) Why should men quarrel: *s*

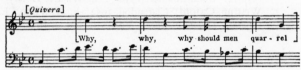

(4e) By ancient prophecies: *a* (4f) If these be they: *sa*

(4g) Their looks are such: *a* (4h) If so, your goodness may your pow'r express: *sa*

(4i)=4a (4j)=4a

[ACT II]

(5) Symphony: *Tpt, 2 Ob, Str*
  (a) [Grave] (b) [Canzona]

(c) [Adagio] (d) [Allegro]

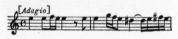

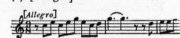

(6a) I come to sing great Zempoalla's story: *a*

(6b) We come to sing great Zempoalla's story: *SATB, Tpt, 2 Ob, Str*

(7ab) What flatt'ring noise is this: *atb, 2 Vn* (7c) Scorn'd Envy, here's nothing: *a*

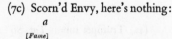

(7d) I fly from the place: *b, 2 Vn*

(7e) = part of 7ab

(7f) Begone, curst fiends of Hell: *a*

(8) First Act tune = 4a

(9a) Symphony: *Tpt, Kdr, Str* (tune = 6)

(9bc) = 6ab

(10) Dance: *Vn*

(11) Second Act tune: Trumpet
tune = 9a: *Str*

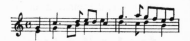

[ACT III]

(12) Dance: *?Vn*

(13a) Ye twice ten-hundred deities: *b, Str*

[*Ismeron*]

Ye twice ten hun-dred de- i-ties,   to whom

(13b) By the croaking of the toad: *b, Str*

(13c) While bubbling
springs: *b*

[*Ismeron*]

By   the croak-ing of the toad

While bub – ling springs

(14) Symphony: 2 *Ob*

(15) Seek not to know: *s, Ob*

[*God of Dreams*]

Seek not to know what must not,what

(16) Trumpet Overture: *Tpt, 2 Vn*
    (a) [Grave]

(b) [Canzona]

[*Canzona*]

M

(c) [Adagio]

(17a) Ah! how happy are we: *at*

[First Aerial Spirit]

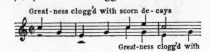

(17bc) We, the spirits of the air: *ss*, [*SATB, Str*]

We the spi-rits of the air

(17d) Greatness clogg'd with scorn: *ss*

Great-ness clogg'd with scorn de-cays

Great-ness clogg'd with

(17e) = 17c   (17f) Cease to languish: *ss*   (17g) = 17c

(17h) I attempt from Love's sickness to fly: *s* (Mrs. Cross)

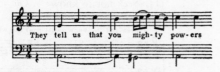

I at-tempt from Love's sick-ness to fly

(17i) = 17c   (17j) = 17d   (17k) = 17e   (17l) = 17f   (17m) = 17g

(18) Third Act tune: *Str*

[ACT IV]

(19) They tell us that you mighty powers:
      s (Mrs. Cross)

They tell us that you migh-ty pow-ers

(20) Fourth Act tune: *Str*

[ACT V]

(21a) Prelude: *Str*

(21b) While thus we bow: *SATB, Str*

While thus,   while thus   we bow

(21c) You who at the altar: *b, SATB*

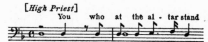

(21d) Prelude: *Str*

(21e) All dismal sounds: *SATB, Str*

(22) Air: *Str*

MSS: 44 (inc), 213, 216 (inc), 313 (inc, Trans), 336 (inc), 338 (inc), 341 (inc), 342, 382, 464 (inc), 677 (inc), 736 (inc), 768 (inc)

Section 1: 22, 50 (inc), 59, 323, 358, 593, 596 (Trans), 774

Section 1b: 406

Section 2: 22, 59, 323, 358, 406, 593, 774

Section 3: 22, 59, 323, 358, 406, 407, 593, 612, 857

Section 3b: 741

Section 4a: 22, 58, 59, 211, 358, 406, 629

Section 4b: 211

Section 4d: 142

Section 4e: 615

Section 4f: 615

Section 4g: 105, 615, 628

Section 4h: 615

Section 5: 412

Section 6: 412

Section 6a: 59, 105, 211, 628

Section 6b: 615

Section 7: 211 (bcdf), 412, 615

Section 7cf: 105

Section 9a: 50, 593

Section 11: 22, 59, 211, 323, 358, 368, 406

Section 12: 22, 60

Section 13: 39, 45, 142, 219, 756, 870

Section 14: 626c (Bass)

Section 15: 45, 142, 219, 310, 460, 623, 626c (Bass)

Section 16: 358, 406

Section 17a: 105, 280, 358

Section 17bc: 50, 211, 406, 615, 629

Section 17h: 211, 598, 624, 628, 866

Section 18: 22, 50, 358, 406, 629

Section 19: 622, 628

Section 20: 211, 358, 406

Section 21: 412

Section 21a: 360, 374

Section 21b: 209, 211, 359, 360, 374, 615

Section 21c: 211, 359, 360, 374, 615

Section 21d: 211, 360, 374
Section 21e: 211, 359, 360, 374
Section 22: 22, 59, 323, 358, 406, 593, 615, 629

EDITIONS: XIX, 1, ?1790b

Sections 1 to 4: 1697a
Section 1b: 1701d
Section 2b: 1701d
Section 4a: 1701d
Section 4b: 1695m, 1702d, 1711b, 1712a, 1721a
Section 4d: 1695m, 1702d, 1711b, 1712a, 1721a
Section 4g: 1695m, 1702d, 1711b, 1712a, 1721a
Section 4h: 1711b, 1712a, 1721a
Section 6: 1695m
Section 7b: 1711b, 1712a, 1721a
Section 7c: 1695m, 1702d, 1711b, 1712a, 1721a
Section 7f: 1695m
Section 11: 1697a
Section 13: 1695m (mnp), 1696g, 1698d, 1700hh, 1700ii, 1705b, 1706a, 1706b, 1710gg, 1720t, 1721a, 1725c, 1726b, 1745c, 1758a, 1805, 1809
Section 15: 1698d, 1706a, 1706b, 1721a, 1745c, 1805
Section 17a: 1695m, 1697a, 1702d, 1711b, 1712a, 1721a, 1805
Section 17bc: 1711b, 1712a, 1721a, ?1755a, ?1790, 1805
Section 17h: 1695d, 1695m, 1698d, 1704a, 1706a, 1706b, 1721a, 1805, 1809
Section 18: 1697a, 1701d
Section 19: 1695m, 1702d, 1711b, 1712a, 1721a
Section 20: 1707g (Mock), 1710dd (Mock), 1714c (Mock), 1719b (Mock)
Section 22: 1697a

COMMENTARY: The date on which this tragedy (first produced at the Theatre Royal, Drury Lane, in January 1664) was converted into an opera is not known, but probably was sometime during 1695, as suggested by the title of the printed collection of songs: ' The Songs in the Indian Queen: As it is now compos'd into an opera ' ... (italics mine). According to Langbaine (1699 edition, p. 75) the play was ' writ in Heroick verse, and formerly acted with general applause at the Theatre Royal, but now turn'd into an opera, and many times of late represented at the same theatre with like success.' The make-up of the cast (all members of the Theatre Royal) indicates that the production took place there. The absence of those members who had seceded with Betterton to Lincoln's Inn Fields in April 1695, shows that the production took place after that date. And the fact that Daniel Purcell composed the ' Additional music ' to The Indian Queen suggests that the production was on the stage when Purcell died. The title-page reads: ' The Additional Musick to the Indian Queen as it is now acted at His Majesties Theatre ' (italics mine). A MS source (British Museum MS Add. 31449) also points to late 1695 as the time of the production. Also, the fact that Heptinstall, May and Hudgebutt had the temerity to bring out an edition unauthorized by Purcell suggests that they might have taken courage to do so during his last illness, or after his death.

Singers mentioned in the early sources include Freeman, ' the boy ' (Jemmy Bowen), Church and Miss Cross. Other members of the original cast (including Mills, Powell, Disney, Leveridge, Mrs. Knight and Mrs. Rogers, among others) may also have sung.

In British Museum MS Add. 24889 (once belonging to Thomas Britton) are to be found the first violin parts for two pieces said to be from The Indian Queen. They are probably not by Purcell:

(No. 2) Indian Queen 1 pts.   (No. 3) Prelude second pt. Indian Queen

The Dance mentioned in the Purcell Society Edition, vol. XIX is not ascribed to *The Indian Queen*, although it is so ascribed in *Apollo's Banquet* (*ca.* 1669). It is unlikely that this was written by Purcell:

The Overture (Section 3) has been transcribed as a keyboard piece (see No. **T690**), as has the Trumpet Tune (Section 4; see No. **T698**). Purcell had used the first three sections of the Symphony (Section 5) in 'Come ye sons of art' (see No. **323/1**), there written in D major. Section 6a appears an octave higher as an instrumental tune in Oxford, Bodleian Library MS C.72, p. 30. The Dance at the beginning of Act III (Section 12) is practically identical to the 'Second Musick' in *The Fairy Queen* (see No. **629/2a**). The text of the song 'Ah how happy are we' as set by Purcell differs from that in the printed edition. The Third Act tune (Section 18) is given as a keyboard piece in Nos. **T677** and **D217**. What may be an additional minuet appears as a keyboard transcription in Oxford, Bodleian Library, MS Mus. Sch. E.397, p. 60 (see **D224**). The song in the Fourth Act, 'They tell us that you mighty powers' is not in the printed editions nor is the additional act, composed by Daniel Purcell and omitted in this catalogue. A selection of 'Mr. Henry Purcells Musick in ye Indian Queen' in Royal College of Music, London, MS 1144 (ff. 50–51v) includes thirteen pieces, among which there is an instrumental transcription of Section 17bc, and the following tune which is also to be found in British Museum MS Add. 35043 and in Goodison's edition.

LITERATURE: G. L. Mayer, 'The Vocal Works of Henry Purcell—A Discography,' *The American Record Guide*, May, 1959.

631. The Tempest, or the Enchanted Isle

(XIX, 111) ?1695; Thomas Shadwell from Shakespeare (or anonymously adapted from D'Avenant and Dryden's adaptation of Shakespeare's play)

Solo: *sabb*   Ob, 2 Vn, Va, Bc   Chorus: *SATB*

(1) Overture: *Str*
  (a) [Grave]   (b) [Canzona]: *Str*

[ACT II]

(2a) Where doth the black fiend
Ambition reside?: *bb*

[First Devil]

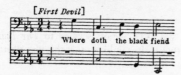

Where doth the black fiend

(2b) In Hell, with flames: *SATB*,
2 *Vn* [*Va*]

In Hell, in Hell, with flames

(2c) Who are the pillars: *bb*

[First Devil]

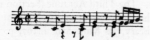

Who are the pil-lars

(2d) Care, their minds when
they wake: *SATB*, 2 *Vn*

(2e) Around we pace: *SATB*,
2 *Vn*

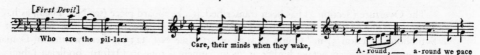

Care, their minds when they wake,

A-round,—— a-round we pace

(3a) Prelude: *Str*

(3b) Arise, ye subterranean winds: *b*, 2 *Vn*

A-rise, a-rise, ye sub——

(4) Dance: *Vn*

[ACT III]

(5ab) Come unto these yellow sands: *s*, 2 *Vn*

[Ariel]

[Come un - to - these yel - - - - low sands]

(5c) Hark the watch-dogs bark:
SATB, *Str*

Hark! hark the watch-dogs bark,

(6a) Prelude: *Bc*

(6b) Full fathom five: *s*

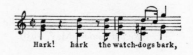

[Ariel]

Full fath-om five thy fa-ther

(6c) Sea-nymphs hourly: *SATB*, 2 *Vn*

Sea - nymphs hour - ly ring_ his_ knell,—

(7a) Dry those eyes: *s, 2 Vn*

(7b) Ritornello: *2 Vn*

(8a) [Prelude]: *Str*

(8b) Kind Fortune smiles: *s*
         [?*Vn, Ob*]

[ACT IV]

(9) Dance of devils: *Vn*

(10) Dear pretty youth: *a*
      (Miss Cross)

[ACT V]

(11a) Great Neptune: *s*

(11b) My dear, my Amphitrite: *b*

(11c) Fair and serene: *b*

(11d) Ritornello: *Str*

(12a) The Nereids and Tritons shall sing:
     SATB, Str

(12b) Ritornello: *Str*

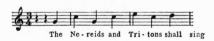

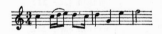

(13) Aeolus, you must appear: *b, Vn*

335

(14a) Your awful voice I hear: *a*

Your aw - ful voice I hear and I o - bey__

(14b) Air: 2 *Vn*

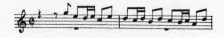

(14c) Come down my blusterers: *a*

Come down, come down, come down

(14d) To your prisons below: *a,*
　　　2 *Vn*

To your pri - sons be - low

(15a) Prelude: *Ob,* 2 *Vn*

(15b) Halcyon days: *s, Ob*

Hal - cyon days, now wars___ are end - ing

(16a) Prelude: 2 *Vn*

(16b) See the heavens smile: *b,* 2 *Vn*

See, the heav - ens smile

(17ab) No stars again shall hurt you: *sb,* [*SATB, Str*]

No stars a - gain shall hurt you, shall hurt you from a - bove

MSS: 214, 339 (with Section 1ab, as shown above, replaced by one composed by Norris), 359 (inc),
　　　381, 393 (inc), 464 (inc), 766 (inc), 788 (bass songs; inc)
　　　Section 1: 59, 408
　　　Section 2e: 212
　　　Section 3b: 212
　　　Section 5ac: 212
　　　Section 6: 212
　　　Section 8ab: 212
　　　Section 10: 219, 310, 628, 633 (inc)
　　　Section 12: 212
　　　Section 13: 789
　　　Section 15: 212
　　　Section 16: 212
　　　Section 17: 212

EDITIONS: XIX, III, 1786 (inc), ?1790b, ?1792, *ca.* 1810

Section 2e: 1805, 1809
Section 3b: 1809
Section 5bc: 1805, 1809
Section 6ab: 1805, 1809
Section 8: 1805
Section 10: 1696e, 1696f, 1698d, 1700n, 1704a, 1705e, 1706a, 1706b, 1721a, 1725c, 1726b, 1745c, 1805
Section 11a: 1805, 1809
Section 12a: 1809
Section 13a: 1805, 1809
Section 14a: 1809
Section 14c: 1809
Section 15b: 1805, 1809
Section 16b: 1805
Section 17ab: 1805

COMMENTARY: According to Downes, Shadwell's operatic version of *The Tempest* was first played at Dorset Garden in 1673. However, Nicoll dates the first production as of April 1674 (the play being printed that same year) and lists revivals for 1676 (bis), 1690, 1695 and 1701. Other revivals are recorded in the Lord Chamberlain's records for 1675 (LC 5/142, p. 81), and for November 15th, 1678 (LC 5/143, p. 162). Later revivals include those for 1702, 1708, 1710, 1714, 1717 and 1729. In 1708 the production included a masque between Bacchus and Cupid. Langbaine (1699 edition) makes no mention of *The Tempest* in his article on Shadwell, but mentions Dryden and D'Avenant's version of 1676, and an anonymous version (though he claims this also for Dryden), which had been 'of late days often acted.' Duffet's *Mock Tempest* was written about this time in competition with these versions. Locke, Draghi, Reggio, Banister, James Hart, Pelham Humphreys and possibly Grabu seem to have contributed music for these early productions.

Purcell's compositions for the opera cannot be dated exactly. The earliest printed source of his music for the play is *Deliciae Musicae* (Book III, dated in 1696, but probably published in 1695), where 'Dear pretty youth' is headed: 'A new Song in *The Tempest*, sung by Miss Cross to her lover who is supposed Dead.' The words of this song are not in the libretto. Nor is the authenticity of the ascription of each piece to Purcell established. The Overture, for instance, is included with this music mainly on the strength of a vague indication in the Royal College of Music, London, MS 990 'Overture in Mr. P. Opera.' The Dance (Section 4) appears to have been taken from Lully's *Cadmus et Hermione* (produced in London in 1686). Purcell's melody is the same as Lully's but he altered the bass. 'Come unto these yellow sands' has been adapted as a mock-song, 'Now comes joyful Peace! A Welcome to the happy Peace. A New Song. The words by Mr. D'Urfey' printed in *The Merry Musician*, I (EDITION 1716c), and in D'Urfey's *Songs Compleat*, II (EDITION 1719a). The Overture has been attached to this music on the flimsiest of evidence. Laurie and Dart believe it to belong to *Dido and Aeneas*, on the grounds that its musical style is too early for 1695. Neither of the two early MS sources in which it is to be found connects it with *The Tempest* in any way. In MS Add. 31450 (f.2) in the British Museum, another Overture is appended to Purcell's songs and tunes for *The Tempest* with the following note: 'N.B. There was no overture in the Original. The following was written by Tho Norris MB of Oxford at the request of Dr. Bever.' (By 'written' the annotator meant 'composed', for the copy is signed at the end: J. P. Hobler Scripsit 1784.') The Overture begins as follows:

337

and continues with four other short and extremely un-Purcellian movements. In this same MS the songs represented by the 6th, 7th and 8th incipits are given to Milcha, Alonzo, and Ferdinand, respectively.

In MS Add. 37027 (f.1), the opening song of the 'First Devil' is preceded by the stage (choreographic?) directions: 'Three Flourishes before the Devils rises (sic) 1st time[:] a good deed for a bad. 2nd time[:] Penitence and bount(y) 3rd time[:] escape is left[;] begin at fiend present.' Opposite the tenor line for the Chorus to this song (Section 2b: 'In Hell, in hell') is the note: 'Viola two notes lower & in the counter tenor cliff.' The cue 'At "O Dismal words for ever"' is written in the margin of f.2v for the song 'Who are the pillars.' 'Arise ye subterranean winds' is preceded in this same MS by the rubric 'In the second Act' indicating that the Act division as given above may be wrong. Further along, on f.8, the cue 'No it begins againe ... flourish' appears for 'Full fathom five' which, like 'Come unto these yellow sands' bears the instruction: 'Once through as a Rittornella.' This MS reverses the above order of the songs 'Kind fortune smiles' and 'Dear pretty youth.' The first ('with oboe and violin') follows after the stage direction 'Flourish at I am faint with Hunger and I must Despair.' 'The Devils Grand Dance' is called for by a stage direction at the beginning of Act 4 (f.11) but is copied in at the end of the work with the direction: 'Second time over second part once, and [then] from the repeat.' Just above this is copied a piece under the heading 'The Salars [sic] Dance—At spirits among us':

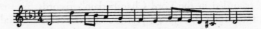

In British Museum MS Add. 37027, dating from the first half of the 18th century, 'The Devils Grand Dance' (which is appended at the end of the work but required by stage directions in the position indicated above) begins as follows:

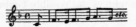

LITERATURE: C. Burney, *A General History of Music*, London: Foulis & Co., Ltd., 1935, II, p. 389; J. Downes, *Roscius Anglicanus* (ed. Montague Summers), London: The Fortune Press, [n.d.], p. 35; J. Hawkins, *A General History of the Science and Practice of Music*, London: Novello, 1853 (discusses Section 13a); A. Lewis, 'Purcell's music for "The Tempest",' *Musical Times*, June, 1959; J. F. Runciman, *Purcell*, London: George Bell, 1909; G. Rylands, 'The Tempest, or the Enchanted Island', *Musical Times*, June, 1959; W. Barclay Squire, 'The Music of Shadwell's "Tempest",' *Musical Quarterly*, 1921.

632. Timon of Athens, the Man-Hater ('The Masque')

(II) 1694(?); Thomas Shadwell, an addition to Shakespeare's *Timon.* ...

Solo: *ssab*   2 *Fl*, 2 *Ob*, [*Ten. Ob.*], *Tpt*, 2 *Vn*, *Va*, *Bc*   Chorus: *SSATB*

(1) Overture: *Tpt, Str*
   (a) [Grave]   (b) [Canzona]: *Tpt, Str*   (c) [Adagio]: *Str*

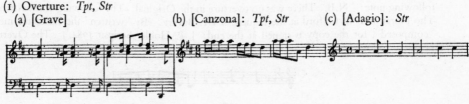

(1d) = 1a   (2) Air: *Tpt, Str*   (3) Jig: *Str*

(4) Air: *Str*   (5) Minuet: *Str*

(6a) Air: *Str*   (6b) Air: *Str*   (7) Minuet

(8) Scotch tune: *Str*   (9) Hornpipe: *Str*

(10a) Prelude: *2 Fl*   (10b) Hark! how the songsters: *ss, 2 Fl*

[George] Hark!   Hark! how the song-sters

Hark!   Hark!

[Jacob]

(11a) Love in their little veins: *s*   (11b) Ritornello: *2 Fl*

[George]

Love in their lit-tle   veins— in-spires

(12) But ah! how much are our delights: *SSB*

(13a) Prelude: *2 Ob*

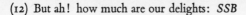

(13b) Hence with your trifling deity: *b, 2 Ob*

(13c) But over us no griefs prevail:
            ATB, 2 Vn [2 Ob, Ten. Ob?]

(14a) Prelude: *2 Vn*

(14b) Come all to me! make haste: *s, 2 Vn*

(15) Who can resist such mighty
      charms?: *SATB, Str*

(16a) Prelude: *2 Ob, 2*
                  Vn(?)

(16b) Return, revolting rebels:
      b, 2 Ob, 2 Vn(?)

(16c) To grief and to care: *b*

(16de) = 16ab

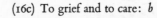

(17) The cares of lovers: *a*

(18a) Prelude: *2 Ob*

(18b) Love quickly is pall'd: *a, 2 Ob*

(19ab) Come let us agree: *sb, SATB*, Str   (20) Curtain tune: *Str*

MSS: 44 (inc), 95 (lacking Sections 1 to 9 and 20), 216 (inc), 217, 298 (inc), 336 (inc), 340 (inc),
342 (inc), 377, 394, 467 (inc), 676, 736 (inc)

Section 1: 22, 50, 358 (anon), 392, 406, 627 (Bass), 637
Section 2: 358 (anon), 368 (in C Major), 406, 627 (Bass)
Sections 2 to 9: 323 (attributed to Paisible)
Section 3: 358 (anon), 406, 627 (Bass)
Section 4: 358 (anon), 406, 627 (Bass)
Section 5: 358 (anon), 406, 627 (Bass)
Section 6: 358 (attributed to Paisible), 406, 627 (Bass)
Section 7: 358 (Paisible), 627 (Bass)
Section 8: 358 (Paisible), 627 (Bass)
Section 9: 358 (Paisible), 627 (Bass)
Section 10: 45
Section 11: 310
Section 13ab: 39, 45
Section 13c: 211
Section 14b: 45
Section 15: 211, 615
Section 16: 39, 45
Section 17: 219
Section 18: 211
Section 19: 45, 211, 310, 361 (Treble), 402, 615
Section 20: 358, 408

EDITIONS: II

Section 10: 1702d, 1711b, 1712a, 1721a, 1809
Section 11: 1700y, 1702d, 1711b, 1712a, 1721a, ?1755a
Section 12: 1702d, 1711b, 1712a, 1721a
Section 13: 1702d, 1711b, 1712a, 1721a, 1805
Section 14: 1702d, 1711b, 1712a, 1721a
Section 16: 1702d, 1711b, 1712a, 1721a, 1805
Section 17: 1695b, 1698d, 1706a, 1706b, 1721a, 1745c, ?1765
Section 19: 1700i, 1700j, 1702a, 1702d, 1705b, 1711b, 1712a, 1721a, 1725c, 1726b, 1737c, 1744,
1745c, 1745d, ?1765, ?1790
Section 20: 1722a (Trans)

COMMENTARY: Shadwell's adaptation of Shakespeare's *Timon of Athens* was first produced some time
on or near January 1677/8, and was printed that same year. Nicoll lists revivals for 1680(?),
1688, 1696 and 1703. In January 1707/8 a production of *The Tempest* was announced ' With all
the original music. To which will be added a Masque compos'd by the late Mr. Henry Purcell,
between Cupid and Bacchus, to be perform'd by Mr. Leveridge, Mrs. Lyndsay and others.
Very likely the masque was that composed by Purcell for *Timon*. Purcell probably composed

music for one of these revivals—or perhaps for one not listed by Nicoll. William Barclay Squire suggests that Grabu may have written music for the earliest production, since his setting of 'Hark how the songsters' was printed in Playford's *Choice Ayres* of 1679. After that date some changes were made in the text, these being retained in the version that Purcell set. Some of the new verses first appeared in *Gentleman's Journal* for May 1693, where Motteux described their origin as follows: 'We have had lately a consort of music, which as it pleased the most nice and judicious lovers of that art, would doubtless have had your approbation; I only speak of the notes which were made by Mr. Franck: As for the words I made 'em in haste, and most of them were design'd for Winter, and set to music then, tho' not seen so that I was forced to alter some lines as well as I could to reconcile 'em to this season. However you have 'em here, tho strip'd of their gay attire, the Notes. Be pleas'd to observe that they are most of them Songs, and some of the words are fitted to the tunes.' Among these are 'The cares of Lovers,' 'Love quickly is pall'd', and 'Come let us agree,' which form the last three numbers of the masque Purcell composed. Squire concludes that Purcell's settings must have been written after this date, since Motteux would not have printed these lines without mentioning an earlier setting by Purcell had one existed. This, plus the fact that 'The cares of lovers' was printed in *Deliciae Musicae* caused him to decide upon 1694 as the most probable date for Purcell's composition. However, none of this evidence is conclusive. The 'Curtain Tune' appears also in transcription for keyboard (see No. **T680**). The overture is the same as that for 'Who can from joy refrain' (see No. **342/1**) and appears in keyboard transcription as No. **T691/1**.

The general style of Purcell's settings does not conform in all points with the elaborate and expressive style of many works from his late period. Furthermore, a broadside in the Boston Public Library dates one of Purcell's songs at least as early as 1680, if the following entry from William Jaggard's *Shakespeare Bibliography* (Stratford-on-Avon: Shakespeare Press, 1911) may be taken at face value:

'A two-part song between Cupid and Bacchus in *Timon of Athens*. Set by Henry Purcell (*ca.* 1680).'

In setting the *Masque*, as printed in the first and all subsequent editions of Shadwell's version of the play, Purcell apparently did not compose music for the last ten sections, of which the first lines are:

'Then hang the dull wretch: Chorus with Haut-boys'
'Go drivel and snore: Nymph'
'With dull aching Noddles: Nymph'
'Better our heads: 1st Bacchus'
'Wine sweetens: 2nd Bacchus'
'Tis love that makes great monarchs: Nymph'
'Tis wine that revels in their vains [sic]: 1st Bacchus'
'Love rules the world: Nymphs and Shepherds'
'Hold, hold our forces: Bacchus'
'Then we with our pipes: General Chorus'

It is strange that Purcell would have omitted to write music for these, in view of his tendency to exploit all such opportunities for climactic endings when he found them in other texts, just as it is odd that he should have added settings of six stanzas which do not appear in the text, including the last three, which, as mentioned above, appear to have been written by Motteux. Perhaps these were added in haste at the last minute to piece out the masque.

Of the instrumental music for *Timon* printed by the Purcell Society, only the Overture and 'Curtain tune' are certainly by Purcell, and even with these we cannot be sure that he intended them for use with *Timon*. The Overture printed by the Purcell Society is authentic, for there is a copy in Purcell's hand in British Museum MS Add. 30934, f.79, where it appears as the Overture to *Who can from joy refrain* (see No. **342/1**). But this same version exists side by side with another (differing from it only in the 'canzona' section which is another piece altogether) in what appears to be a 'fiddler's book' with bass part, British Museum MS Add. 35043 (ff. 69v and 70, respectively). It was also transcribed shortly after, if not during Purcell's lifetime, as a harpsichord piece (see No. **T691**). Yet another version of the Overture is that known as the 'Trumpet Sonata. By Mr. Henry Purcell.' in Royal College of Music, London, MS 822 (f. 131), a straightforward arrangement of the overture for concert performance by trumpet and string orchestra. Except for a few obvious mistakes in the mid-18th century MS of the sonata, the two opening movements of the two versions are identical. The Sonata omits bars 2 to 5 in the Adagio and ends with the direction: 'End with the Allegro.' This is good advice which could well be followed for performing either the Overture or the 'Sonata'. A similar version, followed by a 'Trumpet Aire' from The Married Beau (see No. **603**/7) appears in Fitzwilliam MS C353, p. 93.

Another Overture to *Timon* appears in British Museum Royal Music MS 24.e.13(2), where most of Purcell's music for the masque has been copied in a hand reputedly that of Jeremiah Clarke. The Overture here is in a much later hand, and even in its fragmentary state can be ruled out as far as any resemblance to the well-known Overture is concerned. Its connection with *Timon* is doubtful.

The authenticity of all of the next eight tunes (Sections 2–9 above) is open to question. The last four of these (in F Major) are definitely ascribed to James Paisible in two British Museum MSS: Add. 35043 (on f. 66v under the heading 'Mr. Paisabls (sic) T. in Timon of Athens') and Add. 30839, 39565–7. In the latter source (a set of four instrumental part-books) these four tunes form part of a Suite in F Major beginning on f. 37 in each part-book. In MS Add. 35043, f. 66 also, the first four tunes (i.e. Sections 2–5 above) are ascribed to 'M. Paisible'. In view of the complexity of the problem these various sources present, I have left these tunes in much the same order as they were printed in the Purcell Society Edition pending further investigation of the matter. I have, however, removed the mistaken editorial division of the 6th piece into two, and the camouflaging of the 7th as part of the second—an anomaly which might have persisted had not Westrup discovered it recently in preparing a new edition of *Timon* for the Purcell Society.

In the Chichester MS the rubric 'The Hautboys play the same' is written over the chorus: 'But over us no griefs prevail'. Conversely in R.M. 23.e.13 violins are indicated rather than oboes. After section 16c in the Chichester MS is written: 'As before all the common time.'

The 'Curtain Tune' (Section 20) appears as a Chaconne for Harpsichord (see No. **649**). It also is known in a transcription for violin, evidently first published in the 6th edition of the *First Part of The Division Violin* (see EDITION 1705p). Another source, possibly somewhat earlier, British Museum MS Add. 35043, f. 56v, contains an arrangement for violin and bass under the heading 'Mr. H. Purcell's ground.' No mention is made of any connection with *Timon*.

LITERATURE: B. F. Swalin, 'Purcell's Masque in "Timon of Athens",' *American Musicological Society Papers*, 1941. J. A. Westrup, 'Purcell's Music for "Timon of Athens",' in *Festschrift Karl Gustav Fellerer* (Regensburg, 1962).

GENERAL LITERATURE

J. Bicknell, 'Interdependence of Word and Tone in the Dramatic Music of Henry Purcell,' Unpubl. doctoral dissertation, Stanford University, 1960; E. J. Dent, 'English Opera,' *Proceedings of the Musical Association*, 1926, pp. 71–83; —— *Foundations of English Opera*, Harmondsworth: Penguin Books, 1928; —— 'Purcell on the Stage,' *Athenaeum*, 9th Jan., 1920; J. Downes, *Roscius Anglicanus* (M. Summers, ed.) London: The Fortune Press, n.d.; A. Gray, 'Purcell's Dramatic Music,' *Proceedings of the Musical Association*, 1917, pp. 51–62; D. Grout, *A Short History of Opera* (2 vols.) London: Cumberledge, O.U.P., 1947; A. M. Laurie, 'Purcell's Stage Works,' Unpubl. doctoral dissertation, University of Cambridge, 1962 (submitted); J. Manifold, *The Music in English Drama*, London: Rockliffe, 1956; G. Mayer, 'The Vocal Works of Henry Purcell,' *American Record Guide*, May, 1959, pp. 588–591, 670–687, *passim*;

OPERA, SEMI-OPERAS, ('AMBIGUES'), MASQUE

R. Moore, *Henry Purcell and the Restoration Theatre*, Harvard University Press, 1961; J. Oettel, *Purcells Opern*, Leipzig, n.d.; E. Rendall, 'Purcell's Dramatic Music,' *Music and Letters*, April, 1920; R. Rolland, 'L'opéra anglais au xviie siècle,' *Lavignac's Encyclopédie de la musique I*, Paris: 1913; W. Barclay Squire, 'Purcell's Dramatic Music,' *Sammelbände der Internationalen Musikgesellschaft*, V, 489–564; R. Steglich, 'Die Oper in England bis 1740,' *Handbuch der Musikgeschichte* (G. Adler, ed.) Frankfurt-am-Main: Frankfurter Verlags-Anstalt A.G., 2nd ed., 1929; J. Westrup, 'Purcell and His Operatic Style,' *The Listener*, 22nd Aug., 1940, p. 285; E. W. White, 'Early Theatrical Performances of Purcell's Operas,' *Theatre Notebook*, vol. XIII, No. 2, 1959; —— *The Rise of English Opera*, London: Lehmann, 1951.

KEYBOARD WORKS: HARPSICHORD

Air [rather, Almand in C Major] (VI, 33; See Suite in C, No. 665/2 and Commentary)

Air [in C Major] (VI, 27; See Cibell, Trumpet tune No. T678)

Air [in D Major] (See S120)

Air [in d minor] (VI, 37; See No. T675)

Air [in d minor] (VI, 41; See No. T676)

641. Air [in G Major]

(VI, 49)

MSS: 58

EDITIONS: VI, 49

COMMENTARY: The version occurring in Cambridge, Fitzwilliam Museum MS 52.B.7 (p. 91) is
ornamented differently from that in the Purcell Society Edition. In MS 52.B.7 it is grouped with
Suite I in G Major (see No. **660**).

Air in Gamut (VI, 58; See 'Overture, Air and Jig,' No. T693)

Almand [in a minor] (See D218)

642/1. Almand [in a minor]

(Pauer, 152)

642/2. Corant [in a minor]

(Pauer, 154)

<table>
<tr><td>MSS: 367</td><td>MSS: 367</td></tr>
<tr><td>EDITIONS: Pauer, 152</td><td>EDITIONS: Pauer, 154</td></tr>
</table>

COMMENTARY: The manuscript source for this work, used by E. Pauer for his edition, but withheld from the Purcell Society editor (see VI, ii) is now British Museum MS Add. 41205. Thurston Dart has suggested that Purcell may have intended these two movements as part of a Suite in a minor (see the Commentary for No. 654).

Almand [in B♭ Major] (Pauer, 166; See Suite in B♭ Major, No. 664)

Almand in C Major (See Suite in C Major, No. 665)

Almand and Borry (rather ' Saraband ') in D-sol-re♯ (VI, 55; See D219)

643. Almand (with division) [in G Major]
(VI, 47)

EDITIONS: VI, 47

COMMENTARY: A variation on No. 660/2. The Purcell Society editor has grouped this piece together with Nos. 644, 641, D220 and 651, implying (though not stating) that these might form a suite. There seems no adequate reason for this, although there is likewise no reason why anyone so wishing may not perform them as a suite. There is some room for doubt as to the trustworthiness of the ascription of this ' Suite ' to Purcell, as Thurston Dart has pointed out in his article, ' Purcell's Harpsichord Music ' in *The Musical Times*, June 1959, p. 325. The fact that the opening Almand is padded with some rather tiresome divisions and ornaments suggests that someone like John Reading or William Babell (who often decked out such works with borrowed finery) may have been responsible for this ' Suite '.

Canary [in B♭ Major] (See No. T677)

Chacone (with canon) [in a minor] (See No. T679)

Chacone [in g minor] (VI, 24; See No. T680)

Cibell [in C Major] (See No. T678)

Cibell [in C Major] (See S121)

644. Corant [in G Major]

(VI, 48)

MSS: 58

EDITIONS: VI, 48

COMMENTARY: As for No. **643** above.

Corant [in B♭ Major] (See Suite in B♭ Major, No. 664)

Corant (rather, Saraband) [in B♭ Major] (See Suite in B♭ Major, No. 664)

Gavott [in G Major] (VI, 50; See D220)

Ground [in c minor] (VI, 39; See No. T681)

Ground [in c minor] (VI, 51; See D221)

Ground [in d minor] (See D222)

A new ground [in e minor] (See No. T682)

Ground [in F Major] (See S122)

645. Ground in Gamut

(VI, 33)

MSS: 310, 618

EDITIONS: VI, 33

COMMENTARY: The Purcell Society Edition (VI, viii) gives a variant reading for the last bar. As Thurston Dart has pointed out, the bass is the same as that for the first bars of the theme upon which Bach wrote the Goldberg variations.

Hornpipe [in B♭ Major] (See No. T683)

Hornpipe [in d minor] (See No. T684)

Hornpipe [in e minor] (See No. T685)

Jig [in d minor] (See No. T686)

Jig in Gamut (See 'Overture, Air and Jig in Gamut,' No. T693)

Jig [in g minor] (See D223)

Jig [in g minor] (See S123)

Lesson [in a minor] (See 'Saraband and division in a minor', No. 654)

Lesson [in C Major] (VI, 28; See March [in C Major], No. 647)

646. Lilliburlero. A New Irish tune

(VI, 31) 1689

MSS: 310, 313, 316, 570

EDITIONS: VI, 31, 1686d, 1689c, 1690c, 1695p, 1698f, 1700mm, 1701c, 1703g, 1705a, 1709h, 1711c, 1713b, 1716b, 1719b (Mock, bis), 1721b

COMMENTARY: An arrangement of this piece for strings is in British Museum MS Add. 24889, ff. 23, 48, 68 and 91. For the original tune see Chappell's *Popular Music* (Wooldridge edition, 1893), Vol II, p. 58. The version in EDITION 1686d is anonymous and may not be Purcell's. In fact he probably supplied only a bass and harmonization. The words 'Ho! broder Teague, dost hear de decree?' which sometimes appear with this melody can be found also in a broadside in the Bodleian Library, Oxford, set to a tune called 'Stingo' or, as it appears elsewhere in this catalogue, 'Cold and raw' (see No. **331**/6 and Commentary). Purcell also used the Lilliburlero tune for the bass in No. **597**/5.

647. March [in C Major]

(VI, 28) 1689

EDITIONS: VI, 28, 1689c, 1705a

COMMENTARY: Although printed as a 'Lesson' in the Purcell Society Edition, this piece may more accurately be called a 'March'.

648. March [in C Major]

(VI, 28) 1689

EDITIONS: VI, 28, 1689c, 1705a

COMMENTARY: The Purcell Society Edition (VI, viii) gives a variant reading for the last bar.

March [in C Major] (See No. T687)

March [in D Major] (See 'Trumpet voluntary,' S125)

649. Minuet [in a minor]

(VI, 29) 1689

EDITIONS: VI, 29, 1689c, 1690c, 1705a

COMMENTARY: Untitled in other sources, this piece is called a 'Minuet' in the 1690 edition of *Apollo's Banquet*, although it is printed there anonymously.

650. Minuet [in a minor]

(VI, 29) 1689

MS: 58

EDITIONS: VI, 29, 1689c, 1705a

COMMENTARY: This piece appears as one of several forming a suite in Cambridge, Fitzwilliam Museum MS 52.B.7. The order of movements in this *ad hoc* suite (of which this is the fourth and last) is: Almand, Jig, Air and Minuet. None is ascribed to Purcell.

Minuet [in d minor] (See D224)

Minuet [in d minor] (VI, 32; See No. T688)

New Minuet [in d minor] (VI, 29; See No. T689)

Minuet [in e minor] (See D225)

651. Minuet [in G Major]

(VI, 51)

MSS: 58

EDITIONS: VI, 51

COMMENTARY: The Purcell Society editor implies that this might be part of a suite (see Commentary for No. **643**). He has indicated as his source the 'Cummings' manuscript (now Cambridge, Fitzwilliam Museum MS 52.B.7), where these movements are actually grouped as a suite.

Overture [in A Major] (See D226)

Overture and Canzona [in c minor] (Pauer, 160; See No. T690)

Overture [in D Major] (Pauer, 164; See No. T691)

Overture [in D Major] (Pauer, 162; See No. T692)

Overture, Air and Jig in gamut-♮ (VI, 56; See No. T693)

652. Prelude [in a minor]

(VI, 40)

MSS: 58

EDITIONS: VI, 40

COMMENTARY: The Purcell Society Edition provides an alternative reading for the tenth bar of the piece. Thurston Dart has suggested that Purcell may have intended this as part of a Suite in a minor (see the Commentary for No. **654**).

Prelude [in C Major] (See D240)

653. Rigadoon [in C Major]

(VI, 32) 1689

MSS: 316

EDITIONS: VI, 32, 1689c, 1700mm, 1705a, 1711c

Rigadoon [in d minor] (See D227)

Rondo [in D Major] (See 'Trumpet Voluntary', S125)

Rondo [in d minor] (VI, 38; See 'Hornpipe [in d minor]', No. T684)

654. Saraband with division [in a minor]

(VI, 35)

MSS: 642

EDITIONS: VI, 35

COMMENTARY: In the Purcell Society Edition this piece is called a 'Lesson', for no apparent reason. Thurston Dart suggests that Purcell may have written this as the last movement of a suite beginning with the Prelude in a minor (see No. **652**), and continuing with the Almand and Corant entered above as Nos. **642/1** and **642/2** respectively.

Saraband [in B♭ Major] (See Suite [in B♭ Major], No. 664)

655. Scotch tune (A New Scotch tune) [in G Major]

(VI, 30) 1687

EDITIONS: VI, 30, 1687g, 1689c, 1690c, 1691b, 1693d, 1699e (Mock), 1705a, 1705n (Mock), 1707g (Mock), 1714c (Mock), 1719a (Mock), 1719b (Mock), 1729–31 (Mock), 1731f (Mock), 1731g (Mock)

COMMENTARY: In EDITION 1691b the first note is a fourth higher. The tune is also used as a setting of ' Tom and Will were shepherd swains ' in *Wit and Mirth* (see EDITION 1699e) and of ' Peggy, I must love thee ' in W. Bates's *The Jovial Crew* (1731) to the words: ' How cruel is that parent's care? ' Under this name, the tune found its way into the great stream of Scottish folk-songs, from which Haydn, nearly a century later ventured to fashion it into an ornate setting for 2 violins, 2 voices and continuo (see British Museum MS Add. 35273, f. 89v, a fair copy in the hand of Haydn's amanuensis).

656. Sefauchi's farewell

(VI, 32) 1689

EDITIONS: VI, 32, 1689c, 1690c, 1693d, 1705a

COMMENTARY: Written to commemorate the departure from England in about 1688 of the eminent castrato Giovanni Francesco Grossi, otherwise known as Siface.

Song tune [in C Major] (VI, 28; See No. T694)

Song tune [in C Major] (Dart, *Musick's Handmaid*, 4; See No. T695)

SUITES

660. Suite [in G Major]

(VI, 1: I)

(1) Prelude

(2) Almand

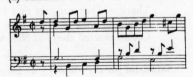

(3) Corant

(4) Saraband

MSS: 58, 364, 774
    Section 1: 345
    Section 2: 345
    Section 3: 345

EDITIONS: VI, 1: I, 1696a, 1699a

COMMENTARY: The Almand appears in a separate version with variations (see No. **643**). In the Purcell Society Edition the last movement is called 'Minuet'. The Prelude appears somewhat altered in the 'Cummings' MS in the Fitzwilliam Museum, Cambridge, MS 52.B.7, p. 89. In the Purcell Society Edition, the Corant begins a major third higher.

Suite [in g minor] (See D228)

661. Suite [in g minor]

(VI, 2: II) 1689

(1) Prelude   (2) Almand

(3) Corant   (4) Saraband

MSS: Section 1: 356

EDITIONS: VI, 2: II, 1696a, 1699a

COMMENTARY: The Purcell Society Edition provides alternative readings for the Almand and the Saraband. The Prelude occurs also in an Organ book, British Museum MS Add. 34695, f. 14.

662. Suite [in G Major]

(VI, 6: III)

(1) Prelude

(2) Almand

(3) Corant

MSS: 642

    Section 1: 356
    Section 2: 345
    Section 3: 345

EDITIONS: VI, 6: III, 1696a, 1699a

COMMENTARY: The Suite seems incomplete, lacking the usual Saraband.

663. Suite [in a minor]

(VI, 10: IV)

(1) Prelude

(2) Almand

(3) Corant

(4) Saraband

MSS: Section 1: 774
   Sections 2 and 4: 345, 686

EDITIONS: VI, 10: IV, 1696a, 1699a

COMMENTARY: Although preferring the (inaccurate) title 'Hornpipe' for the third movement of this suite, the Purcell Society editor has kept the title 'Courante' (Corant) used by E. Pauer.

664. Suite [in B♭ Major]

(Pauer, 156–7, 166)

(1) Almand   (2) Corant

(3) Saraband

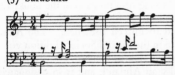

MSS: 367

EDITIONS: Pauer, 156–7, 166

COMMENTARY: The W. A. Barrett manuscript which Pauer used for his edition of this work is now British Museum MS Add. 41205. All three pieces in B♭ are signed as by Purcell, the first with his name in full, the last two with his initials only. The 'Suite' ends with a 'Jigg' in B♭ by Lord Byron.

665. Suite [in C Major]

(Dart: *Musick's Handmaid*, 21–2), 1689

(1) Prelude   (2) Almand

(3) Corant

(4) Saraband

(5) Jigg

MSS: Section 2: 641, 643

EDITIONS: Dart: *Musick's Handmaid*, 21–2, 1689c
      Section 2: VI, 33
      Section 3: 1696a
      Section 4: 1696a

COMMENTARY: Due to a mistake on the part of the printer, in the only known copies of the first edition of *The Second Part of Musick's Handmaid* the existence of this suite was obscured, even though it had been printed in the above order in the 1705 edition of that same publication, and by J. Stafford Smith in his *Musica Antiqua* (vol. II). In his reprint of *Musick's Handmaid*, II (London: Stainer and Bell, 1958), Thurston Dart has sorted out the proper sequence of the pages in the original edition, and has restored the suite to its rightful position in the book, at the same time identifying it as one of Henry Purcell's compositions for keyboard. Three of the movements—the second, third and fourth—are ascribed to Purcell elsewhere. The Almand (published as an ' Air ' in W. Barclay Squire's edition, and in the Purcell Society Edition vol. VI, which he also edited) is ascribed to Purcell in both MS sources (Christ Church, Oxford, MSS 1176 and 1179) and is undoubtedly his. This piece is actually an Almand, and is so designated in *Musick's Handmaid*, II. In Christ Church, Oxford, MS 1176, f. 14, the following anonymous prelude precedes this ' Almand ':

This is ascribed to Purcell in the contents list of the MS, which was made out by Alois Hiff: see D240.

Purcell wrote the following two movements, Corant and Saraband, both of which were published as part of another Suite in C Major by Purcell's widow in 1696. Here a new complication arises: to which suite do these two movements properly belong? When they were composed, they might have belonged to either, for in Purcell's time the form of the keyboard suite was not so strict as it was to become in the next century. Possibly, Frances Purcell may have confused the movements of two different C Major Suites in preparing *A Choice Collection of Lessons for Harpsichord* in 1696. Or she may have borrowed these two inner movements to complete a fragmentary suite for which only the first, second and fifth movements were at hand.

Because Purcell himself edited the earlier collection, and because these five movements seem more convincing as a ' Suite ' than that printed in 1696, I have so entered them here. Of course, there is the alternative possibility, as Thurston Dart suggests, that Purcell himself may have wanted to bring the suite up-to-date. This theory is all the more attractive since the original Prelude is in the old-fashioned French style, whereas all the preludes in the Christ Church MS are in the newer Italian style.

666. Suite in C Major

(VI, 13: V) 1689

(1) Prelude

(2) Almand

(3) Corant (= No. **665**/3)

(4) Saraband (= No. **665**/4)

MSS: 58

Section 1: 234, 281 (another version), 356
Section 4: 570

EDITIONS: VI, 13: V, 1696a, 1699a

Section 3: 1689c

COMMENTARY: The Prelude exists also in a manuscript now in the possession of Lady Jeans (see MS 281), with several variant readings.

667. Suite [in D Major]

(VI, 16: VI) 1689

(1) Prelude

(2) Almand

(3) Hornpipe

MSS: Sections 2 and 3: 345

EDITIONS: VI, 16: VI, 1696a, 1699a

COMMENTARY: The missing bar-line at the beginning of the Prelude (as printed in the Purcell Society edition) is also missing in the *Choice Collection* of 1696. In preparing the suite for publication in this collection, Mrs. Purcell perhaps did not have all the movements at hand. (See Thurston Dart's article 'Purcell's Harpsichord Music' in *The Musical Times* for June, 1959.)

668. Suite [in d minor]

(VI, 18: VII) 1689

(1) Almand (Bell Barr)   (2) Corant

(3) Hornpipe

MSS: Section 1: 345

EDITIONS: VI, 18: VII, 1696a, 1699a

COMMENTARY: The sub-title—a place-name in Hertfordshire—also appears with the song 'I love and I must,' (No. 382), and has not yet been explained satisfactorily. The slight similarity between this bass and that of the song seems hardly to justify the attention some analysts have given it. Purcell used the Hornpipe (Section 3) as the third piece in his music for *The Married Beau* (see No. 603/3). The Purcell Society Edition provides several alternate readings for this Suite, which, as Thurston Dart has pointed out, is 'curiously incomplete', lacking the opening Prelude, and possibly a 'Saraband' as well.

(?) **Suite [in d minor]** (See No. T696)

669. Suite [in F Major]

(VI, 20: VIII) 1689

(1) Prelude

(2) Almand (3) Corant

(4) Minuet

MSS: Section 1: 345
  Sections 2 and 3: 774

EDITIONS: VI, 20: VIII, 1696a, 1699a

COMMENTARY: The minuet, adapted for strings, is in *The Double Dealer* (see No. **592/3**).

Suite [in g minor] (See D228)

670. The Queen's Dolour

MS: 310

COMMENTARY: Although only one source is known at present for this work (Br. Mus. Add. 22099, f. 5v), its inscription may be assumed to be authentic on the strength of the reliable evidence it gives on other Purcell works, until such time as other sources are brought to light.

Toccata [in A Major] (See D229)

Trumpet minuet [in C Major] (See D230)

Trumpet minuet [in D Major] (See D231)

Trumpet tune [in C Major] (VI, 27; See No. T697)

Trumpet tune, called the Cibell (VI, 27; See *Cibell*, No. T678)

Trumpet tune [in C Major] (VI, 24; See No. T698)

Trumpet tune [in C Major] (VI, 37; See S124)

'Trumpet Voluntary' [in D Major] (See S125)

T675. Air [in d minor]
(VI, 37)

MSS: 596

EDITIONS: VI, 37

COMMENTARY: This is a keyboard transcription of a piece associated with *The Indian Queen* music in Oxford, Bodleian Library MS Mus. Sch. e 397, p. 56 (see No. **630**). It occurs in conjunction with another air in a more elaborate version (see No. **T696**/1–2).

T676. Air [in d minor]
(VI, 41)

MSS: 58

EDITIONS: VI, 41

COMMENTARY: This is a transcription of the third minuet in *The Double Dealer* (see No. **592**/7).

T677. Canary [in B♭ Major]

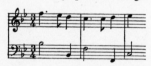

MSS: 236, 570 (also in A Major)

EDITIONS: ?1700

COMMENTARY: This piece for harpsichord appears in two versions in the New York Public Library, MS Drexel 5609 (pp. 168 and 208), as well as in a manuscript in the Euing Library, Glasgow, and in a printed source. The first of the versions in New York Public Library is in B♭ Major, the second, marked 'Slow', is in A Major. The music is the same as that of the 'Curtain tune' in *The Indian Queen* (see No. **630**/18).

T678. [Cibell] Trumpet tune, called the Cibell

(VI, 27) ?1689

MSS: 59, 60, 60 (in D Major), 141, 280, 310, 358, 364, 368 (in F Major), 406, 471, 472, 600, 774

EDITIONS: VI, 27, 1696a, 1699a, 1700l (Mock), 1700m (Mock), ?1700, 1701–2, 1705o, 1705p, 1706d (in F Major), 1709d (Mock), 1719a (Mock), 1719b (Mock), 1730e, 1732 (Mock)

COMMENTARY: D'Urfey adapted this tune to the text 'Crown your bowles, loyal souls' (*Songs Compleat*, II, p. 70). The piece seems originally to have been composed for trumpet and strings, as it is to be found in the Magdalene part-books with parts for these instruments (see MS 59).

LITERATURE: Thurston Dart, 'The Cibell', in *Revue belge de musicologie*, Vol. VI, fasc. 1.

T679. Chacone (with canon) [in a minor]

MSS: 471

COMMENTARY: This 'Canon in 2 parts on a Chacone' appears to have been transcribed from *Dioclesian* (see No. **627**/16). Its source is a manuscript copy bound in at the back of *A Choice Collection of Lessons for the Harpsichord* in the British Museum (Hirsch III, 492, ff. 1–3).

T680. Chacone [in g minor]

(VI, 24) 1689

MSS: 58, 292, 358

EDITIONS: VI, 24, 1696a, 1699a, 1705j, 1705p

COMMENTARY: This is the 'Curtain tune' from *Timon of Athens* (see No. **632**/20). In Cambridge, Fitzwilliam Museum MS 52.B.7 this appears as a part of a suite with three other movements. (See D228.) These may constitute a suite actually written by Purcell or one just made up of various pieces by someone else. Another version, for two violins and bass, was printed in 1705 by Walsh (see EDITION 1705j).

N

T681. Ground [in c minor]

(VI, 39)

MSS: 58, 310, 364, 367, 596

EDITIONS: VI, 39

COMMENTARY: Apparently a transcription of 'With him he brings the partner' in *Ye tuneful Muses* (see No. **344**/11). There are two manuscript versions of this piece. One, in MS 58, served as the basis for the Purcell Society Edition. Another, from Oxford, Bodleian Library MS Mus. Sch. e 397, p. 70, begins as follows:

For other important variants, see the Purcell Society Edition, VI, ix, and D221 (VI, **51**), which is similar in various ways, though on a different ground.

T682. A new ground [in e minor]

(VI, 30) 1689

MSS: 364, 367, 471

EDITIONS: VI, 30, 1689c

COMMENTARY: This piece occurs as an alto solo, 'Here the deities approve' in *Welcome to all the pleasures* (see No. **339**/3). Strangely enough, in view of the fact that he edited the collection, Purcell's name does not appear with this work in *Musick's Handmaid*; but a contemporary ascription to him is to be found in *Orpheus Britannicus* for 'Here the deities approve.' The setting for strings in the 'Magdalene Part-books' (Fitzwilliam Museum, Cambridge, see MS 59) is probably based on the original version in the Welcome Song.

T683. Hornpipe

MSS: 570

COMMENTARY: This is a transcription of the Hornpipe from the incidental music to *Abdelazer* (see No. **570**/8).

T684. Hornpipe [in d minor]

(VI, 38)

MSS: 596

EDITIONS: VI, 38

COMMENTARY: This Hornpipe (called ' Rondo ' in the Purcell Society Edition) is a transcription of the second instrumental piece in the incidental music for *Abdelazer* (see No. **570**/2), also occurring as a ' fiddler's piece ' in British Museum MS Add. 29371, f. 48. Since 1946, it has become widely known as the theme of Benjamin Britten's variations and fugue, ' The Young Person's Guide to the Orchestra ' (op. 34).

T685. Hornpipe [in e minor]

(VI, 47)

MSS: 58

EDITIONS: VI, 47

COMMENTARY: See the ' Hornpipe ' in *The Old Bachelor* (No. **607**/4). This piece appears in company with several other pieces in the ' Cummings ' MS (now MS 58). These other pieces (including those mentioned in the Commentary to No. **643** above) are all in G Major, which renders doubtful the Purcell Society editor's implication that these might form a Suite (see VI, x).

T686. Jig [in d minor]

(VI, 26) 1689

MSS: 58, 310 (in g minor), 364, 774

EDITIONS: VI, 26,   1696a, 1699a, 1701–2 (in d minor)

COMMENTARY: This is a transcription of a Jig from *Abdelazer* (see No. **570**/7).

T687. March [in C Major]

(VI, 23) 1689

MSS: 310, 345

EDITIONS: VI, 23,   1696a, 1699a

COMMENTARY: A transcription of a piece in *The Married Beau* (see No. **603**/8).   A variant reading for bar 5 is to be found in the Purcell Society Edition (VI, vii).

T688. Minuet [in d minor]

(VI, 32) 1689

EDITIONS: VI, 32,   1689c, 1705a

COMMENTARY: This Minuet is a transcription of the ritornello for strings in the St. Cecilia song, *Raise the voice* (see No. **334**/6).

T689. New Minuet [in d minor]

(VI, 29) 1689

EDITIONS: VI, 29, 1689c, 1690c, 1693d, 1705a

COMMENTARY: This is a transcription of the song 'Who can resist such mighty charms' from
 Timon of Athens (see No. **632**/15).

T690. Overture [in c minor]

(Pauer, 160)

(1) [Grave]   (2) [Canzona in c minor]

MSS: 367

EDITIONS: Pauer, 160

COMMENTARY: The Overture is similar to that in *The Indian Queen* (see No. **630**/3a), while the
 Canzona is identical (see No. **630**/3b). E. Pauer's edition derives from the W. A. Barrett
 manuscript which is now British Museum MS Add. 41205.

T691. Overture [in D Major]

(Pauer, 164)

(1) [Grave]   (2) [Canzona in D Major]

MSS: 58, 367, 471, 570

EDITIONS: Pauer, 164

COMMENTARY: This appears to be a transcription of the Overture to *Timon of Athens* (see No. **632**/1), or of the Overture to *Who can from joy refrain* (see No. **342**/1), where it is in C Major. In the manuscript additions to the British Museum copy of *Choice Lessons for the Harpsichord* (Hirsch III, 492) it appears in an anonymous copy entitled 'Overture to Camilla', and in New York Public Library, MS Drexel 5609, p. 206, as a trumpet piece transcribed for keyboard. In his edition, E. Pauer incorporated this Overture and Canzona into one suite with the following pair.

T692. Overture [in D Major]

(Pauer, 162)

(1) [Grave]

(2) [Canzona]

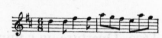

MSS: 367

EDITIONS: Pauer, 162

COMMENTARY: This Overture apparently was taken from the first Symphony in *The Fairy Queen* (see No. **629**/3ab). E. Pauer erroneously edited this as part of a four-movement suite with the foregoing pair of movements.

T693. Overture, Air and Jig in gamut-♭

(VI, 56) 1689

(1) Overture
 (a) [Grave]

 (b) [Canzona]

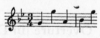

(2) Air

(3) Jig (Morgan)

MSS: 367 (inc), 470

EDITIONS: VI, 56

COMMENTARY: Both parts of the Overture are based on the Overture to *The Virtuous Wife* (see No. **611/1**). The Air appeared also in *Abdelazer* (see No. **570/6**). Both are to be found in *Ayres for the Theatre*, which served as a main collating source for the Purcell Society editor. The Jig is by Morgan (see S123).

Rondo [in d minor] (VI, 38; See Hornpipe, No. T684)

T694. Song tune [in C Major]

(VI, 28) 1689

EDITIONS: VI, 28,   1689c, 1705a

COMMENTARY: See *Ah how pleasant 'tis to love* (No. **353**); it is also somewhat similar to *Aaron thus proposed* (No. **351**).

T695. Song tune [in C Major]

Dart: *Musick's Handmaid*, 4

EDITIONS: Dart: *Musick's Handmaid*, 4,   1689c, 1690c, 1693d

COMMENTARY: This is Purcell's keyboard transcription of his own solo-song, *Sylvia now your scorn give over* (see No. **420**).

T696. (?) Suite [in d minor]

(1) Air

(2) Air

EDITIONS: 1706c

COMMENTARY: The second Air is that mentioned in the commentary to No. **T675**.

T697. Trumpet tune [in C Major]

(VI, 27) 1690

MSS: 471, 570

EDITIONS: VI, 27, 1699a

COMMENTARY: This version was adapted from the 'Trumpet Tune' in *Dioclesian* (see No. **627/21**).

Trumpet tune, called the Cibell (See 'Cibell' No. **T678**)

T698. Trumpet tune [in C Major]

(VI, 24)

MSS: 280, 310, 345, 774

EDITIONS: VI, 24, 1696a, 1699a

COMMENTARY: This trumpet tune occurs also in the prologue to *The Indian Queen* (see No. **630/4a**).

GENERAL LITERATURE

Thurston Dart, 'Purcell's Harpsichord Music,' *The Musical Times*, June 1959; R. Sietz, *Henry Purcell: Zeit, Leben, Werk*, Leipzig: Breitkopf & Härtel, 1955, pp. 183–189; E. Walker, *History of Music in England*, 3rd ed., revised by Westrup, Oxford: Clarendon Press, 1952. See also the Notes to Dart's edition of *Musick's Hand-Maid*, II, London: Stainer & Bell, 1962 (2nd ed.).

ORGAN

Prelude [in C Major] (See D240)

Prelude [in G Major] (VI, 53; See Voluntary, No. 720)

716. A Verse]in F Major]
(VI, 36)

MSS: 345

EDITIONS: VI, 36

Verse in the Phrygian Mode (See S126)

Voluntary [in C Major] (See D241)

717. Voluntary [in C Major]
(VI, 35)

MSS: 643

EDITIONS: VI, 35

COMMENTARY: This work is to be found only in Oxford, Christ Church MS 1179, where the copy is not altogether perfect. McLean's edition gives a revised reading for bars 20–22, along with several other corrections.

Voluntary [in C Major] (VI, 68; See D241ab)

718. Voluntary [in d minor]

(VI, 61)

MSS: 335

EDITIONS: VI, 61

COMMENTARY: This piece occurs without title in British Museum MS Add. 31446, ff. 9v–10v. McLean has made several editorial corrections.

LITERATURE: R. Downes, 'An Organist's view of the Organ Works,' in *Henry Purcell 1659–1695: Essays on His Music* (ed. Imogen Holst) London: O.U.P., 1959, p. 69.

719. Voluntary for double organ

(VI, 64)

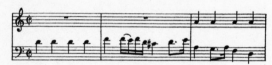

MSS: 346

EDITIONS: VI, 64

LITERATURE: R. Downes, 'An Organist's view of the Organ Works,' in *Henry Purcell 1659–1695: Essays on His Music* (ed. Imogen Holst) London: O.U.P., 1959, p. 69.

720. Voluntary [in G Major]

(VI, 53)

MSS: 356

EDITIONS: VI, 53

LITERATURE: R. Downes, 'An Organist's view of the Organ Works,' in *Henry Purcell 1659–1695: Essays on His Music* (ed. Imogen Holst) London: O.U.P., 1959, p. 71.

Voluntary [in G Major] (See D242)

721. **Voluntary on the 100th Psalm [in A Major]**

(VI, 59)

MSS: 356

EDITIONS: VI, 59

COMMENTARY: See McLean's edition (Henry Purcell, *The Organ Works*, London: Novello, 1957, p. 20) for Blow's Voluntary on this same psalm tune.

GENERAL LITERATURE

See Preface to McLean's edition, *Supra*.

STRINGS
FANTASIAS AND RELATED FORMS

730. Chacony [à 4 in g minor]

(XXXI, 61)

4 parts: Str,

MSS: **324,** 349 (inc)

EDITIONS: XXXI, 61

Cibell [in C Major]. (See No. **T678**) The transcription for Trumpet and Strings in the Magdalene part-books (MS No. 59: Fitzwilliam Museum 23.E.13) may have been the original version of this work.

731. Fantasia. '3 parts upon a ground'

(XXXI, 52)

3 *Fl* (or *Vn*), *Bc*   ?before 1680

(1)

(2)

(3) [Four parts in two]

(4) [Three parts in one]

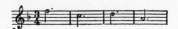

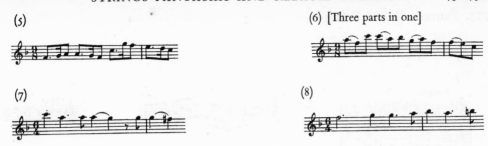

(5)

(6) [Three parts in one]

(7)

(8)

MSS: **326** (fragment), 454

EDITIONS: XXXI, 52

COMMENTARY: A fragment in F Major of the second treble part of this fantasia appears on the back of a correction slip fastened to the autograph copy of *Behold now praise the Lord* (see No. **3**/Comm). This melody (erroneously transcribed by the Purcell Society editor, in vol. XIIIA, note) could easily have been played in the ' violin key ' (D Major) without transposition. The player had but to make mental adjustments for the changes of the clef, key-signatures and accidentals, then play the melody as written. There is also a version in D Major, taken from the copy in Br. Mus. RM MS 20.h.9, which bears the rubric: ' play'd 2 notes higher for the F(lute).' However, it is probable that it was originally written for recorders. The conjectural date given above for this Fantasia, derives from that of *Behold, now praise the Lord.* The case for such an early date is strengthened, moreover, by the fact that the ground (as well as several instructions pertaining to this sort of composition) appears in Christopher Simpson's *A Compendium or Introduction to Practical Music*, London: W. Pearson, 1732, 8th edition, pp. 127–133. Purcell may well have composed this as an advanced exercise at the end of his time as a student of composition.

732. **Fantasia [à 3 in d minor]**

(XXXI, 1: No. 1) *ca.* 1678–80

tr, a, b

(1)

¢: L Add 30930

(2)

Quick

(3)

MSS: **324,** 349 (inc), 569

EDITIONS: XXXI, 1

COMMENTARY: This fantasia appears under the heading (in Purcell's hand): ' Here begineth ye 3 part Fantazia's ' in British Museum MS Add. 30930.

733. Fantasia [à 3 in F Major]

(XXXI, 3: No. 2); *ca.* 1678-80

3 parts: tr, a, b

(1)

(2)   (3)

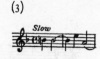

MSS: **324,** 332, 349

EDITIONS: XXXI, 3

COMMENTARY: The numerous revisions in the autograph (see the Purcell Society Edition vol. XXXI, 108) suggest an early date of composition for this fantasia, as does its position in this manuscript.

734. Fantasia [à 3 in g minor]

(XXXI, 5: No. 3) ? before 1680

(1)   (2)

No t-s: L Add 30930

MSS: **324**

EDITIONS: XXXI, 5

COMMENTARY: Purcell also emended several passages in this piece—a fact which suggests a date of composition somewhat earlier than those for the fantasias which follow it in the autograph, most of which are dated.

Fantasia [à 4 in C Major] (See D250)

735. Fantasia [à 4 in g minor]

(XXXI, 7: No. 4) 'June ye 10. 1680'

tr, a, t, b

(1)

(2)

(3)

MSS: **324,** 569

EDITIONS: XXXI, 7

COMMENTARY: In British Museum MS Add. 30930 this is the first work copied in after the heading: 'Here begineth ye 4 part Fantazias,' the first two pages immediately following this heading being blank. It is the earliest of the fantasias actually dated in Purcell's own hand.

736. Fantasia [à 4 in B♭ Major]

(XXXI, 10: No. 5) 'June ye 11. 1680'

tr, m, a, b

(1)

(2)

(3)

(4)

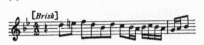

MSS: **324,** 569

EDITIONS: XXXI, 10

737. Fantasia [à 4 in F Major]

(XXXI, 13: No. 6) 'June ye 14. 1680'

tr, m, a, b

(1)

(2)

(3)

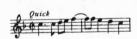

(4)

MSS: **324,** 569

EDITIONS: XXXI, 13

738. Fantasia [à 4 in c minor]

(XXXI, 16: No. 7) 'June ye 19 1680'

tr, m, a, b

(1)

(2)

(3)

(4)

(5)

MSS: **324,** 569

EDITIONS: XXXI, 16

739. Fantasia [à 4 in d minor]

(XXXI, 19: No. 8) 'June ye 19/22. 1680'

tr, m, a, b

(1)

(2)

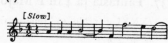

(3)

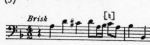

(4)

MSS: **324,** 569

EDITIONS: XXXI, 19

COMMENTARY: Having first written the date 'June ye 19 1680' in the autograph book, Purcell later altered it to read 'June ye 22 1680'.

740. Fantasia [à 4 in a minor]

(XXXI, 22: No. 9) 'June ye 23: 80'

tr, m, a, b

(1)

(2)

(3)

(4)

MSS: **324,** 569

EDITIONS: XXXI, 22

COMMENTARY: Purcell revised the ending of this fantasia after having finished the fair copy in the autograph book (see the Purcell Society Edition vol. XXXI, 109).

741. Fantasia [à 4 in e minor]

(XXXI, 25: No. 10) 'June ye 30. 80'

tr, m, a, b

(1)

(2)

(3)

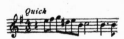

(4)

MSS: **324,** 569

EDITIONS: XXXI, 25

742. Fantasia [à 4 in G Major]

(XXXI, 28: No. 11) 'August ye 18 80'

tr, m, a, b

(1)   (2)   (3)

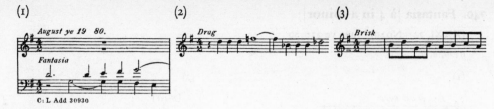

C: L Add 30930

MSS: **324,** 569

EDITIONS: XXXI, 28

COMMENTARY: There is some question about the actual date inscribed by Purcell above the autograph
score of this work.   Under a very powerful glass, it appears that Purcell originally wrote
' August ye 16 80.', then crossed out the upper stroke of the ' 6 ', replacing this with a downward
stroke to make it into ' 9 '.   Then, as if realizing he had put down the wrong date, he scrawled a
rather awkward loop to form an ' 8 '.   It is possible that August 18, 1680, was the date he
intended to write down finally.   Purcell made several corrections after copying the work into
the autograph scorebook.

743. Fantasia [à 4 in d minor]

(XXXI, 31: No. 12) 'August ye 31: 1680'

tr, m, a, b

(1)   (2)

[*Quick*]

₵: L Add 30930

MSS: **324,** 569

EDITIONS: XXXI, 31

COMMENTARY: Again, Purcell corrected his ' fair copy ', in this case lengthening the work by one
bar, as Thurston Dart has pointed out in the Purcell Society Edition.

744. Fantasia [à 4 in a minor]

(XXXI, 94: No. 13) ' Feb. ye 24th 1682/3 '

2 Vn, B.Viol, Bc

₵: L Add 30930

MSS: **324**

EDITIONS: XXXI, 94

COMMENTARY: Purcell probably never finished this fantasia, which is incomplete in the only MS source, without a final double bar-line. It is in the canzona-style associated with the trio-sonatas, and may not have been intended as a fantasia.

745. Fantasia upon one note [à 5 in F Major]

(XXXI, 34) ?before 1680

tr, tr, m, a, b

(1)   (2)

(3)   (4)

MSS: **324,** 569, 629

EDITIONS: XXXI, 34

COMMENTARY: In the autograph, this is the first work which Purcell copied in under the heading: 'Here Begineth ye 5 Part: Fantazies', although seven blank pages intervene.

LITERATURE: H. Rawlinson, 'Fantasia upon one Note for Strings: Henry Purcell,' *The Strad*, Jan. 1948.

Fantasia [à 4 in C Major] (See D250)

746. In nomine [à 6 in g minor]

(XXXI, 37) ? before 1680

tr, s, m, a, t, b

MSS: **324,** 569

EDITIONS: XXXI, 37

COMMENTARY: In the autograph, this work appears under the heading: 'Here Begineth ye 6, 7, & 8 part Fantazia's.'

747. In nomine [à 7 in g minor]

(XXXI, 39) ? before 1680

tr, tr, s, m, a, b, b

C: L Add 30930

MSS: **324,** 569

EDITIONS: XXXI, 39

COMMENTARY: Purcell altered a number of details after copying this work into the score-book (see the Purcell Society Edition vol. XXXI, 110).

748. Pavan [à 3 in A Major]

(XXXI, 46) ? before 1680

2 Vn, Bc

¢: L Add 33236

MSS: 349

EDITIONS: XXXI, 46

COMMENTARY: The suggested date for this composition is based on its comparatively 'early' style, and upon its relative position in British Museum MS Add. 33236. It is also based on the conjecture that this MS may have been copied from a lost 'Mr. Purcell's score-book' which probably contained works composed before the earliest of those appearing in MS Add. 30930.

LITERATURE: M. Wailes, 'Four Short Fantasies by Henry Purcell,' *The Score and I.M.A. Magazine,* June, 1957.

749. Pavan [à 3] in A-re♭

(XXXI, 44)? before 1680

2 Vn, Bc

MSS: 349

EDITIONS: XXXI, 44

COMMENTARY: As for No. **748** above.

LITERATURE: M. Wailes, 'Four Short Fantasies by Henry Purcell,' *The Score and I.M.A. Magazine,*
June 1957.

750. Pavan [à 3] in B♭; 3♯

(XXXI, 49) ? before 1680

2 *Vn, Bc*

¢: L Add 33236

MSS: 349

EDITIONS: XXXI, 49

COMMENTARY: As for No. **748** above.

LITERATURE M. Wailes, 'Four Short Fantasies by Henry Purcell,' *The Score and I.M.A. Magazine,*
June 1957.

751. Pavan [à 3] in Gamut

(XXXI, 42) ? before 1680

2 *Vn, Bc*

¢: L Add 33236

MSS: 349

EDITIONS: XXXI, 42

COMMENTARY: As for No. **748** above.

LITERATURE: M. Wailes, 'Four Short Fantasies by Henry Purcell,' *The Score and I.M.A. Magazine,*
June 1957.

752. Pavan à 4 [in g minor]

(XXXI, 49); ? *ca.* 1677

3 *Vn, Bc*

C: L Add 30930

MSS: **324,** 569

EDITIONS: XXXI, 49

COMMENTARY: The conjectural date above is based on Thurston Dart's apt suggestion that this Pavan may have been a companion piece to the ' Elegy on the death of his worthy companion Mr. Matthew Locke,' who died some time in 1677. The deeply expressive elegiac quality of the Pavane—traditionally a funerary musical form—lends credence to Mr. Dart's hypothesis.

GENERAL LITERATURE

H. Andrews, 'Purcell and 17th Century Chamber Music,' *Music Teacher*, July 1927; F. Bridge, 'Purcell's Fantazias and Sonatas', *Proceedings of the Musical Association*, 1915–16, p. 1; T. Dart, 'Purcell's Chamber Music,' *Proceedings of the Royal Musical Association*, 1958–59, p. 81; A. Holland, ' Purcell's Instrumental Music,' *The Listener*, 13th Nov., 1952; A. Mangeot, ' Some Purcell Fantasias ' (' The Purcell Fantasies and Their Influence on Modern Music ': actual title), *Music and Letters*, vol. VII, No. 2, p. 143; E. Meyer, *English Chamber Music*, London: Laurence & Wishart, 1951; —— ' Form in the Instrumental Music of the 17th Century,' *Proceedings of the Royal Musical Association*, 1938–39, p. 45; —— ' The In Nomine,' *Music and Letters*, vol XVII, No. 1, p. 25; —— *Die mehrstimmige Spielmusik des 17. Jahrhunderts in Nord- und Mitteleuropa*, Kassel: Bärenreiter-Verlag, 1934; A. Pleasants, 'Dissonance in the Fantasias and Sonatas of Henry Purcell,' unpublished doctoral dissertation, Northwestern University, 1953; H. Rawlinson, 'Fantasia Upon One Note for Strings: Henry Purcell,' *The Strad*, Jan. 1948, p. 202; R. Rowen, *Early Chamber Music*, New York: King's Crown Press, 1949; D. Stevens, 'Purcell's Art of Fantasia,' *Music and Letters*, Oct. 1952, p. 314; M. Tilmouth, ' Chamber Music in England,' unpublished doctoral dissertation, University of Cambridge, 1959; P. Warlock ' Purcell's Fantasias for Strings,' *The Sackbut*, May 1927; H. Wessely-Kropik, 'Henry Purcell als Instrumentalkomponist', *Studien zur Musikwissenschaft*, Zweiundzwanzigster Band, p. 85; M. Wailes ' Four Short Fantasias by Henry Purcell,' *The Score*, June 1957. See also the notes and discussions in vol. XXX of the Purcell Society Edition.

SONATAS AND RELATED FORMS

770. Overture and Suite fragment [in G Major]

(XXXI, 68)

2 *Vn, Va*   *Bc*

(1a) [Grave]

Overture

♩: L Add 30930

(1b) [Canzona]

(1c) [Adagio]

(2) [Air]

(3) [Minuet]

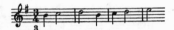

(4) [Jigg]

MSS: **324,** 399 (Section 1 only)

EDITIONS: XXXI, 68

COMMENTARY: As in the Chacony in g minor (see No. **730**), Purcell wrote first the treble and bass lines only of the last three pieces in this suite. However, in this case, he evidently did not finish writing the inner parts. For this reason, as Thurston Dart has pointed out, previous editors have listed these three pieces as a separate 'Suite' for solo violin. Noticing that these pieces, though not labelled, correspond to Overture, Air, [Saraband], Borry, Minuet and Jigg, Mr. Dart filled out the suite with a movement from *Distressed Innocence* (See No. **577**/7) for the Purcell Society Edition. In the original suite, Section 1c is the same as an 'air' from 'The Gordian Knot Unty'd' (See No. **597**/4), and Section 3 is the same as the final minuet in *Distressed Innocence* (See No. **577**/8). Purcell used the 4th movement as a ritornello in *Ye tuneful muses* (see No. **344**/5c).

771. Overture [in d minor]

(XXXI, 76)

2 *Vn, Va*   *Bc*

383

(1a) [Grave]

(1b) [Canzona]

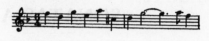

(1c) [Adagio]

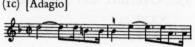

MSS: 454

EDITIONS: XXXI, 76

Overture à 4 in G Major (XXXI, 79; see No. **336**/1ab)

772. Overture à 5 [in g minor]

(XXXI, 82) ?1680

2 *Vn*, 2 *Va*, *Bc*

(1a) [Grave]

(1b) [Canzona]

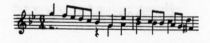

(1c) [Adagio]

MSS: 454

EDITIONS: XXXI, 82

COMMENTARY: The five-part string writing would suggest an early date.

N773. Prelude for solo violin [in g minor]

(XXXI, 93)

EDITIONS: XXXI, 93   1705m, 1708d (a fifth higher, in d minor)

COMMENTARY: This piece was discovered by Mr. Thurston Dart in exemplars of the editions mentioned above which are to be found in the Glen Collection, in the National Library of Scotland, and in the British Museum, respectively.

?Jig [in F Major] (See D257)

?Jig [in G Major] (See D255)

?Jig [in g minor] (See D256)

Mr. Mountfort's Farewell (See D254)

N774. 'Mr. Purcell's Jig'

1687

EDITIONS: 1687g, 1693d

COMMENTARY: See No. **430** ('When first Amintas sued for a kiss ').

780. Sonata [in g minor]

(XXXI, 95)

Vn (and *obbligato* B.Viol?)   *Bc*

(1a) [Grave]   (b) [Canzona]

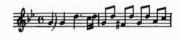

(2) [Largo]   (3) [Vivace]

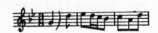

EDITIONS: XXXI, 95

COMMENTARY: According to Sir Frederick Bridge's remarks in one of his Gresham Lectures (see *Musical News*, March 7, 1903, p. 222) Purcell's *Sonata for Solo Violin*, then recently discovered, was found in a book belonging to Mr. Taphouse, of Oxford. It is reported to have been copied by one Mr. Armstrong for a certain Mr. Finch. The owner evidently had bought the MS at Puttick and Simpson's some time before the work was discovered, and he must have allowed it to go abroad before its existence became generally known in England. Sir Frederick was quite incensed that this important work should have been first published by Breitkopf & Härtel in Germany, and went on at great length about the many errors in this edition, which he listed in the next following issue, adding:

'Though the MS in the book Mr. Taphouse lent is quite clear, there are wrong notes in the bass ... and a dozen places where Purcell's harmony is wrongly read.'

In a subsequent issue of the same periodical, Sir Frederick published his own edition of the sonata, which was no doubt better than that he had castigated, even though the modern listener might detect a few instances of questionable taste, not to mention a few 'wrong harmonies', even in this. The justice of his remarks, as well as the authenticity of the work cannot be judged until this unique MS (which still eludes the best of England's musicological sleuths) is brought to light.

From the above account, it is obvious that the MS returned from its trip or journey shortly after the ungratifying edition's appearance. Indeed Sir Frederick mentions several contemporary performances from his own purified version at that time. The fate of this MS during its further sojourn in England has been well summed up by Mr. Thurston Dart, from whose article in the *Proceedings of the Royal Musical Association* (85th Session, 1958/59, p. 85) the following information is taken:

From Mr. Taphouse's collection the MS passed into that of William Cummings, who evidently lent it for an exhibition in 1904. On page 294 of *An Illustrated Catalogue of the Music Loan Exhibition ... 1904* (London: Novello, 1909) the following account of the MS is given:

'Violin Sonata in G minor. Contained in an oblong folio volume of 200 pages, in which are anthems, solos, canons, motets, &c. by Fiocco, Roseingrave, Gasparini, Geminiani, Lully [i.e. Loeillet], Edward Finch, and others. Formerly in the possession of James Bartleman: at the sale of his effects, February 22, 1822, it passed into the collection of George Pigott, of Dublin. Mr. Taphouse purchased the volume when sold by Messrs. Puttick & Simpson, February 21, 1889.' The MS then appears to have been missing for some time, turning up again at a sale of the effects of Miss E. A. Wilmott held by Sotheby's on April 11th, 1936.

LITERATURE: (?) F. Bridge, 'The Recently Discovered Violin Sonata,' *Musical News*, March 17th, 1903, p. 217.

?Sonata fragment [in c minor] (See D251)

?Sonata à 2 [in c minor] (See D252)

SONATAS OF THREE PARTS

790. Sonata I [in g minor]

(V, 1) 1683

2 *Vn, B.Viol, Bc*

(1) [Grave]

(2) Vivace

(3) Adagio

(4) Presto

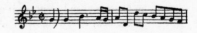

(5) Largo

MSS: 27, 201, 235, 441, 454, 617, 640, 712, 750

EDITIONS: V, 1, 1683c, 1683d

COMMENTARY: The supposed autograph copy of this and other sonatas of the 1683 set (Sibley MS 151841) is not in Purcell's hand, although it is an excellent score of these sonatas, in a neat hand much resembling that of several other late 17th to early 18th century MSS (notably Oxford, Bodleian Library MS Mus. Sch. D3).

791. Sonata II [in B♭ Major]

(V, 9) 1683

2 *Vn, B.Viol, Bc*

(1) [Allegro]

(2) Largo

(3) Presto

(4) Adagio—(Vivace)

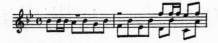

(5) [Allegro]

MSS: 27, 201 (inc), 235, 441, 454, 617, 640, 712, 750

EDITIONS: V, 9, 1683c, 1683d

792. Sonata III [in d minor]

(V, 18) 1683

2 *Vn, B.Viol, Bc*

(1a) [Grave]—(Adagio)

(1b) Canzona

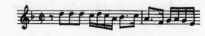

(2) Poco Largo

(3) Allegro

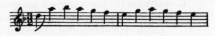

MSS: 27, 235, 441, 454, 617, 640, 712

EDITIONS: V, 18, 1683c, 1683d

793. Sonata IV [in F Major]

(V, 27) 1683

2 *Vn, B.Viol, Bc*

(1a) [Grave]

(1b) Canzona

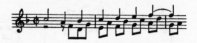

(2) Poco largo

(3) Allegro

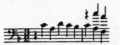

(4) [Adagio]

MSS: 27, 235, 441, 454, 617, 640, 712

EDITIONS: V, 27, 1683c, 1683d

794. Sonata V [in a minor]

(V, 35) 1683

2 *Vn, B.Viol, Bc*

(1) [Allegro]

(2) Adagio

(3) Largo   (4a) Grave   (4b) Canzona—(Adagio)

MSS: 27, 235, 441, 454, 617, 640, 712

EDITIONS: V, 35, 1683c, 1683d

795. VI [in C Major]

(V, 42) 1683

2 *Vn, B.Viol, Bc*

(1a) [Allegro]   (1b) Canzona

(2) Largo   (3) Allegro

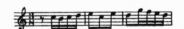

MSS: 27, 235, 441, 454, 617, 640, 712

EDITIONS: V, 42, 1683c, 1683d

COMMENTARY: The opening movement begins as a canon by two-fold augmentation in the 5th and 8th above. The 'theme' is similar to that which Purcell used for his didactic examples in the third part of Playford's *Introduction to the Skill of Music* (12th edition, 1694); see No. **870**.

796. Sonata VII [in e minor]

(V, 51) 1683

2 *Vn, B.Viol, Bc*

(1a) [Grave]   (1b) Canzona

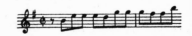

(2) Largo

(3) Grave

(4) Vivace

(5) Adagio

MSS: 27, 235, 441, 454, 617, 640, 712

EDITIONS: V, 51,   1683c, 1683d

COMMENTARY: The Largo (Section 2) begins with the same melodic material as No. **628**/3, although the rhythm differs.   Section 4 is entitled 'Allegro' in the basso continuo part in the 1683 edition (see EDITION 1683c).

797. Sonata VIII [in G Major]

(V, 61) 1683

2 *Vn, B.Viol, Bc*

(1) [Allegro]

(2a) Poco largo

(2b) Allegro

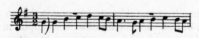

(3) Grave

(4) Vivace

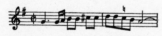

MSS: 27, 235, 441, 454, 570, 617, 640, 712

EDITIONS: V, 61,   1683c, 1683d

798. Sonata IX [in c minor]

(V, 71) 1683

2 *Vn, B.Viol, Bc*

(1) [Grave]

(2) Largo

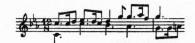

(3) Canzona—(Adagio)

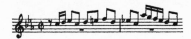

(4) Allegro

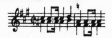

MSS: 27, 235, 441, 454, 617, 640, 712, 750

EDITIONS: V, 71, 1683c, 1683d

799. Sonata X [in A Major]

(V, 82) 1683

2 *Vn, B.Viol, Bc*

(1) [Grave]

(2) Largo

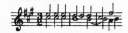

(3) Grave

(4) Presto

MSS: 27, 235, 441, 454, 617, 640, 712

EDITIONS: V, 82, 1683c, 1683d

800. Sonata XI [in f minor]

(V, 88) 1683

2 *Vn, B.Viol, Bc*

(1a) [Grave]

(1b) Canzona

(2) Adagio

(3) Largo

MSS: 27, 235, 441, 454, 617, 640, 712

EDITIONS: V, 88, 1683c, 1683d

801. Sonata XII [in D Major]

(V, 96) 1683

2 Vn, B.Viol, Bc

(1a) [Grave]

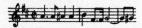

(1b) Canzona

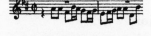

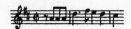

(2) Poco largo

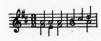

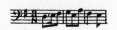

(3a) Grave

(3b) Presto

(4) Allegro—(Adagio)

MSS: 27, 235, 310 (inc, Trans), 441, 454, 617, 640, 712

EDITIONS: V, 96, 1683c, 1683d

SONATAS OF FOUR PARTS

802. Sonata I [in b minor]

(VII, 1)

2 Vn, B.Viol, Bc

(1a)

C: L Add 30930

(1b)

(2)

(3)

(4) Grave

MSS: 235, **324**, 399, 441, 597 (in a minor), 599 (in a minor)

EDITIONS: VII, 1, 1697d

COMMENTARY: Although the date usually associated with this set of Sonatas is that of their publication by Purcell's widow in 1697, the fact is that many of the sonatas are relatively early works. Several of these sonatas of the second set appear in Purcell's hand in British Museum MS Add. 30930, along with the early fantasias, etc. The sonatas are not dated, but the similarity of hand, paper and ink makes it seem unlikely that they were copied long after the fantasias. (See Thurston Dart in *PRMA*, 85th Session (1958/59).) Until further, more concrete evidence comes to light, these works should be listed without dates.

803. Sonata II [in E♭ Major]

(VII, 13)

2 *Vn, B.Viol, Bc*

(1a) [Grave]   (b)

(2)   (3)   (4)

MSS: 63, 235, **324**, 399, 441, 597, 599

EDITIONS: VII, 13, 1697d

804. Sonata III [in a minor]

(VII, 23)

2 *Vn, B.Viol, Bc*

(1) [Grave]   (2) [Largo]   (3)

393

O

(4)　　　　　　　　　　　　　(5) [Allegro]　　　　　　　(6) Grave

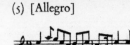　　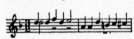　　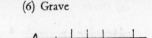

MSS: 235, **324**, 399, 441, 597, 599

EDITIONS: VII, 23,　1697d

COMMENTARY: Much of the continuo is missing in the autograph score, where the sonata ends on a fragment of a folio numbered 37*. On the verso Purcell had copied the first three bars of the violin parts before cutting out the fragment.

805. Sonata IV [in d minor]

(VII, 34)

2 Vn, B.Viol, Bc

(1a) [Grave]　　　　　　　　　　　　　　　　(1b) [Canzona]

(2) [Adagio]　　　　　　　(3) [Vivace]　　　　　　　(4) [Largo]

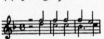　　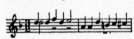　　

MSS: 235, **324** (inc), 399, 441

EDITIONS: VII, 34,　1697d

COMMENTARY: The first few bars of this piece are copied in a small fragment of a correction slip on the back of which is to be found the ending of Sonata No. 3 in a minor (see No. **804** above).

806. Sonata V [in g minor]

(VII, 46)

2 Vn, B.Viol, Bc

(1a) [Grave]　　　　　　　　(1b) [Canzona]　　　　　　(2) [Largo]

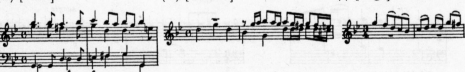

(3) [Adagio]   (4) Presto   (5) Adagio

MSS: 235, 399, 441

EDITIONS: VII, 46, 1697d

807. Sonata VI [in g minor]

(VII, 57)

2 Vn, B.Viol, Bc

[Adagio]

MSS: 235, 309, 441

EDITIONS: VII, 57, 1697d

COMMENTARY: This work is also known as the Great Chaconne in g minor. The ground is the same as that which appears in the 20th piece in *Musick's Handmaid*, II (see the Stainer and Bell edition, first published early in 1958), an anonymous transcription of a song-tune. Since preparing this edition, Mr. Dart has succeeded in identifying this. It is the same composition as that appearing in Br. Mus. Add. MS 22100, f. 77v: ' A Song upon a Ground " Scocca pur, tutti [tuoi] strali " ' by Mr. Baptist. In the index on f. 2v, it is ascribed to Lully, but the actual composer is probably Draghi.

808. Sonata VII [in C Major]

(VII, 70)

2 Vn, B.Viol, Bc

(1) [Vivace]   (2)

C: L Add 30930

(3a)   (3b)

(4)    (5)

MSS: 235, **324**, 399, 441, 612

EDITIONS: VII, 70, 1697d

COMMENTARY: In the autograph (British Museum MS Add. 30930) this piece is copied in the ' spidery hand ' also to be found in connection with other Purcell autographs. If not Purcell's own hand, with another sort of quill, it may be that of some amanuensis (perhaps Mrs. Purcell?) who was in close connection with Purcell throughout most of his career.

809. Sonata VIII [in g minor]

(VII, 82)

2 Vn, B.Viol, Bc

(1a)    (1b) [Canzona]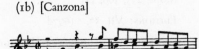

(1c)    (2)   (3)

MSS: 235, **324**, 399, 441, 612

EDITIONS: VII, 82, 1697d

810. Sonata IX (' The Golden ') [in F Major]

(VII, 93)

2 *Vn, B.Viol, Bc*

(1) [Allegro]   (2a)

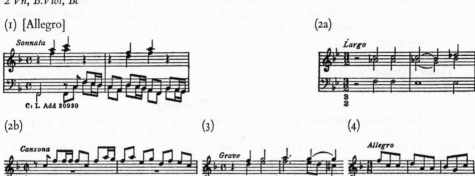

(2b)   (3)   (4)

MSS: 57, 63, 95, 235, **324**, 399, 441, 485, 612, 629, 857, 873

EDITIONS: VII, 93, 1697d, 1704b, 1707b, ?1727 (Section 4: *Vn* I and *Bc* only)

COMMENTARY: Apparently the earliest edition naming this as the ' Golden Sonata ' was that of 1704 (see EDITION 1704b).

LITERATURE: J. Wharton Sharp, ' The Golden Sonata,' *The Strad*, v. 20, No. 233.

811. Sonata X [in D Major]

(VII, 106)

2 *Vn, B.Viol, Bc*

(1a) [Grave]   (1b)

(2)   (3)

(4)

MSS: 235, **324**, 399, 441, 629

EDITIONS: VII, 106, 1697d

COMMENTARY: The first movement of this sonata probably served Daniel Purcell as model for his overture to the Additional Act of *The Indian Queen*, according to Michael Tilmouth in his article 'The Technique and Forms of Purcell's Sonatas,' *Music and Letters*, vol. 40, no. 2, April 1959, p. 110

Tinker's Dance (See D253)

GENERAL LITERATURE

J. F. Bridge, 'Purcell's Fantazias and Sonatas,' *Proceedings of the Musical Association*, 1915–16, p. 1; T. Dart, 'Purcell's Chamber Music,' *Proceedings of the Royal Musical Association*, 1958–59, p. 81; H. Davey, *History of English Music*, London: Curwen & Sons, 1895, p. 357; R. Donington, 'Further Seventeenth- and Eighteenth-Century Evidence on the Performance of Purcell's Works,' [Appendix B] in *Henry Purcell 1659–1695: Essays on His Music* [I. Holst, ed.], London: O.U.P., 1959, p. 123; A. Holland, *Henry Purcell*, London: Penguin Books, 1948, p. 105; S. Lingorow, 'Der Instrumental Stil von Purcell,' Bern: Buchdruckerei Eichner & Co., 1949; W. Newman, *The Sonata in the Baroque Era*, Chapel Hill: University of North Carolina Press, 1959; E. Walker, *History of Music in England*, (3rd edition, rev. by J. A. Westrup), Oxford: Clarendon Press, 1952; W. Whittaker, 'Some Observations on Purcell's Harmony,' *Musical Times*, Oct. 1934.

TRUMPET AND STRINGS

850. Sonata [in D Major]

(XXXI, 86),   ?1694

Tpt, 2 Vn, Va   *Bc*

(1) [Allegro]   (2) Adagio   (3) [Presto]

MSS: 485, 865

EDITIONS: XXXI, 86

COMMENTARY: Michael Tilmouth ('The Technique and Forms of Purcell's Sonatas,' *Music and Letters*, vol. 40, No. 2, p. 109) suggests that this sonata may have been the overture to Purcell's setting of Matthew Prior's New Year's Ode of 1693/4: *Light of the World* (see No. **330**).

Sonata for Trumpet solo (see Overture to *Timon of Athens*/Comm)

WIND CONSORT

860. March and Canzona

XXXI, 92, 1692

4 *Flatt Tpt* [i.e. slide trumpets and trombones] ?*Kdr*

(1) March [Grave]

(2) Canzona

MSS: 632, 679

EDITION: XXXI, 92

COMMENTARY: In Oriel College, Oxford, MS Ua 37/3 is a copy of this work with the heading: 'Queen's Funeral March, sounded before her chariot, Mr. Purcell.' The march was for the funeral of Queen Mary, who died on the 28th of December, 1694, of small-pox. The funeral cortège to Westminster Abbey took place on March 5th, and Purcell's 'March and Canzona' sounded as accompaniment. As Mr. Thurston Dart has pointed out in the preface to his edition of this work (Oxford University Press, 1958) the band of flat trumpets (slide trumpets) and sackbuts (tenor and/or bass trombones) was certainly supported by kettle drums, and perhaps by other percussion instruments. Purcell had already used these compositions as part of the music for *The Libertine* (see No. **600**/2a).

LITERATURE: F. W. Galpin 'The Sackbut, Its Evolution and History,' *Proceedings of the Musical Association*, 33rd Session, 1906/07, p. 1; W. Barclay Squire, 'Purcell's Music for the Funeral of Queen Mary II,' *SIMG*. IV, pp. 225–33.

DIDACTIC EXAMPLES

870. Counterpoint and Canon

(XXXI, 101–7) 1694

A. **Examples in two parts** XXXI, 101–2

(1) 'Fuge in the fourth below'

¢: Introduction to the Skill of Music, 12th Edition

(2) 'Imitation or reports'

(3) 'Double fuge'

(4) 'Per Arsin et Thesin'

(5) 'Per Augmentation'

(6) 'Recte et Retro'

(7a) 'Double Descant'

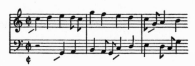

(7b) 'Reply'

(8) Canon in the 8th or 15th

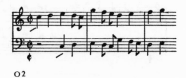

EDITIONS: (XXXI, 101–2), 1694c, 1697b, 1700d, 1718a

LITERATURE: W. Barclay Squire, ' Purcell as Theorist,' *Sammelbände der Internationalen Musikgesell-schaft*, VI, pp. 521–67.

B. Examples in three parts

(1) ' Plain fugeing '

(2) ' Double fugeing '

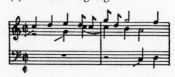

(3) ' Per Arsin & Thesin '

(4) ' Per Augmentation '

(5) ' Recte & Rectro '

(6) ' Double Descant '

(7) Triple fugue

EDITIONS: XXXI, 102–4, 1694c, 1697b, 1700d, 1718a

LITERATURE: W. Barclay Squire, ' Purcell as Theorist,' *Sammelbände der Internationalen Musikgesell-schaft*, VI, pp. 521–67

C. Examples in four parts

(1) ' Plain fugeing '

(2) ' Double fugeing '

(3) 'Per Arsin & Thesin'

(4) 'Per Augmentation'

(5) 'Recte & Retro'

(6) 'Four fugues carried on, interchanging one with another'

D. Canons on Sacred Texts

(1) Gloria Patri, 'A Canon Three Parts in One' (XXXI, 104)

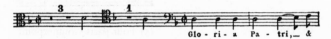

(2) Miserere mei, 'A Canon, Four in Two' (XXXI, 107)

(3) Glory be to the Father, 'A Canon, Four in One' (Playford, p. 141)

EDITIONS: XXXI, 104, 1694c, 1697b

COMMENTARY: Although unsigned, these paradigms in Playford's 12th and 13th (and following) editions of *Introduction to the Skill of Musick* are probably by Purcell. At least they did not appear in previous editions, and are as admissable as the foregoing exercises, which are entered here for the same reasons.

871. Miscellaneous Exercises

(XXXI, *passim*)

(J. Playford: *An Introduction to the Skill of Musick*, Book III, 12th edition, 1694)

(1) 'Several Examples of taking Discords elegantly'

  (a) '. . . taking of Ninths and Sevenths'   (b) '. . . taking the lesser Fourth'

       (p. 95)   (p. 95)

  (c) '. . . taking the Greater Fourth'   (d) '. . . taking two Sevenths in

       (p. 95)   two Parts' (p. 96)

  (2) 'Counterpoint or bass to Tunes or   (3) 'Composition of Three Parts'

     Songs' (p. 101)   (p. 116)

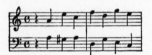 

(4) 'Tune with Second Treble' (p. 116)   (5) Four parts Counterpoint

                                          (p. 130)

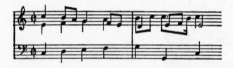 

(6) Elegant [Italianate] Passages

  (a) Sharp and Flat Seventh (p. 131)   (b) 'Flat sixth before a Close' (p. 132)

(c) Third and Fourth Together (p. 132)   (d) [Pedal point] (p. 133)

EDITIONS: XXXI, *passim* 1694c, 1697b, 1700d, 1718a

APPENDIX I: DOUBTFUL ASCRIPTIONS TO PURCELL

ANTHEMS

D1. Awake up my glory

Psalm 57

Verse: *sb*   *Bc* (not indicated)   Chorus: *SATB*

MSS: 40 (Bass only), 411 (Bass only)

COMMENTARY: Both known sources for this work are comparatively late, neither ascription being completely trustworthy. This anthem differs from that by Michael Wise in British Museum MS Add. 30932 and elsewhere.

D2. Glory be to God on high

Luke 2: 14

Verse: *?sb*   Chorus: *?SATB*

(a) Glory be to God: *s*   (b) And on earth peace: *b*

MSS: 98

EDITIONS: 1765b

COMMENTARY: The printed source mentions this anthem as 'taken out of the Communion Service'. The awkward word setting makes this appear a doubtful ascription. In British Museum MS Add. 30478, f. 54, this text (as set by John Foster) is subtitled 'The Thanksgiving after the Holy Communion'.

D3. O be joyful

Psalm 100

MSS: 69

EDITIONS: 1731e, 1765b

COMMENTARY: This anthem is printed anonymously in John Chetham's *A Book of Psalmody*, 1731, beginning on p. 1 of the Appendix (actually the 177th page of the whole volume). At the end appears the direction: 'For the rest of the chorus see page 160.' The *Gloria Patri* printed there is the same as that shown herein as D21.

D4. O God, they that love Thy name

Psalm 5: 11–12

(XXXII, 120)

MSS: 162, 166hi

EDITIONS: XXXII, 120

COMMENTARY: Parts of this incomplete anthem appear in three Durham Cathedral manuscripts: MUS C.28 (a bass book), C.34 (a bass book) and A.33 (an organ book). Until other sources, and the remaining parts for the anthem, are discovered, it must remain in the 'doubtful' category.

D5. O pray for the peace

Psalm 122: 7

MSS: 164b (index only)

D6. Peace be within thy walls

Psalm 122: 6

This anthem was mentioned by Burney (IV, 506), but no copy is known.

D7. Sing we merrily unto God

Verse: *atb*   ?*Bc*   Chorus: *SATB*

MSS: 696

EDITIONS: 1720m, 1723, 1725a, 1725d, 1730d, 1753

COMMENTARY: This anthem is ascribed to Purcell in several undated editions collected and printed by Francis Timbrel in the early part of the eighteenth century. The provisional date, *ca.* 1730, given in one of the volumes in the British Museum Catalogue (press-mark: A.1232.1) is probably wrong. On a back page of the edition, in a contemporary hand, appears the inscription 'Thomas Bradford: Ano Domini 1723,' according to which the date may be advanced to *ca.* 1720 or earlier. The anthem also appears in Michael Broome's *Collection of Church Music* of 1725.

D8. Turn Thee again, O Lord

Psalm 80: 3 (paraphrased)

Full: *SATB*

Turn Thee a - gain, O Lord God.

EDITIONS: 1828[–44]

COMMENTARY: This setting is very similar, though not the same, as one by George Jeffries as shown in British Museum MS Add. 10338, f. 177v.

CANONS AND CHANTS

D15. Alleluia

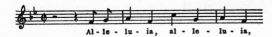

Al - le - lu - ia, al - le - lu - ia,

EDITIONS: 1754a, 1758b

D21. Glory be to the Father

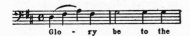

Glo - ry be to the

EDITIONS: 1731e, 1754a, 1758b

COMMENTARY: This is printed as the final chorus to another anthem doubtfully ascribed to Purcell in John Chetham's *A Book of Psalmody*, 1731 (see **D5**/Commentary).

D22. Laudate Dominum (Canon 3 in 1)

Lau - da - te Do - mi - num___ de Coe - lis

MSS: 315

EDITIONS: 1687a, 1688c, 1703e, 1718a, 1733b

COMMENTARY: In Arthur Bedford's *The Excellency of Divine Musick*, London, 1733, p. 62, this canon is printed as ' A Canon for three parts, in the fifth and eighth below, rising a Note every Time . . .' to the words ' O all ye nations of the earth . . .'.

D30. Single Chant [in A Major]

MSS: 141

COMMENTARY: This chant was copied by John Reading, organist of Dulwich College *ca.* 1717. The ascription to Purcell is doubtful because Reading's attributions have not been altogether trustworthy in another instance (see **D33**).

D31. Single Chant [in C Major]

MSS: 648

EDITIONS: 1767a

COMMENTARY: There are several copies of the edition in which this appears (C. and S. Thompson: *Fifty Double Chants*) in the British Museum. In the copy shelved under press-mark E–487 a marginal note in an unidentified hand states: 'This is generally called 'The Grand Chant' and is attributed to Pelham Humfrey.' In Christ Church College, Oxford, MS 1226, this work is so entitled and ascribed to 'Humphries alias Purcell.' In British Museum MS Add. 17784, the Chant is ascribed straightforwardly to Humfrey.

D32. Chant [in G Major]

MSS: 359

D33. Chant [in g minor]

XXX,

MSS: 141, 649, 795d, 850h

EDITIONS: XXX, 1828[–44]

COMMENTARY: Although attributed to Purcell by John Reading in Dulwich College, MS 2, the work is the same as that ascribed to Thomas Purcell, and called the 'Funeral Chant', by Vincent Novello. It was also printed by Burney (Mercer edition, II, 381) who described it as 'the burial chant'.

D34. Chant [in g minor]

MSS: 169

COMMENTARY: The unique source for this chant (Durham Cathedral Library MS D12) provides only the alto part.

D35. Venite. Chant [in G Major]

MSS: 169

COMMENTARY: The alto part alone appears in the manuscript source, Durham Cathedral Library MS D12.

D36. Chant [in g minor]

MSS: 169

COMMENTARY: Only the alto part is given in the MS source, Durham Cathedral Library MS D12.

D37. Chant [in B♭ Major]

MSS: 863

APPENDIX I

D38. Chant [in g minor]

Full: *SATB*

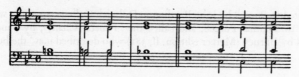

EDITIONS: *A Companion to Congregational Praise*, Congregational Praise Ind. Press, 1951, No. 884, and other similar modern editions.

HYMNS AND PSALMS

D40. Far from me be all false ways

Verse: *ab*   Chorus: *SATB*

Far, far from me be all false ways.

EDITIONS: 1772–4

D41. O God, sole object of our love

O God, sole ob-ject of our love

EDITIONS: 1772–4

D42. O that my grief was throughly weigh'd

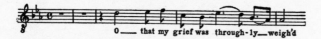

O that my grief was through-ly weigh'd

MSS: Royal College of Music, London, MS 518, reputedly in the hand of Philip Hayes, a source too late for inclusion in Appendix III.

D43. Put me not to rebuke, O Lord

Verse: *atb*   *Bc*

Put me not to re-buke, O Lord.

MSS: 69

D44. The gracious bounty of our God

The gra - cious boun - ty of__ our__ God

EDITIONS: 1772–4

D45. Walsall

Full: *SATB*

MSS: 314

EDITIONS: *ca.* 1721 (see also manuscript additions to *Tunes* ... Engraved by Francis Hoffman: British Museum MS Add. 3433, f. 10).

COMMENTARY: The tune was later used by Christopher Roberts for an organ prelude (published London: Bayley & Ferguson, 1924). He ascribed it to Purcell, and appended the accompanying text:

[When came in flesh th'in - car - nate word]

D46. Westminster Abbey

Full: *SATB*

EDITIONS: *A Companion to Congregational Praise*, Congregational Praise Ind. Press, 1951, No. 237, and other similar modern editions.

SACRED SONGS AND DUETS

D69. Arise, great dead, for arms renown'd

A - rise,_____ great dead

MSS: 758

D70. Arise, my darken'd melancholy soul

(XXX,)

Solo: *t*   *Bc*

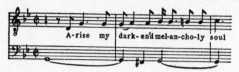

A-rise my dark- en'd mel-an-cho-ly soul

MSS: 343, 348

EDITIONS: XXX,   , 1828[-44]

COMMENTARY: The known manuscript sources with this work give the following ascriptions:

    Br. Mus. Add. 33235, f. 47: Purcell
    Br. Mus. Add. 31460, f. 80ᵛ: Anon.
    Br. Mus. Add. 31460, f. 85v: Blow
    Birmingham, Barber Institute MS M5002, p.60: Blow

    The weight of evidence thus favours Blow.

LITERATURE: H. L. Clarke, *John Blow*, unpublished Doctoral Dissertation, Harvard University, 1947, vol. I, p. 94.

D71. It must be done, my soul

William Norris, ' The Meditation '

Solo: *b*   *Bc*

It must be done, my soul,   it

MSS: 14, 26

EDITIONS: *The Score*, January 4th, 1951

COMMENTARY: This sacred song is ascribed to Purcell in the Barber Institute MS 5002 (p. 138), dating from *ca.* 1700. It also appears in an MS in the library of the Conservatoire Royal de Musique in Brussels (MS 1035), there ascribed to Francis Bragge. The text alone appears in British Museum MS Add. 39316, on f. 57, under the ascription: ' Wm Norris of Bamerton, altered by Catherine Talbot.'

D72. My op'ning eyes are purg'd

' A divine song on the Passion of our Saviour.'

Solo: *s*   *Bc*

My op - 'ning eyes are purg'd, and lo!   a dis-mal

EDITIONS: 1693b, 1714a, 1714b, 1828[–44]

COMMENTARY: This work is anonymous in *Harmonia Sacra*, II, of 1693, and in both editions of that volume which appeared in 1714. Apparently the first ascription of the work to Purcell was made by Vincent Novello. From some of the alterations (corrections?) in his edition (see Vol. III, p. 758) it is possible to suppose that he may have used another source.

D73. O give thanks

Psalm 105

Solo: *t*   Bc

MSS: 69

EDITIONS: 1714b, 1726a, 1750a

COMMENTARY: This work is anonymous in Kings College, Cambridge, Rowe Library MS 20 (p. 249), though indicated as possibly by Barber in the index to that MS. In the catalogue it is ascribed to Purcell. The style of the work, as well as the foregoing evidence, makes this ascription extremely doubtful.

D74. O praise the Lord, laud ye the name

EDITIONS: 1717

COMMENTARY: John Weldon, in his *Divine Harmony*, ascribed this work to one 'Dr. P' without giving any further clue to the identity of the composer. In 1717 'Dr. P' would almost certainly have been understood to be Pepusch.

D75. Praise the Lord, O my soul and all that is within me

MSS: 185

COMMENTARY: In Ely Cathedral Library MS 9 this work is ascribed to Purcell in both the earlier and later manuscripts appended to the volume (though only by means of ditto marks in the first), but has only a pencilled ascription where the composition is copied in.

D76. The Lord, ev'n the most mighty

The Lord,— ev'n the most migh- ty God—

MSS: 764

D77. The night is come

Sir Thomas Browne, 'A Colloquy with God': *Religio Medici*, 1643, (Spurious edition printed 1642)

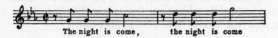

The night is come, the night is come

EDITIONS: 1693b, 1714a, 1828[-44]

COMMENTARY: This work was published anonymously in *Harmonia Sacra*, II, of 1693. Apparently the first ascription to Purcell was made by Vincent Novello in his edition of 1828[-44].

D78. Soon as the morn salutes your eyes

Soon as the morn sa - lutes

EDITIONS: 1772-4

D90. Sanctus

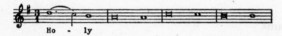

Ho - ly

MSS: 664

COMMENTARY: The only known copy of this piece occurs in an organ book in the Library of Magdalen College, Oxford. The hand in which it is copied (probably dating from the early eighteenth century) is somewhat similar to that of Daniel Purcell.

D91. Te Deum in C

We praise Thee, O Lord.   We praise _____ Thee

MSS: 864, 871

COMMENTARY: The two manuscripts which seem to be the only sources for this work appear to be soprano and bass part-books of a set from which other parts are missing. The manuscripts are late, and are not reliable sources.

CATCHES

D100. Fie, nay prithee, John

XXII, 18, 1685; 'A scolding catch', Anon: H. Playford's *Wit and Mirth*, 1682

Fie, nay pri-thee, John, do not quar-rel, man

MSS: 43, 309, 310, 317, 318, 598, 604 (anon.), 866

EDITIONS: XXII, 18, *ca.* 1680, 1682d (mnp), 1684d (mnp), 1685c, 1686a, 1686d (Trans), 1687e 1687g (Mock), 1693d (Trans, anon.), 1701b, 1703g, 1704c, 1707e, 1707f, 1709e, 1710a, 1711a, 1711c (anon.), 1713b, 1716b, 1720n, 1721b, ?1750, *ca.*1790, 1800c

COMMENTARY: In most of the manuscript sources indicated above, this catch is anonymous. However, in one near contemporary MS, British Museum Add. 22099, it is attributed to John Blow, as it is in MS Add. 30273, dated 1833. In MS Add. 29397, there is a queried ascription to Fishburn, while both he and Blow are mentioned in a pencil note in the copy itself. Otherwise, the work is ascribed to Purcell only in MSS (such as Add. 31463) of the late eighteenth century or later. The catch is also anonymous in all printed editions before that of 1704, after which it is regularly ascribed to Purcell. There are mistakes in the Purcell Society version. Although copied as an anonymous work in Cambridge, Fitzwilliam Museum MS 118, the catch appears in the midst of several other pieces ascribed to Blow.

D101. Hail happy words, abodes of peace

A round

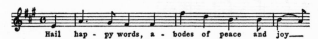

Hail hap - py words, a - bodes of peace and joy——

EDITIONS: 1844

D102. Let's live good honest lives

3 *voices* (16-bar intervals)

Let's live good hon - est lives

MSS: 317, 866

EDITIONS: 1685c, 1701b, 1704c, 1707e, 1707f, 1709e, 1711a, 1720n, 1724c, 1726c, 1731b, 1733a, 1740g, ?1750, 1805

COMMENTARY: According to information given in British Museum MS Add. 29386, this catch was adapted from Cranford by Purcell. In another manuscript source (York Minster library MS 19), it is ascribed to Purcell without qualification. In British Museum MS Add. 31463 (a late source) it is ascribed to Cranford (on f. 16v). In the printed sources, it is anonymous in the first source and ascribed to Purcell, either directly or by implication, in all of the later sources. Hawkins has stated, concerning Cranford: 'He composed that catch in particular to which Purcell afterwards put the words, "Let's live good honest lives".' (IV, p. 613).

D103. Say, good master Bacchus

Say, good mas - ter Bac-chus, a - stride on your butt

EDITIONS: 1691b, 1702f, 1704c, 1707c, 1707e ,1707f, 1709c, 1709e, 1711a

COMMENTARY: This catch appears anonymously in all early sources.

D104. Since women so false and so jiltish are grown

(XXII, 19)

MSS: 309

EDITIONS: XXII, 19

COMMENTARY: This work is to be found only in one unreliable manuscript source, British Museum
MS Add. 19759, f. 40. Until other sources come to light, the ascription to Purcell will remain
doubtful.

D105. The glass was just tim'd

(XXII, 18)

MSS: 317, British Museum Add. 31462 (f. 21) and Add. 31463 (f. 50)

EDITIONS: XXII, 18, *The Catch Club, ca. 1760*

COMMENTARY: All of the known sources for this catch date from the last half of the eighteenth
century. None of these is entirely trustworthy.

D106. Tom, making a mantua for a lass

'Tom the Tailor'

(XXII, 19)

MSS: 45, 317

EDITIONS: XXII, 19, 1702f, 1704c, 1707c, 1709c, 1709e, 1710a, 1711a, 1720n, 1724c, 1726c, 1731b,
1733a, 1740g

COMMENTARY: In the earliest printed sources this catch appears anonymously. In Pearson's
Supplement of New Catches, 1707, and his *Pleasant Musical Companion*, 1720, it is ascribed to
Henry Hall. Manuscript sources (such as British Museum MSS Add. 29386 and 31463) which
ascribe the work to Purcell are not reliable. The text has been bowdlerized in the Purcell
Society Edition.

D107. Well rung, Tom boy

MSS: 317, British Museum MS Add. 31462, and Add. 31463

EDITIONS: 1686a, 1687e, 1701b, 1707ee, 1707f, 1709f, 1720n, 1724c, 1726c, 1731b, 1733a, 1740g

COMMENTARY: Most manuscript sources ascribe this work to the unknown early eighteenth(?) century composer Mr. Miller, while most printed sources give the work as anonymous.

D120. 'Address of the Children of the Chapel Royal to the King, and their master, Capt. Cooke, on his Majesty's birthday, A.D. 1670, composed by master Purcell, one of the children of the said chapel.'

Lost. Said to have been in the possession of Dr. Rimbault. There is the possibility that no such document ever existed, for apparently no one besides Rimbault ever saw the work.

SOLO SONGS

D130. A quire of bright beauties

MSS: 168

COMMENTARY: The text without music is to be found in British Museum MS Add. 28253, f. 65v, where it is entitled 'A Jacobite Song'. The manuscript is undated, but the copy probably originated in the late seventeenth century.

D131. As unconcern'd and free as air

MSS: The 'Cummings' MS (Now in the Nanki Collection?)

EDITIONS: 1706e, 1707g, 1709h, 1720s

COMMENTARY: This song is given anonymously in all the printed sources. The manuscript source is not available for examination, but is said to ascribe this work to Purcell.

D132. Away fond love, thou foe to rest

MSS: 39

COMMENTARY: This song has been catalogued as one of Purcell's compositions in the catalogue of the music in the Fitzwilliam Museum, Cambridge, although it appears in the manuscript as an anonymous work. It almost certainly is not by Purcell.

D133. How peaceful the days are

The Last and Best Edition of New Songs, 1677

How peace - ful the days are

MSS: 309

EDITIONS: 1679, 1696n

COMMENTARY: One verse only was printed anonymously in *Choice Ayres* (1679) Book II.

D134. In Cloe's sparkling eyes

In Clo - e's spark-ling, spark - - - ling

MSS: 870

EDITIONS: 1702b

COMMENTARY: This song was discovered in a manuscript in the York Minster library by the late Gerald Cooper. The manuscript seems to have disappeared since then. In *Mercurius Musicus*, 1702, a setting of the same text is ascribed to William Croft.

D135. Musing, I late on Windsor Terras sate

Thomas D'Urfey: *Musa et Musica, ca.* 1710

Mus - ing, I late on Wind-sor Ter-ras sate

MSS: 358 (anon.)

EDITIONS: 1710hh, 1714c, *ca.* 1715, 1716c

COMMENTARY: In British Museum MS Add. 35043, f. 122, this song appears anonymously as a 'Welsh Air' (the title being written in pencil in a later hand than that which copied the music).

D136. Of noble race was Shinkin

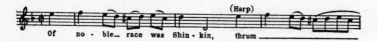

Of no - ble race was Shin - kin, thrum

MSS: 313, 316, 358 (anon.), 598

EDITIONS: 1693k, 1695p, 1698f, 1699e, 1701c, 1703g, 1707g, 1711c, 1713b, 1714c, 1716b, 1716c, 1719b, 1721b, 1729–31

COMMENTARY: The text is ascribed to 'Mr. Jno. Davis, Chaplain to the Earl of Northampton' in British Museum MS Add. 30162. It is there said to have been translated into Greek. Traditionally, the text has been assigned to Thomas D'Urfey. 'Shinkin' is intended to represent the Welsh pronunciation of 'Jenkin'.

D137. One long Whitsun holiday

'The Parson among the Peas', Thomas D'Urfey

One long Whit - sun ho-li-day

MSS: 316, 366, 368

EDITIONS: 1714c, 1716c, 1718b, 1719a, 1719b, 1719c, 1728b

COMMENTARY: Sir John Hawkins (2nd edition, p. 818) relates the anecdote according to which D'Urfey challenged Purcell to set these words 'which left the latter more pains to set with a tune than the composition of his Te Deum.' Nevertheless, the sources all give the work as anonymous, so that it can only doubtfully be ascribed to Purcell, at least at present.

D138. Sunny, rich and fantastic; The Old Tumbler

Thomas D'Urfey: *New Poems*, 1690; and *Miscellany Poems*, 1690

The music is lost

(Also recorded in Day & Murrie as **Smug, rich and fantastic old Fumbler was known**)

EDITIONS: 1719a (mnp), 1719b (mnp)

D140. 'Tis vain to fly like wounded deer

'Tis vain, 'tis vain,— 'tis vain, 'tis vain

MSS: 442

EDITIONS: 1696n

COMMENTARY: This song appears in the Gresham College autograph (MS vi.5.6) with no indication that it is not one of Henry Purcell's own compositions. However, in the year following his death, it was published in *Thesaurus Musicus*, Book V, as a song by Daniel Purcell. Evidence available at present is insufficient to determine who actually composed the work.

D141. View well those stars

View, view well those stars,

MSS: 39

D142. What ungrateful devil makes you come

Gentleman's Journal (July, 1693); Love's Last Shift (1696) mnp

What un-grate-ful— De-vil makes you come?

MSS: 442, 628

EDITIONS: 1696n, 1699e, 1707g, 1714c, 1719b

D143. When first Dorinda's piercing eyes

'The Captive Lover'

Solo: s   Bc

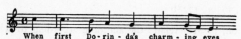

When first Do-rin-da's charm-ing eyes

MSS: 701

EDITIONS: London: Novello & Ewer, 1895

COMMENTARY: The manuscript source has 'piercing' in the index and title, 'charming' in the text of the song. The printed edition gives the sub-title.

D144. While Phyllis is drinking

?Lord Lansdowne, 1696

While Phyl-lis is— drink-ing

MSS: 670, 866

D145. Young Strephon he has woo'd me

Elkanah Settle

Young Stre-phon, he— has woo'd— me

EDITIONS: 1711c, 1714c (ascribed to Daniel Purcell), 1720s

THREE-PART SONGS

D171. A poor blind woman that has no sight at all

'The Blind Beggar's Song'

(XXII, 187)

Solo: ssb

A poor blind wo-man, that has no sight— at all

EDITIONS: XXII, 187, 1744, 1745c, 1745d

COMMENTARY: The caption to this song in Walsh's *Orpheus Britannicus* reads: 'Composed for 3 voices by the late Famous Mr. Henry Purcell, found among some of his old manuscripts and never before published.' These MSS appear to have been lost.

D172. When the cock begins to crow

(XXII, 181)

MSS: 215, 385

EDITIONS: XXII, 181, 1711b, 1712a, 1721a

COMMENTARY: The editor of vol. XXII of the Purcell Society Edition suggests that this was probably intended for insertion in *The Fairy Queen*, reasoning no doubt from a slight similarity of the text to that of Section 5 of that opera. The fact that it did not appear in the earlier editions of *Orpheus Britannicus* makes the ascription to Purcell even more dubious.

D200. [? Neglected Virtue, or the Unhappy Conqueror]

?before 1695; Charles Hopkins, *Tragedy*

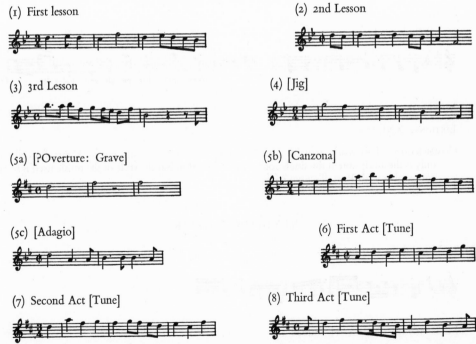

(1) First lesson

(2) 2nd Lesson

(3) 3rd Lesson

(4) [Jig]

(5a) [?Overture: Grave]

(5b) [Canzona]

(5c) [Adagio]

(6) First Act [Tune]

(7) Second Act [Tune]

(8) Third Act [Tune]

(9) Fourth Act [Tune]

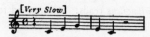

MSS: 358

COMMENTARY: So far the only evidence that links Purcell's name with the music represented above is the heading in British Museum MS Add. 35043, on f. 63v: 'Tunes to Mr. Horden's Play by Mr. P'. The connection appears even more tenuous in view of the fact that Hildebrand Horden (the actor most probably alluded to in the above heading) is not known to have written a play. However, he did write (and deliver) a prologue for *Neglected Virtue*. Horden signed the prologue and, in the course of it, said '... Both myself and my friend, the author of this unsuccessful piece, as we cannot pretend to justify its defects ... &c' The true author of the play appears to have been Charles Hopkins, an obscure dramatist who flourished about the turn of the century.

There are other arguments against the ascription to Purcell. The play was published and, probably, was first acted in 1696, after Purcell's death. Nevertheless, it is just possible that Purcell could have written music for it well in advance of the production. More serious objections spring from the character of the music itself which is not unmistakeably Purcellian in style. Then, too, at the time it would have been unusual for Purcell's name to have been omitted in any production in which his music had a part. The ascription to Purcell in the MS and that in the Hughes-Hughes *Catalogue of Manuscript Music* in the British Museum II: Secular Vocal Music, p. 231 are both extremely doubtful. The pieces are probably by Paisible.

D201. Unidentified Play

(XXI, 171)

(1a) Prelude: 2 *Vn*   (1b) When Night her purple veil: *b, Bc*

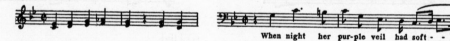

MSS: 758

EDITIONS: XXI, 171

COMMENTARY: This work, actually a small cantata, is almost certainly not by Henry Purcell. Not only is the ascription in the single source most doubtful, but the style of the music itself is scarcely compatible with Purcell's own style.

KEYBOARD WORKS

D218. Almand [in a minor]

MSS: 367 (ascribed to 'H. Purcell').

D219/1. Almand (rather, Gavotte) in D-sol-re♯ **D219/2. Borry (rather, Saraband) in D-sol-re♯**

(VI, 55)   (VI, 55)

MSS: 470   MSS: 470

EDITIONS: VI, 55, 1696a   EDITIONS: VI, 55

COMMENTARY: The source for this piece is a manuscript copy bound into one British Museum copy of *A Choice Collection of Lessons for the Harpsichord* of 1696 (cf. K.1.c.5, pp. 74–6). Their authenticity is doubtful, and their titles wrong.

D220. Gavotte [in G Major]

(VI, 50)

MSS: 58, 141

EDITIONS: VI, 50

COMMENTARY: This piece occurs anonymously within a group of other pieces ascribed to Purcell in Cambridge, Fitzwilliam Museum MS 52.B.7. (See Commentary to No. **643** above.) In Dulwich College, MS 4, the same Gavott, with several extended (and rather trite) variations is ascribed to William Babell. However, this does not necessarily disprove the ascription of the work to Purcell. As may be seen in British Museum MS Add. 39569, Babell so treated several works by Purcell and others.

D221. Ground

(VI, 51)

MSS: 58 (and two missing 'Cummings' MSS)

EDITIONS: VI, 51

COMMENTARY: In the two 'Cummings' MSS described in the Purcell Society Edition vol. VI, Commentary, as 'now missing', this piece appears once anonymously, once with the ascription 'Ground by Mr. Crofts' in which 'Mr. Crofts' has been crossed out and replaced with 'Purcell'. Apart from this evidence, the work is ascribed to Purcell only on the strength of the editor's opinion.

D222. Ground [in d minor]

MSS: 292

EDITIONS: William Barclay Squire (ed.), *Henry Purcell: Original Works for the Harpsichord,* London: Chester, 1918; iv, 24

D223. Jig [in g minor]

EDITIONS: 1706c

COMMENTARY: This Jig is grouped with two Suite movements in d minor (See No. **T696**/1, 2), but is not definitely ascribed to Purcell.

D224. Minuet [in d minor]

MSS: 310 (attributed to Croft), 596

COMMENTARY: In Oxford Bodleian MS Mus. Sch. E.397 this piece is given as a 'Fragment from *The Indian Queen.*' (See No. **630**/Commentary.)

D225. Minuet [in e minor]

MSS: 355

EDITIONS: William Barclay Squire (ed.), *Henry Purcell: Original Works for the Harpsichord,* London: Chester, 1918; iv, 23

D226. Overture [in A Major]

MSS: 58

D227. Rigadoon [in d minor]

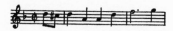

MSS: 570

D228. Suite [in g minor]

(1) [Minuet]

(2) Gavott

(3) Variations

(4) Chacone (See No. **T680**)

MSS: 58

COMMENTARY: The first three movements above are to be found in the Fitzwilliam Museum, Cambridge, MS 52.B.7, forming a suite with the Chacone, which appears among the authentic works in this Catalogue. Apart from the fact that the first piece is ascribed to Purcell in the index of the MS, the grouping of these together with a known Purcell work warrants their admission at least to this 'Doubtful' section.

D229. Toccata

MSS: 312, 335 (attributed to 'Mr. Hen: Purcell'), 356

COMMENTARY: This work has been variously attributed to J. S. Bach, Michelangelo Rossi, and Purcell. The ascription to Bach (see Bach Gesellschaft Edition, vol. 42; 'Appendix of Variants and Dubious Works', pp. 250–4 and SIMG (1900/1), pp. 272 ff.) is impossible; the ascription to Purcell is most unlikely, on stylistic grounds; and the evidence for the ascription to Rossi is shaky. On the title-page of Br. Mus. Add. 24313, the awkward, and rather careless copyist has written: 'Toccatas of Michel Angelo Rossi'; however, the position of the piece at the end of the volume does not establish that it belongs with the title-page.

D230. Trumpet Minuet

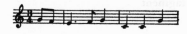

MSS: 58

COMMENTARY: The ascription of this work in the manuscript source appears only in pencil, in a later hand than that of the copyist.

P

D231. Trumpet Minuet

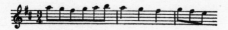

MSS: 570

COMMENTARY: This piece is ascribed to Purcell in pencil, by a later hand, in the manuscript source. Its similarity to No. **607**/7, however, suggests that it might be Purcell's work.

D240. Prelude in C Major

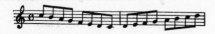

MSS: 641

COMMENTARY: Although this prelude precedes an 'Almand' by Purcell in C Major (see No. **665**/ Comm) in Christ Church, Oxford, MS 1176, f. 14, and is ascribed to him by Alois Hiff, who wrote out the contents list of this MS, the lack of an ascription in the music itself places this work in the doubtful category.

D241a. Voluntary [in C Major]   D241b. Adagio
(VI, 68)

EDITIONS: VI, 68, ?1790b

COMMENTARY: In the earliest known source (Goodison) this work is only 'said to be Purcell's'. On grounds of style the ascription seems unlikely. Mr. Hugh McLean, referring to it as an 'Echo Voluntary', rejected the piece for his edition of Purcell's organ works, suggesting that it may have been written by Daniel Purcell or some other eighteenth-century composer. Since then, Lady Susi Jeans, and Mr. Peter F. Williams (of St. John's College, Cambridge) have discovered the piece in one of the John Reading MSS at Dulwich College, ascribed to Barret. (Presumably the John Barrett who died in 1735.) With all due regard for the fact that Reading's ascriptions are not all reliable, this does seem to confirm that Henry Purcell did not compose the work.

D242. 'The Voluntary Composed by Mr. H. Purcell' Fragment

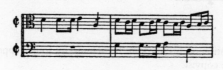

MS: 545

COMMENTARY: This voluntary is represented by only one fragment (given above complete) in a single manuscript in the Nanki Collection. For this information I am indebted to Mr. Hugh McLean of Vancouver, B.C., Canada.

FANTASIAS, SONATAS AND RELATED FORMS FOR STRINGS

D250. Fantasia [à 4 in C Major]

MSS: 848g

COMMENTARY: The only source for this work is a very late eighteenth-century manuscript in the York Minster library. Until such time as a more authoritative source is found, this work must be considered as extremely dubious.

D251. Sonata Fragment [in c minor]

MSS: 601

COMMENTARY: This fragment might be another transcription of a vocal setting, such as that of 'Ye twice ten-hundred deities' (See No. **630**/Commentary), which precedes it in the Bodleian Library, Oxford, MS Mus. C.28. Although four parts have been allowed for, only two (treble and bass) have been copied in.

D252. [Sonata fragment in c minor]

MSS: 592

COMMENTARY: This work is to be found only in one source (in the Bodleian Library, Oxford MS Mus. Sch. C.61), which has only a fragmentary copy giving the first 18 bars. From its style, which is certainly closely akin to that of Purcell, the work might well be the textless melody of a song. [In fact, see No. **473**/2 and ' Addenda '.]

D253. Tinker's Dance

MSS: 55

D254. Mr. Mountfort's Farewell

EDITIONS: ?1700, 1701d

D255. ?Jig

EDITIONS: ?1700

D256. ?Jig

MSS: 408 (*bis* ascribed to ' Mr. P ', and, later, to Mr. Peasable and called ' Pleasure ')

D257. [?Jig]

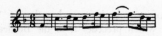

MSS: 592

COMMENTARY: An unnamed piece in Thomas Mace's MS signed only ' H.P.' In the same MS ' My song shall be alway ' and ' Fly swift ye Hours ' are signed only *HP*. In the second part of this ternary work a short bit of text (' And all things in nature are mad ') is underlaid.

INCIDENTAL MUSIC

D571/9. A Fool's Preferment; Here's a health to the king

MSS: 598

COMMENTARY: In the MS source, this song is not ascribed to Purcell, but occurs within a group of Purcell songs. In view of the fact that Purcell did set music for *A Fool's Preferment* and in the absence of any conflicting evidence, the piece may be included among Purcell's doubtful works.

APPENDIX II: SPURIOUS ASCRIPTIONS TO PURCELL

ANTHEMS AND OTHER SACRED WORKS

S1. By the waters of Babylon (P. Humfrey)

(1) Symphony

(2) Verse

MSS: 42, 299, **326**, 540, 850a to h

EDITIONS: 1828[-44]

COMMENTARY: There is a copy of this anthem in Purcell's hand in the so-called 'Flackton MS' (British Museum MS Add. 30932, f. 52) with a note by Philip Hayes to the effect that Purcell had improved and enlarged upon Humfrey's composition. Another copy in Fitzwilliam Museum MS 117 (sometimes called, erroneously, the 'Blow MS') is the same as this in all but a few minor details. However, Tudway's copy (in British Museum MS Harl. 7338, f. 60v) differs considerably from both these. The most important of the differences are as follows:

(1) In place of Humfrey's 'Symphony' of 18 bars, Purcell supplied a condensed introduction for organ, using the theme of the opening tenor solo:

(2) The second, and most of the subsequent Ritornelli Purcell has transcribed for Organ.
(3) Purcell omitted the Ritornello and the prelude which follows it before the chorus: ' Sing us one of the songs of Zion '.
(4) He altered the Ritornello following this in adapting it for organ.
(5) He omitted altogether Humfrey's beginning as follows:

(6) He omitted Humfrey's Ritornello before the verse: ' O daughters of Jerusalem ' as well as the Ritornello between this verse and its chorus.
(7) Throughout, Purcell copied in only fragments of Humfrey's thorough bass, fitting these in where it was convenient to do so.

LITERATURE: J. S. Bumpus, *English Cathedral Music*, London: T. Werner Laurie, [n.d.], I, p. 150.

S2. Christ is risen (E. White)

MSS: 115, 155

S3. *Come honest sexton* (M. Locke)

'The Passing Bell', Anon., 1672 (Variant)

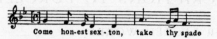

Come hon-est sex - ton, take thy spade

MSS: 1, 309

EDITIONS: 1688c

S4. *God sheweth me His goodness* (William Norris)

Psalm 59: 10–12, 16, 17

Verse: *atb*   ?Bc   Chorus: *S(?)ATB*

God shew-eth me his good-ness

MSS: 334, 773

S5. *Great is the Lord*

Hymn

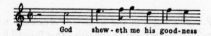

Great is— the— Lord, His

EDITIONS: 1772–4

COMMENTARY: Although ascribed to Purcell in *The Young Gentlemen and Ladies Musical Companion*, this setting is based on the same tune as that for *Hosanna to the Prince of Light* (see **S6**).

S6. *Hosanna to the Prince of light* (? H. Loosemore)

Hymn   'Pensance' C.M.x

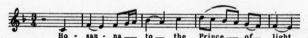

Ho - san - na— to— the Prince— of— light

EDITIONS: ?1798

COMMENTARY: The same tune appears with a setting of the words *Great is the Lord* (see **S5**).

S7. *How pleasant is Thy dwelling place* (Henry Carey) (XXXII, 173)

Hymn   Psalm 84

How pleas - ant is Thy dwell - ing— place

EDITIONS: XXXII, 173, 1789

COMMENTARY: The setting is the same as that for the text 'To celebrate Thy praise O Lord' (see **S18**).

S8. *I am the Resurrection* (Weldon)

I am the Re - sur - rec - ti - on

MSS: 69, 626d, 848c (ascribed to Weldon)

COMMENTARY: However, this work is entitled 'Wanless's Funeral Service' in British Museum Add MS 17820, f. 107v.

S9. *I heard a voice* (Croft)

Full: *SATB*   *Bc*

I heard a voice from Heav'n

MSS: 69, 296

S10. *My heart rejoiceth in the Lord* (William Norris)

I *Samuel* 2: 1–4, 6–8, 10

Verse: *satb*   *Bc*   Chorus: *S(?)ATB*

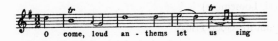

My heart re - joi - [ceth]

MSS: 773

S11. *O come, loud anthems* (M. Cooke)

O come, loud an - thems let us sing

EDITIONS: 1772–4

S12. *O God, wherefore art Thou* (J. Blow)

O God, where - fore art Thou ab - sent
O God,

MSS: 41 (in Purcell's hand), 765 (anon.)

S13. *O Lord God of my salvation* (Vaughan Richardson, Organist of the Cathedral Church of Winchester)

Psalm 88: 1, 2, 3, 4, 13

Full: *SSAB*

O Lord God of my — sal - va - tion

MSS: 200e, 302 (Vaughan Richardson)

EDITIONS: 1765b

COMMENTARY: Although ascribed to Purcell in Aaron Williams' *Royal Harmony*, 1765, this piece was written by Vaughan Richardson, as may be seen in British Museum MS Harl. 7341, f. 133v, and numerous other MSS.

S14. *O Lord, rebuke me not* (Weldon)

Sacred Song

O Lord, re - buke me not in Thine in- [dignation]

MSS: 68, 273, 543

EDITIONS: 1828[-44]

S15. *O miserable man* (Daniel Purcell)

Sacred Song

O O' mi - se - ra - ble man

EDITIONS: 1714a, 1714b, 1828[-44]

S16. *O that mine eyes would melt into a flood* (H. Loosemore)

Hymn   ' An Hymn for Good Friday '

Verse: *sb*   *Bc*   Chorus: *SATB*

O — that mine eyes would melt

MSS: 75, 99, 100 (missing), 101 (chorus only), 102, 326, 347

EDITIONS: 1765b

COMMENTARY: This hymn is clearly ascribed to H. Loosemore in British Museum MS Add. 33234, f. 47, an earlier and far more trustworthy source than any which ascribes the work to Purcell.

S17. The Lord my pasture shall prepare (Henry Carey)

Hymn

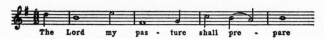

The Lord my pas - ture shall pre - pare

MSS: 352

EDITIONS: 1730g

COMMENTARY: According to the British Museum cataloguer, this work is generally attributed to Henry Carey. In Gawthorn's *Harmonia Perfecta*, 1730, the work is clearly ascribed to Carey.

S18. To celebrate Thy praise, O Lord (Henry Carey) (XXXII, 173)

Psalm

To ce - le - brate Thy praise

EDITIONS: XXXII, 173, 1789

COMMENTARY: The setting is the same as that for *S7*.

S19. Turn Thou us, O good Lord (George Jeffries)

Psalm 80

Verse: *attb*   Chorus: *ATTB*

Turn Thou us, O good Lord

EDITIONS: 1828[–44]

COMMENTARY: This anthem, though attributed to Purcell by Vincent Novello, was definitely composed by George Jeffries, according to the copy in British Museum MS Add. 10338, f. 72, a source which Novello may have used for his edition.

SECULAR VOCAL WORKS

S50. A lass there lives upon the green (R. Courteville)

? Sir Henry Sheers: Southerne's *Oroonoko*, 1690

s   Bc

A lass,___ a lass____there lives up-on the green

433

APPENDIX II

MSS: 341

EDITIONS: 1696g

S51. Cease the rovers (Daniel Purcell)

sb

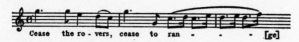

Cease the ro-vers, cease to ran - - - [ge]

MSS: 402 (ascribed to D. Purcell)

EDITIONS: 1744, 1748a, 1767b

S52. Come pull away boys (G. Holmes: catch)

3 voices

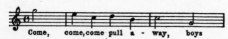

Come,   come, come pull a-way,   boys

MSS: 315, 673 (anon.)

S53. Fill all the glasses (Eccles: catch)

2 voices

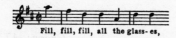

Fill, fill, fill, all the glass-es,

MSS: 45

EDITIONS: 1735b, 1740c, ?1755a, ?1790

S54. Had she not care enough (J. Savile: catch)

3 voices

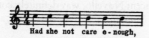

Had she not care e-nough,

EDITIONS: 1667, 1686a, 1687e, 1701b, 1704c, 1707e, 1707f, 1709e, 1710a, ca. 1770

S55. Hang sorrow (W. Lawes)

Sir C[harles] S[edley], W[illiam] D['Avenant] and L. B.: *The New Academy of Complements* 1713,
p. 117 'Song 50'

3 voices

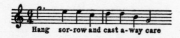

Hang   sor-row and cast a-way care

MSS: 317

S56. Hark the bonny Christ Church bells (H. Aldrich)

3 voices

MSS: British Museum MS Add. 31463, 405, 673 (Purcell)

EDITIONS: 1701b

COMMENTARY: See ' O the bonny Christ-church bells ' in J. Playford's *The Musical Companion* of
1673, which is the same composition with slightly different words. This version also appears in
Royal College of Music MS 1119, f. 5v.

S57. How happy are they (J. Marsh)

s   Bc

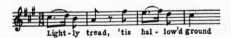

EDITIONS: 1688d (' Mr. Marsh ')

S58. How well doth this harmonious meeting prove (Hugh Bond)

s   *2 Vn, Va, Bc*

MSS: 45 (ascribed to Humfrey), 72, 724

EDITIONS: 1679

S59. Lightly tread, 'tis hallowed ground (M. Wise)

ssb

EDITIONS: London: Duncombe Book & Music Seller, n.d.; [Broad sheet] ' A favorite glee for
Three Voices ' [G. Berg, *ca.* 1795].

S60. Ode to an expiring frog (A. Hutchings)

s   piano

(a) Symphony   (b) [Recit]   (c) [Arioso]

APPENDIX II

EDITIONS: London: Novello, Ewer & Co., 1937

COMMENTARY: A skit by Hutchings published in 1937 as 'The words made by Mrs. Leo Hunter, the music attributed to Mr. Henry Purcell by Arthur Hutchings.'

S61. *Old Chiron thus preached* (M. Wise)

sb   Bc

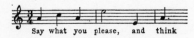

Old Chi-ron thus preached to his pu - pil

MSS: 310, 402, 866

EDITIONS: 1685c, 1686a, 1687e, 1705g, 1737a, 1740e, 1745c, 1745d, 1748a, ?1750, ?1755a, 1775a, ?1786, ?1790

S62. *Say what you please* (W. Turner: catch)

3 *voices*

Say what you please, and think

EDITIONS: 'Two catches for three voices by Mr. W. Turner' [London: ?1710] s. sh. fol.

S63. *Since Cloris the pow'rs*

s   Bc

Since Clo-ris the pow'rs of your charms

MSS: 442

COMMENTARY: This song is anonymous in the so called 'Gresham' MS, and is not in Purcell's hand. There is no reason for ascribing it to him.

S64. *The owl is abroad* (J. C. Smith)

sab   piano

The owl is a-broad,   The bat

EDITIONS: New York: Michael Keane, 1937

S65. *Was ever nymph like Rosamund?* (T. A. Arne)

Addison

s   Bc

Was e - ver nymph like Ro - [samund?]

EDITIONS: 1754b

S66. Why does the morn (J. Blow)

Why does the morn in blush-es rise.

MSS: 318, 347

EDITIONS: 1683b, 1700jj, 1707g, 1714c, 1719b

S67. Hark, Harry, 'tis late (J. Eccles)

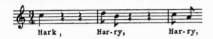

Hark, Har-ry, Har-ry,

MSS: British Museum MS Add. 31463, f. 26v, 673 (Eccles)

EDITIONS: ?1750

COMMENTARY: This work is ascribed to John Eccles in EDITIONS 1693c, 1707ef, 1709f, 1720n, 1724c and 1726c.

S68. Forth from ye dark and dismal cell

Before 1650; ' Tom of Bedlam ', Anon, *Le Prince d'Amour*, 1661

Forth from ye dark and dis - mal cell

MSS: 45, 310, 595

EDITIONS: 1673b, 1675, 1676, 1685c, 1686a, 1686c, 1695p, 1698f, 1699e, 1707g (mnp), 1714c (mnp), 1719b, 1719c, 1720h, 1725c, 1726c, 1745c, ?1780, 1797–1802 (Trans) and *Le Prince d'Amour* . . . with a collection of . . . poems and songs, 1660

COMMENTARY: This song is anonymous in all manuscript sources excepting British Museum MS Add. 22099, where it is ascribed in the index to Henry Lawes, and described in the catalogue as a ' tune taken from an early Gray's Inn Masque, printed for the first time in Playford's *Dancing Master*, 1650.' It is also anonymous in all the printed sources prior to Walsh's *Orpheus Britannicus* (ca. 1725), where it was first ascribed to Purcell. The tune is printed in *The English Dancing Master*, 1650, as ' Graies Inne Maske ', and is certainly not by Purcell.

S69. Sweet tyranness, I now resign (Henry Purcell, Sr.)

(XXII, 186) 1667

Solo: *ssb*

Sweet ty - ran-ness, I now

MSS: 317, British Museum MS Add. 31806

EDITIONS: XXII, 186, 1667, 1673a

COMMENTARY: Burney (Mercer edition, II, 380) who printed this work definitely ascribed it to Henry Purcell the Elder. Furthermore, no-one aged 8 would have been referred to as 'Mr Henry Pursell'; it is certainly by the elder Purcell. Sir Frederick Bridge in his article on Purcell in *Musical News*, January, 1895, claimed that the trio version of *Sweet Tyranness* was written by Henry Purcell the younger. His main argument against its being the work of the elder Purcell is based on the fact that a phrase at the beginning of the second part was almost note for note identical with one in Henry Lawes' music for *Comus*. This hardly explains how this version of the piece came to be ascribed to Purcell the younger.

LITERATURE: Charles Burney, *A General History of Music*, London: Foulis & Co., Ltd., 1935, II, p. 380.

S70. Sweet tyranness, I now resign

(XXV, 170) 1678

S   *Bc*

EDITIONS: XXV, 170, 1678, ?1750, *ca.* 1790

COMMENTARY: If, as is sometimes said, this solo setting is also to be attributed to the elder Henry Purcell, one would then have to question the five Purcell songs which appear with it in *New Ayres and Dialogues* of 1678 (see Nos. **363, 387, 397, 418** and **433**). But since the style of these five is characteristic of the younger Henry Purcell's early style of song-composition, they have been retained among the authentic ascriptions, even though the fact that there is only one source for them leaves their authenticity open to some question. The two settings of 'Sweet Tyranness', on the other hand, are not at all characteristic of the younger Purcell's style, and have therefore been relegated to this appendix of 'Spurious Ascriptions' as the work of Henry Purcell the Elder. In fact, this 'version' is nothing more than a reduction of the trio. (See S**69**.)

DRAMATIC MUSIC

S100. Macbeth

Solo: *s*   2 *Vn, Bc*   Chorus: *SATB*

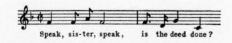

MSS: 62, 212, 216, 290

APPENDIX II

EDITIONS: 1690c (inc), *ca.* 1776

COMMENTARY: Although there are conflicting ascriptions to Purcell and Locke in various other MS and printed sources, the definite attribution to Leveridge in Fitzwilliam MS 87 bears out the association with Leveridge's name in British Museum MS Eg. 2957. Westrup also ascribes the work to Leveridge in his biography of Purcell.

LITERATURE: R. Moore, 'The Music to Macbeth,' *Musical Quarterly*, Jan. 1960, p. 22.

INSTRUMENTAL MUSIC

S120. Air [in D Major] (Jeremiah Clarke)

MSS: 596

COMMENTARY: Although ascribed to Purcell in Oxford, Bodleian MS Mus. Sch. E 397 this work actually was written by Jeremiah Clarke as ' Prince Eugene's March '.

S121. Cibell (Lully)

MSS: 618

S122. Purcell's Ground, or the ' Welsh Ground '

EDITIONS: William Howgill, London: Preston, n.d.

S123. Jig (Morgan)

(VI, 58)

EDITIONS: VI, 58

COMMENTARY: See **T693.**

S124. Trumpet Tune (Clarke)

(VI, 37)

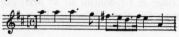

MSS: 596

EDITIONS: VI, 37, ?1700 [Anon]

S125. Trumpet Voluntary (J. Clarke)

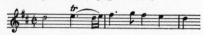

MSS: 345, 364, 774

EDITIONS: 1700b, 1701c, 1703g, 1711c, 1713b, 1716b, 1721b

COMMENTARY: For purposes of authentication, the most important printed source for this work is John Young's *A Choice Collection of Ayres for the Harpsichord or Spinnett* (London, 1700), in which the piece appears on p. 13 as ' *The Prince of Denmark's March*, by Mr. Clarke.' Walsh's *The Third Book of the Harpsichord Master* (London, 1702) provides the same title and ascription. A 17th-century set of four part-books in the British Museum (MSS Add. 30839 and 30365-7), possibly in the hand of James Paisible the elder, also ascribes this tune to Clarke in a 'Suite de Clarke' consisting of nine short movements, of which several (including the 'Trumpet Voluntary', here called a 'Rondeau') appear elsewhere under Clarke's name. A manuscript bequeathed to Mr. H. Watkins Shaw (see Tenbury MS 1508) provides what is probably the earliest source. It gives this work under Clarke's name under the dual title 'Marche' and 'Rondeau' on f. 14v.

There are several anonymous sources. In British Museum MS Add. 31465, it appears simply as a 'Trumpet Tune' without a composer's name. This may have been the MS which Spark used in editing the work as Purcell's Trumpet Voluntary in the late 19th century. The tune also appears anonymously in the 11th edition of *The Dancing Master*, published in 1701. There it is printed as a country-dance tune under the heading 'The Temple'. A MS belonging to Lady Jeans appears to derive from this publication, for it uses the title 'Country dance' and gives the same clumsy version of the tune. The piece turns up again in Gay's *Polly*, where it serves as the finale.

About a century and a quarter later, in the 1870's, William Spark, then Organist of what is now Leeds City Hall, published this work as the first piece in vol. 7 of his series: *Short Pieces for the Organ* (London: Ashdown and Parry, *ca.* 1870) as the *Trumpet Voluntary in D Major, Henry Purcell*. Under this title it achieved public fame three-quarters of a century later as an aid to war-time morale in England, chiefly through the efforts of Sir Henry J. Wood, who published an orchestral version and recorded it for popular use.

S126. Verse in the Phrygian mode (N. Lebègue)

(McLean, 1)

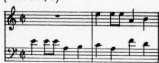

APPENDIX II

MSS: 345, 643

EDITIONS: McLean, 1; N. Lebègue, *Second Livre d'orgue* (*ca.* 1678-9, or 1686)

COMMENTARY: Mr. Hugh McLean, who edited this work for publication in 1957 (*Henry Purcell: The Organ Works*, London: Novello, p. ii) has since advised me of the discovery by Mr. Peter F. Williams (of St. John's College, Cambridge) that N. Lebègue published the same piece in his *Second livre d'orgue* (*ca.* 1678-9, or 1686) under the title: 'Trio du 4e [ton]. Tu solus'. A modern edition is to be found in Guilmant-Pirro: *Archives des Maîtres de l'Orgue*, vol. ix, p. 109, as Mr. Walter Emery has been so kind as to inform me.

APPENDIX III: MANUSCRIPT SOURCES

UNIVERSITY OF CALIFORNIA AT BERKELEY

1: Be M 739745   'May 15, 1716.' (After the last composition in the MS) 'James Ward, His book at ye Crowne in Minories, London.'
2   9   31   33   S3

2: Be M2 C645 Case B   'Organ book.' Late 17th century (?).
19   51

BARBER INSTITUTE, BIRMINGHAM UNIVERSITY

13: **BU 5001**   Score, late 17th century.   Autograph.
19   29   55   142

14: BU 5002   Score, late 17th century.
140   142   143   144   186   191   194   197   200   355   461   482   489   491   511   545
D71

15: BU 5003   Score, 1720.
2   4

RICHARD BORDER COLLECTION
(now dispersed)

20: See 'Private Collections' below.
21: See 'Private Collections' below.
22: See 'Private Collections' below.

BRUSSELS, BIBLIOTHÈQUE DU CONSERVATOIRE

26: BrC 1035   Score, late 17th century.
380   467   490   501   503   508   524   545   572/10ab   D71

27: BrC V.14.981   Score, 18th century.   Said to have been copied from the autograph.
790 to 801

28: BrC L.H.XY 27.174   Score, late 17th century.
487   509   589

CAMBRIDGE, FITZWILLIAM MUSEUM

39: CFM 33   Score, *ca.*1750.
321/12a, 13b   328/8ab, 11b   333/6b   342/4   574/12   628/12, 22, 19a to 27b
629/36a   630/13a   632/13, 16   D132   D141

40: CFM C 39   Score, 1761–2.
                   D1 (Bass only)

     CFM 87   See MS 62 at the end of this section.

41: CFM 88   Score, 'September ye 10th 1682.' Autograph. 'B. Gates, 13th Jan 172$\frac{7}{8}$.

8 11 13B 15 (inc) **17B 25 27** (partly autograph) **35** (inc) **36 37
41 50 51 S12**

42: CFM 117   Score, ' 1683 ' (date of central volume to which additions have been made).
                   Said to be in the hand of John Blow, but not certainly in his hand.
                   6 8 11 13A 19 22 23 26 27 28 35 36 39 50 51 58B 230
                   230 (inc) S1

43: CFM 118   Score, *ca.* 1680.
                   264 279 281 359 370 413 440 482 D100

44: CFM 119   Score, *ca.* 1720.
                   328 (inc), 333 (inc) 335 (inc) 342 (inc) 574 (inc) 583 (inc) 600 (inc)
                   628 (inc) 630 (inc) 632 (inc)

45: CFM 120   Score, *ca.* 1728.
                   242 321/2ab 333/7 335/5a 369 370 380 394 406 413 423 444
                   464 485 486 488 493 494 501 502 503 510 513 514 516 517
                   518 521 522 543 546 571/6 574/15b, 16b, 17 578/1, 3, 6a, 7, 9
                   579 592/10 596 598 601/2 602/1 608 613/1 627/30 628/10bc,
                   15, 26ab, 29, 35, 36, 38 629/4b, 22b, 29 630/13a, 15 632/10, 13b, 14b,
                   16, 19ab D106 S53 S58 S68

46: CFM 152   Score, *ca.* 1720(?). Partially autograph, partially in the hand of John Blow.
                   29 31 (inc) **33** (mainly)

47: CFM C 269   Score. Purcell gathering in late 17th(?) century hand.
                   25

48: CFM C 289   Score. Purcell gathering in late 17th(?) century hand.
                   2

50: CFM C 353   Score, late 17th century. ' Henry Purcell's Airs/Scored(?) Webb.'
                   570/1 to 9 572/1, 2, 5 to 8 574/1 to 7, 9 577/1 to 5, 7, 8 592/4 to 9 597
                   603/2, 3, 6 to 9 (603/7 appears in conjunction with 632/1 shown below)
                   607/2 to 4, 6 to 9 611/2, 3, 5 to 8 627/1, 2b, 4, 19, 24, 25, 34 628/1a, 2, 3,
                   11, 15b, 17b, 18, 28, 31, 40, Appendix 1, 2, 3 629/1ab, 2, 3, 6, 15, 16, 17a,
                   18, 19, 26, 38, 41, 44, 51 630/1a (inc), 9a, 17bc, 18 632/1. (The tune
                   ' Fairest Isle ' from *King Arthur* is copied twice. See **No. 628**/Commentary)

51: CFM C 556   Organ book, early 18th century.
                   36 (has been removed)

52: CFM C 657   Score, late 17th century. Supposed autograph.
                   342

53: CFM C 658   Score, late 17th century. Supposed autograph.
                   335 339

54: CFM C 659   Score, late 17th century. Supposed autograph.
                   333

55: CFM C 660   Score, late 17th century.
                   572 D253

56:    CFM   C 663   Bass part, late 17th century. ' St Cecilia By Mr. Henry Purcel 1696 Bassus Voice.'
$$339$$

57:    CFM   52.B.6   Score, late 17th century. In the hands of John Blow and John Harris, dated on f.2v, ' Saturday, Feb 7th, $170^1/_2$ ' and on f.5v, ' Thursday Feb. 13th 1702 all most 2 a clock ' etc.
$$810$$

58:    CFM   52.B.7   Keyboard book, early 18th century.
574/1abc 628/2 630/4a 641 644 650 651 652 660 666 T676 T680 T681 T685 T686 T691 D220 D221 D226 D228 D230

59:    CFM   25.E.13   Five part-books belonging to Magdalene College, Cambridge, on permanent loan to the Fitzwilliam Museum. Late 17th-century manuscripts in a copyist's hand. The pieces they contain are arranged in sets according to key.
339/3   570/5, 6, 9   574/1ab, 2, 3, 4, 5, 7, 9   607/2, 3, 8, 9   611/3, 4, 6, 7 626/7, 29a 627/1, 21, 24, 31 628/11 629/6, 22b 630/1, 2b, 3, 4a, 6a, 11 22 631/1ab T678

60:    CFM   Music Box II A boxed collection of various late 17th and early 18th-century manuscripts.
430 522 574/15b, 16b, 17 (bass only), 17 595/1 607/4 628/10bc 630/12 T678 T678 (in C Major)

61:    CFM   106 [30.F.21] Keyboard book, ca. 1765. ' Kelway MS.'
T611/9

62:    CFM   87 [23.H.12] Score, ca. 1800. ' John Harris ' (et al).
575 (with a new song—see Section 5) S100

63:    CFM   161 [32.G.18] Score, ca. 1760 (6th gathering).
803 810

CAMBRIDGE, ST. JOHN'S COLLEGE: CHOIR LIBRARY

64a: CJC O 12   Organ book, early to mid 18th century.
2 4 9 19 48 54 57 61

64b: CJC O 14   Organ book, mid to late 18th century.
19 31 33 57 61

CAMBRIDGE, ST. JOHN'S COLLEGE: COLLEGE LIBRARY

65:    CJC Box of unbound, uncatalogued MSS dating from the early or mid 18th century.
2 31

CAMBRIDGE, KING'S COLLEGE CHAPEL LIBRARY

66:    CKCh N Score, mid-18th century.
19

CAMBRIDGE, KING'S COLLEGE: ROWE LIBRARY

67:    CKC 274   Score, late 17th century. ' Nicola Matteis His First & Second Books: David Murray 1693.' (Later manuscript additions.)
627/15, 17

68: CKC 9–17 Score, 18th century (?)
                S14

69: CKC 20   Score, 1750. 'John Walmsley, his book.'
                7 33 58C 61 182 D3 D43 D73 S8 S9

70: CKC 21   Score, *ca.* 1750.
                4

71: CKC 23   Score.
                54 57

72: CKC 24   Score, mid 18th century.
                S58

73: CKC 127 Score.
                120

74: CKC 247 Score, 1685.
                627/15

75: CKC 269 Score, 1763.
                33 61 S16

76: CKC 212 Score, *ca.* 1750.
                578/6b

CANTERBURY CATHEDRAL LIBRARY

77: CC L.15.32 Bass ('Solo book') part-book, apparently once belonging to William Gostling.
                  Late 17th century.
                  4 19 22 31 35 36 57 230ME

78: CC Undesignated Organ book, late 17th century.
                       4 19 52 57

79: CC E.10.2 Contratenor cantoris part-book, 18th century.
                 36 230ME

80: CC E.10.8 Contratenor decani part-book, mid 18th century.
                 4 22 31 33

81: CC E.10.12 Tenor cantoris part-book, mid 18th century.
                  2 4 18 19 31 33 35 36 57 60

82: CC E.10.14 Tenor decani part-book, mid 18th century.
                  2 230 (inc)

83: CC E.10.17 Tenor decani part-book, early 18th century.
                  19 35 36 230

84: CC Undesignated Tenor decani part-book, mid 18th century.
                       2 4 18 19 31 33 35 36

85: CC Undesignated Tenor cantoris part-book, mid 18th century.
                       2 4 18 31 33 35 36 230ME

86: CC E.10.24 Bass decani part-book, mid to late 18th century.
                  2 4 18 19 31 33 35

87: CC E.10.24 Bass decani part-book, late 17th to early 18th century.
                  230ME

CHICHESTER CATHEDRAL LIBRARY

95: ChC 1   Score, late 17th century, 'J° Walter, His Book, 1680' (but copied later).
          195   328/1 to 2a   413   426   471 (inc)   545 (mnp)   632/10 to 19   810

96: ChC 2   Score, late 18th century.
          58C

97: ChC 3   Score, late 18th century.
          31   36   230 (inc)

98: ChC 4   Bass decani part-book, late 18th century.
          19   31   D2

99: ChC 5   Tenor cantoris part-book, late 18th century.
          35   58C   S16

100: ChC 6   Tenor decani part-book, late 18th century.
          S16 (missing)

101: ChC 7   Bass decani part-book, late 18th century.
          S16 (Chorus only)

102: ChC 8   Bass cantoris part-book, late 18th century.
          S16

103: ChC 9   Organ score, late 18th century.
          230E (inc)

(N.B. MSS 2 to 9 above are now on permanent loan in the Chichester Diocesan Records Office.)

CROFT CASTLE COLLECTION

104: See 'Private Collections' below.

EDWARD CROFT-MURRAY COLLECTION

105: See 'Private Collections' below.

DUBLIN, CHRIST CHURCH CATHEDRAL LIBRARY

115: DCC II, 2   Set of 6 part-books.
          230 (inc)   S2

116: DCC III   Set of 8 part-books.
          35   36   37   57   60

117: DCC VI [A]   Organ book.
          57

118: DCC VI [B]   Set of 8 part-books.
          19   33   49

119: DCC VII [A]   Set of 2 part-books.
          19   49   230 (inc)

120: DCC VII [B]   Score, mid 18th century.
          35   36

121: DCC VIII   Organ book.
               2   4   7   19   49   61

122: DCC IX [A]   Set of 2 part-books (Tenor decani; tenor cantoris).
               230E (inc)

123: DCC IX [B]   Score.
               230 (inc)

124: DCC XII   Score.
               57

125: DCC XIII   Organ book.
               36

126: DCC XV   Organ book.
               35

127: DCC XXIV   Score.
               49

DUBLIN, ARCHBISHOP MARSH'S LIBRARY

131: DM Z1.2.25   Score, 18th century.
               7   19   27   33   35   36   232

132: DM Z1.2.28   Score, 18th century.
               31

DUBLIN, TRINITY COLLEGE LIBRARY

138: DT 13   Organ book, mid 18th century.
           7

DULWICH COLLEGE LIBRARY

140: DuC 1   A collection of anthems dated 1717.
            19 (in F Major)   31 (in F Major)

141: DuC 2   Harpsichord lessons, early 18th century.
            120   574/5, 15, 16   T678   D30   D33   D220

14²: DuC 86   Harpsichord lessons, early 18th century.
            339/3ab   583/2   630/4d, 13a, 15

DURHAM CATHEDRAL LIBRARY

149: DrC A 4   Organ book, 1679 and later.
            43

150: DrC A 8   Organ book, *ca.* 1736 to 1738.
            19   31   33   197

151: DrC A 9   Organ book, late 17th century.
            19   33   230M (inc)

152: DrC A 14 Organ book, 1764.
60

153: DrC A 15 Organ book, late 18th century.
19   N67 (has been removed)

154: DrC A 17 Organ book, 1768.
31

155: DrC A 19 Organ book, 1777.
S2

156: DrC A 20 Organ book, 1783 to 1794.
22   35   35   58C

157: DrC A 21 Organ book, late 18th century.
49   138

158: DrC A 25 Organ book, 1684 to 1710. 'Wm Greggs.'
2   14   31   33   40   54   60   61

159: DrC A 26 Organ book, 1768.
4   232 (in C Major)

160: DrC A 28 Organ book, 1741.
2   4   19   22   31   33   35   36   60

161: DrC A 29 Organ book, 1741.
57   230ME (inc)

162: DrC A 33 Organ book, '11 January 1699'.
4   19   22   33   35   36   59   230 (inc)   D4

163a: DrC B 10 Contratenor cantoris part-book, late 17th or early 18th century.
2   4   22   33   35   36   57   60

   b: DrC B 13 Alto cantoris part-book, 1746 to 1774.
9

   c: DrC B 6 Tenor cantoris part-book, 1746 to 1774.
2   4   9   19   22   35   36

   d: DrC B 29 Bass part-book, 1746 to 1774.
4   9   19   22   31   33   35   36   57   60   230ME

   e: DrC B 9v Tenor part-book, 18th century.
2   4   9   19   22   33   35   36   57   60

164a: DrC B 12 Alto cantoris, part-book, 1737 to 1794.
2   4   9   19   22   33   35   36   57   58C   60   230ME (inc)   232/1 (inc)

   b: DrC B 8 Tenor cantoris part-book, 1752 to 1796.
4   230M (inc)   D5 (index only)

(The Durham Cathedral Library catalogue has a number of Purcell works listed for MS B 9, but none of these is to be found in the volume itself.)

   c: DrC B 21 Contratenor cantoris part-book, 1717 to 1772.
7   35   57   230ME (inc)

   d: DrC B 27 Bass part-book, 1716.
2   19   22   33   35   36   232

   e: DrC B 31 Bass cantoris part-book, 1746 to 1791.
9   230ME (inc)

f: DrC   B 32   Bass cantoris part-book, 1736 to 1771.
22   35   36   58C   230ME (inc)

g: DrC   B 33   Bass cantoris part-book, *ca.* 1746.
2   9   60

h: DrC   B 35   Bass decani and cantoris part-book, 1742 to 1791.
9   60   230ME (inc)

i: DrC   B 36   Bass decani part-book, 1738 to 1796.
9   57   230ME (inc)   232

165a: DrC   B 19   Alto cantoris part-book, 1741 to 1771.
230ME (inc)   232

b: DrC   B 5   Tenor decani part-book, 1750 to 1772.
230ME   232

c: DrC   B 7   Tenor cantoris part-book, 1754 to 1799.
230ME   232

d: DrC   B 9   Tenor cantoris part-book, 1749 to 1799.
230ME (inc)

e: DrC   B 28   Bass part-book, 1721 to 1776.
230 (inc)   232

166a: DrC   C 7   Contratenor cantoris part-book, 1640 to 1700.
4   19   22   33   35   36   54   61

b: DrC   C 5   Alto cantoris ('Counter-tenor cantoris' on cover) part-book, 1695.
58B

c: DrC   C 11   Tenor decani part-book, 17th century.
22   43

d: DrC   C 14   Tenor cantoris part-book, 17th century.
4   19   33   35   43

e: DrC   C 15   Tenor part-book, 1691 to 1791.
4   19   22   33   35   36   43   61

f: DrC   C 22   Bass and organ book (Precentor's book).
49

g: DrC   C 27   Tenor part-book, 1716.
2   4   14   15   19   22   23   31   33   35 (inc)   36 (inc)   40   43   53   54   61

h: DrC   C 28   Bass part-book, 1697 to 1794.
2   4   15   19   22   23   31   33   35   36   40   43   53   59   61   D4

i: DrC   C 34   Bass part-book, 1690 to 1727.
4   14   19   22   23   31   33   35   36   40   43   53   59   61   D4

167a: DrC   C 12   Tenor part-book, 1703 to 1793.
22   43

b: DrC   C 19   Bass decani part-book, 1735 to 1737.
7   33   58C   60   230ME (inc)

c: DrC   C 21   Tenor part-book, 1715 to 1742.
9   57   230ME (inc)   232

d: DrC   C 35   Tenor part-book, 1735 to 1772.
7   35   230ME (inc)   232

e: DrC C 26   Bass part-book, 1711 to 1718.
               58B 230ME (inc) 231

f: DrC C 29   Bass cantoris part-book, 1716 to 1739.
               9 57 58B 230ME (inc)

g: DrC C 32   Bass part-book, 1697 to 1705.
               230 (inc)

h: DrC C 30   Bass cantoris part-book, 18th century.
               232

i: DrC C 31   Bass part-book, 1697.
               230 (inc)

j: DrC C 33   Bass part-book, 1691 to 1771.
               230 (inc) 232

168: DrC D 9   Score, late 17th century.
               243 423 626/3a D130

169: DrC D 12 Chants.
               122 (alto only) D34 D35 D36

ELY CATHEDRAL LIBRARY

180: ElC 2   Organ book, ca. 1726.
               2 4 19 33 52 57

181: ElC 3.A   Organ book, ca. 1726(?).
               26 (anon) 31 54 61 230M/3 (inc)

182: ElC 5   Score, ca. 1726(?).
               35 230E

183: ElC 6   Score, ca. 1726(?).
               5 9 17B 18 25 36 49 50

184: ElC 8   Score, 18th century.
               4 9 31 49 54 60

185: ElC 9   Score and organ book, ca. 1726(?).
               23 31 48 60 D75

186: ElC 12   Score, mid 18th century.
               2 28 32 54

187: ElC 15   Score, mid 18th century.
               2 19 57 61

188: ElC 16   Score, late 17th or early 18th century.
               35 56 230

189: ElC 17   Score, before 1726.
               33

191: ElC 19   Score, before 1726. 'James Hawkins, Jr., 1726.'
               32

192: ElC 20   Score, before 1726.
               4 32 54

193: ElC 21   Score, before 1726. 'James Hawkins, Jr., 1726.'
               9 57

194a: ElC 25   Bass part-book, *ca.* 1726(?).
                  2 19 31 57 61

  b: ElC 26   Tenor part-book, *ca.* 1726(?).
                  2 19 31 52 57 61 230MC (inc)

  c: ElC 27   Alto part-book, *ca.* 1726(?).
                  2 19 120 (in b minor) 121

  d: ElC 28   Tenor part-book, *ca.* 1726(?).
                  19 61

  e: ElC 29   Bass part-book, *ca.* 1726 (?).
                  2 60 61 230 (inc)

  f: ElC 30   Alto part-book, *ca.* 1726(?).
                  2 19 31 52 61

  g: ElC 31   Bass part-book, *ca.* 1726(?).
                  2 19 31 33 60

195: ElC 32   Score, mid 18th century.
                  2 4 19 31 57 61

196: ElC 33   Score, 1719.
                  2 4 19 31 54 57 (index only) 61 193

197: ElC 34   Tenor and bass part-book, *ca.* 1726(?).
                  2 19 31 33 60 61

198: ElC 35   Bass and thorough-bass part-book.
                  31 35 61

ETON COLLEGE LIBRARY

200a–e: EtC   A set of Organ books copied at Eton for use in the College Chapel between the years 1681 and 1732. These are copied mainly in the hands of John Walter (organist at Eton, 1681 to 1705) and Benjamin Lamb (organist at Eton, 1705 to 1732).

  a: EtC A   Organ book mainly in the hand of John Walter.
                  230E

  b: EtC C   Purcell's *My song shall be* (No. 31) copied in the hand of John Walter, the remainder in the hand of Benjamin Lamb.
                  2 31 49 (missing) 60

  c: EtC 2   Organ book in the hand of Lamb.
                  33

  d: EtC III   Organ book in the hand of Lamb.
                  60

  e: EtC IV   Organ book in the hand of Lamb.
                  35 36 S13

THEODORE M. FINNEY COLLECTION

201: See 'Private Collections' below.

202: See 'Private Collections' below.

203: See 'Private Collections' below.

FOLGER SHAKESPEARE LIBRARY, WASHINGTON, D.C., U.S.A.

209: F F1.31.45   Score, late 17th century. Supposed autograph.
                        630/21b

210: F 472   Score, early 18th(?) century.
                        629/27 (inc), 28a to 32a

211: F 747.2   Score, 1745.
                        574/11b, 13c, 15a 583/1b, 2, 3ac 600 (inc) 630/4, 6a, 7bcdf, 11, 17bch, 20, 21bcde
                        632/13c, 15, 18ab, 19ab

212: F 747.3   Score and four part-books: Canto principale ('Alto chorus', 'Tenore chorus' —two copies); Tenore principale; Basso chorus (two copies); Tromba I. 'Music Room, Oxford.' Mid 18th century.
                        628/4, 5b, 6, 7, 8, 9a, 10 631/2e, 3b, 5ac, 6, 8ab, 12, 15, 16, 17ab S100

213: F 747.4   Score, late 18th century.
                        583 600 630

214: F 747.42   Score, late 18th century.
                        134 339 572 631

215: F 747.5   Score, late 18th century.
                        321 323/3 489 626/7ab 628 629/5cd D172

216: F 747.6   Score, late 18th century.
                        574 (inc) 583 600 630 (inc) 632 (inc) S100

217: F 770   Score, late 18th century.
                        575 626 (inc) 632

218: F 1064   Score.
                        413

219: F 1634.4   Score, 'Liber Georgij Forman Anno Domini 1721.'
                        31 321/2ab 323/5a 333/7 335/5a 339/3ab 360 362 370 375 380 385 392
                        394 396 406 413 422 423 464 469 485 486 489 490 493 501 502
                        503 510 513 543 570/10 571/6 573 574/17 578/6ab 579 584 585/1 589
                        592/10 596 601/2 603/10 604A 607/11 608 613/1 626/3a 627/35, Appendix
                        2 628/26, 29, 35, 36, 38 629/22b, 40b 630/13a, 15 631/10 632/17

220: F 520630.1   Score, late 17th century.
                        4 19 36 60

GLASGOW UNIVERSITY, EUING LIBRARY

231: GE G.C.21   Score, ca. 1750.
                        502

232: GE Rd 39   Score, ca. 1725.
                        230 (inc)

233: GE Rd 52   Score, ca. 1750.
                        286 290 574/10

234: GE Rd 54   Score, ca. 1730.
                        666/1

235: GE Rd 21   Score, ca. 1780.
                        790 to 801 802 to 811

236: GE Rd 62   Score, ca. 1790.
                        T677

GLOUCESTER CATHEDRAL LIBRARY

245a: GlC A 1 'Counter'—[tenor cantoris] part-book.
    2 9 19 33 57 60 230ME (inc)

  b: GlC A 2 'Counter-Tenor Decani' part-book.
    4 9 35 36

  c: GlC A 3 'Bass Cantoris' part-book.
    2 4 9 19 33 35 36 60 230ME (inc)

  d: GlC A 4 'Bass Decani' part-book.
    9 19 31 33 35 36 53 57 60

  e: GlC [4] 'Bass Decani' part-book, late 18th century.
    2 4 7 9 19 31 33 57 60

246: GlC [2] Organ score, mid 18th century.
    19 35 230ME (inc)

247: GlC [3] Tenor part-book, 'Dec. 7th, 1741.'
    35 57

248: GlC [4] Score, late 17th century (for section containing Purcell's works).
    2 4 9 19 31 33 60

249: GlC [5] Bass part-book, late 17th century. [= MS[2] as designated by Purcell Society editors.]
    31 N67

WILLIAM KENNEDY GOSTLING MANUSCRIPT

255: See 'Private Collections' below.

HAMBURG, STAATS- UND UNIVERSITATS-BIBLIOTHEK

259: HaM $\dfrac{\text{B}}{1847}$ Score, *ca.* 1750–80.
    328

HARVARD COLLEGE, HOUGHTON LIBRARY

270: Hd 1 Score, early 18th century.
    328

JOHN HAUCH COLLECTION

271: See 'Private Collections' below.

HEREFORD CATHEDRAL LIBRARY

272: HeC 30.B.i· ii Organ book, early 18th century.
    4 35 49 61 230ME

273:    HeC   30.B.vii   Organ book, 18th century.
                                   2   33   S14

274:    HeC   30.B.viii   Organ book, late 18th century.
                                     35   36

275:    HeC   30.B.ix   Organ book, early 18th century.
                                     19

276:    HeC   30.B.x   Organ book, ' R. Breton Oct. 30 1731.'
                                     7   19

LADY JEANS COLLECTION

280:    See ' Private Collections ' below.

281:    See ' Private Collections ' below.

LONDON, BRITISH MUSEUM

           L   Stowe 755   (See No. 627/Commentary.)

287:    L   Harl 1270   Score, late 17th to early 18th century. ' Ariette Italiane.'
                                   370

288:    L   Eg 2159   Papers relating to '. . . Mr. Hen Purcell's Music which was performed in the " Victim at the Sacrifice ".' After 1713.

289:   L   Eg 2956   Score, 1689. Autograph.
                                   333

290:    L   Eg 2957   Score, late 17th century.
                                   S100

291:    L   Eg 2958   Score, late 17th century. Supposed autograph.
                                   375

292:    L   Eg 2959   Score, late 17th century. ' Liber Jo: Gostling Ecclesiae St. Pauli apud. Londiniensis. . . .'
                                   T680   D222

293:    L   Eg 2960   Score, late 17th century.
                                   42   43   48   65   291   465   472   486   502   525   572/11ab   586

294:    L   Eg 2969   Score, mid 18th century. ' In the handwriting of Mr. Saville.'
                                   328 (inc)

295:    L   Sloane 3752   Score, ca. 1700.
                                   629 (partial text only)

296:    L   Add 5054   Score, before 1760. (Written by Henry Needler.)
                                   58C   S9

297:    L   Add 5333   Score, early 18th century. Partly in the hand of William Croft (?).
                                   333   600 (inc)   628 (inc)

298:    L   Add 5337   Score, early 18th century.
                                   574 (inc)   632 (inc)

299:    L   Harl 7338   Score, 1715. In the hand of Thomas Tudway.
                                   28   31   57   S1

300: L Harl 7339   Score, 1716. In the hand of Thomas Tudway.
19   25   35   36   48   49   51   230ME (inc)

301: L Harl 7340   Score, 1717. In the hand of Thomas Tudway.
2 (inc)   4   9   33   58C   230 (inc)

302: L Harl 7341   Score, 1718. In the hand of Thomas Tudway.
232   S13 (Vaughan Richardson)

303: L Add 17819   Score, 18th century. In several hands (generally without ritornelli)
2   4   13B   16   25   29   35   36   37   39   42   44   49   50   51   55   57   230 (inc)

304: L Add 17820   Score, 18th century.
6   14 (inc)   18   22   23   28   57   230

305: L Add 17835   Score, 18th century.
321

306: L Add 17840   Score, 18th century.
4   31   33   49   53   232

307: L Add 17842   Score, 18th century.
35   36

308: L Add 17853   Score, late 17th to early 18th century. Dated on f. 34 'May 4, '94.'
331/6c   574/16a   597/5   607/7   629/4b ('Paisible')   630/4a

309: L Add 19759   Score. 'Charles Campleman his book, June ye 9th 1681....'
199 (treble)   253   258   271   279 (treble)   292   359   415   461   D100   D104
D133   S3

310: L Add 22099   Score, ca. 1704 to 1707.
60   134   244   255   265   274   290   321/2, 14   370   406   428B   485   500
502   517   521   570/8   572/9   573   574/1, M6, 10, 15b, 16b, 17   578/3, 7b, 8, 9
596   602/1   T605/2 (attributed to Jeremiah Clarke)   609/10   613/1 (part 2), 2
627/8, T9bc, 16, M21, 22   628/T37, 38   629/4b, 8bcd, 40b, 48   630/15   631/10
632/11, 19   645   646   670   T678   T686   T687   T698   T801   D100   D224
S61   S68

311: L Add 22100   Score, ca. 1682. 'Mr. Dolbin's Book Anno domini 1682'.
340   490 (inc)   541

312: L Add 24313   Organ book(?).
D229

313: L Add 24889   Parts for strings, late 17th to early 18th century.
T576   T605/2   T608 (inc)   627/9a, T9bc, 21   T630 (inc)   646   D136

314: L Add 28864   Score, 18th century.
125 (in a minor)   D45

315: L Add 29291   Score, before 1762, when it belonged to R. Guise.
232/2e   246   D22   S52

316: L Add 29371   Score, 18th century.
T611/9   646   653   D136   D137

317: L Add 29386   Score, ca. 1762. (Mainly written by E. T. Warren Horne)
244   248   253   255   256   262   264   265   270   272   273   274   275   276
277   278   280   281   283   284   286   288   290   292   574/10   D100   D102
D105   D106   D107   S55   S69

318: L Add 29397   Score, ca. 1682 to 1690.
248   251   272   273   282   288   289   292   370   373   406   413   594   D100   S66

319: L Add 29399   Score, early 18th century.
328

320: L Add 29430   Score, early 18th century.
31 (for soprano)

321: L Add 30382   Score, 1678 to 1686. In the hand of H. Bowman.
489 497

322: L Add 30478-9   Tenor cantoris part-book, late 17th century. 'George Davenport (1664)'.
43 (tenor)

323: L Add 30839   Parts, *ca.* 1690.
    (and 39565-7)   574/2, 3, 6 to 9 627/21, T22, 25, 34 628/10a, 15a, MT27, 31, 37 (in G Major),
40 629/1ab, 2, 4a, 6, 17a, 18, T23, 26, 34a, 38, 44 630/1, 2, 3a, 11, 22 632/2
to 9 (Paisible)

324: L Add 30930   Score. Autograph.
13A (inc) **102** (inc) **103ab** **130** **131** **132** **133** **135** **136** **137** (inc) **138**
140 **141** **142** **143** **144** **577/8** **597/4** **730** **732** **733** to **744** **745** **746**
747 **752** **770** **802** **803** **804** **805** (inc) **808** **809** **810** **811**

325: L Add 30931   Score, late 17th century. Partial autograph.
4 **5** **27** (section 2 only) 31 33 (organ score) **45** 54 **58A** 62

326: L Add 30932   Score, late 17th to early 18th century. Partial autograph, partially in the hand
of John Henstridge.
2 (organ score) **3** **6** **28** **64** 185 **731** (fragment) S1 S16

327: L Add 30933   Score, early 18th century. Belonged to the Reverend Joshua Dix in the 19th
century.
51/3b 101 104 105 106 108

328: L Add 30934   Score, 1689. Autograph.
342

329: L Add 31404   Score, 18th century.
19

330: L Add 31405   Score, 18th century.
35 36 56 (inc) 57 339/3ab (inc) 600/1

331: L Add 31420   Score, 19th century.
125

332: L Add 31435   Score, after 1680. 'All the Fanta (*sic*) in this book of Mr. Locks Exad by Mr.
Purcells Score Book.'
733

333: L Add 31443   Score, *ca.* 1700.
51

334: L Add 31444-5   Score, early 18th century.
9 33 48 49 57 58C S4 (Norris) (31444 has only No. 58c)

335: L Add 31446   Organ book, *ca.* 1698.
718 D229

336: L Add 31447   Score, *ca.* 1700.
320 321 327 328 331 333 335 338 340 342 574 (inc) 575 (inc)
583 (inc) 600 (inc) 628 (inc) 630 (inc) 632 (inc)

337: L Add 31448   Score, early 18th century.
328 339 584

338: L Add 31449 Score, after 1696.
630 (inc)

339: L Add 31450 Score, 1784.
626 (inc) 631 (substitute overture by Norris.)

340: L Add 31452 Score, before 1737. Owned by James Kent.
342 574 583 632 (inc)

341: L Add 31453 Score, early 18th century. Dated on f.37v 'Jan. 1699'.
321/2, 5 328 379C 441 574/17 578/6a 603/10 (in c minor) 630 (inc) S50

342: L Add 31455 Part-books, after 1713. Owned by Julian Marshall.
320 (inc) 333 (inc) 574/11 583 600 (inc) 627 (inc) 628/36 630 632 (inc)

343: L Add 31460 Score, 17th to 18th century.
181 189 190 191 193 198 D70

344: L Add 31461 Score, early 18th century.
31 (for soprano)

345: L Add 31465 Score, early 18th century.
660/1, 2, 3 662/2, 3 663/2, 4 667/2, 3 668/1 669/1 T687 T698 716
S125 S126

346: L Add 31468 Organ book, 17th to 18th century.
719

347: L Add 33234 Score. 'Liber Caroli Morgan (?) è Coll. Magd:/Dec^{mo} 6to die 7^{bris} Anno
Domini/1682.'
138 142 144 335/5a 370 413 426 481 482 490 491 541 628/30bcef
S16 S66

348: L Add 33235 Score, late 17th century.
132 138 143 189 191 406 (in a minor) 480 543 545 D70 .

349: L Add 33236 Score, late 17th century.
189 200 369 406 543/1 (ascribed to John Blow) 628/35 730 (inc) 732
(inc) 733 748 749 750 751

350: L Add 33240 Organ book, 1683. Supposed autograph.
339

351: L Add 33287 Score, late 17th century.
322 (inc) 324 325 326 334 (inc) 335 336 337 339 341 343 344 506
508 510 541 542 543 544 628/12

352: L Add 33568 Score, ca. 1768.
S17

353: L Add 34203 Organ score, late 17th century. George Loosemore.
6 ('Mr. Pursol')

354: L Add 34204 Flute book, ca. 1708.
321/4a, 14a M574/6 605/2 (music only)

355: L Add 34609 Organ book, ca. 1759.
D225

356: L Add 34695 Organ book, early 18th century.
661/1 662/1 666/1 720 721 D229

357: L Add 35024 Score, late 18th century.
33 123

358: L Add 35043 Violin or flute book, *ca.* 1694 to 1697. 'John Channing.'
371 406 412 (in C Major) 570/1 to 4, 6, 7, 9 574/1ab 576 578/T7b, 8
588/5 591 592/10 (in d minor) 595/1 602/2 607/10, 11 609/1 to 9 610
611/1, 2, 4 to 6, 8, 9 627/9bc, 18b, 21, 33a 629/4b, 22b, 51 630/1, 2, 3ab,
4a, 11, 16, 17b, 18, 20, 22 (see 'overture' in Commentary); 632/1 to 5 (anon),
6 to 9 (Paisible), 20 (Purcell) T678 T680 D135 (anon) D136 (anon) D200
(N.B. All the foregoing are without text.)

359: L Add 37027 Score, *ca.* 1700. 'Edward Skilton.'
58C 120 121 123 (in a minor) 134 630/21bce 631 (inc) D32

360: L Add 37072-3 Scores, after 1720.
33 36

361: L Add 37232 Treble book.
632/19ab

362: L Add 38189 Treble book, *ca.* 1690.
31

363: L Add 38648 Score, 'John Alcock, London 1734.'
230MCE (inc)

      L Add 39565-7 See Add 30839 (MS 323)

364: L Add 39569 Harpsichord book. 'William Babel, 1702.'
T629/17 660 T678 T681 T682 T686 S125

365: L Add 39868 Organ book. 'John Bennet,' March 25, 1724.
40 (inc)

366: L Add 40139 Score.
628/38 D137

367: L Add 41205 Harpsichord book, mid 18th century.
642/1, 2 664 T681 T682 T690 T691 T692 T693 (inc) D218

368: L Add 47446 Dance book. 'William Pitt, June 12th 1722.'
574/2, 3 T629/12 630/11 632/2 T678 (in F Major) D137

369: L Add 47845 Score, mid 18th century. In the hand of James Kent (?) 1700–1776.
2 20 47 57

370: L Eg 3767 Treble part-book. 'E.C.' early 18th century.
19 31 230/1, 2, 7, 8

LONDON, ROYAL ACADEMY OF MUSIC LIBRARY

373: LAM [1] Score, late 17th century. Theatre holograph. Partial autograph.
629/ (the following sections are autograph or partly autograph) **2a** (partly),
2b, 3a (partly), **6, 26, 35** (partly), **38, 39b** (partly), **49a** (partly), **49bcde**, (?)**51**

374: LAM Misc. 2 Score, late 18th to 19th century.
630/21

375: LAM [3] 'The Books of John Townsend Junr.' 1698/9.
628

376: LAM [4] Score, late 18th (?) century. Bookplate of James Kent.
328

APPENDIX III

377: LAM   N.Pr. [5]   Score, late 18th to 19th century.
574 (inc)   583   632

378: LAM   [6]   Score, late 18th century.
232/1 (The *Jubilate* is copied in a late 19th to 20th century hand.)

LONDON, BRITISH COUNCIL LIBRARY

380: LBC   Chor 220   Score, early to mid 18th century.
327   342   629/27 to 32

381: LBC   Chor 221   Score, mid to late 18th century. ' Sir Watkin Williams Wynn Bart.'
182   184   191   575   631

382: LBC   Chor 222   Score, mid to late 18th century.
630

383: LBC   Chor 233   Score, mid to late 18th century.
333   600

384: LBC   Op. 29   Score, mid to late 18th century.
628

385: LBC   Op. 45   Score, mid to late 18th century. The gathering containing *No. 629* (ff. 1–69) is probably in an early 18th century hand.
574   583/1, 2, 3   629   D172

386: LBC   Coll 79   Score, mid to late 18th century.
16   321   328   334   342

LONDON, ROYAL COLLEGE OF MUSIC LIBRARY

389: LCM   517   Score, late 18th century. Written by E. T. Warren Horne.
13A   103   130   131   132   133   135   136   137   138   140   141   142   143   144

390: LCM   519   Score, 18th century.
322

LCM   520   See Commentary to *King Arthur* (*No. 628*).

391: LCM   810   Score, 18th century.
31

392: LCM   822   Score, 18th century.
323/3   628/2a   629/3   632/1 (Trumpet Sonata)

393: LCM   990   Score, 18th century.
631 (inc)

394: LCM   991   Score, 18th century.
632

395: LCM   993   Score, 1765. Robt Pindar 1765.
323   328   333 (corrupt)   339   583

396: LCM   994   Score, 18th century. Bookplates of John Lucius Dampier and Sir John Dolben, Bart.
320   327   331   338   629/27 to 32

397: LCM   995   Score, 18th century. Bookplates of John Lucius Dampier and Sir John Dolben, Bart.
342   600

398: LCM 996 Score, 18th century. Bookplates of John Lucius Dampier and Sir John Dolben, Bart.
321 326 333 335 575

399: LCM 998-9 Scores, 18th century. '?Copies by Tho. J. Barrow of Westminster Abbey.'
133 140 142 143 770 790 to 801 802 to 811

400: LCM 1056 Score, 18th century.
33

401: LCM 1059 Score, 17th to 18th century.
36 53

402: LCM 1064 Score, 17th to 18th century.
546/3 632/19ab S51 (D. Purcell) S61

403: LCM 1068 Four voice parts (treble, alto, tenor, bass), 17th to 18th century.
2 4 19 33 (supposed autograph; treble missing) 35 36 57 (bass; inc)

405: LCM 1119 Dance book, late 17th century.
253 290 435 442 S56

406: LCM 1144 Score, 17th to 18th century.
570/1 to 9 574/1 to 9 593/1 to 8 607/1 to 9 609/1 to 9 628/10bc, 15a, 17b, 18, 34, 38 629/1ab, 2, 3, 6, 7a, T10a, 15, 16, 17a, 18, 19, 20, 26, 38, 41, 44a T50e, 51, Appendix 4 630/1b, 2, 3, 4a, 11, 16ab, 17bc, 18, 20, 22 632/1 to 9 T678

407: LCM 1147 Score, 1746. Written by John Alcock.
570/1 572/1, 2 574/1 577/1 592/1 597/1 603/1 611/1 627/3 628/2 629/1a, 3, 15, 18a 630/3

408: LCM 1172 Score, 17th to 18th century.
570/6, 7, 9 574/8, 9 577/6 592/8 597/1; 2, 3 609/1 611/1a, 2, 9 628/18 629/6 631/1ab 632/20 D256 (bis, the second attr. to 'Peasable' and called 'Pleasure')

409: LCM 2010 Score, 17th to 18th century.
328

410: LCM 2011 Score, late 17th century.
2 3 16 19 21 29 30 42 47 49 55 63 65

411: LCM 2042 Score. 'Abraham Whorly, His Book 1729.'
35 (bass only; without text) D1 (bass only)

412: LCM 2230 Score. 'William Croft is Booke 1700.'
630/5, 6, 7, 21

LONDON, CHAPEL ROYAL PART-BOOKS

430: LCR RM.23.m.1-6 Set of six part-books, 17th to 18th century. Now in the Music Room of the British Museum.

a: LCR RM.23.m.1 Contratenor decani part-book.
2 4 19 26 31 33 35 36 37 52 57 60 61 230ME

b: LCR RM.23.m.2 Tenor decani part-book.
2 4 18 19 26 31 33 35 36 52 57 60 61 230ME

c: LCR RM.23.m.3 Bassus decani part-book.
2 4 (last chorus) 7 19 26 31 33 35 36 52 57 60 61 230ME

d: LCR RM.23.m.4   Contratenor cantoris part-book.
     2   4   18   19   26   31   33   35   36   37   52   57   61   230ME

e: LCR RM.23.m.5   Tenor cantoris part-book.
     2   4   19   26   31   35   36   52   57   60   61   230ME

f: LCR RM.23.m.6   Bassus cantoris part-book.
     2   4   18   19   26   31   33   35   36   52   57   60   61   230ME

LONDON, GRESHAM COLLEGE LIBRARY

441: LGC VI.4.19   Score, late 18th century.
     790 to 801   802 to 811

442: LGC VI.5.6   Score. Autograph.
     321/9a, 14ab 323/5a (without flutes) **328/4, 6b, 11b 352 354** (inc; voice only) **365 377** (voice only) **382 389 400 404 412 412 425 428A 429 486 570/10** (without bass) **573 576 578/3 580/1 587 592/10 595/2 598 607/10 608 610 613/2 627/Appendix 1, Appendix 2 629/4b, 7, 8bc, 22b** (in F Major), **28** (slightly varied), **39b, 43** (in B-flat), **45** (for soprano), **47, 48** (bass slightly varied), **D140** (not autograph) **D142** (not autograph) **S63** (not autograph)

(N.B. In December, 1958, these MSS were transferred to the Guildhall Library.)

LONDON, KING'S (NOW QUEEN'S) MUSIC LIBRARY

(Music Room, British Museum)

453: LK 20.h.8   Score. Autograph.
     1 (inc; partly autograph) **16 18 19 20** (inc) **21** (index only) **29 30 38** (index only) **42 44 46 47 48** (inc) **49 55 57** (inc) **63 65 181** (inc) **191 200** 320 (inc) 322 (largely not autograph) **324 325 326 329** 332 333 **335 336 337 341** 343 344 **355 362 375** (title only) **380 406** (partly autograph) **422 423 462 468 480 489 490** 493 **497 506 508 510 511 514 516 522 524 541 542 543 544 545 547**

454: LK 20.h.9   Score, late 17th century.
     105   107   109   230ME (inc; *Magnificat* and *Nunc Dimittis* without text)   336/1 731   771   772   790 to 801

455: LK 23.a.17(9)   Score, early 18th century.
     628/12

456: LK 23.g.3   Score, late 18th century.
     578/1, 3

     LK 23.m.1–6   See MS 430 above.

457: LK 24.e.3   Score, 18th century.
     5

458: LK 24.e.4   Score, 1699.
     321

459: LK 24.e.5   Scores, late 17th century.
     (1)   334
     (2)   342 (Owned by John Sale.)

460:	LK	24.e.6	Score, early 18th century.

321/2ab, 5, 14 333/7 335/5a 339/3ab 370 396 485 486 488 501 502 503 573 574/17 578/1, 3, 9 584 589 601/2 602/1 608 609/10 613/1 626/3a 628/26ab, 36 629/4b, 22b, 40b 630/15

461:	LK	24.e.7	Score, early 18th century.

321 (inc) 333 335

462:	LK	24.e.8	Score, early 18th century.

320 327 331 338

463:	LK	24.e.9	Score, 18th century.

328 (in C Major)

464:	LK	24.e.10	Scores, late 18th century.
		(1)	630 (inc)
		(2)	631 (inc)

465:	LK	24.e.11	Score, 18th century.

628

466:	LK	24.e.12	Scores, 18th century.
		(1)	629 (very incomplete)
		(2)	574 (inc)
		(3)	358 376 412 427 595/1

467:	LK	24.e.13	Miscellaneous scores, bound in one volume.
		(1)	Score, 18th century.
			600 (inc; Section 3ab in D Major)
		(2)	Score. In the hand of (?) Jeremiah Clarke, except for the Overture.
			632 (inc)
		(3)	Viola and basso continuo parts, 18th century.
			609/1 611/1ab 627/3
		(4)	Score.
			583 (inc)
		(5)	Score.
			572/1 to 8
		(6)	Score.
			592/1 to 9
		(7)	Score.
			577/7, 8 597/7, 8

468:	LK	24.c.15	Score, mid 18th century.

286

LONDON, MUSIC ROOM, BRITISH MUSEUM

470:	LMR	K.i.c.5	Manuscript additions to *Choice Lessons* . . . 1696. Harpsichord book, late 17th century.

T693 D219

471:	LMR	Hirsch III, 472	*Choice Lessons* . . . 1696. Harpsichord book, late 17th century. Nine pages of manuscript music at the back of this copy, once part of the Taphouse collection.

T678 T679 T682 T691 T697

472:	LMR	d24	Manuscript section bound in at the back of a copy of *Theater Airs* [n.p., n.d.], Sir Griffith Boynton's book, *ca.* 1706.
		1–22	T678

APPENDIX III

LONDON, ST. PAUL'S CATHEDRAL LIBRARY

478: LPC Five part-books, 17th to 18th century. Once owned by John Gostling (?).

(a)   Tenor decani I.
230 (inc)

(b)   Tenor decani II.
19 22 23 24 26 33 52 60

(c)   Counter tenor II.
230 (inc)

(d)   Bass decani I.
19 22 23 24 26 33 52 57 60

(e)   Bass cantoris II.
4 19 22 23 24 26 31 33 52 57 60

LONDON, UNIVERSITY OF LONDON LIBRARY

480: LU Manuscript additions at the back of a copy of *Orpheus Britannicus* I (1698), apparently in a late 18th century hand. ' Bailey Morley, his book 1750.'
583/1b, 4

LONDON, WESTMINSTER ABBEY LIBRARY

481: LWA   Part-books (missing, but mentioned in *Purcell's Sacred Music*, London: Novello, 1828–44, Preface).
10 24 34

482: LWA CJ3(2) Score. ' Finis 1701 Jan.'
627

LOS ANGELES, CALIFORNIA, W. A. CLARK LIBRARY

485: LaC *M401. Manuscript addenda at the back of a continuo book for Purcell's sonata, pub-
P98s Pt 4 lished in 1683. Late 17th to early 18th century.
810 850

486: LaC C6975M4 Twelve volumes of catches, etc., 18th century.
274

487: LaC f0235M4 Score, mid 18th century.
328/8, 9

LEEDS, CENTRAL PUBLIC LIBRARY

489: Le F091/784 Song book, 17th to 18th century.
31 335/5a 578/1, 7b

LICHFIELD CATHEDRAL LIBRARY

500: LfC [1]   Part-books, *ca.* 1700 to *ca.* 1715.
   a: Alto decani.
            2   4   19   22   33   36   53   58C   61   230 (inc)   232
   b: Tenor decani.
            2   4   19   22   33   35   36   53   54   58C   61   230 (inc)   232
   c: Bass decani.
            2   22   33   35   36   53   54   58C   230 (inc)   232
   d: Alto cantoris.
            2   4   19   22   31   33   35   36   53   58C   61   230 (inc)   232
   e: Bass cantoris.
            2   4   9   22   33   35   36   53   54   58C   60   61   230 (inc)   232

501: LfC [2]   Score. ' J. Barker, 1720.'
            2   4   56   57

502: LfC   Missing. ' The First Volume by Mr. Henry Purcell. J. Barker 1750.'

503: LfC [3]   ' The Second Volume by Mr. Henry Purcell, J. Barker 1750.'
            7   9   17A   19   22   25   31   33   35   36   50   60   61   187   230

504: LfC [4]   Score. ' J. Barker, 1750.'
            35

505: LfC [5]   Part-books, mid and late 18th century.
   a: Contratenor decani.
            2   19   22   33   35   36   58C   60   61   230 (inc)   232
   b: Tenor decani.
            2   4   9   19   22   28   31 (inc)   33   35   36   54   57   58C   60   61   230 (inc)   232
   c: Bass decani.
            2   4   9   19   28   33   35   54   57   60   61   230 (inc)   232
   d: Bass I.
            2   4   19   22   33   35   36   60   61   230 (inc)   232
   e: Bass II.
            2   4   9   19   22   28   33   35   36   53   54   57   58C   60   61   230 (inc)   232
   f: Bass III.
            2   4   9   19   22 (page missing)   28   33   35   36   58C   61   230 (inc)   232
   g: Bass IV.
            9

506: LfC [6]   Part-books (counter tenor and bass), mid 18th century.
            2   4   9   19   33   36   61

LINCOLN CATHEDRAL LIBRARY

509: LinC   Four of a set of part-books.
   a: Counter tenor cantoris, ' Examined October/5th, 1685.'
            2   4   9   19   27 (inc)   31   33   35   40   49   52   54   56   61
   b: Tenor decani, ' Examined October the 5th 1685.'
            4   9   19   27 (inc)   33   40   49   52   54   56   60   61

c:		Bass cantoris, 'Examined the 10th of August 1686.'
		2 4 9 19 27 (inc) 31 33 35 40 49 52 54 56 60 61
d:		Bass decani.
		2 4 9 19 27 (inc) 31 33 35 40 49 52 54 56 60 61
510:	LinC	Bass I. Anthem part-book, 'Sept: 26th 1720.'
		2 9 19 33 36 56 61
511a:	LinC	Bass anthem part-book, 'Ex: April ye 8th 1703.'
		2 4 9 19 27 33 49 56 60 61
b:		Tenor anthem part-book, 'Examined Sept. 15th, 1701.'
		2 4 9 19 27 33 49 60 61
512:	LinC	Bass cantoris, anthem part-book, 'September 7th, 1726.'
		35
513:	LinC	Bass cantoris, anthem part-book, 'Exam: Sep: 13. 1737.'
		2 19 33 35 36 56 61
514:	LinC	Bass cantoris, anthem part-book, 'Sep: 17. 1726.'
		4 35 36

LIVERPOOL UNIVERSITY MUSIC LIBRARY

515:	LivU	1 Score, mid 18th century.
		9 56

MANCHESTER PUBLIC LIBRARY

(Henry Watson Music Library)

516:	M	BRm370Bp35 Organ book for anthems by Purcell and Blow, late 17th century. Probably in the hand of John Blow.
		5 7 18 27 48 54 56
517:	M	BRm340Rb15 'The Organ book of William Raylton when under Dr. Croft's tuition.' Late 17th century.
		4 19 35 230ME
518:	M	BRm370CR71 'Josiah Bradbury his Book of Psalms and Anthem tunes.' June 22nd, 1755.
		7 9 19 33 61

MARBURG (FROM THE DEUTSCHE STAATSBIBLIOTHEK, BERLIN)

528:	Ma	Mus 17985 Score, late 18th century.
		134
529:	Ma	Mus 40228 Score, late 18th century.
		286

KENNETH MUMMERY MANUSCRIPT

535:	See 'Private Collections' below.

APPENDIX III

NANKI COLLECTION

540–548: See 'Private Collections' below.

NEW YORK PUBLIC LIBRARY, MUSIC DIVISION

568: NYP Drexel MS 4285.6   Score, mid 18th century.
583

569: NYP Drexel MS 5061   Score, late 17th century.
732 735 736 737 738 739 740 741 742 743 745 746 747
752

570: NYP 5609   Harpsichord book, 18th century.
T570/8 T627/9bc 646 666/4 T677 T677 (in A Major) T683
T691 T697 D227 D231

OXFORD, BODLEIAN LIBRARY

(The number immediately following the letter ' O ' in this list is that assigned to each of the following
MSS in the *Summary Catalogue of Western MSS in the Bodleian Library*)

581: O (16702) **Mus C.26**   Score, late 17th century. Partial autograph.
16 24 192 320 **328** (largely autograph) 339 (inc) 628/35

582: O (16703) Mus C.27   Incomplete set of parts, late 17th century.
328 (inc) 583 (inc) 606/1, 2, 3, 4

583: O (16703*) Mus C.27*   Score, 1695. Autograph.
342

584: O (16708) Mus d.3   Score, 17th to 18th century.
333 600 (inc)

585: O (16677) Mus B.10   Score, 1765, in the hand of J. Awbery.
328

586: O (16847) **Mus A.1**   Score. Autograph.
230M/3 (with fragment of Monteverdi's *Cruda Amarilli* on the back
of a correction slip.)

587: O (26396) Mus Sch D.217   Score, 1689 to 1703.
108 122 193 (ground only)

588: O (26397) Mus Sch C.38   Score, 1700.
232

589: O (26398) Mus Sch C.39   Score, *ca.* 1700. ' Charles Badham.'
2 4 19 22

590: O (26399) Mus Sch C.40   Score, *ca.* 1700. ' Charles Badham.'
7 52 57 (another version) 60 N67

591: O (26400) Mus Sch B.7   Score, *ca.* 1720.
232/1

592: O (26426) Mus Sch C.61   Score, 1688 to 1692. ' Mr. Thomas Mace his book, 1676 '; ' H.
Knight, A.B. è Coll. Wadh.'
31 369 473/2 D257

593: O (26437) Mus Sch C.72   Instrumental parts (2 violins, basso continuo), late 17th century.
574/1, 5 to 9, 15a, 16a   611/1 to 4, 6, 9   630/1, 2, 3, 9, 22

594: O (26439) Mus Sch C.73   Score, late 17th century.
570/4, 5

595: O (26465) Mus Sch C.96   Score, late 17th century.
370   501   517   S68

596: O (26495) Mus Sch E.397   Score, 18th century.
570/2   T630/1   T675   T681   T684   D224   S120   S124

597: O (26545) Mus Sch D.254   Instrumental parts.
802 (in a minor)   803   804

598: O (26896) Mus Sch C.95   Score, early 18th century.
243   248   252   264   265   282   288   289   351   486   571/1 to 7
572/9, 11   574/10   578/6ab   601/1   602/2   605/1   607/10   609/10, 11
M611/7   627/18b, 22, 33a   629/4b, 17abc (inc)   630/17h   D100
D136   D571/9

599: O (26898–901)
     Mus Sch E.400–3   Instrumental parts (2 violins, viola, basso continuo), early 18th century.
802 (in a minor)   803   804

600: O (26905) Mus Sch e 563   Score, early 18th century.
T678

601: O (28973) Mus C.28   Score. Supposed autograph.
130   132   133   136   138   139   140   141   142   143   144   321
332   545   574 (inc)   578 (Part One incomplete; Part Two) D251

602: O (16676) MS b.9   Score, late 18th century.
232

603: O (not yet entered in   Score, 17th century. Probably in the hand of Jeremiah Clarke.
     S.C.) Mus.C.58   4   19   33   35   36   56

604: O (not yet entered in   Scores, 18th century. 'Mr. E. Goddard, No 36 Upper Charlotte
     S.C.) Mus C.107   Street Portland Place.'
574/10   D100 (anon)

605: O (not yet entered in   Flute book. 'Wm. Stakely M.B. ex dono Hen. Heron Ar. 1714.'
     S.C.) Mus e.33   321/2a (in F Major)

606: O (26614) Mus Sch g.614 ? Flute book, 'Anne Burrows, 1694.'
602/2   627/4, T18b   629/17bc

607: O (26615) Mus Sch g.615 Lute and Violin book, early 18th century. 'C. Galoff.' (At reverse
end: 'James Shatterton.')
574/15b, 16b

OXFORD, CHRIST CHURCH LIBRARY

612: OCH 3   Score, late 17th to early 18th century.
570/1   572/1   574/1a   577/1   592/1ab (inc)   597/1   603/1   607/1   611/1a
627/3   628/2   629/3, 18   630/3   808   809   810

613: OCH 22   Score, late 17th (?) century.
27   31   58B   N67 (chorus only)

614:	OCH	23	Score, early 18th century. 'Mr. Richard Goodson, his book.' 134 321/1 to 7, 14ab 482
615:	OCH	32	Score, early 18th (?) century. 328 (inc) 574/11, 13b 583 630/4efgh, 6b, 7, 17bc, 21bc, 22 632/15, 19
616:	OCH	38	Score, 17th to 18th century. 230 (inc)
617:	OCH	39	Score, 17th to 18th century. 790 to 801
618:	OCH	46	Score, late 17th century. 574/16 645 S121
619:	OCH	48	Score, 17th to 18th century. 120
620:	OCH	350	Score, 17th to 18th century. 370 426
621:	OCH	351–2	Part-books (tenor and bass), early 18th century. 570 (inc) 611
622:	OCH	360	Score, late 17th century. 578/7, 9 627/18b 630/19
623:	OCH	363	Score, early 18th century. 570/6 T574/16b 592/5 627/25 628/17a, 26 629/1b, 40b 630/15
624:	OCH	389	Score, 17th to 18th century. 441 584 627/26c 630/17h
625:	OCH	440	Incomplete organ score, mid 18th century. 232 (bass part only, inc; in C Major)
626:	OCH	468–71	Part-books (instrumental and vocal), 1729.
a:		468	Treble and alto instrumental parts: trumpet, violin and oboe. 321 (inc) 627/22, 38b
b:		469	Treble. 'George Jeffries, 1729.' 321 (inc) 627/22
c:		470	Bass. 321 (inc) 334 629/40b 630/14, 15
d:		471	Alto part S8
627:	OCH	482	One of a set of 6 part-books, 17th to 18th century. 632/1 to 9 (bass part only)
628:	OCH	580	Score, late 17th to 18th century. 'Catherine Brooks, her book.' 326/11a (treble and bass) 394 (soprano part only) 414 441 605/2 609/11 613/2 630/4g, 6a, 17h, 19 631/10 D142
629:	OCH	620	Score, before 1702. 'Liber Richard Goodson, Jur.' [sic]. 570/8 572/2, 4, 7 574/4, 6 577/2, 3, 8 592/9 597/3 603/2, 8 (inc) 607/3, 5, 8 611/3 627/9a, 19, 21, 34 628/11, Appendix 1, 3 629/2, 44a 630/4a, 17bc, 18, 22 745 810 811
630:	OCH	628	Score, early 18th century. 103ab 131 132 135 138 140 141 142 143 144
631:	OCH	766	Score, late 17th or early 18th century. 31

632: OCH 794   Score. Bound with several printed works, including Purcell's *Te Deum* and *Jubilate*.
58C 860

633: OCH 960   Score. 'Thomas Ford. d. 1723.'
628/16b (inc) 631/10 (inc)

634: OCH 1109   Score, early 18th century (?).
33

635: OCH 1114   Score, mid 18th (?) century. 'Miss Goodson.'
628/38 (treble part only)

636: OCH 1125   Score, mid 18th century.
627/1

637: OCH 1128   Score, late 17th century.
632/1

638: OCH 1145   Score, 17th to 18th century.
334

639: OCH 1150   Score, late 17th century.
545

640: OCH 1174   Score, late 17th (?) century.
790 to 801

641: OCH 1176   Score, 17th to 18th century.
665/2 D240

642: OCH 1177   Score, before 1714. 'R. Goodson, Sr.'
654 662

643: OCH 1179   Score, 1685 to 1690. 'George Lluellyn.'
665/2 717 S126

644: OCH 1183   Score, 18th century.
627/16

645: OCH 1186   Score, 18th century.
328/1abc

646: OCH 1188–9   Instrumental parts, late 17th century (?).
31

647: OCH 1220–4   Five part-books, 17th century.
  a: 1220   Alto.
4 19 22 33
  b: 1221   Tenor I.
4 19 22 33
  c: 1222   Tenor II.
4 19 22 33 57
  d: 1223   Bass decani.
4 19 22 33
  e: 1224   Bass cantoris.
4 19 22 33 57

648: OCH 1226   Score, 18th century.
19 120 122 D31

649: OCH 1229   Score, 18th century.
57 120 123 D33

650: OCH 1230   Organ score, late 17th century.
                     22   36

651: OCH 1231   Organ score, early 18th century.
                     230ME (inc)

652: OCH 1232   Organ score, early 18th century.
                     35

653: OCH 1235   Organ score, 18th century.
                     19   33

OXFORD, MAGDALEN COLLEGE LIBRARY

664: OMC Book II.2.3   Organ parts of services, *ca.* 1680.
                            D90

665: OMC Anthems No 2   Organ part. (MSS now missing, contents from catalogue.)
                            31   33

666: OMC Organ book No 6   Undated organ book. (MSS now missing, contents from catalogue.)
                            4   33   36   41   49   53 or 54   61   120

667: OMC (Fellows Library)   Manuscript copy inserted into *Harmonia Sacra* I (1688).
          w.3.86   31 (bass part)

OXFORD, MUSIC FACULTY LIBRARY

670: OMF e.1   Score, mid 18th century.
                   370   484   517   574/15b, 16b   589   601/3   627/9b   628/36   629/12,
                   17bc   D144

671: OMF MSL 8.c.4   Scores, early to mid 18th century.
                   232   321

672: OMF MSL 8.b.19   Score, mid to late 18th century.
                   232

673: OMF MSL unnumbered   Score, late 18th to early 19th century.
                   243   253   254   257   259   260   262   266   267   268   270   272   274
                   277   280   282   285   286   288   289   574/10   S52 (anon)   S56 (Purcell)
                   S67 (Eccles)

OXFORD, ORIEL COLLEGE LIBRARY

676: OOC Ua 34   Score, mid 18th century.
                 574   583   632

677: OOC Ua 35   Score, mid 18th century.
                 628   630 (inc)

678: OOC Ua 36   Score, mid 18th century.
                 575

679: OOC Ua 37   Score, mid 18th century.
                 342   860

APPENDIX III

PARIS, BIBLIOTHÈQUE DU CONSERVATOIRE

685: Pa Rés F 202   Score, 18th century.
                                628 (inc; only source for Appendix 4a)

686: Pa Rés 1186 bis, Part I   Keyboard book, 18th century.
                                663/2, 4

PETERBOROUGH CATHEDRAL LIBRARY

691: PC 2   Contratenor cantoris part-book, '1738.'
            31 61

692: PC 4   Tenor cantoris part-book, *ca.* 1760.
            31 61

693: PC 5   Tenor cantoris part-book, '1739.'
            31 61

694: PC 7   Bass part-book, '1717.'
            2 4 19 31 49 57 61 230ME

695: PC 8   Tenor decani part-book, '1754.'
            31 61

696: PC 13   Bass decani part-book, '1747.'
            D7

STANFORD MEMORIAL LIBRARY, PALO ALTO, CALIFORNIA

701: S [1]   Score. Supposed autograph.
            232 D143

SIBLEY LIBRARY, EASTMAN SCHOOL OF MUSIC, ROCHESTER, N.Y., U.S.A.

712: Si 151841   Score, late 17th century. Supposed autograph.
            790 to 801

713: Si M2040; A628 (Vault)   Score, *ca.* 1700.
            25 36 41 45 51

STONLEIGH ABBEY LIBRARY

724: StA [1]   Score, late 17th century. 'The Song Book of Mr. Montriot [?].'
            181 197 321/14ab 370 370 (in B♮ Major) 406 502 503 517 522 525 570/10
            572/11ab 578/1, 3 602/1 608 629/4b S58

TENBURY, ST. MICHAEL'S COLLEGE LIBRARY

735: T 310   Score, *ca.* 1706 to 1709.
            2 19 31 33 57

736: T 338   Score, *ca.* 1735 to 1750. 'John Travers.'
            328 333 574 583 600 628 (inc) 630 (inc) 632 (inc)

737: T 345   Score, *ca.* 1700.
                 9 328/4 379C 609/10

738: T 607   Organ short score, mid 18th century.
                 36

739: T 613   Score, late 18th century.
                 25 29 39 42 44 50 52 55

740: T 712   Organ short score, mid 18th century.
                 232

741: T 785   Score, *ca.* 1700.
                 572/4 574/4, 9 577 (inc) 588 597 603/6 607/6 611/4 628/2 to 4a, 5b to 10
                 629/1a, 18 630/3b

742: T 787   Score, 1685. 'The Score of Mr. John Parson's ffunerall Servis and probably was
                 used at the funeral of Charles the Second.' 'This is in the handwriting of Henry
                 Purcell.' (Signed) 'Joseph Warren.' Supposed autograph.

743: T 789   Score, *ca.* 1700. 'White Kennet, 1725, bought of Mr. John Brown, one of the lay
                 clerks.'
                 2 7 9 (inc) 31 33 40 49 52 61

744: T 797–803 Seven part-books, *ca.* 1715. In the hand of John Gostling. The missing part-book
                 is the Medius decani.
                 22

745: T 805   Score, late 18th century.
                 19 31 36 61

746: T 814–8   Miscellaneous scores.
   a: 814   Score, 18th to 19th century.
                 2 4
   b: 815   Score, late 18th century.
                 57
   c: 816:   Score, late 18th century.
                 4 7 33
   d: 817   Score, 18th to 19th century.
                 35
   e: 818   Score. In the hand of Bartleman (?).
                 31

749: T 1004   Score, late 18th century.
                 28 49 (to text, 'Laudate Dominum') 58A

750: T 1011   Score, *ca.* 1700.
                 790 791 798

751: T 1020   Score, 18th to 19th century.
                 4 33

752: T 1021   Score, late 18th century.
                 7 9 19 33

753: T 1029   Score, mid 18th century.
                 2 4 9 19 28 33 49 61

754: T 1031   Score, mid 18th century. Formerly belonging to Charles Badham.
                 27 28 33

755: T 1034   Score, mid 18th century.
                 2 4 19

756: T 1131   Score, mid 18th century. Formerly belonging to Thomas Bever.
                 578/9 630/13a

757: T 1174   Score, mid 18th century. Formerly belonging to Joseph Warren.
                 230 (inc)

758: T 1175   Score, ca. 1700. Formerly belonging to Wm Hawes (1841), and E. T. Warren
                 Horne. Another note states that this MS was transcribed from the original score,
                 dated 1680, in the handwriting of the author.
                 13A 103ab 130 131 132 133 134 135 136 137 138 140 141 142 143
                 144 182 184 333 574 D69 D201

759: T 1176–80 Five part-books: Medius decani, Contratenor cantoris, Tenor cantoris, Bass
                 cantoris and Organ book. In the hand of John Gostling (?).
                 5 7 9 18 27 35 36 44 48 51 54 56 65

760: T 1181   Organ book. In the hand of John Gostling. (Another book in the foregoing set.)
                 51

761: T 1182   Organ book. In the hand of John Gostling. (Another book in the foregoing set.)
                 35 36

762: T 1183   Score. 'John Smyth, Vic. Cicest. 1731.'
                 19 33 57

763: T 1226   Score, early 18th century.
                 333

764: T 1227[b] Score, early 18th century.
                 54 D76

765: T 1258   Score, early 18th century.
                 35 (full score) 36 (organ score) S12 (anon)

766: T 1226   Score, early 18th century.
                 321 342 626 (inc) 627 631 (inc)

767: T 1276   Score, mid 18th century.
                 609/10

768: T 1278   Score, mid 18th century. ' Mr. Leveridge.'
                 630 (inc; bass part only)

769: T 1287   Score, mid 18th century.
                 28

770: T 1309   A set of 19 vocal and instrumental parts, ca. 1700.
                 328

771: T 1503   Score. 'John Phipps his score-book, Jan 6th 1714–15.'
                 2 19 31 33 38 61

772: T 1504   Score, early 18th century.
                 61

773: T 1505–7 Set of three part-books in late 17th century hand.
                 7 19 33 49 61 S4 S10

774: T 1508   Score. 'Ce livre apartient à G.m Babel 1701 London.'
                 611/9 630/1a, 2b 660 663/1 669/2, 3 T678 T686 T698 S125

TRAVIS AND EMERY MANUSCRIPT

780: See 'Private Collections' below.

APPENDIX III

VIENNA, ÖSTERREICHISCHE NATIONALBIBLIOTHEK

787: V SA.68.A.202   Score, late 18th century.
135

788: V Sm.5675   Score, late 18th century.
631 (bass songs; inc)

789: V 17034   Aria, late 18th century.
631/13

WASHINGTON D.C., LIBRARY OF CONGRESS, MUSIC SECTION

790: W ML 96 H.53   Score, mid 18th century. 'Francis Hopkinson, his book.'
321 629/17 (' By Dr. Purcell.')

791: W ML 96 P.89   Score, late 17th century. Supposed autograph.
516

WIMBORNE MINSTER LIBRARY

795: WM Undesignated   Part-books, anthems and service section.

a: Counter tenor ' A ', early or mid 18th century.
19 33 232

b: Counter tenor, early or mid 18th century.
19 51 232

c: Tenor decani. ' 1737, Reuben Gill, his book.'
19 232

d: Bass, early 18th century.
31 51 D33

796a: WM Undesignated   Tenor part-book (fragmentary), mid or late 18th century.
58C

b: Bass part-book, mid or late 18th century.
19 58C 232

WINDSOR, ST. GEORGE'S CHAPEL, CHAPTER LIBRARY

802: WiG Old MS 1   Organ book, 17th to 18th century.
19 31

803: WiG Old MS 5   Organ book, 17th to 18th century.
2

804: WiG Old MS 7   Organ book, 17th to 18th century.
31

805: WiG Old MS 8   Organ book, 17th to 18th century.
57 60

806: WiG Old MS 10   Organ book, 17th to 18th century.
230ME

807:   WiG   Undesignated   Bass part-book ('Solo book'), mid 18th century (?), solo bass and basso-continuo parts.
                            31

808:   WiG   The First Set   Part-books. anthems and services, early 18th century (?).

  a: Treble decani.
                            2   4   31   33   49

  c: Tenor decani.
                            2

  d: Bass decani.
                            2

  f: Contratenor cantoris.
                            2

  g: Tenor cantoris.
                            2

  h: Bass cantoris.
                            2

809:   WiG   The Second Set   Part-books, anthems and services. The bass decani book is dated on p. 67, 'pd. for Nov. 1744.' The treble cantoris book is perhaps of a later date.

  c: Tenor decani.
                            4   19

  d: Bass decani.
                            4   19

  e: Treble cantoris.
                            35   36

810:   WiG   The Third Set   Part-books, anthems and services, mid 18th century.

  a: Treble decani.
                            2   4   19   31   35   36   49

811:   WiG   The Fourth Set   Part-books, anthems and services. These are 19th century copies for the most part. However, all the contents are by Purcell's near-contemporaries, and the counter tenor decani and bass cantoris books are in an early hand (17th to 18th century), which may indicate that the other part-books were copied as replacements.

  b: Counter tenor decani.
                            35   36

  d: Bass decani.
                            230

  e: Treble cantoris (?).
                            230

  f: Counter tenor cantoris.
                            230

  g: Tenor cantoris.
                            4   19   33   49   57   60   230

  h: Bass cantoris.
                            4   19   31   33   49   57   60   230

812:   WiG   No. 13(?)   Part-books, chants and anthems, mid to late 18th century.

b: Counter tenor decani.
                        35   36   61

f: Counter tenor cantoris.
                        33   35   36   57   61

WORCESTER CATHEDRAL LIBRARY

813:   WoC   A.2.1   Bass cantoris part-book, 1735 to 1755.
                        2   4   9   18   19   33   35   36   57   60   230 ME (inc)   232

814:   WoC   A.2.2   Bass decani part-book, 1741.
                        230ME (inc)   232

815:   WoC   A.2.3   Bass cantoris (?) part-book, 1727 to 1750.
                        2   4   9   19   31   33   57   60

816:   WoC   A.2.4   Bass decani part-book, 1744 to 1748. 'Dean's book.'
                        35   36

817:   WoC   A.2.5   Soprano part-book, ca. 1740.
                        230ME (inc)   232

818:   WoC   A.3.1   Bass cantoris part-book, ca. 1661–1715.
                        2   4   9   14   18   19   31   33   35   49   57   60   61

819:   WoC   A.3.2   Alto decani part-book, 1670 to 1683.
                        14

820:   WoC   A.3.3   Tenor part-book, 1670 to 1700.
                        4   9   15   18   19   31   33   35   49   61   230ME   232

821:   WoC   A.3.4   Alto cantoris part-book, 1695 to 1702.
                        4   9   14   19   31   33   35   36   49   57   61   230ME   232

822:   WoC   A.3.5   Bass decani part-book, ca. 1670 to 1706. 'Dec. 1, 1685.'
                        2   4   9   14   18   19   31   33   35   36   49   57   230ME   232

823:   WoC   A.3.6   Tenor decani part-book.
                        4   9   31   33   35   36   49   63   230ME   232

824:   WoC   A.3.8   Score, 18th century.
                        57

       WoC   A.3.9   See MS 837 below.

825:   WoC   A.3.10   Organ book, 1705 to 1726.
                        4   8   9   11   27   31   41   60

826:   WoC   A.3.11   Bass book, 18th century.
                        4   9   19   33   41   60   230ME

827:   WoC   A.3.12   Tenor cantoris part-book, 1702 to 1706.
                        2   8   11   27   31 (Alleluia; chorus only)   41   57   60

828:   WoC   A.3.13   Alto decani part-book, ca. 1700 to 1760. 'Mr. Forrester's handwriting.'
                        2   8   11   27   41   58C

829:   WoC   A.3.14   Bass decani part-book, ca. 1700 to 1760. 'For the thanksgiving: Jan 27, 1706.'
                        2   8   11   27   41   58C

830:   WoC   A.3.15   Alto decani part-book, ca. 1706 to 1748. Dated on p. 22, 'For the Thanks-
                        giving for the Victory of Rammilies [sic] in Brabant and the Relief of Barce-
                        lona, celebrated Jan 27, 1706.'
                        2   8   11   27   41

| 831: | WoC | A.3.16 | Tenor decani part-book, *ca.* 1706 to 1748. Dated on p. 10, 'For the Thanks-giving, June 17, 1706.' |

2   8   11   27   35   36   41   57   58C   60 (chorus only)

| 832: | WoC | A.3.17 | Alto part-book, *ca.* 1740 to 1770. |

4   9   31   33   57   60   230ME

| 833: | WoC | A.7.6 | Score, 18th century. 'Tho. Pitt.' |

2   3   16   18   19   21   29   30   42   47   55   63   65

| 834: | WoC | Mus B.18 | Score, *ca.* 1720. 'Anthems in Score by Chapel Royal Musicians.' |

19   31   57

| 835: | WoC | Mus B.2.2 | Organ book, mid 18th century. |

19   57   61

| 836: | WoC | Mus B.2.5 | Organ book, mid 18th century. |

2   4   9   31   33   35   36   57

| 837: | WoC | Mus A.3.9 | Score, copied by Rev. Matthew Forrester, probably between 1700 and 1720. |

19   31   33   57

YORK MINSTER LIBRARY

| 847: | YM | [1]* | Single folio score, late 17th (?) century. |

333/7

| 848: | YM | [2]
(M.2/1-11.S) | A set of 11 scores, late 18th century. 'W. Priestley Lightcliffe.' |

a:	Book 1	230ME (inc)
b:	Book 2	2
c:	Book 3	58C S8 (Weldon)
d:	Book 4	7 134
e:	Book 6	9 33 134 182
f:	Book 8	9 33 35
g:	Book 9	D250
h:	Book 11	61 230M/4
i:	Book 7	123

| 849: | YM | [3] | Score, late 18th century. 'W. Priestley Lightcliffe.' |

230ME (inc)

| 850: | YM | [4]
(M.1/1-8.S) | Eight part-books, early 18th century. 'William Gostling.' In the hands of Stephen Bing and John Gostling, *et altri.* |

a: Medius cantoris.
2   10   12   22   33   35   36   39   51   61   230   S1

b: Medius decani.
6   10   19   22   23   33   34   39   43 (inc)   51   60 (index only)   230   S1

c: Contratenor cantoris.
10   19   22   33 (index only)   35   36   39   51   57 (index only)   60 (index only)   230   S1

d: Contratenor decani.
2   6   10   22   23   33   34   39   43 (inc)   51   60   61 (inc)   230   S1

e:			Tenor cantoris.
			2 10 19 22 33 35 36 43 60 230 S1
f:			Tenor decani.
			6 10 23 33 (index only) 34 39 43 51 230 S1
g:			Bass cantoris.
			10 19 (index only) 22 33 (index only) 35 36 (also bass decani part)
			39 51 230 S1
h:			Bass decani.
			2 6 10 19 22 23 33 34 35 (index only) 36 (index only; copied
			into g) 39 43 (inc) 51 60 61 (inc) 230 D33 S1
851:	YM	[5] (M.6.S)	Score, 18th century.
			25 35 36 51 230E
852:	YM	[6a]	Organ score. 'Feb. 2nd 1830.'
			120 (in b minor) 123 124
853:	YM	[6b]	Organ score. 'Feb 2nd 1830.'
			120 (in b minor) 123 124
854:	YM	[7]	Commonplace book, 1743. 'Thomas Gent.'
			416 (w/o text)
855:	YM	[8] (M.8.S)	Score. '7ᵇʳ 1702 John Goldwyn.'
			2 4 9 19 31 56 61
856:	YM	[9]	Score, late 17th (?) century.
			328/2 (inc), 6 (inc)
857:	YM	[10] (M.26.S)	Score, early 18th century.
			629/3 630/3 810
858:	YM	[11]	Score, late 18th century.
			19
859:	YM	[12]	Alto book, ca. 1830.
			230C/5
860:	YM	[13] (M.14.S)	Score, early 18th century.
			49 230E 231
861:	YM	[14] (M.7.S)	Score, 19th century. (Presented by Vincent Novello to replace a copy
			lost in a fire.)
			27 56 231
862:	YM	[15] (M.9.S)	Score, 17th to 18th century. 'Bought of ye Widow of Charles Quarles
			for half a guinea by Will: Knight-January 1717/8.'
			232 328 (inc) 608
863:	YM	[16] (M.11.S)	Score, late 17th century.
			120 121 182 246 485 (soprano only) 486 (soprano only) 501
			(soprano only) 502 (soprano only) 521 578/1 (alto only) 602/1
			613/1 (soprano only) 628/26 (soprano only) D37
864:	YM	[17]	Treble cantoris, late 18th century.
			D91
865:	YM	[18] (M.15.S)	Score, late 17th (?) century.
			850
866:	YM	[19] (M.12.S)	Score, late 17th (?) century. In the same hand as MS [16] above.
			241 243 244 245 247 248 253 254 255 259 262 264 265 267

270 272 273 274 275 276 280 281 284 286 287 288 289 290
291 338/9a 342/2d 513 574/10 591 627/35 628/35 630/17h
D100 D102 D144 S61

867: YM [20] (M.5/1–3,5) Part-books. 'Harrison.' '1688.'
189 199

868: YM [21] (M.21.S) Score.
18

869: YM [22] (M.32/1.S) Score, mid 18th century.
608

870: YM [23] (M.75) Score, mid 18th century.
503 571/6 608 630/13a D134

871: YM [24] (M.161) Score, late 18th to early 19th century.
125 (bass only) D91

872: YM [25] (M.87) Score, late 18th century.
134 (inc; corrupt)

873: YM [26] (M.57/1–3) Part-books, early 18th century.
810

* The numbers in square brackets above are from a provisional finding-list for Purcell works in York Minster Library. Those in round brackets are the press-marks devised by Mr. Jack Pilgrim, who has recently undertaken the task of cataloguing the whole of the library. Still more recently, Mr. George Dodgson, Assistant Librarian at York Minster has completed and co-ordinated the catalogue.

PRIVATE COLLECTIONS

RICHARD BORDER COLLECTION

(Sold at Sotheby's, April 9–10, 1962)

20: Late 17th century book of bass parts of anthems. Chapel Royal part-book with arms of Charles II stamped on the cover. Signed inside the back cover: 'William Croft, 1697.'
28 N68 (chorus bass part only)

21: Bass parts of services. Late 17th century. 'Bespoke of a child of the King's Chappel.'
230ME (inc)

22: Score, *ca.* 1710, 'A Collection of Airs Cosisting [*sic*] of Overtures, Preludes, Chacones, Sarabands, Marches, Trumpet Tunes, Psalm Tunes, Slow Airs, Minuets, Grounds, Rondeaus, Jiggs, Dances and other Act Tunes; Compos'd by Henry Purcell for the Theatres: Being the Instrumental Music in Score to the following Operas and Plays. . . .' 'Monson.'
570/1 to 9 572/1 to 8 574/1 to 9, 16b 575/5 577/1 to 8 592/1 to 9 597/1 to 5, 7, 8 603/1 to 9 607/1 to 9 627/1, 2b, 3, 4, 9a, 19, 21, 25, 34 628/1a, 2ab, 3, 15a, 17b, 18, 28, 31, 40, app. 1, 2, 3 629/1ab, 2ab, 3ab, 6, T10c, 15, 16, 17a, 18, 19, 26, 38, 41, 44a, 51, App. 4 630/1ab, 2, 3, 4a, 11, 12, 17a, 18, 22 632/1abc

CROFT CASTLE COLLECTION

104: Score. 'James Bowman 1765.'
33 58C

EDWARD CROFT MURRAY COLLECTION

105: Manuscript additions at the back of a copy of the first edition of *Orpheus Britannicus* I (1698).
31 33/2a 328/11b 600/3b 627/13b, 22 629/48b 630/4g, 6a, 7c, 7f, 17a

APPENDIX III

THEODORE M. FINNEY COLLECTION

201: Anthem book. Late 17th to early 18th century.
9/6 19 27 60/11 N69 790 791 (inc)

202: Anthem book. Late 18th century.
4 19 31 57

203: Anthem book. Late 18th century.
2 4 7 19 33

WILLIAM KENNEDY GOSTLING MANUSCRIPT

255: The so-called ' William Kennedy Gostling MS,' said to be in the hand of John Gostling, now in private hands and ' unavailable.' Sold by Sotheby's, London, in 1935.
2 5 7 9 31 33 44 48 52 54 56 60

A description of ten of the seventeen anthems by Purcell in this MS appeared in the *Musical News* for May 23, 1903. The information it contains, as well as the fact that it is rather inaccessible there, makes it worth while to print the pertinent entries here:

> ' There are contained in it 64 Anthems; 17 by Henry Purcell, 23 by Dr. John Blow, 3 by Mr. Lock, 4 by Pelham Humphreys, 4 by Mr. William Turner, 1 by Dr. Child, 2 by Dr. Aldrich, 3 by Mr. Tudway, 4 by Mr. Jeremiah Clark, 1 by Mr. J. Peggott, and 1 by Mr. Bird and Dr. Aldrich, and 1 is anonymous. . . .
>> " Behold I bring you glad tidings." Mr. Henry Purcell, Christmas, 1687.
>> " Blessed are they that fear the Lord." Mr. Henry Purcell. For the Thanksgiving appointed in London and 12 miles round upon Her Majesty being with child, and on the 29th following over England.
>> " Praise the Lord, O my Soul." Mr. Henry Purcell, 1687.
>> " Thy way, O God, is Holy." Mr. Henry Purcell, 1687.
>> " O sing unto the Lord." Mr. Purcell, 1688.
>> " Blessed is the man that feareth the Lord." Purcell. Anthem for the Charterhouse sung upon the Founder's Day by Mr. Barincloe and Mr. Bowman. This is a duet, but an extra part for the tenor is inserted in the book.
>> " O give thanks unto the Lord." Mr. Purcell, 1693.
>> " The Way of God is an undefiled Way," Mr. Purcell, Nov. 11th, 1694. (King William then returned from Flanders.)
>> " Sing unto God." Henry Purcell Composuit, 1687.
>> " The Lord is King, the earth may be glad." Mr. Henry Purcell, 1688. . . .'

JOHN HAUCH COLLECTION

271: Score, mid 18th century.
35 36

LADY JEANS COLLECTION

280: Score, *ca.* 1710 to 1715.
488 570/8 574/2 607/1 611/8 628/Appendix 3 630/17a T678 T698

281: Score, early 18th century.
666/1 (different version)

APPENDIX III

KENNETH MUMMERY MANUSCRIPT

535: Violin or flute part-book, late 17th century French MS containing song tunes and instrumental pieces from operas by Lully, Purcell, *et al.* (Now in the possession of the author of this Catalogue.)
629/1, 2, 3, 6, T10, 15, 16, 17a, 18, 19, 26, 38, 45, 46b

NANKI COLLECTION

540: Nanki Library Catalogue, page 12, Item 10 (Unidentifiable in Cummings Sale Catalogue).
Late 17th-century book of anthem bass parts, probably from the scattered Chapel Royal set dating from the time of Charles II. (*cf.* MSS nos. 22 and 430.)
33   52 ('Alleluia' and 'Amen' choruses only)   N66   N68   S1 (ascribed to P. Humphrey)

541: Nanki Library Catalogue, page 12, Item 9 (Cummings Sale Catalogue: 448(a)).
Tenor part-book, early 18th-century. 'William Hawes' *et altri.*
230/M1, 2

542: Nanki Library Catalogue, page 12, Item 6 (Cummings Sale Catalogue: 24).
Score of anthems, early 18th-century. W. H. Cummings book-plate, with a fragment of an alleluia in the autograph of John Blow, dated 1683, pasted inside front board.
36

543: Nanki Library Catalogue, page 12, Item 4 (Cummings Sale Catalogue 904b).
Scores of sacred and secular songs, early to mid-18th century, with catches copied into remaining spaces, *passim*, by a later hand.
257   259   260   263 (without music)   272   273   277   280   282   283   284   289   290   485   486   488   502   517   522   579   602/1   628/36   S14

544: Nanki Library Catalogue O-1-54 (Cummings Sale Catalogue 1401). Song-book with scores of songs in English, Italian, and Latin. Late seventeenth-century MS from the pages of which Joseph Warren removed sheets of printed music that had been pasted over.
138   143   144   492   497

545: Nanki Library Catalogue, page 9, Item 3 (r-1) (Cummings Sale Catalogue 1399).
Keyboard book, with some songs and miscellaneous pieces, early 18th century. 'William Raylton/ His [Book]/170[0]' 'William Raylton/a favorite [*sic*] pupil of Dr. Wm. Croft/App^d Organist of Canterbury/Cathedral 1736. Died 1757.... This book, partly in his/handwriting (see page 14) was given him by Mr. Croft/March 31 170[0].'
D242

546: Nanki Library h 31 3. Parts, late 17th–early 18th century (3MS, 2 printed).
790–801

547: Nanki Library o.5.12   Score, 18th century.
626

548: Nanki Library c. 4. 9.   Score, 'P. Chetwin, London, 1674'.
S100

TRAVIS AND EMERY MANUSCRIPT

780: Score, mid 18th century. Theatre copy with directions. 'WHC i. J. C. Jackson.'
628 (inc)

APPENDIX IV: EDITIONS

1667

1667:   *Catch that Catch Can, or The Musical Companion* . . . To which is now added a second book containing dialogues, glees, ayres, and ballads . . . Printed by W. Godbid for J. Playford, London, 1667.

       S54 S69

1673

1673a: *The Musical Companion*, In Two Books. The First Book containing Catches and Rounds for Three Voyces. The Second Book containing Dialogues, Glees, Ayres and Songs for Two, Three and Four Voyces. Collected and Published by John Playford, Practitioner in Musick. London, Printed by W. Godbid for John Playford, at his Shop in the Temple near the Church, 1673.

       253 S69

1673b: *Choice Songs and Ayres* for One Voyce to Sing to a Theorbo-Lute, or Bass-Viol Being most of the Newest Songs sung at Court, and at the Publick Theatres. Composed by Several Gentlemen of His Majesties Musick. The First Book. London, Printed by W.G. . . . sold by John Playford . . . and John Ford . . . 1673.

       S68

1675

1675:   *Choice Ayres, Songs & Dialogues to Sing to the Theorbo-Lute or Bass-viol.* Being most of the newest ayres, and songs, sung at court and at the publick theatres. Composed by several gentlemen of his majesties musick, and others. The second edition corrected and enlarged . . . Printed by W. Godbid . . . sold by John Playford, London, 1675.

       436 S68

1676

1676:   *Choice Ayres* . . . Newly reprinted with large additions. Printed by W. Godbid . . . sold by John Playford . . . [London] 1676.

       436 S68

1678

1678:   *New Ayres and Dialogues Composed for Voices and Viols* of Two, Three and Four Parts: Together with lessons for viols or violins, by John Banister . . . and Thomas Low . . . Printed by M.C. for H. Brome, London, 1678.

       363 387 397 418 419 433

1679

1679:   *Choice Ayres and Songs to Sing to the Theorbo-lute or Bass-viol.* Being most of the newest ayres and songs sung at court and at the publick theatres . . . The second book . . . Printed by Anne Godbid . . . sold by John Playford . . . London, 1679.

       356 386 468 470 471 D133 S58

1680

1680: *Theodosius: or The Force of Love.* Acted by their Royal Highnesses servants at the Duke's Theatre. Written by Nat. Lee, with the musick betwixt the acts . . . Printed for R. Bentley and M. Magnes, London, 1680.

> 606/1, 2, 5, 6, 8, 9

c1680: *Lessons for the Recorder*: [*ca.* 1680 Engraved s.sh.fol.]

> D100

1681

1681: *Choice Ayres and Songs to Sing to the Theorbo-lute or Bass-viol.* . . . The third book . . . Printed by A. Godbid and J. Playford Junior . . . Sold by John Playford, London, 1681.

> 357   374   388   407   416   432   606/5, 8, 9

1682

1682a: *Hail to the Knight of the Post.* Titus Tell-troth: or the plot-founder confounded . . . To the tune of 'Hail to the myrtle shades' [from Purcell's *Theodosius*] Printed for Allen Banks by R. B[ride] London, 1682. s.sh.fol.

> M606/8

1682b: *Musick's Recreation on the Viol Lyra-way.* The second edition printed by A.G. and J.P. for J. Playford . . . London, 1682.

> 606/T5, T9

1682c: *The Compleat Swearing-Master*: a Rare new Salamanca Ballad. To the Tune of Now, now the fight's done. London: Printed for Allen Banks, 1682.

> M606/5

1682d: *Wit and Mirth.* An Antidote against Melancholy. Compounded of Ingenious and witty Ballads, Songs and Catches and other Pleasant and Merry Poems. London, Printed by A.G. and J.P. and sold by Henry Playford . . . 1682.

> 253(mnp)   484(mnp)   D100(mnp)

1683

1683a: *An Introduction to the Skill of Musick* . . . [Book III]: *A Brief Introduction to the Art of Descant, or Composing of Musick in Parts* . . . Printed by A.G. and J.P. for John Playford . . . London, 1683.

1683b: *Choice Ayres and Songs to Sing to the Theorbo-lute or Bass-viol* . . . The fourth book . . . Printed by A. Godbid and J. Playford Junior . . . sold by John Playford . . . and John Carr . . . [London], 1683.

> 195   370   390   411   413   415   435   581   S66

1683c: *Sonnata's of III. Parts: two viollins and basse: to the organ or harpsechord* . . . I. Playford and I. Carr for the author . . . London, 1683 [Violino Primo].

> 790 to 801

1683d: *Sonnata's of III. Parts: two viollins and basse* . . . [?the second issue] . . . Printed for the author and sold by I. Playford and I. Carr . . . London, 1683.

> 790 to 801

1683e: *A New Collection of Songs and Poems* . . . by Thomas D'Urfey. . . . London: Printed for Josaph [sic] Hindmarsh, at the Black Bull in Corn hill: 1683.
589

1683f: [*The Second Part of Youth's Delight on the Flagelet*, or the Young Gentlewoman's Recreation; being a Choice collection of Songs, tunes, and ayres, composed by several able masters, and set to the flagelet, By the author of the first part. Printed for John Clarke: London, 1683.] obl. 8º.
606/5, 8

1683g: The Newest Collection of the Choicest Songs, As they are sung at Court, Theatre, Musicke-Schools, Balls, &c . . . London, Printed by T. Haly for D. Brown, at the Black Swan and Bible without Temple-Bar, and T. Benskin, in St. Bride's Church-Yard, Fleet-Street; 1683.
292 (in B-flat, printed as a ' song ').

1684

1684a: *A Musical Entertainment perform'd on November XXII, 1683* It being the Festival of St. Cecilia, a great patroness of music . . . Printed by J. Playford Junior . . . sold by John Playford . . . and John Carr . . . London, 1684.
339

1684b: *Choice Ayres and Songs to Sing to the Theorbo-Lute or Bass-viol* . . . The fifth book . . . Printed by J. Playford Junior . . . sold by John Playford . . . and John Carr . . . London, 1684.
359 361 372 384 424 466 519

1684c: *A Century of Select Psalms*, And Portions of the Psalms of David, Especially those of Praise . . . The Second Ed. Corrected . . . For the use of the Charterhouse, London. By John Patrick, Preacher there. London: printed by MF for R. Royston, Bookseller to the King['s] most excellent Majesty . . . 1684.
132(mnp) 133(mnp) 136(mnp) 137(mnp) 138(mnp) 139(mnp) 141(mnp) 142(mnp) 143(mnp)

1684d: *Wit and Mirth*, 2nd ed., 1684.
240(mnp) 246(mnp) 253(mnp) 261(mnp) 264(mnp) 271(mnp) 288(mnp) 484(mnp) 594(mnp) 601(mnp) D100(mnp)

1685

1685a: *A Choice Collection of 180 Loyal Songs*, all of them written since the two late plots (viz.) The horrid Salamanca Plot in 1678; and the Fanatical Conspiracy in 1683. Intermixt with some new love songs . . . The third edition with many additions. Printed by N.T. . . . London, 1685.
606/M8(mnp) M9

1685b: *A Third Collection of New Songs, Never Printed Before.* The words by Mr. D'Urfey., Set to music by . . . Dr. John Blow, Mr. Henry Purcell, Senior Baptist [*et altri*] . . . with thorow-basses for the theorbo and bass-viol . . . Printed by J.P. for Joseph Hindmarsh . . . London, 1685.
463 509 589

1685c: *Catch that Catch Can: or the Second Part of the Musical Companion*: being a collection of new catches, songs, and glees never printed before . . . Printed by J. P[layford Jr.] for John Playford.
240 246 250 253 258 261 271 279 281 283 288 292 484 514 594 D100 D102 S61 S68

1685d: *The Theater of Music*: or A Choice Collection of the newest and best songs sung at the court and public theaters . . . A theorbo-bass to each song for the theorbo or bass-viol . . . The first book . . . Printed by J. Playford for Henry Playford and R.C. . . . London, 1685.

       368   385   393   399   443

1685e: ——————— The second book . . . London, 1685.

       290   367   378   398   409   422   437   510   520

1686

1686a: *The Second Book of the Pleasant Musical Companion*: Being a new collection of select catches, songs, and glees for two and three voices. The second edition, corrected and much enlarged . . . Printed for John Playford . . . London, 1686. [But note manuscript inscription in the British Museum copy: A.412.d: 'The gift of Mr. John Playford to John Jackson—Oct. 8 *1685*'.]

       240 246 248 249 253 264 276 277 279 280 281 283 285 286 287 288 289

       290 292 484 494 507 514 522 594 D100 D107 S54 S61 S68

1686b: *The Theater of Music* . . . The third book . . . Printed for Henry Playford and R.C. . . . sold by Henry Playford . . . and John Carr . . . London, 1686.

       438   481   483   498   512

1686c: *The Dancing-Master*: Or, Directions for dancing Country Dances, with Tunes to each Dance for the Treble-Violin. The 7th Edition, with Addition of several new Dances, never before printed. London, Printed by J.P. and sold by John Playford, at his Shop near the Temple Church, 1686.

       S68

1686d: *The Delightful Companion or Choice New Lessons for the Recorder or Flute* . . . London: John Playford . . . 1686.

       T253   646   DT100

1687

1687a: *An Introduction to the Skill of Music* . . . (Book III): *The Art of Descant, or Composing of Musick in Parts in a more Plain and Easie Method than any heretofore Published*. By John Playford. The eleventh edition, corrected and enlarged. Printed by Charles Peregrine for Henry Playford . . . London, 1687.

       109   D22

1687b: *A Pastoral Elegy on the Death of Mr. John Playford*. London, printed for Henry Playford, 1687. The words by Mr. Tate. Set by Mr. Henry Purcell.

       464

1687c: *Comes Amoris; or the Companion of Love*. Being a choice collection of the newest songs now in use. With a thorow-bass to each song for the Harpsichord, theorbo, or Bass-viol. The first book . . . Printed by Nat. Thompson for John Carr and Sam. Scott . . . sold by John Carr . . . London, 1687.

       282   406   430   487   505

1687d: *The Theater of Music* . . . The fourth and last book . . . Printed by B. Motte for Henry Playford . . . London, 1687.

       355 362 406 430 431 487 492 495 497 505

1687e: *The Second Book of the Pleasant Musical Companion* . . . [Another issue, see EDITION 1686a] . . . a new additional sheet to the catch book . . .

       240 246 248 249 253 264 276 277 279 280 281 283 285 286 287 288 289

       290 292 484 494 509 514 522 594 D100 D107 S54 S61

1687f: *Vinculum Societatis, or the Tie of Good Company.* Being a choice collection of the newest songs now in use. With thorow-bass to each song for the Harpsichord, theorbo or bass-viol. The first book of this character . . . Printed by F. Clark, T. Moore, and J. Heptinstall, for John Carr and R.C. . . . sold by John Carr . . . and Sam. Scott . . . London, 1687.

      287   391   417

1687g: *Apollo's Banquet*: Containing Instructions & Variety of New Tunes, Ayres, Jiggs and several New Scotch Tunes for the Treble-Violin . . . John Playford. The 5th Edition with New Additions. London [Printer's name obliterated], 1687.

      655   MD100   N774

1688

1688a: *A Fool's Preferment, or the Three Dukes of Dunstable.* A comedy. As it was acted at the Queen's Theatre in Dorset-Garden by Their Majesties Servants. Written by Mr. D'Urfey . . . compos'd by Mr. Henry Purcell . . . Printed for Jos. Knight and Fra. Saunders . . . London, 1688. [Another title-page for the songs]: *New Songs Sung in The Fool's Preferment, or the Three Dukes of Dunstable.* In the Savoy: Printed by E. Jones for Jos. Knight and Fran. Saunders . . . 1688.

      571/1 to 4, 6 to 8

1688b: *Comes Amoris: or the Companion of Love.* Being a choice collection of the newest songs now in use . . . The second book . . . printed by Tho. Moore for John Carr . . . and Sam Scott . . . London, 1688.

      331/6(bass)

   Head title on sig. H1: *A Small Collection of the newest Catches for 3 Voices:*

      260   262   275   277

1688c: *Harmonia Sacra; or Divine Hymns and Dialogues*: with a thorow-bass for the theorbo-lute, bass-viol, harpsichord, or organ. Composed by the best masters of the last and present age . . . The first book . . . Printed by Edward Jones for Henry Playford . . . London, 1688.

      181   184   186   188   189   190   191   193   197   198   199   200   D22   S3

1688d: *The Banquet of Musick*: or a collection of the newest and best songs sung at court, and at publick theatres. With a thorow-bass for the theorbo-lute, bass-viol, harpsichord, or organ. Composed by several of the best masters . . . The first book . . . Printed by E. Jones for Henry Playford . . . London, 1688.

      262   275   423   491   493   543   S57 (Mr. Marsh)

1688e: ———————— The second book . . . London, 1688.

      353   395   408   420

1688f: *Vinculum Societatis* . . . The second book with a small collection of flute tunes . . . Printed by T. Moore and J. Heptinstall, for John Carr . . . and Sam. Scott . . . London, 1688.

      267   351   353   420

1689

1689a: *Comes Amoris* . . . The third book . . . London, 1689.

      469   501   503

1689b: *The Banquet of Musick* . . . The third book . . . London, 1689.

      255   517

1689c: *The Second Part of Musick's Hand-maid*: Containing the newest Lessons, grounds, sarabands, minuets, and Jiggs, set for the virginals, harpsichord, and spinet . . . Printed on copper-plates for Henry Playford . . . London, 1689.

337/5c (in C Major) 646 647 648 649 650 653 655 656 665 666/3 T682 T688
T689 T694 T695

?1689: *An Opera Perform'd at Mr. Josias Priest's Boarding School at Chelsey.* By Young Gentlewomen.
The words by Mr. Nat. Tate. The Music composed by Mr. Henry Purcell.
626(mnp)

1690

1690a: *The Songs in Amphitryon* with the Musick composed by Mr. Henry Purcell, London: Printed
by J. Heptinstall for Jacob Tonson ... 1690.
572/9, 10ab, 11ab

1690b: *The Banquet of Musick* ... The fourth and last book ... London, 1690.
256 469 501 503

1690c: *Apollo's Banquet* ... The sixth edition, with new additions. E. Jones, for Henry Playford:
[London], 1690.
T606/9 T629/12 646 649 655 656 T689 T695 S100(inc)

1690d: *New Poems, consisting of Satyrs, Elegies and Odes* ... London: printed for J. Bullord and A.
Roper, 1690.
626/Epilogue.

?1690: *Youth's Delight on the Flageolet,* the Second part ... 9th edition with additions ... also a scale
of the Gammut the violin way ... John Clarke [London].
430 629/17[MS]

1691

1691a: *Amphitryon; or the Two Sosia's* ... Printed for J. Tonson and M. Tonson ... London, 1691
... Appendix *The Songs in Amphitryon, with the Musick.* Composed by Mr. Henry Purcell ...
Printed by J. Heptinstall for Jacob Tonson ... London, 1691.
572/9, 10ab, 11ab

1691b: *Apollo's Banquet:* Containing variety of the newest tunes, ayres, jiggs, and minuets, for the
treble-violin, now in use at publick theatres, and at dancing-schools, being most of them within
the compass both of the flute and flagelet. To which is added some new songs and catches.
The second book ... Printed by E. Jones for Henry Playford ... London, 1691.
341/4b 403 572/2, 4, 5, 6, 7, 9, 10ab, N12 597/2, 5, 7 599 607/2, 3, 4 T612/4
627/18, 33 628/10bc, 15a, T21, T27, 37, 38 655 D103

1691c: *Sound, Fame, thy brazen trumpet.* A song in Dioclesian. London, *ca.* 1691. s.sh.fol.
627/22

1691d: *Tell me why, my charming fair.* A dialogue in the Prophetess. [T. Cross jun. sculp.] ff. 2 fol
London, c1691.
627/35

1691e: *The Banquet of Musick*: or a collection of ... songs ... most of them within the compass of
the flute ... The fifth book ... Printed by Edw. Jones ... and sold by Henry Playford ...
and Sam. Scott ... London, 1691.
291 502 525

1691f: *The Vocal and Instrumental Musick of the Prophetess, or the History of Dioclesian.* Composed by
Henry Purcell, Organist of Their Majesties Chappel, and of St. Peters Westminster. Printed
by J. Heptinstall for the author ... sold by J. Carr ... London, 1691.
627(inc)

1691g: *Vinculum Societatis* ... The third book; with several new airs for the flute or violin ...
        Printed by T. Moore and J. Heptinstall for John Carr ... London, 1691.

        588/3   599   607/3, 4

1692

1692a: [*Philomela, or The Vocal Musitian*: being a collection of the best and newest songs; especially
        those in the two operas, The ' Prophetess ' and ' King Arthur ' written by Mr. Dryden: and
        set to musick by Mr. Henry Purcell. Printed on copper plates; and sold by T. Cross ... and
        J. Man ... London, 1692.] Entered in *Term Catalogues*, Trinity, 1692. No entry in *Stationer's
        Register*. cf. Day & Murrie, *English Song Books*.

        627(inc)   628(inc)

1692b: *Some Select Songs as they are Sung in the Fairy Queen.* Set to musick by Mr. Henry Purcell ...
        Printed by J. Heptinstall for the author ... sold by J. Carr ... [and] Henry Playford. ...
        London, 1692.

        629/10a, 12, 13, 17, 22b, 23, 25a, 33b, 34b, 44b

1692c: *The Banquet of Musick* ... The sixth and last book ... Printed by Edw. Jones ... sold by John
        Carr ... and by Henry Playford ... London, 1692.

        369   405   486   516   588/4   598   612/1, 3, 4

1692d: *The Fairy-Queen: an Opera.* Represented at the Queen's-Theatre by Their Majesties' Servants
        ... Printed for Jacob Tonson ... London, 1692.

        629(mnp)

1692e: *The Gentleman's Journal* ... January, 1692. Printed and ... sold by R. Baldwin ... London,
        1692. (on p. 37): *Stript of their green our groves appear.*

        444

1692f: ———————————— June, 1692, p. 27: *If musick be the food of love* (first version).

        379A

1692g: ———————————— August, 1692, p. 27: *Ah me! to many deaths decreed.*

        586

1692h: ———————————— October, 1692, p. 32: *Let us dance, let us sing.*

        627/Appendix 3

1692i: ———————————— December, 1692, p. 27: *Corinna is divinely fair.*

        365

1692j: *Your hay it is mow'd.* A new song in the dramatick opera [*King Arthur*] written by Mr. Dryden.
        London, *ca.* 1692. s.sh.fol.

        628/37

?1692: *A Scotch-Song* Sung by Mrs Ayliffe at the Consort in York Buildings. Mr. Henry Purcell.

        412

c1692: *The Dialogue in the last Opera, call'd the Fairy Queen.* n.d., n.p. [in British Museum MS
        Add. 35043, f.1, a book belonging to John Channing in 1694. ? Engraved by Thomas
        Cross.]

        629/22b

1693

1693a: *Comes Amoris* ... The fourth book ... Printed by J. Heptinstall for John Carr, and Samuell
        Scott ... London, 1693.

        263   331/6(bass)   379B   385   576   580/1   602/2   627/Appendix 3   629/50c

1693b: *Harmonia Sacra; or Divine Hymns and Dialogues . . . The second book . . .* London, 1693.

   134 182 183 192 196 D72 D77 S15

?1693c: *Joyful Cuckoldom, or the Love of Gentlemen and Gentlewomen,* A collection of new songs with ye musick for ye lute, violin, flute, or Harpsichord by Henry Purcell, Dr. John Blow, Mr. John Eccles, et altri . . . Printed by J. Heptinstall for Henry Playford . . . sold by Daniel Dring . . . 1671. [So dated on the manuscript title-page, presumably by error of the copyist. The volume is a collection of single-sheet songs, probably published between 1690 and 1696. One of the numbers (a dialogue by J. Eccles from ' The Richmond Heiress ' has at the end: ' Printed and sold by R. Cross . . . and by Mr. Man . . . 1693.' See in that year for another entry.]

   243 257 259 331/6 (bass) 403 572/9, 10ab 574/10 576 580/1 582 587 595/1
   601/1 602/2 607/10 612/1, 2, 3 627/9bc, M21, 31a, 33a, Appendix 1, Appendix 2
   628/10bc 629/10a, 12, 17, M17, 23, 34b, 44b

1693d: *The First Book of Apollo's Banquet:* Containing instructions, and variety of new tunes, ayres, jiggs, minuets, and several new Scotch tunes for the treble-violin. To which is added, the tunes of the newest French dances now in use at court and in dancing-schools. The 7th edition corrected . . . with new additions. Printed by E. Jones for Henry Playford . . . London, 1693.

   T567 601/T1, T3 629/6, T10, T12, T17, T23, 26, 44bc 655 656 T689 T695
   N775 TD100(anon)

1693e: *The Gentleman's Journal,* January, 1693, p. 29 [misprinted ' 27 ']: *Tell me no more . . .* ; p. 31 [misprinted ' 29 ']: *Though you make no return . . .*

   601/1, 3

1693f: ———————————— February, 1693, p. 68 [misprinted ' 32 ']: *No watch, dear Celia, just is found.*

   401

1693g: ———————————— April, 1693, p. 133: *Kindly treat Maria's day.*

   321/14ab 321(mnp)

1693h: ———————————— June, 1693, p. 205; *We now, my Thyrsis.*

   427

1693i: ———————————— September, 1693, p. 315: *I envy not a monarch's fate.*

   376

1693j: ———————————— December, 1693, p. 421: *Since from my dear Astrea's sight*; p. 426: *When first I saw the bright Aurelia's eyes.*

   627/Appendix 1, Appendix 2

1693k: *Thesaurus Musicus:* Being a collection of the newest songs performed at Their Majesties Theatres; and at the consorts in Villier-street in York-Buildings, and in Charles Street Covent-Garden. With a thorow-bass to each song for the harpsichord, theorbo, or bass-viol. To which is annexed a collection of aires composed for two flutes, by several masters. The first book . . . Printed by J. Heptinstall for John Hudgebut . . . sold by John Carr . . . and by John Money . . . and at most musick shops in town. London, 1693.

   247 333/7ab 601/1, 3 D136

1693l: ———————————— The second book.

   579 582 592/10 627/Appendix 1, Appendix 2 628/26

1693m: *'Tis nature's voice.* A song set by Mr. Henry Purcell and sung by himself at St. Cecilia's Feast, and exactly engraved by Tho. Cross. . . . London, *ca.* 1693. s.sh.fol.

   328/4

1693n: *A Song Sung by himself at St. Caecilia's Feast.* Tho: Cross. London, *ca.* 1693. ' *Tis Nature's Voice.*

   328/4

1693o: *The Fairy-Queen*: An Opera ... with Alterations, Additions and several new songs ... Printed for Jacob Tonson ... London 1693.
        629(mnp)

1694

1694a: *A Collection of One Hundred and Eighty Loyal Songs.* All written since 1678. And intermixt with several new Love songs. To which is added the notes ... The fourth edition with many additions ... Printed and sold by Richard Butt ... London, 1694.
        606/M8(mnp), M9

1694b: *A Collection of Some Verses out of the Psalms of David* ... composed in two parts, cantus and bassus ... collected by Daniel Warner ... revised by Mr. Henry Purcell ... Printed by E. Jones, London, 1694.

1694c: *An Introduction to the Skill of Musick* ... (Book III) *The Art of Descant* ... The twelfth edition. Corrected and amended by Mr. Henry Purcell ... Printed by E. Jones for Henry Playford ... London, 1694.
        109   870   871

1694d: *Comes Amoris* ... The fifth book ... Printed by J. Heptinstall for John Carr ... London, 1694
        321/2ab, 10b, 14ab   429   518   573   596   629/4b, M22b

1694e: *Lads and lasses blithe and gay.* A Scotch song in the second part of the play (by T. D'Urfey) call'd Don Quixote, sung by Mrs. Hudson and set to musick by Mr. Henry Purcell. London, 1694(?) s.sh.fol.
        578/8

1694f: *Let the dreadful engines* ... T. Cross, London, 1694.
        578/3

1694g: *The Gentleman's Journal* ... January and February 1694 ... p. 33: *Sawney is a bonny lad.*
        412

1694h: ——————————— March, 1694, p. 65: *The danger is over.*
        595/1

1694i: ——————————— April, 1694, p. 101: *There's not a swain* (The words fitted to the tune by N. Henley, Esq.); p. 104: *Ask me to love no more.*
        358, 587

1694j: ——————————— May 1694, p. 137: *Strike the viol, touch the lute.*
        323/5a

1694k: ——————————— July, 1694, p. 213: *Celia's fond, too long I've lov'd her.*
        364

1694l: ——————————— October and November, 1694, p. 277: *Dulcibella* ... [Indexed as 'Castabella, a song set by Mr. Purcell'].
        485

1694m: *Thesaurus Musicus* ... The second book ... Printed by J. Heptinstall for Henry Playford ... sold by Henry Playford ... and John Money ... and at most musick-shops ... London, 1694.
        412   579   582   592/10   627/Appendix 1, Appendix 2   628/26

1694n: ——————————— [Another issue] ... Printed by J. Heptinstall for John Hudgebutt, and ... sold by John Money ... and at most Musick-shopes in town. 1694.

1694o: *The Songs to the New Play of Don Quixote.* As they are sung at the Queen's Theatre in Dorset Garden. Part the first ... Printed by J. Heptinstall for Samuel Briscoe ... London, 1694.
        578/1 to 5

1694p: *The Songs to the New Play of Don Quixote.* Part the first. . . . [Another issue of the above.]
        578/1 to 5

1694q: *The Songs to the New Play of Don Quixote* . . . Part the second . . . Printed by J. Heptinstall for
Samuel Briscoe . . . London, 1694.
        578/6, 7, 8

1694r: [*Two Songs from The Double Dealer*] . . . Printed by J. Heptinstall for John Hudgebutt . . . sold
by Jo. Money . . . and at most musick-shops in town . . . London, 1694(?).
        592/10

1695

1695a: *Deliciae Musicae:* Being a collection of the newest and best songs sung at court and at the
publick theatres, most of them within the compass of the flute. With a thorow-bass, for the
theorbo-lute, bass-viol, harpsichord, or organ. Composed by several of the best masters. The
first book . . . Printed by J. Heptinstall for Henry Playford. . . . London, 1695.
        396   410   414   441   601/2   610   613

1695b: ——————— The second book . . .
        379C   521   600/3b   632/17

1695c: *Fair Cloe my breast so alarms.* T. Cross, London, *ca.* 1695.
        486

1695d: *I attempt from love's sickness to fly.* A song in the Indian Queen. Thomas Cross, London,
ca. 1695.
        630/17h

1695e: *If love's a sweet passion.* [Song from *The Fairy Queen.*] London, *ca.* 1695, s.sh.fol.
        629/17

1695f: *I see she flyes me.* [Song from *Aureng-Zebe.*] Thomas Cross, London, *ca.* 1695. s.sh.fol.
        573

1695g: *Lucinda is bewitching fair.* A new song sung in Abdelazar. London, *ca.* 1695.
        570/10

1695h: *Now the maids and the men.* [Song from *The Fairy Queen.*] Thomas Cross, London, 1695.
        629/22b

1695i: *See where repenting Caelia lies.* [Song from *The Married Beau.*] London, 1695.
        603/10

1695j: *The New Treasury of Musick:* or a collection of the choicest and best song-books for these
twenty years last past. The words composed by the most ingenious wits of this age, and set to
musick by the greatest masters in that science. With a thorow-bass to most songs, for the
theorbo, lute or bass-viol, harpsichord or spinnet . . . Printed for Henry Playford . . . London,
1695. [This volume consists of Books I, II and IV of the ' Theatre of Music ' (1685-7); Books
IV and V of ' Choice Ayres and Songs ' (1683-4), with the above new title-page. See these
entries for contents.]

1695k: *Thesaurus Musicus* . . . The third book . . . Printed by J. Heptinstall for John Hudgebutt . . .
sold by John Carr . . . and John Money . . . and at most musick-shops . . . London, 1695.
        371   578/8   591   595/2   603/10

1695l: ——————— The fourth book . . . sold by John Carr and Daniel Dring . . . and at most
musick-shops . . . London, 1695.
        410   570/10   628/29

1695m: *The Songs in the Indian Queen*: As it is now compos'd into an opera. By Mr. Henry Purcell ... Printed by J. Heptinstall ... sold by John May ... and for John Hudgbutt at Tho. Dring's ... London, 1695.

        630/4bdg, 6, 7cf, 13(mnp), 17ah, 19

1695n: *The Songs in the Tragedy of Bonduca*. Set by Mr. Henry Purcell. Excellent musick-books lately printed for, and sold by Henry Playford ... London, 1695(?).

        574(inc)

1695o: *Three Elegies upon the Much Lamented Loss of Our Late Most Gracious Queen Mary*. The words of the two first by Mr. Herbert. The latter out of the Oxford Verse; and sett to musick by Dr. Blow and Mr. Henry Purcell ... Printed by J. Heptinstall for Henry Playford ... London, 1695.

        383   504

1695p: *The Dancing Master*: Or directions for Dancing Country Dances, with tunes to each Dance for the Treble-Violin. The Ninth Edition Corrected; with Additions of several new Dances and Tunes never before printed ... Printed by E. Jones for H. Playford ... 1695.

        403(w/o text) 646 D136 S68

1695q: *A New Song* the words by Mr. Congreve Set to Music by Mr. Henry Purcell and engraven exactly by Tho. Cross: *Pious Celinda goes to pray'r*.

        410

1696

1696a: *A Choice Collection of Lessons for the Harpsichord or Spinnet* Composed by ye late Mr. Henry Purcell Organist of his Majesties Chappel Royal, & of St. Peters Westminster ... Printed on copper plates for Mrs. Frances Purcell, Executrix of the Author ... sold by Henry Playford ... London, 1696.

        660 661 662 663 665/3, 4 (see Commentary) 666 667 668 669 T678 T680 T686 T687 T698

1696b: *A Collection of Songs Set to Musick by Mr. Henry Purcell & Mr. John Eccles*. Printed and sold by Tho. Cross ... and ... at the musick shops. London, 1696.

        328/4 500 598 604A 627/22

1696c: *Ah! how sweet it is to love*. [Song from *Tyrannick Love*.] London, ca. 1696.

        613/2

1696d: *Celia has a thousand charms*. [Song from *The Rival Sisters*.] Tho. Cross, London, 1696.

        609/10

1696e: *Dear pretty youth*. [Song from *The Tempest*.] London, ca. 1696.

        631/10

1696f: *Deliciae Musicae* ... The third book ... Printed by J. Heptinstall, for Henry Playford ... The fourth book will be publish'd next term, which will make the first volume compleat. London, 1696.

        574/10, 17 605/1, 3 609/10, 11, 12 628/35 631/10

1696g: ———————— The fourth book.

        584 630/13a S50

1696h: *Deliciae Musicae* ... The first volume compleat ... London, 1696. [This is the date of a title-page printed especially for this volume, which consists of the several books of 'Deliciae Musicae' which had appeared earlier. See these individual items for the contents of the whole volume.]

1696i: *New Songs in the Third Part of the Comical History of Don Quixote* . . . Being the last piece set to musick by the late famous Mr. Henry Purcell . . . Engrav'd on copper-plates . . . Printed for Samuel Briscoe . . . London, 1696.
578/9

1696j: *O lead me to some peacefull gloom.* [Song from *Bonduca.*] London, 1696.
574/17

1696k: [*Songs and Ayres set by Dr. Blow, Mr. Henry Purcell, Mr. James Hart, Mr. William Turner, Mr. Michael Wise, and several other eminent masters* . . . Printed for C. Brome . . . London, 1696. Entered in *Term Catalogue,* East. 1696 (II. 579). No entry in *Stationers' Register.* No copies recorded.]

1696l: *Take not a woman's anger ill.* [Song from *The Rival Sisters.*] London, 1696.
609/11

1696m: [*The Complete Flute Master: Or the Whole Art of Playing on the Recorder Laid Open* . . . The second edition, with additions of several new lessons, made by the late famous Mr. Henry Purcell. Sold by John Walsh . . . London. Advertised in the London Gazette for Feb. 27–March 2, 1695 (i.e. 1696), but no extant copies are recorded.]

1696n: *Thesaurus Musicus* . . . The fifth book . . . Printed by J. Heptinstall for John Hudgbutt . . . sold by Samuel Scott . . . and Daniel Dring . . . and at most music-shops . . . London, 1696.
394   574/15b, 16b   D133   D140   D142

1696o: *'Twas within a fourlong of Edenborough town.* [Song from *The Mock Marriage.*] London, 1696.
605/2

1696p: *Whilst I with grief.* [Song from *The Spanish Friar.*] London, ca. 1696.
610

1696q: ——————— [Another edition] engr. for I. Walsh, 1696.
610

1696r: *The Second Part of the Dancing Master* . . . All new Dances, never before printed. Printed for Henry Playford, 1696.
605/T2, T3   609/2, 3, T11   611/9

1696s: *A Collection of New Songs, set by Mr. N. Matteis* . . . John Walsh, London, 1696.
M517

1697

1697a: *A Collection of Ayres, Compos'd for the Theatre, and upon Other Occasions.* By the late Mr. Henry Purcell . . . Printed by J. Heptinstall, for Frances Purcell . . . sold by B. Aylmer . . . W. Henchman . . . and Henry Playford . . . London, 1697.
570/1 to 9   572/1 to 8   574/1 to 9   577/1 to 7   592/1 to 9   597   603/1 to 9   607/1 to 9   611/1 to 8   627/1ab, 2b, 3ab, 4, 15, 19, 24, 25, 34   628/1a, 2, 3, 10a, 11, 15a, 17b, 18, 28, 31, 34, 40, Appendix 3   629/1ab, 2ab, 3ab, 6, 10d, 15, 16, 17a, 18ab, 19, 26, 38, 41, 44a, 51, Appendix 4   630/1ab, 2ab, 3ab, 4a, 11, 17a, 18, 22

1697b: *An Introduction to the Skill of Musick* . . . (Book III) *The Art of Descant* . . . made very plain and easie by the late Mr. Henry Purcell. The thirteenth edition . . . Printed by E. Jones for Henry Playford . . . London, 1697.
109   870   871

1697c: *Te Deum et Jubilate, for Voices and Instruments made for St. Cecilia's Day, 1694.* Perform'd before the Queen, Lords, and Commons, at the Cathedral-Church of St. Paul, on the thanksgiving day for the glorious successes of Her Majesty's army the last campaign. Compos'd by the late famous Mr. Henry Purcell. The second edition . . . Sold by J. Walsh . . . J. Hare . . . and P. Randall . . . London, 1697.

232

1697d: *Ten Sonata's in Four Parts.* Compos'd by the late Mr. Henry Purcell . . . Printed by J. Heptinstall for Frances Purcell . . . sold by B. Aylmer . . . W. Henchman . . . and Henry Playford . . . London, 1697.

802 to 811

1697e: [*The Harpsicord Master.* Containing plain and easy instructions for learners on the spinnet or harpsicord; written by the late famous Mr. Henry Purcell, at the request of a particular friend, and taken from his own manuscript, never before publish'd, being the best extant, together with a choice collection of the newest aires and song-tunes, compos'd by the best masters, and fitted for the harpsicord, spinnet, or harp by those that compos'd them, all graven on copper plates . . . sold by J. Walsh . . . and J. Hare . . . London, 1697(?). (Advertised in *The Post Boy*, Oct. 21–3, 1697; and entered in *Term Catalogues*: III, Feb. 1698; but no copies known.)]

1697f: *Thy Genius lo!* [Song from *The Massacre of Paris*.] Tho. Cross, London, 1697.

604B

1697g: *Youth's Delight on the Flagelet* the third Part containing the newest lessons with easier Directions . . . being the 11th edition with additions . . . Printed for . . . and sold by John Hare . . . 1697.

430 T609/11

1698

1698a: [*A New Sheet of Catches.* Set by the late Mr. Henry Purcell . . . Printed for H. Playford . . . London, 1698. (Entered in *Term Catalogues*: Mich. 1698 (III. 94), but no extant copies are recorded.)]

1698b: *New reformation begins thro the nation.* A Song in the Campaigners [by D. Purcell], the words by Mr. Tho. D'Urfey, to a tune of Mr. Henry Purcel's and exactly engrav'd by Dan: Wright. London, *ca.* 1698. s.sh.fol.

M611/7

1698c: ———————————————————— [Another edition] . . . 1698.

M611/7

1698d: *Orpheus Britannicus.* A collection of all the choicest songs for one, two, and three voices. Compos'd by Mr. Henry Purcell. Together with such symphonies for violins or flutes as were by him design'd for any of them: and a thorough-bass to each song; figur'd for the organ, harpsichord or theorbo-lute. All which are placed in their several keys according to the order or the gamut . . . Printed by J. Heptinstall for Henry Playford . . . London, 1698.

321/2ab 323/5a 328/4 333/7ab 335/5a 339/3ab 360 362 369 370 375
379C 380 387 392 394 396 406 413 422 423 428B 444 464 470 485 486 488
493 501 502 503 510 513 514 517 521 522 543 570/10 571/6 573 574/17
578/1, 3, 6, 9 579 580/1 584 585/1 586 589 592/10 596 598 601/2 602/1
603/10 604A 608 609/10 610 613 626/3a 627/35, Appendix 1, Appendix 2
628/26, 29, 35, 36, 38 629/4b, 22b, 40b 630/13, 15, 17h 631/10 632/17

1698e: [*The Second Part of the Musical Companion*; containing all Mr. Purcell's new catches: to which is added a sheet more, never printed in the former editions . . . Printed for H. Playford . . . London, 1698. (Entered in *Term Catalogues*: H. II, 1698 (III. 54). Not entered in *Stationer's Register*. Probably a re-issue of the 1694 edition (q.v.) including the sheet which was sold separately.)]

1698f: *The Dancing Master* 10th edition . . . Printed by J. Heptinstall for Samuel Sprint at the Bell in Little Britain and H. Playford . . . 1698.

646 D136 S68

1698g: —————————— The Second Part: The Second Edition with Additions: printed for Henry
Playford, 1698.
570/8 605/T2, T3 609/3, T11, 12 611/9

1699

1699a: *A Choice Collection of Lessons for the Harpsichord or Spinnet* . . . The third edition with additions
. . . Printed on copper plates for Mrs. Frances Purcell . . . London, 1699.
660 661 662 663 665/3, 4 (see Commentary) 666 667 668 669 T678 T680
T686 T687 T697 T698

1699b: *Mercurius Musicus*: Or The Monthly Collection of New Teaching Songs, compos'd for the
theatres and other occasions; with a thorow-bass for the harpsichord, or spinett: The songs
being transpos'd for the flute at the end of the book. For January . . . Printed by William
Pearson . . . for Henry Playford and sold by him . . . and J. Hare . . . and at all other musick-
shops . . . London, 1699.
434

1699c: *The Whole Volume of the Monthly Collections, intituled, Mercurius Musicus* [For the year 1699]
. . . Printed by William Pearson . . . for Henry Playford . . . and sold by him . . . and J. Hare
. . . and J. Young . . . London, 1699.
434 D144

1699d: *Odes and Dialogues* [Running title] Book I. [Two songs by Paisible and H. Purcell, the second
incomplete.] (The only extant copy now in Harvard College Library.)
584

1699e: *Wit and Mirth: Or Pills to Purge Melancholy*; Being a Collection of the best Merry Ballads and
Songs, Old and New . . . Printed by Will. Pearson, for Henry Playford . . . London, 1699.
379B 412 430 578/8 595/1 601/3 602/2 605/2, 3 606/8 609/11 628/10bc, 15bc
629/10ab, 17bc M655 D136 D142 S68

1699f: [*The Second Collection of New Songs and Ballads* . . . Thomas D'Urfey, 1699. (Entered in *Term
Catalogues* for Trinity, 1699, and advertised in *The Post Boy*, No. 658, June 27, 1699.) Two
leaves from this edition are probably contained in the Harvard College Library: Mus.
512.23F*, ff. 607, 610. See Cyrus Day: *The Songs of Thomas D'Urfey*, Harvard University
Press, 1933, p. 42.]
584

1700

1700a: *A Choice Collection of Lessons for the Harpsichord or Spinnet* . . . [Another issue of EDITION
1699a. See this for contents.]

1700b: *The Second Book of the Harpsichord Master* . . . lessons for the harpsichord or spinnette . . . By
Dr. Blow, Mr. Courtivall, Mr. Clark, Mr. Barrett & Mr. Crofts. To which is added plain
rules for learners. The whole fairly engraven . . . Printed for I. Walsh . . . London, 1700.
S125

1700c: *And in each track of glory.* Tho. Cross Jr. *ca.* 1700.
333/7ab

1700d: *An Introduction to the Skill of Music* . . . the fourteenth edition . . . printed by William Pearson
. . . for Henry Playford . . . London, 1700.
[See EDITION 1697b for contents.]

1700e: *As soon as the chaos.* [Song from *The Marriage-Hater Matched.*] London, *ca.* 1700.
602/1

1700f: *Behold the man that with gigantick might.* The mad dialogue. [From *The Richmond Heiress.*] London, *ca.* 1700.
608

1700g: *Celebrate this festival.* A song sung before the late Queen. London, *ca.* 1700. s.sh.fol.
321/2ab

1700h: *Celemene, pray tell me.* A dialogue in the second part of the Conquest of Granada . . . Tho. Cross, London, *ca.* 1700.
584

1700i: *Come let us agree.* A two-part song between Cupid and Bacchus. [From *Timon of Athens.*] London, *ca.* 1700.
632/19

1700j: —————— [Another edition.] *ca.* 1700.
632/19

1700k: *Come let us leave the town.* [Song from *The Fairy Queen.*] London, *ca.* 1700.
629/4b

1700l: *Crown your bowles:* An ode on the King's happy return from abroad, the words by Mr. Durfey. To a sebell of Mr. Henry Purcell. London, *ca.* 1700. s.sh.fol.
MT678

1700m: —————— [Another issue.]
MT678

1700n: *Dear pretty youth.* [Song from *The Tempest.*] London, *ca.* 1700.
631/10

1700o: *Fairest isle.* A song in the dramatick opera [*King Arthur*] . . . London, *ca.* 1700.
628/38

1700p: *Fear no danger to ensue.* [As altered by C. Gildon for *Measure for Measure.*] London, *ca.* 1700.
626/7ab

1700q: *From rosie bow'rs.* [Song from *Don Quixote* Part III.] London, *ca.* 1700.
578/9

1700r: —————— [Another edition.] The las [sic] song the Author sett, it being in his sickness. [pp. 38–41 of a part of a larger collection.] London, *ca.* 1700.
578/9

1700s: *Genius of England.* [Song from *Don Quixote* Part II.] London. *ca.* 1700.
578/7

1700t: *I'll sail upon the dog-star.* [Song from *A Fool's Preferment.*] Tho. Cross, jr. London, *ca.* 1700.
571/6

1700u: *I see she flyes me.* [Song from *Aureng-Zebe.*] Tho. Cross, London, *ca.* 1700.
573

1700v: *Let the soldiers rejoyce.* A new song in the ' Prophetess ' . . . the words by Mr. Betterton . . . sung by Mr. Freeman. *ca.* 1700. s.sh.fol.
627/9bc

1700w: —————— [Another edition.] London *ca.* 1700.
627/9bc

1700x: *Lost is my quiet for ever.* A song for 2 voices . . . London, *ca.* 1700. s.sh.fol.
502

1700y: *Love in our little veins.* A song [from *Timon of Athens*] sung by the boy . . . Tho. Cross, London. *ca.* 1700.
632/11

1700z: *My dearest, I languish.* A dialogue between Mr. Cooke and Mrs. Hudgson ... [From *Pausanias.*] London, *ca.* 1700.
    585/2

1700aa: *New reformation begins thro' the nation* ... Tho. Cross, London, *ca.* 1700. s.sh.fol.
    M611/7

1700bb: *Sound fame, thy brazen trumpet.* A song in 'Dioclesian'. London, *ca.* 1700.
    627/22

1700cc: *Take not a woman's anger ill.* [Song from *The Rival Sisters.*] London, *ca.* 1700.
    609/11

1700dd: *Three catches for 3 voices.* London, *ca.* 1700.
    256 272 351

1700ee: *Thus to a ripe consenting maid.* A song in the comedy call'd 'The Old Batchelor' ... London, *ca.* 1700.
    607/10

1700ff: *Two Catches for Three Voices, set by Mr. Willis, also a song* [Fear no danger] *in the play call'd 'Measure for Measure'.* set by Mr. Henry Purcell. London *ca.* 1700.
    626/7ab

1700gg: *When my Acmelia smiles.* A song ... exactly engrav'd by Tho. Cross, London, *ca.* 1700.
    434

1700hh: *Ye twice ten hundred deities.* The conjurers song or The croaking of the toad ... within the compass of the flute. [Song from *The Indian Queen.*] London, *ca.* 1700.
    630/13

1700ii: ———————————— [Another edition.] Sung by Mr. Leveridge. London, *ca.* 1700.
    630/13

1700jj: *Wit and Mirth,* or Pills to Purge Melancholy; being a Collection of the best Merry Ballades and Songs, Old and New. Fitted to all Humours, having each their proper Tune for either voice or Instrument, many of the Songs being new Set. With Several New Songs by Mr. D'Urfey ... The Second Part ... London: Printed by William Pearson, for Henry Playford, 1700.
    572/9, 10b 606/9 627/9bc, 18b, 31ab, 33a S66

1700kk: *The Love's of Dido and Aeneas,* a Mask in Four Musical Entertainments. [From the 1700 Quarto of Gildon's *Measure for Measure.*] London: printed for D. Brown and R. Parker, 1700.
    626(mnp)

1700ll: *The Saylors Song,* Set by Mr. Henry Purcell Sung by Mr. Wiltshire, in the Play call'd *Measure for Measure* and exactly engraved by Tho: Cross.
    626/29bc

1700mm: *Airs de Danses Angloises, Hollandoises, A Deux Parties.* Nouvellment recueillies par Antoine Pointel. A Amsterdam, Dans le Nest, proche le long-Pont. Imprimez A Pares. Chez Christophe Ballard, Seul Imprimeur du Roy pour la Musique, rue S. Jean de Beauvais au Mont-Parnasse. MDCC. Avec priv. du Roy.
    611/9 ('St Martin's Lane') 629/6 (called 'The Old Bachelor') 646 ('Lirbourler' [sic]) 653

?1700:   *? Apollo's Banquet. Choice New Tunes, Ayres, and Jiggs for the Treble Violin.* n.d., n.p. [Unique copy in Royal College of Music Library.]
    331/6 (bass) 570/2, 3 574/2, 3, 6 (in A Major) 597/2 603/8 611/6 628/18 T677 T678 D254 D255 S124 (anon.)

1701

1701a: *The Whole Volume of ... Mercurius Musicus ...* London, 1701. [See EDITION 1699c for contents.]

1701b: *The Second Book of the Pleasant Musical Companion ...* The fourth edition, corrected and much enlarged. William Pearson, for Henry Playford. London, 1701.
> 240 241 242 243 244 245 248 249 252 253 254 255 256 257 259 260 262 263 264 265 266 267 268 269 270 272 273 274 275 276 277 280 281 282 283 284 285 286 287 288 289 290 291 292 351 574/10 594 599 D100 D102 D107 S54 S56

1701c: *The Dancing Master ...* 11th edition corrected, with the Add'ns of new Dance Tunes, the whole printed in new character.
> 570/7, 8 605/T2, T3 607/4 609/2, 3, 9, T11 611/9 646 D136 S125

1701d: *Apollo's Banquet* newly reviv'd: containing new and easie instructions for the treble-violin, with ... ayres, tunes, jiggs, minuets, sarabands, chacones and cybells, etc. (The eighth edition) entirely new. Printed by W. Pearson, for Henry Playford: London, 1701.
> 570/3 574/2, 3 611/6 628/18 630/1b, 2b, 4a, 18 D254

1701–2

1701–2: *50 Airs Anglois ... Livre premier ...* ed. George Bingham: Estienne Roger, Amsterdam, 1701–2.
> 572/2 574/6 (in d minor) 607/7 T678 T686 (in d minor)

1702

1702a: *Come let us agree.* [Song from *Timon of Athens.*] ... Printed for John Cullen, London, *ca,* 1702.
> 632/19

1702b: *The Whole Volume of ... Mercurius Musicus ...* London, 1702. The contents are the same as for EDITION 1699c with the addition of D134.

1702c: *Mr. Henry Purcel's Te Deum ...* Printed for and sold by J. Walsh ... and J. Hare ... London. 1702.
> 232

1702d: *Orpheus Britannicus ... Book II ...* William Pearson, for Henry Playford ... London, 1702.
> 321/3, 7, 9a 328/3b, 8ab 331/6 (bass), 7a 333/3b, 4ab, 6b, 11b 335/2, 3 338/9a, 10a 342/2b, 2e, 3a, 4b, 6 352 381 402 405 410 421 434 473 499 500 516 518 520 525 546 572/11ab 574/12, 13b 578/7 583/2 590 600/3b 607/11 627/22, 30, Appendix 3 629/7b, 8bcd, 21a, 29, 31, 33b, 34b, 35, 36a, 39b, 43, 45b, 47b, 48b 630/4bdg, 7c, 17a, 19 632/10, 11a, 12, 13b, 14, 16, 19

1702e: *Sound a parley.* A two part song in 'King Arthur' ... Printed for John Cullen, London, *ca.* 1702.
> 628/26

1702f: *Supplement of New Catches, to The Second Book of the Pleasant Musical Companion ...* William Pearson for Henry Playford ... and J. Hare, London, 1702.
> 258 D103 D106

1702g: *The Third Book of the Harpsicord Master.* Being a collection of choice lessons ... at the end of the book is added plain and easy rules for learners, made by the late famous Mr. Hen. Purcell , ... Printed and sold by J. Walsh ... London, 1702.

1702h: *The Whole Volume Compleat Intituled The Monthly Masks of Vocal Musick* . . . [Purcell's Harpsicord Rules mentioned in the advertisement.]

1703

1703a: *An Introduction to the Skill of Musick* . . . The fifteenth edition. London, 1703.

1703b: *A prince of glorious race.* Song on the Duke of Gloucester's Birthday sung . . . by Mr. Robert exactly engrav'd by T. Cross, London, *ca.* 1703.
     342/3a

1703c: *Cinthia frowns.* A song in the ' Double Dealer ' . . . sung by Mrs. Ayliff and exactly engrav'd by Tho. Cross. London, *ca.* 1703.
     592/10

1703d: *From rosie bow'rs.* [Song from *Don Quixote* Part III.] London, *ca.* 1703.
     578/9

1703e: *Harmonia Sacra.* The first book. The 2nd edition . . . enlarged and corrected; also four . . . anthems of the late Mr. Henry Purcell's, never before printed . . . William Pearson for Henry Playford . . . and John Sprint . . . London, 1703.
     7 19 31 33 181 184 186 188 189 190 191 193 197 198 199 200 D22

1703f: *Julia your unjust disdain.* A song for two voices . . . exactly engravd by Tho. Cross, London, *ca.* 1703.
     500

1703g: *The Dancing Master* . . . The whole work Revised and much more correct than any former editions . . . Printed by J. Heptinstall for H. Playford . . . [London] 1703.
     570/7, 8 605/T2, T3 607/4 609/2, 3, 9, T11 611/9 646 D100 D136 S125

1704

1704a: *A Choice Collection of Songs by Severall Masters.* Francis Horton, 1704.
     328/4 486 573 574/17 578/3 584 603/10 604A 609/10 613/2 627/22 629/4b, 22b
     630/17h 631/10

1704b: *That excellent sonata in F. for violins* . . . *the Golden sonata* . . . London, 1704.
     810

1704c: *The Jovial Companion, or Merry Club* . . . catches . . . by the late Mr. Henry Purcell & Dr. Blow . . . I. Walsh & P. Randall . . . London, n.d. [1704].
     241 243 245 248 253 255 262 264 265 267 268 270 274 275 277 280 284
     286 290 291 574/10 D100 D102 D103 D106 S54

1704d: [*The Second Book of The Pleasant Musical Companion* . . . published chiefly for the . . . musical societies, which will be speedily set up in all the chief cities and towns in England. Composed by Dr. Blow, the late Mr. Henry Purcell . . . The fourth edition corrected and much enlarged. (Entered in *Term Catalogues* Trin. 1703 III, 358–9. No entry in *Stationers' Register*.)]

1705

1705a: *A Choice Collection of Lessons* . . . by . . . Dr. John Blow, and the late Mr. Henry Purcell . . . Printed for H. Playford, London, 1705.
     646 647 648 649 650 653 655 656 T688 T689 T694

1705b: *A Collection of the Most Celebrated Songs and Dialogues Composed by the Late Famous Mr. Henry Purcell.* Printed for R. Mears, London, *ca.* 1705.

321/2ab 333/7ab 369 370 485 502 521 571/6 574/17 578/3, 6ab, 7, 9 608
609/10 627/22, 35 628/26 629/22b 630/13 632/19

1705c: *Celladon when spring came on.* A song in the comedy call'd The Country Miss with her Furbeloe, the words made by Mr. Tho: D'Urfey. [From *The Old Mode and the New.*] London, *ca.* 1705.
M574/6

1705d: *Celebrate this festival.* London, *ca.* 1705.
321/2ab

1705e: *Dear pretty youth.* London, *ca.* 1705.
631/10

1705f: *If music be the food of love.* [Third version] I. Walsh [plates from *Orpheus Britannicus*] London, *ca.* 1705.
379C

1705g: *Old Chiron thus preach'd.* London, *ca.* 1705.
S61

1705h: *O lead me to some peacefull gloom.* [Song from *Bonduca.*] London, *ca.* 1705.
574/17

1705i: *Since times are so bad.* A dialogue. [From *Don Quixote* Part II.] ... London, *ca.* 1705.
578/6a

1705j: *The First Part of the Division Violin* ... The sixth edition, corected [sic] and enlarged with Aditions [sic] of the newest divisions ... I Walsh, London, 1705.
T680

1705k: *When Myra sings* ... London, 1705.
521

1705l: *Within an arbor of delight.* A Poole at Pickett. [Song] The words made and set to a tune ['Lads and Lasses'] by H. Purcell ... by Mr. D'Urfey. London, 1705.
M578/8

1705m: *Select Preludes or Voluntarys for ye Violin.* Walsh and Hare, London, 1705.
N773

1705n: *Wit and Mirth* ... The 2d Edition Corrected with Additions, and Printed on the new Tyed Note ... Printed by W. Pearson, for H.P. ... London, 1705.
M655

1705o: *The Second Part of the Division Violin* ... the Fourth Edition corected [sic] and enlarged with Additions of the newest Chacons Allmands Preludes and Choice Cibells composed by the best Masters ... I. Walsh ... and I. Hare ... : London, 1705.
T678

1705p: [*The 1st and 2nd Parts of the Division Violin*, consisting of the most celebrated Grounds and Divisions for the Violin. These Editions are enlarged with Additions of the newest Grounds, Chacoons, Allemands, Preludes and Choice Cibels, compos'd by the best masters of the age. Printed for J. Walsh ... and J. Hare ... (presumably a re-advertisement of EDITIONS 1705j and 1705o in *The Post Man*, Nov. 6–8, 1705.)]

1706

1706a: *Orpheus Britannicus* ... The second edition with large additions ... Printed by William Pearson, and sold by John Young, London, 1706.
321/2ab, 6b, 11, 12, 13ab 323/3, 5a 325/8a 328/4, 6, 9, 11b 333/7ab, 9, 10, 13a 335/5a

339/3ab 344/11a 360 365 369 370 379C 389 392 394 396 423 428B 465 470
485 486 488 489 496 501 502 503 513 514 517 521 522 523 570/10 571/6
573 574/15b, 16b, 17 578/1, 3, 4h, 6a, 9 579 580/1 584 585/1 586 589 592/10 595/2
596 598 600/1b, 1d 601/2 602/1 603/10 604A 608 609/10 610 613 626/3a
627/6b, 13b, 35, Appendix 1, Appendix 2 628/9a, 12bc, 16b, 19, 20, 21, 22, 26ab, 29,
35, 36, 38 629/4b, 22b, 40b 630/13, 15, 17h 631/10 632/17

1706b: ———————— The second edition with large additions ... Printed by William Pearson
and sold by John Cullen ... London, 1706.
See EDITION 1706a for contents.

1706c: *The Lady's Banquet* ... London, 1706.
T696 D223

1706d: *The Second Part of the Division Flute* ... London, I. Walsh [? 1706].
T678 (in F Major)

1706e: *Wit & Mirth, or Pills to Purge Melancholy*; being a choice collection ... carefully corrected by
Mr. J. Lenton. Vol. IV. Printed by William Pearson, London, 1706.
331/6 (bass) 395 403 408 M574/6 576 582 587 588/4 601/1 605/1 607/11
609/12 M611/7 612/2, 3, 4 628/38 629/12, M17, 23, 34b D131

1707

1707a: *From rosie bow'rs.* Song from 'Don Quixote' Part III. Tho. Cross, London, *ca.* 1707.
578/9

1707b: *Harmonia Mundi.* Consisting of six favorite sonata's [for two violins and bass] collected out
of the choisest works of six most eminent authors, viz. Signr. Torelli, Mr. H. Purcell, Signr.
Bassani, Mr. Pepusch, Signr. Albinoni, & Signr. Pez. The first collection engraven and carefully corrected. Printed for I. Walsh ... I Hare ... and P. Randall. London, 1707. [The
British Museum copy has a slip bearing the imprint 'John Young' pasted over the original
imprint of the violino primo part.]
810

1707c: *Supplement of New Catches* ... Printed by William Pearson, London, 1707.
258 D103 D106

1707d: *Te Deum et Jubilate* ... The second edition ... J. Walsh ... I. Hare ... and P. Randall ...
London, 1707.
232

1707e: *The Second Book of the Pleasant Musical Companion* ... The fifth edition ... Printed by William
Pearson for Henry Playford ... London, 1707.
240 241 242 243 244 245 248 249 252 253 254 255 256 257 258 259 260
262 263 264 265 266 267 268 269 270 272 273 274 275 276 277 280 281
282 283 284 285 286 287 288 289 290 291 292 351 574/10 594 599 D100
D102 D103 D107 S54

1707f: ———————————————————— The fifth edition, corrected and much enlarged.
[See EDITION 1707e for contents.]

1707g: *Wit and Mirth* ... The third edition, Vols. I–IV. William Pearson, London, 1707.
(Copy in British Museum): 371 379B 412 430 572/9, 10b 578/8 M578/8
591(mnp) 595/1 601/3 602/1 605/2, 3 606/8, 9 609/11(mnp) 627/9bc, 18b, 31ab,
33a 628/10bc, 15bc, 37 629/10, 17 M630/20 M655 D136 D142 S66 S68(mnp)
(Copy in New York Public Library): 331/6 (bass) 359 371 372 379B 384 395
403 408 412 519 572/9, 10ab 574/M6, M17 576 578/2, M8 582 587 588/4

591(mnp) 601/1 602/1 605/1 606/8, 9 607/11 609/11(mnp), 12 M611/7 612/2, 3, 4
627/9bc, 18b, 33a 628/10bc, 15bc, 37, 38 629/12, 17, M17, 23, 34b M360/20 M655
D131 D136 D142

1708

1708a: *[Miscellaneous Operas . . . (including) . . . ' Opera of Dioclesian ' Compos'd by the late Mr. Henry Purcell.* (Advertised in the *Daily Courant*, January 15, 1708, but there is no known extant copy. Walsh may merely have re-issued Heptinstall's edition of 1691.)]

1708b: *Te Deum et Jubilate . . .* The second edition [either advertised or re-issued]. London, 1708.
232

1708c: *The Monthly Mask of Vocal Music . . .* January, 1708.
M611/7

1708d: *Select Preludes and Vollentarys for the Flute.* Walsh and Hare, London, 1708.
N773 (in d minor)

1709

1709a: *Celladon when spring came on . . .* London, *ca.* 1709.
M574/6

1709b: *Mercurius Musicus . . .* for ye year 1708 [1709]. Publish'd for January (February) (April) (June) (October) (November) (December) . . . Printed for J. Walsh, (and P. Randall) . . . and J. Hare. London (1708, 1709).
In the British Museum copy there is a table with a list of ' Books of Instrumental and Vocal Musick Printed in the year 1709 ' in which are mentioned: ' A Cantata by Mr. Purcell ' (No. 315 in W. C. Smith's *Bibliography of John Walsh*); ' Finger's and Purcell's Sonatas for the Violin ' (No. 329); ' Finger's and Purcell's Solos for the Flute ' (No. 329). The latter two, certainly, and the first one, probably, were written by Daniel Purcell.

1709c: *Supplement of Catches . . .* London, 1709.
258 D103 D106

1709d: *The Bottle Companions, or Bacchanalian Club* being a choice collection of merry drinking songs and healths . . . I. Walsh . . . & P. Randall . . . and I. Hare. London (n.d.).
MT678

1709e: *The Jovial Companions . . .* Printed for I. Walsh & P. Randall . . . and I. Hare, London, (1709).
241 243 245 248 253 255 262 264 265 267 268 270 274 275 277 280 284
286 288 290 291 574/10 D100 D102 D103 D106 S54

1709f: *The Pleasant Musical Companion . . .* The fifth edition . . . Printed by William Pearson, . . . sold by John Young, London, 1709.
[See EDITION 1707e for contents.]

1709g: *The Whole Volume Compleat Intituled The Monthly Masks . . .* I. Walsh, London, 1709. 'A cantata by Mr. Purcell ' [probably Daniel Purcell]. [Advertisement mentioned in Walsh Catalogue.]

1709h: *Wit and Mirth . . .* The second edition with additions . . . Vol. IV. Printed by William Pearson, London, 1709.
(Copy in British Museum): 395 M574/6 587 601/1 605/1 609/12, M611/7 646
(Copy in New York Public Library): 331/6 (bass) 395 403 408 M574/6 576 582
587 588/4 601/1 605/1 607/11 609/12 M611/7 612/2, 3, 4 628/38 629/12, M17,
23, 34b D131

1710

1710a: *[A Collection of Catches on Single Sheets*, without title-page]. London, *ca.* 1710.
           242 258 260 264 265 267 273 274 277 280 286 287 290 292 351 D100
           D106 S54

1710b: *Ah! how sweet it is to love.* [Song from *Tyrannick Love.*] London, *ca.* 1710.
           613/2

1710c: *And in each track of glory.* London, *ca.* 1710.
           333/7ab

1710d: *Behold the man that with gigantic might.* London, ? 1710.
           608

1710e: *Celebrate this festival.* London, *ca.* 1710.
           321/2ab

1710f: *Celia has a thousand charms.* [Song from *The Rival Sisters.*] London, *ca.* 1710.
           609/10

1710g: *Come if you dare.* A Song in the Dramatick Opera (of *King Arthur*) . . . London, *ca.* 1710.
           628/10bc

1710h: *Drunk was I last night* . . . [Tho. Cross, Jr.] London, *ca.* 1710.
           M574/6

1710i: *Dulcibella, when e'er I sue for a kiss.* [Tho. Cross, jr.] [J. Walsh.] London *ca.* 1710.
           485

1710j: *Fair Chloe my breast so alarms* . . . Tho. Cross, jr. London, ? 1710.
           486

1710k: *Fair Iris and her swain.* [Tho. Cross jr.] London, *ca.* 1710.
           572/11ab

1710l: *Fly swiftly ye hours.* Set by Mr. Henry Purcell and sung by Mrs. Tofts in the subscription
           musick. Jno. Cullen . . . London, *ca.* 1710.
           369

1710m: *Fly swift ye hours* . . . London, 1710.
           369

1710n: *For folded flocks and fruitful plains* . . . London, *ca.* 1710.
           628/36

1710o: *From rosie bowers* . . . [p. 6–7 of an unidentified collection.] London, ? 1710.
           578/9

1710p: *From silent shades* . . . ' Bess of Bedlam ' . . . London, *ca.* 1710. [pp. 14–15 of an unidentified
           collection.]
           370

1710q: *Genius of England* . . . London, *ca.* 1710. [pp. 16–17 of an unidentified collection.]
           578/7

1710r: *I call you all.* [Song from *King Arthur.*] London, *ca.* 1710.
           628/9a

1710s: *I see she flyes me* . . . J. Walsh, London, *ca.* 1710. [Printed from the same plates as Walsh's
           ' Orpheus Britannicus '.]
           573

1710t: *Jack thou'rt a toper.* A catch sung by the Roman soldiers in the tragedy of Bonduca. London, *ca.* 1710.
        574/10

1710u: *Let the dreadful engines* . . . London, ?1710.
        578/3

1710v: *Lost is my quiet* . . . London, *ca.* 1710.
        502

1710w: *Sound a parley.* A two-part song [in *King Arthur.*] . . . London, *ca.* 1710
        628/26ab

1710x: *Sound, Fame, thy brazen trumpet* . . . London, ?1710.
        627/22

1710y: *Stript of their green our groves appear.* London, *ca.* 1710. [Listed under ' Courteville, Raphael,' in British Museum Catalogue.]
        444

1710z: *The fife and all the harmony of war* . . . [Song from *Ode for St. Cecilia's Day.*] London, *ca.* 1710.
        328/11b

1710aa: *To arms, and Britons strike home.* [Two songs from *Bonduca.*] London, *ca.* 1710.
        574/15b, 16b

1710bb: *Two daughters of this aged stream.* A two-part song [from *King Arthur*] . . . London, *ca.* 1710.
        628/29

1710cc: *Were I to cure three nations fears.* (Set to the tune of ' Were I to choose the greatest bliss '.) A song for two voices by a Person of Honour. London, *ca.* 1710.
        M517

1710dd: *When Sylvia in bathing.* A song on a lady's going into the bath, made by Mr. Thomas D'Urfey . . . exactly engrav'd by Tho. Cross. London, *ca.* 1710.
        M630/20

1710ee: *When Myra sings.* A song for two voices . . . Tho. Cross Jr. London, *ca.* 1710.
        521

1710ff: *Within an arbor of delight* . . . London, *ca.* 1710.
        M578/8

1710gg: *Ye twice ten-hundred deities* . . . London, *ca.* 1710.
        630/13

1710hh: *Musa et Musica or Humour & Musick* . . . Pleasant and merry humours with Scotch & Love Songs, the words by Mr. D'Urfey etc: Pippard: London, *ca.* 1710.
        D135

1711

1711a: *Catches for Flutes*; or a collection of the best catches contriv'd and fitted for 1:2:3: or 4 flutes, to be performed in the nature of catches, which makes a compleat consort of flutes, being the first of the kind yet publish'd . . . Printed for J. Walsh . . . & J. Hare. London, [1711].
        241 243 248 252 253 255 262 265 267 270 274 275 280 284 286 288 290
        291 574/10 D100 D102 D103 D106

1711b: *Orpheus Britannicus* . . . the second book . . . The second edition with additions. Printed by William Pearson, for S.H. Sold by J. Young . . . and J. Cullen. London, 1711.

The contents are the same as for EDITION 1702d with the following additions: 328/10b, 515, 578/4b, 627/8, 628/6c, 629/50e, 630/4h, 7b, 17bc D172.

1711c: *A Hundred & Twenty Country Dances for the Flute*: Being a choice collection of the Pleasant & most Airy Tunes out of all the Dance Books: London: Printed for & Engr. by L. Pippard at ye sign of Orpheus . . . where are new Books of Sonatas & Solos & new songs of all sorts.
611/9 (in a minor) 646 653 D100 (anon) D136 D145 S125

1712

1712a: *Orpheus Britannicus* . . . the second book . . . The second edition . . . [Another issue.] London, 1712.
[See EDITION 1711b for contents.]

1712b: *The Monthly Mask of Vocal Music or the newest Songs Made for the Theatre* . . . publish'd for Aprill. Printed for and sold by I. Walsh and I. Hare, London, 1712.
573

1712c: *Wit and Mirth* . . . With several new songs by Mr. D'Urfey. The third edition, Vol. III . . . Printed by William Pearson . . . and sold by J. Young . . . London, 1712.
359 372 384 519 574/M6, M17 578/2

1713

1713a: *An Introduction to the Skill of Musick* . . . The sixteenth edition, corrected and done on the new-ty'd note. Printed by William Pearson, for John Sprint . . . London, 1713.

1713b: *The Dancing Master* . . . Fifteenth edition . . . The whole work revised and done on the new-ty'd note, and much more correct than any former editions . . . London: printed by W. Pearson and sold by John Young . . . 1713.
570/8 605/T2, T3 609/2, 3, 9, T11 611/9 646 D100 D136 S125

1714

1714a: *Harmonia Sacra* . . . Book II, the second edition, very much enlarg'd and correct'd. Printed by William Pearson for S.H. London, 1714.
134 182 183 192 196 D72 D77 S15

1714b: *Harmonia Sacra* . . . Books I & II. The third edition . . . Printed by William Pearson for S.H. London, 1714.
7 19 31 134 181 182 183 184 186 188 189 190 191 192 193 196 197 198 199 200 D72 D73 S15

1714c: *Wit and Mirth* . . . The fourth edition . . . Vols. I–V . . . Printed by William Pearson . . . sold by John Young . . . London, 1714.
The contents are as for EDITION 1707g (British Museum copy), with the following additions: D135, D137, D145 (Daniel Purcell).

1715

1715a: *A Collection of New Songs*, with a through bass to each song for the harpsicord, compos'd by several masters. London: I. Walsh (n.d.). ?1715.
M574/6 605/2

1715b: *Celia has a thousand charms.* Song from *The Rival Sisters.* London, ca. 1715.
609/10

1715c: *Musing I late on Windsor Terras* . . . s.sh.fol. ca. 1715.
D135

1716

1716a: *[Mr. Purcell's Lessons with Instructions for the Harpsicord.* J. Walsh and J. Hare . . . London, before 1716. (Advertised as Walsh publication No. 499 in 'The 4th Book of the Ladys Entertainment.') No extant copy is known.]

1716b: *The Dancing Master* . . . The sixteenth edition containing 358 of the Choicest . . . tunes . . . London: printed for W. Pearson and sold by John Young . . . 1716.
[See EDITION 1713b for contents.]

1716c: *The Merry Musicians.* or a cure for the Spleen . . . Part I . . . printed by H. Meers for I. Walsh . . . & I. Hare . . . 1716.
D135   D136   D137

1717

1717: *Divine Harmony.* The 2d Collection being Select Anthems for a Voice alone . . . Composed by Several Eminent Authors . . . Printed for I: Walsh and I: Hare. &c. London, 1717.
D74

1718

1718a: *An Introduction to the Skill of Musick* . . . The seventeenth edition . . .
109   870   871   D220

1718b: *The Dancing Master*: Vol. the Second, the 3rd Edition, containing 360 of the Choicest Old and new Tunes . . . London: Printed by W. Pearson, and sold by John Young . . . 1718.
603/6   D137

1718c: *A Book of Psalmody, containing a Variety of Tunes for all the Common Meters* . . . John Cheltham, 1718.
125

1719

1719a: *Songs Compleat, Pleasant and Divertive*; set to musick by Dr. John Blow, Mr. Henry Purcell . . . Written by Mr. D'Urfey. Five vols. Printed by William Pearson for J. Tonson. London, 1719.
Vols I and II: 291   320/2a(mnp)   333/2(mnp), 7ab   405   M430   463   465(mnp)   481   509(mnp)   578/1(mnp), 2, 3(mnp), 6a(mnp), 7, 9(mnp)   584(mnp)   589(mnp)   602/1(mnp), 2   608(mnp)   M611/7   627/22(mnp)   M655   MT678   D137   D138(mnp)

1719b: *Wit and Mirth* . . . Printed by William Pearson for J. Tonson . . . Five vols. London, 1719.
(Copy in British Museum): 291   320/2a(mnp)   333/2, 7ab   359   371   372   379B   405   407   412   430   463   465(mnp)   481   489   509(mnp)   572/9, 10   M574/6   578/1(mnp), 2, 3(mnp), 6a(mnp), 7, 8, M8, 9(mnp)   584(mnp)   589(mnp)   591(mnp)   595/1   601/3   602/1(mnp), 2   605/3   606/8, 9   608(mnp)   609/11   M611/7   627/9bc, 18b, 22(mnp), 31ab, 33a   628/10, 15bc, 37   629/10   M630/20   M646   M646   M655   MT678   D135   D136   D137   D138(mnp)   D142   S66   S68
(Copy in New York Public Library): 290   320/2a(mnp)   333/2, 7ab   359   371   372   379B   384   405   407   412   430   M430   443   463   465(mnp)   481   489   509(mnp)   519   572/9, 10   574/M6, M17(mnp)   578/1(mnp), 2, 3(mnp), 6(mnp), 7, 8, M8, 9(mnp)   584(mnp)   589(mnp)   591(mnp)   595/1   601/3   602/1(mnp), 2   605/1, 2, 3   606/8, 9   608(mnp)   609/11   M611/7   627/9bc, 18b, 22(mnp), 33a   628/10, 37   629/10, 17   M630/20   M655   MT678   D135   D136   D137   D138(mnp)   D142   S68(mnp)

1719c: ——————— Another issue of Vol. I.

291 320/2a(mnp) 333/2, 7ab 405 578/1(mnp), 3(mnp), 6a(mnp), 7, 9(mnp) 584(mnp) 589(mnp) 602/1(mnp), 2 608(mnp) 627/22(mnp) D137 S68

1720

1720a: *A Collection of Sea Songs on Several Occasions* . . . I. Walsh . . . and I. Hare . . . (n.d.), London, ?1720.

571/6

1720b: *And in each track of glory.* London, *ca.* 1720.

333/7ab

1720c: *Bess of Bedlam* [i.e. ' From silent shades.'] London, *ca.* 1720.

370

1720d: ——————— [Another issue, from an unidentified collection.] London, *ca.* 1720.

370

1720e: ——————— [Another issue, from an unidentified collection.] London, *ca.* 1720.

370

1720f: *Celia has a thousand charms.* [Song from *The Rival Sisters.*] London, *ca.* 1720.

609/10

1720g: *For love ev'ry creature is form'd.* A two part song. London, *ca.* 1720.

488

1720h: *Forth from my dark and dismal cell* . . . London, *ca.* 1720.

S68

1720i: *From rosy bowers* . . . London, *ca.* 1720.

578/9

1720j: *Go tell Amynta gentle swain.* A two part song. London, *ca.* 1720.

489

1720k: *Let Caesar and Urania live.* A two part song. [From *Sound the trumpet.* p. 33 of an unidentified collection.]

335/5a

1720l: *Te Deum et Jubilate* . . . J. Walsh [n.d.], London, ?1720.

232

1720m: *The Divine Musick Scholar's Guide* . . . [ed. Francis Timbrell], London, *ca.* 1720.

D7

1720n: *The Pleasant Musical Companion* . . . The sixth edition . . . Printed by William Pearson . . . sold by J. Young. London, 1720.

240 241 242 243 244 245 248 249 252 253 254 255 256 257 258 259 260 262 263 264 265 266 267 268 269 270 272 274 275 276 277 280 281 282 283 284 285 286 287 288 289 290 291 292 351 574/10 594 599 D100 D102 D106 D107

1720o: *To arms* . . . Will Cluer, London, 1720.

574/15b

1720p: ——————— *& Britons strike home.* Tho. Cross Jr. London, 1720.

574/15b, 16b

1720q: *To this place we're now come.* A song for two voices . . . London, *ca.* 1720.

N526

1720r: *Were I to choose the greatest bliss.* London, 1720.
      517

1720s: *Wit and Mirth* . . . The sixth and last volume . . . William Pearson for J. Tonson, London, 1720.
      331/6 (bass) 395 403 M403(mnp) 408 576 582 587(mnp) 588/4 601/1 M606/5(mnp) 607/11 609/12 612/2, 3, 4 628/M30bc(mnp), 38 629/12, M17, 23, 34b D131 D144 D145

1720t: *Ye twice ten hundred deities.* Song from 'The Indian Queen'. London, 1720.
      630/13

1720u: *Come follow me.* London, *ca.* 1720.
      628/14abc

1721

1721a: *Orpheus Britannicus* . . . The third edition with large additions . . . Books I and II . . . Printed by William Pearson for S.H. London, 1721.
      Book I: 321/2ab, 6b, 11b, 12a, 13b 323/3, 5a 325/8a 328/3b, 4, 6, 8, 9, 11b 333/7, 9, 10, 13a 339/3ab 344/11a 360 365 369 370 379C 396 425 428A 465 469 485 486 488 489 496 503 513 514 515 517 521 522 523 571/6 573 574/15b, 16b, 17 578/1, 3, 4h, 6a, 9 579 580/1 584 585/1 586 589 592/10 595/2 596 598 600/1bd 601/2 602/1 603/10 604A 608 609/10 610 613 626/3a 627/6ab, 13b, 35, Appendix 1, 2, 3 628/9a, 12, 16b, 19b, 20b, 21, 22, 26, 29, 35, 36, 38 629/4b, 22b, 40b 630/13, 15, 17h 631/10 632/17
      Book II: The contents are the same as for EDITION 1702d with the following additions: 328/10b, 578/4b, 627/8, 628/6c, 629/50e, 630/4h, 7b, 17bc, D172; and with the following omission: 472

1721b: *The Dancing Master:* Vol. the First . . . The 17th Edition . . . London: Printed by W. Pearson, and sold by John Young . . . 1721.
      [See EDITION 1731b for contents.]

1721c: *Anchor's Collection of Psalm Tunes.* London, *ca.* 1721.
      D45

1722

1722a: *The First Part of The Division Violin* . . . 6th Edition: London: I. Walsh . . . & I. Hare . . . n.d.
      T632/20

1722b: *The Pleasant Musical Companion.* The seventh edition . . . Printed by William Pearson? London, ?1722.
      Contents unknown; probably as in EDITION 1720n.

1723

1723:   *A Book of Psalmody* . . . Robert and John Barber, London: William Pearson . . . 1723.
      D7

1724

1724a: *Musica Sacra* or Select Anthems in Score . . . To which is added, The Burial Service. William Croft. (2 vols.) Published by Walsh, London, 1724.
      58C

1724b: *An Introduction to the Skill of Musick* . . . The eighteenth edition . . . Printed by William Pearson for John and Benj. Sprint . . . London, 1724.
> [For contents, see the editions of 1713 and 1718.]

1724c: *The Pleasant Musical Companion.* The eighth edition . . . Printed by William Pearson for John and Benj. Sprint . . . London, 1724.
> [See EDITION 1720n for contents.]

1724d: *An Introduction to the Skill of Musick* . . . & Anthems, Hymns, Psalm-Tunes, in Several Pts. By Edward Betts, Organist of Manchester. London: Pr. by William Pearson . . . 1724.
> 2 19 60

1725

1725a: *Michael Broom's Collection of Church Musick,* for the use of his scholars. London: 1725.
> D7

1725b: *I spy Celia, Celia eyes me.* A song for two voices set by Mr. Purcell. London, ca. 1725.
> 499

1725c: [*Orpheus Britannicus.*] *Mr. Hen^r Purcell's Favourite Songs out of His Most Celebrated Orpheus Britannicus* and the rest of his works, the whole fairly engraven and carefully corrected. Printed for In^o Walsh, London, ca. 1725.
> 321/2ab 333/7ab 369 370 379C 485 486 501 502 521 571/6 573 574/15b, 16b, 17 578/1, 3, 6ab, 7, 9 598 608 609/10 613/2 627/22, 35 628/26 629/4b, 22b 630/13 631/10 632/19 S68

1725d: *The Divine Musick Scholar's Guide* . . . F. Timbrell. Engraved by Will Cluer Dicey. London, 1725.
> D7

1726

1726a: *Harmonia Sacra* . . . The first book, the third edition very much enlarg'd and corrected; also four excellent anthems of the late Mr. H. Purcell's, never before printed . . . Printed by William Pearson for S.H. London, 1726.
> 7 19 31 D73

1726b: [*Orpheus Britannicus.*] *Mr. Hen^r. Purcell's Favourite Songs out of His Most Celebrated Orpheus Brittanicus* [*sic*] and the Rest of His Works the whole fairly engraven and carefully corrected. The second edition with additions . . . Printed for and sold by In^o. Walsh . . . and In^o. and Joseph Hare . . . London, ?after 1726.
> The contents are the same as in EDITION 1725c with the following additions: 335/5a, 428A, 444, 584, 602/1, 628/38; and with the following omissions: 574/16b, 578/6b, 608/1.

1726c: *The Pleasant Musical Companion* . . . The nineth [*sic*] edition, 1726.
> [See EDITION 1720n for contents.]

?1727

?1727: *Medulla Musicae:* Being a Choice Collection of Airs . . . in 2 Vols . . . Colligit R.M. Philomusicus. London: Cluer, [?1727].
> 810/4 (Vn 1 and Bc only)

1728

1728a: *A Choice Collection of Twenty-four Psalm-Tunes*, all in four parts, and fifteen anthems, set by different authors, for 2, 3, and 4 voices; with their names to each tune . . . The whole collection engraved and printed by Michael Broome, music and copperplate printer in Column Row . . . Birmingham, *ca.* 1728.
>> N110

1728b: *The Dancing Master.* Vol. the Second . . . The 4th Edition . . . London: Printed by W. Pearson and Sold by John Young . . . 1728.
>> 603/6 D137

?1728: *The Merry Musicians*: Or a Cure for the Spleen . . . vol. III . . . London: printed for I. Walsh . . . Jos: Hare . . . & I. Young.
>> 444

1729–31

1729–31: *The Musical Miscellany*: being a collection of choice songs set to the Violin and Flute . . . London: John Watts, 1729–31, 6 vols.
>> M655 MD136

1730

1730a: *An Introduction to the Skill of Musick* . . . The nineteenth edition . . . Printed by William Pearson for Benjamin Sprint . . . London, 1730.
>> [For contents, see the editions of 1713 and 1718.]

1730b: *Hark, my Daridcar.* A two-part song [from Purcell's music to *Tyrannick Love*]. London, *ca.* 1730.
>> 613/1

1730c: *Harmonia Sacra* or Select Anthems in Score. Compos'd by the late Henry Purcell. I. Walsh, London, (n.d.). [?1730.]
>> 7 19 31 33 57 60

1730d: *The Divine Musick Scholar's Guide or the Timbrel New Tun'd*, in three books. The first is a compleat introduction to ye grounds of musick, with the famous Mr. Henry Purcels directions for playing on ye spinnet, harpsichord or organ . . . Collected and printed by F. Timbrel . . . Will. Cluer Dicey, London and Northampton, *ca.* 1730.
>> D7

1730e: *The First & Second Division Violin* . . . Daniel Wright, London, *ca.* 1730.
>> T678

1730f: *To arms & Britons strike home* . . . London, *ca.* 1730.
>> 574/15b, 16b

1730g: *Harmonia Perfecta*: A Complete Collection of Psalm Tunes in Four Parts . . . Taken from the most Eminent Masters . . . chiefly Mr. Ravenscroft . . . London: Wm. Pearson . . . and Nathaniel Gawthorn at the Black Peruke in Rood Lane, Fenchurch Street, 1730.
>> 125 S17

1730h: *The Lover.* Opera As it is performed at the Theatre-Royal by His Majesty's Servants By Mr. Chetwood . . . The Third Edition, with Alterations. And the Musick Prefix'd to each. London Printed for John Watts at the Printing Office in Wild Court near Lincoln's Inn Fields. 1730.
>> 605/2 628/27 (2nd stanza)

1731

1731a: *Te Deum & Jubilate* . . . J. Walsh . . . J. Hare . . . and P. Randall . . . London, 1731.
232

1731b: *The Catch Club or Merry Companions*, being a choice collection of the most diverting catches for three and four voices. Compos'd by the late Mr. Henry Purcell, Dr. Blow, (et altri) . . . Two books. Printed for I. Walsh, London, *ca.* 1731.
240 241 242 243 244 245 248 249 252 253 254 256 257 259 260 262 263
264 265 266 267 268 269 270 272 274 275 276 277 280 282 283 284 285
286 288 290 291 292 351 574/10 599 D102 D106 D107

1731c: *The Modern Musick-Master, or the Universal Musician*, containing . . . I. An Introduction to Singing . . . (Note this second treble was never printed before.) London, 1731.
333/7ab

1731d: *The Musical Miscellany*, being a collection of choice songs . . . John Watts, London, ?1731.
628/38

1731e: *A Book of Psalmody* containing variety of Tunes for all Common Metres . . . & Thirteen Anthems . . . 4th edition with Additions. By John Chetham, London: Printed by William Pearson . . . 1731.
N110 D3 D21

1731f: *The Highland Fair*; Or Union of Clans. An Opera. As it is Performed at the Theatre Royal . . . written by Mr. Mitchell With Musick, which wholly consists of . . . Scot's tunes . . . London . . . J. Watts, 1731.
M655

1731g: *The Jovial Crew, A Comic Opera as it is Acted at the Theatre Royal* . . . [by W. Bates]. . . . London: Pr. for J. Watts, 1731.
602/2 628/27 (2nd stanza) M655

1732

1732: *The Merry Mountebank, or the Humourous Quack-Doctor* . . . compiled . . . by Timothy Tulip, of Fidlers-Hall in Cuckholdshire, Esq . . . Vol. I: . . . Printed by William Pearson, London, 1732.
MT678

1733

1733a: *The Catch Club, or Merry Companions* . . . First part . . . I. Walsh, London, 1733.
See EDITION 1731b for contents.

1733b: *The Excellency of Divine Musick* . . . Arthur Bedford . . . London, 1733.
D22

1733c: *The New Flute Master for the year 1733.* London: n.p., 1733.
629/6

1735

1735a: *Fair Cloe my breast so alarms.* [p. 20 from an undesignated collection.]
486

1735b: *Fill all the glasses.* A two-part song in the play call'd Harry the Fifth . . . within the compass of the flute. J. Simpson, London, *ca.* 1735.
S53

1735c: *Genius of England.* [Song from *Don Quixote* Part II.] Printed for Elizabeth Hare . . . London, *ca.* 1735.
     578/7

1735d: *The Divine Musick Scholar's Guide* . . . F. Timbrel . . . Will. Cluer Dicey, London and Northampton, *ca.* 1735 . . . with the famous Mr. Henry Purcels directions for playing on the spinnet, harpsicord, or organ. [Another edition of the above dated *ca.* 1735 in the British Museum Catalogue has been removed to *ca.* 1720 (see EDITION 1720m) on the evidence of a manuscript note in the back of the volume, which reads: 'Thomas Bradford's Book/Tho Bradford Ejus Liber Ano. Domini 1723.']

1735e: *To arms & Britons strike home* and *Genius of England.* (A trumpet song.) London, *ca.* 1735.
     574/15b, 16b   578/7

1736

1736a: *The Musical Entertainer,* Engrav'd by George Bickham junn^r.   ol. I . . . Printed for & sold by George Bickham . . . London, ?1736.
     370   578/9

1736b: *King Arthur, or Merlin, the British Enchanter* as it is performed at the Theatre in Goodman's Fields. The Musick by Mr. Purcell . . . London: Printed by R. Walker, 1736.
     628 (mnp)

1737

1737a: *The Musical Entertainer,* engrav'd by George Bickham, jun^r.   Two volumes . . .
     370   574/15b   578/9   S61

1737b: *The Universal Musician, or Songster's Delight* . . . London, (n.d.) [?1737–8].
     370   578/9

1737c: *Divine Recreations.* Being a Collection of Psalms, Hymns, and Canons in Two, Three, and Four Parts: With Easy, Grave, and Pleasant Tunes adapted to each of them . . . London: Printed by A. Pearson . . . Part II: For the Easter Quarter: 1737.
     230M/2d   632/19

1740

1740a: [*Two catches:*] *A three voice catch* ['Jack thou'rt a toper'] *and a four voice catch* ['Soldier, take off thy wine']. London, *ca.* 1740.
     274   574/10

1740b: *Come let us leave the town.* London, *ca.* 1740.
     629/4b

1740c: *Fill all the glasses.* [Song from *Harry the Fifth*; No. 21 from an unidentified collection.] London, 1740.
     S53

1740d: [*Four catches for three and four voices.*] London, *ca.* 1740. Probably contained *Nos.* 269 and 276.

1740e: *Old Chiron thus preach'd.* [p. 45 of an unidentified collection.] ?1740.
     S61

1740f: *Sing all ye muses.* A song sung at the knighting of Don Quixote. [pp. 51–55 of an unidentified collection.] London, *ca.* 1740.
     578/1

1740g: *The Pleasant Musical Companion.*
         [See EDITION 1720n for contents.]

1740h: *Three catches.*
         273   274

1740i: *Three sheets of catches*: (1) Three catches. London, *ca.* 1740.
                      273   274
                 (2) Four catches. London, *ca.* 1740.
                      264   265
                 (3) Four catches. London, *ca.* 1740.
                      269   276

1740j: *To arms & Britons strike home.* [p. 33 of an unidentified collection.] London, ?1740.
         574/15b, 16b

1740k: *Would you know how we met.* A catch for three voices; and *'Tis too late or the coach.* A catch for 3 voices. London, *ca.* 1740.
         280   290

1744

1744:   *Thesaurus Musicus.* A collection of two, three, and four part songs ... To which are added some choice dialogues. Set to musick by ... D. Blow, H. Purcell, Handel, Dr. Green, Dr. Purcell, Eccles ... The whole revis'd by ... [James Oswald.] Vol. I. Printed for John Simpson, London, [1744].
         333/7ab   335/5a   485   517   572/11ab   574/15b   578/1, 6a   602/1   607/11   627/30
         628/26, 36   629/4b   632/19   D171   S51

1745

1745a: *Celia has a thousand charms.* [Song from *The Rival Sisters.* p. 9 of Walsh's ' Orpheus Britannicus '.] London, *ca.* 1745.
         609/10

1745b: *My dearest I languish.* A dialogue ... [from *Pausanias.* Two pages from Walsh's ' Orpheus Britannicus '.] London, *ca.* 1745.
         585/2

1745c: *Orpheus Britannicus*: A collection of choice songs for one, two and three voices with a through bass for the harpsichord. Printed for I. Walsh. London [*ca.* 1745].
         321/2ab   333/7ab   335/5a   369   370   379C   394   423   428A   444   485   486   488
         489   501   502   513   514   517   521   522   750/10   571/6   572/11ab   573   574/15b, 16b, 17
         578/1, 3, 4h, 6a, 7, 9   579   580/1   584   585   592/10   595/2   596   598   600/1b   601/2
         602/1   604A   608   609/10   610   613/2   627/6ab, 13b, 22, 35, Appendix 1   628/26, 29,
         35, 36, 38   629/4b, 22b   630/13, 15   631/10   632/17, 19   D171   S61   S68

1745d: *Thesaurus Musicus,* a collection of two, three, and four part songs, several of them never before printed. To which are added some choice dialogues set to musick by the most eminent masters, viz. Dr. Blow, H. Purcell, Handel, Dr. Green, Dl. Purcell, Eccles, Weldon, Leveridge, Lampe, Carey &c ... John Simpson, London, 1745.
         333/7ab   335/5a   485   503   517   574/15b, 16b   578/1, 6a   602/1   607/11   627/30
         628/26, 29, 36   629/4b, 8bcd   632/19   D171   S61

1746

1746a: *Calliope, or English Harmony*, a collection of the most celebrated English and Scots songs . . . London, engraved by Henry Roberts, (n.d.) [?1746].
609/10

1746b: *Universal Harmony*, or the Gentlemen & Ladie's social companion . . . London, J. Newberry, 1746.
628/38

1747

1747:   *An Introduction to Singing* . . . by Peter Prelleur. London: J. Simpson, (n.d.) [1747].
574/15b, 16b

1748

1748a: *Musarum Brittanicarum Thesaurus*: or A Choice collection of English Songs, dialogues, and catches for two, three, and Four voices in score . . . William East: Waltham, Leicestershire, 1748.
245 275 333/6ab 486 574/10 628/35 629/22b S51 S61

1748b: [British Melody] *Proposals for printing by subscription a new musical entertainment entitled British Melody*; or the Monthly Musical Magazine: consisting of an accurate . . . collection of . . . songs of one, two, and three parts . . . musick by . . . H. Purcell and other eminent masters . . . Number 2. W. Brett: London, (1748) fol.
389 596

1750

1750a: *Sacred Melody* being a choice collection of Anthems . . . selected by Abraham Milner, London (n.d.) [1750].
9 D73

1750b: *The second edition of the first book of The Voice of Melody*. With great additions. ed. William Corbett, collected printed and sold by William East of Waltham, Leicestershire, and by Whiteman Stationers in Grantham. 1750.
33 N110

?1750:   *A Collection Revival and refining (from the more gross & obscene songs) of the old catch book* together with a variety of two, & three part songs . . . by Abraham Milner. London: Milner.
241 262 269 270 274 275 281 284 286 287 333/6ab 419 486 500 502 517
520 521 525 546 574/10 585/2 628/26, 36 D100 D102 S61 S67

1753

1753:   *David's Harp well Tuned* . . . Robert Barber: London, Brown, 1753.
D7

1754

1754a: *A choice collection of eleven anthem's* . . . ed. John Bishop of Winchester. Collected, engraved printed for and sold by Michael Broome, Birmingham, 1754.
D15 D21

1754b: *The Muse's Delight* . . . Liverpool: Sadler, 1754.
        S65

1755

?1755a: *A Collection of Songs for Two & Three Voices taken from Orpheus Britannicus* . . . Printed by John Johnson, London, ?1755.
        323/3 333/7ab 335/5a 485 486 488 489 490 499 501 502 503 517 520 521
        N526 546 572/11ab 574/15b 578/1, 6a, 7 585/2 602/1 607/11 608 613/1 627/30
        628/26, 29, 36 629/4b, 8bcd, 22b 630/17bc 632/11ab S53 S61

1755b: *Te Deum and Jubilate.* Boyce's version with instrumental parts.
        232

1756

1756:   *Apollo's Cabinet* or the Muses Delight, an accurate collection of English and Italian songs, cantatas, and duets set to music for the harpsichord, violin, german-flute &c. with instructions for the voice, violin, harpsichord or spinet, german-flute, common-flute, hautboy, french-horn, bassoon, and bass-violin. Also a compleat Musical Dictionary, and several hundred English, Irish and Scots songs. Liverpool: John Sadler, 1756.
        574/16b S65

1758

1758a: *Clio and Euterpe*, or British Harmony. A collection of celebrated songs and cantatas . . . London, Henry Roberts, 1758.
        574/15b, 16b 578/7 630/13

1758b: *Divine Harmony* . . . collection of anthems set by John Bishop, Mr. Henry Purcell and Mr. Hine etc. Collected, printed and sold by Michael Broome, Birmingham, 1758.
        D15 D21

1760

c1760:   [From] *Rosy bowers.* The last song that was set by . . . Mr. Henry Purcell, It being in his sickness. In *Chloe*, or the Musical Magazine, etc. No. 68 [*ca.* 1760] fol.
        578/9;
    and in No. 11: 629/17

1763

1763:   *Social Harmony* Consisting of a Collection of Songs and Catches. In two, three, four and five Parts from the Works of the most eminent Masters To which are added Several Choice Songs on Masonry. By Thomas Hale of Darnhall Cheshire 1763. [Engraved by] Morrison.
        335/5a 503 578/1 628/30ef, 36 629/4b

1765

1765a: *Church Music Reformed or the Art of Psalmody* . . . by John Arnold, Philo-Musicae . . . R. Brown, London, 1765.
        120 (anon) 125

1765b: *Royal Harmony or the Beauties of Church Music* . . . ed. Aaron Williams, printed for J. Johnson, London, *ca.* 1765.
  7 33 D2 D3 S13 S16

?1765: *Harmonia Anglicana*; or English Harmony Reviv'd. [London . . . ?1765.]
  335/5a 485 486 517 521 574/15b, 16b 578/1 602/1 613/1 628/26, 29, 30ef
  632/17, 19

1767

1767a: *Fifty Double and Single Chants* . . . Printed for C. & S. Thompson, London, *ca.* 1767.
  120 123 D31

1767b: *The Essex Harmony* being a choice collection of the most celebrated songs and catches . . . by John Arnold. 3rd ed., London: Robert Brown, 1767.
  274 287 574/10, 15b 585/2 S51

1768

1768: *Cathedral Music being a Collection in Score of the Most Valuable and Useful Compositions for that Service* . . . Selected and carefully Revis'd by Dr. William Boyce. vol. ii Printed for the editor, London, 1768.
  4 35 36 37 60

1769

1769a: *Six Select Anthems in Score* . . . London, printed for Messrs. Birchall and Andrews at Handel's Head. London 1769.
  54

?1769b: *Six Select Anthems in Score* . . . Printed by Wm. Randall, London, ?1769.
  2

1770

1770a: *Harmonia Sacra* . . . ed. R. Williamson (n.d.) London, [1770].
  19

1770b: *King Arthur, or the British Worthy.* A Masque By Mr. Dryden, As it is performed at the Theatre-Royal in Drury-Lane, By His Majesty's Company. The Music by Purcell and Dr. Arne. The Scenes by French and Carver. A New Edition, London: Printed for W. Strathan, L. Hawes and Co. T. Davies, T. Lownds, T. Beckett, and W. Griffin. 1770. (Music not published.)
  628(mnp)

1770c: *The Musical Magazine* or Compleat Pocket Companion . . . London: T. Benner and W. Bingley: 1767–72. Vol IV for the year 1770.
  628/38

1770d: *The songs airs duets & choruses in the masque of King Arthur,* as perform'd at the Theatre Royal in Drury Lane compos'd by Purcell and Dr. Arne. John Johnston: London, *ca.* 1770.
  628(inc)

c1770: *Had she not care enough* (ascribed to Purcell and included with *Let ambition fire thy mind*, Weldon). R. Falkener, London, *ca.* 1770 s.sh.fol.
  S54

1771

1771:   *Vocal Music*, or the songster's companion ... London: Robert Horsfield ... [1771].
      628/38

1772–4

1772–4:   *The Young Gentlemen and Ladies Musical Companion*, or Sunday's Amusement: for the Organ, harpsicord, piano forte, Ger: flute, and violin. (J. Wilson) by Thomas Chapman. London: Straight and Skillern [1772].
      125 195 D40 D41 D44 D78 S5 S11

1773

1773:   *Cathedral Music* ... ed. Dr. William Boyce, vol iii. London, 1773.
      2 33 57 61 230

?1773:   *The songs* ... &c in King Arthur, compos'd by Purcell and Dr. Arne. London, Longman & Lukey (n.d.) [?1773].
      628(inc)

1774

1774a: [*Roxburghe Ballads: Vol II*] Ancient Songs and Ballads: Written on Various Subjects, And printed between the Years 1555 & 1700 Chiefly Collected by Robert Earl of Oxford, and Purchased at the Sale of the late Mr. West's Library in the Year 1773 ... in Two Volumes: ... London: Arranged and Bound in the Year 1774. Vol. II.
      572/M9 606/M5, M8(*bis*) 627/M9b, M18b(*bis*) 629/M17bc

1774b: *The New Musical and Universal Magazine* ... London: printed for R. Snagg. No. 29 Pater Noster Row ... (n.d.) [1774].
      494 495

1775

1775a: *A choice collection of two, three, & four part songs* compos'd by Purcell, Blow, Handell, Dr. Green and several other eminent masters. Book 2nd. London: Chas. and Saml. Thompson [1775].
      274 574/10, 15b 578/6a S61

1775b: *The Cathedral Magazine*, or Divine Harmony ... vol i, Printed for J. French (n.d.) London, 1775.
      49

1776

c1776:   *The Original Songs, Airs, and Choruses which were Introduced in the Tragedy of* Macbeth *in score*. By Matthew Lock, Chapel organist to Queen Catharine, Consort to King Charles II. Revived & Corrected by D. Boyce. (Ded. to David Garrick.) London: Longman & Broderip.
      S100

1778

1778:   *The Psalm Singers Assistant or a Key to Psalmody* ... By John Crompton of Southwold, Suffolk. Printed for the author by G. Bigg, London 1778.
      7 232/1

1779

1779a: *The Complete Psalmodist*, or the Organist's Parish-clerks, and Psalm-singer's Companion . . .
By John Arnold. 7th ed. G. Bigg, London 1779.
33   49   230M

1779b: *The Hibernian Magazine*, February, 1779, Dublin.
628/29

?1779: *A Select collection of the most admired songs, duetts &c* [London]: Corri, ?1779.
286   370

1780

1780: *Harmonia Coelestis* . . . a collection of . . . anthems . . . ed. Thomas Williams. Printed by the
editor, London, 1780.
33

?1780: *Miscellaneous collection of songs.* p. 99, ' Forth from my dark.'
S68

c1780: *The favorite songs, duetts and chorusses . . . in Bonduca* . . . Sung . . . at the Theatre Royal Drury
Lane. (Score.) J. Bland: London, [*ca.* 1780] fol.
335/5a   574/11, 13b, 14, 15b, 16b, 17   578/7

1781

1781: *King Arthur, or the British Worthy*, A Masque Altered from Dryden by David Garrick, Esq.
And now performed at the Theatre Royal in Drury-Lane. The Music by Purcell and Dr.
Arne. The Scenes by French and Carver, London: Printed for W. Strahan, T. Lowndes,
T. Calson, and S. Bladon. 1781. (Music not published.)
628(mnp)

?1781: *Six Select Anthems* . . . printed by Birchall & Andrews, at Handel's Head, (n.d.) London,
[?1781].
54

1784

1784: *Te Deum et Jubilate* . . . Wright & Co. etc. London *ca.* 1784.
232

1785

1785a: *Harmonia Sacra* or Divine and moral songs with hymns and anthems . . . [a reprint of R.
Williamson: 1770] Longman and Broderip, *ca.* 1785.
19

1785b: *Purcel's Celebrated Te Deum and Jubilate* . . . H. Wright, London, *ca.* 1785.
232

1786

?1786: *Calliope* or English Harmony A Collection of the most Celebrated English and Scots Songs
Neatly Engrav'd and Embellish'd with Designs . . . Vol I . . . Oct ?1786.
609/10   S61

1786:   *The musick in the Comedy of the Tempest* in score composed by Henry Purcell. London: Harrison [1786].
       631(inc)

1788

1788:   *The Prophet,* an Opera . . . composed by [or rather, selected from the works of] Sacchini, Purcell, *et al.* Longman and Broderip: London (1788).
       M626/7ab

1789

1789:   *Select Psalms of David* . . . ed. Stamford, printed W. Harrod, London 1789.
       S7 S18

c1789–
  1798:   *Six Select Anthems* in Score Never before published . . . London: Preston and Song, (n.d.).
       54

1790

1790a: *Cathedral Music* . . . Selected and Carefully Revis'd by Dr. Samuel Arnold . . . Printed for the Editor, London 1790 vol. i.
       5

?1790b: *Goodison's edition of Purcell.* B. Goodison, London, ?1790.
       4 5 19 35 45 65 321 327 333 583 628 630 631 D241

1790c: *Psalms of David* . . . London: Dr. Miller, 1790.
       125

1790d: *Musicae vocalis deliciae* being a collection of scarce and celebrated Madrigals, catches, &c. London: Skillern (1790).
       280

1790e: *Poor Thomas Day* A collection of Catches, canons, and Glees . . . Composed, selected & arr. by J. W. Calcott, BM.
       574/10 628/38

?1790:   *A Collection of Songs* for two and three voices taken from ' Orpheus Britannicus '. Composed by Henry Purcell. London: John Johnson, (n.d.) [?1790].
       333/6ab 335/2, 5a 485 486 489 499 501 502 503 517 520 521 N526 546 572/11ab 574/15b, 16b 578/1, 6a, 7 585/2 602/1 607/11 608 613/1 627/30 628/26b, 29, 30ef, 36 629/4b, 8bcd, 22b 630/17bc 632/19 S53 S61

c1790:   *Apollonian Harmony*: a collection of . . . glees, catches, madrigals, canzonetts, rounds & canons . . . by Aldrich, Arne . . . Purcell . . . and other . . . masters . . . The words consistent with female delicacy. 6 vols. Printed for S.A. & P. Thompson: London, [*ca.* 1790].
       230M/2f 262 267 274 275 419 495 523 574/10 578/1 605/3 609/11 626/7ab 628/16b, 30ef, 36, 38 D100

1791

c1791:   *The Psalms of David in metre* . . . the words selected from the new version of Tate & Brady . . . & others . . . Also an appendix containing select hymns . . . The music consisting of the tunes in present use, with additional ones by Handel, Purcell, Boyce, Nares, Howard, &c. The whole selected and adapted by Hugh Bond, etc. Preston & Sons: London, [*ca.* 1791].
       191/2

1792

1792:   *The Divine Harmonist* ... ed. Thomas Busby, printed W. Locke, London, 1792.
     60   61   182

?1792:   *A new edition of the celebrated music in the Tempest* composed by Henry Purcell, revised and corrected by Doctor Busby. London: Broderip & Wilkinson. (n.d.) [?1792].
     631

1795

1795:   *Sacred Harmony* ... in parts, anthems and church services ... ed. Robert Willoughby. Printed for the Editor, London:
     33   232

1796

?1796:   *The Psalms of David in Metre* ... H. Bond, ... 1796.
     191/2

1797–1802

1797–
1802:   *The Pianoforte Magazine*, vol II. London: Harrison & Co. [1797–1802].
     574/15, 16   TS68

1798

?1798:   *The Village Harmony*, or New England Repository of Sacred Music. published by West & Richardson, Boston, Mass. [?1798].
     125   S6

1799

1799:   *The Hymns, Te Deum Laudamus, and Jubilate Deo*, in English 3rd edition, ed. T. Skillern, London, 1799.
     232

1800

1800a: *Ancient Church Music* ... Psalm-tunes ... carefully collated and set in three parts by Richard Sampson ... London: Caldbin: 1800.
     125 (see Commentary)

1800b: *Harmonia Sacra*, Collection of Anthems in Score ... John Page of St. Paul's Cathedral. Printed and Published for the Editor. 2 vols, London, 1800.
     7   19   45

1800c: *Vocal Pocket Companion* ... catches, glees and duets ... G. Smart, London: for Smart ... [?1800].
     262   290   626/7ab   D100

1805

1805:   *The Beauties of Purcell* in Two Volumes .... arranged with a separate accompaniment for the Pianoforte ... by Jos. Corfe ... Printed and Sold for Mr. Corfe by Preston, London, 1805.

134 184 191 253 256 274 276 281 286 288 290 321/2ab 327/7 333/10 335/5a
355 370 405 485 486 487 498 499 501 502 503 517 521 522 546 571/6
574/12, 14, 15b, 16b, 17 578/1, 3, 6a, 9 600/1bd 602/1 604A 609/10 613 626/7ab
627/5bc, 18b, 30, 32b, 35, 38, 19 to 27 628/10, 12, 13, 16b, 19, 20b, 21, 22, 23, 24, 25,
26, 29, 36, 38 629/8bcd, 29 630/13, 15, 17abch 631/2e, 5bc, 6ab, 8, 10, 11a, 13a, 15b,
16b, 17ab 632/13b, 16 D102

1809

1809: *The Beauties of Purcell* ... Selected, adapted and Arranged for the Pianoforte ... by John
Clarke. vol. i, Printed and Sold by Rt. Birchall, London, 1809.
321/2ab 370 517 521 574/11b, 12, 14, 15b, 16b, 17 578/3, 9 604A 613/1 628/10,
12, 13, 29, 38, 19b to 25a 630/13, 17h 631/2e, 3b, 5bc, 6ab, 11a, 12a, 13a, 14a, 14c.
15b 632/10b

1810

c1810: *The Original Music in the Tempest* as composed by Purcell, Dr. Arne & Linley now performing
at the Theatre Royal in Covent Garden ... The Overture & Addnl. new music composed
and the whole Arranged by John Davey. London: W. Turnbull.
631

1828

1828[–44]: *Musical Antiquarian Edition. The Cathedral Services, Anthems Hymns and other Sacred Pieces
composed by Henry Purcell.* Edited by Vincent Novello. J. Alfred Novello, London [1828],
1832 and 1844, 4 vols.
2 3 4 5 6 7 8 9 11 13B 15 16 18 19 21 22 23 25 26 27 28 29 30
31 32 33 34 (Preface only; mnp) 35 36 37 38 39 40 41 42 43 44 45 47
48 49 50 51 52 54 55 56 57 58C 60 61 62 63 64 65 101 103ab 104 105
106 108 120 123 125 130 131 132 133 134 135 136 137 138 139 140
141 142 143 181 182 183 184 185 186 188 189 190 191 192 193 196
197 198 199 200 230 231 232 D8 D33 D70 D72 D77 S1 S14 S15 S16
(N67 and N68 are mentioned in the 'Preface' as missing.)

[There is no real difference between the versions of 1828 and 1842, although the sequence of
pieces is altogether different, and the indexes to contents have been altered in some ways not
affecting the contents of the volumes themselves. The same plates were used throughout,
without significant alteration other than pagination &c.]

1831

1831: *Christian Psalmody* ... Cotterill, 1831.
125

1841

1841a: *Musica Antiqua II.* Piano Forte Part to ... *Dido and Aeneas.* Compressed from the Score by
G. Alex Macfarren ... Printed and Sold by Chappell, London, 1841.
626

1841b: *Musica Antiqua XI. Dido and Aeneas* ... Now first Printed. Edited by G. Alex Macfarren.
Printed for the Members of the Musical Antiquarian Society by Chappell. London 1841.
626

S

1842

1842: *Bonduca*, A Tragedy Altered from Beaumont & Fletcher The Music Composed A.D. 1695, by Henry Purcell, Edited & Preceded by an Historical Sketch of Early English Dramatic Music, by Edward F. Rimbault, FSA. London: Printed for Members of the Musical Antiquarian Society by Chappell . . . 1842.

574

1843

1843: *King Arthur* An Opera in Five Acts Written by John Dryden, Composed by Henry Purcell and Now First Printed. Edited by Edward Taylor . . . London: Printed for the Members of the Musical Antiquarian Society . . . 1843.

628

c1843: *Dido and Aeneas.* A Tragic Opera in Three Acts Composed Anno 1675 by Henry Purcell Now First Printed Edited by G. Alexander MacFarren, London: Printed for the Members of the Musical Antiquarian Society, Chappell, n.d.

626

1847

1847: *Musica Antiqua XII. Ode Composed for the Anniversary of St. Cecilia's Day A.D. 1692* . . . now first printed and Edited from a Cotemporary MS by Edward F. Rimbault . . . Printed for the Members of the Musical Antiquarian Society by Chappell. London, 1847.

328

1848

1848: *Ode Composed for the Anniversary of St. Cecilia's Day, A.D. 1692* by Henry Purcell. Now first printed and edited from a Cotemporary MS by Edward Rimbault. London: Printed for the Members of the Musical Antiquarian Society, Chappell, 1848.

328

Undated publications

1: *Musical Library*, London, n.d. (From a copy in the Biblioteca del Conservatoria Luigi Cherubini, Florence.)

4/6

2: *Sacred Music for One, Two, Three & Four Voices.* Vol I. ed. R. J. Stevens, London. Printed for the editor, Charterhouse, n.d.

4/6   58C

3: *94 Songs* by Henry Purcell, D. Purcell, Blow, Bryce, Eccles . . . *et altri* . . . Cardiff Public Library.

N526

4: *Harmonia Perfecta*, . . . Nathaniel Gawthorn [? early 18th century].

125

ADDENDA

(The contents of the following will be inventoried and cross-referenced in a later edition of this catalogue.)

1699–1700

Recueil d'airs à 4 parties tirez des Opera [sic] *Tragédies & Comédies de Mono.* Henry Purcell, [Book I[–II], Amsterdam: Estienne Roger, [1699–1700]. (Unique copies of all the parts for this apparently pirated edition are to be found in the Uppsala University Library, Utl. Instr. mus. tr. 80:3.)

1700

A Collection of Songs set to Musick by Mr. Henry Purcell and Mr. John Eccles. London: Tho. Cross. [*ca.* 1700].

1708

The Second Part of the Division Flute. Containing the newest divisions upon the choicest grounds for the flute . . . London: J. Walsh, J. Hare, & P. Randall, [1708].

1709

Duos anglais de différents maitres à 2 flutes ou violons. Livre second.—Amsterdam: P. Mortier, [*ca.* 1709].

1715

A Collection of the Choicest Songs and Dialogues composed by the Most Eminent Masters of the Age. London: J. Walsh, [*ca.* 1715].

1716

The Merry Musician; or, *A Cure for the Spleen being a Collection of the Most Diverting Songs and Pleasant Ballads, set to musick* . . . Vol. I[–IV]. London: J. Meere for J. Walsh, 1716[–1733].

1719

Love in A Riddle. A pastoral. As it is acted at the Theatre Royal . . . Written by Mr. Cibber, London: J. Watts, 1719[–1729].

1722

The Compleat Musick-master: being plain, easie and familiar rules for singing, and playing on the . . . violin, flute, haut-boy, bass-viol, treble-viol, tenor-viol. Containing likewise . . . choice tunes . . . fitte to each instrument, with songs for two voices . . . The third edition, with additions. London: W. Pearson, 1722.

1728

The Beggar's Opera. As it is acted at the Theatre Royal in Lincolns-Inn-Fields. Written by Mr. Gay . . . To which is added, the musick engrav'n on copperplates. London; J. Watts, 1728.

The Quaker's Opera. As it is perform'd at Lee's and Harper's great theatrical Booth in Bartholomew-Fair. With musick prefix'd to each song. London: J. W. W[atts] . . . J. Roberts . . . 1728.

1729

Momus Turn'd Fabulist: or, Vulcan's Wedding. An opera; after the manner the Beggar's opera . . . With musick prefix'd to each song. London: J. Watts, 1729

The Cobler's Opera . . . To which is added, the musick engrav'd on copper-plates. London: T. Wood, 1729.

The Wedding: a Tragi-comi-pastoral-farcial Opera . . . *With an Hudibrastick Skimmington.* By Mr. Hawker . . . To which is prefix'd the overture by Dr. Pepusch. With an addition of the musick to each song . . . London: W. Mears (S. Birt), 1729.

1732

A Collection of Original Scotch Songs, with a thorough bass to each song, for the harpsicord. London: J. Walsh, [*ca.* 1732].

1733

The Livery Rake, and Country Lass. An opera as it is perform'd at the new theatre in the Hay-market with the musick prefix'd to each song. London: J. Watts, 1733. I.

1734

Don Quixote in England. A comedy . . . as it is acted at the new theatre in the Hay-market. By H. Fielding. London: J. Watts, 1734.

The British Musical Miscellany, or Delightfull Grove. Being a collection of celebrated English and Scotch songs. By the best masters. Set for the violin, german flute, the common flute and harpsichord. Vol. I–IV . . . London: J. Walsh, 1734–38. 6 vols.

1735

The Merry Cobler: or, *The Second Part of The Devil to Pay.* A farcical opera in one act . . . by Mr. Coffee, author of the first part. London: J. Watts, 1735.

1736

The Lover His Own Rival. A ballad opera. As it is perform'd at the new theatre in Goodman's-Fields. By Mr. Langford. London: J. Watts, 1736.

Divine Recreations, being a collection of psalms, hymns, and canons, in two, three, and four parts: with easy, grave, and pleasant tunes adapted to each of them. To be continued quarterly. Part 1[–III]. London: A. Pearson, 1736–37.

1738

The Universal Musician, Songster's Delight. Consisting of the most celebrated English and Scotch songs, favourite cantata's &c. Vol. 1. London: W. Lloyd, 1738.

1739

Calliope, or English Harmony. A collection of the most celebrated English and Scots songs . . . with the thorough bass and transpositions for the flute . . . London: H. Roberts, 1739. 2 vol.

Calliope or English Harmony. A collection of the most celebrated English and Scots songs . . . London: J. Simpson. Engraved by H. Roberts, 1739/1746. 2 vols.

1740

A Choice Collection of Twenty-four Psalm-tunes, All in Four Parts, and Fifteen Anthems . . . by different authors, for 2, 3, and 4 voices; . . . also some of the most favourite tunes set by Dr. Croft . . . with . . . lessons . . . for . . . beginners . . . with . . . nine psalm tunes . . . and one anthem by Jeremiah Clark . . . and a Te Deum . . . by Henry Hall . . . Collected, engraved and printed by Michael Broome . . . [*ca.* 1740].

The Catch Club, or *Pleasant Musical Companion.* Birmingham, [*ca.* 1740].

1742

Harmonia Anglicana. A collection of two, three, and four part songs several of them never before printed, to which are added some choice dialogues set to musick by the most eminent masters viz. Dr. Croft, H. Purcel, Eccles, Dr. Blow . . . London: J. Simpson, *ca.* 1742.

The Modern Music Master . . . London: W. Dicey & J. Simpson, *ca.* 1742. 7 vols.

Thesaurus Musicus. A collection of two, three, and four part songs, several of them never before printed to which are added some choice dialogues set to musick by the most eminent masters . . . Dr. Blow, H. Purcell, Handel, Dr. Green, Dl. Purcell, Eccles, Weldon, Leveridge, Lampe, Carey, etc. . . . London: J. Simpson, [*ca.* 1742].

1752

The Psalm-singer's Compleat Tutor and Divine Companion . . . Containing a collection of curious psalm-tunes, hymns and canons . . . The second edition Vol. II. London: for the author, [1752].

1754

The Muses Delight. An accurate collection of English and Italian songs, cantatas and duets set to musick for the harpsichord, violin, german-flute . . . London: H. Purcell, 1754.

1759

The Free Masons Songs. With chorus's in three & four parts . . . Edinburgh: R. Brenner, *ca.* 1759.

1760

[*The Muses Delight.*] *The Compleat Tutor*; or familiar instructions for the voice, violin, harpsichord, german-flute, hautboy, french-horn, common-flute, basson and bass violin . . . Liverpool: J. Sadler, *ca.* 1760.

1762

Clio and Euterpe or British Harmony. A collection of celebrated songs and cantatas . . . in three volumes . . . London: H. Roberts, 1762.

The Catch Club, or *Merry Companion.* A collection of favourite catches for three and four voices by H. Purcell, Dr. Blow, and the most eminent authors. BookI[–II] London: J. Walsh, [1762].

1763

Social Harmony . . . a collection of songs and catches in two, three, four, and five parts from the works of the most eminent masters to which are added several choice songs on Masonry. London: J. Lewer, 1763.

A First [*-Thirty-second*] *Collection of Catches, Canons, and Glees for Three, Four, Five and Nine Voices Never Before Published*, selected by Thomas Warren. London: P. Welcker, [1763–94].

Thesaurus Musicus, a collection of two, three and four part songs, several of them never before printed. To which are added some choice dialogues set to musick by the most eminent masters, viz Dr. Blow, H. Purcell . . . etc. The whole revise'd carefully corrected and figured by a judicious master. London: R. Bremner, [1763].

1765

Fifty Double and Single Chants, being the most favourite as perform'd at St. Paul's Westminster and most cathedrals . . . London: C. & S. Thompson, [*ca.* 1765].

Harmonia Sacra; or divine and moral songs with hymns and anthems . . . [London: R. Williamson, *ca.* 1765].

The Catch Club or Merry Companions . . . Compos'd by Dr. Henry Purcell, Dr. Blow, and the most eminent authors. Selected by C. I. F. Lampe. Book I[–II] London: J. Walsh, [*ca.* 1765].

Thesaurus Musicus a Collection of Two, Three and Four Part Songs, Several of Them never before printed. To which are added some choice dialogues set to musick by the most eminent masters viz. Dr. Blow, H. Purcell . . . etc . . . the whole revis'd carefully corrected and figur'd by a judicious master. London: R. Bremner, [*ca.* 1765].

1770

Divine Harmony: being a choice collection of six cathedral anthems ... Birmingham: M. Broome, [*ca.* 1770].

Divine Harmony: being a collection of two hundred and seven double and single chants ... London: T. Vanderman, 1770.

1774

The Essex Harmony ... Vol. 1, The fourth edition, with large additions. London: R. and M. Brown, 1774.

1775

A Choice Collection of the Most Favourite Catches ... as they are sung at the catch clubs. Dublin: S. Lee [*ca.* 1775].

A Collection of Voluntaries, for Organ or Harpsicord. Composed by Dr. Green, Mr. Travers & several other eminent masters. Book I[–IV]. London: Longman, Lukey & Co., [*ca.* 1775–1780].

Social Harmony, consisting of a collection of songs and catches in two, three, four, and five parts ... London: Longman, Lukey & Co., [*ca.* 1775].

The New Merry Companion, or Complete Modern Songster: being a select collection of the most celebrated songs, lately sung at the theatres, Vauxhall, Ranelagh, &c. London: J. Wheble, [*ca.* 1775].

1778

The New Merry Companion; or *Vocal Remembrances*; being a select collection of the most celebrated songs lately sung at the theatres Vauxhall, Ranelagh ... London: Wallis & Stonehouse, J. Bew, W. Davenhill, Cornhill & Longman, Lukey & Broderip, [*ca.* 1778].

1780

A Collection of Catches, Canons, Glees, Duettos ... Selected from the works of the most eminent composers antient and modern. Vol. I[–IV] Edinburgh: J. Sibbald, and Co., [*ca.* 1780].

A Collection of the Most Admired Glees and Catches for Three, Four and Five Voices. Selected from the works of all the celebrated authors. Book I[–IV]. Dublin: Anne Lee, [1708].

The Songsters Favourite, or new collection containing forty ... songs, duets, trios, &c. Adapted to the voice, harpsichord, and german flute. Edinburgh: for the Compiler, [1780].

1782

The Convivial Songsters; being a select collection of the best songs in the English language humourous, satirical, bachanalian ... London: J. Fielding, [1782].

1783

A Select Collection of English Songs. In three volumes [Edited by J. R. Ritson]. London: J. Johnson, 1783.

The New Musical Magazine; or compleat library of vocal and instrumental music ... The whole accompanied with a universal dictionary of music. London: Harrison & Co, 1783–86.

1784

The Beauties of Music and Poetry, Vol. I[–VI]. London: J. Preston, [1784].

1785

Amusement for the Ladies, being a selection of favorite catches, glees and madrigals, several of which have gained the prize medals of the noblemen & gentleman's catch club ... London: Longman & Broderip, *ca.* 1785–95, 9 bks. in 3 vols.

Amusement for the Ladies, being a selection of favorite catches, glees and madrigals, several of which have gained the prize medals of the noblemen & gentlemen's catch club ... London: Longman & Broderip, *ca.* 1785–93. 9 bks. in 3 vols.

Anacreontic Songs for 1, 2, 3, & 4 voices composed and selected by Doctor Arnold, London: J. Bland, 1785.

1787

Bland's Collection of Catches, Glees &c. Selected from the works of the most eminent composers ... London: J. Bland, [1787].

Elements of Thorough Bass and Composition, in which the rules of accompaniment for the harpsichord or piano-forte are rendered amusing ... by Edward Miller Mus. D. Opera quinta. London: Preston, [1787].

The Ladies Collection of Catches, Canons, Canzonets, Madrigals &c. Selected from the works of the most eminent composers. London: J. Bland, [*ca.* 1787–1796].

1790

A Choice Collection of Catches and Glees, Adapted for a Violin and Violoncello, to which are added some favorite airs with variations by Mr. Agus, London: Fentum, [*ca.* 1790].

A Collection of Catches, Canons, Glees, Duets ... selected from the works of the most eminent composers, Vol. I[–IV]. London: Longman and Broderip, [*ca.* 1790].

A Collection of Psalms and Hymns for the Use of Parish Churches ... The music compos'd & harmoniz'd by P. Hellendaal Senr ... Cambridge: the editor, [1790].

A Select Collection of Catches, Canons, and Glees, among which are several never before published. The whole composed, selected and arranged by J. W. Alcott, London: Goulding and Co., [1790].

1795

Amusement for the Ladies, being a selection of the favorite catches, canons, glees and madrigals ... London: Preston, [*ca.* 1795].

A Collection of Duets, Rotas, Canons, Catches & Glees, selected for, and most respectfully inscribed to the members of the Bristol Catch Club and the Cecilian Society by the editor. Bristol: [?Robert Broderip], 1795.

Select Collection of the Most Admired Songs, Duetts, &c. from the operas ... In four books ... By D. Corri, London: Corri, Dussek & Co., [*ca.* 1795].

Skillern's Select Collection of Catches and Glees for Three and Four Voices. London: T. Skillern, [*ca.* 1795].

The Massachusetts Compiler of Theoretical and Practical Elements of Sacred Vocal Music ... Boston: I. Thomas, and E. T. Andrews, 1795.

The School of the German-flute ... Book the first containing ... 56 ... Italian, English, Scotch, and French Airs ... London: the author, [1795].

1796

A Miscellaneous Collection of Songs, Ballads, Canzonets, Duets, Trios, Glees, & Elegies; in two vols ... by F. A. Hyde, London: Longman & Broderip ... 1796–1798.

1797

The Vocal Magazine. Containing a selection of the most esteemed English, Scots, and Irish songs, vols. I–III, Edinburgh: [n.p.] 1797–1799.

A Second Volume to the Rev. Dr. Addington's collection of Psalm and Hymn Tunes.... [Ed. by S. Hawes] London: T. Condor Bucklersbury and C. Logan, [*ca.* 1797].

A Select Collection of new Favourite and Popular Songs, by the Most Celebrated Composers. London: Harrison, [*ca.* 1797].

1798

L. Lavenu's Musical Journal or Pocket Companion. Containing a great variety of opera dances, single airs, duets, waltz's . . . arranged for the flute or violin. London: L. Lavenu, [1798], 2 vols.

Sacred Music for One, Two, Three & Four Voices from the works of the most esteemed composers Italian & English, selected, adapted and arranged by R. J. Stevens. London: the editor, [*ca.* 1798–1802].

1799

Cahusac's Pocket Companion for the German Flute . . . containing a selection of two hundred favorite airs properly adapted for that instrument . . . London: T. & W. M. Cahusac, [*ca.* 1799] 4. vols.

Harmonia Coelestis: a collection of church music, in two, three, and four parts. With the words adapted to each, comprehending not only the metres in common use, but the particular metres in the Hartford collection of hymns; the tunes correctly figured for the organ and harpsichord . . . Chiefly collected from the greatest masters in Europe, and never before printed in America. By Jonathan Benjamin. Northampton: A. Wright, 1799.

1800

A Choice Collection of Catches, Canons, Glees, Duetts . . . selected with the greatest care from the most esteemed compositions, most respectfully dedicated to the right honourable Lady Jane Mountgomerie. Glasgow: A. MacGoun, [*ca.* 1800].

Amusement for the Ladies, being a selection of the favorite catches, canons, glees and madrigals; as performed at the noblemen & gentlemen's catch club . . . London: Broderip & Wilkinson, [*ca.* 1800].

Appollonian Harmony: a collection of scarce & celebrated glees, catches, madrigals, canzonets, rounds & canons antient and modern, with some originals . . . Vols. I[–IV]. London: Thompson's music warehouse, [*ca.* 1800].

Nine Vocal Trios Arranged from the Most Favourite Airs and Duetts of Purcell, Wise, Travers, Hayden, & Harrington. [ed. by J. Corfe] London: Boderip & Wilkinson, [*ca.* 1800].

Social Harmony, being a choice collection of catches, glees, songs, &c. for two, three, & four voices by eminent composers . . . selected by R. Willoughby . . . (London): the editor, [*ca.* 1800].

The Flowers of Harmony, being a collection of . . . catches, glees, & duets . . . selected from the most eminent composers . . . London: G. Walker, [*ca.* 1800] 4 vols.

The Ladies Collection of Catches, Glees, Canons, Canzonets, Madrigals, Selected from the Works of the Most Eminent Composers by John Bland, . . . Vol. I[–IV]. London: F. Linley, (R. Birchall), [*ca.* 1800].

The Ladies Collection of Catches, Glees, Canons, Canzonets, Madrigals . . . Vol. I[–IV]. London: F. Linley (R. Birchall), [*ca.* 1800].

APPENDIX V: CHRONOLOGY

DATED WORKS (See note on p. 535)

UNDATED WORKS

In the first part of this chronology, Purcell's works are listed by dates ascertainable from MS or printed sources, or from documentary evidence relating to a first performance. Many of these dates should be prefixed by the works 'not later than'. Some collected works are listed together under the date of original publication, even though many of the individual pieces would obviously have been composed earlier. Within each section, works are listed alphabetically.

APPENDIX VI

LIST OF WORKS BY OTHER COMPOSERS COPIED OUT BY PURCELL

Anonymous

Holy, holy [Organ score] Fitzwilliam MS 152, p. 54
Unidentified instrumental movement in e minor [four parts] Fitzwilliam MS 88, f.26ᵛ

Batten, Adrian

Hear my prayer, O God [Score: Full anthem] Fitzwilliam MS 88, f.118rev.

Blow, John

Christ being risen from the dead [Score: Verse anthem] Fitzwilliam MS 88, f.93ᵛrev.
Cry aloud [Score: Verse anthem] Fitzwilliam MS 88, f.28ᵛ
God is our hope [Score: Full anthem with verse] Fitzwilliam MS 88, f.141rev.
My God, my soul is vex'd [Score: Verse anthem] Fitzwilliam MS 88, f.108rev.
O God, wherefore art Thou? [Score: Full anthem with verse] Fitzwilliam MS 88, f.138rev.
O Lord God of my salvation [Score: Verse anthem] Fitzwilliam MS 88, f.99rev.
O Lord, I have sinned [Score: Verse anthem] Fitzwilliam MS 88, f.142ᵛrev.
O pray for the peace [Score: Verse anthem] British Museum Royal MS 20.H.8, f.16
O sing unto the Lord [Score: Verse anthem] Fitzwilliam MS 88, f.9ᵛ
Save me, O God [Score: Verse anthem] Fitzwilliam MS 88, f.134ᵛrev.
Sing we merrily [Score: Verse anthem] Fitzwilliam MS 88, f.14ᵛ

Bull, John

Miserere mei [Score: Canon 8 in 4 on the plainsong] MS formerly in the collection of the late Dr. Boris Ord.

Byrd, William

Bow Thine ear, O Lord [Score: Full anthem] Fitzwilliam MS 88, f.129rev.
O Lord, make Thy servant [Score: Full anthem] Fitzwilliam MS 88, f.125rev.
Prevent us, O Lord [Score: Full anthem] Fitzwilliam MS 88, f.126rev.

Carissimi, Giacomo

Crucior in hac flamma [Score: Duet] British Museum Royal MS 20.H.8, f.127rev.

Child, William

Sing we merrily [Score: Full anthem] Fitzwilliam MS 88, f.114ᵛrev.

Gibbons, Orlando

Almighty and everlasting God [Score: Full anthem—only the first few measures have been copied, although there is space for continuation; anonymous] Fitzwilliam MS 88, f.112rev.
Gloria [Organ score, anonymous] Fitzwilliam MS 152, f.1ᵛ (not foliated)
Hosanna to the son of David [Score: Full anthem] Fitzwilliam MS 88, f.136rev.
Lift up your heads [Score: Full anthem] Fitzwilliam MS 88, f.124rev.

Giles, Nathaniel

O give thanks [Score: Full anthem] Fitzwilliam MS 88, f.119^{v}rev.

Humfrey, Pelham

By the waters of Babylon [Score: Verse anthem] British Museum Add. MS 30932, f.52 [See Appendix II, S1 for commentary.]

Lift up your heads [Score: Verse anthem] Fitzwilliam MS 88, f.23^v

Like as the hart [Score: Verse anthem] Fitzwilliam MS 88, f.7

Lord, teach us to number [Score: Verse anthem] Fitzwilliam MS 88, f.21

O Lord, my God [Score: Verse anthem] Fitzwilliam MS 88, f.4

O praise the Lord [Score: Verse anthem] Fitzwilliam MS 88, f.1

Locke, Matthew

I will hear what the Lord will say [Score: Verse anthem] Fitzwilliam MS 88, f.40^v

Lord, let me know mine end [Score: Verse anthem] Fitzwilliam MS 88, f.133^{v}rev.

Sing unto the Lord [Score: Verse anthem] Fitzwilliam MS 88, f.31

The Lord hear thee [Score: Verse anthem] Fitzwilliam MS 88, f.38^v

Turn Thy face from my sins [Score: Full anthem with verse] Fitzwilliam MS 88, f.131rev.

When the Son of man [Score: Verse anthem] Fitzwilliam MS 88, f.36^v

Monteverdi, Claudio

Cruda Amarilli [Fragment of a scored transcription of the madrigal, without words] Bodleian MS Mus.a.1, p. 2

Mundy, William

O Lord, I bow the knee [Score: Full anthem] Fitzwilliam MS 88, f.122^{v}rev.

Tallis, Thomas

I call and cry [Score: Full anthem] Fitzwilliam MS 88, f.127^{v}rev.

Tomkins, Thomas

O Lord, I have loved [Score: Full anthem] Fitzwilliam MS 88, f.120^{v}rev.

INDEX I

INDEX OF FIRST-LINES, TITLES AND SUB-TITLES

T

INDEX II

INDEX OF INSTRUMENTAL FORMS AND TITLES

Adagio (see also Overture, Sonata,
or Symphony) 323/1c; 328/1c, e; 331/1c;
337/1c; 342/1c; 572/1c; 574/1c; 588/1c;
592/1c; 593/5c; 597/1c; 607/1c; 609/1c;
627/3c; 629/27e; 630/5c, 16c; 632/1c;
770/1c; 771/1c; 772/1c; 790/3; 791/4;
792/(1a); 793/4; 794/2, (4b); 796/5;
798/(3); 800/2; 801/(4); 802/1a; 803/2;
804/3; 805/2; 806/3, 5; 807; 808/5;
809/1a; 850/2; D200/5c; D241b

Air 570/3, 4, 6, 9; 572/5; 572/4, 6, 8; 577/2, 3
(Slow Air), 4; 592/4, see 6 (Minuet), 8, 9;
597/2, 4, 7; 603/2 (Slow Air), 4; 607/3
(Slow Air); 609/2, 4, 6, 8, 9; 611/3 (Slow
Air), 4; 628/3; 629/2a (see also Second
Music), 38 (Fourth Act Tune); 630/1ab (see
also First Music), 22, Comm; 631/14b;
632/2, 4, 6a, 6b; 641; T675; T676;
T693/2; T696/1, 2; 770/2; S120 (Clarke)

Allegro (see also Overture, Sonata,
or Symphony) 328/1d; 629/27d, f; 630/5d;
791/1, 5; 792/3; 793/3; 794/1; 795/1a, 3;
797/1, 2b; 798/4; 801/4; 804/5; 808/4;
810/1, 4; 811/4; 850/1

Almand 642/1; 643 (with division); 660/2
661/2; 662/2; 663/2; 664/1; 665/2; 666/2;
667/2; 668/1 (Bell Barr); 669/2; D218;
D219/1 (rather Gavotte)

Bell Barr (see Almand)

Borry (Borrée, Bourrée) 572/8; 607/7 (Borrée);
D219/2 ('Borry', rather, Saraband)

Canaries (Canary) 627/34; T677

Canon 629/15 ('Four in Two': see also
Dance for the followers of the Night);
T680/Comm (in two parts on a Chacone);
795/1a; 870/8

Canzona (see also Overture, Sonata, or Symphony)
1/1b, 5; 2/1b; 3/1b; 5/1b; 18/1b, 5;
19/1b; 20/1b, 7b; 30/1b, 5b; 31/1b, 7b;
42/1b, 8; 44/1b; 46/1b; 47/1b, 5; 48/1b,
7b; 55/1b, 4; 57/1b; 63/1b; 65/1b, 5;
320/1b; 321/1b; 322/1b (Overture); 323/1b;
324/1b; 325/1b; 326/1b; 327/1b; 328/1b;
329/1b, 6b; 331/1b; 332/1b; 333/1b, 8b;
334/1b; 335/1b; 336/1b; 337/1b; 338/1b;
339/1b; 340/1b; 341/1b; 342/1b; 343/2b;
344/1b; 506/1b; 510/1b, 3; 541/1b; 543/1b;
544/1b; 547/1b; 570/1b (Allegro); 572/1b;
574/1b; 577/1b; 588/1b; 592/1b; 593/5b;
597/1b; 603/1b; 607/1b; 609/1b; 611/1b;
626/1b; 627/3b; 628/2b, 4b; 629/3b, 18b,
27b; 630/3b, 5b, 16b; 631/1b; 632/1b;
T690/2; T691/2; T692/2; T693/1b; 770/1b;
771/1b; 772/1b; 780/1b; 792/1b; 793/1b;
794/4b; 795/1b; 796/1b; 798/3; 800/1b;
801/1b; 802/1b; 803/1b; 804/4; 805/1b;
806/1b; 808/3b; 809/1b; 810/2b; 811/1b;
860/2; D200/5b

Chacony (Chacone, Chaconne) 335/7; 342/7;
597/6; (see 626/Comm: Dance Gittars
Chacony) 627/16; 628/1ab (see also First
Music); 629/51 (see also Dance for the
Chinese Man and Woman; T679 (with
canon); T680; 730 (Chacony); 807 (Great—
in g minor); D228/4

Cibell (Trumpet Tune) T678; S121 (Lully)

Corant 642/2; 644; 660/3; 661/3; 662/3;
663/3; 664/2; 665/3; 666/3; 668/2; 669/3

Counterpoint and Canon 870

Curtain Tune 630/20

Dance 627/36, 37d; 628/15a, 24c; 630/10, 12,
Comm; 631/4
of Antics 578I/Comm

INDEX III

AUTHORS, TRANSLATORS, PARAPHRASERS, AND SOURCES OF TEXTS

INDEX IV

GENERAL INDEX

PRINTED IN GREAT BRITAIN
BY ROBERT MACLEHOSE AND CO. LTD
THE UNIVERSITY PRESS, GLASGOW

FEB 2 1 1964

798561